NEW TEST
COMMENTARY

GEOFFREY B. WILSON

VOLUME ONE:

ROMANS – EPHESIANS

THE BANNER OF TRUTH TRUST

THE BANNER OF TRUTH TRUST
3 Murrayfield Road, Edinburgh EH12 6EL, UK
P.O. Box 621, Carlisle, PA 17013, USA

*

© Geoffrey B. Wilson 2005

ISBN 0 85151 898 2
(Volume 1)

*

Typeset in 11/14 pt Adobe Caslon
at the Banner of Truth Trust

Printed in the U.S.A. by
Versa Press, Inc.,
East Peoria, IL

*

Except where noted, Scripture quotations are from
the American Standard Version (1901)

CONTENTS

Romans

INTRODUCTION

*P*aul's introduction to the Roman Epistle is a consummate blend of authority and tact. Since he was personally unknown to the Christians at Rome he took particular pains to explain his motives in writing to them. It was because he had been hindered from paying them a personal visit that he determined to write this letter. In the wisdom of God, Paul was prevented from going to Rome at the time and in the manner he had planned. The apostle longed to see his fellow-Christians there in order to impart to them 'some spiritual gift', but God had devised something better. Rather than permit Paul to make the desired journey, God inspired him to instruct the Roman Christians in the doctrines of grace by means of this epistle.

Thus the providential frustration of Paul's laudable design led to the permanent enrichment of the whole church of God. This letter has preserved the authoritative and systematic teaching of the apostle to the Gentiles and it still provides the infallible norm by which every presentation of the gospel must be judged. Instead of simply establishing the believers at Rome by oral teaching, a far greater honour was reserved by God for his servant; for every Christian who desires to become firmly grounded in the faith must still sit at the feet of Paul of Tarsus, and receive with all humility that 'gospel of God' which was first committed to him 'by the revelation of Jesus Christ' [*Gal.* 1:12].

CHAPTER ONE

1: Paul, a servant of Jesus Christ, called to be an apostle, separated unto the gospel of God,

Paul, a servant of Jesus Christ: Paul introduces himself to the church at Rome as 'a servant of Jesus Christ'. The word *bond-slave* expresses his complete submission to the lordship of Christ. This relationship is not unique to Paul, but is shared by all true Christians. Therefore he begins by confessing his own interest in the gospel. This shows that there can be no valid exercise of authority where there is no personal experience of Christ's redeeming power. Those who are still the 'servants of sin' cannot work for Christ, however many titles and offices they may temporarily usurp. To all such Christ will say one day, 'I never knew you: depart from me, ye that work iniquity' [*Matt.* 7:23]. Rebels must be first subdued by Christ, for only then can they serve him acceptably. The conquest of Christ's grace inevitably precedes Paul's commission for service; compare Acts 9:5 with Acts 26:16. Further, those who confess 'Jesus is Lord' must also make a credible avowal that they are indeed his servants by their daily obedience to his commandments. Thus, before everything else, Paul is a Christian.

Called to be an apostle: Paul now passes to that which distinguishes him from other Christians. He is not only a participant in a common faith, he has been elevated to the apostolate. It is in virtue of that unique authority bestowed upon him by the risen Christ that he addresses the church at Rome.

The word 'apostle' means 'sent one' or 'messenger' but unlike the Twelve Paul had not been a witness of the earthly ministry of the Lord, hence he described himself as 'one born out of due time' [*Acts* 1:21, 22; *1 Cor.* 15: 8]. And though the former persecutor of God's church was 'the least of the apostles', he admitted no inferiority in regard to the authority of his commission or the scope and effectiveness of his labours [*1 Cor.* 15: 9, 10].

The unique function of the apostles as witnesses of the resurrection and as the inspired and authoritative interpreters of the will of the Lord constitutes the sole foundation for all genuine discipleship [*1 Cor.* 3:10, 11; *Eph.* 2:20; *Rev.* 21:14].

Since their office is essentially unrepeatable the only 'apostolic succession' known to the New Testament is continuing fidelity to that sacred deposit of truth which was once for all delivered to the church by them. By contrast, the defection of Judas supplies impressive proof that an external call is no substitute for regenerating grace [*Acts* 1:16–26; *John* 6:70, 71].

Separated unto the gospel of God: The immediate and enduring effect of Paul's call to apostleship is his separation to the gospel of God. The once zealous Pharisee (separated one) became totally dedicated to the gospel, when God's eternal purpose reached the beginning of its historical fulfilment on the road to Damascus [*Gal.* 1:15; *Phil.* 3:5, 6; *Acts* 26:16–18]. This 'good news' proclaimed by Paul is no mere human innovation – it is the gospel of God.

The dominant place that God occupied in Paul's thought and affections is evidenced by the heavenly 'digression' which naturally follows the first mention of the divine name. As God's ambassador he is never happier than when he is speaking of the excellences of his sovereign.

2: which he promised afore through his prophets in the holy scriptures,

The gospel is no novelty, no after-thought on the part of God. Indeed it was foreshadowed in the Old Testament provisions for worship and was 'promised afore through his prophets'. Paul constantly emphasized the fact that the Old Testament revelation reached its supreme climax in the gospel. He was always able to endorse the voice of prophecy without any sense of incongruity. Augustine's celebrated dictum, that the New Testament is concealed in the old, and that the Old Testament is revealed in the New, well expresses the apostle's thought here.

As antiquity is in itself no guarantee of reliability, this prophetic testimony has been preserved without error 'in the holy scriptures'. Christ himself declared that the 'scripture cannot be broken' [*John* 10:35], and his apostles held to the same exalted conception of the Old Testament. The scriptures are described as 'holy' because they must be received and reverenced for what they are, God's august self-disclosure to sinful man. The prevalent modern view of 'limited inspiration' is recklessly put forward despite the apostolic anathema, for did not Paul passionately aver, 'Yea, let God be found true, but every man a liar'? [*Rom.* 3:4]

3: concerning his Son, who was born of the seed of David according to the flesh,

Concerning his Son: This gospel of God, which was promised of old, is perfectly summed up in God's Son, who is the brightness of the Father's glory 'and the express image of his person' [*Heb.* 1:3]. The One who is co-eternal and co-equal with the Father, is the very Christ whom all Christians worship [cf. the confessional 'our' of verse 4: 'even Jesus Christ our Lord'].

Who was born of the seed of David according to the flesh: This is the first of the two successive stages of the Messianic vocation. As to the flesh, Christ was born, though not begotten, of David's line in fulfilment of the ancient promise [*Isa.* 7:14, AV; *Luke* 1:32; *Acts* 2:30; *2 Tim.* 2:8]. The expression 'of the seed of David' implies Christ's willing subjection to mortality for the redemption of his people, a point made explicit in the phrase which follows, 'by the resurrection from the dead.' [cf. *Acts* 2:24–32] On the cross the 'Sun of Righteousness' was eclipsed during those awful hours in which he suffered the penal infliction of divine wrath against sin [*Gal.* 3:13]. The essential glory of Christ became obscured, when he voluntarily descended into that profound abyss of shame and suffering, which marked the lowest point of his humiliation [*Phil.* 2:8].

4: who was declared to be the Son of God with power, according to the spirit of holiness, by the resurrection from the dead; even Jesus Christ our Lord,

Who was declared to be the Son of God with power: This verse describes how the abasement of the Son gave place to the glory of his exaltation. Paul does not say that the resurrection 'made' Christ the Son of God, but that it 'declared' or marked his appointment as 'the Son of God *in power*'. The contrast he draws is between the Son's earthly life of subordination to the Father's will as the 'Servant of the Lord', 'and the heavenly instatement by which he entered upon a new phase of sonship characterized by the possession and exercise of unique supernatural power' (Geerhardus Vos).

According to the Spirit of holiness (RSV): This enthronement inaugurated the age of the Spirit, whose descent on the day of Pentecost conclusively proved Christ's claim to eternal equality with the Father, for none but the Son of God could send forth the Holy Spirit [*John* 16:7; cf. *1 Cor.* 15:45; *2 Cor.* 3:17].

By the resurrection from the dead: The resurrection is that pivotal point in the Incarnate life, which marks the end of Messianic suffering, and the beginning of the transcendent lordship of the Mediator [*Acts* 2:36; *Phil.* 2:9–11]. Moreover, the future resurrection of all believers is guaranteed by this triumph of the 'firstborn from the dead' [*Col.* 1:18; *1 Cor.* 15:20].

Even Jesus Christ our Lord: Since the gospel of God is centred upon his Son, its entire content is expressed in the names that denote the functions he fulfils. The personal name 'Jesus' recalls the historic sacrifice by which he became the Saviour of his people; the official title 'Christ' shows that this gracious design was accomplished in obedience to the Father's will; while 'Lord' denotes the universal sovereignty to which he has been advanced by the resurrection. It is this common confessor in the *present* lordship of God's Son over all things, notwithstanding all appearances to the contrary, that unites the apostle with his readers.

5: through whom we received grace and apostleship, unto obedience of faith among all the nations, for his name's sake;

Through whom we received grace and apostleship: In the experience of Paul, the grace of God in conversion and the call to apostleship coalesced in his encounter with the exalted Mediator through whom he received the double boon [*1 Tim.* 1:11–14]. In this second reference to his office [cf. verse 1] he brings out the roving nature of his commission as the apostle to the Gentiles.

Unto obedience of faith among all the nations: It is this revelation to Paul of the universal lordship of Christ which explains his unceasing endeavours to bring men of every nation to recognize the reality of that divine rule in their lives [compare *Psa.* 2:8 with *Matt.* 28:19, 20]. Such obedience to Christ is the fruit of faith in him; whereas the refusal to trust him for salvation is the worst form of disobedience [*John* 16:9].

For his name's sake: It was not primarily to benefit the nations that Paul engaged in this evangelism, but for the sake of 'the name which is above every name' [*Phil.* 2: 9]. His paramount concern was not philanthropic but Christocentric. Above all else he sought the honour and glory of his Lord, and in this he faithfully reflected the antecedent design of God.

6: among whom are ye also, called to be Jesus Christ's:

Among whom are ye also: Paul assigns no special place of honour to the Roman church, and his right to address it rests upon its evident inclusion within the terms of his divine mandate to proclaim the faith 'among all the nations' [*Rom.* 16:26].

Called to be Jesus Christ's: i.e. they belong to Christ by predestination, redemption, and calling. The apostle never leaves his readers to imagine that they became believers just by voluntary choice, but always traces their salvation back to the effectual calling of God [*Rom.* 8:30, 11:29; *1 Cor.* 1:9; *2 Tim.* 1:9f].

7: to all that are in Rome, beloved of God, called to be saints: Grace to you and peace from God our Father and the Lord Jesus Christ.

To all that are in Rome, beloved of God, called to be saints: Paul recognizes no distinctions in discipleship, for all believers are beloved of God, and all are called to be saints. This is at once a gift and a demand. The distinguishing love of God confers the status of 'sainthood' upon all believers, but it remains their constant vocation to progress in holiness, even though 'sinless perfection' lies beyond this present life [7:21].

Grace to you and peace: Paul combines the Greek and Hebrew forms of greeting in this characteristic salutation. Grace is God's undeserved kindness in the gospel. Christ's propitiatory death provides the only basis for a restoration of fellowship between God and man. It is the subjective appropriation of that great objective fact of the gospel, which produces that 'peace of God which passeth all understanding' [cf. 5:1; *Eph.* 2:13, 14; *1 John* 4:10].

From God our Father and the Lord Jesus Christ: The juxtaposition of these names is further proof that the absolute deity of Christ was of the very essence of Paul's gospel.

Although the Judaizers persistently opposed Paul's doctrine of grace there is no evidence to suggest that they ever challenged his teaching on this crucial issue. 'The same phenomenon appears everywhere in the Pauline Epistles – the tremendous doctrine of the person of Christ is never defended, but always assumed'(J. G. Machen).

8: First, I thank my God through Jesus Christ for you all, that your faith is proclaimed throughout the whole world.

First, I thank: All Paul's epistles, except that to the Galatians, begin with thanksgiving to God for the faith of his readers. He does not congratulate the Romans upon their faith, but fervently thanks God for it. Hence faith must be God's gift to them [*Phil.* 1:29; *2 Pet.* 1:1].

My God: The knowledge that Paul had of God was neither abstract nor speculative, but living and personal. He could also speak of 'my gospel' because it was first his by experience, and the commission to preach it stemmed from this relationship [2:16, 16:25].

Through Jesus Christ: Every approach to God must be made through the merits of the Mediator, for in order to know God as Father, it is necessary to recognize Christ as Lord and Saviour [*John* 14:6; *1 Tim.* 2:5]. The solemn truth revealed by Scripture is that, apart from Christ, God is a consuming fire [*Heb.* 10:26–29, 12:29].

For you all: The apostle's genuine and undisguised affection for all believers, without respect of persons, was his artless method of securing their reverent attention.

That your faith is proclaimed throughout the whole world: That a witness was maintained in the very capital of the Empire was a great encouragement to Christians everywhere. This reminder of the widespread influence of their example was a stimulus to their continuing fidelity to the gospel.

9: For God is my witness, whom I serve in my spirit in the gospel of his Son, how unceasingly I make mention of you, always in my prayers

For God is my witness: As the believers in Rome could not know of his intense interest in their spiritual welfare, he commends himself to them by drawing their attention to the perfect knowledge which God has of his heart. It is almost an oath. Although God is very far from the thoughts of the wicked, the Christian is constantly conscious of the divine oversight, and he regulates his conduct accordingly [*Psa.* 10:4, 139].

Whom I serve in my spirit: All true service is spiritual, as befits the nature of God [*John* 4:24]. These words show that unlike 'some ungracious pastors', Paul's piety kept pace with his exhortations, for his own service was without reservation of any kind [12:1, 2; Philippians 4:9]. It follows that no bodily service is acceptable to God, which is not informed and animated by a renewed spirit [8:1–14; *Col.* 3:10]. That false mysticism which confines itself to inactive religious veneration is also condemned here, because spiritual worship is ever expressed in rational service [contrast 1:25].

In the gospel of his Son: Despite the general reluctance to believe it, the only 'good news' God has for mankind is to be found 'in the gospel of his Son' [*Luke* 2:10, 11].

How unceasingly I make mention of you, always in my prayers: Paul may be 'unknown by face unto' the church at Rome, but the Christians there are no strangers to his prayers. Their spiritual welfare has a familiar place among the apostle's urgent petitions for the growth and establishment of the whole church of God. If prayer does not 'change things', it is, nevertheless, the appointed means by which God bestows promised blessings upon his people. Ardent prayer is a certain index that such answers of grace are at hand [*Ezek.* 36:37]. 'To pray without labouring is to mock God: to labour without prayer is to rob God of his glory' (Robert Haldane).

10: making request, if by any means now at length I may be prospered by the will of God to come unto you.

The specific burden of Paul's prayer was that he might be given the opportunity to visit Rome, yet he consciously subjected this desire to the will of God. Luke's account of the unexpected manner in which his request was fulfilled, and his final arrival in Rome as a 'prisoner of Jesus Christ,' reads like a triumphal progress, which indeed it was [*Acts* 28].

In the pursuit of every lawful project there must be a humble acknowledgement of the divine proviso, 'Thy will be done,' for as Charles Hodge remarks, God's 'providence is to be recognized in reference to the most ordinary affairs of life' [*James* 4:15].

11: For I long to see you, that I may impart unto you some spiritual gift, to the end ye may be established;

Paul now turns to the purpose of his long-awaited visit. As he also expects to be enriched by their meeting together [verse 12], it seems clear that no particular gift is in mind; what he desires is that the Romans might be strengthened in their faith (James Dunn). Hence he gladly acknowledges the reality of a faith which he only seeks to confirm, and in his modest use of the passive form 'he hides himself by expressing the result' (A. W. Pink). God's purpose in the bestowal of individual gifts is achieved in the building up of the whole community. And the glory of the divine prerogative in thus establishing the church is in no way diminished by his use of human instruments to accomplish it.

12: that is, that I with you may be comforted in you, each of us by the other's faith, both yours and mine.

To avoid giving the impression that the benefits will be all one-sided, Paul assures his readers that he too will be blessed through his fellowship with them. He is not coming to Rome as an aloof benefactor, for he knows that while he is among them ('in you') he will be strengthened and encouraged by their faith. 'There is none so poor in the Church of Christ who may not impart to us something of value' (Calvin).

However, it is to be carefully noted, that a common faith is the uniting factor in such a fellowship. There can be no mutual edification where there is no mutual faith. John Fawcett gave inimitable expression to this fact of Christian experience in the first verse of his famous hymn. It is only 'the fellowship of kindred minds' which binds hearts together in Christian love. Today many would make 'fellowship' the means of securing a 'common faith', but this is nothing less than a wilful inversion of what is ever the biblical order [*2 John*].

13: And I would not have you ignorant, brethren, that oftentimes I purposed to come unto you (and was hindered hitherto), that I might have some fruit in you also, even as in the rest of the Gentiles.

And I would not have you ignorant, brethren: Paul's characteristic way of underlining what he is about to say. See also 11:25; *1 Cor.* 10: 1, 12:1; *2 Cor.* 1:8; *1 Thess.* 4:13.

That oftentimes I purposed to come unto you (and was hindered hitherto): They must understand that it was not because of indifference that the apostle had not yet made the journey to Rome. But so far he had been hindered from paying them the desired visit, presumably by the need to fulfil his missionary work in the East before turning to the West [cf. 15:22–24].

That I might have some fruit in you also: The quest for spiritual fruit was the mainspring of all the apostle's activity. No doubt it was because Paul saw Rome as an important missionary centre, that he specially wished to strengthen the witness there by a personal visit.

Even as in the rest of the Gentiles: Evidently the church at Rome was predominantly Gentile in character.

14: I am debtor both to Greeks and to Barbarians, both to the wise and to the foolish.

A study of Paul's sermons in Acts shows that he adapted his presentation of the gospel to suit the particular needs of his listeners [cf. *Acts* 14:15 ff. with 17:22ff.]. The apostle was always careful to take account of differences in national character and cultural development (or the lack of it), yet he knew that beneath these superficial classifications, there was the most fundamental division of all, that between the saved and the lost.

Since Paul's unremitting labours were not inspired by those to whom he was sent, but by his abiding sense of the divine obligation which rested upon him, he was not deterred by the unfavourable response his message so often excited. For he knew that all men everywhere needed the gospel, and the solemn fact that they do not by nature desire it had no bearing on his responsibility to make full proof of his ministry [*1 Cor.* 9:6].

15: So, as much as in me is, I am ready to preach the gospel to you also that are in Rome.

'As far as he was concerned, he was willing to preach in Rome; but whether he should do so or not, rested not with him, but with God' (Hodge).

16: For I am not ashamed of the gospel: for it is the power of God unto salvation to every one that believeth; to the Jew first, and also to the Greek.

For I am not ashamed of the gospel: Although the apostle is proud of the gospel, he is not unaware of the general contempt in which it is held, and so he prefers to say that he is not ashamed of it. The unpopularity of a crucified Christ has prompted many to present a message which is more palatable to the unbeliever, but the removal of the offence of the cross always renders it ineffective [*Gal.* 5:11]. An inoffensive gospel is also an inoperative gospel. Thus Christianity is wounded most in the house of its friends.

For it is the power of God unto salvation to every one that believeth: This gives the reason for Paul's pride in the gospel: 'It is the power of God for salvation to every one who has faith' (RSV). As Anders Nygren makes clear, this does not mean that faith is the *condition* of salvation, as though the gospel really depended upon man's response for its power to save; for in fact the *capacity* to believe is given through the operation of God's power in the gospel (cf. comment on 'I thank', verse 8). This means that whenever the gospel is preached, the power of God is at work for the salvation of men, delivering them from the dominion of darkness, and bringing them into the new age which was ushered in by the appointment of Christ as 'the Son of God *in power*' [verse 4; cf. *Luke* 11:21, 22].

To the Jew first, and also to the Greek: The gospel is for Jews and Gentiles alike ('Greek' here has this wider meaning). It is sent 'first' to the Jew, a priority always recognized by Paul in his missionary practice. But by insisting that it is 'also' for the Gentiles, he 'maintains the radical religious *equality* already proclaimed in the words: "To every one that believeth"' (F. Godet). [*Gal.* 3:26–29].

17: For therein is revealed a righteousness of God from faith unto faith: as it is written, But the righteous shall live by faith.

For therein is revealed a righteousness of God: The gospel is 'the power of God unto salvation' for in it there is the *dynamic* revelation of a *unique* righteousness. Unlike the legal righteousness by which man vainly seeks to attain a right standing before God *through* personal obedience to the law [10:3; *Phil.* 3:9], the divine righteousness is that status which God confers upon believers *without* personal obedience because he reckons or imputes to them the obedience of Christ. As the knowledge of such a salvation could never be derived from the natural operation of human reason, this extraordinary righteousness calls for a special revelation in which the unimaginable provision of grace is not only objectively communicated (in the Word of God, whether written or preached) but also subjectively applied (in the experience of believers).

From faith unto faith: 'He saith not, from faith to works, or from works to faith; but "from faith to faith," i.e. only by faith' (M. Poole). Salvation from first to last is by faith in the justifying righteousness of Christ.

As it is written, But the righteous shall live by faith: As Paul is propounding nothing new, he confirms his doctrine by an appeal to the Old Testament [*Hab.* 2:4, also cited in *Gal.* 3:11 and *Heb.* 10:38]. In this quotation the prophet contrasts the Chaldean invader, whose boastful self-sufficiency shows that he is not upright in heart, with the 'righteous' man who shall live (or be saved) by his faith in the promise of God's deliverance. Thus the faith of the man whom God approves and accounts as righteous [cf. *Gen.* 15:6, cited in *Gal.* 3:6] is the opposite of the spirit of pride which disregards God and invokes his judgment. And it is because salvation always consists in this reliance upon God's righteous intervention in history that it is not an artifice of exegesis for the apostle to find the basis for the ensuing argument in this text.

18: For the wrath of God is revealed from heaven against all ungodliness and unrighteousness of men, who hinder the truth in unrighteousness;

This verse begins a terrifying indictment of human sin. The apostle turns first to the sins of those who are without the light of special revelation [verses 18–32]. God will judge the heathen by the light of nature, which is common to all men, and this is sufficient to leave them without excuse [verse 20]. It may seem strange to some that Paul devotes nearly three chapters to an exhaustive examination of the problem of sin. However, slight views of sin never lead to a fervent appreciation of grace. Man is ever ready to excuse himself. He wears his sins lightly, and tends to dismiss them as mere peccadilloes. In his view they offer no barrier to blessing. After all, forgiveness is God's business! ('God will pardon me, it is his trade', were the last words of the poet Heinrich Heine.)

For the wrath of God: Paul therefore insists that the gravity of sin must be measured by the strength of the divine reaction it provokes. God is not indifferent to sin. It continually calls forth his holy abhorrence. Sin is an affront to the holiness of God, it is a direct assault upon his majesty, and 'the wrath of God' is an expression which indicates the righteous outflow of divine disfavour upon the sinner. This wrath is not an automatic judgment upon sin by an anonymous cosmic computer, nor can it be entirely explained by the feelings produced in the sinner who is punished. Rather, the phrase 'the wrath *of God*' points to the most intense, personal response to sin within the divine being, though this is without those unworthy human emotions which are normally associated with this word.

Is revealed from heaven: These words do not demand any supernatural manifestation of God's wrath from heaven. They assert the fact that God's retributive justice is evident in history [*Isa.* 10:5]. God is no idle spectator of world events; he is dynamically active in human affairs. The commission of sin is constantly punctuated by divine judgment. Truly, 'The history of the world is the judgment of the world' (Friedrich Schiller).

Against all ungodliness and unrighteousness of men: The stress here lies on the abstract qualities of ungodliness and unrighteousness rather than upon the personal agents through whom they find expression, because God would not punish men if it were not for their sin. The order is also significant. Impiety towards God results in injustice towards men. The derangement in man's primary relationship leads naturally to disturbances in all his transactions with his fellowmen.

Who hold down the truth in unrighteousness (RV): Man unavoidably knows God, for everywhere in the created order he is confronted by 'his everlasting power and divinity' [verse 20]. But it is because man also knows that he is a sinner that he always seeks to suppress or stifle this true knowledge of God. For though sin has not destroyed man's religious capacities, it has turned them away from the living God, so that he now prefers to worship the finite deities of his own invention [verse 23].

19: because that which is known of God is manifest in them; for God manifested it unto them.

As Calvin says, Although God is in his essence 'incomprehensible, utterly transcending all human thought,' yet he is inescapably revealed within all men through their knowledge of 'the things that are made' [verse 20], this 'manifestation of the Godhead being too clear to escape the notice of any people, however obtuse' [cf. *Acts* 14:17, 17:27–29].

20: For the invisible things of him since the creation of the world are clearly seen, being perceived through the things that are made, even his everlasting power and divinity; that they may be without excuse:

God's revelation of himself in creation is perspicuous, for there is in it a most glorious display of his divine power. The word translated as 'divinity' (*theiotes*) occurs only here in the New Testament. On this R. C. Trench wrote, 'It is not to be doubted that St Paul uses this vaguer, more abstract, and less personal word, just because he would affirm that men may know God's power and majesty from his works.' This knowledge of God's creative power renders men responsible, and thus leaves them without excuse.

But the knowledge of God's redeeming grace is mediated to mankind solely through his Son in whom 'dwelleth all the fullness of the *Godhead* bodily' [*Col.* 2:9]. Paul there uses the word *theiotes* to express the essential deity of the Son, for he 'is declaring that in the Son there dwells all the fullness of absolute Godhead; they were no mere rays of divine glory which gilded him, lighting up his person for a season with a splendour not his own; but he was, and is, absolute and perfect God.'

21: because that, knowing God, they glorified him not as God, neither gave thanks; but became vain in their reasonings, and their senseless heart was darkened.

Because that, knowing God, they glorified him not as God: It is because 'the *unseen* things of God are *clearly seen*' that men cannot plead ignorance for not glorifying him as God (Bengel). The seriousness of this charge lies in the final thrust, 'they glorified him not *as God*'. It shows that all men are destitute of true piety, for all their religious pretensions are based upon a false image they have formed of God. If it is impossible for man to add to the essential glory of God, it yet remains his obligation as God's image-bearer willingly to ascribe unto him that glory which is due to his name.

Neither gave thanks: Since man does not like to retain the knowledge of God *as God*, he cannot see him as the benevolent author of all his good. Instead he chooses to live independently in a world of uncertainty, which leaves him free to celebrate his 'good luck', or to praise his superior foresight, as the fancy takes him.

But became vain in their reasonings: The second part of the verse emphasizes the fact that when men reject the truth, they embrace lies in its place. The absence of truth always ensures the presence of error. Men must think something, and when truth is banished, the light that is within them becomes darkness [*Matt.* 6:23].

In thus refusing the true knowledge of God, their understanding 'became vain', an evident allusion to the heathen infatuation with idols, those 'vanities' which are devoid of any correspondence with the truth [*Deut.* 32:21; *Acts* 14:15].

In the New Testament 'reasonings' bears an unfavourable sense, and denotes the unregulated activity of the mind 'in the service of a corrupt heart' (Godet) [*Luke* 5:2, 22]. Here it indicates reliance upon the speculative powers of reason to provide a firm basis for religious faith. It is fatal to mistake philosophical enlightenment for spiritual illumination. Every form of heathen gnosis is but a variety of that false fire which ever ends in eternal despair [*Isa.* 50:11].

And their senseless heart was darkened: 'The heart' in the Bible stands for the complete selfhood of man; it is the moral centre of all his intellectual, emotional, and volitional activity. A heart which is destitute of spiritual understanding is in a condition of darkness which affects the whole man. This gives the *coup de grâce* to the modern myth of man's unaided ascent from primitive animism to the lofty summit of monotheism. It is only in the biblical record of man's fall from his original state of integrity that his present abnormal condition receives an adequate explanation [*Eccles.* 7:29].

22: Professing themselves to be wise, they became fools,

The effect of sin upon the mind of man is to turn his fancied wisdom into foolishness [*1 Cor.* 1:17–27]. Calvin observed 'that when miserable men do seek after God, instead of ascending higher than themselves, as they ought to do, they measure him by their own carnal stupidity ... Hence, they do not conceive of him in the character in which he is manifested, but imagine him to be whatever their own rashness has devised.' The folly of idolatry is therefore the logical result of this corrupt imagination (verse 23). However when God declares man's wisdom to be foolishness, the whole question of the validity of human knowledge is raised. It is because man 'holds down the truth in unrighteousness' that he becomes a problem to himself. It was by receiving the devil's lie, 'Ye shall be as gods,' that man first fell into sin [*Gen.* 3: 5].

He aspired to an equal ultimacy with God, and thus denied the most basic fact of his own existence, namely, his creature-hood. By refusing to know God *as God*, he lost the only means of identifying *himself!* Every 'problem' in philosophy stems from this primal apostasy. The profound opening sentence of Calvin's *Institutes* expresses this inseparable relationship with unique clarity. 'Our wisdom, in so far as it ought to be deemed true and solid wisdom, consists almost entirely of two arts: the knowledge of God and of ourselves.' It is the loss of the true knowledge of God, which makes the Socratic injunction, 'Know thyself,' an impossible requirement.

No independent knowledge is possible for man. Everything he knows, he knows from God. It is because man refuses to acknowledge this source, and insists upon the originality of his own interpretation of the 'brute facts' of the universe, that his knowledge is poisoned by the fatal error of his fundamental religious presupposition, which is, that there is no self-existent Creator to whom he is indebted for every breath which he draws [*Acts* 17:16–31].

23: and changed the glory of the incorruptible God for the likeness of an image of corruptible man, and of birds, and fourfooted beasts, and creeping things.

In words drawn from Psalm 106:20 Paul cites man's preference for idolatry as the supreme evidence of his folly. For he thus exchanged the glory of the immortal God for the unreal copy of the figure of mortal man, and even of birds, four-footed beasts, and serpents! But because such an image only represents the deity, idolaters do not regard themselves as idol worshippers. They invoke their god by means of the image; they do not bow down to the image itself.

This sophistry is still favoured by Rome in her vain attempt to justify her wilful departure from the Word of God, yet this is that very thing which the Bible condemns root and branch. Aaron made a golden calf, but he did not have the slightest intention of leading the people to worship this image. He said, 'Tomorrow is a feast *to the Lord* [*Exod.* 32:5]. The calf was simply an aid to devotion, but God's judgment of the matter was very different. 'They made a calf in Horeb, and *worshipped a molten image.* Thus they changed their glory for the likeness of an ox that eateth grass' [*Psa.* 106:19, 20].

God has written ICHABOD across the elaborate solemnities of all idolaters, whether pagan or 'Christian', for the glory has departed from them [*1 Sam.* 4:21, 22; cf. *Isa.* 40:18ff, 44:10ff].

It needs to be further noted that idolatry may not be limited to the mere worship of graven images, it also extends to the unlawful deification of any aspect of created reality, for to break the greatest commandment is still the greatest sin [*Matt.* 22:37, 38; *1 John* 5:21].

24: Wherefore God gave them up in the lusts of their hearts unto uncleanness, that their bodies should be dishonoured among themselves:

'Wherefore' points to God's justice in giving up those who had dishonoured him to the dishonouring of their own bodies. Three times in five verses the terrible sentence rings out: 'God gave them up' [verses 24, 26, 28]. In this handing of them over without restraint to the self-degradation wrought by their own lusts, they receive that 'recompense of their error which was due' [verse 27; cf. *Psa.* 81:12]. As R. C. H. Lenski says, 'Men who so love the cesspool of sin are sent into it by justice; what they want, they shall have.'

25: for that they exchanged the truth of God for a lie, and worshipped and served the creature rather than the Creator, who is blessed for ever. Amen.

This verse re-echoes the thought of verse 23, but it is in no sense a mere repetition of it. Paul's first concern is to vindicate the apparent severity of God's judgment upon idolaters [verse 24] by emphasizing the heinous nature of their sin. Then again, it might seem from verse 23 that man had successfully detracted from the essential glory of God by his idolatry, but Paul's fervent ascription of praise here is also a statement of the transcendent blessedness of the Creator. Indeed it is quite impossible for man actually to succeed in his sinful attempt to diminish God's glory. If this were possible, the dividing line between the Creator and the creature would cease to exist, and God would no longer be God. Later in the epistle Paul shows that no creatures can escape paying their tribute to the revenue of the Creator's glory, whether willingly or unwillingly, whether in mercy or in wrath [9:22, 23; *Rev.* 4:11].

26: For this cause God gave them up unto vile passions: for their women changed the natural use into that which is against nature:

What was hinted at in verse 24 is now specified in verses 26, 27. The moral degeneracy of the ancient world is exhibited in this awful catalogue of sexual vice, which pagan religion, so far from restraining, actively promoted.

Today the increasing prevalence of those sexual perversions, which are complacently regarded by the avant-garde as 'interesting variants', is a dreadful mark of God's wrath upon a civilization which glories in its 'post-Christian' character.

'Paul first refers to the degradation of females among the heathen, because they are always the last to be affected in the decay of morals, and their corruption is therefore proof that all virtue is lost' (Hodge).

27: and likewise also the men, leaving the natural use of the woman, burned in their lust one toward another, men with men working unseemliness, and receiving in themselves that recompense of their error which was due.

The honourable nature of the married state is grounded in the creative ordinance of God, while the illegitimate desire here described derives its proper name from the city of Sodom, which was destroyed because of it [*Heb.* 13:4; *Gen.* 19:5]. Poole comments, 'How meet was it that they who had forsaken the Author of nature, should be given up not to keep the order of nature.' So that the frightful physical and moral consequences of indulging these unnatural lusts was the due recompense for their 'error' in 'wandering away' from the true God (verses 21–23).

28: And even as they refused to have God in their knowledge, God gave them up unto a reprobate mind, to do those things which are not fitting;

Although all men have a knowledge of God, their refusal to acknowledge him shows that they are determined atheists at heart. Paul's word-play is preserved in Charles Williams' translation, 'As they *did not approve* of fully recognizing God any longer, God gave them up to minds that He *did not approve.*' Originally the word translated as 'reprobate' was applied to metals which failed to pass the assayer's test. Here a 'reprobate mind' refers to the mind that God cannot approve and must reject because of its folly in dispensing with its greatest good – the knowledge of Himself.

This blinding of the highest faculty in man constitutes the greatest judgment upon man. The religious orientation of man is unmistakably mirrored in his consciousness, and this finds its practical expression in his conduct. Thus man's thoughts can never be regarded as purely theoretical; for it is his mental attitude towards God which determines the quality of his actions towards his fellowmen. What Paul is saying is that man's 'unrighteousness' is the natural consequence of his 'ungodliness', the guilt of which he has just proved.

29: being filled with all unrighteousness, wickedness, covetousness, maliciousness; full of envy, murder, strife, deceit, malignity; whisperers,

This is the longest list of sins to be found in Paul's letters (verses 29–31). And though it does not furnish an exhaustive catalogue of vice, it certainly conveys a horrifying impression of those sins which enslaved the heathen world in moral chaos. In this verse the inward disposition of apostate mankind is first described in terms of *general motivation* ('being filled with all unrighteousness, wickedness, covetousness, maliciousness') and then of *specific desires* ('full of envy, murder, strife, deceit, malignity'). For 'whisperers' see the next verse [cf. *Mark* 7:21–23].

30: backbiters, hateful to God, insolent, haughty, boastful, inventors of evil things, disobedient to parents,

How this evil character manifested itself in daily conduct is next set forth in an apparently random list, which begins with 'whisperers' and extends to the end of verse 31.

Haters of God (ASV margin): 'And so God-murderers. Forasmuch as sinners are God-haters, and could wish there were no God, that they might never come to judgment' (John Trapp). In those who speak of the 'Death of God', the wish is father to the thought. Secularism seeks to murder God.

Inventors of evil things: New sins must be discovered by those with jaded palates, and new words must be coined for them. A relevant verdict on the restlessness of present-day society [*Isa.* 57:20].

31: without understanding, covenant-breakers, without natural affection, unmerciful:

Without natural affection: Man's inhumanity to man affords striking proof of the biblical doctrine of total depravity. The common practice of infant exposure is a single instance of the senseless brutality which was rife in the ancient world. Nevertheless, modern life is not without its own impressive parallels [cf. Paul's prophecy, *2 Tim.* 3:3]. Those who impudently break the first commandment are not likely to be restrained by the second, an unhappy sequence which is fully documented by the history of the present century [*Matt.* 22:37–39]. No ultimate moral values can be retained by those who reject belief in God as an anachronistic survival of medieval superstition. Humanistic ethics are doomed to shameful failure because they try to build on sand.

32: who, knowing the ordinance of God, that they that practise such things are worthy of death, not only do the same, but also consent with them that practise them.

The fact that the law of God is ineradicably stamped upon man's consciousness means that he can never sin with a clear conscience. But this knowledge of his just exposure to the sentence of death, as only God can inflict it, does not deter him from sinning because he is in love with his lusts. Hence men not only continue to commit sin themselves, but also 'consent' to it in others, that is, they actually applaud those who do the things which they *know* to be wrong! Paul's examination of the sin of the Gentiles reaches its damning climax in this awful statement. Nothing could exceed the enormity of the concluding indictment. Men enjoy sin simply because it is evil, and they delight to observe others in the same state of condemnation as themselves [*Psa.* 10:3; *Prov.* 2: 14].

CHAPTER TWO

1: Wherefore thou art without excuse, O man, whosoever thou art that judgest: for wherein thou judgest another, thou condemnest thyself; for thou that judgest dost practise the same things.

As Paul has established the guilt of the Gentiles he now deals with the case of the Jew, who is not actually named until verse 17. One reason for Paul's use of the generic term 'man' is his concern to prove the strict impartiality of God's judgment [verses 1–11]. Another is that he would gain a sympathetic hearing, and his earnestness is evident in the entreaty, 'O man'. The Jew is nonetheless identified in the first verse by the national pastime – censoriousness!

'Wherefore' expresses the apostle's conclusion in advance of his argument. The reasoning appears to be as follows: 'In judging others, you also condemn yourself, as you are guilty of the very same sins; THEREFORE you are without excuse, O man.' The Jew could heartily endorse the condemnation of the Gentile world, but this verse, which reproduces the Lord's teaching in Matthew 7:1–3, is nicely calculated to unmask his hypocrisy.

2: And we know that the judgment of God is according to truth against them that practise such things.

If the Jew commits the same sins as he condemns in the Gentiles, let him not imagine that either privilege or profession can secure him against the just condemnation of God. Paul says 'we know' that God's judgment is strictly in accord with the facts of the case. The word for 'truth' is defined by Cremer as 'the reality lying at the basis of an appearance'.

Man must judge by the outward aspect, and he is often deceived by it; it is otherwise with God who looks upon the heart [*1 Sam.* 16:7].

Paul is no dissembler, no mute patron of error, and his loyalty to God is the clearest proof of his sincere love for man [*Gal.* 2:11]. It is never a 'kindness' to conceal the truth from men, for as long as they are allowed to indulge a false hope, they must remain strangers to the only hope which 'putteth not to shame' [5:5]. In the kingdom of God, those who would build for eternity, must first dig deep [*Luke* 6:48].

3: And reckonest thou this, O man, who judgest them that practise such things, and doest the same, that thou shalt escape the judgment of God?

Not content with an abstract statement of an invariable spiritual principle [verse 2], Paul presses home its personal application with remorseless logic. If you condemn the Gentiles for these sins, then

how can *you* expect your privileged position [*Matt.* 3:8, 9] to secure
your immunity from God's judgment when you are practising the same
sins yourself? For to be guilty of such works of darkness when enjoying
much greater light is far more deserving of blame.

**4: Or despisest thou the riches of his goodness and forbearance and
longsuffering, not knowing that the goodness of God leadeth thee to
repentance?**

The Jew imagined that his experience of God's goodness meant that
God would not judge him as strictly as the heathen. Not realizing that
this kindness was intended to lead him to repentance, he was guilty of
holding God in contempt. For he mistook the mercy that suspended
judgment in the interests of salvation for a moral indifference to sin
[*Eccles.* 8: 11]. And the same fatal mistake is made by anyone who
presumes that time given for the turning *from* sin is a divine patronage
of the sinner *in* sin. 'There is in every wilful sin an interpretative
contempt of the goodness of God' (Matthew Henry).

**5: but after thy hardness and impenitent heart treasurest up for thyself
wrath in the day of wrath and revelation of the righteous judgment of
God;**

The Jew not only fails to benefit from the opportunities for
repentance given him by God's longsuffering, but by his continued
impenitence he is 'amassing, like hoarded treasure, an ever-
accumulating stock of Divine wrath, to burst upon him in the day of
the revelation of the righteous judgment of God' (David Brown)
[James 5:3].

Although the present age is not without its tokens of God's righteous
judgment, the full manifestation of it is reserved until 'the day of wrath'
when the complete equity of God's proceedings will be made plain to all
his creatures – angels, demons, and men [cf. *Psa.* 7:11 with *Rev.* 6:17].

'There is no judgment of God which is not according to strict justice;
there is none that is a judgment of mercy. Mercy and justice are
irreconcilable except in Christ, in whom mercy is exercised consistently
with justice' (Haldane).

6: who will render to every man according to his works:

Since the deeds of men afford an infallible index of their character, these acts provide the public evidence by which God judges them [*Prov.* 24:12; *Matt.* 16:27; *2 Cor.* 5:10; *Rev* 22:12]. It must be remembered that this is not an exposition of Paul's gospel, though it is an essential preliminary to it. The apostle is preaching the full rigour of the law to those who sought to be justified by it [10:1–3]. The application of this principle is unfolded in the following verses [7–10].

'The wicked will be punished on account of their works, and according to their works; the righteous will be rewarded, not on account of, but according to their works' (Hodge).

The believer's union with Christ is shown by his good works, the reward of which is the reward of God's grace [*Isa.* 26:12; *John* 15:5].

7: to them that by patience in well-doing seek for glory and honour and incorruption, eternal life:

The righteous are now described in terms of the principle stated in the preceding verse. In this passage it does not fall within the scope of the apostle's purpose to explain the dynamic from which these good works spring [for that, see 3:21ff].

His present design is to prove to the Jew the complete impartiality of the divine administration. When this section is interpreted as teaching salvation by works, Paul's teaching becomes involved in a hopeless self-contradiction. Against this, it is sufficient to note that the heavenly aspirations which characterize the righteous are not found in a hard and impenitent heart [verse 5]. They are the fruit of a restored relationship [*Ezek.* 36:26, 27]. It is true that many idly dream of glory and honour and immortality, but obedience and perseverance are the invariable marks of those who cherish a living hope [*Col.* 1: 22, 23]. Such continuance in well-doing is the indispensable condition for the attainment of eternal life [*Matt.* 24:13; *Heb.* 3:14].

8: but unto them that are factious, and obey not the truth, but obey unrighteousness, shall be wrath and indignation,

Next the works of the wicked are reviewed. It is better to understand the 'factious' as those who are motivated by that spirit of 'base self-seeking' which thinks only of the immediate gains of sin, and so does not seek after glory, honour and immortality [verse 7]. Hence they refuse to obey the truth and choose to obey unrighteousness, because they are bent on enjoying the pleasures of sin for a season. As all unrighteousness is *sin* and sin is lawlessness [*1 John* 5: 17; 3:4], such a course of action is a direct attack upon the authority of the Lawgiver and calls forth his righteous reaction of 'wrath and indignation.'

9: tribulation and anguish, upon every soul of man that worketh evil, of the Jew first, and also of the Greek;

'*Tribulation and anguish*' will be the terrible effects of the overflowing of God's 'wrath and indignation' upon all evildoers on judgment day. Paul is not content to say that this unimaginable punishment will be the portion of Jew and Greek alike, but he insists that the Jew has an unenviable priority in the order and degree of his condemnation. For like many professing Christians, the Jew thought that the mere possession of his spiritual privileges was in itself a certain insurance against divine retribution. But when such advantages are scorned, preeminence in condemnation is secured and the debt to justice proportionately increased [*Amos* 3:2; *Matt.* 11:22; *Luke* 12:47].

10: but glory and honour and peace to every man that worketh good, to the Jew first, and also to the Greek:

This completes the application of the principle stated in verse 6. Paul here repeats two of the terms used in verse 7 but replaces 'incorruption' with 'peace'. For instead of the 'anguish' felt by the lost, 'peace' is that state of eternal blessedness which is the portion of 'every man that worketh good'. Once more the emphasis falls not on a man's pedigree or pretensions but on his performance. But again the priority of the Jew, whether in condemnation or salvation, neither exempts the Greek from judgment nor excludes him from glory.

11: for there is no respect of persons with God.

The inevitable conclusion to be drawn from the foregoing argument is that God is no respecter of persons [*Deut.* 10:17; *Acts* 10:34]. It is impossible to bribe this judge, whose sentence is strictly in accord with character and is not affected by 'outward state and condition, as country, sex, wealth, wisdom, etc' (Trapp). Hence the Jew could expect no special treatment on the grounds that he was a member of the chosen race.

12: For as many as have sinned without the law shall also perish without the law: and as many as have sinned under the law shall be judged by the law;

Thus God will 'render to every man according to his works' [verse 6]. The very fact that such a judgment reveals any who are righteous, demands the gospel to explain their existence. Paul's very precise statement of principle leaves room for this, but an explanation of the gospel is quite alien to his present purpose, and so he does not disclose the basis of their righteousness. In this part of the epistle his object is not only to establish the guilt of the Jew, but also to vindicate the complete equity of the divine procedure in a judgment of condemnation. This restricted design certainly does not require a consideration of justification by faith, but it does demand convincing proof of man's guiltiness before God.

Accordingly, the apostle now shows that the judgment of God will be commensurate with the light enjoyed by men. The Gentiles who are without the benefit of special revelation will be judged by the light of nature, their disobedience to which is sufficient to secure their condemnation. On the other hand, the Jew who has been blessed with the written law of God will be judged according to the greater light which he has enjoyed. Great privilege always brings greater responsibility, and if neglected, greater liability to punishment. The heathen are not so blameworthy as the Jew. Nevertheless, both are guilty and both shall perish [*Luke* 12:47, 48].

13: for not the hearers of the law are just before God, but the doers of the law shall be justified:

Another uncomfortable fact, conveniently forgotten by the Jew, is rammed home by Paul. It was not enough to be a diligent hearer of the law; it enjoined undeviating obedience to all its precepts. He who seeks justification *by* the law must be perfectly obedient *to* the law. And the implication is that such an exact conformity to its demands is beyond the achievement of sinful man, a fact which receives explicit confirmation in the devastating accusation that begins at verse 17 [*James* 1:22, 2:10]. The manner in which the word 'justified' here makes its first appearance, affords striking evidence of its forensic character.

14: (for when Gentiles that have not the law do by nature the things of the law, these, not having the law, are the law unto themselves;

The heathen are not in possession of the written law [verse 12], yet their own judgments and actions are an acknowledgment that the moral law has been stamped upon their constitution by the Creator. For whenever they attempt to follow the dictates of conscience, they are confronted with the obligation to bring their conduct into conformity with this law that is revealed within them.

This partial and external obedience to 'the things of the law' is not said to be a fulfilment of the law, and should not be confused with the spiritual and perfect obedience that Paul attributes to the 'doers' of the law in the previous verse. As W. G. T. Shedd observes, the phrase denotes a fractional obedience to particular parts of the law, and not the law as a whole. The pagan does not obey the law in its entirety. It is obvious that such a piecemeal 'obedience' cannot please God, when it even fails to silence the witness of an 'accusing' conscience (verse 15).

15: in that they show the work of the law written in their hearts, their conscience bearing witness therewith, and their thoughts one with another accusing or else excusing them;)

There is a close resemblance between the English and the Greek words for 'conscience'. The literal sense of the latter is given by W. E. Vine as 'a knowing with', and hence 'co-knowledge with oneself'. Conscience is that innate faculty to distinguish between right and wrong which passes its independent judgment on a man's conduct. It is regarded by John Murray as 'an evidence of our indestructible moral nature, and is proof of the fact that God bears witness to himself in our hearts'.

The conscience of the natural man is blurred, though not extinguished, by sin, but in the Christian it is enlightened by the Word of God, and quickened by the Holy Spirit. That this verse refers to the activity of conscience in the unregenerate is finely brought out by Murray's perceptive remark, 'Paul does not say that the law is written upon their hearts.' It is true that the law of God is indelibly written in their hearts, but it has not been engraved by grace upon their hearts [cf. *Jer.* 31:33]. If then the imperfect witness of the conscience of the natural man convicts him of his sinfulness, how much more will the Author of conscience condemn it?

16: in the day when God shall judge the secrets of men, according to my gospel, by Jesus Christ.

Paul now sums up the whole paragraph by showing that the principle laid down in verse 6, that God 'will render to every man according to his works', will be exhibited on the day of judgment to the eternal confusion of those who only 'glory in appearance'. For it was through trusting in the perfunctory performance of an external code that Jewish hypocrisy was fostered. And it is to warn against such a delusive confidence in appearance that the apostle reminds his kinsmen of the Day when the 'secrets of men' will be infallibly judged [verses 28, 29; *1 Cor.* 4:5]. Moreover, the Judge of all men is Jesus Christ, whose ability to discern the hidden depths of every heart supplies further proof of his deity [*Acts* 17:31; *2 Cor.* 5:10]. 'According to my gospel' registers Paul's conviction that he was not only commissioned to preach the gospel of grace, but also to warn of 'the judgment to come' [*Acts* 24:25].

17: But if thou bearest the name of a Jew, and restest upon the law, and gloriest in God,

What follows proves that it is not the hearers, but the doers of the law who shall be justified [verse 13]. Having reached this point in the argument, Paul is ready to identify the man he is addressing [verse 1], and here begins an ironical rehearsal of the privileges in which the Jew gloried [verses 17–20].

The Jew bore his name proudly for it was the theocratic title of honour which marked him out as a member of the chosen race. He rested upon the law, confident that his salvation was assured by the mere possession of it. Worst of all, in boasting that his nation was the sole recipient of the divine favour he transferred to himself the glory that belonged to God alone [cf. *Jer.* 9:24].

18: and knowest his will, and approvest the things that are excellent, being instructed out of the law,

The superior discernment of the Jew and his mental approval of the divine will were the results of his possession of the written Word of God in which he was instructed from childhood. But unlike the Psalmist, he failed to see that this light was given to guide his steps into the path of obedience [*Psa.* 119:105].

19: and art confident that thou thyself art a guide of the blind, a light of them that are in darkness,

The Jew was proud of his knowledge and looked with contempt upon the Gentiles who were given over to idolatry. Although those who were sickened by the excesses of heathen worship were generally welcome as proselytes, there was always the danger that these converts from paganism would be corrupted by the inconsistencies they constantly observed in their guides [*Matt.* 15:14; 23:15, 16].

20: a corrector of the foolish, a teacher of babes, having in the law the form of knowledge and of the truth;

The Jew took great pride in his ability to correct and teach these Gentile converts, because he knew that in the law he possessed the 'form', the correct embodiment, of absolute knowledge and truth. Paul does not contest the claim, but next shows that the Jew's failure to do what he knew to be right was far more inexcusable than the heathen ignorance he despised [verses 21–24].

21: thou therefore that teachest another, teachest thou not thyself? thou that preachest a man should not steal, dost thou steal?

This series of rhetorical questions reaches a crescendo of searing indignation as Paul compares the profession of the Jew with his practice. For in teaching others, he had failed to teach himself [*Matt.* 23:31] and in these verses he is accused of theft, adultery, and sacrilege. Thus the Jew is himself found guilty of the very sins he professed to abhor in others. On his proneness to theft and adultery, see *Psa.* 50:18, *Jer.* 5:8.

22: thou that sayest a man should not commit adultery, dost thou commit adultery? thou that abhorrest idols, dost thou rob temples?

Plainly this is a list of such glaring inconsistencies as would excite the contempt of the heathen [verse 24]. And this was especially the case when the well-known Jewish hatred of idolatry was overcome by a rapacity which did not scruple to steal idolatrous objects or offerings, notwithstanding the ban imposed by Deuteronomy 7:25f. So that by the violation of his professed abhorrence of all idols, the Jew destroyed his own distinctiveness and in fact became a practising pagan!

23: thou who gloriest in the law, through thy transgression of the law dishonourest thou God?

The final antithesis announces the astonishing verdict. The Jew who glories in the law is the very person who is dishonouring God by his transgression of the law.

'God is dishonoured by the transgressions of his people, in a manner in which he is not dishonoured by the same transgressions in the wicked, who make no profession of being his' (Haldane).

24: For the name of God is blasphemed among the Gentiles because of you, even as it is written.

The conclusion Paul draws from this damning indictment is that the religious perversity of the Jew caused the Gentiles to blaspheme the name of God, for they judged the character of the Deity by the conduct of those who claimed to be his people. Unbelievers who have ample opportunity to observe the sins which are committed by professors are not thereby encouraged to assume the mantle of true religion themselves.

So far from the Gentiles having a monopoly in sin, Paul has proved from Scripture that the guilt of the Jew is aggravated by the fact that he always sins against the light [*Isa.* 52:5].

25: For circumcision indeed profiteth, if thou be a doer of the law: but if thou be a transgressor of the law, thy circumcision is become uncircumcision.

The Jew had one last hope left, and that was his unbounded confidence in circumcision as a sufficient security against condemnation. Paul proceeds to demolish this false hope by arguing against the Jew on his own terms. In such a context it was not germane to the apostle's purpose to speak of circumcision as a sign of the covenant of grace. As such it would be spiritually profitable to all those who share in Abraham's justifying faith.

However, the Jew placed his reliance upon his physical descent from Abraham, and he trusted in the law of Moses [*Matt.* 3:9; *John* 8:39]. 'Very well,' says Paul, 'even on that basis circumcision is profitable, but only if you keep the law. Should you fail to do this, the sign is nullified by your disobedience.' In effect Paul only mentions the possibility of keeping the law in order to dismiss it. The Jew looked for his deliverance in the law, but in reality it sealed his doom [5:20; 10:5; *Gal.* 3:19–22].

Hodge's practical remark on this verse is worthy of note: 'Whenever true religion declines, the disposition to lay undue stress on external rites is increased . . . The Christian Church, when it lost its spirituality, taught that water in baptism washed away sin. How large a part of nominal Christians rest all their hopes on the idea of the inherent efficacy of external rites!'

26: If therefore the uncircumcision keep the ordinances of the law, shall not his uncircumcision be reckoned for circumcision?

Since the privilege of circumcision was cancelled by Jewish disobedience, it logically followed that the disadvantage of uncircumcision was removed by Gentile obedience. The obedience that Paul has in view is not the pagan's sporadic observance of 'the things of the law' [verse 14], but the believer's fulfilment of the law's righteous requirements through the power of the indwelling Spirit [cf. *Rom.* 8: 4]. Hence the apostle is referring 'to those many Gentiles converted to the gospel who, all uncircumcised as they are, nevertheless fulfil the law in virtue of the spirit of Christ, and thus become the *true* Israel, *the Israel of God, Gal.* 6:16' (Godet).

27: and shall not the uncircumcision which is by nature, if it fulfil the law, judge thee, who with the letter and circumcision art a transgressor of the law?

Therefore if those who remain in their naturally uncircumcised state are to fulfil the law, it is evidence that their obedience will condemn the Jew who, despite the advantage of the written law and circumcision, is still a transgressor of the law [*Matt.* 12:41, 42]. As Paul here relentlessly insists, the Jew's failure to profit from these privileges only served to increase his guilt. For the law engraved on tables of stone finds no accomplishment in a stony heart of unbelief, and its unfulfilled commands thus become a swift witness against the transgressor [cf. *2 Cor.* 3:6, 7]. And though circumcision, like the New Testament ordinances of Baptism and the Lord's Supper, was of divine appointment, yet there was no value in the 'outward and visible sign' unless it was accompanied by 'inward and spiritual grace'.

28–29: For he is not a Jew who is one outwardly; neither is that circumcision, which is outward in the flesh: but he is a Jew who is one inwardly; and circumcision is that of the heart, in the spirit, not in the letter; whose praise is not of men, but of God.

In passing this crushing verdict upon the spiritual bankruptcy of Judaism, the apostle completely reverses the Jew's own ideas of his Jewishness. For he boasted of his birth, trusted in external rites, and like all who are content with an outward show, he expected the praise of men [*Matt.* 6:5; *John* 5:44]. In denying the validity of this confidence, Paul makes a play on the word 'Jew', which means 'praise'; 'whose praise is not of men, but of God'. Moreover, the spiritual significance of circumcision was clearly taught by the prophets [*Deut.* 10:16, 30:6; *Jer.* 4:4, 9:26]. Therefore the true circumcision is that of the heart which is renewed by the Holy Spirit. It is true that the doctrine of the Spirit finds no formal place in this part of the letter, but Paul's veiled reference to the results of believing the gospel demands such an acknowledgment of the Spirit's regenerating activity. Matthew Henry effectively transposes the verse into Christian terms:

'He is not a Christian, that is one outwardly, nor is that baptism, which is outward in the flesh; but he is a Christian, that is one inwardly, and baptism is that of the heart, in the spirit, and not in the letter; whose praise is not of men, but of God.'

CHAPTER THREE

1: What advantage then hath the Jew? or what is the profit of circumcision?

If the 'privileges' of the Jew served only to increase his condemnation, then it would appear that they were a serious liability which he could well do without. Paul anticipates and answers the objections which his teaching in the previous chapter would raise in the Jewish mind.

In the same way, a nominal Christian when faced with God's rejection of his empty profession, will always ask what the advantage of his creed and baptism is if they cannot save him from condemnation? (Godet).

2: Much every way: first of all, that they were intrusted with the oracles of God.

This verse sheds a remarkable light on Paul's view of Scripture. He does not here complete his enumeration of the spiritual blessings of the Jews [for that see, *Rom.* 9:4, 5], but sums them all up in this one supreme privilege. 'First of all', before everything else, God conferred upon them the dignity of being the depositaries of the divine oracles [*Acts* 7:38]. Indeed the Jews would not have so carefully preserved the written record of God's dealings with their race in judgment as well as grace, apart from the sustained conviction that such a special revelation had been entrusted to them by God. And as a true son of Israel, the apostle shared that conviction in full measure.

'For Paul the *written* Word is God's speech, and God's speech is conceived of as existing in the form of a "trust" to Israel; divine oracles have fixed and abiding form . . . And Paul was not afraid of being accused of bibliolatry when he thus assessed the inscripturated Word' (John Murray). But when the Jews were thus assured that the message of salvation was in their hands, it was all the more tragic that they failed to see the fulfilment of the Messianic promises in the One whom they had despised and rejected [cf. *Isa.* 53].

3: For what if some were without faith? shall their want of faith make of none effect the faithfulness of God?

It may seem surprising that Paul refers to the Jews' widespread rejection of the gospel as the unbelief of 'some'. But though the 'some' are many, they are not the whole. This 'some' therefore points to the other 'some' in whom God's purpose according to the election of grace is fulfilled [cf. 11:1–7].

As we also live in a world which appears largely indifferent if not actively hostile to the Word of God, it is important to remember that this Word always accomplishes the purpose for which he sends it forth [*Isa.* 55:11], for he will never permit the want of faith in 'some' to nullify his own faithfulness.

4: God forbid: yea, let God be found true, but every man a liar; as it is written,
That thou mightest be justified in thy words,
And mightest prevail when thou comest into judgment.

Not content with the negative answers implied in the preceding questions, Paul dismisses any suggestion of God's unfaithfulness with total abhorrence. For God must be found true, even though every man should turn out to be a liar [cf. *Psa.* 116:11]. The falsehoods of men are so often said to invalidate the veracity of God that the apostle's vehement protest is exactly to the point. And this is our warrant to defend the unchanging truthfulness of God's Word against all the objections of unbelief, whether voiced in the form of apostate science, philosophy, or theology! 'Whenever, then, the Divine testimony is contradicted by human testimony, let man be accounted a liar' (Haldane).

This affirmation is confirmed by an appeal to Psalm 51:4: 'That Thou mayest be justified when Thou speakest, and win the case when Thou enterest into judgment' (F. F. Bruce). The image is that of a court in which God condescends to plead his case against men so that his Word may be publicly vindicated. It is clear that God must always emerge the victor from such a contest. For when men argue with God they only succeed in covering themselves with shame.

5: But if our unrighteousness commendeth the righteousness of God, what shall we say? Is God unrighteous who visiteth with wrath? (I speak after the manner of men.)

However, it may be objected that if man's unrighteousness thus serves to show forth the righteousness of God, is it not therefore unjust of God to reward this contribution to his glory with the infliction of his wrath? Paul's indignant disclaimer, 'I speak after the manner of men', indicates that his reluctant statement of this sinful mode of reasoning was only in order to refute it with all the energy at his command.

6: God forbid: for then how shall God judge the world?

Paul's repugnance to this impiety is again expressed in the exclamation, 'God forbid'. It is a folly that does not deserve a reply, though he provides one in the form of a question. This announces a truth which would command the assent of his imaginary Jewish objector, for clearly a God divested of rectitude would be quite unable to judge the world [cf. *Gen.* 18:25]. It is because God is righteous that he is bound to punish evildoers who have no intention of serving him, even though the actions which evoke his wrath may also unwittingly redound to his glory [verse 5]. It should be noted that Paul does not try to prove the fact of universal judgment; he simply asserts it as a fundamental element of the revelation which has been entrusted to him. According to John Murray, the significance of the apostle's answer is that it shows what must always be true in regard to the ultimate facts of revelation: 'These facts are ultimate, and argument must be content with categorical affirmation. The answer to objections is proclamation.'

7: But if the truth of God through my lie abounded unto his glory, why am I also still judged as a sinner?

In this more vivid re-statement of the cavil raised in verse 5, Paul now plays the part of the ungodly objector. In the boldness of its questioning of God's rectitude, it reveals an attitude of mind that constitutes the very essence of ungodliness.

8: and why not (as we are slanderously reported, and as some affirm that we say), Let us do evil, that good may come? whose condemnation is just.

The most outrageous application of this principle is found in the lawless perversion of the gospel which was slanderously attributed to the apostle by his enemies [cf. 6:1]. 'By reducing the reasoning of the Jews to a conclusion shocking to the moral sense he thereby refutes it ... Any doctrine, therefore, which is immoral in its tendency or which conflicts with the first principles of morals, must be false, no matter how plausible may be the arguments in its favour' (Hodge).

By contrast Ignatius Loyola taught his followers to suppress their own moral feelings. 'If anything shall appear white to our eyes which the Church has defined as black, we likewise must declare it to be black' (cited by L. Boettner). The enthusiastic adoption of such a system of moral casuistry made the name of 'Jesuit' infamous throughout Europe.

Paul's concurrence with God's judgment of condemnation is based on the recognition that this verdict is just, and is therefore not to be deprecated. It must be acknowledged that the apostles of Christ were unacquainted with the all-pervasive moral anaemia which nowadays is euphemistically described as Christian tolerance. R. L. Dabney points out 'that the inspired men of both Testaments felt and expressed moral indignation against wrong-doers, and a desire for their proper retribution at the hand of God . . . Sympathy with the right implies reprobation of the wrong.'

9: What then? are we better than they? No, in no wise: for we before laid to the charge both of Jews and Greeks, that they are all under sin;

This verse begins the apostle's summing up of what he has separately demonstrated, namely, that the Gentiles and the Jews are alike guilty before God. Although Paul has insisted upon the value of the privileges enjoyed by the Jew [verse 2], he vigorously denies that these advantages enhance their standing before God. Those gripped by sin are also under its condemning power. The guilty have no 'rights'; they must sue for grace [verses 19–26].

10: as it is written, There is none righteous, no, not one;

This community in condemnation is confirmed by an impressive chain of Old Testament quotations, appropriately headed by a free rendering of Psalm 14:3, which denies the possibility of finding even one righteous man. What unites all men is their solidarity in guilt, for every man lacks the righteousness which God demands. 'Righteousness is the criterion by which sin is judged and the absence of righteousness means the presence of sin' (John Murray).

11: There is none that understandeth, There is none that seeketh after God;

Once again the thought, rather than the precise words of the Psalmist, is reproduced by Paul [*Psa.* 14:2, 53:3]. It is because man's mind has been blinded by sin, that there is no movement of his will towards God. God is man's greatest good; it is man's inability to recognize and act upon this truth which reveals the extent of his depravity [*Eph.* 4:18].

12: They have all turned aside, they are together become unprofitable; There is none that doeth good, no, not so much as one:

This is an exact quotation of *Psa.* 14:3, 53:4 from the Greek version of the Old Testament. It diagnoses the condition of mankind as one of universal apostasy [cf. 1:21]. All have turned aside from God the source of life, with the result that humanity has become soured, corrupted, and completely unprofitable to God. Not a single soul does anything that is good, because 'all are rotten to the core' [*Psa.* 14:3, NEB].

13: Their throat is an open sepulchre;
   With their tongues they have used deceit:
   The poison of asps is under their lips:
14: Whose mouth is full of cursing and bitterness:

The vices of the tongue are next described in words which are again taken from the Psalms [cf. 5:9, 139:4, 10:7]. Perhaps nothing more vividly demonstrates the wickedness of man than his vile debasement of the noble faculty of speech, 'for out of the abundance of the heart the mouth speaketh' [*Matt.* 12:34]. First, the *throat* is likened to an open grave, which may either suggest the desire to devour its intended victim, or the pollution that is spread by the foul odours of corruption. By contrast the deceitful *tongue* accomplishes its evil designs with sugared words of flattery. The third figure compares the calumny and falsehood which emerges from malignant *lips* with the serpent's infusion of its deadly poison. Finally, the *mouth* is said to be full of the cursing and bitterness that manifests the hatred of a heart bent on murder (Godet).

15: Their feet are swift to shed blood;
16: Destruction and misery are in their ways;
17: And the way of peace have they not known:

These verses are from Isaiah 59:7, 8. This hatred is also expressed in deeds; only the feet are mentioned because they carry the body and its members on their campaigns of violence. The horrifying picture is drawn in three graphic strokes: ruthless, devastating feet crushing and shattering; leaving trails of destruction and wails of misery in their wake; and all because they have not known the one way of peace, which is only followed by those who obey the Prince of peace [*Matt.* 5:9] (Lenski).

18: There is no fear of God before their eyes.

The final quotation is taken from Psalm 36:1. Practical atheism is the root cause of man's unrighteousness. In the natural man there may be a theoretical belief in God's existence, but his behaviour constantly belies his profession. In his conduct he is neither constrained by reverential awe, nor restrained by the fear of future punishment. All the evils described in the preceding verses are but the logical outcome of the truth set forth here. 'The absence of this fear means that God is excluded not only from the centre of thought and calculation but from the whole horizon of our reckoning; God is not in all our thoughts. Figuratively, he is not before our eyes. And this is unqualified godlessness' (John Murray).

19: Now we know that what things soever the law saith, it speaketh to them that are under the law; that every mouth may he stopped, and all the world may be brought under the judgment of God:

It is an indisputable axiom that those who are 'under the law' are obliged to render a perfect obedience to it. The charge has a particular relevance to the Jew who did not realize that his sinfulness made the law the instrument of his own condemnation. It is plain that Paul's use of the word 'law' here includes the whole of the Old Testament, for his quotations were drawn from the Psalms and Isaiah. However, the fact that the Gentiles have not received the written Word does not place them beyond the scope of its condemnation, for their failure to live up to the light of nature leaves them without excuse [2:14, 15].

Man's conduct is in mournful conformity with the character given to him in the Word of God, and he is therefore justly exposed to the wrath of God.

The condemnation of all men is the inevitable consequence of a broken law, which passes impartial judgment upon all transgressors. The purpose of the law is to bring the whole world *under judgment* (*hupodikos*). The word appears only here in the New Testament. It describes the plight of an accused person who has no hope of averting the sentence of condemnation because he cannot refute the charge brought against him. Every mouth is silenced by the law; it leaves man without a word to utter in his own defence [*Job* 40:4; *Psa.* 130:3].

20: because by the works of the law shall no flesh be justified in his sight: for through the law cometh the knowledge of sin.

In language borrowed from Psalm 143:2 this gives the reason for the preceding assertion. The guilt of all men must be established *because* no man can be declared just on the basis of his deeds when 'the law calls nothing obedience, but perfect obedience' (Shedd). Certainly if any man could perfectly obey the law, he would be justified by that obedience [2:13]. But in fact this theoretical possibility is never realized, for 'there is none righteous, no, not one' [verse 10]. The cause of this universal failure resides in the inability of the 'flesh' to fulfil a 'spiritual' law. For however much the 'flesh' may impress its own kind, it shall not 'be accounted righteous in his sight' (ASV Margin). The verse states the inescapable conclusion to be drawn from the foregoing arguments. The sin which disqualifies man from all hope of being justified by his personal obedience to the law of God, also condemns him for his total inability to meet its righteous demands.

But this negative conclusion is not without positive value, 'for through the law cometh the knowledge of sin'. A correct understanding of the true function of the law is an essential element in the effective proclamation of the gospel. The heart of man must be deeply furrowed by the sharp plough of God's law before there can be a profitable reception of the seed of life. Paul's doctrine of grace is firmly based upon an adequate doctrine of sin, because he knew that it is only the convicted sinner who desires an interest in the Saviour from sin. Thus the proper use of the law is to convince man of his guilt before God, for no unawakened heart is able to appreciate gospel grace [*Gal.* 3:22].

21: But now apart from the law a righteousness of God hath been manifested, being witnessed by the law and the prophets;

The whole of Paul's gospel is embraced in the antithesis between the 'then' of man's misery and the 'now' of God's grace [cf. *Eph.* 2:12, 13]. Here his emphatic 'but now' rivets the attention upon the dramatic change effected by the action of God. For now 'apart from the law' – that is, taking no account whatever of man's abortive attempts to comply with its demands – God's righteousness has been revealed (for this, see comment on 1:17). Moreover, what is now so clearly manifested was also attested by the law and the prophets. The entire

Old Testament gave witness to this 'righteousness without works'; it was foreshadowed in the rites of the law, and foretold in the promises of the prophets [cf. *Luke* 24:27, 44].

22a: even the righteousness of God through faith in Jesus Christ unto all them that believe;

Man is put into possession of a divine righteousness through (*dia*) the instrumentality of faith. The preposition used shows that faith is not a meritorious work; it is simply the hand that lays hold of the merits of Another. Here for the first time in the epistle, Paul directly relates the righteousness of God with the redemptive achievement of Christ. As this statement *limits* the gift of righteousness to the faith which is specifically directed to Jesus Christ, so it also *includes* all those who exercise such faith in him – it is 'unto all and upon all them that believe' (ASV margin). This fullness of expression emphasizes the fact that the same blessing is extended to every believer. It is the glory of the gospel that 'there is no discrimination among believers – the righteousness of God comes upon them *all* without distinction' (John Murray).

22b: for there is no distinction;
23: for all have sinned, and fall short of the glory of God;

There is also no distinction between Jew and Gentile in regard to their common need of an interest in Christ, because they are both equally guilty before God. 'For all sinned and (do) come short of the glory of God' (David Brown). 'The sinning of each man is presented as an historical fact of the past' (II. A. W. Meyer, cited by Hodge). Dr Hodge's own comment here is, 'The sinning is represented as past; the present and abiding consequence of sin is the want of *the glory of God*' [cf. 5:12]. The natural result of the disfiguration of God's image in man through sin, is found in man's complete ethical disablement. All men do constantly fall short of the glory of God, because all have sinned in Adam, and all are sinners by practice.

24: being justified freely by his grace through the redemption that is in Christ Jesus:

After the digression of verses 22b and 23, the present participle, 'being justified', shows how God's righteousness is even now conferred upon all believers [verse 22a]. God at once declares them righteous by putting the righteousness of Christ to their account. The double description used by Paul safeguards the character of justification as an absolute grant to the undeserving. Those who are 'freely' justified 'by his grace' clearly must receive it as God's gift. The total incapacity of man to make any contribution to this divine donation could not be more strongly emphasized. The riches of God's grace and the imaginary 'merits' of man cannot he allowed to co-exist together for one moment. Church history has proved that the maintenance of this truth is the crucial element in the preservation of Paul's gospel from corruption. It was the recovery by Martin Luther of the doctrine of God's free justification of the ungodly which heralded the greatest revival of true religion since the days of the apostles. It is the verdict of history that Christianity languishes whenever this doctrine is obscured.

The cost of this 'free' justification is met by the One who gave his life 'a ransom for many' [*Matt.* 20:28]. Paul used the original word in its strengthened form, which, as Trench points out, does not signify a mere recall from captivity, 'but recall of captives from captivity through the payment of a ransom for them'. Thus redemption in the New Testament may not be reduced to the idea of simple deliverance; for the emancipation of which it speaks is the purchase of Christ's blood [*Eph.* 1:7; *Col.* 1:14; *1 Pet.* 1:18, 19]. And there can be no experience of redemption apart from a personal knowledge of the Redeemer in whom 'this redemption resides in its unabbreviated virtue and efficacy' (John Murray).

> 25: whom God set forth to be a propitiation, through faith, in his blood, to show his righteousness because of the passing over of the sins done aforetime, in the forbearance of God;

> 26: for the showing, I say, of his righteousness at this present season: that he might himself be just, and the justifier of him that hath faith in Jesus.

These verses provide the clearest statement of God's method of salvation to be found in the whole of Scripture. Such a revelation of what the cross means to God is obviously of supreme importance to man, since it unalterably determines the content of saving faith. The cross is not an unexplained symbol, a mysterious event which saves irrespective of the kind of response it evokes in man: for salvation literally depends upon receiving God's interpretation of its significance.

Whom God set forth to be a propitiation: The heart of the gospel is that on the cross God publicly set forth Christ as a 'propitiatory offering', that is, as the appointed means by which God's wrath against sinners is averted.[1] Having proved at length that the wrath of God rests upon 'all ungodliness and unrighteousness of men' [1:18], Paul now points every convicted sinner to the one sacrifice which satisfied all the claims of divine justice. The dreadful reality of God's wrath against sin required appeasement, but the magnitude of God's love was manifested in the very provision of that propitiation which sin demanded [*1 John* 4:10]. This means that faith must find its pardon in Christ's sufferings for the guilty. For there can be no pacification of man's conscience apart from a believing interest in the blood which pacified God's wrath.

> *If Thou hast my discharge procured,*
> *And freely in my room endured*
>   *The whole of wrath divine,*
> *Payment God cannot twice demand*
> *First at my bleeding Surety's hand,*
>   *And then again at mine.*
>
>   Augustus M. Toplady

Through faith, in his blood: These two clauses further define the concept of propitiation: 'Propitiation does not take place except through faith on the part of the saved, and through blood on the part of the Saviour' (Godet). The first limits the propitiatory power of Christ's sacrifice to those who exercise faith in him; the second locates that power in the blood that was poured out in a violent death, vicariously borne to save sinners from receiving the wages they had earned by their disobedience [6:23].

---

[1] Recent energetic attempts to make 'propitiation' mean 'expiation' – a sinister feature of many modern translations – have been ably refuted by Leon Morris in his important linguistic study, *The Apostolic Preaching of the Cross* (Tyndale, 1965). On this passage he says that more than expiation is required, for to speak of expiation is to deal in sub-personal categories (cf. Bushnell: 'We propitiate only a person, and expiate only a fact, or act, or thing'), 'whereas the relationship between God and man must be thought of as personal in the fullest sense.' p. 201.)

To show his righteousness because of the passing over of the sins done aforetime, in the forbearance of God: God's purpose in setting forth Christ as a propitiation was to demonstrate his judicial righteousness by punishing sin with the severity it deserved. Such a vindication of God's character was necessary, because his forbearance in passing over sins in former times was widely misinterpreted by sinful men as an indifference to the claims of justice [*Acts* 14:16, 17:30]. However, this was only the suspension and not the revocation of the punishment which was due; payment of the debt was postponed, but the charges were not cancelled. And though that delay in the day of reckoning then ministered to a false sense of security in sin, no such illusion can now be entertained when the cross exhibits God's determination to avenge every breach of his law.

For the showing, I say, of his righteousness at this present season: God's past forbearance in passing over sins without exacting their proper penalty was only possible because he had in view the demonstration of his righteousness 'at this present season', that is, the epoch of Christ's manifestation as the propitiation for the sins of the world [*1 John* 2:2]. 'And the implication is, that apart from this sacrifice, the justice of God would have no more allowed "forbearance" and delay of penalty, in the instance of mankind, than it did in that of the fallen angels' (Shedd). And with respect to the future, this manifestation of God's righteousness at Golgotha was for the purpose of providing a righteous pardon for his people.

That he might himself be just, and the justifier of him that hath faith in Jesus: God's provision of Christ as a 'propitiatory offering' was the public vindication of his justice, and at the same time the means of justifying (declaring just) the ungodly [4:5]. If God had executed judgment upon the guilty he would have shown himself to be just, but he could not justify the ungodly by inflicting upon them what his justice demanded. Thus for God both to vindicate his own righteousness, and put righteousness within the reach of the sinful, it was necessary that instead of executing this judgment upon sinners he should provide a propitiation for their sins (Denney). Hence the cross exhibits the unfathomable wisdom of God, for it is only in the penal sufferings of his Son that his inflexible determination to punish sin, and his sovereign will to exercise mercy are seen to harmonize [*Psa.* 85:10; *Gal.* 3:13; *2 Cor.* 5:21].

Paul's final words again stress the indispensable rôle of faith in justification, and specifically, of faith 'in Jesus'. Here the human name 'Jesus' becomes a poignant reminder of the cost of the Christian's 'free' justification [*Heb.* 2: 9].

> 27: Where then is the glorying? It is excluded. By what manner of law? of works? Nay: but by a law of faith.

> 28: We reckon therefore that a man is justified by faith apart from the works of the law.

Now that Paul has explained God's way of putting sinners right with himself [verses 21–26], he asks, 'What room is left for boasting in this gospel?' The question is applicable to all men, though it has particular point for the Jew who gloried in his privileges and boasted of his works [cf. 2:17–25; *Luke* 18:9–12; *Phil.* 3:4–6]. His answer is, 'It is entirely shut out.' The law (or principle) which for ever excludes such boasting is not that of works but of faith. And this is because: 'Faith is *self*-renouncing; works are *self*-congratulatory. Faith looks to what God does; works have respect to what we are' (John Murray).

The apostle therefore concludes that a man is justified by the faith which receives the gift of God's righteousness, quite apart from 'the works of the law'. Since these principles are mutually exclusive, it is impossible for a man to be justified by faith, while he seeks righteousness by his own obedience to the law. Hence Luther was true to the spirit of the passage when he insisted that justification is by faith *alone*. 'Here St Paul shows himself a pure Lutheran' (Trapp).

> 29: Or is God the God of Jews only? is he not the God of Gentiles also? Yea, of Gentiles also:

> 30: if so be that God is one, and he shall justify the circumcision by faith, and the uncircumcision through faith.

Paul further shows that the old racial distinctions have been abolished in the gospel of God's free grace [cf. *Eph.* 2:11–18]. As all Jews know there is but one God [*Deut.* 6:4], it follows that he is God of both Jews and Gentiles [*Isa.* 45:21, 22]. Then since this one God is the same for all, he cannot have two ways of declaring men righteous, one for Jews and another for Gentiles (Lenski). In the matter of their acceptance with God, Jews therefore enjoy no superiority over Gentiles. Salvation is neither guaranteed by circumcision, nor precluded by uncircumcision, because anyone whom God justifies is justified 'by' or 'through' faith (a difference in expression which warrants no distinction in meaning). Such a recognition of faith as the decisive factor in salvation depends upon the realization that all men have been reduced to the same common level of need by sin [3:23].

31: Do we then make the law of none effect through faith? God forbid: nay, we establish the law.

Finally, Paul asks whether this insistence upon faith does away with the law. Is not God's commandment made void by the claim that no contribution is made to justification by any works of legal obedience? Recoiling from the suggestion in disgust, he shows that the righteousness of faith does not abrogate but actually establishes the law. For by faith 'we attain a perfect righteousness, we are interested in the most complete obedience of Christ to the moral law; and that hereby every type, promise, and prophecy is fulfilled; see *Matt.* 5:17; *Luke* 16:17' (Poole).

CHAPTER FOUR

1: What then shall we say that Abraham, our forefather, hath found according to the flesh?

Paul has claimed that his gospel is but the manifestation of what was foretold in the law and the prophets [1:2, 3:21].

Now he shows that the fundamental continuity which exists between the promises and their fulfilment also extends to the justification of believers in Old Testament times. The apostle's appeal to the experience of Abraham and David provides confirmation of the fact that believers in both dispensations are justified in exactly the same way, by faith in God's promise. The precise interpretation of the verse depends on whether the phrase 'according to the flesh' goes with 'forefather' or 'hath found'. Those who favour the latter alternative take the question to mean: What did Abraham obtain according to the flesh? Did the patriarch gain righteousness by any works of his own? [cf. *Phil.* 3:3, 4] If the former construction is adopted the question would be: What then shall we say of the case of Abraham, our forefather according to the flesh? It seems better to understand the phrase in this physical sense, 'because the contrast with another kind of fatherhood belonging to Abraham is already in the apostle's thoughts: see verse 11' (Denney).

2: For if Abraham was justified by works, he hath whereof to glory; but not toward God.

3: For what saith the scripture? And Abraham believed God, and it was reckoned unto him for righteousness.

A Jewish objector to the teaching that men are justified by faith alone would naturally appeal to the case of his illustrious ancestor. And certainly *if* Abraham had been justified on the basis of his works he would have had a ground for boasting. But he was not justified by works as is seen from the fact that he had no such ground of boasting before God; an assertion which the apostle proves by citing the testimony of Scripture, *Gen.* 15:6.

This states that Abraham simply believed God, he rested on the bare promise of God [verses 18–22], 'and it was reckoned unto him *for* (*eis*) righteousness'. As the whole weight of Paul's argument is directed against justification by works [verses 4, 5], it is obvious that 'faith' is not to be understood as a work which is reckoned as righteousness by God. The preposition (*eis*) must rather mean that faith is *unto* righteousness; it is the instrument through which the believer becomes personally interested in the justifying righteousness of Christ.

Righteousness was reckoned to Abraham as a matter of grace and not of debt [v. 4]. It was not acquired by his own merit, but conferred upon him by sovereign grace. There is, however, nothing fictional or unreal about this gracious act of imputation by which the sinner is justified. For God declares none righteous save those whom he constitutes righteous in Christ. Hence the unrighteous can be judged righteous only because Christ's perfect righteousness is actually put to their account.

4: Now to him that worketh, the reward is not reckoned as of grace, but as of debt.

5: But to him that worketh not, but believeth on him that justifieth the ungodly, his faith is reckoned for righteousness.

Despite legalistic assumptions to the contrary, the case of Abraham cannot be compared with that of a worker, whose pay is never allotted by grace but is 'reckoned according to debt' – a phrase which aptly applies to the Jewish recording of merits (cf. *TDNT*, vol. 4, p. 291). For whenever merit-mongers seek to accumulate a credit balance with God, they only succeed in putting themselves hopelessly in the red!

Having indicated the impossibility of attaining righteousness by works, Paul sets forth God's method of grace in an antithesis which absolutely excludes boasting [v. 5]. It is a general statement of the principle that holds good in the case of every sinner who is justified. The significance of the singular is well brought out by Hodge's remark, 'God does not justify communities.' When a man has been brought to realize his own ungodliness, he no longer tries to work for his acceptance by God. He abandons the ground of merit as a lost cause, and instead believes on him who justifies 'the ungodly'. The strength of Paul's paradox serves to magnify the miracle of God's grace in freely justifying the ungodly. 'The man is taken as ungodly, "just as he is", and is forgiven. He is not first made perfectly holy, and then pronounced just. Neither is he first made imperfectly holy or partially sanctified, and then pardoned. Pardon and justification is the very first act (after election, 8:30) which God performs in reference to the "ungodly"' (Shedd). And he is justified in spite of his ungodliness, 'because his *faith* is reckoned for righteousness' (cf. comment on v. 3).

In the Old Testament judges are instructed to 'justify the righteous, and condemn the wicked,' but in the gospel it is God's unique prerogative to justify the 'ungodly' and that without injustice, as Romans 3:26 makes clear [*Deut.* 25:1]. But once the sinner *is* justified he neither remains ungodly [*1 Cor.* 6:11], nor is barren of the 'works' by which he is later 'justified' [*James* 2:20ff]. As such deeds are the *consequence* of God's transforming verdict it is obvious they can add nothing to it, but they do afford the visible proof of the reality of the saving change that has taken place.

6: Even as David also pronounceth blessing upon the man, unto whom God reckoneth righteousness apart from works,

7: saying, Blessed are they whose iniquities are forgiven,
And whose sins are covered.

8: Blessed is the man to whom the Lord will not reckon sin.

The fundamental importance of Genesis 15:6 in showing that faith is 'reckoned' for righteousness is confirmed by the use which is made of the same word in Psalm 32:1, 2. As John Murray observes, it is particularly pertinent to Paul's purpose that the man whom David pronounced blessed is not the man who has good works put to his account 'but whose *sins* are *not* laid to his account'. And the apostle rightly interprets this non-reckoning of sin as the positive imputation of righteousness. For though justification embraces much more than the remission of sin [cf. 5:17–21], he is able to take the part for the whole, because God's forgiveness necessarily implies the complete reinstatement of the sinner.

9: Is this blessing then pronounced upon the circumcision, or upon the uncircumcision also? for we say, To Abraham his faith was reckoned for righteousness.

10: How then was it reckoned? when he was in circumcision, or in uncircumcision? Not in circumcision, but in uncircumcision:

Paul now asks, Is this blessedness of which David spoke confined to those who are circumcised? He has already denied that circumcision is necessary to justification [3:29–31], but here reverts to the example of Abraham to explain why this rite must not be imposed upon Gentile believers [verses 9–12].

Circumcision was a question of critical importance in the early church. In the Jewish mind it was not a sign of God's grace, but the first meritorious act of obedience to the law, which became a symbol of an adherence to a scheme of salvation by works. It had taken pride of place in Paul's repentant recital of his former self-righteousness [*Phil.* 3:5]. Judaizers, who claimed to be Christians, constantly dogged the apostle's footsteps and endeavoured to force his Gentile converts to submit to circumcision. Paul sternly warned the Galatians that to consent to this demand was to fall from grace, for it became a token of their debt to fulfil the whole law [*Acts* 15:9, 10, 24; *Gal.* 5:1–4; *Phil.* 3:2, 3].

According to the indisputable testimony of Scripture Abraham's faith 'was reckoned for righteousness', but it must be farther asked, How – i.e. under what circumstances – was his faith thus reckoned to him?

Was it when he was in the state of circumcision or uncircumcision? That it was when he was still uncircumcised is the answer that lies on the very surface of the Old Testament record. 'Abraham's justification is narrated in Genesis 15, his circumcision not till Genesis 17, some fourteen years later: hence it was not his circumcision on which he depended for acceptance with God' (Denney).

> 11: and he received the sign of circumcision, a seal of the righteousness of the faith which he had while he was in uncircumcision: that he might be the father of all them that believe, though they be in uncircumcision, that righteousness might be reckoned unto them;

> 12: and the father of circumcision to them who not only are of the circumcision, but who also walk in the steps of that faith of our father Abraham which he had in uncircumcision.

In correcting the Jews' misplaced confidence in circumcision, Paul is careful not to discredit its real value as an ordinance of divine appointment. It was given to Abraham by God as a sign and seal of his *faith*. It was the external mark (sign) which was the authentication (seal) of the righteousness that was his by faith while he was still virtually a Gentile. As the visible token of his justification, it assured Abraham of the genuineness of his faith. But it added nothing to that faith, nor did it dispense with its necessity. Consequently it was no more of an automatic passport to salvation for unbelieving Jews, than are the sacraments today for unbelieving Gentiles.

Moreover, it was in the purpose of God that Abraham was justified by faith before he was circumcised since he thus became 'the father of all them that believe'. This shows that spiritual kinship and not physical descent is the determining factor. It is only those who share Abraham's faith, who are accounted his spiritual heirs. All uncircumcised believers are appropriately included among the children of Abraham, because the righteousness which was reckoned to him in that state, is also imputed to them upon exactly the same terms.

On the other hand, it must not be supposed for a moment that circumcision is a hindrance to faith. The circumcised who also share Abraham's 'uncircumcision-faith' may equally claim him as their father. 'Circumcision is not an excluding factor and neither is it a contributing factor to that by which we become the children of Abraham. All who are of faith "these are the sons of Abraham" [*Gal.* 3:7]' (John Murray).

13: For not through the law was the promise to Abraham or to his seed, that he should be heir of the world, but through the righteousness of faith.

Having shown that Abraham was justified by faith alone [verses 1–8], and that this 'uncircumcision-faith' made him the father of all believers [verses 9–12], Paul now confirms his argument by another consideration, namely, 'that law and promise are mutually exclusive ideas'. (Denney) For it was 'not through law' (ASV margin) *of any kind* that the promise was given to Abraham. John Murray points out that the absence of the article here serves to emphasize that the Mosaic economy is not in view, but simply law as law demanding obedience. God had acted unilaterally in giving Abraham a great promise, which was not suspended upon his obedience to any law, for that would have ruled out its fulfilment as the unconditional bestowment of grace. The promise is antithetical to law.

The gracious provisions of the promise apply not only to Abraham but also to his seed, who are his *spiritual* offspring, i.e. all believers [cf. verses 16, 17; whereas in Gal. 3:16 the 'seed' is Christ]. The words 'that he should be heir of the world' are not an exact quotation but a summary of the promises God made to Abraham [cf. *Gen.* 12:3, 18:18, 22:18].

Abraham was saved by his faith in the promise, but it is evident that neither he nor his seed have yet inherited the world. Hence this ultimate fulfilment of the promise still awaits Christ's return in glory [cf. *Matt.* 5:5; *2 Pet.* 3:13].

14: For if they which are of the law be heirs, faith is made void, and the promise is made of none effect:

Faith is made void and the promise is nullified if the inheritance is to be earned by an obedience to law, whether written upon the conscience or inscribed upon tables of stone. Paul here exposes the futility of Jewish unbelief in seeking righteousness by means of law, because law rules out both faith and the promise on which it rests (Lenski). Thus the man who seeks justification by works has substituted trust in his own ability for faith in the promise. But the true heirs rest upon the promise, for they know that they could never *merit* God's great salvation [cf. 10:1–10].

15: For the law worketh wrath; but where there is no law, neither is there transgression.

Paul now reveals the real result of this false faith to dash all hope of inheriting by law. For instead of producing the expected blessing, law works nothing for sinful men but wrath! This is the wrath of God which is called forth by man's constant contradiction of his law [1:18]. Without law there would be no sin, for sin is any lack of conformity to the demands of law [*1 John* 3:4]. As these demands are always spurned by man's transgressions, law unavoidably works wrath. 'The sin is as wide as the law; and the law has been shown to be as wide as the race [2:12–16]' (Shedd). Therefore justification by law is an impossibility [*Gal.* 3:10–12].

16: For this cause it is of faith, that it may be according to grace; to the end that the promise may be sure to all the seed; not to that only which is of the law, but to that also which is of the faith of Abraham, who is the father of us all

This states the conclusion that must be drawn from the preceding argument. Since an adherence to law only brings conviction of sin and ministers wrath, the one way in which sinners may receive the inheritance is through the faith which embraces the provisions of grace. 'Faith and grace cohere; law and the promised inheritance are contradictory' (John Murray).

God's purpose in determining that the inheritance should be 'of faith' was to make the promise sure to all the seed; not only to believers who are 'of *the* law' (i.e. those born under the Mosaic economy, Jews), but also to believing Gentiles having Abraham's faith if not his blood (Shedd). In describing Abraham as 'the father of us all', the apostle makes a unit of the two groups because their common faith has made them members of the same family [cf. *Gal.* 3:9].

17: (as it is written, A father of many nations have I made thee) before him whom he believed, even God, who giveth life to the dead, and calleth the things that are not, as though they were.

The parenthetical appeal to Genesis 17:5 proves that Abraham's spiritual fatherhood extends to Gentiles as well as Jews, for this quotation from the Greek version of the Old Testament renders 'nations' by the same word that Paul uses for 'Gentiles' = *ethne* (so C. K. Barrett).

Who is the father of us all . . . before him whom he believed: The connection is with the preceding verse. Abraham is our father because he is so before God. In the eternal purpose of God Abraham was destined to be the spiritual prototype of all who believe. For Abraham this purpose of God was as certain when it was expressed in the form of promise as if it had already passed into the sphere of accomplishment, and herein lies the distinctive character of his faith. As the promise given to Abraham appeared to face insuperable difficulties, it demanded an omnipotent God for its fulfilment. It was to just such a God that Abraham's faith was directed [verse 20].

First, he is the God 'who giveth life to the dead'. The promise of an heir to this aged couple called for nothing less than the supernatural impartation of life [verse 19]. Similarly, all spiritual vivification belongs to God alone [*Eph*. 1:19, 20].

Secondly, he 'calleth the things that are not, as though they were'. 'The word "call" is used of God's effectual word and determination' (John Murray). God's decree gives a certain future to those things which are without present existence. Because Abraham believed that the declared purpose of God must come to pass, he received the promise as though it were the fulfilment [cf. *Heb*. 11:1].

18: Who in hope believed against hope, to the end that he might become a father of many nations, according to that which had been spoken, So shall thy seed be.

'Who in hope believed against hope' is a striking description of Abraham's faith. 'It was both contrary to hope (as far as nature could give hope), and rested on hope (that God could do what nature could not)' (Denney). And Abraham so believed against every evidence to the contrary, in order that God's declared purpose might be fulfilled through him. He faced the obstacles that stood in the way of his becoming a father at all without any weakening of faith [verse 19], because every time he looked at the stars in the heavens he was reminded of the Promiser's creative power (though Paul quotes only part of Genesis 15:5, Lightfoot says 'his readers would mentally continue it'). 'It is the nature of faith to believe God upon his bare word . . . It will not be, saith sense; it cannot be, saith reason; it both can and will be, saith faith, for I have a promise for it.' (Trapp)

19: And without being weakened in faith he considered his own body now as good as dead (he being about a hundred years old), and the deadness of Sarah's womb;

In order to show that the fulfilment of God's promise was strictly supernatural in character, Abraham and Sarah were denied an heir until all natural hope was extinguished. 'This explains why, in the life of Abraham, so many things proceed contrary to nature . . . Abraham was kept childless until an age when he was "as good as dead", that the divine omnipotence might be evident as the source of Isaac's birth [*Gen.* 21:1–7; *Rom.* 4:19–21; *Heb.* 11:11; *Isa.* 51:2].' (Geerhardus Vos, *Biblical Theology*, p. 81).

The omission of 'not' in the best texts is important (cf. AV: 'he considered *not* his own body now dead'). For it shows that though Abraham was not blind to the empirical facts of the situation, he did not allow them to have an adverse effect upon his faith in the promise. He faced up to his own and his wife's 'deadness' without doubting God's Word.

20: yet, looking unto the promise of God, he wavered not through unbelief, but waxed strong through faith, giving glory to God,

21: and being fully assured that what he had promised, he was able also to perform.

It was because Abraham's attention was fixed upon the promise, that he was not inwardly torn by distrust; but was rather strengthened in faith, giving glory to God. Believing God's Word always gives glory to God. It honours *his promises* by taking him at his word, and it honours *his power* by acknowledging his ability to do the impossible [*Mark* 10:27]. Unlike the unbelieving [1:21], Abraham glorified God as God, by recognizing him as the all-powerful Creator who could not fail to keep his covenanted word (so Barrett).

22: Wherefore also it was reckoned unto him for righteousness.

'Wherefore also' indicates the consequence of the faith described in verses 20, 21. Abraham's specific and unqualified reliance on God's promise was the necessary condition, but not the ground of his justification. Since this unwavering faith glorified God by reckoning upon his faithfulness, God also reckoned it to Abraham for righteousness [*Gen.* 15:6, see also comment on verse 3].

23: Now it was not written for his sake alone, that it was reckoned unto him;

24: but for our sake also, unto whom it shall be reckoned, who believe on him that raised Jesus our Lord from the dead,

25: who was delivered up for our trespasses, and was raised for our justification.

In conclusion Paul drives home the lesson to be learned from the history of Abraham [cf. *1 Cor.* 10:11]. For the same divine reckoning by which Abraham was justified will be reckoned to all who believe after the pattern of his faith. This identical method of reckoning shows that Abraham was not justified by a faith which was radically different from that of the Christian. In fact there is an identity of belief which makes his example of abiding significance for the Christian. 'He believed in God as quickening the dead, that is, as able to raise up from one as good as dead, the promised Redeemer' (Hodge). Therefore Christ declared, 'Abraham rejoiced to see my day; and he saw it, and was glad' [*John* 8:56]. However, the Christian enjoys the fulfilment of that which Abraham only received in the form of promise, for Paul succinctly describes this as believing 'on him that raised Jesus our Lord from the dead'. In the New Testament, belief in the gospel is frequently expressed as a belief in the resurrection, because this climactic event is at once the ultimate vindication of Christ's claim to be the Son of God, and the decisive proof of God's acceptance of his redeeming work [10:9; *Acts* 1:22, 4:33, 17:31; *1 Cor.* 15].

It should be noticed that Paul knows nothing of a 'Jesus' worship, which would force God the Father into the background of men's minds. He explicitly states that saving belief is focused on him who 'waked' Jesus. As Geerhardus Vos says, The Father's power was exercised in the resurrection of Jesus, so that through him it may work upon others.

Who was delivered up for our trespasses, and was raised for our justification. In this brief sentence of profound import and eloquent simplicity, there is distilled the very sum of saving knowledge. It is best to take both expressions as having prospective reference: 'He was delivered up on account of our offences – to make atonement for them; and he was raised on account of our justification – that it might become an accomplished fact' (Denney). Christ's death and resurrection are inseparable because they form one redemptive act; neither makes sense without the other, so that whenever one is mentioned the other is always implied. Here again our attention is directed to the action of God the Father in delivering up his Son to make atonement for our sins [8:32; *Acts* 2:23], and in raising him for our justification [6:4; *Acts* 3:15; *Gal.* 1:1]. And we are thereby taught to ascribe all the glory of our salvation to God who designed, provided, and executed this great work of redemption.

Paul here says that Christ was raised for our justification, for though the work of atonement was finished on the cross, the righteousness by which we are justified is forever embodied in the living Lord through whom this grace is mediated to us [John Murray; cf. 5:2, *1 Cor.* 1:30]. But it would have been equally legitimate to say that he died for our justification, since his redeeming death is the basis of our reinstatement before God [cf. 5: 9; *Eph* 1:7]. However, the verse as it stands, serves to show that Paul never thought of the cross by itself, for 'he knew Christ only as the Risen One who had died, and who had the virtue of his atoning death ever in him' (Denney).

CHAPTER FIVE

In what follows Paul expounds the blessed consequences that flow from Christ's having been raised for our justification. As Nygren puts it, All who have this new life in Christ are free from wrath [ch. 5], free from sin [ch. 6], free from law [ch. 7], and free from death [ch. 8].

1: Being therefore justified by faith, we have peace with God through our Lord Jesus Christ;

Although 'let us have peace with God' (RV) is the better attested reading, it is rejected by most scholars because it is inconsistent with the context. Exhortation is entirely out of place in a passage where Paul is speaking of the objective benefits of justification [verses 10, 11], and there can be no doubt that his meaning is 'we *have* peace with God' (as in AV, ASV, RSV).

'Therefore' introduces the conclusion to be drawn from the preceding argument [cf. 12:1]. '*Therefore,*' says the apostle, 'having been justified by faith, we have peace with God.' This means that God's wrath no longer threatens us, because we are accepted in Christ [verse 9]. What is indicated is not a change in our feelings, but a change in God's relation to us. And this objective peace with God is not only the purchase of Christ's blood but also the fruit of his continued mediation. 'All spiritual blessings are *in* Christ. But they are also enjoyed *through* Christ's continued mediatory activity' (John Murray).

2: through whom also we have had our access by faith into this grace wherein we stand; and we rejoice in hope of the glory of God.

It is also through the mediation of Christ that we have had our 'introduction' by faith into this grace of justification in which we have come to stand. The idea suggested by the word is that of introduction to the presence-chamber of the king. As Sanday and Headlam observe, 'The rendering "access" is inadequate, as it leaves out of sight the fact that we do not come in our own strength but need an "introducer" – Christ.' Having once been ushered into this state of grace and favour, it is our immutable privilege to enjoy unhindered communion with the Father.

It would be strange if these blessings did not promote within the believing heart a lively sense of assurance and confident hope. Indeed the word translated as 'rejoice' really means an exultant boasting, which is inspired by the certainty that 'we have peace with God' [verse 1]. This glorying is faith's present anticipation of the glory to be revealed at the consummation of God's eternal purpose in Christ, when our chief end shall be realized as we 'glorify God and enjoy him for ever' [cf. 8:17–25; *2 Cor.* 3:18; *Col.* 3:4; *1 John* 3:2].

3: And not only so, but we also rejoice in our tribulations: knowing that tribulation worketh stedfastness;
4: and stedfastness, approvedness; and approvedness, hope:

But our boasting is not confined to the hope of future glory; we also see our present trials as a cause for exultation! This glorying in tribulation is a fruit of faith, for as Calvin says, 'This is not the natural effect of tribulation, which, as we see, provokes a great part of mankind to murmur against God, and even to curse him.' It is only the knowledge that these tribulations are the appointment of his heavenly Father, which enables the Christian to rejoice in them, for in themselves they are evil, grievous and not joyous [*Heb.* 12:6; *Rev.* 3:19]. Paul's own experience was in line with his teaching, 'that we must through much tribulation enter into the kingdom of God' [*Acts* 14:22]. There is no short cut to glory. The believer must follow the path marked out for him by his Saviour, for the cross always precedes the crown [*Phil.* 1: 29, 30].

We can glory in tribulation because we have come to know that it works in us a spirit of brave endurance. It is by the exercise of this grace that the Christian approves himself and shows that he is no fair-weather professor [*Matt.* 13:21]. Hence the endurance of these trials provides the Christian with subjective evidence of his own sincerity. His Christian character is proved by his patience in tribulation, which in turn assures him of the genuineness of his hope [*1 Pet.* 1:7]. John Murray draws attention to the fact that the apostle has described a circle which begins and ends in hope. He insists that 'glorying in tribulations is subordinate – they subserve the interests of hope'. Accordingly, the believer's present trials must always be viewed in the light of their eternal sequel [*1 Pet.* 4:12, 13].

5: and hope putteth not to shame; because the love of God hath been shed abroad in our hearts through the Holy Spirit which was given unto us.

This is the one hope that is well founded, and so, unlike those who have embraced a delusory hope, we are not put to shame [cf. *Psa.* 25:20]. On the contrary, it is the hope in which we glory even in the midst of our afflictions. Haldane here points out the connection between the Christian's hope and his power to witness; 'Just in proportion as his hope is strong, will he make an open and bold profession of the truth . . . This shows the great importance of keeping our hope unclouded. If we suffer it to flag or grow faint, we shall be ashamed of it before men.'

We are able to sustain this hope in such straits, 'because the love of God has been poured out in our hearts through the Holy Spirit who was given to us.' It is evident from the context that Paul refers to God's love for us [verse 8], and not our love for him as Romish expositors maintain on dogmatic grounds following Augustine (cf. Nygren's vigorous protest). It is not without significance that in this verse both the love of God and the Holy Spirit are mentioned for the first time in the epistle, for only he can communicate to us the sense of God's love. This is in fact a concise statement of the theme which is fully developed by Paul in Chapter 8. 'Poured out' indicates the lavish diffusion of this love which carries with it the irrefragable assurance of salvation [cf. *Acts* 2:17, 18, 33, 10:45; 'poured out upon us richly,' *Titus* 3:6]. The sphere of the Spirit's operation is the heart to which he has immediate access; it being his special work to apply the benefits of redemption to those for whom the Saviour suffered. 'Who was given to us' harks back to the time of conversion, for it is only in the Spirit that a man can savingly confess 'Jesus is Lord' [1 Cor. 12:3; cf. 8:9].

'Though sinners should hear ten thousand times of the love of God in the gift of his Son, they are never properly affected by it, till the Holy Spirit enters into their hearts, and till love to him is produced by the truth through the Spirit' (Haldane).

6: For while we were yet weak, in due season Christ died for the ungodly.

The supreme demonstration of the love of God is seen in Christ's death for the ungodly. This love is at once original and unmerited, for it is extended to those who are completely powerless to help themselves. 'Sinful' seems to be the meaning of 'weak' here, for 'while we were yet weak' is almost synonymous with 'while we were yet sinners' (verse 8). It was therefore while we were under the condemning power of sin, while we were wholly disabled by sin, that Christ died for our benefit. God could find nothing in the 'ungodly' to constrain his love [cf. 4:5]. The amazing character of God's love thus lies in the fact that it was exercised towards those whose natural condition was absolutely repugnant to his holiness. And it is only as we are taught by grace to acknowledge this unpalatable truth that the boundless nature of God's love begins to dawn upon us. 'In due season' means that Christ died at the time appointed by God, and in accordance with his eternal purpose [*John* 8: 20, 12:27, 17: 1; *Gal.* 4:4; *Heb.* 9: 26].

7: For scarcely for a righteous man will one die: for peradventure for the good man some one would even dare to die.

8: But God commendeth his own love towards us, in that, while we were yet sinners, Christ died for us.

It is not likely that Paul is drawing a contrast between a righteous and a good man, and it is better to understand both epithets as describing the same individual. As John Murray explains it, 'In the human sphere scarcely for a *righteous* and *good* man will one die but God exhibits and commends *his* love in that it was for *sinners* Christ died.' It is obvious that 'righteous' and 'good' are used *relatively* of man's judgment, for the universal dominion of sin has already been proved at length. A man may indeed be prepared to make the ultimate sacrifice to save someone whom he *deems* to be worthy of it, but God gave up his Son to the death of the cross for those whom he *knew* to be utterly vile and worthless! The comparison thus brings out the unique character of God's love, which reached its zenith in Christ's death for sinners [*John* 3: 16; *1 John* 4:10]. From this it follows that conviction of sin is the essential prerequisite to an interest in Christ [*Mark* 2: 17]. Hence those who imagine that they are without sin necessarily exclude themselves from all the blessings which Christ purchased for sinners by his death [*1 John* 1:8–10]. 'While we were yet sinners' implies that the readers are no longer in that state of condemnation [cf. 1:7], 'for he died to save us, not *in* our sins, but *from* our sins; but we were yet sinners when he died for us' (Matthew Henry). [*Matt.* 1:21].

9: Much more then, being now justified by his blood, shall we be saved from the wrath of God through him.

The Christian faith is not groundless optimism, but a confident hope based upon cogent reasoning. The argument is that if Christians were justified by the death of Christ when they were lost in sin, how much more shall they be saved from wrath now that they are restored to God's favour. In this section the one-sided nature of God's action in salvation is strongly brought out by Paul's graphic description of man's plight. In verse 6, 'powerless' (NEB) indicates a total inability to obey God's commands while 'ungodly' points to the inevitable connection which exists between godlessness and the lack of godliness. In verse 8 the word 'sinners' describes those who are by nature and by inclination addicted to disobedience, and in verse 10 'enemies' means those who hate God, and who are by reason of their sin, hateful to God. Thus, it was for man, helpless and hopeless, that Christ died. Paul 'assumes that Christ's death put sinners on a new footing, a new standing before

God; in a word, that it rectified their relation. And then he argues: "If justified as sinners by his blood, much more shall we as friends be saved from wrath through him'" (Smeaton).

The hope of glory necessarily includes the assurance that through Christ we shall be saved from the wrath to come [*John* 3:36]. 'It was a virile conception of God that the apostle entertained and, because so, it was one that took account of the terror of God's wrath. Salvation from the future exhibition of that terror was an ingredient of the hope of glory' (John Murray). [2:5, 8; *1 Thess.* 1:10, 5:9]

10: For if, while we were enemies, we were reconciled to God through the death of his Son, much more, being reconciled, shall we be saved by his life;

The argument of this verse is based on the two states of Christ, for if reconciliation was made by means of his humiliating death, then how much more shall his glorious resurrection life ensure the final salvation of those for whom he suffered.

As Denney rightly insists, 'enemies' must be given the passive meaning it undoubtedly has in 11:28. We were *God's* enemies, not merely ourselves hostile to God, but in a real sense the objects of his hostility by reason of our sin. This meant that our restoration to divine favour depended entirely upon God, the Offended One, taking the initiative in reconciling the offenders to himself. And this he did by removing the sin, which was the ground of that enmity, through the death of his Son.

Therefore to suggest that what is in view is the laying aside of our hostility is to miss the point of the whole passage. 'Paul is demonstrating *the love of God*, and he can only do it by pointing to what God has done, not to what we have done . . . The subjective side of the truth is here completely, *and intentionally*, left out of sight; the laying aside of *our* hostility adds nothing to God's love, throws no light on it; hence in an exposition of the love of God it can be ignored' (Denney).

'Much more' indicates an indissoluble connection between Christ's death and resurrection, because it assures all who are reconciled to God by Christ's death of their perseverance to glory by virtue of his endless life.

11: and not only so, but we also rejoice in God through our Lord Jesus Christ, through whom we have now received the reconciliation.

Having spoken in the previous verse of reconciliation in terms of its objective accomplishment, the apostle now describes the glorying in God which attends its subjective application. The knowledge that God is a reconciled Father in Jesus Christ suffuses the believing heart with exultant joy. Salvation is a present reality for the Christian. And as God was reconciled by the death of the Mediator, even so believers receive this reconciliation *through* the mediation of their exalted Redeemer. As the concluding words of the verse unmistakably show, reconciliation 'is not a change in our disposition toward God, but a change in his attitude toward us. We do not *give* it (by laying aside enmity, distrust, or fear); we *receive* it, by believing in Christ Jesus, whom God has set forth as a propitiation through faith in his blood. We take it as God's unspeakable gift' (Denney).

12: Therefore, as through one man sin entered into the world, and death through sin; and so death passed unto all men, for that all sinned:

The Puritan Thomas Goodwin said, 'In God's sight there are two men – Adam and Jesus Christ – and these two men have all other men hanging at their girdle strings' (cited by F. F. Bruce). This passage makes it clear that Paul regarded Adam as the first man, whose disobedience to God's commandment had far-reaching consequences for the human race. But for those modern scholars who regard the Fall as a mythical statement of what is nevertheless a valid religious truth, Adam becomes a sort of religious Everyman. It would be frivolous to reproduce such a view as an exposition of the apostle's teaching in this place. The right to be regarded as a serious interpreter of Paul's gospel rests upon a willingness to remain within the boundaries of his thought. It does not consist in expounding what the apostle would have taught if only he had been better informed! According to Paul, Adam is a type of Christ, but only by way of complete contrast. Adam's transgression involved the whole race in sin, condemnation and death, whereas Christ's obedience purchased righteousness, justification, and life for his people. His design is to show that God's justification of the ungodly proceeds on the same principle by which Adam's sin was imputed to his posterity. Therefore a rejection of solidarity in sin is also a denial of solidarity in grace.

Unhappily the big guns of modern 'science' have persuaded most scholars today to make a strategic withdrawal from the front line of biblical supernaturalism to take up a position which they imagine can be more easily defended against the attacks of unbelief. However, J. G. Vos has pointed out the consequences of this capitulation to the prevailing climate of scepticism: 'This argument of Paul in Romans 5 depends absolutely for its validity on the fact that as Jesus was a historical person so Adam was a historical person. There cannot be a proper parallel between a mythical Adam and an historical Christ. Adam is as essential to the Christian system of theology as Jesus Christ is. Christ is, indeed, called in Scripture "the second Adam" or "the last Adam". Any theory which tends, as the common form of evolution does, to eliminate Adam as a real historical person, is destructive of Christianity. Yet this very thing is done by the common form of evolutionary theory. It has no more room for a real Adam than it has for a real fall of mankind into sin. And if Christ as the second Adam came to undo the harm done by the first Adam, then we must needs continue to believe in the reality of the first Adam' (*Surrender to Evolution: Inevitable or Inexcusable?*, p. 20).

Therefore, as through one man sin entered into the world, and death through sin: How much of the preceding context is summed up in this 'therefore' is a matter of dispute. Nygren does not take it to refer to any particular verse or statement, but to the presupposition which underlies all that Paul has said. It introduces an explicit statement of what has so far only been implied, namely, that Adam and Christ are the respective heads of the two ages; Adam is the head of the old age of *death*, and Christ is the head of the new age of *life*. 'As' begins a comparison which has no corresponding 'so' to complete it. This is because the extraordinary content of the verse called for an explanatory parenthesis [verses 13–17]. John Murray notes that each part of the verse has a distinct emphasis. 'In the first half the accent falls upon the *entrance* of sin and death through *one man*. In the second part the accent falls upon the universal *penetration* of death and the sin of *all.*'

Adam was not the originator of sin, 'for the devil sinneth from the beginning,' but humanity was introduced to sin by Adam's failure to obey God [*1 John* 3:8]. As the image-bearer of God, Adam's life consisted in communion with his Maker, so separation from God resulted in Adam's death [*Gen.* 2:17, 3:19]. Sin meant that Adam could no longer live in fellowship with God in the garden. 'The root of death is in having been sent forth from God' (Vos). Death is not natural to the constitution of man, but is the penal consequence of sin [6:23]. If Adam had not sinned, he need not have died. In that case it is probable that eternal life would have been imparted to him by means of the tree of life [*Gen.* 3:22]. 'After man should have been made sure of the attainment of the highest life, the tree would appropriately have been the sacramental means for communicating the highest life' (Vos, *Biblical Theology*, p. 28). But by disobeying God he partook instead of the sacrament of death (James Philip).

And so death passed unto all men for that all sinned: Although it is possible to understand this statement as referring to the voluntary sins of all men, the context clearly forbids this interpretation, because Paul, no less than five times, explicitly states that the universal sway of death is due to the single sin of one man [verses 15, 16, 17, 18, 19]. The only satisfactory solution to the problem is to be found in the representative relation which Adam sustained to the race. 'In Adam all die' [*1 Cor.* 15:22] can only be explained by the fact 'that in Adam all sin'. Sin is traced back to Adam, 'because we are in Adam in a peculiar manner, not only as our seminal root but also as our representative head' (John Murray, *The Imputation of Adam's Sin*, p. 82).

> **13: for until the law sin was in the world; but sin is not imputed when there is no law.**
>
> **14: Nevertheless death reigned from Adam until Moses, even over them that had not sinned after the likeness of Adam's transgression, who is a figure of him that was to come.**

The purpose of Paul's parenthesis is to prove his statement that 'death passed unto all men' through the single sin of Adam. This is made evident by the fact that sin was in the world up to the time that the law was given by Moses. But in accordance with the principle already stated in 4:15, the presence of sin always implies the existence of some kind of law, for the simple reason that 'sin is not imputed when there is no law'. Yet from Adam to Moses death reigned 'even over them that had not sinned after the likeness of Adam's transgression', i.e. over those who unlike Adam stood outside the pale of special revelation and did not therefore openly and willingly violate the positive command of God. Paul's assumption is that *this universal reign of death cannot be explained except by the transgression of an expressly revealed commandment*, and since that cannot be laid to the charge of each and every member of the race, the only sin that can account for it is the sin of Adam and the participation of all in that sin (so John Murray).

In the concluding clause of verse 14 Adam is said to be 'a figure of him that was to come'. It is because Adam's one act of disobedience is imputed to others, whose activity was not personally and voluntarily engaged in its performance, that he is here described as a type of Christ. For as the sin of Adam was the ground of our condemnation, so the righteousness of Christ is the ground of our justification. Adam's one sin sufficed to ruin the race, but Christ's obedience conferred righteousness upon his people. Just as 'death reigned over those who did not sin after the similitude of Adam's transgression' so the apostle is 'chiefly interested in demonstrating that men are justified who do not act righteously after the similitude of Christ's obedience' (John Murray).

15: But not as the trespass, so also is the free gift. For if by the trespass of the one the many died, much more did the grace of God, and the gift by the grace of the one man, Jesus Christ, abound unto the many.

Verses 15–17 qualify the final clause of the previous verse, 'who is a figure of him that was to come,' so that Paul does not complete the comparison begun in verse 12 until verse 18. This verse begins with an emphatic negation, calculated to dispel any illusion that there is an exact correspondence between the sin of Adam and the work of Christ. Certainly the free gift is not like the transgression, for we gain far more in Christ than ever we lost through Adam [cf. *Eph.* 2:4–7]. As the 'much more' indicates, we have here another *a fortiori* argument which extols the munificence of God's grace in our salvation [cf. verses 9, 10, 17]. It was through the trespass of the *one* that *the many* died ('many' is used for the sake of emphasis, though of course all mankind is meant). But grace not only annuls the sentence of condemnation, it also abounds unto justification and life! John Murray draws attention to the piling up of expressions which throws into relief the free grace of God. God's gratuitous favour is manifested in the free gift of righteousness [verse 17], which is the gift by the grace of the one man

Jesus Christ. In speaking of the smaller company who are thus blessed, Paul probably alludes to Isaiah 53:11, 'where the Servant of the Lord justifies "the many"' (F. F. Bruce).

16: And not as through one that sinned, so is the gift: for the judgment came of one unto condemnation, but the free gift came of many trespasses unto justification.

Another compressed statement serves to introduce a fresh point of contrast. The gift far exceeds one man's sinning. For through the single sin of one man the judgment of condemnation came upon all men, but the free gift took account of many transgressions which were all embraced in the one verdict of justification. This is the amazing grace that not only reverses our just condemnation in Adam, but also declares us righteous because Christ has completely satisfied the claims of divine justice on our behalf [2 *Cor.* 5: 21]. 'Christ has done far more than remove the curse pronounced on us for the one sin of Adam; he procures our justification from our own innumerable offences' (Hodge).

17: For if, by the trespass of the one, death reigned through the one; much more shall they that receive the abundance of grace and of the gift of righteousness reign in life through the one, even Jesus Christ.

The final contrast shows that the terrible consequences of the Fall are more than overcome through the justifying righteousness of Christ which is freely put to our account ('imputed not infused' – Sanday and Headlam; cf. 3:21, 22, 10: 3; *Phil.* 3:9). If Adam's one trespass brought the whole race *under the reign* of death, then how much more shall they who receive the abundance of grace and the gift of righteousness *reign in life*, both now and in the glory to come, through the continuous mediation of the one, Jesus Christ. 'If the union with Adam in his sin was certain to bring destruction, the union with Christ in his righteousness is yet more certain to bring salvation' (Shedd).

18: So then as through one trespass the judgment came unto all men to condemnation; even so through one act of righteousness the free gift came unto all men to justification of life.

This verbless summary brings the parallel which was begun in verse 12 to a striking conclusion: 'So then as through one trespass – unto all men condemnation; even so through one act of righteousness – unto all men to justification of life.' If the second 'all' is coextensive with the first, then the passage teaches a universalism that is contrary to the total testimony of Scripture. What Paul has in view is not the numerical extent of those saved; he is showing what the respective acts of Adam and Christ mean for those they represent. All who are condemned are condemned through the *one trespass* of Adam, and all who are justified are justified because of the *one righteous act* of Christ. Christ's whole earthly course, culminating in the death of the cross, is here referred to as a single act, because his complete obedience purchased for his people a righteousness as indivisible as that seamless robe which once he wore [cf. *Matt.* 3:15; *John* 8:29; *Gal.* 4:4; *Phil.* 2:8]. The phrase 'justification of life' means 'justification entitling to, and issuing in, the rightful possession and enjoyment of life' (David Brown).

19: For as through the one man's disobedience the many were made sinners, even so through the obedience of the one shall the many be made righteous.

As it is by the imputation of Adam's disobedience that many are 'constituted sinners', so it is through the imputation of Christ's obedience that many are 'constituted righteous'. 'Viewed from the standpoint of personal, voluntary action the disobedience in the one case is that of Adam and the obedience is that of Christ. But the effect of the "constituting" act is that others, not personally and voluntarily engaged, come to have property, indeed propriety, in the personal, voluntary performance of another' (John Murray, *The Imputation of Adam's Sin*, p. 88). As the representative head of his people, Christ came to render a perfect obedience to all the *precepts* of the law in order to fulfil all righteousness on their behalf [cf. verse 18]. But because a broken law also called for the willing endurance of the *penalty* it pronounced against its transgressors, it was necessary for the Surety of a sinful people to exhaust that penalty in his own body on the tree [*1 Pet.* 2:24]. Only Christ could render such a perfect obedience to God, and this he did for those he represented [*John* 17: 2].

Our being placed in the category of the righteous is the blessed consequence of Christ's 'one act of righteousness'. This is not a bare declaration; it is also a constitutive act. Justification means that our participation in the benefits of Christ's righteousness is as real as was our involvement in the misery of Adam's sin. And this is because the same principle is at work in each of the 'constituting' acts. The future tense does not mean that justification is an act which is reserved for the consummation, but that it continues as an operative principle to the end of the age in order to include all who shall be justified by Christ's obedience. This doctrine was given beautiful expression by the writer of the Epistle to Diognetus, 'O the sweet exchange, O the inscrutable creation, O the unlooked for benefits, that the sin of many should be put out of sight in one Righteous Man, and the righteousness of one should justify many sinners!' (quoted by F. F. Bruce).

20: And the law came in besides, that the trespass might abound; but where sin abounded, grace did abound more exceedingly:

21: that, as sin reigned in death, even so might grace reign through righteousness unto eternal life through Jesus Christ our Lord.

In making his comparison between Adam and Christ, Paul has already referred to the Mosaic law [verses 13, 14], and now he explains its particular bearing upon the situation that was brought into being through Adam's trespass. In the purpose of God it 'came in alongside' in order that the trespass might abound. 'Adam's trespass was disobedience to expressly revealed commandment. When the law came in through Moses, there was henceforth a multiplication of the kind of transgression exemplified in Adam's trespass, that is to say, transgression of clearly revealed commandment.' (John Murray) So though the Jews imagine the law to be the very citadel of sanctity, it is in fact the divine searchlight that not only shows up sin for what it is, but also arouses the enmity of the heart so that it actually provokes further transgressions [cf. 7:8, 11, 13]. Such a 'law-work' is a necessary preparation for the profitable reception of the gospel, for it is only through the work of the law that a man becomes convinced of his need of an interest in the Saviour from sin.

But where sin abounded, grace did abound more exceedingly: This superabounding provision of grace does not apply to *all* who have abounded in sin; it is 'particular, and peculiar to the elect; to them only the grace of God is superabundant after that they have abounded in sin, and by how much the greater is their guilt, by so much the greater is the grace of God in the free forgiveness thereof' (Poole).

That, as sin reigned in death, even so might grace reign through righteousness unto eternal life: This wholly unexpected boon was the result of the divine design. For it was God's purpose that the benefits of redemption should vastly exceed the evils of man's rebellion. 'The issues of a *divine* act working salvation are much more sure, than the issues of a *human* act working ruin' (Philippi). Adam's sin had introduced the seemingly interminable reign of death, but God savingly intervened to strip sin of its sovereignty [6:23]. He made provision for the reign of grace, even the grace that reigns *through righteousness* unto eternal life. The righteousness contemplated is that which was wrought out by the Second Adam, whose complete obedience purchased a title to eternal life for all he represented. 'Grace did not, could not, deliver the lawful captives without paying the ransom. It did not trample on justice, or evade its demands. It reigns by providing a Saviour to suffer in the room of the guilty. By the death of Jesus Christ, full compensation was made to the law and justice of God' (Haldane).

Through Jesus Christ our Lord: Paul's reverence for his exalted Lord is very evident here, and is consistent with apostolic usage. The human name 'Jesus' may suffice to describe or emphasize the humiliation of the Incarnate life, but the undimmed glory of his Resurrection life demands the full title, 'Jesus Christ our Lord'. As the Christian's life is 'hid with Christ in God', his gaze must ever be directed to the beatific vision of the glorified Lord [*Col.* 3:1–4]. Eternal life, together with every other spiritual blessing, is conveyed to believers *through* the continual mediation in heaven of their enthroned Priest-King.

CHAPTER SIX

1: What shall we say then? Shall we continue in sin, that grace may abound? God forbid.

A grace which superabounds over sin may prompt a carnal heart to reason, 'The more I sin, the more God's grace is glorified in my justification.' Paul puts the objection in the form of a question, 'partly to show his dislike that his doctrine should be so perverted, and partly to show the peace of his own conscience, that he was far from such a thought' (Poole). This licentious inference is at once energetically rejected by the apostle as an abuse of grace.

2b: We who died to sin, how shall we any longer live therein ?

The absurdity of supposing that Christians can live in sin is exposed by giving the reason for its rejection in the form of a question. They are not only 'dead to sin' (as the AV inadequately translates) but they 'died' to it in the past – the tense pointing to a definitive, once-for-all act. Thus the question is, 'We, being as we are persons who died to sin, how shall we any longer live therein?' The impossibility of the believer living in sin is this way asserted in the strongest possible manner. The force of Paul's thought and the foundation of the ensuing argument is the fact that *believers have died to sin*, and it is this decisive breach with sin which constitutes their identity.

Therefore, 'the person who has died to sin no longer lives and acts in the sphere or realm of sin . . . There is a kingdom of sin, or darkness, and of death. The forces of iniquity rule there. It is the kingdom of this world and it lies in the wicked one [cf. *2 Cor.* 4:3, 4; *Eph.* 2:1–3; *1 John* 5:19]. The person who has died to sin no longer lives there; it is no more the world of his thought, affection, will, life, and action. His well-springs are now in the kingdom which is totally antithetical, the kingdom of God and of his righteousness' (John Murray, *Principles of Conduct*, pp. 204–5). [*Gal.* 1:4; *Col.* 1:12, 13; *1 Pet.* 4:1–4].

3: Or are ye ignorant that all we who were baptized into Christ Jesus were baptized into his death?

Another question at once serves to substantiate the apostle's thesis and to reprove his readers for failing to grasp the implications of their baptism (the same method is used extensively in 1 Corinthians, see for example *1 Cor.* 3:16, 6:15). As Denney says, 'There is no argument in the passage at all, unless all Christians were baptized.' In accordance with the command of Christ and the practice of the apostles, all who were converted by the preaching of the gospel in the early church confessed their faith in Christ in baptism [*Matt.* 28:19; *Acts* 2:38].

The force of the question therefore lies in its appeal to what all believers know from experience, viz. baptism 'into Christ' signifies union with Christ in his death. But they must further recognize that this not only means that they died with him, but that in doing so *they also died to sin!*

4: We were buried therefore with him through baptism into death: that like as Christ was raised from the dead through the glory of the Father, so we also might walk in newness of life.

This verse shows that baptism not only sets forth the union of believers with Christ in his death, but that it also has the positive purpose of identifying them with him in his resurrection life. 'They were, in fact, "buried" with Christ when they were plunged in the baptismal water, in token that they had died so far as their old life of sin was concerned; they were raised again with Christ when they emerged from the water, in token that they had received a new life, which was nothing less than participation in Christ's own resurrection life' (F. F. Bruce). And the terms in which this truth is expressed impressively illustrate the glory and dignity of the new life which is theirs in Christ. For just as Christ was raised by the Father's glorious power, so they have been raised to walk 'in a new state, which is life.' (Lightfoot) [cf. *Eph.* 1:19, 20; 2:1].

Although the New Testament commonly refers to believers as those for whom Christ died, a number of passages also state that they died in Christ [6:3–11; *2 Cor.* 5:14, 15; *Eph.* 2:4–7; *Col.* 3:3]. 'All for whom Christ died also died in Christ. All who died in Christ rose again with Christ. This rising again with Christ is a rising to newness of life after the likeness of Christ's resurrection. To die with Christ is, therefore, to die to sin and to rise with him to the life of new obedience, to live not to ourselves but to him who died for us and rose again. The inference is inevitable that those for whom Christ died are those and those only who die to sin and live to righteousness' (John Murray, *Redemption – Accomplished and Applied*, p. 70).

5: For if we have become united with him in the likeness of his death, we shall be also in the likeness of his resurrection;

The preceding reference to our new life in Christ is proved by the fact that identity with him in the likeness of his death must be followed by identity with him in the likeness of his resurrection. On the word 'likeness', John Murray says that it shows Paul is not speaking of '*our* physical death and resurrection; he is dealing with our death to sin and our resurrection to spiritual life.' To denote the certainty of this the apostle uses the future tense ('we shall be'). The verse is therefore 'another reminder that the death and resurrection of Christ are inseparable. Those for whom Christ died are those for whom he rose again and his heavenly saving activity is of equal extent with his once-for-all redemptive accomplishments' (op. cit., p. 71).

6: knowing this, that our old man was crucified with him, that the body of sin might be done away, that so we should no longer be in bondage to sin;

An appreciation of this argument should lead us to acknowledge that 'our old man was crucified with him'. This means that the old man *no longer lives*, our unregenerate self was crucified with Christ. Paul speaks of a completed act and not of a continuing process. It is because the old man is dead and buried that the believer's struggle with indwelling sin cannot be explained in terms of an antithesis between the old man and the new man. 'The believer is a new man, a new creation, but he is a new man not yet made perfect. Sin dwells in him still, and he still commits sin. He is necessarily the subject of progressive renewal . . . But this *progressive* renewal is not represented as the putting off of the old man and the putting on of the new' (John Murray, *Principles of Conduct*, p. 219; for a detailed consideration of *Col.* 3:9, 10 and *Eph.* 4:20–24, see pages 214–218 of his book).

The apostle's teaching is that in virtue of his vital union with Christ the believer enjoys *the inalienable status of a man who has been sanctified by a definitive act*. It is this act which provides the basis for his increasing conformity to Christ, as it also affords the guarantee of his complete glorification [*2 Cor.* 3:18; *Phil.* 1:6]. This lays the solemn responsibility upon him to live like the new man he is, for the old man is dead and so can no more be blamed for his sins [cf. the awful warning of *1 Cor.* 6:15, 16].

Paul further states that this took place in order that 'the body of sin' ('that body of which sin has taken possession' – Sanday and Headlam) might be done away. He does not use the word 'body' to suggest a materialistic conception of sin, as though the body were the source and seat of sinfulness, but because sin finds its concrete expression through 'the body as conditioned and controlled by sin' (John Murray). Thus sin is not the controlling factor in the Christian, because the old man has been crucified.

The final clause sets forth the purpose for which this was effected. It was in order to terminate our bondage to sin. This introduces the theme of freedom from the bondservice of sin that is developed in the following verses. For having been marvellously delivered from our compulsory serfdom to sin, we must not voluntarily continue to render service to it.

7: for he that hath died is justified from sin.

'Justified' does not here refer to our acquittal from sin's guilt, but to our being 'quit' of sin's power. The thought is that sin has no power over a dead man. For as death clears men of all claims, so 'it clears us, who have died with Christ, of the claim of sin, our old master, to rule over us still' (Denney). Hence Christians are to realize and reckon on the fact that they have been delivered from their former servitude to sin in order to become the servants of righteousness [6:11ff].

8: But if we died with Christ, we believe that we shall also live with him;

Paul here prepares the way for the personal application of the truth that believers have died to sin [cf. verses 3, 5]. The 'if' of reality denotes the certainty of our identity with Christ in his death. If that is true (as it is), then it must follow that we shall also live with him. Although this living with Christ doubtless includes the future resurrection state of glory, the primary reference is to our present participation in the resurrection life of Christ. As Christians cannot live at all without Christ, 'we believe' expresses the assurance of faith that we shall so live in union with him.

9: knowing that Christ being raised from the dead dieth no more; death no more hath dominion over him.

This assurance is grounded upon the finality of the resurrection, which is the guarantee that believers must continuously share in Christ's resurrection life. In that state of glory, 'death hath no more dominion over him,' but this implies that he was once under its power. For in assuming the burden of sin he became subject to the penalty of sin. Yet in the death he died the price was paid which forever broke death's lordship over his people. So his resurrection is the pledge that this victory over sin will be repeated in the experience of every believer.

10: For the death that he died, he died unto sin once: but the life that he liveth, he liveth unto God.

The once-for-all character of Christ's death is stressed in this verse, and this is an emphasis which is frequent in the New Testament [*Heb.* 7:21, 9:12, 28, 10:10; *1 Pet.* 3:18]. By taking the form of a servant for our salvation Christ entered into the state of humiliation that was conditioned by the sin with which he was vicariously identified (John Murray). But this connection with sin was terminated by his atoning death, and in his resurrection he entered upon a state of life that was not conditioned by sin. His death thus completely severed his relationship *to sin*, so that the life which he now lives in glory he lives *to God*. This is of course no reflection on the fact that the whole of Christ's earthly course was marked by his total devotion to God. The contrast drawn is between his vicarious relation to sin on earth, and his lack of any connection with sin in heaven. 'As Christ, then, once entered upon this life and glorious activity, does not depart from it to return back again, so the believer, once dead to sin and alive to God in Christ, cannot return to his old life of sin. Verse 11 explicitly draws this conclusion, held in suspense since verse 8, and prepared for in verses 9 and 10' (Godet).

11: Even so reckon ye also yourselves to be dead unto sin, but alive unto God in Christ Jesus.

It should be noted that it is only after Paul has unfolded the full implications of union with Christ that doctrine at last gives place to exhortation. The content of the command presupposes what has already been proved. For if believers are not dead to sin, they could not reckon to be true what was in fact not the case. Two acts of reckoning are called for, the first being preparatory to the second. It is because we can reckon on having died to sin that we can also reckon on being alive to God. And this we are 'in Christ Jesus'. This is the first time in the epistle that Paul uses this pregnant phrase, which here points to the divine initiative in our salvation. For we are 'in Christ' only through the gracious act of God that put Christ's righteousness to our account (C. E. B. Cranfield). 'We may forget what we should be; we may also (and this is how Paul puts it) forget what we *are*. We are dead to sin in Christ's death; we are alive to God in Christ's resurrection; let us regard ourselves as such *in Christ Jesus*' (Denney).

12: Let not sin therefore reign in your mortal body, that ye should obey the lusts thereof:

This command must be understood in the light of the assurance that 'sin shall not have dominion over you' [verse 14]. Sin does not lord it over believers, and it is only because this is true that the command, 'Let not sin therefore reign,' becomes meaningful. 'To say to the slave who has not been emancipated, "Do not behave as a slave" is to mock his enslavement. But to say the same to the slave who has been set free is the necessary appeal to put into effect the privileges and rights of his liberation. So in this case the sequence is: sin does not have the dominion; therefore do not allow it to reign' (John Murray).

On the other hand, the exhortation would be pointless if sin did not exist in the believer. For though he died to sin and his life is hid with Christ in God [*Col.* 3:3], his mortal body is still very much alive to the pull of those unlawful physical and mental desires, by which sin seeks to regain the mastery over his life. But he is to realize that through Christ he now has the power to resist the prohibited cravings he once helplessly indulged. It is probable that Paul refers to the body as 'your *mortal* body' to illustrate the incongruity of any yielding to its sinful demands on the part of those who are 'alive from the dead' [verse 13].

13: neither present your members unto sin as instruments of unrighteousness; but present yourselves unto God, as alive from the dead, and your members as instruments of righteousness unto God.

Since believers have died to sin, they must not go on presenting their bodily members to sin as the 'weapons of unrighteousness' (ASV margin) to wage warfare in its service. 'Sin is regarded as a sovereign (who reigns, verse 12), who demands the military service of subjects (exacting obedience, verse 12), levies their quota of arms (weapons of unrighteousness, verse 13), and gives them their soldier's-pay of death (wages, verse 23)' (Lightfoot). But they are to present themselves and their members *once for all* to God as befits those who are 'alive from the dead'. For as the radical renewal of the whole man involves his total dedication to God, this necessarily includes the surrender of his faculties and members to God's service. These are now to be used as the 'weapons of righteousness' in the fight against their former master. That the apostle took no quiescent view of the Christian life is shown by his frequent use of military metaphors, which reflect the seriousness of the struggle that no good soldier of Jesus Christ can avoid [cf. *Eph.* 6:10ff].

14: For sin shall not have dominion over you: for ye are not under law, but under grace.

The encouragement to fulfil these imperatives is provided by the promise given in the first part of the verse. This future should not therefore be taken as a disguised exhortation; it rather expresses the certainty of the fact asserted. We can indeed so present ourselves and all our members to God for his service, because sin *shall not* have lordship over us. For to come under the government of redeeming grace in Christ is to be freed from the dominion of sin. This is neither freedom from sinning nor freedom from conscious sin. 'Sin as indwelling and committed is a reality; it does not lose its character as sin. It is the contradiction of God and of that which a believer most characteristically is. It creates the gravest liabilities. But by the grace of God there is this radical change that it does not exercise the dominion. The self-condemnations which it evokes are the index to this fact. It is this destruction of the power of sin that makes possible a realized biblical ethic' (John Murray, *Principles of Conduct*, pp. 220-1).

We owe this deliverance to the fact that we are no longer under law but under grace. 'Under law' (no article) does not mean 'under the Mosaic economy', for many who lived under the dispensation of law were the recipients of grace. To be under law is to be under its commands, and under its condemnation for every failure to meet its righteous demands. This means that law can do nothing to justify law-breakers; it simply confirms them in their helpless bondage to sin. But by Christ's mighty rescue we are placed under the sovereignty of grace instead. As 'under grace' indicates, independence is not an option that is open to man. For it is through the justifying provisions of grace that we are filled with the spiritual power which enables us 'to trample unrighteousness under foot and to work righteousness' (Lenski) [cf. 13:8–10; *Gal.* 5:6].

15: What then? shall we sin, because we are not under law, but under grace? God forbid.

As Paul is aware of the way in which such spiritual teaching can be perverted by blind logic, he now returns to consider the question raised in verse 1 from a different point of view. There his reference to superabounding grace had prompted the false inference of continuing in sin that it might abound all the more. Here the removal of the restraint of law could be misconstrued as a free licence to sin, and again the suggestion is summarily rejected by his 'God forbid'. For though in 'one sense the believer is not "under law", in another sense he is [cf. *1 Cor.* 9: 21]' (John Murray). The monstrous nature of this reasoning is exposed in the following verses.

16: Know ye not, that to whom ye present yourselves as servants unto obedience, his servants ye are whom ye obey; whether of sin unto death, or of obedience unto righteousness?

Paul's readers know or certainly *ought* to know that they have been released from the bondage of sin for the service of righteousness [verse 3]. No absolute freedom is conferred upon the Christian, *for his position is simply that of a slave who has changed masters* (Nygren). Formerly he was the slave of sin, rendering willing obedience to the lusts that bring death in their train. But now that he has become the slave of righteousness [verse 18], he must see to it that his obedience in its service is equally wholehearted [cf. *Luke* 16:13].

17: But thanks be to God, that, whereas ye were servants of sin, ye became obedient from the heart to that form of teaching whereunto ye were delivered;

The Christians in Rome clearly do not owe their deliverance to the power of their own choice. For as Nygren well says, 'Paul does not *praise* them for having made a better and happier choice; he *thanks* God for taking them out of the old bondage.' It was through the exercise of divine power that they who *were* the slaves of sin, *became* obedient to the pattern of teaching to which they were delivered [cf. *2 Tim.* 1:13]. The apostolic gospel is here likened to a pattern or mould into which molten metal is poured to set. This mould is the authoritative norm that shapes the thought and conduct of all who are delivered up to its teaching. One would expect doctrine to be handed over to the hearers, rather than the hearers to the doctrine. But

Christians are not the masters of a tradition like the Rabbis, for they are created by the Word of God and they remain in subjection to it (so Barrett). As an ex-Pharisee Paul knew better than anyone else the frustration and futility of an external obedience. But Christianity is not legalism because it renders to God that heart obedience which is the mark of the new creation.

18: and being made free from sin, ye became servants of righteousness.

These passives again point to the action of God in releasing us for his service: 'and having been liberated from sin, you were enslaved to righteousness'. This paradoxical way of expressing the truth shows that the effectual call of God makes our commitment to righteousness as absolute as was our former slavery to sin. 'The striking thought is the fact that our emancipation is a new enslavement. In verse 20 we are shown what a sad liberty we enjoyed when we were slaves of sin; here we are shown what a glorious liberty we obtained when we were made slaves to righteousness' (Lenski).

19: I speak after the manner of men because of the infirmity of your flesh: for as ye presented your members as servants to uncleanness and to iniquity unto iniquity, even so now present your members as servants to righteousness unto sanctification.

In thus speaking of believers being 'enslaved to righteousness' Paul has illustrated the truth in a figure drawn from human relations. This is in order to meet the weakness of their spiritual understanding [cf. *1 Cor.* 3:1]. But this illustration requires further explanation, for 'enslavement to righteousness' could look as if holiness were a matter of sheer compulsion. 'It is not so; *'for* as you once willingly and entirely surrendered yourselves to sin, and were in *this* way slaves of sin, so now willingly and entirely surrender yourselves to righteousness, and be in *this same* voluntary manner slaves of righteousness'" (Shedd). Paul's point is that though their service is now of a different kind and is directed to a different end, yet it calls for *the same dedication* they once showed in the service of sin. 'Unto holiness' (AV) is better fitted to convey 'the once-for-all breach with sin and commitment to righteousness' than 'sanctification' which is often used to denote a process (John Murray).

20: For when ye were servants of sin, ye were free in regard of righteousness.

As an incentive to obedience Paul now bids his readers consider the unprofitable nature of their former course [verses 20, 21]. At that time they were 'free in regard of righteousness'. As responsible subjects they were not exempt from the claims of righteousness upon them, but they were devoid of righteousness and they gloried in their supposed freedom from its restraints. But this was a spurious liberty since it involved them in the guilt which was the inevitable consequence of their iniquity. 'Sinful *inclination* (which is as really inclination as holy inclination) is *false* freedom, because it conflicts with the moral law, and is forbidden by it' (Shedd).

21: What fruit then had ye at that time in the things whereof ye are now ashamed? for the end of those things is death.

The question Paul asks implies the negative reply, 'No fruit whatever!' As sinners they had then imagined that there was some gain in their sin, but as believers they know that there was no fruit in the things of which they are now ashamed. In that state of sin they could bear no fruit unto God, because they were infatuated with 'the unfruitful works of darkness' whose only end is death [cf. *Gal.* 5:22; *Eph.* 5:9]. 'As soon as the godly begin to be enlightened by the Spirit of Christ and the preaching of the Gospel, they freely acknowledge that the whole of their past life, which they lived without Christ, is worthy of condemnation. So far from trying to excuse themselves, they are in fact ashamed of themselves. Indeed, they go farther, and continually bear their disgrace in mind, so that the shame of it may make them more truly and willingly humble before God' (Calvin).

22: But now being made free from sin and become servants to God, ye have your fruit unto sanctification, and the end eternal life.

From the fruitlessness, shame, and condemnation of that bondage of death, Paul gratefully turns to contemplate the glorious transformation wrought in them by the grace of God. 'But now, you have been liberated from sin and enslaved to God, you have your fruit unto holiness, and the end eternal life.' Paul's conclusion thus proves that grace can never minister to licence, for it always produces fruit which leads to holiness and issues in eternal life [cf. *Heb.* 12:14].

23: For the wages of sin is death; but the free gift of God is eternal life in Christ Jesus our Lord.

Having explained these two contrasting forms of bond service, Paul now sums up their respective results in a final statement that leaves nothing more to be said. On 'wages' H. W. Heidland makes three significant comments. 1. As 'wages' were paid to meet the costs of living, sin is here shown to be the deceiver that promises life but pays out death. 2. Because these 'wages' are not confined to a single payment, the shadow of the final penalty already overhangs this present life. For just as eternal life is the present possession of the believer, so sin already offers its slaves deadly poison from the cup of death. 3. Since 'wages' is a legal term, this shows that man has rights only in regard to sin, and these rights become his judgment (*TDNT*, vol. 5, p. 592). This death has the same duration as the life that belongs to the future age. Both are endless because the future age is endless. The term 'death' does not therefore point to the annihilation of the sinner. 'To pay any one is not to put him out of existence; it is rather to make him feel the painful consequences of his sin, to make him reap in the form of corruption what he has sowed in the form of sin [*Gal.* 6:7, 8; *2 Cor.* 5:10]' (Godet).

Although Paul has referred to the fruit borne by believers, he does not regard this as meriting eternal life. This is the free gift of God in Christ Jesus our Lord; it is given to us in Him who has merited it for us [cf. *1 Cor.* 1: 30]. For unlike sin, righteousness is not self-originated; consequently its reward must be gracious. Eternal life is a gift 'because the imputed righteousness of a believer is a gratuity, and his inherent righteousness is the product of the Holy Spirit moving and inclining his will' (Shedd). Pen and ink cannot conceal the apostle's exultant joy as he thus celebrates the triumph of God's grace in our salvation.

CHAPTER SEVEN

1: Or are ye ignorant, brethren (for I speak to men who know the law), that the law hath dominion over a man for so long time as he liveth?

Having proved that believers have died to sin [ch. 6], Paul next explains the way in which they have become dead to the law [ch. 7]. He had touched on this topic in his reference to the fact that believers are not under law [6:14], but the immediate need to refute the false inference that might be drawn from this proposition had then prevented his positive exposition of how this came about. But now the Christians in Rome have their attention turned to this subject, whose importance is impressed upon them by the pastoral concern which is reflected in the repeated address of 'brethren' [verses 1, 4]. The apostle begins his discussion by reminding them that the law only has authority over a man for as long as he lives, and he is confident that this general principle will be self-evident to everyone who knows anything about law.

2: For the woman that hath a husband is bound by law to the husband while he liveth; but if the husband die, she is discharged from the law of the husband.

3: So then if, while the husband liveth, she be joined to another man, she shall be called an adulteress: but if the husband die, she is free from the law, so that she is no adulteress, though she be joined to another man.

To illustrate this general principle Paul refers to the law of marriage. If during the lifetime of her husband the woman marries another man, she is guilty of adultery. However, if her husband dies, the marriage tie is dissolved and she is legally free to marry again [*1 Cor.* 7:39]. As a wife she was under the law regarding husbands, but as a widow she is altogether free of that law. The comparison suits Paul's purpose very well, because it shows that a person can be set free from a law without the overthrow of the law itself. For it is clear that the law regarding husbands continues in full force, though she is herself freed from it. The point is that this death not only ends one relationship, but it legally opens the way for her to enter into another union. 'So we Christians, no longer under law, are now in a most blessed new relation: under grace [6:14, 15]. Paul's illustration is perfectly chosen' (Lenski).

4: Wherefore, my brethren, ye also were made dead to the law through the body of Christ; that ye should be joined to another, even to him who was raised from the dead, that we might bring forth fruit unto God.

Those who try to turn this simple illustration into a complex allegory or parable accuse the apostle of confusion of thought because the parallel is not exactly carried through in this verse. But this is to mistake his purpose, for in fact he here confines himself to a single point of comparison. *And this is the principle that legal obligation is severed by death.*

As the husband's death released his wife from the marriage bond, so there is a death by which we are freed from the law. *For through Christ's death we have received our discharge from all the claims of the law upon us.* 'We were made dead to the law through the body of Christ,' i.e. through his vicarious endurance of the law's curse on our behalf [*Gal.* 3:13].

The positive purpose of our severance from the law was that we should be joined to another, 'even to him who was raised from the dead'. Christ having been thus raised from the dead dies no more [6: 9], and it is by our participation in his endless life that the permanence of this new union is secured [*John* 14: 19]. The great end served by this union with Christ is 'that we might bring forth fruit unto God' [cf. 6:22; *Gal.* 5:22, 23]. Had Paul wished to continue the marriage metaphor 'bear offspring' would have been a more suitable word than 'bear fruit', in addition to which this fruit is borne 'for God' and not 'for Christ', as a woman bears children for her husband. This fruit-bearing is the unexpected sequel to our severance from the law that confounds all legalists, who think that the relinquishing of law is fatal to the production of good works; we next see what it does produce (so Lenski).

5: For when we were in the flesh, the sinful passions, which were through the law, wrought in our members to bring forth fruit unto death.

This verse shows why such fruitfulness was impossible under the law. Here for the first time in the epistle Paul uses the expression 'in the flesh' to describe the old unregenerate life of sin in contrast to the new life 'in the Spirit' [verse 6]. The basis for this usage is doubtless to be found in the distinction made by our Lord: 'that which is born of the flesh is flesh; and that which is born of the Spirit is spirit' [*John* 3:6]. 'The *reason* why we are naturally generated in sin is that, whenever we begin to be, we begin to be as sinful because of our solidarity with Adam in his sin . . . Natural generation we may speak of, if we will, as the means of conveying depravity, but, strictly, natural generation is the means whereby we come to be and depravity is the correlate of our having come to be' (John Murray, *The Imputation of Adam's Sin*, pp. 92–3). To be 'in the flesh' is therefore to be in that condition in which it is impossible to please God [8:8].[1]

---

[1] Since 'the Word became flesh, and dwelt among us, it is impossible to suppose that sinfulness belongs to the flesh as flesh. However, it must be remembered that

While we were in that sinful state the law aroused in us those sinful passions, which were powerfully at work in our members to bring forth 'fruit' – well, yes, if you wish to call it that, but it was *fruit for death!* According to the apostle to be 'in the flesh' and 'under the law' is a sure prescription for death, because the law kindles in a corrupt nature the very desire it is supposed to suppress. For as he presently explains, its holy prohibitions are then the incitement to transgression [verses 7–13]. Thus lawlessness is the paradoxical result of being under the law! This in no way conflicts with what Paul says elsewhere on the function of the law in exercising a restraint upon evil-doers [13:3, 4; *1 Tim.* 1:9, 10], for though the fear of punishment restrains the criminal passions, it does not eradicate them and only restrains to a degree, and even then not always. As Denney says, 'Death is personified here as in verse 17: this tyrant of the human race is the only one who profits by the fruits of the sinful life.'

6: But now we have been discharged from the law, having died to that wherein we were held; so that we serve in newness of the spirit, and not in oldness of the letter.

But now we have been discharged from the law – a bondage which was terminated through our having died to the law! *With the result* that we are now serving in newness of the Spirit, and not in oldness of the letter (cf. 6:4 which states the *purpose* of our being raised with Christ). The 'newness' of this service consists in the life, power, and effectiveness which it derives from its Author, the Holy Spirit. Before his conversion Paul had vainly tried to serve God 'in oldness of the letter', but it was a service which he later described as a 'confidence in the flesh' [*Phil.* 3:3, 4].

Christ's entry into the world was as unique as his departure from it. 'The knowledge of the virgin birth is important because of its bearing upon our view of the solidarity of the race in the guilt and power of sin. If we hold a Pelagian view of sin, we shall be little interested in the virgin birth of our Lord; we shall have little difficulty in understanding how a sinless One could be born as other men are born. But if we believe, as the Bible teaches, that all mankind are under an awful curse, then we shall rejoice in knowing that there entered into the sinful race from the outside One upon whom the curse did not rest save as he bore it for those whom he redeemed by his blood' (Gresham Machen, *The Virgin Birth of Christ*, p. 395). The validity of the title 'the last Adam' as applied to Christ really rests upon the supernatural fact of the virgin birth.

What is set out below gives more simply the substance of a note by Shedd:

THE TWO KINDS OF SERVICE

The 'oldness of the letter' is a service of bondage, a mechanical and false obedience enforced by a fearful spirit of servitude, which seeks to perform by an effort of will the letter of the law. Here the law is written *in* the heart [*Rom.* 2:15], and is therefore external to the will.	The 'newness of the Spirit' is a service of liberty, a spontaneous and real obedience inspired by a joyful spirit of adoption, which actually fulfils by an inward inclination the intent of the law. Here the law is written *upon* the heart [*Jer.* 31:33] and is therefore internal to the will.

'For the letter killeth, but the Spirit giveth life'
[*2 Cor.* 3:6].

7: What shall we say then? Is the law sin? God forbid. Howbeit, I had not known sin, except through the law: for I had not known coveting, except the law had said, Thou shalt not covet:

As Paul has insisted that the law cannot deliver the sinner but merely makes his bondage more bitter, some might be ready to infer that the law itself was sinful; a suggestion that meets with his customary expression of intense aversion. On the contrary, he emphatically rejects this false idea by an appeal to his own experience of the law's real effect. For it was through the law that he came to realize that he was himself a sinner. If then the law shows up sin for what it really is, it cannot itself be sinful.

In the second part of the verse Paul describes how the law brought this knowledge of sin home to his heart. He had imagined himself to be 'blameless' for as long as he was able to entertain the notion that external obedience could satisfy the demands of the law [*Phil.* 3:6]. Conviction of sin came to him with the realization that the law condemned not only outward breaches of the commandments but also the first secret stirrings of sinful desire within the heart [*Matt.* 5: 21–30].

8: but sin, finding occasion, wrought in me through the commandment all manner of coveting: for apart from the law sin is dead.

The word here rendered 'occasion' (*aphorme*) 'was used to denote a base of operations in war , so Paul is saying that the law provided sin with the base it needed for mounting its attack against him (Vine). So that instead of being crushed by the commandment which forbade coveting, he found that it stimulated in him all kinds of covetousness. 'The more the light of the law shines upon and in our depraved hearts, the more the enmity of our minds is roused to opposition, and the more it is made manifest that the mind of the flesh is not subject to the law of God, neither can be' (John Murray, *Principles of Conduct*, p. 185). Hence it was Paul's experience that apart from the law sin was dead. This means that he had no consciousness of sin until the law aroused within his heart every sort of sinful desire. 'By means of this poker in the hands of sin the slumbering fire in Paul was stirred to shoot out all its flames' (Lenski).

9: And I was alive apart from the law once: but when the commandment came, sin revived, and I died;

Paul was 'alive' in his own self-esteem until his conscience was awakened by the commandment. His intimate acquaintance with the letter of the law could not puncture his proud self-righteousness, but when the law was powerfully applied to his heart by the Holy Spirit he lost that good opinion of himself. The hopeless nature of Paul's plight was revealed by the law, which not only condemned his sin, but what was still more alarming, stimulated the once dormant depravity of his heart to vigorous activity; thus when sin 'revived' Paul 'died'.

10: and the commandment, which was unto life, this I found to be unto death:

When Paul discovered within himself this violent contradiction of the law's demands, he found that the commandment which promised life upon obedience had become for him nothing more than a sentence of death [*Lev.* 18:5]. 'How vain therefore is it to expect salvation from the law, since all the law does, in its operation on the unrenewed heart, is to condemn and to awaken opposition! It cannot change the nature of man' (Hodge).

11: for sin, finding occasion, through the commandment beguiled me, and through it slew me.

However, this tragic result was not the fault of the law. For it was really sin that took advantage of the law to 'beguile' Paul, and through it slew him [cf. *2 Cor.* 11:3]. This word recalls Eve's deception by Satan, who made the commandment seem an unreasonable obstacle to the gratification of a harmless desire, from which no evil but only good could come [*Gen.* 3:1–13]. Such forbidden fruit always seems sweet in prospect, but bitter experience proves that death is always the aftermath of disobedience. In Eve's case it brought death upon the race [5:12]; in Paul's case it brought the fact of his already existing deadness home to his consciousness.

12: So that the law is holy, and the commandment holy, and righteous, and good.

Paul now states the conclusion to be drawn from the preceding verses [verses 7–11]. As the law is holy, so each of its stipulations including that mentioned in verse 7 'is holy, and righteous, and good'. Thus in spite of the bad use that sin makes of the law, the apostle insists that the resultant misery is no fault of the law itself [verse 13]. For the adjectives used point to the fact that the law perfectly reflects the character of its divine author. Hence John Murray observes, 'As "holy" the commandment reflects the transcendence and purity of God and demands of us the correspondent consecration and purity; as "righteous" it reflects the equity of God and exacts of us in its demand and sanction nothing but that which is equitable; as "good" it promotes man's highest well-being and thus expresses the goodness of God.'

13: Did then that which is good become death unto me? God forbid. But sin, that it might be shewn to be sin, by working death to me through that which is good; – that through the commandment sin might become exceeding sinful.

Since Paul 'died' when the commandment came [verses 9, 10], was this mournful result to be attributed to the good law? The very wording of the question shows what the answer must be, for no good thing can bring about the death of anybody (Lenski). But not content to leave the inference to be drawn, he again utters his strong exclamation of denial. No, the real culprit for this tragic reversal of his expectations is sin, which is shown up in its true character by working evil through that which is good! However, the final purpose clause makes it plain that the perversity of sin in abusing the law was not outside the scope of God's redemptive design. For he has ordered the operation of the law to be the means of impressing upon the sinner the excessive sinfulness of sin. Accordingly, when sin wields the law as a weapon of death, the sinner's false sense of security is shattered and the hopelessness of his situation is agonizingly revealed.

These verses are therefore an instructive account of Paul's experience before conversion as they explain how the law of God was used to bring conviction of sin to his heart [verses 7–13]. Nowadays when such birth pangs are distinctly unfashionable it is worth recalling the practical remark of Charles Hodge on this passage: 'If our religious experience does not correspond with that of the people of God, as detailed in the Scriptures, we cannot be true Christians.'

14: For we know that the law is spiritual: but I am carnal, sold under sin.

The clue to the interpretation of this controversial passage is to remember the purpose for which it was written [verses 14–25]. In this chapter the apostle's theme is freedom from the law, but this truth is conditioned by the fact that the believer is not only 'in Christ' but he is also still 'in the flesh'. And this inevitably means that there is a dualism in his present experience between the 'now' and the 'not yet'. The paradoxical consequences of living in this state of tension are well drawn out by Nygren:

Chapter 6: We are *free from sin* – yet we must battle against it.

Chapter 7: We are *free from the law* – yet we are not righteous according to its criterion.

Chapter 8: We are *free from death* – yet we long for the redemption of our bodies.

When this distinction is understood there is no difficulty in referring Paul's persistent use of the present tense in these verses to a present conflict within himself. There is here no indulgence in self-analysis for its own sake, but a practical concern to prove that the law can neither justify nor sanctify. For as the law was powerful to convict but powerless to save the sinner [verses 7–13], so it is quick to detect but impotent to remove the sin that remains in the believer [verses 14–25]. From this it follows that the law can never be the means of salvation, neither in its attainment nor in its retention. The believer's righteousness is not of the law, but is nothing less than the righteousness of God in Christ [*Phil.* 3:9].

For we know that the law is spiritual: The reason Paul here uses the plural 'we' is to associate all believers with this judgment, which is an evaluation of the law that is peculiar to the regenerate. They know that the law is spiritual because they can discern that it is inspired and indited by the Holy Spirit. This statement therefore refers to the divine origin and character of the law.

But I am carnal, sold under sin. This contrasts the spirituality of the law with the inner contradiction of its holy perfection which marks the life that is lived in the flesh. When Paul thus confesses that he is 'carnal', or 'fleshly', this must not be confused with the condition of the unregenerate, who are as to their *state*, 'in the flesh' [7:5, 8:8], whose *conduct* is after the flesh' [8:4, 5], and whose *thought* is governed by a 'carnal mind' [8:6, 7]. But 'fleshly' certainly does point to a condition of life that falls far short of the absolute holiness of the law. It frankly indicates a participation in the weakness that inescapably belongs to the flesh. For though the apostles claimed infallibility for their teaching, and could exhort believers to follow their example, even they never claimed to be sinlessly perfect [cf. *Gal.* 2:11; *1 Cor.* 9: 26, 27; *Phil.* 3:12–14; *1 John* 1: 8]. As set against the standard of God's holiness, Paul in common with all other believers is not completely holy [cf. *Job* 40:4; *Psa.* 38:1–10, 40:12, 51:1–12, 69:5, 90:7, 8, 119:96, 120, 176; *Isa.* 6:5; *Matt.* 26:41; *Rom.* 8:23; *Eph.* 6:12; *Heb.* 12:1].

'He is still to some extent, and he feels it to be no small extent [verse 2], ruled by *flesh*. But he is not wholly and completely ruled by it. He is inwardly inclined to good [verses 15, 19, 21]; is disinclined to, and hates evil [verses 15, 16, 19]; "delights in the law of God" [verse 22]; and "serves the law of God" [verse 25]. The natural man is not thus described in Scripture. That a regenerate man may be called "carnal" is proved by *1 Cor.* 3:1, 3' (Shedd).

As the strong expression 'sold under sin' recalls Elijah's word to Ahab, some have contended that it could not describe a regenerate person. But there is an important difference between what is passively experienced and what is actively determined. Paul complains that he *has been sold* under sin, whereas it is said of Ahab that he *sold himself* to do that which is evil in the sight of the Lord [*1 Kings* 21: 20]. Paul thus finds himself taken captive by a power that forces his members to serve sin against his will, but he knows that this is only because no good thing dwells 'in his flesh' [verse 18]. And though constantly betrayed by the flesh, he also knows that he is no longer the slave of sin but the willing servant of righteousness [6:17, 18]. Hence we should not fail to appreciate the fact that the force of the apostle's language is due to the intensity of his feeling against this *partial bondage of the flesh* (which is not the same thing as his former absolute bondage to sin).

15: For that which I do I know not: for not what I would, that do I practise; but what I hate, that I do.

This substantiates the indictment of the previous verse. 'For that which I do *I know not*,' i.e. Paul does that which he *does not love and delight in* [cf. 'know' in *Psa.* 1:6, 36: 10; *Amos* 3: 2; *Matt.* 7:23; *John* 10:14; *1 Cor.* 8:3; *2 Tim.* 2:19]. The second 'for' explains that his actions are a strange contradiction of his affections. For what commands the consent of *his inmost will*, he fails to practise; but what he hates with a holy detestation, that he does. As Paul represents himself as doing that which he does not will, the passage presents something of a psychological problem, since no act can be performed without the motivation of the will. Moreover, it is equally evident that he does not claim coercion as an excuse to evade the moral responsibility for his actions [cf. verse 24]. But as already hinted above, Paul is here using 'will' in the 'highly restricted sense of that determinate will to the good, in accordance with the will of God, which is characteristic of his deepest and inmost self, the will of "the inward man" [verse 22]. It is that will that is frustrated by the flesh and indwelling sin. And when he does the evil, he does what is not the will of his deepest and truest self, the inward man. This explains both types of expression, namely, that what *he wills* he does not do and what *he does not will* he does' (John Murray). Furthermore, as the same author says, it is not to be supposed that in thus delineating the conflict between these carnal and spiritual principles Paul is giving a '*statistical* history of the outcome' or that 'his determinate will to the good came to no effective fruition in practice'.

16: But if what I would not, that I do, I consent unto the law that it is good.

What Paul does that is contrary to his inward inclination evokes the self-condemnation which really amounts to an endorsement of the spirituality of the law [verse 14]. As Calvin indicates in his commentary, it is quite illegitimate to draw a parallel between Ovid's confession, 'I see what is better and approve of it; I follow what is worse,' and what is taught here, for such similarities are purely verbal. The heathen could never 'consent unto the law that it is good'. That is the testimony of the regenerate heart! 'There is no conflict between the law and the believer; it is between the law and what the believer himself condemns' (Hodge).

17: So now it is no more I that do it, but sin which dwelleth in me.

This is yet another declaration which could only be made by a regenerate man. Paul now regards the sin that he commits as so foreign to his renewed *ego* that he can say that it is *no longer* 'I that do it, but sin which dwelleth in me' [verse 20]. This is not a convenient method of escaping the blame for the sin; it is an affirmation that in the struggle against sin, the self stands on God's side. For there are not two egos in Paul contending for the mastery. There is but one acting subject, the new man in whom sin has been deposed from its regency, though not yet expelled from its residency. So that sin is now a 'squatter', and not the true inhabitant, the figure being taken from a house into which an intruder has crowded (Shedd). 'There is a total difference between surviving sin and reigning sin, the regenerate in conflict with sin and the unregenerate complacent to sin. It is one thing for sin to live in us: it is another for us to live in sin' (John Murray, *Redemption – Accomplished and Applied*, p. 145).

18: For I know that in me, that is, in my flesh, dwelleth no good thing: for to will is present with me, but to do that which is good is not.

The preceding statement is now confirmed by a further explanation of this strange duality. Paul knows from personal experience that in him, *that is*, in his flesh, there dwells nothing good. His care in distinguishing 'in me' from 'in my flesh' is significant. It provides an additional proof that he is speaking of *his present experience as a believer,* for a man who is unregenerate is nothing but flesh! So Paul cannot let the statement stand without qualification. For he is also a man in whom the Holy Spirit dwells. Hence it would be untrue to say that there was no holiness in him. But that aspect of the truth is alien to his present purpose, which is to show that his remaining sin ('dwells' looks back to verse 17) prevents him from fulfilling what he desires to do.

Thus what Paul wills he fails to accomplish in practice. 'He does not mean that he has nothing but an ineffectual desire, but he denies that the efficacy of his work corresponds to his will, because the flesh hinders him from the exact performance of what he is doing' (Calvin). The new man cannot completely carry out the desires of his heart, for he is frustrated by the flesh in two ways. 1. Even when he obeys, which is his general habit, he never comes perfectly up to the ideal of the law which is *spiritual* [verse 14]. 2. He sometimes yields to inward corruption, and actually transgresses the law (so Shedd).

19: For the good which I would I do not: but the evil which I would not, that I practise.

In this repetition of the thought of verse 15, the thing willed is defined as the 'good' and that which is not willed but practised as the 'evil'. It must not be forgotten that it is in the light of God's law that Paul makes this evaluation of himself [verse 14]. It is precisely because the Christian is painfully aware of the 'spiritual' nature of the law of God that he realizes the impossibility of ever bringing 'the flesh' into conformity with its demands. Thus the practical importance of the passage for us lies in its disclosure of the apostle's experience of this inner conflict that is characteristic of and restricted to the regenerate.

20: But if what I would not, that I do, it is no more I that do it, but sin which dwelleth in me.

How much Paul deplores this inability is shown by his repeated disavowal of the sin that still lodges in his flesh [verse 17]. Regenerate Paul is forced to live with it, but he will neither recognize it nor come to terms with it. This is not a denial of responsibility for the obedience that sin coerces from his members, but it is a refusal to acknowledge its right to do this [verse 23]. For after the city of Mansoul has been liberated by King Emmanuel, the forces of Diabolus continue their resistance to his rule, though they no longer have any real claim to the city (See John Bunyan's instructive allegory, *The Holy War*).

21: I find then the law, that, to me who would do good, evil is present.

22: For I delight in the law of God after the inward man:

23: but I see a different law in my members, warring against the law of my mind, and bringing me into captivity under the law of sin which is in my members.

As 'then' indicates, Paul is now ready to sum up the condition described in the preceding verses [verses 14–20]. 'I find, then, this law in operation, that when I desire to do what is good, evil lies ready to hand.' (F. F. Bruce) 'The law' has nothing to do with the Mosaic law as this translation clearly shows; it is 'the law of sin' [verse 23] which habitually opposes Paul's will to do good.

Hence John Owen observes: *'Believers have experience of the power and efficacy of indwelling sin.* They *find* it in themselves; they find it as a *law.* It hath a self evidencing efficacy to them that are alive to discern it. They that find not its power are under its dominion. Whoever contend against it shall know and find that it is present with them, that it is powerful in them. He shall find the stream to be strong who swims against it, though he who rolls along with it be insensible of it' (Treatise on 'The Remainders of Indwelling Sin in Believers', *Works*, vol. 6, p. 159).

What Paul predicates of himself in verse 22 is unquestionably the utterance of a regenerate man. For no one who is a stranger to the grace of God can say, 'I *joyfully* agree with the law of God' (Arndt-Gingrich). So far he has used only 'I' in his struggle to explain what he essentially is, but now he adds the term 'the inward man'. This points to the transformation which has brought about his delighted concurrence with the divine will. 'The inward man' is therefore 'the "new man" in Christ that is daily being renewed in the Creator's image [cf. *2 Cor.* 4:16; *Col.* 3:10]' (F. F. Bruce).

But though Paul thus delights in God's law, he sees 'a different law' – 'the law of sin' – that is constantly at war with his wholehearted assent to 'the law of God', which he calls 'the law of my mind'. This spiritual discernment is the fruit of regeneration, for the natural man cannot even *see* the things of God, let alone describe them as the law of his mind [cf. *John* 3:3; *1 Cor.* 2:14]. The reference is to the governing principle of his life, since 'the mind' here includes both the understanding and the will. 'The understanding is enlightened, and the will is enlivened by the Holy Spirit, who dwells in the *mind*, thus regenerated, as the source and support of its divine life.' (Shedd)

However, the apostle's complaint is that he finds the law of his mind opposed by the law of sin in his members. He finds this rebellious principle warring against his allegiance to God and bringing him into captivity. These participles point to an unceasing warfare, but because they are present and not aorist participles they tell us nothing of the ultimate success of the campaign [cf. *1 Pet.* 2:11; *James* 4: 1]. Hence this captivity cannot be regarded as a permanent condition which has been secured by a decisive victory. Moreover, the fact that Paul *twice* refers to the law of sin *in* his members shows that this is no longer the law *of* his members. He speaks of a foreign power that forces his members to revolt against the rule of his mind which they would otherwise obey [cf. 6:19]. But just as no sovereign in his capital can view an insurrection in his provinces with complacency, so Paul deeply deplores this violent contradiction of his regenerate will in his members as the next verse eloquently demonstrates.

24: Wretched man that I am! who shall deliver me out of the body of this death?

In thus giving expression to the real distress he feels as he watches the course of this conflict, Paul is not giving way to blank despair. For though he condemns himself in such unsparing terms, he remains confident that his cry for deliverance will be heard [verse 25]. This is neither the wail of a lost soul, nor the bewildered appeal of a man under conviction but without hope. 'He does not inquire who is to deliver him, as if he were in doubt, like the unbelievers, who do not understand that there is only one deliverer. His language is that of a man who is panting and almost fainting, because he sees that his help is not close enough' (Calvin). What he longs for is the redemption of his body [8:23], which will end the struggle that he knows will go on for as long as he inhabits 'the body of this death', i.e. the physical body in whose members the law of sin is still operative. It is precisely because the believer's present emancipation from the thraldom of sin is not a deliverance to a state of absolute sinlessness that his final salvation remains a matter of hope [8:24].

25: I thank God through Jesus Christ our Lord. So then I of myself with the mind, indeed, serve the law of God; but with the flesh the law of sin.

I thank God through Jesus Christ our Lord. The groan for deliverance from 'the body of this death' is answered by this triumphant thanksgiving which looks forward to the resurrection hope of all believers [*1 Cor.* 15:56, 57]. 'Paul does not say that he already has this deliverance. It has been confused with our deliverance. It has been confused with our deliverance from the guilt of sin in justification. This has led to the mistaken idea that Paul is here dramatizing his past unregenerate state. This converts Paul into a show actor' (Lenski).

So then I of myself with the mind, indeed, serve the law of God; but with the flesh the law of sin. Such is the situation that continues until the glorious day of consummation [8:11]; until then this strange duality remains. Paul however is careful to emphasize his personal responsibility for all the acts he has described; he does not shift the blame for his forced surrender to the law of sin upon an old ego! But it should also be noted that in placing 'I myself' next to the law of God, he shows 'that he regards this as the prominent fact of his present experience and moral state . . . Paul does not serve sin so much as he serves holiness' (Shedd). Haldane therefore justly concludes: 'Beyond this no child of God can go while in this world; it will ever remain the character of the regenerate man . . . In every believer, and in no one else, there are these two principles, – sin and grace, flesh and spirit, the law of the members and the law of the mind. This may be perverted by the opposer of divine truth into a handle against the gospel, and by the hypocrite to excuse his sin. But it gives ground to neither. It is the truth of God, and the experience of every Christian.'

CHAPTER EIGHT

1: There is therefore now no condemnation to them that are in Christ Jesus.

From the contradiction of 'the flesh' which believers still find within themselves, Paul now turns to the determinative aspect of their experience by explaining the full implications [verses 1–11] of what was summarily stated in 7:6 (cf. comment there). They have been discharged from the law, having died to its *condemning* power, because the sentence of condemnation which they deserved was fully borne by Christ on their behalf. So that there is now no condemnation of any kind for those who are 'in Christ Jesus' [6:3–11]. This means that they have not only been liberated from all liability to punishment, but also that in Christ they have been delivered from the enslaving power of sin in order that they might serve God 'in newness of the spirit'.

2: For the law of the Spirit of life in Christ Jesus made me free from the law of sin and of death.

'For' advances the reason for the assurance just given. This is the last time that Paul sets forth his own experience ('me') to illustrate the experience of all believers. He was freed once for all from the lordship of 'the law of sin and death' when the power of God brought him under the governance of another principle, 'the law of the Spirit of life in Christ Jesus'. Although the tense of the verb shows that this liberation was effected in his justification, the apostle's purpose is not to revert to justification but to advance to the blessed life-giving consequences that flow from it.

Sin was able to turn God's holy law into the law of death [7:10, 11], but thanks to the grace which delivered him from all condemnation that same law is now the rule of his life [7:23: 'the law of my mind']. The Spirit's law of life is *qualitatively* different, but it is not *quantitatively* different in the sense that the Holy Spirit impels to any action not already prescribed by the law of God (see note on 7:6 and compare 13:8–10). It must be acknowledged that life in the Spirit is not an external obedience to a killing code, but neither is it a formless mysticism which has no relation to the revealed will of God. 'After his liberation Paul freely adopts and obeys God's law, and sin's law is deposed and is able to disturb him only from the outside through his members' (Lenski). When the Holy Spirit thus puts a man 'in Christ' the reign of sin is broken, but even this 'victorious' chapter does not relieve him of the necessity of putting to death the deeds of the body [8:13]! Is this then so very different from the struggle described [7:23–25] in the previous chapter of 'defeat'?

3: For what the law could not do, in that it was weak through the flesh, God, sending his own Son in the likeness of sinful flesh and for sin, condemned sin in the flesh:

This second 'for' traces the Spirit's work in the believer back to its objective basis, i.e. to the act by which God condemned sin in the flesh. What God did establishes what the law could not do; it was unable to condemn 'sin in the flesh' because 'it was weak through the flesh'. The law could condemn the sinner but it could not break the dominion of sin. For though sin had no place in the original constitution of man, once he fell a prey to this alien power, the law could only confirm its usurped lordship, since all breakers of the law lie helplessly under the curse [*Gal.* 3:10]. Sin consigns man to the debtor's prison, and then makes the law his gaoler. 'Verily I say unto thee, Thou shalt by no means come out thence, till thou hast paid the last farthing' [*Matt.* 5:26].

God, sending his own Son: This points to the pre-existence of the Son. He was God's own Son before he was sent into the world. Here, as always in Scripture, God the Father is represented as taking the initiative in the salvation of mankind. 'His own Son' (see also verse 32) is the Pauline equivalent to the Johannine title, 'only begotten Son' and both point to an eternal and essential relationship [*John* 1:14, 18, 3:16, 18; *1 John* 4:9].

In the likeness of sinful flesh: Paul sails between the Scylla of denying the reality of Christ's humanity ('in the likeness of flesh') and the Charybdis of compromising his sinlessness ('sinful flesh'). He uses this unique and exact expression to show us that the incarnation brought the Son into the closest connection with our sinful condition, short of actually becoming sinful himself. And his meaning is that when the Son entered into our lot he overcame sin in the flesh, i.e. in the same realm which sin had made its own.

And for sin: To introduce the idea of a 'sin-offering' (RV) here is an unwarranted restriction of the apostle's thought. The whole purpose of God's sending his own Son in the likeness of sinful flesh was to judge and destroy *sin!* For apart from sin there would have been no need for his coming at all.

Condemned sin in the flesh: Although the law is powerful to condemn sin in the flesh in a purely declarative sense, it is impotent to destroy sin's power over the flesh. But it was in the flesh of Christ that God both pronounced and executed his sentence upon sin [8:1]. 'In that same nature which in all others was sinful, in that very nature which in all others was dominated and directed by sin, in that nature assumed by the Son of God but free from sin, God condemned sin and overthrew its power. Jesus not only blotted out sin's guilt and brought us nigh to God. He also vanquished sin as power and set us free from its enslaving dominion. And this could not have been done except in the "flesh". The battle was joined and the triumph secured in that same flesh which in us is the seat and agent of sin' (John Murray).

4: that the ordinance of the law might he fulfilled in us, who walk not after the flesh, but after the Spirit.

In order that the just requirement of the law might be fulfilled in us (RSV): This statement does not refer to the justifying righteousness of Christ, but to the work of the Holy Spirit within the believer. According to Jeremiah, God's promise to write his law upon the hearts of his people was to be a distinguishing feature of the New Covenant of which he prophesied [*Jer.* 31:31–34, see also *Ezek.* 36:26–28]. This 'New Covenant is not indifferent to law. It is not contrasted with the old because the old had law and the new has not. The superiority of the new does not consist in the abrogation of that law but in its being brought into more intimate relation to us and more effective fulfilment in us' (John Murray, *The Covenant of Grace*, p. 29). Paul speaks of such a fulfilment in this verse. The righteous requirement of the law is fulfilled in believers through 'the law of the Spirit of life in Christ Jesus' [verse 2]. 'That their obedience is not *perfect* is no more a truth than that it is a *real* and *acceptable* obedience through Christ' (David Brown).

Who walk not after the flesh, but after the Spirit. The apostle has all believers in view [cf. verse 9]! Negatively, they are described as those whose life-style is no longer determined by the dictates of the flesh. Positively, they are shown to be those who are willingly walking (a walk is a voluntary progress!) under the gracious direction of the Holy Spirit. 'For Paul, the human spirit is dormant or dead until it is aroused to life by the Spirit of God; hence to "walk . . . after the *pneuma*" implies the action of the human spirit in response to the guidance of the divine Spirit' (F. F. Bruce). This contrast between the flesh and the Spirit is the theme of the next section [verses 5–13].

5: For they that are after the flesh mind the things of the flesh; but they that are after the Spirit the things of the Spirit.

Paul now proceeds to explain the difference between these two mutually exclusive ways of living. To walk after the flesh [verse 4] is the course of conduct that naturally results from a life which is determined by the flesh ('after the flesh'), and a mind which is therefore set upon the things of the flesh. The man who is thus dominated by the flesh has no capacity to discern the things of the Spirit, which are foolishness to him because he is dead towards God [1 Cor. 2:14]. On the other hand, the believer is no longer of the flesh for he has been divinely quickened; his life is under the direction of the Spirit so that he fixes his mind upon spiritual things. It must be realized that an absolute distinction is in view here. The apostle is not contrasting the lower nature of the flesh with the higher nature of the spirit in one individual; he is insisting that men are *either* 'in the flesh' *or* 'in Christ'.

6: For the mind of the flesh is death; but the mind of the Spirit is life and peace:

The natural man has the mind of the flesh; the believer the mind of the Spirit. To have the mind of the flesh is to exist in that state of spiritual death which reaches its culmination in the second death, the eternal death which is the wages of sin [6:23; *Eph.* 2:1]. But to have the mind of the Spirit is to enjoy the first-fruits of life now, and to reap the full harvest hereafter [verse 11]. This life is therefore spiritual life and the peace that accompanies it is the feeling of inward tranquillity that results from a restored relationship with God [5:1].

7: because the mind of the flesh is enmity against God; for it is not subject to the law of God, neither indeed can it be:

This verse gives the reason why 'the mind of the flesh is death'. It is 'enmity against God', the author of life! 'Alienation from him is necessarily fatal' (Denney). This hostility is actively expressed in its total opposition to the declared will of God. As if this were not enough, Paul adds that it is *incapable* of submission to the law of God. Because *self-will* is enthroned in the 'mind of the flesh' it cannot obey the will of its Creator, Sustainer, and Judge! This is a constitutional impossibility which neither the promise of reward nor the threat of punishment can remove. 'The expulsion of the sinful inclination, and the origination of the holy inclination, in the human will, is a revolution in the faculty which is accomplished only in its regeneration by the Holy Spirit. Self-recovery is not possible to the human will, though self-ruin is [*Hosea* 13:9]' (Shedd).

8: and they that are in the flesh cannot please God.

This re-states the thought of verse 7 in more personal terms, and so paves the way for Paul's direct address to the readers in verse 9. 'The mind of the flesh' is not an abstraction; it belongs to those who cannot please God. They *ought* to please God, but they *cannot* please him. This total inability of the natural man is due to his total depravity – his 'natural' aversion to God [verse 7]. Those who object to this doctrine, which has its basis in this passage, often do so because they think that total depravity means absolute depravity. It is however a term 'of *extensity* rather than *intensity*. It is opposed to *partial* depravity; to the idea that man is sinful in one moment and innocent or sinless in another; or sinful in some acts and pure in others. It affirms that he is all wrong, in all things, and all the time. It does not mean that man is as bad as the devil, or that every man is as bad as every other, or that any man is as bad as he may possibly be, or may become. But there is no limit to the universality or *extent* of evil in his soul. So say the Scriptures, and so says every awakened conscience' (Tayler Lewis, quoted by Alexander Whyte in his *Commentary on the Shorter Catechism*, p. 40).

9: But ye are not in the flesh, but in the Spirit, if so be that the Spirit of God dwelleth in you. But if any man hath not the Spirit of Christ, he is none of his.

Paul here thankfully turned to the believers in Rome who are 'not in the flesh, but in the Spirit'. By the grace of God they now belong to an entirely different realm. But though they have been delivered from the dominion of the flesh, they are still living in a body which is subject to death because of sin [verse 10]. And this means that they are called to resist the unceasing attempts of the flesh to re-assert its authority over them [verses 12, 13]. It is the Holy Spirit who initiates this conflict and sustains the believer in it, because a man is nothing but flesh until he is in the Spirit and the Spirit is in him. There is a quietism that tends to equate peace with the absence of all strife, and there is an enthusiasm that can neglect the duty of putting to death the deeds of the body. But this constant struggle with the flesh is a surer evidence of the presence of the indwelling of the Spirit!

The apostle does not doubt that this is the experience of his readers, but the 'if so be' which qualifies his assurance shows that this is to be confirmed by self-examination [2 Cor. 13:5]. Because if any man has not the 'Spirit of Christ' [John 16:7], he is none of his [Jude 19]. As any man who lacks the Spirit is no Christian, so every man who belongs to Christ is indwelt by his Spirit. Consequently all believers are 'Spiritual' and no distinction can be made between those who are 'in the Spirit' and those who are not 'in the Spirit' (John Murray).

10: And if Christ is in you, the body is dead because of sin; but the spirit is life because of righteousness.

But the Spirit is life because of righteousness (AV). This is a reference to the Holy Spirit and not to the human spirit, for we contribute nothing to this life which is given to us through the justifying righteousness of Christ. 'If then Christ dwells in your heart through the Spirit, though your body is doomed to die because of sin, you have life in the Spirit because of righteousness.' Eternal life is our present possession on account of the righteousness of God, accomplished for us by Christ and applied to us by the Holy Spirit, who will also quicken even our mortal bodies on that great day when our salvation shall be consummated [verse 11]. 'Now, if all men die on account of sin, as the apostle here teaches, then no man can have life by his own righteousness' (Haldane).

11: But if the Spirit of him that raised up Jesus from the dead dwelleth in you, he that raised up Christ Jesus from the dead shall give life also to your mortal bodies through his Spirit that dwelleth in you.

The spiritual resurrection of believers is the guarantee of their participation in the resurrection of the body, for the Spirit through whom God raised Jesus from the dead already dwells in their hearts. 'It should be noticed how significantly Paul varies in this connection the name of Christ. First he speaks of the raising of *Jesus* from the dead. Here the Saviour comes under consideration as to himself, his own human nature. Then he speaks of the raising of *Christ Jesus* from the dead. Here the Saviour comes under consideration as the Messiah in his representative capacity, which furnishes a guarantee that his resurrection must repeat itself in that of the others' (Geerhardus Vos, *The Pauline Eschatology*, p. 163). What an incentive such a glorious prospect affords believers for mortifying the deeds of the body!

12: So then, brethren, we are debtors, not to the flesh, to live after the flesh:

All Christians are perpetual debtors to grace, but they owe no debt to the flesh. Hence those who are the temples of the Holy Spirit must no longer obey the insistent demands of the flesh [*1 Cor.* 3:16]. The conclusion is drawn in negative terms in order to underline the utter inconsistency of such a course. The positive implication is that all who are so graciously indwelt by the Spirit will yield themselves without reserve to his government of their lives.

13: for if ye live after the flesh, ye must die; but if by the Spirit ye put to death the deeds of the body, ye shall live.

The paradoxical nature of this utterance strikingly sets forth the reason why believers are under no obligation to the flesh: To *live* after the flesh brings on *death;* to put to *death* the deeds of the body preserves *life!*

For if ye live after the flesh, ye must die: Eternal death is the inevitable consequence of living after the flesh. It is because this cause can never be separated from its death-dealing effect that believers must never think that it is safe to yield to the lusts of the flesh. Anyone who thinks otherwise has clearly mistaken a false sense of security *in* sin for a true experience of salvation *from* sin. 'Let not that man think he makes any progress in holiness who walks not over the bellies of his lusts. He who doth not kill sin in his way takes no steps towards his journey's end' (John Owen).

But if the Spirit: This essential qualification rules out all asceticism, all fleshly ideas of mortifying the flesh [cf. *Col.* 2:18–23]. 'Mortification from a self-strength, carried on by ways of self-invention, unto the end of a self-righteousness, is the soul and substance of all false religion in the world' (John Owen).

Ye put to death the deeds of the body, ye shall live: As the only true life is spiritual life, believers must put to death the deeds of the body, i.e. the *physical* body that sin still uses as its ally in its war against the soul [cf. 7:23: 'the law of sin which is in my members']. It is not spiritual to overlook the fact that sin comes to its concrete expression through the body. Having been freed from the law of sin and death [verse 2], believers are now under an abiding obligation to deny sin this use of the body for its development to the detriment of their life [*Col.* 3:5]. As John Owen says, 'Be killing sin or it will be killing you.' And this is a work which is peculiar to believers, for those who are still under the dominion of sin cannot be called upon to mortify particular sins but are first to be summoned to saving interest in Christ (cf. Owen, *Of the Mortification of Sin in Believers*, ch. 7).

14: For as many as are led by the spirit of God, these are sons of God.

Those who faithfully engage in this daily work of mortifying the flesh enjoy the assurance that they are indeed sons of God. '*For* as many as are being led by the Spirit of God, *these* are the sons of God.' The believer's submission to the leading of the Spirit in the fight against indwelling sin is thus a sure mark of true sonship. Paul 'had pointed to the very fact of this conflict as a banner of hope. For he identifies the fact of the conflict with the presence of the Holy Spirit working in the soul; and in the presence of the Holy Spirit is the earnest of victory. The Spirit would not be found in a soul which was not purchased for God and in the process of fitting for the heavenly Kingdom. Let no one talk of living on the low plane of the seventh chapter of Romans. Low plane, indeed! It is a low plane where there is no conflict. Where there is conflict with the Spirit of God as one party in the battle – there is progressive advance towards the perfection of Christian life. So Paul treats it' (B. B. Warfield, 'The Spirit's Testimony to Our Sonship' in *Faith and Life*, pp. 189–90).

This leading of the Spirit can *never* contradict the testimony of God's Word but is *always* in conformity with it. It 'excludes all fanaticism, all auto-suggestion, all hearing fictitious, imaginary inward voices. We have the *written* Word with which to test every inward Word that we have absorbed' (Lenski). It is of the greatest importance to note that the Spirit who led Jesus into the wilderness to be tempted also helped him to gain the victory over the devil by bringing God's *written* Word to his remembrance [cf. *Luke* 4:1, 4, 8, 12, 14; *Eph.* 6:17].

15: For ye received not the spirit of bondage again unto fear; but ye received the spirit of adoption, whereby we cry, Abba, Father.

'Ye received' is in the aorist tense and it looks back to the time when Paul's readers became Christians. You did not then receive the Holy Spirit as a spirit of bondage 'again unto fear' [cf. *Gal.* 4:1–9]. Their former state was characterized by a slavish dread of punishment. 'They were then not under grace, but under law [6:14]; and "the law worketh wrath" [4:15]. The legal spirit has nothing genial or spontaneous in it: no enjoyment. This wretched spirit, or frame of mind, was not introduced a second time, by the reception of the Holy Ghost' (Shedd). For it is the function of the Spirit to bring men into a state of liberty and not bondage [*2 Cor.* 3:17].

In the second part of the verse the verb is repeated for the sake of emphasis. On the contrary, you received in conversion the Holy Spirit as the Spirit of adoption through whom you were assured of your acceptance into the family of God! This is the adoption of grace whereby those who were God's enemies are not merely made his friends but are advanced by him to the status of sons [*1 John* 3: 1]. 'Adoption confers the *name* of sons, and a *title* to the inheritance; regeneration confers the *nature* of sons, and a *meetness* for the inheritance' (Haldane) [*John* 1:12, 13].

And it is because they have not only the *status* but also the *heart* of sons that they are impelled to cry, 'Abba, Father!' (Denney). This crying recalls the urgent invocation of God which is frequently found in the Psalms (Cranfield notes that the same word is used more than forty times in the Greek translation of this book, e.g. *Psa.* 3:4, 18:6, 34:6 etc.). But here it is the Spirit of adoption who moves us to call upon God as our Father. As Mark 14:36 shows, Abba is the Aramaic word which Jesus used to address his Father in prayer, and it is probable that the prayer he taught the disciples began with this word [*Luke* 11:2]. Since this was the familiar title used by Jewish children to address their earthly father, its application by Jesus to God was revolutionary in its implications, suggesting the intimacy of a Father-child relationship not found in Judaism (Kittel, *TDNT*, vol. 1, p. 5). When we realize that the spiritual experience of *every* believer is summed up in this *one* word, we are not surprised that it was preserved in transliteration by Greek-speaking Christians for the permanent enrichment of the church universal.

16: The Spirit himself beareth witness with our spirit, that we are children of God:

This shows that there is a double testimony to our adoption. The first is the witness borne *by our spirit* as we are prompted by the Holy Spirit to cry, Abba, Father; the second is the witness borne by the Holy Spirit *to our spirit* to assure us that we are indeed children of God. As John Murray points out, This is a witness to our spirit so that we are not to understand it in terms of a direct revelation to the effect, 'Thou art a child of God.' It is rather an inward certitude which is made particularly clear in sealing to our hearts the promises that belong to us as the heirs of God and in generating in us the assurance of the Father's adopting love.

Paul gives absolutely no hint that he is here speaking of a higher experience of assurance which might be unknown to some of his readers. Indeed his words cannot be understood of a coming of the Spirit subsequent to conversion, as the *parallel passage* in Galatians clearly shows: 'To prove that you are sons, God has sent into our hearts the Spirit of his Son, crying, "Abba! Father!" You are therefore no longer a slave but a son, and if a son, then also by God's own act an heir' [*Gal.* 4:6, 7, NEB].

The Galatians ceased to be slaves when they received the filial spirit of sons in their conversion [cf. 3:1: 'Did you receive the Spirit by keeping the law or by believing the gospel message?' (NEB)]. And it is not without significance that Paul confidently makes this appeal to their *experience* of the Spirit as the proof of the genuineness of their faith in Christ [cf. verses 9, 14]. Perhaps if modern evangelism were less obsessed with conversion without feeling – 'Do not doubt your salvation even though you do not *feel* any different' – there would be less emphasis upon post-conversion experiences!

17: and if children, then heirs; heirs of God, and joint heirs with Christ; if so be that we suffer with him, that we may be also glorified with him.

And if children, then heirs: Those who are children must also be heirs.

By their adoption believers are entitled to an eternal inheritance. 'As the birthright of a child confers a title to the property of its father, and so distinguishes such property from what the child may acquire by industry and labour, so also is the case with adoption. Here we see the difference between the law and the gospel. The law treats men as mercenaries, and says, Do, and live; the gospel treats them as children, and says, Live, and do' (Haldane).

Heirs of God, and joint-heirs with Christ: The possession of the Holy Spirit is the earnest or deposit which assures believers that they will receive the promised inheritance [*Eph.* 1:14; cf. verse 23]. This divine gift enables them to embrace the stupendous thought that they are heirs of God and fellow-heirs with Christ. In its broadest manifestation the inheritance is the kingdom of God, but the sum of its bliss will be the eternal enjoyment of God himself [*Psa.* 16:5f; 73:25, 26; *Lam.* 3:24]. As the natural Son of the Father Christ is the proper heir; believers being sons by adoption are only heirs in virtue of their union with him. Christ has already entered into the glory which was won for his people by his obedience unto death, and this exaltation is the pledge that they shall follow him there.

If so be that we suffer with him, that we may be also glorified with him: But just as the cross preceded the crown in the experience of Christ, so his people must first suffer with him before they can be glorified with him. Their identification with Christ inevitably involves believers in suffering for his name's sake, and in this sense they suffer with him [*John* 15:18; *Phil.* 1:29; *1 Pet.* 4:13]. These sufferings are both internal and external, and they result from taking their stand with Christ against the world, the flesh, and the devil. And though such sufferings contribute nothing towards the cost of their salvation which was wholly borne by him [*Isa.* 53:5], they are a necessary part of the refining process that prepares them for glory [*1 Pet.* 1:6, 7].

18: For I reckon that the sufferings of this present time are not worthy to be compared with the glory which shall be revealed to us-ward.

The reference to future glory leads the apostle to enlarge upon this expectation. He brings forward a threefold testimony to confirm suffering believers in their hope: 1. Creation itself groans for deliverance, verses 19–22; 2. Christians groan for glory, verses 23–25;

3. The Spirit himself groans with them in their longing, verses 26–27.

In the light of faith Paul reckons that the sufferings of the present age are not worthy to be compared with the glory of the age to come. His calculation is comprehensive in its scope. It covers every kind of suffering we may experience in this age of distress as well as that which is endured for Christ's sake [verse 17]. 'We need comfort and assurance not only when we suffer for Christ but also and often much more when we endure other suffering' (Lenski). The glory to be revealed already exists in the person of the glorified Christ, but it shall then reach unto us. It 'is to be bestowed upon as, so that we become the actual partakers; it is not a glory of which we are to be mere spectators' (John Murray).

19: For the earnest expectation of the creation waiteth for the revealing of the sons of God.

As W. J. Grier explains, 'All nature, now groaning under the curse pronounced at the Fall, awaits a deliverance and renovation corresponding to the deliverance of the redeemed' (*The Momentous Event*, p. 65) [*Gen.* 3:17; *Matt.* 19:28; *Acts* 3:21; *2 Pet.* 3:13; *Rev.* 21:1]. In thus attributing to inanimate creation a longing that properly belongs to rational creatures, Paul vividly shows that the restoration of the material world is intimately bound up with the fulfilment of God's redemptive purpose.

For the revealing of the sons of God: 'Their status as sons of God with all privileges attached, such as freedom and heirship, existed before, but had not been openly demonstrated. Not their celestial body, but their supreme sonship was in hiding. It is this *status* that will be revealed, and this revelation will be accomplished, by laying upon them the glory, the medium for whose manifestation, to be sure, is the body of the resurrection' (Geerhardus Vos, *The Pauline Eschatology*, p. 198).

20: For the creation was subjected to vanity, not of its own will, but by reason of him who subjected it, in hope

When God cursed the ground for man's sake, the whole creation was subjected to vanity through no fault of its own. The sin of Adam involved the created order in a judgment which condemned it to the futility and frustration of falling short of its original purpose. But as

God's sentence upon sin did not cut off man from the hope of redemption, creation was made a sharer in his hope as well as his punishment.

'When the curse is completely removed from man, as it will be when the sons of God are revealed, it will pass from creation also; and for this creation sighs. It was made subject to vanity on the footing of this hope; the hope is latent, so to speak, in the constitution of nature, and comes out, in its sighing, to a sympathetic ear' (Denney).

21: that the creation itself also shall be delivered from the bondage of corruption into the liberty of the glory of the children of God.

The content of this hope is that creation shall at length be delivered from its slavery to corruption to share in the liberty of the glory that belongs to the children of God. 'Corruption' explains 'vanity' by showing that the failure of creation to reach its goal is due to the principle of decay and death which ends everything. But failure is not God's final word for creation. 'It is, and always shall be, the world which God Almighty has created, which He, in spite of all the sins of angels and of men, has in its broad dimensions upheld and maintained, and which at the time of the end He will so bring out to a perfect form of life, that it will perfectly correspond to His purpose of creation, and which, in spite of the sins of angels and of men shall make his original plan – now no more susceptible of corruption – shine forth resplendently in fullness and richness of form' (Abraham Kuyper, *The Revelation of St John,* p. 344).

22: For we know that the whole creation groaneth and travaileth in pain together until now.

'For' confirms this miserable state by showing that the whole creation is groaning together in what Philippi calls 'a grand symphony of sighs'. Nevertheless, these groans are not seen as the death-throes of creation, but as the birth-pangs that point to its restoration. 'Because the creatures are subject to corruption, not through their natural desire, but by God's appointment, and also because they have a hope of being freed hereafter from corruption, it follows that they groan like a woman in labour until they have been delivered. This is a most appropriate comparison to inform us that the groaning of which he speaks will not be in vain or without effect. It will finally bring forth a joyful and happy fruit' (Calvin).

23: And not only so, but ourselves also, who have the firstfruits of the Spirit, even we ourselves groan within ourselves, waiting for our adoption, to wit, the redemption of our body.

This 'groaning for glory' is consciously shared by the Christian who longs for the consummation of his salvation in the 'redemption of the body' [*2 Cor.* 5:2]. This full and final deliverance from all the consequences of sin is here called the 'adoption' because the resurrection will constitute the supreme manifestation of the sonship. The possession of the 'firstfruits of the Spirit' not only points to the certainty of the final harvest, but also arouses within the Christian 'a painful sense of hunger', since present 'partial enjoyment' has only 'whetted the appetite for the true food in its abundance'. The same idea is present in the description of the Spirit as the 'earnest' or 'pledge' of future glory [*2 Cor.* 1:22, 5:5; *Eph.* 1:14]. 'The present possession of the Spirit is regarded in the light of an anticipation. The Spirit's proper sphere is the future aeon (age); from thence he projects himself into the present, and becomes a prophecy of himself in his eschatological (or final) operations' (Vos, op. cit., pp. 40, 165).

24: For in hope were we saved: but hope that is seen is not hope: for who hopeth for that which he seeth?

For in hope were we saved: Salvation as a present reality of the believer's experience cannot be an object of hope, 'for who hopeth for that which he seeth?' 'In hope' therefore refers to the 'redemption of the body' mentioned in the previous verse. The context makes it clear that the Christian hope does not terminate in the heavenly bliss of the soul in the intermediate state, but eagerly anticipates the final fulfilment of the promise of the resurrection of the body unto life eternal.

25: But if we hope for that which we see not, then do we with patience wait for it.

The patient endurance of present trials is a fruit of hope, for as Calvin remarks, 'All that the gospel promises concerning the glory of the resurrection vanishes away, unless we spend our present life in bearing with patience the cross and tribulations' [*1 Thess.* 1: 3]. 'Impatience spells dispute and dissatisfaction with God's design . . . Expectancy and hope must not cross the bounds of history; they must wait for *the end*, "the liberty of the glory of the children of God"' (John Murray) [cf. *2 Cor.* 4:18, 5: 7].

26: And in like manner the Spirit also helpeth our infirmity: for we know not how to pray as we ought; but the Spirit himself maketh intercession for us with groanings which cannot he uttered;

Although the believer is even now a child of God, his present state is characterized by weakness and infirmity. This verse provides the comforting assurance that the exigencies of this situation are met by the ministry which the Holy Spirit exercises within the hearts of believers. The Christian is not crushed under an abounding sense of his own infirmity, because the Holy Spirit graciously shares with him in the bearing of this burden.

For we know not how to pray as we ought: Inability in prayer is not only an illustration of the weakness of the believer but also an explanation of it. He neither knows what to pray for, nor how to present his petitions as he ought. Hence the necessity for the illumination and the inspiration of the Spirit, who is the true author of prevailing prayer.

But the Spirit himself maketh intercession for us with groanings which cannot be uttered: The children of God are represented by two advocates. Their glorified Redeemer ever lives to make intercession for them in heaven, and the Holy Spirit condescends to plead for them from within their own hearts [*John* 14:16, 26, 15:26, 16:7; *Heb.* 7:25; *1 John* 2:1]. This is 'not an intercession through us as mere conduits, unengaged in the intercession ourselves; it is an intercession made by the Spirit as our helper and not as our substitute . . . The Spirit intercedes for us then by working in us right desires for each time of need; and by deepening these desires into unutterable groans. They are our desires, and our groans. But not apart from the Spirit. They are his; wrought in us by him' (B. B. Warfield, 'The Spirit's Help in Our Praying' in *Faith and Life*, pp. 199–200).

27: and he that searcheth the hearts knoweth what is the mind of the Spirit, because he maketh intercession for the saints according to the will of God.

Since this groaning is nothing less than the expression of 'the mind of the Spirit', it has not only a meaning, but also that meaning is perfectly discerned by God, the searcher of hearts [*Psa.* 139:1, 23; *Jer.* 17:10]. It further follows that this intercession of the Spirit must be in perfect harmony with 'the will of God'. The strong encouragement which this passage offers to believers is that when God searches their hearts he finds in the groanings of the Spirit a perfect reflection of his own loving purpose for them. 'Both the intercession of Christ and the intercession of the Spirit are represented in the New Testament as made on behalf of those who are in Christ – saints, the Church, not mankind in general' (Denney) [*John* 17:9].

28: And we know that to them that love God all things work together for good, even to them that are called according to his purpose.

This verse is the climax of the chapter. 'We know' is not the language of tentative conjecture, but of experimental certainty. Paul is very far from saying that everything is for the best in the best of all possible worlds, for this sublime assurance is limited by a double qualification. It is only the children of God who can claim this promise. Nothing will be found to work for the final good of the wicked, but all things must work together for the ultimate blessing of those who love God and are called according to his purpose [see for example: *Gen.* 50:20; *Acts* 8:4; *Phil.* 1:12].

'If all things work together for good, there is nothing within the compass of being that is not, in one way or other, advantageous to the children of God. All the dispensations of Providence, whether prosperous or adverse, all occurrences and events – all things, whatsoever they be – work for their good. They do not work thus of themselves: It is God that turns all things to the good of his children. The afflictions of believers, in a peculiar manner, contribute to this end [*Psa.* 119:67, 71]. Even the sins of believers work for their good, not from the nature of sin, but by the goodness and power of him who brings light out of darkness. That it is turned to good, is the work of God, and not ours [cf. *Luke* 22:31–34]. We ought no more to conclude that on this account we may sin, than that wicked men do what is right when they persecute the people of God, because persecutions are overruled by him for good. That all things work together for good to them who love God, establishes the doctrine of the perseverance of the saints; for if all things work together for their good, what or where is that which God will permit to lead them into condemnation?' (Haldane).

Those who thus love God are 'the called'; and they are called because they were first chosen. Charles Hodge points out that 'called' is 'never, in the epistles of the New Testament, applied to those who are the recipients of the mere external invitation of the gospel. It always means *effectually called*, i.e., it is always applied to those who are really brought to accept the blessings to which they are invited . . . This call is not according to the merits of men, but according to the divine *purpose*.' [*Rom.* 9:11; *Eph.* 1:11; *2 Tim.* 1:9]

In Romans 8:28–30 Paul describes 'an unbreakable chain of events proceeding from God's eternal purpose in foreknowledge and predestination to the glorification of the people of God. It is impossible to remove calling from this setting. The called are called according to purpose; the purpose is antecedent to the calling' (John Murray, *Redemption – Accomplished and Applied,* pp. 156–157).

29: For whom he foreknew, he also foreordained to be conformed to the image of his Son, that he might be the firstborn among many brethren:

For whom he foreknew: This word may not be reduced to mean the mere foresight of faith by God; it is virtually the equivalent of foreloved [cf. *Psa.* 1:6, 144:3; *Jer.* 1:5; *Amos* 3:2; *Hos.* 13:5; *Matt.* 7:23; *1 Cor.* 8:3; *Gal.* 4:9]. 'God has always possessed perfect knowledge of all creatures and of all events. There has never been a time when anything past, present, or future was not fully known to Him. But it is not His knowledge of future events (of what people would do, etc.) which is referred to in Romans 8:29, 30, for Paul clearly states that those whom He *foreknew* He predestined, He called, and He justified. Since all men are *not* predestined, called, and justified, it follows that all men were *not foreknown* by God in the sense spoken of in verse 29 . . . Although God knew *about* all men before the world began, He did not *know* all men in the sense that the Bible sometimes uses the word "know", i.e., with intimate personal awareness and love. It is in this latter sense that God fore*knew* those whom He predestined, called, and justified' (Steele and Thomas, *Romans – An Interpretive Outline,* pp. 132, 134).

He also foreordained to be conformed to the image of his Son: As 'Whom he foreknew' draws our attention to the distinguishing love of God, so 'he also foreordained' informs us of the high and holy destiny for which the elect are appointed by God. Since this destination is their conformity to the image of their incarnate and glorified Redeemer, it is nothing less than their conformity to the image of the eternal Son of God [cf. *2 Cor.* 3:18; *Eph.* 1:4, 5; *Phil.* 3:21]. Therefore a true understanding of what is involved in election can never lead to careless security in sin [*2 Pet.* 1:1–12].

That he might be the firstborn among many brethren: This shows us that the divine decree has for its ultimate end the exaltation of Christ. 'The term "firstborn" reflects on the *priority* and the *supremacy* of Christ [cf. *Col.* 1:15, 18; *Heb.* 1:6; *Rev.* 1:5] . . . The fraternal relationship is subsumed under the ultimate end of the predestinating decree, and this means that the pre-eminence of Christ carries with it the eminence that belongs to the children of God. In other words, the unique dignity of the Son in his essential relation to the Father and in his messianic investiture enhances the marvel of the dignity bestowed upon the people of God. The Son is not ashamed to call them brethren [*Heb.* 2:11]' (John Murray).

30: and whom he foreordained, them he also called: and whom he called, them he also justified: and whom he justified, them he also glorified.

The eternal purpose of God for his children finds its historical expression in their calling and justification, and these acts are the earnest of their future glorification, the certainty of which is indicated here by the use of the past tense. No such assurance would be conveyed to believers if 'calling' depended upon the will of man, for no chain is stronger than its weakest link [*John* 1:13]. However, it must be noted that throughout the passage Paul speaks of salvation exclusively in terms of God's action. Those whom he foreloved are none other than those whom he glorified.

Thus God's foreknowledge, predestination, calling, justification, and glorification of his people form five links in an unbreakable chain of salvation. The invincibility of God's purpose is the guarantee that those whom he has quickened to new life in Christ shall not fall short of future glory, for that which has been forged upon the anvil of God's grace cannot be thwarted by the will of the creature. By means of this revelation made through the apostle, the Christian's vision transcends the frontiers of time. Eternal election is the spring of grace and eternal glory is its consummation. Present trials are only seen in their true proportions when they are viewed within the context of these eternal vistas of grace.

Paul does not mention the believer's present experience of sanctification 'because the difference between sanctification and glory is one of degree only, not one of kind. Sanctification is progressive conformity to the image of Christ here and now [cf. *2 Cor.* 3:18; *Col.* 3:10]; glory is perfect conformity to the image of Christ there and then. Sanctification is glory begun; glory is sanctification completed' (F. F. Bruce).

31: What then shall we say to these things? If God is for us, who is against us?

The argument concluded, Paul turns to a triumphant application of the teaching. The note of victory is immediately struck in the challenging question, 'What then shall we say to these things?' It covers all the apostle has taught in the epistle. And it serves to introduce four rhetorical questions whose purpose is to assure all who are 'in Christ' of their impregnable security so that they might enjoy an invincible confidence in God [verses 31, 33, 34, 35]. Each question really answers itself, but Paul is not content to leave it at that. He uses these questions as pegs on which to hang this glorious paean of praise to God's sovereign grace. 'If God is for us, who is against us?' 'If' implies no doubt, but states a condition of reality. Since God is for us, then all our adversaries are of no account, for who can frustrate his saving purpose? Indeed, the fact that God is for us was supremely demonstrated in the sacrifice of his Son on our behalf [verse 32].

32: He that spared not his own Son, but delivered him up for us all, how shall he not also with him freely give us all things?

He that spared not his own Son: Paul's language here appears to be taken from the Greek version of Genesis 22:12. The willingness of Abraham to offer up Isaac provides only a faint analogy of the Father's ultimate self-sacrifice in refusing to spare his own Son.

'He would have spared his Son had he wished to execute upon us the punishment we had incurred. He would have spared his Son, and removed the cup of suffering from him, had he not purposed to confer upon us all conceivable good. But, in love to us, he spared not his own Son. He removed not the cup from him, that it might never be presented to us. This scripture connects the Christian's safety under divine protection with the fact that God spared not his own Son, – a phrase which implies that he spared not the Surety, that he might rescue us' (George Smeaton, *The Apostles' Doctrine of the Atonement*, p. 181).

But delivered him up for us all: 'Spared not' is negative; 'delivered up' is positive. It was the Father who delivered up his Son to the damnation and dereliction of that death which sin merited [*Mark* 15:34]. It was the Father who delivered up his Son to all the powers of darkness and the hands of wicked men, so that he might endure and exhaust the sentence of doom on behalf of those for whom he vicariously bore it [*Luke* 22:53; *Acts* 2:23]. 'Who delivered up Jesus to die? Not Judas, for money; not Pilate, for fear; not the Jews, for envy; but the Father, for love!' (Octavius Winslow).

Hence Calvary was the fulfilment of Zechariah's prophecy, 'Awake, O sword, against my shepherd, and against the man that is my fellow, saith the LORD of hosts' [*Zech.* 13:7; *Matt.* 26:31]. This is not the sword of judicial power as in *Rom.* 13:4, but the sword of divine justice. For behind the farce of his earthly trial, there was the reality of his arraignment as the appointed sin-bearer of a sinful people before the heavenly tribunal [*Isa.* 53:4–7]. 'The sheep had deserved the blow, but the shepherd bares his own bosom to the sword, and is wounded for the sins of his people, and bears those sins in his own body on the tree' (T. V. Moore).

As Poole comments, 'for us all' refers to 'such persons as he had before mentioned, such as God foreknew, predestinated, called, etc., which is not all men in general, but a set number of persons in particular: it is an expression both of latitude and restriction; of latitude, in the word *all*; of restriction, in the word *us*.'

How shall he not also with him freely give us all things? As Lenski says, 'The argument is not merely from the greater to the less but a statement of the impossibility of not completing what God began at so tremendous a cost to himself.' For it is inconceivable that God should thus give his Son up to death, even the death of the cross, and then withhold the lesser gifts of grace which his people will need to finish their pilgrimage of faith in triumph.

33: Who shall lay anything to the charge of God's elect? It is God that justifieth;

Those who press charges against believers are doomed to disappointment, for they fight against God's decree. It is impossible to curse, still less to condemn, those whom God has determined to bless [*Num.* 23:19, 20]. Paul's intention in tracing every blessing to its ultimate source in God's sovereign choice, is to lay the only foundation for a genuine sense of Christian assurance, even as he demolishes all possibility of pride in the creature. If imaginary merit could never constrain God's love, neither could real demerit extinguish it. All the glory and all the praise belong to God alone. Election is never taught in Scripture as a speculative dogma, but as a practical reality of Christian experience. Those who know that they have been 'loved with everlasting love' will not surrender this precious truth simply because it arouses the antipathy of carnal minds.

It is God that justifieth: The answer shows that God cannot fail to justify those whom he has chosen to be the free recipients of his loving kindness. The term 'justify' is significant, for it indicates that God's love is never exercised at the expense of God's law. 'If justice is not satisfied, there can be no justification, no peace of conscience, no security either for salvation or for the moral government of God. The Bible knows nothing of mere pardon. There can be no pardon except on the ground of satisfaction of justice. It is by declaring a man just, (that is, that justice in relation to him is satisfied), that he is freed from the penalty of the law, and restored to the favour of God' (Hodge) [*Isa.* 50:8, 9].

34: who is he that condemneth? It is Christ Jesus that died, yea rather, that was raised from the dead, who is at the right hand of God, who also maketh intercession for us.

The confidence that it is God who justifies prompts this further challenge. The answer shows that Christ's finished work and his present heavenly ministry of intercession guarantee the security of his people, who are thereby assured that nothing shall be able to separate them from the love of Christ [verse 35].

It is Christ Jesus that died: Paul simply states the fact of Christ's death, for he has fully explained its purpose earlier in the epistle [3:21–26, 4:25, 5:8–11, 6:4–10, 8:3,4]. 'The terseness at this point draws attention to the stupendous significance of the death of Christ in the series of redemptive facts instanced in this verse. That Christ Jesus should have died is in itself so arresting a fact that the simple statement summons us to reflection on the implications' (John Murray).

Yea rather, that was raised from the dead: The efficacy of the death resides in the reality of the resurrection, for a dead Saviour is a contradiction in terms. The testator lives again to become his own executor, thus personally ensuring that all the beneficiaries of the will actually receive the benefits of his death [*Heb.* 9:16, 17].

Who is at the right hand of God: The glorious exaltation of the Mediator to the place of supreme authority and power in heaven is itself an assurance that his people shall follow him there [*John* 14:2, 3]. Since the heavens have now received the bodily presence of the Lord 'until the times of restoration of all things', it therefore follows that there can be no corporeal manifestation in the Lord's Supper, whatever priestly pretensions are made to the contrary [*Acts* 3:21].

Who also maketh intercession for us: 'His session denotes his *power* to save us; his intercession, his *will* to do it' (Bengel). Calvin warns against the danger of measuring this intercession by carnal judgment, 'for we must not think of him as humbly supplicating the Father on bended knee and with outstretched hands'. It must rather be understood as his claim that 'the efficacy of his death should be made good to the uttermost' after the style adopted in his great high priestly prayer, 'Father, I *will* that they also whom thou hast given me be with me where I am' (David Brown) [*John* 17:24; *Heb.* 7:24, 25].

35: Who shall separate us from the love of Christ? shall tribulation, or anguish, or persecution, or famine, or nakedness, or peril, or sword?

36: Even as it is written,
For thy sake we are killed all the day long;
We were accounted as sheep for the slaughter.

In the final question 'the love of Christ' refers to Christ's love for his people, and not their love to him, because no assurance could be derived from the latter [cf. verse 37]. Here Paul returns to the thought of 'the sufferings of this present time' [verse 18]. The world always sees these afflictions as the proof that Christ has removed his favour from us, whereas in fact they serve to bring us into even closer fellowship with him [*Phil.* 3:10].

As Denney points out, 'For thy sake' is the crux of the quotation which comes from Psalm 44:22. 'This is what the Psalmist could not understand. That men should suffer for sin, for infidelity to God, was intelligible enough; but he and his countrymen were suffering because of their faithfulness, and the psalm is his daring expostulation with God. But the apostle understood it. To suffer for Christ's sake was to enter into the fellowship of Christ's sufferings, and that is the very situation in which the love of Christ is most real, near, and sure to the soul' [cf. 5:3].

37: Nay, in all these things we are more than conquerors through him that loved us.

In view of the accumulated evils which are faced and overcome by the Christian warrior, 'conquer' is far too weak a word for Paul to use. Only the word in its heightened form can do justice to this conquest which is snatched out of seeming defeat. Nay, in all these afflictions which come upon us for the sake of the name we confess, we are *more than* conquerors! Overwhelming victory is ours because we are given the strength to endure 'through him who did love us' [cf. *Col.* 2:15]. For he who loved us unto the death of the cross, loves us still and we stand fast in our faith through his matchless grace!

38: For I am persuaded, that neither death, nor life, nor angels, nor principalities, nor things present, nor things to come, nor powers,

39: nor height, nor depth, nor any other creature, shall be able to separate us from the love of God, which is in Christ Jesus our Lord.

In the magnificent conclusion Paul affirms his God-given persuasion that nothing can ever sever the Christian from the love of God [*Jude* 24, 25]. Men have been wrongly persuaded of many things, but the apostle states the abiding reality of Christian experience.

Neither death nor life: As we must either live or die, these cover every eventuality that can befall us. If our last enemy death cannot separate us because Christ has vanquished it and robbed it of its sting [*1 Cor.* 15:55f.], then we are assured that nothing which precedes that final crisis will be any more successful [*Matt.* 10:29, 30].

Nor angels, nor principalities: The evil angels and hostile principalities [*Eph.* 6:12], who would be glad to separate us from Christ, have been stripped of their power to effect their malevolent design by Christ's great victory on the cross [*Col.* 2:14].

Nor things present, nor things to come: As therefore Christ has made all history his own, the Christian must neither yield to the temptation to despair in present affliction, nor entertain any fearful foreboding of what the future might hold for him [verse 28].

Nor powers: If taken together with angels and principalities as in the AV, 'powers' would likewise refer to these cosmic forces of evil. But its separation in the best texts lends weight to John Murray's suggestion that 'no mighty work or miracle [cf. especially *2 Thess.* 2:9] can be effective in separating from Christ'.

Nor height, nor depth: These were technical terms in astrology, and if Paul had this meaning in mind, the reference would be to the movements of the planets which were thought to control the destinies of mortals. 'But fate, whether real or imaginary, has no power over those whose lives are "hid with Christ in God" [*Col.* 3:3]' (F. F. Bruce).

Nor any other creature: Paul doubtless adds this to include any other aspect of created reality he has omitted to mention. He thus leaves no loophole for any contradiction of the sublime confidence that is expressed in his concluding words. *Nothing* 'shall be able to separate us from the love of God, which is in Christ Jesus our Lord!' Denney finely says, 'The love of Christ is God's love, manifested to us in him; and it is only in him that a divine love is manifested which can inspire the triumphant assurance of this verse.' So ends one of the most glorious chapters in the whole of Scripture. It should surely prompt our praise: *Hallelujah, for the Lord God Omnipotent reigneth!*

CHAPTER NINE

Paul now moves to the pressing problem of Israel's present unbelief, which he proceeds to show is 'neither total nor final' (Hodge). The present rejection of the gospel by the majority of his kinsmen after the flesh is not to be interpreted as an abrogation of the divine promises, nor does it indicate any abdication of divine power. Whatever present appearances may say to the contrary, Paul will not permit any compromise on the question of God's sovereignty, for capitulation at this point marks the abandonment of belief in the living God. Chapters 9–11 are in no sense a parenthesis, but must be understood as the natural culmination of the apostle's doctrinal teaching in this epistle, for he is jealous to maintain and vindicate the purpose of God in history, and this remains a matter of paramount importance in the church today.

1: I say the truth in Christ, I lie not, my conscience bearing witness with me in the Holy Ghost,

2: that I have great sorrow and unceasing pain in my heart.

Although he was hated bitterly by his own people, Paul's conversion had only intensified his natural affection for them, and he regards their continuing unbelief with unceasing anguish. He confirms this revelation of his inward feelings with a most solemn oath. Paul is not only united by faith to Christ who is himself the truth, but he is also indwelt by the Holy Spirit who endorses the testimony of his conscience. Therefore his readers may rest assured that his confession is without a vestige of dissimulation. His grief for Israel is not feigned, it is the constant burden of his heart.

3: For I could wish that I myself were anathema from Christ for my brethren's sake, my kinsmen according to the flesh:

So deep is his feeling for his brethren 'according to the flesh' that Paul could wish himself accursed for their sake. 'The expression is evidently hypothetical and conditional, "I could wish, were the thing allowable, possible, or proper"' (Hodge) [cf. *Exod.* 32:32]. 'In this we may discern a characteristic of a Christian. He who has no sorrow for the perishing state of sinners, and especially of his kindred, is not a Christian. No man can be a Christian who is unconcerned for the salvation of others' (Haldane).

4: who are Israelites; whose is the adoption, and the glory, and the covenants, and the giving of the law, and the service of God, and the promises;

5: whose are the fathers, and of whom is Christ as concerning the flesh, who is over all, God blessed for ever. Amen.

This impressive enumeration of the religious privileges of the Jews serves to emphasize the tragedy of their repudiation of Christ, the fulfiller of all the promises made to them. The title 'Israelites' marks their descent from Jacob whose name was changed to 'Israel' in 'honour of his prevailing faith which would not let God go until God had blessed him' (Lenski) [*Gen.* 32:28]. 'The adoption' refers to their theocratic election by which they were separated from the heathen nations to become God's peculiar people [*Exod.* 4:22, 19:5; *Hos.* 11:1]. 'The glory' was the visible sign of God's presence with them; it was seen in the pillar of cloud that guided them through the wilderness, and in the cloud of glory that rested on the tabernacle and upon the mercy seat [*Exod.* 29:43, 40:34; *Lev.* 16:2]. 'The covenants' is plural because God's covenant was progressively revealed and confirmed to the patriarchs, and publicly ratified at Sinai. It was here that God signally favoured them by 'the giving of the law', thus leaving all other nations to walk in the vanity of their mind. And as their worship was also instituted by God, 'the service of God' was with them the worship of the true God in the true way. But what gave all these privileges their *saving content* were 'the promises' that related to the Messiah, and it was *through faith* in these promises that the saints of the old dispensation laid hold of eternal life [cf. *Heb.* 11].

In verse 5 the phrase 'whose are the fathers' no doubt refers to Abraham, Isaac, and Jacob, the fathers of faith of whom they might be proud [*Exod.* 3:6; *Luke* 20:37]. But Israel's greatest glory consists in Christ's consenting to be their kinsman 'as concerning the *flesh*', even he 'who is over all, God blessed for ever. Amen.' It is not piety that has prompted the Unitarians and their fellow travellers to contend that this is a doxology to God (cf. RV margin, RSV, NEB), but the anxiety to avoid Paul's plain ascription of the title 'God' to Christ. Oscar Cullmann has shown that it is not a true independent doxology (these always begin with 'Blessed', cf. *2 Cor.* 1:3; *Eph.* 1: 3), but a doxological apposition; and that the reference to Christ's flesh requires a continuation which goes beyond flesh, after the fashion of the analogous formula in *Rom.* 1:3, 4 (*The Christology of the New Testament*, p. 313). Moreover, the idea that this is a doxology to God is ruled out by the context. For as Lenski says, 'What makes the grief of Paul so poignant is the fact that God should have favoured Israel so highly. To say the least, if Paul were to insert a doxology to God at this point, it would be out of place, the incongruity would be evident.' It is, however, highly appropriate for Paul to show that the Christ the Jews rejected and crucified is the One 'who is over all, God blessed for ever' – a statement to which we are also glad to add our own emphatic *AMEN!*

6: But it is not as though the word of God hath come to nought. For they are not all Israel, that are of Israel:

'The reason why the rejection of the Jews involved no failure on the part of the divine promise, is, that the promise was not addressed to the mere natural descendants of Abraham. "For they are not all Israel which are of Israel," i.e., all the natural descendants of the patriarch are not the true people of God, to whom alone the promises properly belong' (Hodge) [*Isa.* 55:10, 11].

7: neither, because they are Abraham's seed, are they all children: but, In Isaac shall thy seed be called.

This shows that natural descent from Abraham is no guarantee of spiritual kinship with Abraham. Ishmael was also Abraham's child, but he did not belong to the line of faith which God established in Isaac. The true seed of Abraham all embrace the promise of God, so that it is useless to claim Isaac's inheritance without sharing Isaac's faith in the promise. As Abraham was compelled by God to disown Ishmael, the child who was conceived in unbelief [*Gen.* 16:2, 21:12], so none but those who share his justifying faith in the promise shall be acknowledged by God as his seed [4:16–25; *Gal.* 4:28]. As the Puritan John Flavel put it, 'If Abraham's faith be not in your hearts, it will be no advantage that Abraham's blood runs in your veins.'

8: That is, it is not the children of the flesh that are children of God; but the children of the promise are reckoned for a seed.

It is because 'that which is born of the flesh is flesh' that a fleshly pedigree, far from ensuring salvation, actually excludes it [*John* 3:1–10]. God has never recognized the children of the flesh as his own, but ever and only the children of the promise, who are brought forth from the tomb of their unbelief by the regenerating power of the promise [*1 Pet*. 1:23; *James* 1:18]. Thus the true children of Abraham are those 'who are born after the manner of Isaac, by the word and promise of God' (Poole).

9: For this is a word of promise, According to this season will I come, and Sarah shall have a son.

As the accent here falls upon the *creative power* of God's promise [cf. 4:17], so what follows serves to define its *elective purpose* [verses 10–13]. God gave the promise of a son to Abraham and Sarah when they were beyond all hope of an heir. That promise did not fall short of its appointed fulfilment, because it was accompanied by the power to make it good. 'Is any thing too hard for the LORD?' was the rebuke Sarah received from the Lord for the laughter of unbelief with which she first greeted this announcement of the divine purpose [*Gen*. 18:10, 14]. Hence Isaac was literally the child of promise, for it was evident that he owed his existence to nothing but the power of God's Word.

10: And not only so; but Rebecca also having conceived by one, even by our father Isaac –

As it might be argued that there was good reason for God to choose Isaac in preference to the resentful son of a slave, this is added to prove the unconditional nature of God's sovereign choice. For there was no such disparity between Esau and Jacob, 'either in birth or in works: they had both one and the same mother; Rebecca conceived with them at one and the same time, and that by no other person than our father Isaac; and yet the one of these is chosen, and the other refused. This now was an undeniable proof, that the promise belongs not to all the children of Abraham, or of Isaac, according to the flesh; all the seed of neither are the children of the promise' (Poole).

11: for the children being not yet born, neither having done anything good or bad, that the purpose of God according to election might stand, not of works, but of him that calleth,

God made known his will concerning the children before their birth in order to show that his choice was not based on works, for his preference was expressed long before there could be any manifestation of their character. 'As for original sin, they were both alike tainted therewith' (Poole) [*Eph*. 2:3].

Not of works, but of him that calleth: 'This doctrine is alone consistent with Christian experience. "Why was I made to hear thy voice?" No Christian answers this question by saying, Because I was better than others' (Hodge) [cf. comment on 8:28; *1 Tim.* 1:9].

12: it was said unto her, The elder shall serve the younger.

Those who believe that the election spoken of in this passage is national and not personal are quick to point out that Jacob was never personally served by Esau. However, it cannot be gainsaid that in a spiritual sense Esau did in fact 'serve the younger', for he forfeited his birthright, and therefore 'in reference to the highest interests, Esau was placed below Jacob, as much as Ishmael was below Isaac. This is the real spirit of the passage' (Hodge) [*Gen.* 25:23].

13: Even as it is written, Jacob I loved, but Esau I hated.

It cannot be denied that in this quotation from Malachi 1:2,3 the prophet has in view the nations of Israel and Edom, but it must not be assumed that their respective destinies can be considered in isolation from that difference which God first made between their respective heads. As the election of Jacob is the proof of God's love, so the rejection of Esau is the evidence of God's hatred. The two aorists look back to the acts which caused these twins to differ. Both were hateful on account of Adam's sin, so that it is in fact easier to explain God's hatred of Esau than his love for Jacob. For as Warfield well says, 'When all deserve death it is a marvel of pure grace that any receive life; and who shall gainsay the right of him who shows this miraculous mercy, to have mercy on whom he will, and whom he will to harden?' Certainly Jacob deserved this mercy no more than Esau. But God sovereignly chose Jacob in Christ, whereas he just as sovereignly passed by Esau. Hence God hated Esau for no other reason but his sin for God hates nothing but sin – and this holy hatred of sin may not be defined in terms of a loving less, as some commentators try to do. 'Nothing, then, is said of Esau here that might not be said of every man who shall finally perish' (Haldane).

14: What shall we say then? Is there unrighteousness with God? God forbid.

As usual Paul proposes an objection to his teaching in order emphatically to repudiate it. It is the very height of madness for men to charge God with injustice because he elects some and rejects others [*Gen.* 18:25; *Job* 33:13].

15: For he saith to Moses, I will have mercy on whom I have mercy, and I will have compassion on whom I have compassion.

Paul justifies his strong denial by an appeal to Scripture [*Exod.* 33:19]. As all deserve nothing but wrath, none can claim mercy as a right. Hence God is not unjust when he leaves some to reap the due reward of their deeds. For though he is bound to punish sin, he is under no obligation whatever to exercise mercy. Since, then mercy is not a debt which God owes to man, he is free to dispense it on *whomsoever* he pleases. Such distinguishing mercy is *pure* mercy, because it is not called forth by any mitigating factors in those to whom it is extended. Men therefore have no just ground for complaint if God gives some more than they earned [cf. 6:23], 'Is it not lawful for me to do what I will with mine own?' [*Matt.* 20:15]

16: So then it is not of him that willeth, nor of him that runneth, but of God that hath mercy.

From this it follows that 'God's election is not of Jacob's, or of any other man's, willing or running; i.e. it is not from his good desires or deeds, his good inclinations or actions, or from the foresight thereof; but it is of God's mere mercy and good pleasure. This text wounds Pelagianism under the fifth rib' (Poole).

17: For the scripture saith unto Pharaoh, For this very purpose did I raise thee up, that I might show in thee my power, and that my name might be published abroad in all the earth.

The choice of some unto eternal life inevitably implies the rejection of others, and this is confirmed by the example of Pharaoh [*Exod.* 9:16]. The verse states that God brought this implacable adversary on to the stage of history for the express purpose of providing the world with an unforgettable demonstration of the fate that awaits all those who set themselves up to oppose the fulfilment of his promise of grace and mercy.

'It was not the not yet existent Scripture that made this announcement to Pharaoh, but God himself through the mouth of his prophet

Moses. These acts could be attributed to "Scripture" only as the result of such a habitual identification, in the mind of the writer, of the text of Scripture with God as speaking, that it became natural to use the term "Scripture says", when what was really intended was "God, as recorded in Scripture, said"'(B. B. Warfield, *The Inspiration and Authority of the Bible*, pp. 299–300).

18: So then he hath mercy on whom he will, and whom he will he hardeneth.

The apostle now affirms the general principle which is to be drawn from this particular example. Since God is sovereign in the exercise of his mercy, the case of Pharaoh illustrates his determination to pass by others, whom he leaves to perish in their sins for the manifestation of his justice (cf. *Canons of Dort*, 1:15). This doctrine of reprobation is the counterpart of the doctrine of election, for the election of some inevitably implies the reprobation of others [cf. *Matt.* 11:25, 26; *1 Pet.* 2: 8; *Jude* 4]. 'In fact, every passage of Scripture which teaches that any will be finally lost, teaches at the same time, by necessary implication, if the doctrine of election be true, that they were eternally reprobated or left out of the number of the elect. The two doctrines stand or fall together' (J. H. Thornwell, *Collected Writings*, vol. 2, p. 144).

And whom he will he hardeneth: Paul 'as explicitly affirms the sovereignty of reprobation as of election, – if these twin ideas are, indeed, separable even in thought: if he represents God as sovereignly loving Jacob, he represents Him equally as sovereignly hating Esau; if he declares that He has mercy on whom He will, he equally declares that He hardens whom He will' (B. B. Warfield, *Predestination*).

19: Thou wilt say then unto me, Why doth he still find fault? For who withstandeth his will?

Paul anticipates a plausible objection of the carnal mind. If God hardens whom he will, why does he still find fault? If God is sovereign then man can no longer be held responsible for the result.

For who withstandeth his will? that is, his decretive will, and the answer implied in the question is, No-one. However, with regard to the preceptive will of God, man can and does withstand it, and for this he is justly held responsible by God. 'It was the preceptive will of God that the Jews should not crucify the Lord Jesus Christ. They acted in this manner contrary to God's command, and were therefore guilty; still, it was the decretive will that the Saviour should be crucified, for the Jews and Roman soldiers did only what "his hand and his counsel determined before to be done." The preceptive will of God is the rule of duty to us; the decretive will, the plan of operations, to himself. The distinction is plainly just, natural and scriptural. The preceptive will of God is sometimes called his *revealed* will, and his decretive called his *secret* will . . . The preceptive will is the sole rule of duty to man, as its name shows; and fearful guilt is always incurred when the commands of God are disregarded or despised. It is not my business to inquire whether God has a secret decree – that I shall or shall not, in point of fact, comply with his injunctions; it is enough that I am bound to do so, and am justly held punishable if I do not obey. Whatever rule of operations he may prescribe to himself, the one which he has given to me is plain and intelligible, and his unrevealed purposes will afford me no shelter if I neglect or disregard it' (Thornwell, op. cit., pp, 163–5) [*Deut.* 29:29].

In a most helpful discussion of the very difficult question, 'God and evil', Gordon Clark has this to say on the subject of human responsibility: 'Although the betrayal of Christ was foreordained from eternity as a means of effecting the atonement, it was Judas, not God, who betrayed Christ. The secondary causes in history are not eliminated by divine causality, but rather they are made certain. And the acts of these secondary causes, whether they be righteous acts or sinful acts, are to be immediately referred to the agents; and it is these agents who are responsible.' (*Religion, Reason and Revelation*, p. 239)

20: Nay but, O man, who art thou that repliest against God? Shall the thing formed say to him that formed it, Why didst thou make me thus?

Here all who are tempted to echo this sinful suggestion are vigorously taken to task by the apostle. His first question rebukes the reckless impiety of the man who replies against God, while the second logically refutes the creature's self-assumed right to complain against his Creator. For it is indisputable that 'God has the Creator's right to do what he will with those whom he has himself moulded and fashioned' (Sanday and Headlam) [*Isa.* 45:9].

21: or hath not the potter a right over the clay, from the same lump to make one part a vessel unto honour, and another unto dishonour?

Paul employs the familiar Old Testament figure of the potter and the clay to illustrate the authority of God over his creatures [cf. *Isa.* 2,9:15, 16; 64: 8, 9; *Jer.* 18:1–6]. He argues from the less to the greater, for if a potter has power over his clay, to form it as he pleases, then God has much more power over his creatures, to form or order them as he chooses. God's authority over his creature is greater than that of a potter over his clay. The potter made not his clay; but both clay and potter are made by God (Poole).

From the same lump: Both types of vessel are fashioned from the same lump, which represents human nature ruined by the Fall. As Warfield says, 'The body out of which believers are chosen by God's unsearchable grace is the mass of justly condemned sinners, so the destruction to which those that are passed by are left is the righteous recompense of their guilt. Thus the discrimination between men in the matter of eternal destiny is distinctly set forth as taking place in the interests of mercy and for the sake of salvation: from the fate which justly hangs over all, God is represented as in his infinite compassion rescuing those chosen to this end in his inscrutable counsels of mercy to the praise of the glory of his grace; while those that are left in their sins perish most deservedly, as the justice of God demands' (*Predestination*).

22: What if God, willing to show his wrath, and to make his power known, endured with much longsuffering vessels of wrath fitted unto destruction:

As the future manifestation of God's wrath will perfectly reveal his righteous character, it is therefore the most flagrant folly to mistake his present longsuffering for an unholy indifference to sin [cf. verse 17; *Eccles.* 8:11]. Although it is perfectly true that the non-elect fit themselves for destruction by their own wickedness, it must not be too hastily assumed that this is the apostle's meaning in this place. The verse '*does not* say the vessels of wrath *fitted themselves*, nor does it say they are *fit for* destruction; instead, it declares they are "fitted *to* destruction", and the context shows plainly it is *God* who thus "fits" them – objectively by his eternal decrees.' (Arthur Pink, *The Sovereignty of God*, p. 120) [cf. verses 20, 21].[1]

---

[1] As Gerhard Delling insists, '*fitted* unto destruction' here means *foreordained for destruction*', and not merely '*ready* or *ripe* for destruction' as B. Weiss and H.A.W. Meyer suggest without philological justification (*TDNT*, vol. 1, p. 476).

23: and that he might make known the riches of his glory upon vessels of mercy, which he afore prepared unto glory,

'The elect differ from the reprobate only in the fact of their deliverance from the same gulf of destruction. This, moreover, is by no merit of their own, but by the free goodness of God. It must, therefore, be true that the infinite mercy of God towards the elect will gain our increasing praise, when we see how wretched are all those who do not escape his wrath' (Calvin).

24: even us, whom he also called, not from the Jews only, but also from the Gentiles?

If the rejection of ethnic Israel is demonstrated by their unbelief, then the calling of the Gentiles indicates their inclusion within the scope of the divine promise. Since those who are the subjects of God's promise are also called by God, this gift of faith provides a proof of election. 'None of the Jews or Gentiles were vessels of mercy, except those whom he had effectually called to himself. This verse incontestably proves, contrary to the erroneous glosses of many, that the apostle is here speaking of the election of individuals, and not of nations' (Haldane).

25: As he saith also in Hosea,

I will call that my people, which was not my people;
And her beloved, that was not beloved.

The conversion of the Gentiles from heathendom exhibits on a far grander scale the same principle which was set forth in Hosea's message of mercy to apostate Israel [*Hos.* 2:23, which is applied to the church in *1 Pet.* 2:10].

26: And it shall be, that in the place where it was said unto them, Ye are not my people,

There shall they be called sons of the living God.

God's promise to restore a rejected people is here applied by Paul to the calling of the Gentiles. In this case, the phrase 'in the place where' is best taken as referring to 'every place, where the people had been regarded as aliens, they should be called the children of God' (Hodge). For the believing Gentiles are now recognized by God in the very place where previously they had been regarded as 'aliens from the commonwealth of Israel' [*Eph.* 2: 12]. Consequently under the new covenant no place is more sacred than any other, for a change of heart makes a change of locality as unnecessary as it renders pilgrimages irrelevant [*John* 4:20–24].

27: And Isaiah crieth concerning Israel,

If the number of the children of Israel be as the sand of the sea, it is the remnant that shall be saved:

28: for the Lord will execute his word upon the earth, finishing it and cutting it short.

As the apostle quoted Hosea [verses 25, 26] to prove the election of a part of the Gentiles, so he now cites Isaiah to prove the reprobation of a part of the Jews [*Isa.* 10: 22, 23]. Calvin comments, 'His description of Isaiah as *exclaiming*, and not speaking, is deliberately intended to arouse greater attention. The words of the prophet are plainly designed to prevent the Jews from boasting excessively in the flesh. It is a terrible thing to learn that only a small number out of an incalculable multitude shall obtain salvation.'

Cutting it short: 'If only a remnant of the Jewish Church, God's own people, were saved, how careful and solicitous should all professors of religion be, that their faith and hope be well founded' (Hodge).

29: And, as Isaiah hath said before,
Except the Lord of Sabaoth had left us a seed,
We had become as Sodom, and had been made
like unto Gomorrah.

This citation of Isaiah 1:9 is in agreement with the prophet's previous statement [verses 27, 28]. For unless the Lord of Hosts had left us a seed, Israel would have been long since visited with the same annihilating judgment that fell upon Sodom and Gomorrah. 'That only a remnant is saved points up the severity and extent of the judgment executed. That a remnant is saved is the evidence of the Lord's favour and the guarantee that his covenant promise has not failed' (John Murray).

30: What shall we say then? That the Gentiles, who followed not after righteousness, attained to righteousness even the righteousness which is of faith:

31: but Israel, following after a law of righteousness did not arrive at that law.

What are we to conclude? We are faced with the paradoxical result that Gentiles who did not pursue righteousness, attained it; while Israel, pursuing a law of righteousness, did not attain to that law. This was because unrighteous Gentiles were glad to embrace 'the righteousness of faith' [3:22ff.], whereas Israel's pride in their possession of a law, which prescribed but could not bestow righteousness, was at the root of their vain attempts to catch up with its impossible demands. It is not the function of the law to justify, but to bring sinners under the conviction of their utter failure to reach its standard of perfection [3:20].

'Error is often a greater obstacle to the salvation of men than carelessness or vice. Christ said that publicans and harlots would enter the kingdom of God before the Pharisees. In like manner the thoughtless and sensual Gentiles were more susceptible of impression from the gospel, and were more frequently converted to Christ, than the Jews, who were wedded to erroneous views of the plan of salvation . . . Let no man think error in doctrine a slight practical evil. No road to perdition has ever been more thronged than that of false doctrine. Error is a shield over the conscience, and a bandage over the eyes' (Hodge).

32: Wherefore? Because they sought it not by faith, but as it were by works. They stumbled at the stone of stumbling;

Such an unexpected result obviously calls for an explanation. As Denney says, 'Everything in religion depends on the nature of the start. You may start *from faith*, from an utter abandonment to God, and an entire dependence on him, and in this case a righteousness is possible which you will recognize as *God's righteousness*, God's own gift and work in you; or you may start *from works*, which really means in independence of God, and try to work out, without coming under obligation to God, a righteousness of your own, for which you may subsequently claim his approval, and in this case, like the Jews, all your efforts will be baffled. Your starting point is unreal, impossible.'

Thus it was because the Jews were infatuated by this imaginary self-righteousness that they refused the real faith-righteousness which was offered to them in the gospel. A gratuitous salvation is always an offence to those who desire to earn it by their own efforts; hence the Christ, whom believers regard as the chief corner stone, became to them the stone of stumbling [*1 Pet.* 2:6–8]. The offence of the cross, 'at which they stumbled, is not simply the fact that it *is* a cross, whereas they expected a Messianic throne; the cross offended them because, as interpreted by Paul, it summoned them to begin their religious life, from the very beginning, at the foot of the Crucified, and with the sense upon their hearts of an infinite debt to him which no "works" could ever repay' (Denney).

33: even as it is written,

Behold, I lay in Zion a stone of stumbling and a rock of offence:
And he that believeth on him shall not be put to shame.

In this verse Paul combines two passages from Isaiah 8:14 and 28:16. Poole remarks, 'Jesus Christ is properly a corner-stone, elect and precious; but accidentally and eventually a stumbling-stone, *Luke* 2:34.' Consequently an encounter with the One who is the great Divider of mankind cannot be avoided. Those who do not find him to be their rock of refuge will be ruined by stumbling on the stumbling-stone [*John* 16: 9]. As it is the summation of all wickedness to find in Christ nothing but a rock of offence, so believers are assured that all who put their trust in him shall never be ashamed or confounded.

CHAPTER TEN

1: Brethren, my heart's desire and my supplication to God is for them,
that they may be saved.

Brethren: This affectionate address to those who are Paul's brethren in the Lord is intended to focus their attention upon his earnest desire for the salvation of those who are only his kinsmen according to the flesh. He is not discussing Israel's unbelief with any sense of academic detachment, for he longs that they might be brought to faith in Christ. And no doubt remembering his former blindness, he prays that the Lord might remove the veil of unbelief from their heart [*2 Cor.* 3:14–16]. The comments of John Murray on this verse deserve the closest consideration for they are of the utmost importance in preserving the balance of truth: 'In the preceding chapter the emphasis is upon the sovereign and determinative will of God in the differentiation that exists among men. God has mercy on whom he wills, and whom he wills he hardens. Some are vessels for wrath, others for mercy. And ultimate destiny is envisioned in destruction and glory. But this differentiation is God's action and prerogative, not man's. And, because so, our attitude to men is not to be governed by God's secret counsel concerning them. It is this lesson and the distinction involved that are so eloquently inscribed on the apostle's passion for the salvation of his kinsmen. We violate the order of human thought and trespass the boundary between God's prerogative and man's when the truth of God's sovereign counsel constrains despair or abandonment of concern for the eternal interests of men.'

2: For I bear them witness that they have a zeal for God, but not according to knowledge.

Zeal is always misdirected when it is misinformed. In his speech before Agrippa, Paul confessed, 'I verily thought with myself, that I ought to do many things contrary to the name of Jesus of Nazareth' [*Acts* 26:9–11]. In thus condemning his former course the apostle has for ever laid bare the categorical imperative which governs every unregenerate heart. This is only to be expected, for all who are not ruled by Christ do that which is right in their own eyes, but zeal can never make it right to do those things which are contrary to that Name which is above every name. And where there is no submission to the will of Christ, there can be no knowledge of the mind of Christ [*Acts* 9:6, 7]. Hence nothing is known as it should be known, for every truth coheres in him who is the truth ('What is truth? said jesting Pilate; and would not stay for an answer' – Bacon). Today the measure of man's guilt before God is demonstrated by his determination to discover self-existent 'truths'. The quest for knowledge apart from Christ is the supreme evidence of arrogant unbelief, for it directly opposes God's plan to sum up all things in Christ. There are no neutral 'facts' in a theistic universe!

3: For being ignorant of God's righteousness, and seeking to establish their own, they did not subject themselves to the righteousness of God.

If the Jews had not known of God's righteousness, their ignorance would have been excusable. But this was a willing ignorance which refused the instruction of God's word in favour of *their own* inventions. They preferred, as Poole observes, 'a home-made righteousness' of their own spinning, for 'they will not go abroad for that which they think they have, or may have, at home. They will not be beholden to another for that which they suppose they have in themselves. They have righteousness enough of their own working; and therefore they reject and withdraw themselves from that which is of God's appointing.'

This is not simply a Jewish mistake; it is the cardinal delusion in the religion of the natural man. He always seeks to justify himself and may succeed before men, but he remains a stranger to God's justification [*Luke* 16:15, 18:9–14]. 'All legal endeavour is hostility to evangelical requirement. He who would work out a personal righteousness rejects Christ's righteousness. The "worker" excludes the "believer" [4:4, 5]' (Shedd).

4: For Christ is the end of the law unto righteousness to every one that believeth.

Since God gave his law to a people redeemed by grace, they did not imagine that his favour could be earned by their obedience, even though the continued enjoyment of blessing was suspended upon it. It should be remembered that Paul's polemic was directed against that false interpretation of the law which had erased the whole concept of grace from the Old Testament. According to the Judaizers, salvation was gained by a meritorious obedience to the law. Such was Paul's former course, and his kinsmen are still blinded by the same error [*Phil.* 3:9]. Unbelievers expect to attain righteousness by the works of the law, but this relationship to the law has been terminated by Christ for all believers, who therefore no longer regard it as the instrument of their justification. 'There is *no* believer, *Gentile or Jew,* for whom law, *Mosaic or other,* retains validity or significance as a way to *righteousness,* after the revelation of the righteousness of God in Christ' (Denney).

5: For Moses writeth that the man that doeth the righteousness which is of the law shall live thereby.

The principle enunciated in Leviticus 18: 5 became a sentence of condemnation when it was artificially isolated from the context of grace in which it was originally set. Hence the relevance of its testimony against those who sought after righteousness by the deeds of the law. Paul quotes it again in Galatians 3:12.

6: But the righteousness which is of faith saith thus, Say not in thy heart, Who shall ascend into heaven? (that is, to bring Christ down:)

Paul finds an admirable description of the 'righteousness of faith' in Deuteronomy 30:11–14. In his farewell discourse Moses warns the people against giving way to a spirit of unbelief, for God has drawn near to them in the covenant of grace, and everything which pertains to their temporal and eternal good has been clearly revealed to them. If the light afforded by the old dispensation then made unbelief inexcusable, what shall be said of those who remain in darkness now that the Light of the world has been fully manifested? Thus the appropriateness of the apostle's application is evident. Paul interprets the first question as a denial of the reality of the Incarnation. It is quite beyond man's power to scale the heights of heaven either by legalistic endeavour or by speculative philosophy, and there is now no necessity to make the attempt, for 'the Word became flesh and tabernacled among us' [*John* 1:4, ASV margin]. The sheer perversity of unbelief is shown by the many who prefer to undertake an impossible Odyssey rather than put their trust in an accessible Christ.

7: or, Who shall descend into the abyss? (that is, to bring Christ up from the dead.)

It is equally futile to attempt a descent into the abyss or grave to discover the truth. The reality of life after death is not to be proved by the unlawful attempts of the Spiritists to communicate with the souls of the departed [*Deut.* 18:9–12; *Isa.* 8:19, 20]. One came back from the realm of the dead in all the splendour of his resurrection life as the first-fruits of them that slept [*1 Cor.* 15:20]. Death holds no terrors for the Christian for the keys of death have been committed to him who broke its dominion over mankind through his glorious victory over all the powers of darkness [*1 Cor.* 15:55–57; *Eph.* 4:9; *Rev.* 1:18].

8: But what saith it? The word is nigh thee, in thy mouth, and in thy heart: that is, the word of faith, which we preach:

In this quotation of Deuteronomy 30:14, Paul identifies the word spoken of by Moses with the 'word of faith, which we preach'. As the word was the means by which grace was ministered to the hearts of God's people in the period of promise, so the preached word of the gospel now conveys the justifying righteousness of Christ to all who receive it by faith and thus take it into their mouths and hearts. But as then many of the Jews only received the law outwardly, not taking the gospel promise it contained into their hearts, so now the majority had rejected the gift of righteousness that was openly offered to them in the preaching of the gospel.

9: because if thou shalt confess with thy mouth Jesus as Lord, and shalt believe in thy heart that God raised him from the dead, thou shalt be saved:

In this description of the essence of saving faith, Paul places confession before belief to correspond with the order followed in Deuteronomy 30:14 [verse 8], and then inverts them in the next verse to show the order of experience.

Because if thou shalt confess with thy mouth Jesus as Lord: This word of the gospel saves 'because' it has Christ himself for its content. The complications of later theological development are often adversely compared with the apparent simplicity of the earliest Christian confession of faith, 'Jesus is Lord.' However, the significance of this credal formula is not to be judged by the conciseness of its expression, for the supernatural character of its content demands nothing less than a supernatural faith to embrace it [*1 Cor.* 12:3]. In this identification of the historical Jesus with his subsequent exaltation to supreme lordship and universal dominion, all the facts of the gospel are presupposed [cf. *Phil.* 2:5–11].

This was the consistent emphasis of the apostolic proclamation, and no preaching which fails to do justice to Christ's present sovereignty is faithful to the authoritative pattern laid down in the New Testament. Open confession of his name before men is an indispensable condition for all authentic discipleship. 'Those who are ashamed or afraid to acknowledge Christ before men, cannot expect to be saved. The want of courage to confess, is decisive evidence of the want of heart to believe' (Hodge) [*Matt.* 10:32; *Luke* 12:8; *1 John* 4:15].

And shalt believe in thy heart that God raised him from the dead, thou shalt be saved: The part is put for the whole, for to believe that 'God has raised Christ from the dead, involves the belief that Christ is all that he claimed to be, and that he has accomplished all that he came to perform' (Hodge) [1:4, 4:24, 25]. The term 'heart' stands for the whole man in the unity of his selfhood. Man is more than an artificial agglomeration of thought, feeling, and will. The modern notion which equates the 'heart' with the emotions is not sanctioned by the use of this word in Scripture.

Haldane draws attention to Paul's sustained use of the second person. 'If *thou* shalt confess with *thy* mouth, and shalt believe in *thine* heart, *thou* shalt be saved. He speaks of every one, so that all may examine themselves, for to every one believing and confessing, salvation is promised; thus teaching each one to apply the promise of salvation to himself by faith and confession.'

10: for with the heart man believeth unto righteousness; and with the mouth confession is made unto salvation.

Paul again underlines the fact that there is no salvation without confession and faith, but here they are exhibited in their true order: 'faith being the root, confession the branch, *Matt.* 12:34; *2 Cor.* 4:13' (Shedd). The Jews knew very well that it was necessary to attain righteousness in order to be saved, but in seeking to attain it by the works of the law they simply sentenced themselves to failure and rejection. For nothing but heart-faith can receive the righteousness which ensures salvation, and such faith is glad to confess its indebtedness to Christ for this priceless boon.

11: For the scripture saith, Whosoever believeth on him shall not be put to shame.

Paul again invokes the testimony of Isaiah 28:16 to confirm his doctrine [9:33], but here substitutes 'whosoever' for 'he that believeth' as he wishes to stress the universality of the gospel offer of salvation. This good news must be preached to all men, because the promise is that 'whosoever' puts his trust in Christ shall never be put to shame. Hence a man's natural birth neither qualifies nor hinders him from receiving the righteousness which is of faith.

12: For there is no distinction between Jew and Greek: for the same Lord is Lord of all, and is rich unto all that call upon him:

13: for, Whosoever shall call upon the name of the Lord shall be saved.

Paul has already stated that there is no distinction in regard to guilt [3:22]; now he affirms that there is no distinction in regard to grace! The Jews believed otherwise and maintained that there *was* a distinction which was entirely in their favour, one that required that a Gentile become a Jew before he could be saved [cf. *Acts* 15:1–31]. But instead of compelling a Greek to become like a legalistic Jew, the Jew must drop his legalism and become like a believing Greek (Lenski). There are not two gospels, one for Jews and another for Gentiles, because both are under the same condemnation and so both have the same need. There is therefore but *one* gospel which promises that the same Lord, who is Lord of *all*, is abounding in wealth toward *all* who call upon him. The immediate context makes it clear that 'Lord' is to be referred to the exalted Christ, and this is confirmed by the use of this expression elsewhere in the New Testament [cf. verses 9, 12, 13: See *Acts* 7:59, 60; 9:14, 21; 10:36; 22:16; *1 Cor.* 1:2; *Phil.* 2:11; *2 Tim.* 2:22].

The words of verse 13 are taken from Joel 2:32, which is also quoted by Peter in his sermon on the day of Pentecost [*Acts* 2:21]. David Brown remarks, 'This is but one of many Old Testament passages of which *Jehovah* is the subject, and which in the New Testament are applied to *Christ* – an irrefragable proof of his proper divinity.' And as there is salvation in no other Name [*Acts* 4:12], all who refuse to call upon that Name thereby exclude themselves from his kingdom of grace and glory.

14: How then shall they call on him in whom they have not believed? and how shall they believe in him whom they have not heard? and how shall they hear without a preacher?

15: and how shall they preach, except they be sent? Even as it is written, How beautiful are the feet of them that bring glad tidings of good things!

Paul has proved that salvation depends on calling on Christ, but Israel refuses to recognize him as Lord. How is this mystery to be explained? Paul runs through the chain that leads to faith and confession: 1. There can be no calling on him in whom one does not believe; 2. there can be no believing in him of whom one has not heard; 3. there can be no hearing without a preacher; 4. there will be no preachers unless God sends them (Nygren). What, then, is the reason for Israel's failure to confess Christ as Lord? Beginning with the last point, he works backwards and shows from Scripture that Israel cannot plead ignorance as an excuse for their unbelief. For God has certainly sent forth the heralds of salvation to preach the good news to Israel [*Isa.* 52:7]. The prophet pictures the joy with which the exiles receive the news of their release from the Babylonian captivity, but the approach of the messengers who run with the news of a far richer deliverance is not welcomed by Israel. Unhappily, their dust-covered feet are not 'beautiful' to them!

16: But they did not all hearken to the glad tidings. For Isaiah saith, Lord, who hath believed our report?

This poignant understatement heightens the tragedy of Israel's refusal to give heed to the glad tidings they undoubtedly heard. 'Not all' but nearly all repudiated the gospel, and so failed to receive the righteousness which was offered to them in the Word [verse 3]. It is very significant that the prophet's lament, which is echoed by Paul, appears at the head of the clearest prediction of Christ's sufferings in the whole of Scripture [*Isa.* 53:1]. 'The very heart of the gospel Israel would not believe, neither then nor thereafter, not even after the Messiah had already come' (Lenski).

17: So belief cometh of hearing, and hearing by the word of Christ.

The result of this reasoning is now presented in summary form: 'So faith comes from what is heard, and what is heard comes by the preaching of Christ' (RSV). If Israel had not heard this preaching of Christ there would have been an excuse for their unbelief. Hence Paul immediately goes on to show that such is not the case.

18: But I say, Did they not hear? Yea, verily,
Their sound went out into all the earth,
And their words unto the ends of the world.

The plea of ignorance is decisively dismissed in the words of Psalm 19:4. For the message has been so widely diffused among the Diaspora (the Jews dispersed among the Gentiles) that Paul can appropriately describe its universal proclamation in terms of the general witness of creation to its Creator. 'There is not a synagogue which has not been filled with it; not a Jew in the world who can justly plead ignorance on the subject' (Godet).

19: But I say, Did Israel not know? First Moses saith,

I will provoke you to jealousy with that which is no nation,
With a nation void of understanding will I anger you.

Thus Israel has heard the message through which faith comes, and yet has not trusted in him of whom it speaks [verse 14]. To bring out the reason for this, Paul adds another question: Can it be that Israel did not *understand* the gospel? He has a two-fold answer ready to hand from both the law and the prophets. First, there is Moses' testimony against Israel's forthcoming apostasy for which they would be rejected by God in favour of a 'no nation' [*Deut.* 32:21]. As a people who are insensible of God's mercies will provoke him to jealous anger by their idolatry, so he in turn will arouse the same feelings in them by blessing a senseless people with his salvation. Paul sees this prophecy has been fulfilled in the calling of the 'foolish' Gentiles who had both heard and understood the gospel, to the jealous fury of the Jews who above all people ought to have understood it [cf. *Acts* 17:5, 13].

20: And Isaiah is very bold, and saith,

I was found of them that sought me not;
I became manifest unto them that asked not of me.

Finally, in applying the testimony of Isaiah to the calling of the Gentiles, Paul draws attention to the boldness of the prophet, for the Jews vainly imagined that they alone enjoyed the monopoly of God's grace and favour [*Isa.* 65:1].

21: But as to Israel he saith,

All the day long did I spread out my hands unto a disobedient and gainsaying people.

In Isaiah 65:2 the prophet eloquently contrasts God's patient entreaties and continued loving-kindness with Israel's stubborn refusal to yield to the overtures of his mercy. 'The arms outstretched all the day long are the symbol of that incessant pleading love which Israel through all its history has consistently despised. It is not want of knowledge, then, nor want of intelligence, but wilful and stubborn disobedience, that explains the exclusion of Israel (meanwhile) from the Kingdom of Christ and all its blessings' (Denney).

CHAPTER ELEVEN

1: I say then, Did God cast off his people? God forbid. For I also am an Israelite, of the seed of Abraham, of the tribe of Benjamin.

It is in view of Israel's continuing unbelief that Paul now asks, 'Did God cast off his people?' Although the form of the question demands a negative reply, he emphatically rejects the suggestion with his usual expression of abhorrence. Because even now there is a believing remnant to which Paul is proud to belong, for though he was specially called to minister to the Gentiles, he does not permit his readers to forget that he is himself an 'Israelite'. 'Paul was a Jew by descent from Abraham, and not merely a proselyte; and he was of one of the most favoured tribes. Judah and Benjamin, especially after the exile, were the chief representatives of the theocratical people' (Hodge).

2a: God did not cast off his people which he foreknew.

It is evident that 'his people which he foreknew' refers to *the nation* of Israel and not to the elect from among the Jews, because it would be inconceivable that God should cast off *his elect* (Alford). On the subject of God's foreknowledge Warfield says: 'According to the Old Testament conception, God foreknows only because he has pre-determined, and it is therefore also that he brings it to pass; his foreknowledge, in other words, is at bottom a knowledge of his own will, and his works of providence are merely the execution of his all-embracing plan' (*Predestination*).

2b: Or know ye not what the scripture saith of Elijah? how he pleadeth with God against Israel,

3: Lord, they have killed thy prophets, they have digged down thine altars: and I am left alone, and they seek my life.

4: But what saith the answer of God unto him? I have left for myself seven thousand men, who have not bowed the knee to Baal.

The quotation is apposite to Paul's purpose, for Elijah's angry prayer against Israel in a time of general apostasy received a surprising rejoinder [*1 Kings* 19:10, 14, 18]. 'Notwithstanding the apostasy of Israel as a whole, yet there was a remnant, though only a remnant, whom God had kept for himself and preserved from the idolatry of Baal's worship. This example is adduced to prove that God had not cast off Israel as his chosen and beloved people. The import, therefore, is that the salvation of a small remnant from the total mass is sufficient proof that the people as a nation had not been cast off' (John Murray).

5: Even so then at this present time also there is a remnant according to the election of grace.

It should be remembered that the first converts to Christianity were Jews, and though the great mass of Israel rejected the gospel, the existence of an elect remnant proved that God's plan had not miscarried. Times of religious declension make it evident that the believing remnant 'is a remnant according to the election of grace' [cf. *1 Cor.* 4:7].

6: But if it is by grace, it is no more of works: otherwise grace is no more grace.

David Brown remarks, 'The general position here laid down is fundamental, and of unspeakable importance. It may be thus expressed: There are but two possible sources of salvation – men's works and God's grace; and these are so essentially distinct and opposite, that salvation cannot be of any combination or mixture of both; it must be wholly either of the one or of the other' [*Eph.* 2:8, 9].

7: What then? That which Israel seeketh for, that he obtained not; but the election obtained it, and the rest were hardened:

At present then, Israel as a nation has not obtained the righteousness it sought, 'because they sought it not by faith, but as it were by works' [9:32]. That they entertained such a false hope was the result of a self-hardening which was judicially confirmed by God [verse 8]. However, some Jews have attained to the righteousness of faith, because these had been elected unto eternal life [verse 5]. Paul uses the abstract noun 'the election' to place the emphasis upon the sovereignty of God's choice. 'When men are saved they are saved by the sovereign grace of God, and when they perish, it is by the appointment of God, *Jude* 4, through their own fault' (Haldane).

8: according as it is written, God gave them a spirit of stupor, eyes that they should not see, and ears that they should not hear, unto this very day.

The language here is taken from Isaiah 29:10 and Deuteronomy 29:4 and it is probably not improper to detect in it an echo of the thought of Isaiah 6:9. 'The design of such citations frequently is to show that what was fulfilled partially in former times, was more perfectly accomplished at a subsequent period. The Jews had often before been hardened, but at no former period were the people so blinded, hardened, and reprobate, as when they rejected the Son of God, and put him to an open shame. It had often been predicted that such should be their state when the Messiah came. The punitive character of the evils here threatened, cannot escape the reader's notice. This blindness and hardness were not mere calamities, nor were they simply the natural effects of the sins of the people. They were punitive inflictions. They are so denounced. God says, I will give you eyes that see not. It is a dreadful thing to fall into the hands of the living God. The strokes of his justice blind, bewilder, and harden the soul' (Hodge).

9: And David saith,

Let their table be made a snare, and a trap,
And a stumblingblock, and a recompense unto them:
10: Let their eyes be darkened, that they may not see,
And bow thou down their back always.

These words are from Psalm 69:22, 23. J. A. Alexander comments, 'The imprecations in this verse and those following it are revolting only when considered as the expression of malignant selfishness. If uttered by God, they shock no reader's sensibilities, nor should they, when considered as the language of an ideal person, representing the whole class of righteous sufferers, and particularly Him who, though he prayed for his murderers while dying [*Luke* 23:34], had before applied the words of this very passage to the unbelieving Jews [*Matt.* 23:38], as Paul did afterwards [*Rom.* 11:9, 10]. The general doctrine of providential retribution, far from being confined to the Old Testament, is distinctly taught in many of our Saviour's parables. See *Matt.* 21:41, 22:7, 24:51' (*Commentary on Psalms*, p. 295.)

11: I say then, Did they stumble that they might fall? God forbid: but by their fall salvation is come unto the Gentiles, to provoke them to jealousy.

12: Now if their fall is the riches of the world, and their loss the riches of the Gentiles; how much more their fullness?

This question introduces a new section in which the apostle shows that the fall of Israel *as a nation* is not final. The present preservation of an elect remnant is the earnest of their future restoration. Meanwhile even their fall is not without its beneficent consequences for the world at large. Paul argues that if the 'stumbling' of Israel has brought salvation to the Gentiles, then their 'fullness' must bring untold blessing to mankind [verse 15]. Moreover, the realization that the covenant favour of God has been extended to the Gentiles is designed to provoke Israel earnestly to seek after an interest in the same salvation. 'The Jews, even those who were professors of Christianity, were, in the first place, very slow to allow the gospel to be preached to the Gentiles; and in the second, they appear almost uniformly to have desired to clog the gospel with the ceremonial observances of the law. This was one of the greatest hindrances to the progress of the cause of Christ during the apostolic age, [which] would, in all human probability, have been a thousandfold greater, had the Jews, as a nation, embraced the Christian faith. On both these accounts, the rejection of the Jews was incidentally a means of facilitating the progress of the gospel. Besides this, the punishment which befell them on account of their unbelief, involving the destruction of their nation and power, of course prevented their being able to forbid the general preaching of the gospel which they earnestly desired to do' (Hodge) [*Acts* 13:46].

13: But I speak to you that are Gentiles. Inasmuch then as I am an apostle of Gentiles, I glorify my ministry;

14: if by any means I may provoke to jealousy them that are my flesh, and may save some of them.

Paul does not regard his ministry to the Gentiles as a work which is hostile to Jewish interests, but as one whose constant tendency is to promote the spiritual good of his kinsmen. The strength of his feeling for them may be gauged by the description given in verse 14, 'them that are my flesh'. He hopes that when they see the blessings brought to the Gentiles through his labours 'some of them' will be saved. What is here implied will be explicitly stated presently, namely, that the love and compassion which their great apostle exercised towards the unbelieving Jews is an example which should be followed by all Gentile believers.

The shameful failure of the church to heed the plain teaching of Paul on this matter is without doubt one of the greatest blots upon its history. The address adopted in verse 13 gives the impression that the church in Rome was largely a Gentile community [cf. 1:13].

15: For if the casting away of them is the reconciling of the world, what shall the receiving of them be, but life from the dead?

The Gentiles need not fear that the future conversion of Israel will impoverish them. On the contrary, it will bring unimaginable blessing to the world. From the first God designed to bless mankind through the seed of Abraham [*Gen.* 28: 14]. Now if the fall of the Jews has resulted in the 'reconciling of the world', what shall their restoration be, but 'life from the dead'? David Brown comments: 'The meaning seems to be that the reception of the whole family of Israel, scattered as they are among all nations under heaven, and the most inveterate enemies of the Lord Jesus, will be such a stupendous manifestation of the power of God upon the spirits of men, and of his glorious presence with the heralds of the cross, as will not only kindle devout astonishment far and wide, but so change the dominant mode of thinking and feeling on all spiritual things as to seem like a resurrection from the dead.'

16: And if the firstfruit is holy, so is the lump: and if the root is holy, so are the branches.

Israel's consecration to God is now illustrated by two metaphors. As the offering of the first part of the dough consecrated the whole lump, so the dedication of the root to God ensures the 'holiness' of the branches [*Num.* 15:17–21]. Hodge is careful to point out that in this verse the word 'holy' does not mean 'morally pure', but is used to describe the special separation of the Jews from the rest of the world for the service of God. The application of both figures to the consecration of the patriarchs appears to be confirmed by verse 28. The final restoration of Israel is therefore guaranteed by the distinguishing love of God for Abraham, Isaac, and Jacob.

17: But if some of the branches were broken off, and thou, being a wild olive, wast grafted in among them, and didst become partaker with them of the root of the fatness of the olive tree;

18: glory not over the branches: but if thou gloriest, it is not thou that bearest the root, but the root thee.

Since the Gentiles have been made profitable only by a supernatural act of divine grace, they have no occasion to boast against those natural branches which have been broken off through unbelief. They have contributed nothing, and received everything. All their spiritual vitality is derived *from the root* of the cultivated olive tree, 'for salvation is of the Jews' [*John* 4:22]. As the purpose of all grafting is to impart new life and vigour *to the root*, it is plain that Paul is here pointing a spiritual analogy, which has no exact parallel in the natural realm [cf. verse 24: 'contrary to nature'].

19: Thou wilt say then, Branches were broken off, that I might be grafted in.

Contempt for those who have fallen through unbelief, and a sense of pride in the present possession of gospel privileges, are both reflected in this imaginary Gentile objection. To describe such an attitude is the best argument against its adoption. 'I' is given emphatic expression by the word *ego* which, as John Murray observes, underlines the 'egoism and vainglory of this boasting'.

20: Well; by their unbelief they were broken off, and thou standest by thy faith. Be not highminded, but fear:

It should be noted that Paul does not represent fear as an emotion which is incompatible with the exercise of faith, for those who truly trust God also have learned wholly to distrust themselves. Self-confidence and confidence in God are polar opposites. On more than one occasion the apostle puts forward the fear of failure as a proper stimulant to Christian endeavour [*1 Cor.* 2:3; *Eph.* 6:5; *Phil.* 2:12. cf. *Heb.* 4:1; *1 Pet.* 1:17]. 'Seest thou thy brother shipwrecked! look well to thy tackling' (Trapp) [*1 Cor.* 10:12].

21: for if God spared not the natural branches, neither will he spare thee.

Those who commit the same fault may expect to share the same fate. There is no respect of persons with God. If Israel's natural privileges afforded no protection against God's righteous judgment, then the Gentiles must know what surely awaits them if they do not continue in God's goodness [verse 22].

22: Behold then the goodness and severity of God: toward them that fell, severity; but toward thee, God's goodness, if thou continue in his goodness: otherwise thou also shalt be cut off.

This is an invitation to contemplate God in the character in which he has been pleased to reveal himself. It is the goodness of God which justifies his existence in the eyes of most men, for they are unwilling to admit that the Deity has any higher purpose than the advancement of their own good. On the other hand, the severity of God is a most distasteful concept to autonomous man, because it is at once a denial of man's independence and an unequivocal assertion of God's sovereignty. 'Men generally form in their imagination the character of God according to their own inclination. It is the duty of the Christian to take God's character as it is given by himself. His goodness is no evidence that he will not punish the guilty; and the most dreadful punishment of the guilty is consistent with the existence of supreme goodness in the divine character' (Haldane).

The exhortations to persevere in the faith, which are found throughout the New Testament, are not inconsistent with the promise of divine preservation unto life eternal. Rather it is by giving heed to such admonitions that Christians are brought to glory. 'God graciously causes a man to persevere in willing. That is the whole truth . . . the true doctrine is not that salvation is certain if we have once believed, but that *perseverance in holiness* is certain if we have truly believed' (A. A. Hodge, *The Confession of Faith*, pp. 234–5) [*Acts* 13:43].

23: And they also, if they continue not in their unbelief, shall be grafted in: for God is able to graft them in again.

This verse marks a smooth transition from warning to hope, for if unbelief separates, it is equally true that faith is the bond of union. Paul has said that if the Gentiles lose their faith, they shall be broken off. Conversely, if Israel does not remain unbelieving they shall be grafted in again. Since such an event is not likely to occur after the 'natural' order of events, it is here expressly attributed to the power of God. And it is a representation which is entirely consonant with the supernatural character of faith. Faith is not self-originated; it is the gift of God. It is his prerogative to remove the veil of unbelief from the heart, and to bestow the capacity to respond to the gospel.

24: For if thou wast cut out of that which is by nature a wild olive tree and wast grafted contrary to nature into a good olive tree; how much more shall these, which are the natural branches, be grafted into their own olive tree?

Now if such foreign branches have been so unexpectedly incorporated into the good olive tree, how much more likely is the restoration of the natural branches to what is after all their own olive tree? The emphasis rests upon the fitness of such a restoration. There is no derogation of the power which would be required to accomplish it.

Contrary to nature: 'Therefore nature contributes nothing toward the work of conversion' (Trapp) [*Eph.* 2:3].

25: For I would not, brethren, have you ignorant of this mystery, lest ye be wise in your own conceits, that a hardening in part hath befallen Israel, until the fulness of the Gentiles be come in;

For I would not, brethren, have you ignorant of this mystery: Spiritual ignorance is dispelled only by divine revelation. This characteristic form of address is designed to secure the readers' close attention to the important statement which is to follow it [cf. 1:13; *1 Cor.* 10:1; 12:1; *2 Cor.* 1: 8; *1 Thess.* 4:13]. This is not a mystery 'in the pagan sense of an esoteric doctrine known only to the initiated, but in the Christian sense of a doctrine that requires a divine revelation in order to be known. Compare Romans 16:25; 1 Corinthians 2:7–10, 15:51; Ephesians 3:4, 5' (Shedd).

Lest ye be wise in your own conceits: 'Ignorance of the Scriptures is the cause of high-mindedness in Christians' (Haldane).

That a hardening in part hath befallen Israel, until the fulness of the Gentiles be come in: This amounts to a divine disclosure of what could not have been naturally anticipated. There is to be a spiritual restoration of Israel as a nation, but this will not take place 'until the fulness of the Gentiles be come in'. The gathering into the kingdom of the majority of the *elect* Gentiles will mark the terminus of Israel's unbelief. This expectation is not inconsistent with Paul's prediction of the widespread apostasy which will occur in connection with the revelation of the Man of Sin, for as Geerhardus Vos is careful to point out, 'The coming in of the Gentiles does not preclude the falling away again from the Gentiles of considerable groups' (*The Pauline Eschatology,* p. 133) [cf. *2 Thess.* 2:3].

Although the central thrust of the apostle is unmistakable, the manner of its accomplishment remains obscure, and no doubt this is intentional. As Hodge wisely observes, 'Prophecy is not proleptic history. It is not designed to give us the knowledge of the future which history gives us of the past. Great events are foretold; but the mode of their occurrence, their details, and their consequences, can only be learned by the event. It is in the retrospect that the foreshadowing of the future is seen to be miraculous and divine.'

26: and so all Israel shall be saved: even as it is written, There shall come out of Zion the Deliverer;
He shall turn away ungodliness from Jacob:

27: And this is my covenant unto them,
When I shall take away their sin.

The context makes it certain that 'Israel' must refer to the nation of Israel, but the word 'all' gives no warrant for believing that every individual Jew is to be saved. It simply means the nation as an elect body. Paul quotes from Isaiah 59:20 and Jeremiah 31:33 to prove that he is propounding no novelty, but is only bringing to more explicit expression what has been long foretold in Scripture. It is in harmony with the miraculous nature of the event predicted that the accent in these prophecies 'falls upon what God will do' (John Murray).

28: As touching the gospel, they are enemies for your sake: but as touching the election, they are beloved for the fathers' sake.

With regard to the gospel the Jews are now enemies through their temporary unbelief, though this alienation has been the means of bringing the Gentiles into the sphere of blessing. However, this present enmity cannot impair their election of God, for the people of Israel 'are beloved for the fathers' sake'. God's attitude to the nation of Israel may not be gauged by their present rejection, but is to be viewed in the light of the promises made to the patriarchs. Thus Israel's exclusion is not final, and their eventual restoration is guaranteed.

29: For the gifts and the calling of God are not repented of.

'These words, considered simply and abstractedly, afford this truth; that the special gifts of God, his election, justification, adoption, and in particular, effectual calling, are irrevocable. God never repents of giving, nor we of receiving them. It is otherwise with common gifts and graces, *1 Sam.* 15:11. But if you consider these words relatively, as you respect what went before, the sense seems to be this; that "the gifts and calling of God," whereby he was pleased to adopt the posterity of Abraham, and to engage himself by covenant to them, are inviolable, and are such as shall never be reversed or repented of' (Poole)

30: For as ye in time past were disobedient to God, but now have obtained mercy by their disobedience,

31: even so have these also now been disobedient, that by the mercy shown to you they also may now obtain mercy.

As the disobedient Gentiles have obtained mercy through the disobedience of Israel, even so Israel shall find mercy through the Gentiles' experience of God's mercy. If God has brought good out of that which is in itself evil, what may he not bring out of that which is good?

32: For God hath shut up all unto disobedience, that he might have mercy upon all.

Defenders of the doctrine of election are sometimes accused of dwelling too much upon the severities of chapter 9 without taking due account of the closing stages of Paul's argument. But Warfield has well said, 'We do not escape from the doctrine of predestination of the ninth chapter in fleeing to the eleventh.' And of this verse, he remarked: 'On the face of it there could not readily be framed a more explicit assertion of the divine control and the divine initiative than this; it is only another declaration that he has mercy on whom he will have mercy, and after the manner and in the order that he will' (*Predestination*).

As there can be no exercise of mercy where there is no disobedience, God has shut up both Jew and Gentile in this common prison in order that his mercy might be bestowed upon both without distinction. 'The apostle is not here dealing with individuals, but with those great divisions of mankind, Jew and Gentile. And what he here says is, that God's purpose was to shut up each of these divisions of men to the experience, first, of an unhumbled, condemned state, without Christ, and then to the experience of his mercy in Christ' (David Brown).

33: O the depth of the riches both of the wisdom and the knowledge of God! how unsearchable are his judgments, and his ways past tracing out!

This survey of the divine purpose in history has evoked in Paul a profound feeling of awe and adoration. When finite understanding encounters Infinite Wisdom the only proper response is one of unqualified wonder and worship. John Murray makes the important point that this doxology was not prompted by what was unknowable in God, but by the incomprehensibility of that which God has revealed! It is a revelation which it is completely beyond our capacity to fathom, and therefore we must cry with the apostle, 'O the depth!' 'It is not the reaction of painful bewilderment but the response of adoring amazement, redolent of joy and praise. When our faith and understanding peer to the horizons of revelation, it is then our hearts and minds are overwhelmed with the incomprehensible mystery of God's works and ways' (John Murray).

34: For who hath known the mind of the Lord? or who hath been his counsellor?

35: or who hath first given to him, and it shall be recompensed unto him again?

These quotations from the Old Testament are taken from Isaiah 40:13 and Job 41:11. 'As it is the tendency and result of all correct views of Christian doctrine to produce the feelings expressed by the apostle at the close of this chapter, those views cannot be scriptural which have a contrary tendency; or which lead us to ascribe, in any form, our salvation to our own merit or power' (Hodge).

36: For of him, and through him, and unto him, are all things. To him be
the glory for ever. Amen

'Here we have the grand truth which lies at the foundation of all
religion. All things are *of God*, for he is the Author of all; his will is the
origin of all existence. All things are *through him*, for all things are
created by him as the grand agent. All things are likewise *to him*, for
all things tend to his glory as their final end' (Haldane).

CHAPTER TWELVE

1: I beseech you therefore, brethren, by the mercies of God, to present
your bodies a living sacrifice, holy, acceptable to God, which is your
spiritual service.

I beseech you therefore, brethren, by the mercies of God: This eloquent
appeal proves that acceptable obedience is always the grateful response
of redeemed hearts to the multiplied mercies of God. That Paul should
choose to entreat rather than command underlines the voluntary nature
of the response which a real experience of these compassions should
constrain. Paul knows that if his readers have truly understood his
exposition of the doctrines of grace, this knowledge will be clearly
exhibited in a holy walk. Christian doctrine is never taught to provide
a species of intellectual enlightenment but to promote practical
obedience. For if theology is *grace*, then ethics is *gratitude*
(F. F. Bruce).

To present your bodies: Christianity sanctions no unnatural dichotomy
between the spirit and the body, and the realism of the apostle is very
evident in this requirement. A sanctification which does not extend to
the body is essentially spurious [*1 Thess.* 5:23, 24]. The same body
through which sin once found its concrete expression must now be
presented to God as the vehicle of righteousness [6:19].

A living sacrifice, holy, acceptable to God: It is the great reality of Christ's
sacrifice which 'has swept all dead victims from off the altar of God'
(David Brown). Thus it is the body as raised to new life in Christ which
is to be presented to God [6:13]. Such living sacrifices are holy and
acceptable to God solely through the efficacy of Christ's redemptive
travail. Believers find their acceptance with God through his beloved
Son in whom he is well pleased. 'The sacrifice of the mass not being
appointed by God, and actually subversive of the sacrifice of the cross,

instead of being agreeable to God, must be odious in his sight' (Haldane).

Which is your reasonable service (AV): This dedication of the body to the service of God is to be informed and directed by the mind, for it is here described as 'your rational worship'. The superiority of the new covenant is shown in the replacement of the ritual offering of a dead body by the rational consecration of the living body. 'The lesson to be derived from the term "rational" is that we are not "Spiritual" in the biblical sense except as the use of our bodies is characterized by conscious, intelligent, consecrated devotion to the service of God' (John Murray).

> **2: And be not fashioned according to this world: but be ye formed by the renewing of your mind, that ye may prove what is the good and acceptable and perfect will of God.**

"'Do not fall in," says the apostle, "with the fleeting fashions of this world, nor be yourselves fashioned to them, but undergo a deep abiding change by the renewing of your mind, such as the Spirit of God alone can work in you" [cf. *2 Cor.* 3:18]' (Trench). The inward transformation of the mind is the only effective preservative against outward conformity with the spirit of this present age.

Since Christians properly belong to the 'high mountain-land above' they must refuse to descend to the level of those whose minds are blinded by the god of this world and whose outlook is consequently circumscribed by that which is temporal [*2 Cor.* 4:4, 18].

That ye may prove what is the will of God, even the thing which is good and acceptable and perfect (ASV margin): The purpose of this renewal of the mind is that Christians may be able to test and approve in practice what is the will of God. The three adjectives serve to show that God's will defines the morally good, prescribes what is well pleasing to him, and provides a standard which is ethically complete [*Matt.* 5:48]. 'No one discovers the line of action which from possessing these characteristics can be identified as the will of God unless he is transformed from his native affinity to the world by the renewing of his mind by the Holy Spirit' (Denney).

> **3: For I say, through the grace that was given to me, to every man that is among you, not to think of himself more highly than he ought to think;**

but so to think as to think soberly, according as God hath dealt to each a measure of faith,

Paul begins this exhortation to humility by reminding his readers that every gift, including that of apostleship, is the bestowal of God's grace which therefore excludes all boasting. Christians are neither to over-value nor to under-estimate their talents but must seek to assess them realistically, 'according as God hath dealt to each man a measure of faith'.

Paul's play on words is well brought out by David Brown: 'Not to be high-minded above what he ought to be minded, but so to be minded as to be sober-minded' [*Phil.* 2:3, 5].

4: For even as we have many members in one body, and all the members have not the same office:

5: so we, who are many, are one body in Christ, and severally members one of another.

This familiar Pauline figure perfectly conveys the idea of diversity in unity; there are many members but only one body [*1 Cor.* 10:17; 12:27]. It is necessary to recognize the true value of these spiritual endowments and the proper sphere in which they are to be exercised, for the gifts which are peculiar to each member only promote the well-being and harmony of the whole body when they are practised in a spirit of genuine humility. Those who do not hold to the Head can have no fellowship with the members; hence a desire for pre-eminence spells death to all spiritual usefulness [*Col.* 2:19, *3 John* 9]. Meekness is the mint-mark of all true followers of the Lamb.

6: And having gifts differing according to the grace that was given to us, whether prophecy, let us prophesy according to the proportion of our faith;

7: or ministry, let us give ourselves to our ministry; or he that teacheth, to his teaching;

8: or he that exhorteth, to his exhorting: he that giveth, let him do it with liberality; he that ruleth, with diligence; he that showeth mercy, with cheerfulness.

No particular order is followed here, for this is not a list of offices, but a series of examples which show how various gifts are to be exercised within the body of Christ. 'It is quite obvious that the apostle is not distinguishing offices, but gifts. Every gift does not require a different office. Many of the gifts required no office at all' (Haldane).

Paul's definite instruction to those with the gift of prophecy, 'to prophesy in agreement with the faith' (Arndt-Gingrich), indicates their subordination to apostolic authority [1 Cor. 14:37]. They must not exceed their brief, nor fall short of its commission. This principle holds good whether 'prophecy' refers to those miraculous gifts which flourished in the early church or whether, as Calvin prefers, 'he is referring simply to ordinary gifts which remain perpetually in the Church'. In either case, no revelation or exposition is valid which departs from the infallible norm established by the apostolate. Every human utterance is subject to, and must be tested by the supreme authority of Scripture, which is the inspired record of 'the faith which was once for all delivered unto the saints' [Jude 3].

Ministry, teaching, and exhortation are to be faithfully practised by those who are thus gifted. 'Ministry' may refer either to the ministry of the Word or to the office of a deacon. 'Teaching is addressed to the understanding; exhortation, to the conscience and feelings' (Hodge). These must always go together, for if teaching gives exhortation its content, exhortation gives teaching its force. Giving is to be graced by liberality. Those who have freely received must freely give without ulterior design for gain, or ostentatious desire for fame. Those entrusted with responsibility in the government of the church are to be diligent, and not negligent, in the performance of their duties. Finally, the ministry of mercy is to be distinguished by a cheerful spirit. Kindly acts must be seen to stem from a loving concern for the sufferer, for 'if he observes gloominess on the face of those who help him, he will take it as an affront' (Calvin).

> **9: Let love be without hypocrisy. Abhor that which is evil; cleave to that which is good.**
>
> **10: In love of the brethren be tenderly affectioned one to another; in honour preferring one another;**

From 'gifts' Paul now passes to 'love' [cf. verses 3–8 with 1 Cor. 12; verses 9–21 with 1 Cor. 13]. Although Christians are bound to acknowledge the supremacy of love, they must not allow their profession of it to run ahead of their real feelings for others, for those who do are guilty of hypocrisy [*2 Cor.* 6:6; *1 Pet.* 1:22]. A new concept of love needed a new word to describe it, and *agape* 'is a word born within the bosom of revealed religion' (Trench). 'Christian love, whether exercised toward the brethren, or toward men generally, is not an impulse from the feelings, it does not always run with the natural inclinations, nor does it spend itself only upon those for whom some affinity is discovered' (Vine), and this is because Christian love is ever patterned upon an experience of the self-giving love of God, a love which has no regard for the worthiness of its objects [cf. 5:8].

The Christian's attitude towards good and evil must be violently partisan. He cannot look upon evil with benevolent neutrality, nor can he regard it as something which is 'less good'. His rejection of it must be unqualified and total [*Psa.* 119:104; *Amos* 5:15; *Jude* 23]. On the other hand, he must steadfastly 'cleave to that which is good'. This does not indicate a slight preference for the good, it means to 'be glued to it'. The same word is used to signify the permanence of the marriage relation [*Matt.* 19:5].

'In honour preferring one another' is the method recommended by Paul for the maintenance of a spirit of brotherly love (verse 10). 'As there is nothing more opposed to brotherly concord than the contempt which arises from pride, while each esteems others less and exalts himself, so modesty, by which each comes to honour others, best nourishes love' (Calvin) [*Phil.* 2:3].

11: in diligence not slothful; fervent in spirit; serving the Lord;

The progression of thought in this trio of exhortations is well noted by Lenski. First, Christians must be marked by diligence in devotion that does not lag behind. This effectively enjoins the prompt performance of present duty. Secondly, this zeal is to be maintained by ensuring that their spiritual temperature remains on the boil [*Acts* 18:25]. 'A man's spirit must move him to diligence; when enough steam is generated in the boiler, the engine speeds over the rails' (Lenski). Thirdly, this energy is to be expended in serving the Lord. 'Many are diligent enough, some have fanatical zeal; many glow and literally boil over in their spirit; but so much of the busy effort and the steam back of it is not at all work for the Lord' (Lenski). 'Serving the Lord' really means working as a slave in his service, taking orders only from him and obeying them implicitly.

12: rejoicing in hope; patient in tribulation; continuing steadfastly in prayer;

The summons to be 'patient in tribulation' is significantly sandwiched between the call to rejoice in hope and to continue instant in prayer. The Christian does not sink under present trials, because he is buoyed up by the hope of future glory and the divine strength which is imparted to him through prayer. Those who are without God in the world are necessarily destitute of hope, for hope belongs only to those who know God [*Eph.* 2:12]. Believers therefore ought to enjoy the assurance of their salvation and eagerly anticipate its consummation, but exhortation is required if they are to live up to the level of their spiritual privileges in Christ Jesus [*Heb.* 6:11; *1 Pet.* 1:8]. 'The measure of perseverance in the midst of tribulation is the measure of our diligence in prayer. Prayer is the means ordained of God for the supply of grace sufficient for every exigency and particularly against the faint-heartedness to which affliction tempts us' (John Murray).

13: communicating to the necessities of the saints; given to hospitality.

These are two ways in which the brotherly love enjoined in verses 9 and 10 is to be given practical expression. The poverty and persecution which made these injunctions especially relevant in the early church also gave the opportunity for an impressive demonstration of the true meaning of Christian fellowship [*Heb.* 13:2; *1 John* 3: 17].

14: Bless them that persecute you; bless, and curse not.

This Pauline echo of the Lord's teaching was also faithfully reproduced in his own life, for those who bear Christ's image are partakers of his sufferings and must meet them in the same spirit [*Matt.* 5:44; *Luke* 6:28; 23:34; *John* 5:20; *1 Cor.* 4:12, 13]. The inflexible determination of the natural man to persecute the righteous affords the most striking proof of his total depravity [*Gal.* 4:29]. The young man Saul first learned the difference between the achievements of law-righteousness and the triumph of grace through Stephen's memorable obedience to this 'impossible' demand. It should be noted that the command freely to forgive the persecutor and to call down blessings upon his head does not involve the Christian in the obligation to approve actions which are morally wrong. Christians cannot approve the *character* of their persecutors, even though they are required to love their *persons*. Thus Stephen cried, 'Lord, lay not *this sin* to their charge' [*Acts* 7:60]. 'When Jesus Christ commands us to love our enemies, it is with the love of benevolence and compassion . . . This love of benevolence for the person of a bad man ought to be, in the Christian, the finite reflection of what it is in God, limited only by the higher attribute of righteousness' (R. L. Dabney, *Discussions*, vol. 1, p. 717). This distinction by no means lessens the difficulty of such an obedience, but it does show that this obedience is not inconsistent with the demands of righteousness.

15: Rejoice with them that rejoice; weep with them that weep.

As divided joy is doubled, so divided sorrow is halved (Lenski). It is because Christians are members of one body that they must share in the joys and sympathize with the sorrows of their fellow-members [*1 Cor.* 12:2,6]. 'Respecting this injunction, Chrysostom remarks that it is easier to weep with those that weep, than to rejoice with those that rejoice; because nature itself prompts the former, but envy stands in the way of the latter' (Shedd).

16: Be of the same mind one toward another. Set not your mind on high things, but condescend to things that are lowly. Be not wise in your own conceits.

Differences in gifts and capacities among Christians offer no excuse for any differentiation within the Christian fellowship [*Phil.* 2:2; 4:1]. Christians are here warned against the ambition and conceit which would turn these differences, which are ordained of God, into occasions of strife, envy, or vain-glory. The fellowship of believers is to be distinguished by that love which 'seeketh not its own' but rather seeks the good of others [*1 Cor.* 13: 5]. 'Be not wise in your own conceits' is taken from Proverbs 3:7. To state this danger is to exhibit its folly. 'Just as there is to be no social aristocracy in the Church so there is to be no intellectual autocrat' (John Murray).

17: Render to no man evil for evil. Take thought for things honourable in the sight of all men.

'Public reparation is when the magistrate, according to the justice and mercy of the divine law, sentences an evil person who has injured his fellow. Private revenge is when those who are not magistrates take matters into their own hands and retaliate against those who have wronged them. The former is clearly permitted, for an apostle declared the magistrate is "the minister of God" for executing judgment upon evil-doers; the same apostle as expressly forbids retaliation: "Recompense to no man evil for evil"' (Arthur Pink, *The Sermon on the Mount*, p. 116).

Take care to preserve an honourable testimony in the sight of all (Bruce): This is a quotation of the Greek version of Proverbs 3:4. Christians are to avoid disgracing their profession by maintaining a standard of conduct which will commend itself to the consciences of their unbelieving neighbours. That the conscience of the natural man is sufficiently enlightened to acknowledge such a standard is also the condemnation of his own failure to conform to it [*2 Cor.* 8:21; *Phil.* 4: 8; *1 Pet.* 3:16].

18: If it be possible, as much as in you lieth, be at peace with all men.

This exhortation to live peaceably with all men is introduced by a double limitation. 'If it be possible' implies that it will not always be possible. When truth is the price of peace, then peace is bought at too dear a rate. 'We are never to seek to maintain peace, either with the world or with Christians, by the sacrifice of any part of divine truth. A Christian must be willing to be unpopular, that he may be useful and faithful. To whatever obloquy or opposition it may expose him, he ought earnestly to contend for the faith which was once delivered unto the saints' (Haldane). However, as the second qualification indicates, a relish for discord is no part of Christian virtue and the Christian, so far as it depends on him, must make every effort to preserve and promote peace with his fellowmen [*Heb.* 12:14].

19: Avenge not yourselves, beloved, but give place unto the wrath of God: for it is written, Vengeance belongeth unto me; I will recompense, saith the Lord.

'Beloved' mirrors Paul's awareness of the difficulty of this require-ment. Christians are not to avenge themselves, but are to leave room for the wrath of God. For it is his right to punish wrong-doers whom he has promised to repay in full measure [*Deut.* 32: 35]. 'The idea is not that instead of executing vengeance ourselves we are to abandon the offender to the more tremendous vengeance of God; but this – that God, not injured men or those who believe themselves such, is the maintainer of moral order in the world, and that the righting of wrong is to be committed to him' (Denney).

20: But if thine enemy hunger, feed him; if he thirst, give him to drink: for in so doing thou shalt heap coals of fire upon his head.

21: Be not overcome of evil, but overcome evil with good.

But the Christian must not only refuse to avenge himself, he is also to repay enmity with every form of kindness. Verse 20 is a quotation of Proverbs 25:21, 22, which is to be taken in a good sense. As Derek Kidner remarks, 'The "coals of fire" represent the pangs which are far better felt now as shame than later as punishment.' Evil is not vanquished by retaliation, but it may be conquered by kindness. 'The true victory over evil consists in transforming a hostile relation into one of love by the magnanimity of the benefits bestowed. Thereby it is that good has the last word, that evil itself serves it as an instrument: such is the masterpiece of love' (Godet).

CHAPTER THIRTEEN

1: Let every soul be in subjection to the higher powers: for there is no power but of God; and the powers that be are ordained of God.

The first seven verses of this chapter define the Christian's duty to the state. Paul begins by showing that the state lawfully claims the obedience of 'every soul' because the power it wields is of God. There can be no exercise of power apart from God [*Isa.* 10:5–7, 45:1; *Dan.* 5:26]. The admission of this truth establishes the important principle that the authority of the state is a delegated, and not an absolute authority. It is only the recognition of this principle which prevents the state from usurping supreme power over the souls of men. Thus when the demands of the state are in conflict with the law of God, resistance to them becomes a positive duty for the Christian [*1 Kings* 21:3; *Dan.* 3:18, 6:12; *Mark* 12:17; *Acts* 4:19, 5:29; *Heb.* 11:23].

History has shown that when theism comes to its rights, human liberty is assured, while the natural tendency of atheism is ever towards totalitarianism. However, at the time this letter was written the systematic persecution of Christians by the state had not yet begun, and therefore this inference is not drawn by the apostle, but when Caesar later demanded the things which belonged to God, Christians could not doubt that he had exceeded his just claims upon their obedience.

'Some have supposed that the right or legitimate authority of human government has its foundation ultimately in "the consent of the governed", "the will of the majority," or in some imaginary "social compact" entered into by the forefathers of the race at the origin of social life. It is self-evident, however, that the divine will is the source of all government; and the obligation to obey that will, resting upon all moral agents, the ultimate ground of all obligation to obey human governments' (A. A. Hodge, *The Confession of Faith*, p. 293).

2: Therefore he that resisteth the power withstandeth the ordinance of God: and they that withstand shall receive to themselves judgment.

'When Paul insists that every soul should be subject to the powers that be, he is evidently removing from the individual judgment any question as to a *de jure* as opposed to a *de facto* government . . . The powers that be, i.e., the actually existing powers are ordained of God' (Gordon Clark, *A Christian View of Men and Things*, p. 140). Therefore those who resist the civil government resist the ordinance of God and consequently incur the judgment of God, who will punish this disobedience.

Yet this passage does not provide rulers with a *carte-blanche* authority to exercise unlimited powers. These powers are limited by the nature of the authority which is committed to the civil magistrate. It was Paul's object to establish the simple principle 'that magistrates are to be obeyed. The extent of this obedience is to be determined from the nature of the case. They are to be obeyed as magistrates, in the exercise of their lawful authority. When Paul commands wives to obey their husbands, they are required to obey them as husbands, not as masters, nor as kings; children are to obey their parents as parents, not as sovereigns; and so in every other case' (Hodge). Thus the crown rights of the Redeemer lie well beyond the sphere of the state's sovereignty.

3: For rulers are not a terror to the good work but to the evil. And wouldest thou have no fear of the power? do that which is good, and thou shalt have praise from the same:

Unrestrained freedom results in anarchy, for then every man does that which is 'right in his own eyes' [*Judg.* 21: 25]. The state is ordained by God to meet the exigencies of the situation created by sin. The fabric of society is preserved from total corruption by the authority of the magistrate. 'It is with the deed that the magistrate is concerned. Paul speaks of the good and evil work. It is not the prerogative of the ruler to deal with all sin but only with sin registered in the action which violates the order that the magistrate is appointed to maintain and promote' (John Murray) [*1 Pet.* 3:13].

Charles Hodge draws the following conclusions from verses 3–7. 'The design of civil government is not to promote the advantages of the rulers, but of the ruled. They are ordained and invested with authority, to be a terror to evil doers, and a praise to them that do well. They are the ministers of God for this end, and are appointed for "this very thing". On this ground our obligation to obedience rests, and the obligation ceases when this design is systematically, constantly, and notoriously disregarded. Where unfaithfulness on the part of the government exists, or where the form of it is incompatible with the design of its institution, the governed must have a right to remedy the evil. But they cannot have the moral right to remedy one evil, by the production of a greater. And, therefore, as there are few greater evils than instability and uncertainty in governments, the cases in which revolutions are justifiable must be exceedingly rare.'

4: for he is a minister of God to thee for good. But if thou do that which is evil, be afraid; for he beareth not the sword in vain: for he is a minister of God, an avenger for wrath to him that doeth evil.

Christians should regard the preservation of law and order as an incalculable good, for the impartial administration of justice protects and promotes the highest interests of religion.

But if . . . : The state is described as 'the minister of God' because 'it is charged with a function which has been explicitly forbidden to the Christian [12:17a, 19]' (F. F. Bruce). It is to be 'an avenger for wrath to him that doeth evil,' and this infliction is regarded by Paul as an expression of the wrath of God. In order effectively to discharge this duty the state is armed with the sword. In these degenerate days when the poison of humanism has directed sympathy to the criminal instead of the victim, it ought to be particularly noted that the apostle describes the restraints imposed by the law in terms of retributive vengeance. As John Murray says, 'Nothing shows the moral bankruptcy of a people or of a generation more than disregard for the sanctity of human life. And it is this same atrophy of moral fibre that appears in the plea for the abolition of the death penalty. It is the sanctity of life that validates the death penalty for the crime of murder' (*Principles of Conduct*, p. 122) [*Gen.* 9:6].

The state is also armed with the sword in order to defend its frontiers and the lives of its citizens against the aggressor. Gordon Clark aptly remarks, 'Christ said, "Render unto Caesar the things that are Caesar's." Of course, the immediate reference was taxes, but Christ knew that Caesar had an army. He did not refuse to pay taxes to Rome on the ground that some of the tribute would be used to support that army' (*What Do Presbyterians Believe?* p. 208). Pacifism receives no encouragement from the New Testament. It is true that harlots are commanded to go and 'sin no more', but soldiers are not asked to resign from the army! [cf. *Luke* 3:14].

5: Wherefore ye must needs be in subjection, not only because of the wrath, but also for conscience' sake.

It is because the civil government is ordained by God that the Christian must obey its demands as a matter of conscience, and not simply to escape threatened punishment. Hence when the supremacy of God is recognized, every subordinate relationship is transformed and the performance of every duty is ennobled [*Eph.* 6:1–9; *1 Pet.* 2: 13, 14].

6: For this cause ye pay tribute also; for they are ministers of God's service, attending continually upon this very thing.

This verse is to be understood as an explanatory statement rather than a command. Even if the rulers do not consciously fulfil the role assigned to them by God, they are nevertheless God's servants, and therefore Christians should not scruple to pay the taxes necessary to maintain the government God has appointed to office. 'This very thing' refers to the collection of these taxes by God's 'ministers' – *leitourgos*, a term which in the New Testament, is almost invariably used to describe religious service [15:16]. Furthermore, these lawful dues are collected to defray public expenditure and not to satisfy private greed, a point which is well taken by Calvin: 'It is right, however, that they should remember that all that they receive from the people is public property, and not a means of satisfying private lust and luxury. We see the uses for which Paul appoints the tributes which are paid, viz. that heads of state may be furnished with assistance for the defence of their subjects.'

7: Render to all their dues: tribute to whom tribute is due; custom to whom custom; fear to whom fear; honour to whom honour.

This sums up what Paul has to say on the duty of Christians towards the state. They are to pay their rulers their lawful dues, in direct taxes and in the taxes levied on goods, also rendering to them the reverence and honour that is due to their office.

But as the *temporal* state is not the *eternal* kingdom, 'the duty of obedience to secular authorities is a temporary one, for the present period of "night" [verse 12]; in that "day" which is "at hand" a new order of government will be introduced, when "the saints shall judge the world." [*1 Cor.* 6:2] The state is to "wither away" (on this Paul and Karl Marx agree); "the city of God remaineth"' (F. F. Bruce).

8: Owe no man anything, save to love one another: for he that loveth his neighbour hath fulfilled the law.

Owe no man anything: The verbs which begin verses 7 and 8 are both in the imperative mood. The Christian is not only to render obedience to the state, but also faithfully to discharge his obligations to society. First and foremost, he must shun the stigma of unpaid debts, for transparent honesty is to characterize all his transactions with his fellow-men. The conscientious observance of this very practical axiom is the essential prelude to all effective witness-bearing [*Psa.* 37:21].

Save to love one another: The Christian's love for his neighbour is but the visible reflection of his love for God. It is his consistent obedience to the second great commandment which affords the most convincing proof of his unqualified commitment to the first [*Mark* 12:30, 31]. Although the unregenerate commonly interpret 'love' in terms of acquisitive desire, the recipients of free grace have learned a better definition, for they know that it is 'more blessed to give than to receive' [*Acts* 20:35]. While Christian love enriches every human relationship, the love which seeks its own leads only to impoverishment.

For he that loveth his neighbour hath fulfilled the law: The modern disjunction between law and love is quite foreign to Paul's thought, for Christian love is not exercised in a void but in accordance with revealed commandment. Law gives love its content; love gives law its fulfilment. 'We may speak, if we will, of the law of love. But, if so, what we must have in view is the commandment to love or the law which love fulfils. We may not speak of the law of love if we meant that love is itself the law. Love cannot be equated with the law nor can law be defined in terms of love . . . Law prescribes the action, but love it is that constrains or impels to the action involved' (John Murray, *Principles of Conduct*, pp. 22, 24).

9: For this, Thou shalt not commit adultery, Thou shalt not kill, Thou shalt not steal. Thou shalt not covet, and if there by any other commandment, it is summed upon in this word, namely, Thou shalt love thy neighbour as thyself.

Paul now gives four examples from the second table of the law to illustrate the way in which this love is to be manifested. This appeal to the Decalogue exhibits the abiding validity of the moral law and proves that there is no abrogation of it under the new covenant. The negative form of these commandments is eloquent of the havoc which sin has wrought, and points to the absolute necessity of deliverance from its enslaving power.

The whole of the second table is summed up in the command, 'Thou shalt love thy neighbour *as thyself*' [*Lev.* 9:18]. Here legitimate self-love is made the searching standard by which love for others is to be measured [*Eph.* 5:29]. But no such limitation is placed upon the love which the first commandment demands. 'The love of God is supreme and incomparable. We are never asked to love God as we love ourselves or our neighbour as we love God. To God our whole being in all relationships must be captive in love, devotion, and service. To conceive of such captivity to our own selves or to any creature would be the essence of ungodliness' (John Murray) [*Mark* 12:30, 31].

10: Love worketh no ill to his neighbour: love therefore is the fulfilment of the law.

Love worketh no ill to his neighbour: Nothing less than positive love for others can prompt such an abstention from all ill-doing.

Love therefore is the fulfilment of the law: 'If we may use the metaphor, love fills to the brim the cup which the law puts into our hands. Love is the first drop; it is the last drop; and it is all the drops in between. From start to finish it is love that fulfils the law. When love is all-pervasive and inclusive, then the fulfilment of the law is completed' (John Murray, *Principles of Conduct*, p. 23).

11: And this, knowing the season, that already it is time for you to awake out of sleep: for now is salvation nearer to us than when we first believed.

Knowing 'the season' (the critical nature of the time in which they are living: the period that precedes the end) must spur Christians to live as they ought! This consciousness of moving towards the final goal invests time with a special significance for believers, and provides them with a powerful stimulus to regulate their conduct in the light of that hope [cf. *Heb.* 10: 24f.].

Hence Paul says that it is already time for his readers in Rome to awake out of sleep; not as though they were completely asleep, but that they should shake off all sleepiness and face the present situation with the urgency it demands [cf. *1 Thess.* 5:6–8]. For the consummation of our salvation is now nearer than when we first believed the gospel! He thus encourages the imminent expectation of Christ's return, while avoiding any specific reference to the *chronological* nearness of that event [*Acts* 1: 7; *2 Pet.* 3: 8].

12: The night is far spent, and the day is at hand: let us therefore cast off the works of darkness, and let us put on the armour of light.

The knowledge that 'the day is at hand' is here presented as the grand incentive to Christian obedience. It is natural for those who are of the night to commit 'the works of darkness', but those upon whom the Sun of righteousness has arisen must discard the former lusts of their ignorance and don 'the armour of light' [cf. *Eph.* 6:11–18; *1 Thess.* 5:8].

13: Let us walk becomingly, as in the day; not in revelling and drunkenness, not in chambering and wantonness, not in strife and jealousy.

'The day' has not yet dawned [verse 12], but because believers belong to it they are to behave as if it had. So though the night still surrounds them, they must shun the deeds which evil men love to practise under its cloak, and are to walk with as much decorum as men do in the full light of day. As then daylight and decency go together, all intemperance, impurity, and discord must be renounced.

14: But put ye on the Lord Jesus Christ, and make not provision for the flesh, to fulfil the lusts thereof.

As Hodge says, 'All Christian duty is included in putting on the Lord Jesus; in being like him, having that similarity of temper and conduct which results from being intimately united to him by the Holy Spirit' [*Gal.* 3:27] This union forbids the indulgence of all sinful propensities. Salvation is *from* sin, and *to* holiness.

CHAPTER FOURTEEN

1: But him that is weak in faith receive ye, yet not for decision of scruples.

Here for the first time in the epistle Paul turns to deal with a particular problem on which the Christians in Rome needed clear guidance. This was the relation between the 'weak' and the 'strong' in regard to their respective attitudes towards 'things indifferent'. That this was not a matter of indifference to the apostle is indicated by the length of his masterly discussion which extends to 15:13.

But him that is weak in faith: i.e. 'not "him that is weak in the truth believed," but "him whose faith wants that firmness and breadth which would raise him above small scruples"' (David Brown). Agreement with the cardinal truths of the gospel is assumed, for without this there is no basis for Christian fellowship at all. It is evident that the 'weakness' envisaged here was not associated with any departure from the faith, and this accounts for the irenical tone adopted by the apostle, whereas the motive which prompted the ascetic observances which are so unsparingly condemned in the Galatian and Colossian epistles was a subversion of the gospel itself.

Receive ye: Those who have a clearer conception of Christian liberty are to welcome without reserve those who have not yet been emancipated from conscientious scruples concerning food and the observance of special days.

John Murray points out that the 'weak' brother is described as a total abstainer from certain kinds of food, and that there is therefore no case for applying Paul's teaching in this place to the intemperate. The 'weakness' of those who go to excess 'is iniquity and with those who are guilty of this sin Paul deals in entirely different terms. Drunkards, for example, will not inherit the kingdom of God [*1 Cor.* 6:10] and Paul enjoins that if any one called a brother is a drunkard, with such an one believers are not to keep company or even eat [*1 Cor.* 5:11]. How different is Romans 14:1: "Him that is weak in faith receive ye"' (John Murray, 'The Weak Brother,' Appendix E, *Commentary*, vol. 2, p. 260).

Yet not for decision of scruples: The 'weak' brother was not to be received for the deciding of doubts or scruples, i.e. 'not for the purpose of arguing him out of them, which indeed usually does the reverse; whereas to receive him to full brotherly confidence and cordial interchange of Christian affection is the most effectual way of drawing them off' (David Brown).

2: One man hath faith to eat all things: but he that is weak eateth herbs.

Perhaps it is the fear of eating meat which has been previously dedicated to idols which prompts the 'weak' believer to restrict himself to a vegetarian diet, but the Christian who is fully instructed realizes that all food laws have been abolished under the gospel. There is no virtue or value in going without meat on Fridays, and it is certainly not sinful to drink tea and coffee!

3: Let not him that eateth set at nought him that eateth not; and let not him that eateth not judge him that eateth: for God hath received him.

Paul warns both the 'strong' and the 'weak' against giving way to the particular temptation to which each was especially prone, in order to prevent their difference from providing sin with an opportunity to introduce a division within the Christian fellowship. The 'strong' must not despise the 'weak' for refusing to eat, and the 'weak' must not judge the 'strong' for using his liberty in eating.

For God hath received him: That God is specifically stated to have received 'him that eateth' must be taken to imply the divine approval of his action, and thus marks the impropriety of his condemnation by him who is 'weak'. 'Though the weak are accepted with God through the righteousness of Christ, this weakness is not acceptable to him. It is an error, and cannot be pleasing to God. And accordingly the strong, and not the weak, are here said to be accepted' (Haldane).

4: Who art thou that judgest the servant of another? to his own lord he standeth or falleth. Yea, he shall be made to stand; for the Lord hath power to make him stand.

This reproof is directed to the 'weak' who condemned the 'strong' for their liberty in eating all things. By assuming the right to judge another's servant they exceeded their prerogative and were therefore to blame. Such judgments are irrelevant and impertinent, because it is obvious that the opinions of others can neither impair nor improve the standing of a servant before his own master [*1 Cor.* 4:39].

Yea, he shall be made to stand: This makes it clear that even the 'strong' do not stand in their own strength. The power to stand is imparted to every believer by Christ himself, apart from whom all would inevitably and irrevocably fall. It is the Lord Christ who grants persevering strength, and who also maintains the present standing of his servants despite the unjust censures of those who are completely unqualified to judge them.

5: One man esteemeth one day above another: another esteemeth every day alike. Let each man be fully assured in his own mind.

It is evident that this verse has no bearing on the weekly observance of the Lord's day since this was not regarded in the early church as a matter of human opinion, but of divine obligation. The meaning is rather that those who were 'weak' would still think that they ought to observe the feast days of the old economy, while the 'strong' would realize that all such distinctions now belonged to the past. 'Let each man be assured in his own mind' shows that an enforced conformity has no place in the fulfilment of the Christian ethic which demands the unfettered freedom of the individual conscience before God.

6: He that regardeth the day, regardeth it unto the Lord: and he that eateth, eateth unto the Lord, for he giveth God thanks; and he that eateth not, unto the Lord he eateth not, and giveth God thanks.

'The true criterion of Christian character is found in the governing purpose of the life. He that lives unto the Lord, i.e., he who makes the will of Christ the rule of his conduct, and the glory of Christ his constant object, is a true Christian, although from weakness or ignorance he may sometimes mistake the rule of duty, and consider certain things obligatory which Christ has never commanded' (Hodge).

7: For none of us liveth to himself, and none dieth to himself

8: For whether we live, we live unto the Lord; or whether we die, we die unto the Lord: whether we live therefore, or die, we are the Lord's.

What Paul is saying in verse 7 is made clear in verse 8. His thought is not that our actions affect others, but that whatever we do is done in relation to the Lord. Since our whole life and even our death gathers its meaning from our union with him, how can we think of making an exception in regard to such non-essentials as the food one eats or does not eat? Paul refuses to indulge in moral casuistry. He does not make a definite ruling which would satisfy legalists. Instead he lifts the whole discussion to the highest level, so that each may determine these matters in the light of this fundamental relationship. He brings in our death in order to put these small questions into their proper perspective. 'When they are placed in the light of our end, so many things shrivel into the trivialities they really are' (Lenski).

9: For to this end Christ died and lived again, that he might be Lord of both the dead and the living.

Paul's previous statement, 'we are the Lord's', is now explained. Believers belong to Christ because they have been bought with a price [*1 Cor.* 6:20]. Christ died and rose again in order to secure the lordship which he exercises over his people. It is a lordship which therefore belongs to the sphere of redemptive accomplishment. As the triumphant Mediator he has been invested with absolute sovereignty over both the dead and the living. Since all believers live in virtue of the resurrection-life of Christ, it also follows that the death of the body cannot dissolve this vital union with their Redeemer, for 'it would be absurd to suppose that he reigns over them as mere insensible matter' (Haldane) [*Matt.* 22:32]. Poole says, 'As God, he hath a universal dominion over all; but as Mediator, he hath a more special dominion over all the Father gave to him: this dominion he purchased at his death, and he had the full exercise of it when he rose again, *Matt.* 28:18; *Phil.* 2:9, 10.'

10: But thou, why dost thou judge thy brother? or thou again, why dost thou set at nought thy brother? for we shall all stand before the judgment-seat of God.

These questions, addressed respectively to the 'weak' and the 'strong', are vibrant with rebuke. The repetition of the word 'brother' not only indicates the equality of their standing but is also a timely reminder that their relationship should be distinguished by that mutual love which delights to cover a multitude of faults. Paul here prefers to speak of 'the judgment-seat of God' in order to prepare for the quotation of Isaiah 45:23 in the following verse, and the inference to be drawn from it in verse 12 ('to God'). But *2 Cor.* 5:10 shows that 'the judgment-seat of God' is also 'the judgment-seat of Christ,' which means that all believers shall be judged by God in Christ [cf. 2:16; *Acts* 17:31]. Therefore instead of anticipating that solemn assize by their presumptuous mutual criticism, the 'weak' and the 'strong' should rather take the present opportunity to correct their conduct towards one another before it is too late to make amends.

11: For it is written,

As I live, saith the Lord, to me every knee shall bow,
And every tongue shall confess to God.

'The passage, as it stands in the prophet, has no immediate reference to any "day of judgment," but is a prediction of the ultimate subjugation to the true God (in Christ) of every soul of man; but this of course implies that they shall bow to the award of God upon their character and actions' (David Brown) [*Isa.* 45:23, which is again quoted by Paul in *Phil.* 2:10,11].

12: So then each one of us shall give account of himself to God.

'As, therefore, God is the supreme judge, and we are to render our account to him, we should await his decision and not presume to act the part of judge over our brethren' (Hodge).

13: Let us not therefore judge one another any more: but judge ye this rather, that no man put a stumbling block in his brother's way, or an occasion of falling.

The following verses make it evident that the 'strong' are now addressed. Paul insists that the greater liberty of conscience which they enjoy must be limited by the superior demands of love, for freedom which is exercised without regard to the scruples of those who are 'weak' places a stumbling block in their path. The conduct of the 'strong' is not to provide the 'weak' brother with 'an occasion of falling'. Cain's indignant disclaimer, 'Am I my brother's keeper?' thus demands an affirmative response from those who own a stronger bond than natural brotherhood. There is a play on the word 'judge' in this verse, which Hodge renders as, 'Do not *judge* one another, but *determine* to avoid giving offence.'

14: I know, and am persuaded in the Lord Jesus, that nothing is unclean of itself: save that to him who accounteth anything to be unclean, to him it is unclean.

The first part of the verse is concessive. The 'strong' are right in their belief that moral evil cannot reside in things [*Titus* 1:15]. The typical service rendered by the ceremonial law was no longer required when the Antitype himself appeared. Christ fittingly abolished its restrictions by showing that the true source of all defilement was found within man, and therefore nothing from without could make him unclean [*Mark* 7:1–23]. It is not to be supposed, however, that Paul has gleaned this knowledge with difficulty through hearing the teaching of Jesus at second-hand, for the familiar formula, '*in* the Lord Jesus,' points to an unshakeable conviction which is enjoyed in virtue of his vital union with Christ. But all men are not in possession of the great liberating truth, and the man who believes 'anything to be unclean, to him it is unclean' [*1 Cor.* 8:4, 7]. 'Persons in ignorance ought to be instructed, but they ought never to be encouraged to do what they themselves judge to be contrary to the will of God' (Haldane).

15: For if because of meat thy brother is grieved, thou walkest no longer in love. Destroy not with thy meat him for whom Christ died.

Christ's dying love for the 'weak' brother is here strongly contrasted with that loveless abuse of liberty which would tempt him to sin against his conscience. This arresting language is not intended to suggest that any man could actually rob Christ of the fruit of his passion, but it is designed to remind strong believers of their very real responsibility towards their weaker brethren [*1 Cor.* 8:11]. David Brown remarks, 'The word "meat" is purposely selected as something contemptible, in contrast with the tremendous risk run for its sake . . . Whatever tends to make any one violate his conscience tends to the destruction of his soul; and he who helps, whether wittingly or no, to bring about the one is guilty of aiding to accomplish the other.'

16: Let not then your good be evil spoken of.

'Do not so use your liberty, which is good and valuable, as to make it the occasion of evil, and so liable to censure' (Hodge). In practice Christian liberty is limited by the higher claims of Christian love, for love teaches us that this freedom must never be exercised to the spiritual detriment of another [verses 20, 21; *1 Cor.* 10:23, 24].

17: for the kingdom of God is not eating and drinking, but righteousness and peace and joy in the Holy Spirit.

In the interests of their weaker brethren the 'strong' may indeed abstain from certain foods without loss, because the kingdom of God does not consist in carnal things like meat and drink, but in the enjoyment of those blessings of which the Holy Spirit is the author. Righteousness peace, and joy are therefore to be regarded as the subjective experience of the objective salvation which was fully expounded in the doctrinal section of the epistle. In other words, they must first be received as blessings from above before they can be manifested as virtues among men. 'That the religious import ought to be put in the forefront is shown by *joy in the Holy Spirit* which is a grace, not a virtue. In comparison with these great spiritual blessings, what Christian could trouble the Church about eating and drinking? For their sake, no self-denial is too great' (Denney).

18: For he that herein serveth Christ is well-pleasing to God, and approved of men.

He who in this way serves Christ (i.e. by putting first things first: spiritual blessings before food and drink), is well-pleasing to God and approved by the consciences of his fellow-men. For Christians must always conduct themselves in a manner which should constrain the admiration of the unbelieving, and so deprive them of any occasion for just criticism. Paul's habit of passing almost imperceptibly from God to Christ, and vice versa, is all the more striking because it provides an incidental disclosure of his attitude towards Christ. The Deity of the Saviour was the fundamental axiom of Paul's thought, and the very heart of his religious experience.

19: So then let us follow after things which make for peace, and things whereby we may edify one another.

This exhortation to the 'strong' is based upon the whole of the preceding argument [verses 19–22]. Those who are members of the body of Christ must constantly seek to promote peace within that body, and play their full part in the mutual edification of their fellow-members [*1 Cor.* 10: 23].

20: Overthrow not for meat's sake the work of God. All things indeed are clean; howbeit it is evil for that man who eateth with offence.

The lack of any connective makes this command all the more impressive [cf. verse 15b]. Let not the 'strong' find themselves pulling down God's work just for the sake of meat! 'The apostle sees in whatever tends to violate a brother's conscience the *incipient* destruction of God's work (for every converted man is such) – on the same principle as "he that hateth his brother is a murderer" [*1 John* 3:15]' (David Brown).

Paul again acknowledges that all food is clean [verse 14], but he points out that not all eating is without offence. 'The strong are to consider these two facts: eating despite giving dangerous offence – refraining from eating to avoid offence. A strong Christian will have little difficulty in making a choice between the two. Who would want to place a stumbling block into the path of anyone?' (Lenski).

21: It is good not to eat flesh, nor to drink wine, nor to do anything whereby thy brother stumbleth.

In a useful note on Christian liberty, Steele and Thomas write: 'It must be emphasized that by its very nature *Christian liberty is limited to things not sinful in themselves.* There is danger of confusion at this point, for Paul, in Romans 14:21, uses wine as an *example* of the type of thing which should be given up IF its use offends others. The danger of confusion lies in the fact that many Christians today think that drinking wine is a sin in itself. Some think that the Bible forbids its use even in moderation; others mistakenly identify drinking wine with drunkenness and thus wrongly conclude that because the latter is a sin so is the former. But inasmuch as Paul uses wine as an example of the kind of thing that a Christian is *free to use, unless it offends others*, it is evident that its use is not itself a violation of God's law and therefore is not a sin. Note carefully that Romans 14:21 *does not read*: "It is right not to eat meat or *get drunk* or do anything that makes your brother stumble." The reason is evident; *getting drunk is a sin* whether it offends a brother or not, whereas *drinking wine is not wrong unless* it results in drunkenness or causes others to stumble. "So, whether you eat or drink, or whatever you do, do all to the glory of God. Give no offence to Jews or to Greeks or to the church of God" [*1 Cor.* 10: 31, 32]' (*Romans – An Interpretive Outline*, pp. 117–118).

22: The faith which thou hast, have thou to thyself before God. Happy is he that judgeth not himself in that which he approveth.

Paul first insists that the 'strong' are not to indulge in the unloving exercise of their liberty to the spiritual detriment of others. So though the conviction they rightly hold may not be waived to confirm the wrong ideas of the 'weak', they are forbidden to flourish it in a way which causes their brethren to stumble.

In the second part of the verse Paul lays down the principle by which Christians are to be guided in 'things indifferent'. In all cases where believers are without a plain commandment to follow, they are to obey the dictates of their own conscience. This principle is first stated positively for the 'strong' [verse 22b], and then negatively for the 'weak' [verse 23a]. Thus the 'faith' of the 'strong' is to be 'a firm and intelligent conviction before God that one is doing what is right, the antithesis of feeling self-condemned in what one permits oneself to do' (F. F. Bruce).

23: But he that doubteth is condemned if he eat, because he eateth not of faith; and whatsoever is not of faith is sin.

On the other hand, the 'weak' believer who emulates the liberty of the 'strong' without sharing their convictions, stands condemned not only by his own conscience but also by God. Therefore the 'strong' must not tempt the 'weak' to violate their consciences by expecting them to act as if they also had no scruples about eating.

Hence Paul concludes that 'whatsoever is not of faith is sin'. This means that 'whatsoever is not done with a conviction that it is agreeable to the will of God, is sinful in the doer, although it should be right in itself. This is the generalization of the preceding doctrine. It applies not merely to meats, but to everything. If any person be convinced that a thing is contrary to God's law, and yet practises it, he is guilty before God, although it should be found that the thing was lawful' (Haldane).

CHAPTER FIFTEEN

1: Now we that are strong ought to bear the infirmities of the weak, and not to please ourselves.

2: Let each one of us please his neighbour for that which is good, unto edifying.

In this chapter the same subject of Christian forbearance is continued. Paul identifies himself with the 'strong' and says we are under an obligation to use our strength in bearing the infirmities of the 'weak'. For even a lawful liberty is not to be enjoyed at the expense of a weak brother. Wilful *self-pleasing* must not be allowed to masquerade under the disguise of Christian principle. Nor, as verse 2 indicates, is such self-pleasing to be sacrificed in the interests of *men-pleasing*, which would be inconsistent with fidelity to Christ [*Gal.* 1:10; *Eph.* 6:6]. The aim is the spiritual advantage of the neighbour, his building up in the faith.

3: For Christ also pleased not himself; but, as it is written, The reproaches of them that reproached thee fell upon me.

In this verse Paul reminds his readers that those who bear Christ's name must also follow Christ's example. The assertion that Christ did not please himself is corroborated by an appeal to Psalm 69:9, which shows that Christ attracted the reproaches of men by his unswerving fidelity to the Father's will. 'Men, even the most wicked, approve of morality and acts of kindness to the human race. They hate Christ and Christians only because of their holding forth the character of God, which they dislike' (Haldane). This reflection upon the cost of Christ's obedience affords an astonishing contrast with the slight sacrifice the 'strong' are here exhorted to make in the interests of the 'weak'. 'This Psalm is so frequently quoted and applied to Christ in the New Testament, that it must be considered as directly prophetical. Compare *John* 2:17, 15:25, 19:28; *Acts* 1: 20' (Hodge).

4: For whatsoever things were written aforetime were written for our learning, that through patience and through comfort of the scriptures we might have hope.

The important principle now adduced explains the apostle's frequent appeals to the Old Testament in confirmation of his doctrine. It is the preservation of the Word of God in permanent form which constitutes proof of its abiding purpose and therefore of its contemporary relevance. Since nothing which God has revealed and recorded is superfluous, no part of that testimony can be neglected without spiritual loss [*1 Cor.* 10:6, 10; *2 Tim.* 3:16, 17]. The instruction imparted by the Scriptures not only sustains believers under their present trials but also informs and inspires their hope for the future [8:23–25].

5: Now the God of patience and of comfort grant you to be of the same mind one with another according to Christ Jesus:

6: that with one accord ye may with one mouth glorify the God and Father of our Lord Jesus Christ.

This beautiful prayer sums up what Paul desires for both the 'strong' and the 'weak'. He first directs them to God as the author of that patience and comfort which is ministered to their hearts through his Word of truth [verse 4; cf. *John* 17:7].

Grant you to be of the same mind one with another according to Christ Jesus: His request is that they may be given that unity of mind and purpose which is according to the divine norm established for them by

Christ Jesus, their exalted Redeemer and covenant Head. This serves to remind us that unanimity on the horizontal level can be secured only as each believer realizes the implications of his vertical relationship with Christ. Fellowship depends upon what Christ Jesus has done for his people and what he is for them as the consequence of that work. Fellowship is therefore that corporate experience which results from an individual participation in him who 'is made unto us wisdom, and righteousness, and sanctification, and redemption.' [*1 Cor.* 1: 30].

That with one accord: As Heidland observes, 'with one accord' is a term which is used in the New Testament to emphasize the inner unanimity of the community. For though there were many personal and material tensions in the first congregations, these tensions were continually transcended as the church addressed itself to the glorifying of the one Lord. Hence constant worship is the key to continuing unanimity. [*Acts* 2:46] (*TDNT*, vol. V, p. 186)

Ye may with one mouth glorify the God and Father of our Lord Jesus Christ: Where there is such oneness of mind there is also this oneness of mouth. Unity of belief leads to unity in praise; the order is significant because the latter can never be attained without the former! In the gospel God is glorified by the worship that acknowledges him in the character in which he has been pleased to reveal himself to us, i.e. as 'the God and Father of our Lord Jesus Christ'. This majestic designation is in fact a compressed confession of faith [cf. *2 Cor.* 1:3; 11:3; *Eph.* 1:3; *1 Pet.* 1:3]. For to say this is to express our belief in the reality of the incarnation (God is 'the God' of Christ *as man*); the eternal Deity of the Son (God is 'the Father' of Christ *as God*); and the efficacy of his redeeming work ('*our* Lord Jesus Christ').

7: Wherefore receive ye one another, even as Christ also received you, to the glory of God.

This verse serves a dual function. It concludes the apostle's discussion of the problem of the 'strong' and the 'weak' [14:1–15:6], and it prepares the way for his wider application of the same principle to relations between Jewish and Gentile believers [verses 8–13]. When Christ has received all believers without distinction, then clearly they must not allow unimportant differences to cause divisions within the church. Therefore we must receive one another, even as Christ received us to the glory of God's faithfulness and mercy [verses 8, 9]. As God is glorified by Christ's reception of us, so he is to be glorified by that mutual fellowship which transcends all individual and accidental diversities. For what does not matter to Christ should not matter to us!

8: For I say that Christ hath been made a minister of the circumcision for the truth of God, that he might confirm the promises given unto the fathers,

Paul now proceeds to explain how the mixed congregation of Jews and Gentiles in Rome glorifies God. For God's veracity is vindicated in the conversion of Jews, and his mercy is magnified in the salvation of Gentiles [verse 9]. For the sake of God's truth Christ has become a minister of the circumcision in order to fulfil the promises which God gave to the patriarchs.

Moreover, it is Christ who continues to exercise this ministry in the present proclamation of the apostolic gospel throughout the world, and Paul sees a convincing proof of God's faithfulness in the many Jews who have already hailed Christ as the Messiah who suffered and triumphed for them.

9: and that the Gentiles might glorify God for his mercy; as it is written,
Therefore will I give praise unto thee among the Gentiles,
And sing unto thy name.

Paul now proves that the inclusion of the Gentiles within the scope of God's mercy was no afterthought, by introducing a chain of testimonies from the Old Testament [verses 9–12]. The first of these is from Psalm 18:49 in which David resolves to celebrate his victories over the Gentiles by confessing the Name of God in their midst. He thus saw his military conquest of the surrounding nations as an opportunity to dispel their heathen darkness by bringing them into a knowledge of the one true and living God.

10: And again he saith,
Rejoice, ye Gentiles, with his people.

The second quotation is from Deuteronomy 32:43 according to the LXX or Septuagint (Greek version of the Old Testament). The invitation it extends to the Gentiles to share in Israel's rejoicing in what Jehovah has done for them is really an inducement to join them in the sharing of these covenant blessings.

11: And again,
Praise the Lord, all ye Gentiles;
And let all the people praise him.

Although the third testimony is taken from the shortest Psalm [*Psa.* 117:1], the importance of a message may not be measured by its length! And this missionary summons to all Gentiles to praise the Lord manifests an astonishing insight into Israel's role as 'the mediator of saving truth' to the other nations on the face of the earth (H. C. Leupold).

It is Messianic in the sense that it is prophetic of the spread of the gospel throughout the world [cf. *John* 4:22].

12: And again, Isaiah saith,
There shall be the root of Jesse,
And he that ariseth to rule over the Gentiles;
On him shall the Gentiles hope.

The climax is reached in this quotation of Isaiah's prediction of Christ's lordship over the Gentiles [*Isa.* 11:10, LXX]. It is indeed astounding that a descendant of Jesse, David's father, a mere shoot of a defunct Jewish royal line should be elevated to this position of precedence so that the Gentiles would come to hope in him (Lenski). Even as Paul wrote these words he was conscious of their fulfilment in the multitudes throughout the empire who were flocking to Christ as he was lifted up before them in the preaching of the gospel.

13: Now the God of hope fill you with all joy and peace in believing, that ye may abound in hope, in the power of the Holy Spirit.

Paul concludes his teaching on Christian forbearance, and the main body of the epistle, with a brief prayer for his readers in Rome. He commends them to God who, as the author of this gospel hope [verse 12], is able to fill them with all joy and peace in believing, so that they abound in hope by the power of the Holy Spirit. And we are thereby taught that this objective hope is ours in subjective possession solely through the agency and power of the Holy Spirit.

14: And I myself also am persuaded of you, my brethren, that ye yourselves are full of goodness, filled with all knowledge, able also to admonish one another.

15: But I write the more boldly unto you in some measure, as putting you again in remembrance, because of the grace that was given me of God,

Before concluding the letter Paul wishes to make it clear that he has not written to the church at Rome because he thought that the believers there were either lacking in their Christian experience or deficient in their knowledge of divine truth. He tactfully points out that the design of his letter is not to introduce them to any new doctrine, but rather to remind them of the truth which they already possessed. The warmth of his address has not been inspired by any desire for self-aggrandizement, but stems from the grace of apostleship which had been given to him by God. It is therefore as the apostle to the Gentiles that he claims the right to minister to this predominantly Gentile congregation [verse 16].

16: that I should be a minister of Christ Jesus unto the Gentiles, ministering the gospel of God, that the offering up of the Gentiles might be made acceptable, being sanctified by the Holy Spirit.

To be a minister of Christ Jesus to the Gentiles in the priestly service of the gospel of God, so that the offering of the Gentiles may be acceptable (RSV): 'There is in the Christian Church no real priesthood, and none but figurative sacrifices. Had it been otherwise, it is inconceivable that the 16th verse of this chapter should have been expressed as it is. Paul's only priesthood and sacrificial offerings lay, first, in ministering to them, as "the apostle of the Gentiles," not the sacrament, with the "Real Presence" of Christ in it, or the sacrifice of the mass, but "the Gospel of God," and then, when gathered under the wing of Christ, presenting them to God as a grateful offering, "being sanctified (not by sacrificial gifts, but) by the Holy Spirit"'(David Brown) [cf. *Heb.* 13:9–16].

Being sanctified by the Holy Spirit: 'There were some, no doubt, who maintained that Paul's Gentile converts were "unclean", because they were not circumcised. To such cavillers Paul's reply is that his converts were "clean," because they were sanctified by the Holy Spirit who had come to dwell within them [cf. verse 19, "by the power of the Spirit of God"]'(F. F. Bruce).

17: I have therefore my glorying in Christ Jesus in things pertaining to God.

18: For I will not dare to speak of any things save those which Christ wrought through me, for the obedience of the Gentiles, by word and deed,

Having received such a divine commission Paul does not hesitate to glory in it, but this glorying is limited to those things which Christ has wrought through him [*1 Cor.* 1:31; *2 Cor.* 10:17]. There is no need for him to claim the credit for another's work. He has abundant cause for rejoicing in the fruit of his own labours for Christ. The aim of Paul's ministry was to make the Gentiles obedient 'by word and deed', for he well knew that the absence of such a grateful response meant that there had been no true experience of gospel grace. In opposing *legalism* the apostle made no concessions to *lawlessness*. He did not preach a cheap and easy 'believism,' because Christ will not admit to being the Saviour of those who refuse to follow him as Lord [*2 Thess.* 1:8].

19: in the power of signs and wonders, in the power of the Holy Spirit; so that from Jerusalem, and round about even unto Illyricum, I have fully preached the gospel of Christ;

It was by the remarkable assistance of the Spirit of God that Paul had fulfilled his apostolic commission within the boundaries mentioned in this verse [*1 Cor.* 2:4]. Hodge points out that the expression 'fully preached' means 'to bring the gospel (i.e. the preaching of it) to an end, to accomplish it thoroughly; see *Col.* 1:25. In this wide circuit had the apostle preached, founding churches, and advancing the Redeemer's kingdom with such evidence of the divine co-operation, as to leave no ground of doubt that he was a divinely appointed minister of Christ.'

20: yea, making it my aim so to preach the gospel, not where Christ was already named, that I might not build upon another man's foundation;

The function of the apostolate was to establish churches in those areas where Christ was unknown, and Paul's missionary strategy was based upon this principle. The apostle therefore refused to build upon another man's foundation, because he had limited himself to this pioneer work in accordance with the distinctive commission he had received [*1 Cor.* 3:10].

> 21: but, as it is written,
> They shall see, to whom no tidings of him came,
> And they who have not heard shall understand.

Paul sees this preaching of the gospel in places where Christ's name was not known as a fulfilment of Isaiah 52:15, which promises the Suffering Servant a world-wide dominion as the necessary sequel to his humiliation. So it happens that Gentiles now see what they had not before been told about the Messiah, and they who had not previously heard now understand in true faith.

> 22: Wherefore also I was hindered these many times from coming to you:
> 23: but now, having no more any place in these regions, and having these many years a longing to come unto you.
> 24: whensoever I go unto Spain (for I hope to see you in my journey, and to be brought on my way thitherward by you, if first in some measure I shall have been satisfied with your company) –

The pressure of Paul's missionary work had so far prevented his eagerly anticipated visit to the church at Rome, but now that he had concluded his ministry around Illyricum, he is planning a journey to Spain. On his way there he hopes to have the opportunity to enjoy a season of fellowship and refreshment with the Christians in Rome. These verses make it evident that Paul would not permit his personal desire to visit Rome to interrupt his missionary programme. We do not know if Paul ever reached Spain, but when he came to Rome it was under very different circumstances from those contemplated when these words were written.

> 25: but now, I say, I go unto Jerusalem, ministering unto the saints.
> 26: For it hath been the good pleasure of Macedonia and Achaia to make a certain contribution for the poor among the saints that are at Jerusalem.

But before Paul can set sail for Spain he has one last service to accomplish. It is to deliver the contribution which the Gentile

Christians have made for the relief of the hard-pressed community of Jewish believers in Jerusalem. Paul's insistence upon accompanying the Gentile delegates to Jerusalem shows how much importance he attached to this mission, for as F. F. Bruce explains, he regarded it as an act of worship which was to mark the climax of his Aegean ministry in 'the outward and visible sign of that "offering up of the Gentiles" which crowned his priestly service as apostle of Jesus Christ.'

27: Yea, it hath been their good pleasure; and their debtors they are. For if the Gentiles have been made partakers of their spiritual things, they owe it to them also to minister unto them in carnal things.

Since the Gentiles owed their spiritual enrichment to the Jews, it was only natural that they should seek to repay this moral debt by ministering to the material necessities of their Jewish brethren in Christ. Nevertheless their contribution was quite voluntary. 'Charity is an obligation but it is not a tax' (John Murray).

28: When therefore I have accomplished this, and have sealed to them this fruit, I will go on by you unto Spain.

As soon as Paul has completed this mission of mercy he intends to fulfil his promise to visit the Roman Christians *en route* to Spain. 'And have sealed to them this fruit' indicates why he thought it necessary to deliver in person the gift which was the fruit of his ministry among the Gentiles. He clearly regarded this collection as the visible authentication of his mission to the Gentiles, and hoped that this fruit of the Spirit would convince the Jewish believers in Jerusalem of the common bond which united them with their Gentile brethren in Christ [*Eph*. 1:13].

29: And I know that, when I come unto you, I shall come in the fulness of the blessing of Christ.

Paul's confidence that he would come to them 'in the fulness of the blessing of Christ' was amply justified by the event, even though he was to come to Rome as a prisoner. Christ brought him there in the most wonderful way 'in order to witness in Rome as he had witnessed in Jerusalem, which meant among *Jews* in Rome, and at once upon his arrival He opened the door to *the Roman Jews* for him [*Acts* 28:17–31]' (Lenski).

30: Now I beseech you, brethren, by our Lord Jesus Christ, and by the love of the Spirit, that ye strive together with me in your prayers to God for me;

In conclusion Paul beseeches his brethren in Rome to strive together in prayer for him, as those who are doubly motivated by 'our Lord Jesus Christ' and by the love wrought in their hearts by 'the Spirit'. 'What Paul asks is that they should join him in striving with all their might – in wrestling as it were – against the hostile forces which would frustrate his apostolic work' (Denney).

31: that I may be delivered from them that are disobedient in Judaea, and that my ministration which I have for Jerusalem may be acceptable to the saints;

32: that I may come unto you in joy through the will of God, and together with you find rest.

33: Now the God of peace be with you all. Amen.

Paul asks them to pray that he might be delivered from the unbelieving Jews who hated him for seeking to convert them to the faith he had once persecuted, and that the collection might be acceptable to the believing Jews who might scorn a gift from the Gentiles because of slanderous reports about the way in which he was receiving them into the church [cf. *Acts* 21:17]. In verse 32 he looks hopefully beyond the hazards of his present undertaking to the joy of his meeting with the Christians in Rome. John Murray notes that 'the will of God' is here 'his decretive will realized through providence . . . it was not part of God's revealed will to Paul that he would go to Rome. Hence the reserve of submissiveness to what God determined his providence for Paul would prove to be.' The apostle concludes with the brief but comprehensive prayer that the God of peace would be with all his people in Rome.

CHAPTER SIXTEEN

1: I commend unto you Phoebe our sister, who is a servant of the church that is at Cenchreae:

2: that ye receive her in the Lord, worthily of the saints, and that ye assist her in whatsoever matter she may have need of you: for she herself also hath been a helper of many, and of mine own self.

Paul closes his letter by greeting all the believers in Rome. He sends his personal greetings to the friends he had met elsewhere in the course of his labours, and he salutes the leaders of the five groups in whose 'houses' the church met together for worship [verses 5, 10, 11, 14, 15].

The most likely explanation of the apostle's commendation of Phoebe is that she was the bearer of this letter. The Christians in Rome are asked to 'receive her in the Lord' and to help her in whatever way they can, for she has been of great assistance to many, including Paul himself. From this it would appear that Phoebe, like Lydia, was a woman whose wealth and position enabled her to render such service to others. Although the question cannot be decided with certainty, the fact that she is introduced as 'a servant' *of the church* at Cenchreae lends support to the view that she served it in the official capacity of 'deaconess' (ASV margin).

3: Salute Prisca and Aquila my fellow-workers in Christ Jesus,

4: who for my life laid down their own necks; unto whom not only I give thanks, but also all the churches of the Gentiles:

Paul first greets his former hosts at Corinth, Prisca and Aquila, now living in Rome, and thankfully recalls an otherwise unrecorded occasion when they risked their lives on his behalf, an act of courage which has also earned the gratitude of all the Gentile churches, for 'his preservation redounded to the benefit of them all' (Poole) [*Acts* 18:1–3].

5: and salute the church that is in their house. Salute Epaenetus my beloved, who is the firstfruits of Asia unto Christ.

In the early days of Christianity there were no church buildings and so believers gathered for worship with a family whose house was suitable for this purpose. Usually there would be several such house-churches in a city, as there were also in Rome. Aquila and Priscilla were a couple whose house was always at the disposal of the Lord, whether they lived in Corinth or Rome [cf. *1 Cor.* 16:19]. As Epaenetus was the first convert to Christ in the Roman province of Asia it was natural that Paul would feel a special bond of affection for him. The discovery of an Ephesian with this name on a Roman inscription is very interesting (Denney).

6: Salute Mary, who bestowed much labour on you.

Of the others Paul greets here nothing further is known, but perhaps Mary was one of the founder members of the church in Rome. It is possible that the apostle had learned of her outstanding service through Aquila and Priscilla. Denney notes that 'for you' is much better supported than 'for us' (AV), and says, 'There is something finer in Paul's appreciation of services rendered to others than if they had been rendered to himself.'

7: Salute Andronicus and Junias, my kinsmen, and my fellow-prisoners, who are of note among the apostles, who also have been in Christ before me.

Andronicus and Junias are, like Paul, of Jewish descent, and evidently they were once his fellow-prisoners for the sake of the gospel. Apparently they are missionary-preachers of note in the church (using 'apostles' in its wider meaning as in *Acts* 14:14), and were believers before Paul, who seems to envy them this priority in the faith. And truly if to be 'in Christ' is the 'most enviable human condition, the earlier the date of this blessed transition the greater the grace of it' (David Brown).

8: Salute Ampliatus my beloved in the Lord.

Ampliatus was a name common among Roman slaves. An inscription found on a tomb in the cemetery of Domitilla makes it probable 'that a person of this name was conspicuous in the earliest Roman church, and may have been the means of introducing Christianity to a great Roman house'(Denney). This man is beloved of Paul as a brother 'in the Lord'.

9: Salute Urbanus our fellow-worker in Christ, and Stachys my beloved.

Urbanus is also a slave name which means city-bred. The fact that Paul greets him as 'our' rather than as 'my' [verse 3] 'fellow-worker' may suggest that all Christian workers had a common helper in him (Denney). Stachys is a Greek name which means an 'ear of corn.'

10: Salute Apelles the approved in Christ. Salute them which are of the household of Aristobulus.

'Approved' means that the faith of Apelles had been proved genuine by some conspicuous trial [*James* 1:12]. Paul salutes the Christian slaves

[*1 Cor.* 1: 26–31] who belong to the household of Aristobulus, whom Lightfoot identified as the grandson of Herod the Great. It is probable that he had died before this letter was written, in which case his household, though continuing to bear his name, would have been transferred to the Imperial palace.

11: Salute Herodion my kinsman. Salute them of the household of Narcissus, that are in the Lord.

'My kinsman' shows that Herodion was a Jew. His name suggests that he was a slave in the household of Aristobulus (verse 10). Paul also here greets the Christian slaves who belonged to the household of Narcissus. This man was probably the influential freedman of Claudius. He committed suicide shortly before this letter was written. On his death his slaves would become the Emperor's property while continuing to bear the designation, 'those of Narcissus'. Lightfoot suggests that these were among the saints 'of Caesar's household' whom Paul mentions in Philippians 4:22.

12: Salute Tryphaena and Tryphosa, who labour in the Lord. Salute Persis the beloved, who laboured much in the Lord.

These women may have been twin sisters, but it is certain that they did not live up to their names. They were not too 'Dainty' or 'Delicate' to work for the Lord! Another woman, Persis the beloved, is here honoured for the hard work she has done for the Lord,

13: Salute Rufus the chosen in the Lord, and his mother and mine.

As Mark probably wrote his gospel in Rome, it is almost certain that this Rufus was the son of Simon of Cyrene, who bore the cross for Jesus [*Mark* 15:21]. 'The chosen in the Lord' does not refer to his election, for that is true of every Christian; it means that he is a distinguished Christian (cf. Denney: 'that choice Christian'). Paul also greets his mother as 'his mother and mine', a tender touch that gratefully recalls an occasion when she had performed the part of a mother to him.

14: Salute Asyncritus, Phlegon, Hermes, Patrobas, Hermas, and the brethren that are with them.

Although nothing is known of these five men, their names suggest that they were slaves, and it is likely that they were the members of a Christian fellowship within some nobleman's household.

15: Salute Philologus and Julia, Nereus and his sister, and Olympas, and all the saints that are with them.

Philologus and Julia are evidently husband and wife, and it seems that a large group of believers met for worship in their home. Presumably Nereus and his sister (for whom A. F. Walls suggests the name Nereis) and Olympas (or Olympiodorus) were prominent members of that house-church. Thus Paul sends greetings to twenty-six Christians in Rome, of whom eight are women, and only five or six are Jews (Aquila and Prisca, Andronicus, Junias, Herodion, and possibly Mary).

16: Salute one another with a holy kiss. All the churches of Christ salute you.

As Hodge remarks, 'It does not follow, because a custom prevailed in the early churches, and received the sanction of the apostles, that we are obliged to follow it. These customs often arose out of local circumstances and previous habits, or were merely conventional modes of expressing certain feelings, and were never intended to be made universally obligatory. As it was common in the East, (and is so, to a great extent, at present, not only here, but on the continent of Europe), to express affection and confidence by "the kiss of peace", Paul exhorts the Roman Christians to salute one another with a holy kiss; i.e. to manifest their Christian love to each other, according to the mode to which they were accustomed. The exercise and manifestation of the feeling, but not the mode of its expression, are obligatory on us. This is but one example; there are many other things connected with the manner of conducting public worship, and with the administration of baptism and the Lord's Supper, common in the apostolic churches, which have gone out of use. Christianity is a living principle, and was never intended to be confined to one unvarying set of forms.'

As they salute one another in this way, Paul wishes them to know that all the churches with which he is associated join with him in sending a united greeting to their brethren in Rome.

17: Now I beseech you, brethren, mark them that are causing the divisions and occasions of stumbling, contrary to the doctrine which ye learned: and turn away from them.

As Lenski points out, this admonition is an integral part of the whole letter. It is entirely natural that after having expounded the unified doctrine at length and extended these uniting salutations [verses 3–16], Paul should now warn them against giving heed to any contrary doctrine which would break their unity in the faith. 'Mark them' does not imply that false teachers are already at work in Rome [cf. verse 19]; it means 'look out for them,' be on your guard against those who cause divisions and occasions of stumbling by introducing their own ideas. The true doctrine is *one*; the divisions of error are *many!* Believers are to turn away from such men; they are to avoid them as they would the plague. This apostolic injunction is in striking contrast with the advice of certain present-day church leaders who urge us to have fellowship with them! To identify exactly those whom Paul had in mind is not so important [but see *Phil.* 3:1ff]; what is vital is that we should avoid those who are fracturing the true unity of the church in their quest for a false unity.

18: For they that are such serve not our Lord Christ, but their own belly; and by their smooth and fair speech they beguile the hearts of the innocent.

Here such false teachers are shown up for what they really are in order that innocent Christians may not be deceived by their flattering and deceitful speeches. For they do not serve our Lord Christ but their own belly [cf. *Phil.* 3:19]. It would seem that the allusion is to the Judaizers whose insistence upon the Gentile observance of Jewish food laws is unsparingly condemned as a service of the belly. And indeed all who peddle the corruptible doctrines of men [*Col.* 2:22] in preference to the incorruptible gospel of God are mere belly-worshippers! Therefore let no Christian be deceived by their fair speeches which disguise the poison of deadly error [cf. *Gen.* 3:1–6; *2 Cor.* 11:3; *Eph.* 4:14].

19: For your obedience is come abroad unto all men. I rejoice therefore over you: but I would have you wise unto that which is good, and simple unto that which is evil.

In giving them this exhortation Paul is not suggesting that they have already succumbed to false doctrine; 'for *your* obedience is come abroad unto all men [1: 8]. Over *you* therefore I rejoice.' The Roman church was free of doctrinal error and needed guidance only in connection with 'things indifferent' [ch. 14]. Nevertheless, Paul would have them to be wise towards the good, which in this context must mean the doctrine they had learned [verse 17], and 'simple' or 'unmixed' towards the evil teaching which is contrary to the truth [cf. *Matt.* 10:16]. 'That is what Paul "wants", and we know how he laboured for this. Today many frankly do *not* want this. Error does not stink in their nostrils; to them it has a holy smell. Although they offend and insult the true church they embrace open errorists, they are not as Paul says "unmixed", unadulterated with regard to the bad, but "mixed," adulterated, and often, sad to say, proud of the fact' (Lenski).

20: And the God of peace shall bruise Satan under your feet shortly. The grace of our Lord Jesus Christ be with you.

'We are to be wise and unmixed, but we depend upon God for the victory.' Hence they must look to the Author and Preserver of peace to maintain their peaceful unity in the doctrine they had learned [verse 17]. For behind the work of errorists who cause divisions and death-traps stands Satan the father of lies [*Gen.* 3:5], whom God will swiftly crush under their feet [*Gen.* 3:15]. Paul here reveals the source of all falsehood so that no believer may be deceived as Satan's dupes go about their deadly work of destroying the souls of men. For the day will soon come when all who make and all who love lies shall be cast with Satan into the lake of fire for ever [*Rev.* 20:10, 15, 21:8, 22:15]. Every Christian should therefore pray: 'Help me, O God, that I may never even unconsciously lend even my little finger to Satan for this work of spreading error!' (Lenski). The benediction fittingly concludes this important paragraph.

21: Timothy my fellow-worker saluteth you; and Lucius and Jason and Sosipater, my kinsmen.

22: I Tertius, who write the epistle, salute you in the Lord.

23: Gaius my host, and of the whole church, saluteth you. Erastus the treasurer of the city saluteth you, and Quartus the brother.[1]

[1] The American Standard Version omits the repeated benediction of verse 24.

Paul's friends at Corinth now send their greetings to the Christians at Rome. Timothy heads the list, and is followed by the names of three Jewish believers. It is impossible to identify Lucius, but it is possible that the other two are mentioned in Acts, Jason in 17:5 and Sosipater in 20:4. Tertius who acted as the apostle's amanuensis was evidently also a Christian. Paul had himself baptized Gaius [*1 Cor.* 1:14], who is noted for his hospitality, and he is probably to be identified with Titius Justus of *Acts* 18:7. It is significant that Paul should choose to associate the greeting of an otherwise unknown Christian, Quartus, with that of the distinguished treasurer of the city of Corinth, Erastus. The apostle knew nothing of a Christianity which recognized class distinctions! [*Gal.* 3:28].

25: Now to him that is able to establish you according to my gospel and the preaching of Jesus Christ, according to the revelation of the mystery which hath been kept in silence through times eternal,

26: but now is manifested, and by the scriptures of the prophets, according to the commandment of the eternal God, is made known unto all the nations unto obedience of faith;

27: to the only wise God, through Jesus Christ, to whom be the glory for ever. Amen.

Paul concludes his greatest epistle with a magnificent doxology which summarizes its leading themes [verses 25–27]. He commends the Christians in Rome to God who is able to establish them [1:11] in his gospel [2:16], that preached message whose subject is Jesus Christ [1:3, 4], which is the unveiling of the mystery kept secret for long ages but now disclosed [11:25; *Eph.* 3:3ff; *Col.* 1:26f].

The revelation of this age-old secret is made to the nations through 'the scriptures of the prophets'. Until Christ came, their message had been confined to Israel, but Christ's fulfilment of the Old Testament hope made their words meaningful to the whole world [cf. *1 Pet.* 1:10–12]. And this great change came about in accord with the command of the eternal God in the pursuance of his eternal purpose, namely, that the gospel should be proclaimed to all the nations to bring them to the obedience of faith [1:5].

The One who devised this great plan of salvation is 'the only wise God', and it is in virtue of having this character that he is able to establish the Romans according to Paul's gospel (Denney). It is therefore to him, through the mediation of Jesus Christ, that all glory is to be ascribed for ever. Amen.

SOLI DEO GLORIA

BIBLIOGRAPHY AND ACKNOWLEDGEMENTS

The author expresses his grateful thanks to the following authors and publishers who have kindly given permission to reproduce quotations from their copyright works.

BRUCE, F. F., *Commentary on Romans* (Tyndale, 1963).

BRUCE, F. F., *An Expanded Paraphrase on the Epistles of Paul* (Paternoster, 1965).

CALVIN, JOHN, *Commentary on Romans* (Oliver & Boyd, 1961) (translated by Ross Mackenzie).

CLARK, GORDON, *Religion, Reason and Revelation* (Presbyterian & Reformed, 1961).

KITTEL, GERHARD, AND FRIEDRICH, GERHARD, *Theological Dictionary of the New Testament (TDNT)* (translated by Geoffrey W. Bromiley) vols. 1–9 (Eerdmans, 1964–74).

KUYPER, ABRAHAM, *The Revelation of St John* (Eerdmans, 1964).

LENSKI, R. C. H., *The Interpretation of St Paul's Epistle to the Romans* (Augsburg, 1961).

MORRIS, LEON, *The Apostolic Preaching of the Cross* (Tyndale, 1965).

MURRAY, JOHN, *The Epistle to the Romans* (Eerdmans, 1960, 1965) (NIC).

—— *Principles of Conduct* (Tyndale, 1957).

—— *The Imputation of Adam's Sin* (Eerdmans, 1959).

STEELE, D. N. AND THOMAS, C. C., *Romans – An Interpretive Outline* (Presbyterian & Reformed, 1963).

VINE, W. E., *Expository Dictionary of New Testament Words* (Oliphants, 1958).

VOS, GEERHARDUS, *The Pauline Eschatology* (Eerdmans, 1961).

VOS, J. G., *Surrender to Evolution: Inevitable or Inexcusable?* (Geneva Tracts)

In addition to these, the following books were consulted:

ALEXANDER, JOSEPH ADDISON, *Commentary on the Psalms* (Zondervan, n.d.)

ALFORD, HENRY, *The Greek Testament* (Rivingtons, 1859).

ARNDT, W. F. AND GINGRICH, F. W., *A Greek-English Lexicon of the New Testament* (University of Chicago Press, 1957).

BARRETT, C. K., *A Commentary on the Epistle to the Romans* (A & C Black, 1957).

BOETTNER, LORAINE, *Roman Catholicism* (Banner of Truth, 1966).

BROWN, DAVID, *Romans* (JFB) (Collins, 1874).

BUNYAN, JOHN, *The Holy War* (many editions).

CALVIN, JOHN, *The Institutes of the Christian Religion* (translated by Henry Beveridge) (James Clarke, 1957).

CLARK, GORDON, *A Christian View of Men and Things* (Eerdmans, 1952).

—— *What Do Presbyterians Believe?* (Presbyterian & Reformed, 1965).

CRANFIELD, C. E. B., *Romans,* vol. I, I–VIII (New ICC) (T. & T. Clark, 1975).

CULLMANN OSCAR, *The Christology of the New Testament* (SCM 1963).

DABNEY, R. L., *Discussions: Evangelical and Theological* (Banner of Truth, 1967).

DAVIDSON, F. AND MARTIN, RALPH P., *Commentary on Romans* (NBC) (Inter-Varsity Press, 1970).

DENNEY, JAMES, *Commentary on St. Paul's Epistle to the Romans* (EGT) (Hodder & Stoughton, 1912).

DOUGLAS, J. D. (Editor), *The New Bible Dictionary* (IVF, 1962).

DUNN, JAMES D. G., *Jesus and the Spirit* (SCM, 1975).

GODET, F., *Commentary on Romans* (T. & T. Clark, 1881).

GRIER, W. J., *The Momentous Event* (Banner of Truth, 1970).

HALDANE, ROBERT, *Commentary on Romans* (Banner of Truth, 1958).

HENRY, MATTHEW, *Commentary on the Holy Bible* (various editions).

HODGE, A. A., *The Confession of Faith* (Banner of Truth, 1958).

HODGE, CHARLES, *Commentary on Romans* (Banner of Truth, 1972).

KIDNER, DEREK, *The Proverbs* (Tyndale, 1964).

LEUPOLD, H. C., *Exposition of the Psalms* (Baker, 1961).

LIGHTFOOT, J. B., *Notes on the Epistles of St Paul* (Zondervan, 1957).

LLOYD-JONES, D. M., *Romans: An Exposition,* vols. 1–14 (Banner of Truth, 1970–2003).[1]

MACHEN, J. G., *The Origin of Paul's Religion* (Eerdmans, 1965).

—— *The Virgin Birth* (Presbyterian & Reformed, 1965).

MOORE, T. V., *Commentary on Zechariah* (Banner of Truth, 1958).

MURRAY, JOHN, *The Covenant of Grace* (Tyndale, 1956).

—— *Redemption – Accomplished and Applied* (Banner of Truth, 1961).

NYGREN, ANDERS, *Commentary on Romans* (Fortress Press, 1972).

OWEN, JOHN, *Works,* vol. 6 (Banner of Truth, 1966).

PHILIP, JAMES, *The Epistle to the Romans* (Didasko Press, n.d).

PINK, ARTHUR W., *Gleanings in Paul* (Moody Press, 1967).

—— *The Sermon on the Mount* (Baker, 1959).

PINK, ARTHUR, W., *The Sovereignty of God* (Baker, 1965).

POOLE, MATTHEW, *Commentary on the Holy Bible,* vol. 3 (Banner of Truth, 1963).

SANDAY, W. AND HEADLAM, A. C., *A Critical and Exegetical Commentary on the Epistle to the Romans* (ICC) (T. & T. Clark, 1881).

SHEDD, W. G. T., *A Critical and Doctrinal Commentary upon the Epistle of St Paul to the Romans* (Scribners, 1879).

SMEATON, GEORGE, *The Apostles' Doctrine of the Atonement* (Banner of Truth, 1991).

THORNWELL, JAMES HENLEY, *Collected Writings,* vol. 2 (Banner of Truth, 1974).

TRAPP, JOHN, *Commentary on the New Testament* (Sovereign Grace Book Club, 1958).

TRENCH, R. C., *Synonyms of the New Testament* (James Clark, 1961).

VAN TIL, CORNELIUS, *The Defence of the Faith* (Presbyterian & Reformed, 1955).

VOS, GEERHARDUS, *Biblical Theology* (Banner of Truth, 1975).

WARFIELD, B. B., *Biblical and Theological Studies* (Presbyterian & Reformed, 1952).

—— *The Inspiration and Authority of the Bible* (Marshall, Morgan & Scott, 1959).

WARFIELD, B. B., *Faith and Life* (Banner of Truth, 1974).

WHYTE, ALEXANDER, *A Commentary on the Shorter Catechism* (T. & T. Clark, 1961).

---

[1] The series is now complete in 14 vols. Full details are available from the publisher.

1 Corinthians

INTRODUCTION

After the destruction of the old city of Corinth in 146 BC by the Romans under Lucius Mummius, the site remained unoccupied until a century later when it was refounded as a Roman colony by Julius Caesar. New Corinth soon became an important political and commercial centre with a large cosmopolitan population. Unfortunately the revival of its civic eminence was marred by the same vices which in former days had made its name a byword for immorality even in the ancient world.

Paul came to Corinth about AD 51. The opposition and indifference which he had encountered in Macedonia and Athens were not calculated to inspire the hope that his reception in Corinth would be any more favourable to the gospel, but encouraged by the Lord in a vision he persevered in the work for eighteen months [*Acts* 18:1–18]. Although the church thus founded was the crowning achievement of the second missionary journey, its further advance was hindered by troubles which almost overwhelmed him with grief.

It appears from 1 Corinthians 5:9 that while Paul was at Ephesus he had occasion to reprove the Corinthians for their moral laxity in a 'previous' letter which has not been preserved. Some time later 'Chloe's people' brought disturbing news of divisions within the church [1:11], and he also received an official letter asking for guidance on particular matters of faith and practice (note the repeated 'now concerning': 7:1; 7:25; 8:1; 12:1; 16:1; 16:12). It may well be that Paul wrote this Epistle over a period of several weeks, dealing first with the emotive issues raised by what had been told him of the state of the church [chapter 1–6], and then replying to the questions put to him by the Corinthians in their letter [chapter 7and following].

Whether or not this letter was delivered by the church leaders mentioned in 1 Corinthians 16:17, their welcome visit doubtless supplied him with additional information on the problems they were facing. The Epistle that is known to us as 'First' Corinthians was the Apostle's inspired reply to the varied demands of this dangerous situation. It was in bringing the light of the cross to bear upon a great diversity of subjects that Paul attained a marvellous unity in his letter, and showed the only way in which harmony could be restored at Corinth. The unique authority of the deliverance assures the people of God in every age that a consistent application of the same gospel principles which were first laid down for them by a 'wise masterbuilder' is fully adequate to deal with every difficulty that would arrest their progress in the Christian Way.

CHAPTER ONE

In greeting the church at Corinth, Paul reminds this community of his own calling as an apostle, and of their call to be saints. He thanks God for their rich spiritual endowments, and encourages them with the assurance that God will keep them to the end [verses 1–9]. Paul begins by appealing for unity, for he has heard that their fellowship is fractured by party strife. As these sinful divisions were caused by the folly of glorying in men, Paul is glad that he had baptized so few of them personally, because this showed he could not be charged with having baptized in his own name [verses 10–16]. For Christ had not sent Paul to baptize, but to preach the unadorned word of the cross. And though the wisdom of the world rejects this message as foolishness, believers have found it to be the power and the wisdom of God. Hence the Corinthians must not glory in that wisdom which was confounded by God in their own calling. Thus the fact that they owe their salvation solely to the grace of God must teach them to glory only in the Lord [verses 17–31].

1: Paul, called to be an apostle of Jesus Christ through the will of God, and Sosthenes our brother,

According to his usual practice, Paul invests the normal form of greeting with a distinctively Christian content which subtly prepares his readers for what is to follow it. Since Paul's authority is in dispute [9:1], he begins by reminding the Corinthians that he is 'a called apostle'. Because his conversion coincided with this commission, he could never refer to the powers he exercised as an apostle without recalling that great watershed in his spiritual experience. Consequently the validity of his subsequent career rested entirely upon the reality of this encounter with the person of the exalted Christ [*Acts* 26:9–20]. Moreover, the eternal purpose of God for his life was revealed to him in the call of Christ [*Gal.* 1:15, 16]. Thus Paul's right to command the obedience of the church in Corinth is based on the unshakeable conviction that he was appointed to this high office by the direct intervention of God.

And Sosthenes the brother (ASV margin)*:* It is impossible to say for certain whether this is the Sosthenes referred to in Acts 18:17. But whoever he was, it is clear that Paul is glad to associate himself with an honoured colleague who is evidently well known to the readers, and whose brotherly concern for them is witnessed by his wholehearted approval of the apostle's message, though he plainly had no part in its composition. For 'he did not stand in any position of authority, he has no special connexion with the contents of the Epistle, and does not reappear again directly or indirectly, but the Apostle at once returns to the singular, "I thank my God" [1:4]', (J. B. Lightfoot). Ever since the Christian experience of forgiveness first brought a new wealth of meaning to the word 'brother', the sons of grace have been distinguished by their unfeigned love for the brethren [*1 Pet.* 1:22; *1 John* 3:14].

2: unto the church of God which is at Corinth, even them that are sanctified in Christ Jesus, called to be saints, with all that call upon the name of our Lord Jesus Christ in every place, their Lord and ours:

Despite glaring imperfections which merited the sternest reproofs, Paul does not hesitate to address this group of people as 'the church of God which is at Corinth'. The word 'church' (*ekklesia*) was originally used of any secular assembly (e.g. the Ephesian concourse, *Acts* 19:32, 39, 41), but Christians probably made it their own because it is used of 'the congregation' of Israel in the Greek version of the Old Testament [cf. *Acts* 7:38, RSV]. As the word itself suggests, the church consists of those whom God has 'called out' from the world into fellowship with himself. But if God designs to separate his people from the world, the establishment of the church in pagan Corinth proves that it is not his will immediately to remove them from it [cf. 5:10; *Matt.* 5:14; *John* 17:15]. The apostle who had no wish to encourage the Corinthians to be unmindful of either the faith or the needs of other Christian communities, nevertheless recognized the existence of the church of God in all its fullness at Corinth. For wherever two or three are gathered together in Christ's name, he is truly present in the midst [*Matt.* 18:20].

Even them that are sanctified in Christ Jesus (cf. 1:30): The church is further defined as consisting of those whom God has set apart for himself '*in* Christ Jesus'. The preposition shows that it is solely through the work of Christ that this consecration is initiated and sustained. 'The Corinthians are not born saints but they are sanctified by virtue of an act of God in Jesus, the consequences of which last till the present' (F. W. Grosheide).

Called to be saints: The designation expresses the purpose for which they have been set apart by God. As Paul is a 'called apostle', so the Corinthians are 'called saints'. Unless 'sainthood' were first bestowed, it could never be acquired. But the ethical demand for holy living is inseparable from what is freely given in the gospel, and so it is the vocation of those who have been made saints by God to become in daily obedience what they are 'in Christ Jesus' [*1 Pet.* 1:15]. Therefore, to remind them of their calling is also to rebuke them for their sin.

With all that call upon the name of our Lord Jesus Christ in every place: Although what Paul has to say in this letter is addressed to the Corinthians, he wants to make them conscious of their spiritual kinship with all other believers wherever they may live. This is the true antidote for an insular faith. We are not to isolate ourselves from our fellow believers, for we are members together with all the saints of God [14:36]. Matthew Poole rightly observes that this 'is an eminent place to prove the Divine nature of Christ; he is not only called *our Lord,* our common Lord, but he is made the object of invocation and Divine worship' so that 'none but such as call upon the name of Jesus Christ our Lord, are fit matter for a gospel church'. This of necessity excludes all who 'deny the Godhead of Christ' from any place in the church of God, whatever pretensions are made to the contrary [*1 John* 5:20; *2 John* 7].

Their Lord and ours: This afterthought corrects any possible misunderstanding of the word 'our'. For, adds Paul, he is not only *our* Lord but also *their* Lord! There is here 'a covert allusion to the divisions in the Corinthian church, and an implied exhortation to unity' (Lightfoot).

3: Grace to you and peace from God our Father and the Lord Jesus Christ.

Grace to you and peace: The appearance of this phrase throughout the New Testament suggests that it was the common form of greeting among Christians, and the 'password' by which they recognized one another. The order of the words is always the same, for without an experience of the grace of God there can be no knowledge of the peace of God. But to enjoy the unmerited favour of God in Jesus Christ is to be made a partaker of that peace which ensures the spiritual prosperity of the whole man.

From God our Father and the Lord Jesus Christ: These blessings flow down to men from above. The linking together here of 'God' and 'Lord' under a common preposition ('from') is an indication of their essential equality. This disclosure of Paul's attitude toward Christ is all the more impressive because it is incidentally revealed rather than formally defined.

4: I thank my God always concerning you, for the grace of God which was given you in Christ Jesus;

As in secular correspondence the greeting is followed by the thanksgiving, though in Paul's Epistles the form is never used to win the readers' goodwill but rather to thank God for their faith (with the exception of Galatians where the apostle saw no such cause for thanksgiving, cf. *Gal.* 1:6). Since Paul is here referring to his prayers for the Corinthians, it is quite wrong to suggest that this thanksgiving is tinged with irony, for at the outset of a letter filled with rebuke, he is at pains to assure them that the very existence of the church in a place like Corinth calls for constant thanksgiving to God.

Because the apostle delights to extol the grace of God in its essential character as an absolute grant to the undeserving, he underlines the fact that this was given them 'in Christ Jesus'. This objective salvation which is theirs in Christ is the basis upon which all the other spiritual graces and gifts that he enumerates are bestowed [verses 5–7].

5: that in everything ye were enriched in him, in all utterance and all knowledge;

The Corinthians have been made rich by the grace of God, so that they abound 'in all utterance and all knowledge'. The use of a single preposition shows that this spiritual wealth consisted in a thorough understanding of the gospel together with the power to give it eloquent expression. It is significant that Paul singles out the gifts upon which they set the greatest store. Yet he can no more refrain from rejoicing in these lavish endowments of God's grace than from censuring the Corinthians – and most justly so – for their sinful abuse of them [8:1ff.; 12:8; 13:1ff.].

6: even as the testimony of Christ was confirmed in you:

This enrichment resulted from the spiritual quickening which was produced in their hearts through the testimony which Paul had borne to Christ in their city. The truth of what the apostle declared to them was confirmed in them by the Holy Spirit. All preaching must rely for its success upon the Spirit's work in confirming the truth of the message in those who hear it, for eloquence without power is idle rhetoric [cf. 2:4].

7: so that ye come behind in no gift; waiting for the revelation of our Lord Jesus Christ;

The shower of spiritual blessings which followed the conversion of the Corinthians leads to the conclusion that they do not come short of any gift of grace. The reference must not be restricted to the special gifts that were exercised in Corinth, but rather includes all spiritual endowments.

Although all the early Christians lived in eager expectation of Christ's appearing, in Corinth this hope had been dimmed by a spirit of sinful complacency with present good [4:8], and the airing of doubts concerning the resurrection [15:12]. The Corinthians therefore needed to be reminded of the great end of their calling, for only those who are looking for the Lord's return will live as they ought for him [*Titus* 2:12, 13; *1 John* 3:2, 3; *2 Pet.* 3:11, 12]. 'It is the character of Christians, that they wait for Christ's second coming; all our religion hath regard to that: we believe it and hope for it, and it is the business of our lives to prepare for it, if we are Christians indeed' (Matthew Henry).

8: who shall also confirm you unto the end, that ye be unreprovable in the day of our Lord Jesus Christ.

'Who' refers to Christ [verse 7], who acts on God's behalf. Christ has not only saved the Corinthians, but he will also keep them to the end. As the appointed Judge of all men [*Rom.* 2:16], Christ will then declare his people to be 'unreprovable'. The word 'implies not merely acquittal, but the absence of even a charge or accusation against a person' (W. E. Vine). Yet now they are far from being beyond reproach, for the apostle is himself about to level grave charges against them. But they will be 'exempt from accusation' in the day of judgment [*Rom.* 8:33; *Col.* 1:22], because then their subjective state will perfectly correspond with the objective standing which is already theirs in Christ. Thus F. Godet remarks, 'If then they are no longer subject to any accusation, it will not be only, as during their earthly career, in virtue of their justification by faith, it will be in virtue of their thenceforth perfected sanctification.'

In the day of our Lord Jesus Christ: This affords another striking proof of the Deity of Christ. It is because God has revealed his purpose to judge the world by Jesus Christ that the Old Testament 'day of Jehovah' is now spoken of as the 'day of Christ'.

9: God is faithful, through whom ye were called into the fellowship of his Son Jesus Christ our Lord.

Since God has called the Corinthians to salvation through Christ, his faithfulness is the guarantee that he has not called them in vain [10:13; *Phil.* 1:6; *1 Thess.* 5:24]. The call that came to them through the preaching of the gospel is an effectual calling, because it took place in accordance with God's antecedent purpose of grace [*Acts* 18:10; *Rom.* 8:30; *2 Tim.* 1:9]. It is by this creative intervention of God that they have been brought into fellowship with his Son. The meaning is not that they partake of the divine essence after the manner of the pagan mystery religions, but that their final glorification is certified by the faith-union which has made them present sharers in Christ's resurrection life [cf. *Col.* 3:4].

10: Now I beseech you, brethren, through the name of our Lord Jesus Christ, that ye all speak the same thing, and that there be no divisions among you; but that ye be perfected together in the same mind and in the same judgment.

The apostle begins with an urgent appeal for unity. The adversative 'now' is in painful contrast with the thanksgiving, for the existence of factions within the church is a flagrant contradiction of that 'fellowship' to which the Corinthians were called by God [verse 9]. The inconsistency of these divisions is also implied by the affectionate address 'brethren'.

Through the name of our Lord Jesus Christ: In the first ten verses Christ's name occurs no less than ten times. This emphatic repetition is meant to remind them that the church belongs to Christ and not to men. Here the 'appeal to the one Name is an indirect condemnation of the various party names' (Robertson-Plummer) [verse 12].

That ye all speak the same thing: As the meaning of this classical expression is 'to make up differences' (Lightfoot), Paul is calling for something more than mere unanimity of utterance. But since there can be no such restoration of harmony unless all do say the same thing, the admonition obviously demands the abandonment of party slogans which can only foster strife within the church.

And that there be no divisions among you: Negatively, there must be an end to the cleavages which were caused by partisan preferences for individual leaders. For though the whole community still met together for worship [11:17ff.], these internal 'dissensions' were threatening to tear it apart.

But that ye be perfected together in the same mind and in the same judgment: Positively, these breaches in the fellowship are to be healed. The order is experimental. Unity of judgment is not to be expected until they share the same frame of mind. 'He is urging them to give up, not erroneous beliefs, but party-spirit' (Robertson-Plummer).

11: For it hath been signified unto me concerning you, my brethren, by them that are of the household of Chloe, that there are contentions among you.

Although the elders of the church did not see fit to mention these divisions in their letter to Paul, he had been informed of the seriousness of the situation by members of Chloe's household. They were probably slaves who had visited the apostle in Ephesus while on business for their mistress [verse 26]. We do not know whether she was herself a Christian, but she was evidently known to the Corinthians.

12: Now this I mean, that each one of you saith, I am of Paul; and I of Apollos; and I of Cephas; and I of Christ.

What Paul roundly condemns is the factious spirit which has led to the formation of these parties within the church; he gives no hint of any doctrinal deviation from the faith. Apollos may have been the unwitting cause of the trouble, for some in Corinth found his polished speech more to their taste than the plain preaching of Paul. Those who regarded this as a challenge to their loyalty to the apostle would be provoked to counter it with the cry, '*I* am of Paul.' Presumably Jewish believers were responsible for dismissing the rival claims of the Paul-party and the Apollos-party with the retort, 'But *I* am of Cephas.' It is unnecessary to assume that Peter had visited Corinth in order to account for the existence of this group. Finally, those who were disgusted with the unseemly conflict over personalities would say, 'I belong to *Christ!*' The apostle's total rejection of these opposing cliques is explained in chapter 3:22f. For the groups who chanted these slogans erred by showing a sinful partiality for the human leaders whom God had given for the benefit of the whole church. But as Paul's indignant rejoinder makes clear ('Is Christ divided?'), the error of those whose watchword made Christ their own private property was even more grievous.

13: Is Christ divided? was Paul crucified for you? or were ye baptized into the name of Paul?

Moffatt renders the question, 'Has Christ been parcelled out?' and adds that 'though this protest covers all the groups, it starts from the sectional claim of the last-named clique'. In the second and third questions Paul in deference to the other leaders tactfully uses his own name to make the point. Since Paul was not crucified for the Corinthians and they were not baptized into his name, it is obvious that they do not belong to him but to Christ who bought them with his blood [6:20]. For when all Christ's members owe their salvation to his death for them, it is clear that no man can usurp the unique position which he now occupies as their exalted Lord [*Phil.* 2:11]. In this indirect but forceful way the Corinthians are reminded that it was upon Christ's authority that they were baptized into his name, and so declared themselves to be his property [cf. 3:23].

Crucified . . . baptized: 'The cross and baptism claim us for Christ. The correlatives are, redemption and self–dedication' (J. A. Bengel).

14: I thank God that I baptized none of you, save Crispus and Gaius;

15: lest any man should say that ye were baptized into my name.

In view of what had happened since he left Corinth, Paul regards it as a happy providence that he baptized so few while he was there. Crispus was the ruler of the synagogue where Paul began his mission [*Acts* 18:8], and Gaius is probably to be identified with Titus Justus who opened his house to the preaching of the gospel after the Jews had rejected it [*Acts* 18:7; *Rom.* 16:23]. As a result, the Corinthians could neither say that they stood in any special relation to the apostle as their baptizer, nor deny the fact that they belonged to the Christ into whose name they had been baptized. 'The outrageous idea which Paul combats throughout is that men or any man should in any way be substituted for Christ in the church' (R. C. H. Lenski).

16: And I baptized also the household of Stephanas: besides, I know not whether I baptized any other.

On second thoughts, Paul remembers or is perhaps reminded by his amanuensis that he also baptized the house of Stephanas, the first family in Achaia won to Christ. C. K. Barrett candidly concludes that though the meaning of 'household' cannot be decided with complete precision, 'it should be noted that at 16:15 *the household . . . of Stephanas* are said to *have set themselves for service to the saints.* This could hardly be said of children, and the presumption is that in using this word Paul is thinking of adults.' (C. K. Barrett, *The First Epistle to the Corinthians*, p. 48). On this temporary lapse of memory, Charles Hodge remarks that inspiration 'rendered its recipients infallible, but it did not render them omniscient. They were preserved from asserting error, but they were not enabled either to know or to remember all things.'

17: For Christ sent me not to baptize, but to preach the gospel: not in wisdom of words, lest the cross of Christ should be made void.

That Paul had baptized so few in Corinth was not surprising: 'For Christ did not send me to baptize, but *to evangelize*' (G. G. Findlay). As an apostle it was not an essential part of his commission to baptize; his primary task was to make disciples through the preaching of the gospel [*Acts* 9:15. 22:14, 15; *1 Tim.* 2:7]. In consequence he usually delegated the baptizing to an assistant, and following Christ's own practice, it is likely that the other apostles did the same [*John* 4:1, 2; *Acts* 10:48]. 'Baptizing required no special, personal gifts, as preaching did. Baptism is not disparaged by this; but baptism presupposes that the great charge, to preach the gospel, has been fulfilled' (Robertson-Plummer) [*Matt.* 28:19].

Not in wisdom of words: Paul now begins to lay bare the root of the sinful divisions in the Corinthian church. The existence of these parties was not due to his activity in their midst, for he had been faithful both to the letter and the spirit of his commission. Not only did he evangelize without personally baptizing, but he also refused to embellish his message with 'cleverness in speaking' (Arndt-Gingrich). He confined himself to a simple proclamation of the facts of the gospel [15:1ff].

Lest the cross of Christ should be made void: The apostle had shunned this style of speech lest the cross of Christ should be emptied of its real significance. For though a dazzling display of rhetoric might impress the intellect, it would not lead the conscience to appropriate a divine salvation. 'The nucleus of the apostolic preaching was a *fact* – Christ crucified. To preach it as a philosophic system would be to empty it of its saving power, a truth which finds abundant and lamentable illustration in the history of the Church' (M. R. Vincent).

18: For the word of the cross is to them that perish foolishness; but unto us who are saved it is the power of God.

Paul here exhibits 'the utter folly of trying to improve the word of the cross by casting it into the word of human wisdom in order to get rid of its apparent "foolishness" for a certain class of people' (Lenski).

For the word of the cross is to them that are perishing foolishness (ASV margin): Those who regard the message of a crucified Christ as foolishness are not merely in the process of perishing; they are 'the perishing', i.e. those whose perdition is certain, for 'the perfective force of the verb implies the completion of the process of destruction' (Vine). It is not only because the unbelieving are spiritually dead that they are on the way to eternal ruin [*2 Thess.* 1:9]. They also sentence themselves to this future doom by rejecting the only word which could deliver them from their present condition.

But unto us who are being saved it is the power of God (ASV margin):
The 'word of the cross' divides mankind into two classes only, the saved
and the lost [cf. *2 Cor.* 2:15f.]. That the apostle and his readers are, by
the grace of God, among those who 'are being saved' is indicated by
the word 'us'.

'In the language of the New Testament salvation is a thing of the
past, a thing of the present, and a thing of the future ... It is important
to observe this, because we are thus taught that "salvation" involves a
moral condition which must have begun already, though it will receive
its final accomplishment hereafter' (Lightfoot). So those whom God
has declared righteous are in the process of being made holy, and this
increasing conformity to Christ will be perfected in their glorification
[*1 John* 3:2f.].

It would have been true to say that the message which the lost dismiss
as 'foolishness' is in fact 'the wisdom of God' [verses 24, 30], but before
ever men can admire the infinite wisdom of the gospel they must
experience its saving power [*Rom.* 1:16]. For nothing less than 'the
power of God' could suffice to save those 'who were dead in trespasses
and sins' [*Eph.* 2:1]. 'But only that gospel is the power of God which
proclaims that the cross was the propitiation for sin, the sole ground
of pardon . . . let anything else be substituted for the cross, and
preaching is denuded of its efficacy, and stripped of this power' (George
Smeaton).

19: For it is written,

I will destroy the wisdom of the wise,
And the discernment of the discerning will I bring to nought.

The quotation is from Isaiah 29:14. The prophet predicts that God
will nullify the worldly wisdom of Judah's politicians who hoped to
counter the threat of Assyrian aggression through an alliance with
Egypt. As this lack of trust in God exposed the hollowness of his
people's worship [verse 13], God will act in such a marvellous way
that the folly of their reliance upon human wisdom will be decisively
demonstrated [verse 14]. 'This "wisdom" of Hezekiah's advisers was
exactly like that which was trying to magnify itself in Corinth. It
emanated, not from God, but from godless thinking. The "prudence"
of their tricky scheming failed to take into account God's promise and

his power and was thus fit only to be cast aside and to be utterly forgotten. Paul would have his readers conclude from this quotation that what God did with this kind of wisdom in the days of old he does with all wisdom of this kind: he will destroy it and bring it to nought' (Lenski).

20: Where is the wise? where is the scribe? where is the disputer of this world? hath not God made foolish the wisdom of the world?

Where is the wise? The first question is drawn from Isaiah 19:12. Pharaoh's counsellors, for all their false pretensions to wisdom, could not foresee, much less frustrate the judgment of Jehovah upon Egypt. The quotation is apt because the Greeks also gloried in their wisdom, but God will clearly show the futility of every form of reasoning that fails to reckon with him.

Where is the scribe? The second question alludes to Isaiah 33:18. After God's deliverance of his people from the Assyrian danger, men will ask in astonishment, 'What has become of the scribe who was to tabulate the tribute to be taken from a conquered nation?' He is nowhere to be seen! In a similar way the salvation of God has made foolish the vaunted learning of the Jewish scribes. 'Knowledge of the Scriptures does not help if it is not accompanied by a believing submission to the word of the cross, the wisdom of God' (Grosheide) [cf. *John* 5:39].

Where is the disputer of this age? (ASV margin): Paul now adds a question of his own. The third term 'disputer' would apply equally well to the dialectical subtlety of the Greek and to the legal casuistry of the Jew. Moreover, the construction indicates that 'disputer', 'scribe', and 'wise', are all 'of this age'. Consequently their wisdom cannot transcend it. It is a wisdom which belongs to a world-order that is perishing. 'It is the gospel alone which connects us with the era to come, and this gospel is the truth which all the wise of this world reject as long as they remain only worldly-wise' (Lenski).

Hath not God made foolish the wisdom of the world? The world and God are opposed, because each regards the other's wisdom as folly [verses 18, 25]. But in the preaching of Christ crucified, God actually turned to foolishness all the imagined wisdom of the world [verses 21–25].

21: For seeing that in the wisdom of God the world through its wisdom knew not God, it was God's good pleasure through the foolishness of the preaching to save them that believe.

It was in accordance with God's plan that the world failed to gain the knowledge of God by its own wisdom. For it was his eternal purpose to save sinners through the cross of Christ, and the fulfilment of this wise decree demonstrated the folly of what the world accounted wisdom. This wisdom is always self-frustrating because it is essentially hostile to God. Those blinded by sin make God in their own image, and so fail to see that the 'God' thus made is merely an expression of their self-love. Men are delivered from this fatal reliance upon their own wisdom only when they are brought to recognize that they must receive 'the reconciliation' which God in his wisdom has provided through Christ crucified. "'Through its (Greek) wisdom the world *knew not* God," as through its (Jewish) righteousness it *pleased not* God . . . The intellectual was as signal as the moral defeat; the followers of Plato were "shut up", along with those of Moses, "unto the faith which should afterwards be revealed" [*Gal.* 3:22f]' (Findlay).

It was God's good pleasure through the foolishness of the thing preached to save them that believe (ASV margin): What the world regards as foolishness is not simply the act of preaching, but the content of the message thus proclaimed. 'To announce as the Saviour of the world one who died the vile death of a criminal on the cross seems, indeed, to be the acme of foolishness. To expect that this announcement will do what all the world with its mighty effort of wisdom failed to do, namely, actually to lift man up again into communion with God, only intensifies the impression of utter foolishness' (Lenski). But the rejection of the word of the cross is not universal, because it is the good pleasure of God to save those who 'believe'. The tense of the verb shows that it is not enough to have once believed, for in the New Testament it is only a living faith that saves [cf. *John* 3:36: 'He that *believeth* on the Son hath everlasting life'].

22: Seeing that Jews ask for signs, and Greeks seek after wisdom;

This verse explains why the world deems God's wisdom to be foolishness. The national characteristics of both races 'are hit off to perfection in the words "ask" and "seek". To the Jews God has already spoken; and they, from the proud eminence of their divinely sprung religion, "demand" of all upstart religions their proofs and credentials [cf. *Matt.* 12:38, 16:1; *John* 6:30]. The Greeks, on the other hand, are seekers; and they seek, as they worship, they know not what. They can only give it the general name of wisdom or truth' (T. C. Edwards). The paradoxical result was that those who were opposed in every other respect found themselves united in their rejection of the preaching of Christ crucified, for it neither satisfied the Jewish expectation of a carnal kingdom nor rewarded the Greek quest for a philosophical explanation of the universe. As it was then, so it is now. It is because the gospel contradicts the presuppositions which underlie both the religion and the reasoning of the unregenerate that the world still continues to despise it.

23: but we preach Christ crucified, unto Jews a stumbling block, and unto Gentiles foolishness;

If no message was less welcome, none was more needed than this! 'Christ crucified' expresses more than the mere fact of his crucifixion, for the perfect tense indicates 'the *permanent character* acquired by it, whereby he is now a Saviour [*Gal.* 3:1]' (A. R. Fausset). Since the Jews anticipated the advent of a victorious prince who would liberate them from the oppressor's yoke, nothing could have been more repugnant to them than the scandal of a *crucified* Messiah [*Deut.* 21:23; *Gal.* 3:13]. It was the doctrine on which they stumbled and fell [*Rom.* 9:33; *1 Pet.* 2:8]. 'To Jews "the word of the cross" announced the shameful reversal of their most cherished hopes; to Greeks and Romans it offered for Saviour and Lord a man branded throughout the Empire as amongst the basest of criminals; it was "outrageous", and "absurd"' (Findlay).

24: but unto them that are called, both Jews and Greeks, Christ the power of God, and the wisdom of God.

'*But unto the called themselves*' (ASV margin) stresses the contrast between those who receive the gospel and those who reject it. It is only the effectual calling of God which accounts for the difference between these two groups. The fact that some Jews and Greeks do 'believe' [verse 21] the message of salvation is not explained by Paul in terms of their 'free will'; he attributes their faith to nothing but the gracious initiative of God. 'The apostle exalts the divine act in salvation; he sees God's arm laying hold of certain individuals, drawing them from the midst of those nationalities, Jewish and Gentile, by the call of preaching; then, when they have believed, he sees the Christ preached and received, unveiling himself to them as containing exactly all that their countrymen are seeking, but the opposite of which they think they see in him' (Godet). For the doctrine of the Cross was to the Jews a stumbling block, and to the Gentiles foolishness [verse 23].

Christ the power of God, and the wisdom of God: 'Crucified' is omitted here, because when the offence of the cross is overcome, 'Christ' is received not only in his cross, but also in the power of his resurrection life. God thus puts his people in possession of a 'salvation, which is at once the mightiest miracle in the guise of weakness and the highest wisdom in the guise of folly' (Edwards). The order of the words teaches us that before men can admire the wisdom of God in Christ, they must first experience the divine power of Christ in vanquishing their sins.

25: Because the foolishness of God is wiser than men; and the weakness of God is stronger than men.

Literally, Paul speaks of 'the foolish thing' and 'the weak thing' of God. By using neuter adjectives he 'avoids ascribing the abstract qualities of foolishness and of weakness to God as though they were two of his actual attributes' (Lenski). The reference is to the apparent foolishness and weakness of a particular act of God, namely, the death of Christ [cf. *2 Cor.* 13:4]. 'For it is surely a foolish and a weak thing to let God's own Son die miserably on the cross . . . And yet this foolish and this weak thing outranks and absolutely outdoes all the wisdom and all the power of men . . . If men were asked how God should proceed to save the world they would certainly not say by sending his Son to the cross. Yet this is what God did, and, behold this act saves! So wise is this foolish thing, so powerful this weak thing' (Lenski).

26: For behold your calling, brethren, that not many wise after the flesh, not many mighty, not many noble, are called.

That God is resolved to reduce the world's wisdom to foolishness is now confirmed by an appeal to their own experience of his grace. For in Corinth not many of those who were great by worldly standards had been effectually called by God to faith in Christ; a humbling thought which is softened by the affectionate address, 'brethren'. Nothing could more clearly demonstrate the folly of their infatuation with human wisdom than a consideration of the divine reversal it received in their own calling. Thus they must learn that 'the things which elevate man in the world, knowledge, influence, rank, are not the things which lead to God and salvation' (C. Hodge).

27: but God chose the foolish things of the world, that he might put to shame them that are wise; and God chose the weak things of the world, that he might put to shame the things that are strong;

But God chose the foolish and the weak things of the world, so that the wise who pride themselves on their wisdom, and the strong who glory in their strength might be 'put to shame'. In this and the following verse Paul is emphasizing the *creative character* of God's electing grace. For though God has chosen the foolish and the weak, it is in order to make them truly wise and strong: wise with his wisdom, and strong in his strength. 'Facing the disdainful attitude of the world the church may be comforted to know that God himself has called and elected her. Therein the church bears the character of the crucified Christ [*Isa.* 42:1f.; *Matt.* 21:42; *1 Pet.* 2:6f.]' (Grosheide).

28: and the base things of the world, and the things that are despised, did God choose, yea and the things that are not, that he might bring to nought the things that are:

The Corinthian church was the living proof that God's love did not stop short at the foolish and the weak; it even extended to those whom the world despised as base, whether by birth ('not *many* noble', 1:26) or by behaviour ('And such *were* some of you . . .', 6:11). Paul is not simply carried away by rhetoric when he adds that God has chosen 'the things that are not, that he might bring to nought the things that are' [cf. *Rom.* 4:17]. His words are full of meaning, as his readers ought to be the first to acknowledge. 'When God set his plan in motion there was no church in Corinth, save in his intention; notwithstanding opposition (and its own weakness), it now existed. God's wisdom in the gospel had already been validated by its effect, and will in the end be completely vindicated by the totality of the new creation' (Barrett).

29: that no flesh should glory before God.

'Glory not *before* him, but *in* him' (Bengel). Here Paul turns to his aim, to warn them that the preachers in whom they gloried had no ground for glorying in themselves; so the hearers ought to glory not in them, but in the Lord [3:21; 4:6]' (Fausset).

30: But of him are ye in Christ Jesus, who was made unto us wisdom from God, and righteousness and sanctification, and redemption:

Paul intends to leave the Corinthians in no doubt whatsoever that they owe their salvation entirely to God's act. It is all 'of him' that they are now 'in Christ Jesus'. Such a gratuitous salvation evidently excludes all boasting in the flesh [*Rom.* 3:27].

Who became to us wisdom from God: Everlasting wisdom belonged to the eternal Son [*Prov.* 8:22–31], but he 'became' the wisdom of God 'to us' when he entered into our lot. For it is God's wisdom to provide righteousness, holiness, and redemption for destitute sinners through Christ crucified, and these three terms define the nature of this objective achievement.

That is to say, righteousness and sanctification and redemption:

1. This *righteousness* was secured by the perfect obedience which Christ rendered to God in life and death. He fulfilled the law of God in his life, and exhausted its penalty in his death [*Rom.* 3:25, 26]. Now believers are thus 'righteous, not in themselves, but in Christ [cf. *2 Cor.* 5:21]. Christ is not only their justification, but also the ever–abiding cause of their remaining justified; that is, he is their righteousness' (Edwards).

2. This *sanctification* almost has the same meaning as 'righteousness', for Paul refers to the *status* of holiness which God confers upon believers in Christ [cf. 6:11], and not to the *process* of sanctification in which their co–operation is enlisted. 'We must go back to the Jewish worshippers, and the severe prohibition against coming before God if not purified according to the preparation of the sanctuary; for persons defiled were without access, and debarred from fellowship with Jehovah and other worshippers. But, when sprinkled by the blood of sacrifices, they were readmitted to the worship. They were then a holy people. The blood of sacrifice was their sole ground of access. Even so, by means of the one ever valid sacrifice of Calvary, sinners excluded on

account of sin have access in worship and boldness to approach a holy God. In that sense Christ crucified was made of God to us sanctification' (Smeaton).

3. *Redemption* 'is the first gift of Christ to be begun in us, and the last to be brought to completion. For salvation begins when we are extricated from the labyrinth of sin and death. In the meantime however we sigh for the final resurrection day, yearning for redemption, as it is put in Romans 8:23. But if someone asks how Christ has been given to us for redemption, I reply that he made himself the price of redemption' (Calvin).

31: that, according as it is written, He that glorieth, let him glory in the Lord.

The Corinthian church was torn by party strife because its members were glorying in men. They were guilty of extolling the human agents through whom they had received their salvation instead of exulting in the divine Author of it [3:21, 22]. Paul's free citation of Jeremiah 9:23, 24 is therefore especially apposite, since it not only reveals their duty but also condemns their sin. They are to glory only 'in the Lord'; that is, in Christ 'the Lord of glory' [2:8]. In ascribing this divine honour to Christ, the apostle again points to Deity.

CHAPTER TWO

Paul defends his ministry among the Corinthians by reminding them that they did not owe their conversion to his own powers of persuasion, but to the power of God in blessing the preaching of a crucified Christ to their hearts [verses 1–5]. Although he had repudiated the world's wisdom, he insists that his message is the true wisdom, for now God's once hidden purpose of grace is revealed in the gospel and received through the Spirit [verses 6–13]. But though this wisdom is foolishness to the natural man who has no capacity to discern it, the spiritual man is able to form a judgment about all things because believers have the mind of Christ [verses 14–16].

1: And I, brethren, when I came unto you, came not with excellency of speech or of wisdom, proclaiming to you the testimony of God.

It was in accordance with this principle [1:31] that Paul had abstained from presenting his message in a manner which would have commended itself to human wisdom. He disdained any show of superiority in the form ('speech') or content ('wisdom') of his teaching. He neither varnished the gospel by elaborate language ('Corinthian words'), nor distorted it by philosophical subtlety. The simple fact that Paul 'came' to Corinth proved that the church he planted there was no spontaneous growth, but a supernatural work of grace. In their admiration for later teachers the Corinthians had forgotten that their believing was the consequence of his coming [Rom. 10:14f].

Came . . . proclaiming to you the testimony of God: As they very well know, this was Paul's policy from the moment of his arrival in Corinth [1:6]. This is the testimony 'which God gives and which has God as its contents. Paul holds a mandate from God and he speaks of no one else but God. God has revealed himself and the centre of this revelation is the work of Christ. To speak of God is to speak of Christ. Here is a complete surrender to God and a giving up of all that is human. All this is expressed in the contrast between *I* at the beginning and *God* at the end of the verse' (Grosheide).

2: For I determined not to know anything among you, save Jesus Christ, and him crucified.

'Paul does not say that, when he came to Corinth, he adopted a new evangelistic approach, and there is no suggestion that he had accommodated his message of "Christ and him crucified" to his hearers at Athens and now regretted it' (N. B. Stonehouse, *Paul before the Areopagus*, p. 36). The reason why Paul recalls the character of his ministry among the Corinthians is that those who were now enamoured of human wisdom needed an urgent reminder of the content of the gospel they had professed to believe. 'The plea that our age demands certain modifications of the gospel captivates many today, and they do not decide as Paul did. Of course, they intend to lose nothing of the gospel but only to aid it in finding more ready and widespread acceptance among men. But such good intentions on our part reflect on the Lord's intentions, who originally made the gospel what it is' (Lenski).

Jesus Christ, and him crucified: 'Paul's only design in going to Corinth was to preach Christ; and Christ not as a teacher, or as an example, or as a perfect man, or as a new starting point in the development of the race – all this would be mere philosophy; but Christ *as crucified,* i.e. as dying for our sins. Christ as a propitiation was the burden of Paul's preaching. It has been well remarked that *Jesus Christ* refers to the person of Christ, and *him crucified,* to his work; which constitute the sum of the gospel' (Hodge).

3: And I was with you in weakness, and in fear, and in much trembling.

This includes whatever contributed to his sense of weakness. Paul felt quite unequal to the magnitude of the task which faced him in Corinth. Everything seemed to militate against the success of his mission, and heightened his own feeling of personal and bodily weakness. Hence the Lord's timely encouragement of his hard–pressed servant was by no means superfluous [*Acts* 18:9, 10]. 'Each word is an advance upon the other. The sense of weakness produced fear. The fear betrayed itself in much trembling . . . The expression denotes the Apostle's nervous apprehension that he might not fulfil his ministry aright: i.e. fear and trembling in the sight of God rather than of man' (Lightfoot) [cf. *Phil.* 2:12].

4: And my speech and my preaching were not in persuasive words of wisdom, but in demonstration of the Spirit and of power:

'Speech' (or 'word') harks back to 'the word of the cross' [1:18], i.e. the gospel, while 'preaching' is the apostle's proclamation of it. Thus in neither the substance of his message nor in the manner of its presentation did Paul resort to 'persuasive words of wisdom' to make it more palatable to the natural man. 'My' is emphatic; 'contrasting his Message with the dogmas of philosophers, his method with theirs' (Edwards).

But in demonstration of the Spirit and of power: Instead he relied entirely upon the Spirit of God to provide an indisputable proof of this testimony within the hearts of men. As in 1 Thessalonians 1:5, Paul's first reference to the Spirit in this Epistle is linked to the 'power' which attended his preaching of the gospel. It was the Spirit who demonstrated the truth of the message by convicting the hearers of their need of Christ. And because that power did not proceed from himself [verse 3] but from God [verse 18], the Corinthians have no cause to glory in men [cf. 1:31].

5: that your faith should not stand in the wisdom of men, but in the power of God.

'That' points to the purpose of God in so dispensing with the wisdom of men. For a faith that depends upon clever reasoning may be demolished by a more acute argument, but the faith which is produced by the power of God can never be overthrown. Hence 'faith' is more than a mere intellectual conviction of the truth. 'It is trust in God; and this saving trust grows out of the all–powerful activity of the Divine Spirit' (Edwards) [verse 12; *2 Cor.* 4:6, 7].

6: We speak wisdom, however, among them that are fullgrown: yet a wisdom not of this world, nor of the rulers of this world, who are coming to nought:

But though faith does not depend upon the wisdom of men [verse 5], the Corinthians must not think that 'the word of the cross' [1:18] is devoid of wisdom, for in common with all true preachers of the gospel ('we') Paul speaks the highest Wisdom. Some take the 'fullgrown' to be Christians of mature understanding as distinguished from the 'babes' of 3:1, but this view is not favoured by the context which contrasts 'the called' or converted with the unbelieving who reject the gospel as foolishness [1:23, 24]. When contrasted with the unsaved it is appropriate to refer to all believers as the 'perfected' or the 'mature' because they alone 'have reached Christ crucified as the goal' (Lenski).

Although many commentators argue that 'the rulers of this world' is a reference to demonic powers, the apostle would not have expected his readers to grasp such an idea without a word of explanation, and it is preferable to take his words in their natural meaning [*Acts* 3:17]. So these rulers 'are to be understood as great men according to the world's estimate of greatness', whether in *intellect* ('wise'), *power* ('mighty'), or *rank* ('noble') as in 1:26 (Lightfoot). 'The word "rulers" must not be taken of magistrates only, since Paul has in mind all those who set the pattern of this world, including the rulers in the sphere of science and art. Of all of them it holds true that they *are coming to nought*' (Grosheide).

7: but we speak God's wisdom in a mystery, even the wisdom that hath been hidden, which God foreordained before the worlds unto our glory:

But the wisdom we speak is diametrically opposed to the spurious wisdom of the world [verses 5, 6]. For it is God's wisdom, and this wisdom has been fully manifested in the gospel. Since nothing but the gospel can enrich the Corinthians with all the riches of God, they must not continue to hanker after that wisdom which leads only to final and fatal impoverishment. When Paul speaks 'wisdom among the mature' he is not setting forth a secret doctrine different from that preached to beginners, but the same 'word of the cross' – for he knows nothing greater or higher [*Gal.* 6:14] – in its inner meaning and larger implications (Findlay).

In a mystery, even the wisdom that hath been hidden: 'The Christian "mystery" according to Paul is not something that is to be kept secret on principle, like the mysteries of Eleusis, but it is something which, though it was formerly hidden in the counsels of God, is now to be made known to all. Some, it is true, may never be able to receive it. But that which is necessary in order that it may be received is not "gnosis" or an initiation. It is rather acceptance of a message and the holy life that follows. "If you would know the deep things of God," Paul says to the Corinthians, "then stop your quarrelling." We find ourselves here in a circle of ideas quite different from that of the mystery religions' (J. G. Machen, *The Origin of Paul's Religion*, p. 273) [*Rom.* 16:25, 26; *Eph.* 3:3–6; *Col.* 1:26].

Which God foreordained before the ages (ASV margin): 'Before man was formed, before the first phosphor light of his little wisdom began to glow, God's wisdom was complete, God's decision was fixed as to the object and as to the result of that wisdom' (Lenski).

Unto our glory: Our eternal glory is thus the result of God's eternal decree. 'The wisdom of the great men of the world ends in their destruction; God's wisdom leads, not only to our salvation, but to our glory' (Edwards). Moreover, those who are destined to share in the glory of 'outward exaltation' [*Rom.* 8:17, 18] are none other than those who even now enjoy the glory of 'inward enlightenment' [*2 Cor.* 3:18]. For as fellowship with God on earth is glory begun, so fellowship with God in heaven is glory consummated [*Psa.* 73:23–26].

8: which none of the rulers of this world hath known: for had they known it, they would not have crucified the Lord of glory:

None of the rulers of this world knew God's wisdom. '"Had they discerned, as they did not, they would not have crucified, as they did." It is manifest from this that the "rulers" are neither demons nor angels, but the rulers who took part in crucifying the Christ' (Robertson-Plummer).

Crucified the Lord of glory: This shows that Paul regarded Jesus, even in the days of his flesh, as the 'Lord to whom glory belongs as his native right' (B. B. Warfield, *The Lord of Glory*, pp. 223–4). The expression strongly contrasts the essential glory of the Lord with the shame of his suffering. 'We see that the person of Christ may be designated from his divine nature, when what is affirmed of him is true only of his human nature . . . Whatever is true either of the soul or body may be predicated of a man as a person; and whatever is true of either the divine or human nature of Christ may be predicated of Christ as a person. We need not hesitate therefore to say with Paul, the Lord of glory was crucified; or even, in accordance with the received text in Acts 20:28, "God purchased the church with his blood." The person who died was truly God, although the divine nature no more died than the soul of man does when the breath leaves his body' (Hodge).

9: but as it is written,

Things which eye saw not, and ear heard not,
And which entered not into the heart of man,
Whatsoever things God prepared for them that love him.

'Not only was God's wisdom unknown to the princes of this world, but those things in which it manifests itself are in their nature such that their inner meaning cannot be known without a revelation of the Spirit within' (Edwards). Here Paul freely selects certain scriptural expressions from Isaiah 64:4 and 65:17, which he arranges in an ascending scale in order to show the absolute necessity of a divine disclosure of this mystery. 'By combining the three terms *seeing, hearing,* and *entering into the heart,* the apostle wishes to designate the three means of natural knowledge: sight, or immediate experience; hearing, or knowledge by way of tradition; finally, the inspirations of the heart, the discoveries of the understanding proper. By none of these means can man reach the conception of the blessings which God has destined for him' (Godet). The Corinthians prided themselves on their spiritual knowledge, but Paul does not say that these inconceivable blessings have been prepared for those who know God, but rather for those who love him [cf. 8:3]. 'Not *gnosis* but love is the touchstone of Christian maturity and spirituality' (Barrett).

10: But unto us God revealed them through the Spirit: for the Spirit searcheth all things, yea, the deep things of God.

But in the goodness of God, what could never be discovered by human reason has been revealed to Christians by the Holy Spirit. 'Searcheth all things' expresses the 'intra–divine activity of the Holy Spirit' (Godet). Since his knowledge of God is infinite, the fathomless depths of God hold no mysteries for him. And it is because he alone 'fathoms everything' (Arndt-Gingrich) that only he can reveal the hidden wisdom of God to men [verse 7]. Thus the passage proves the personality and divinity of the Spirit by ascribing intelligent activity and omniscience to him.

11: For who among men knoweth the things of a man, save the spirit of the man which is in him? Even so the things of God none knoweth, save the Spirit of God.

As no one can know the things of a man except the spirit of the man that is 'in him', so no one can understand the things of God apart from the Spirit of God. The omission of 'in him' from the second part of the verse shows that Paul's analogy must not be pressed beyond its immediate purpose: 'for in the case of ourselves, we and our own spirit are *numerically one*; whereas in this very passage – and in every other place where the Holy Spirit is spoken of – there is observed *a distinction of conscious personality* between "God" on the one hand and the "Spirit of God" on the other' (David Brown).

12: But we received, not the spirit of the world, but the spirit which is from God; that we might know the things that were freely given to us of God.

But *we* received, not that spirit of human wisdom which permeates a fallen world, but rather the Spirit which is of God. For 'to whatever degree of power this spirit of the world may rise, it cannot give man the knowledge of the divine plans, nor make an apostle even of the greatest genius' (Godet). The aorist tenses of the verbs show that until the Spirit is imparted in regeneration there can be no personal participation in the blessings of the gospel. Hence Findlay remarks that the historic gifts of God to men in Christ 'would have been idle boons without the Spirit enabling us to "know" them' [cf. *Eph.* 1:17ff.].

13: Which things also we speak, not in words which man's wisdom teacheth, but which the Spirit teacheth; combining spiritual things with spiritual words.

Paul here refers to himself and the nature of his ministry in Corinth: 'which things we speak out, not in words taught by man's wisdom, but in those words which are taught by the Spirit'. The apostle could not proclaim a spiritual message in words of natural wisdom, and this was why he preached as he did. The Corinthians found his speech insipid because it lacked the savour of worldly wisdom, but their complaint merely showed that they still had a carnal palate [3:1; *2 Cor.* 10:10]. For no words but those which are instinct with the divine life of the Spirit have the power to vivify the spiritually dead.

Combining spiritual things with spiritual words: In short, not only has the Spirit revealed these things to Paul, but he also ensures that they are exactly transmitted to others through the very words which he teaches. 'Both the spiritual things and the spiritual words that convey them emanate equally from the Spirit, and the apostles combine the two accordingly. This is Paul's definition of Verbal Inspiration' (Lenski).

14: Now the natural man receiveth not the things of the Spirit of God: for they are foolishness unto him; and he cannot know them, because they are spiritually judged.

Now the natural man: This man may be of the noblest character and attainments in the estimation of the world, yet he lacks the one thing needful. He is described as the natural man because his nature is unchanged by grace. As a stranger to the new birth [*John* 3:3–8], he is 'one who lives on the purely material plane, without being touched by the Spirit of God' (Arndt-Gingrich). Hence he not only lacks the capacity to receive the things of the Spirit, but he also rejects them as foolishness [cf. *Rom.* 8:7].

Because they are spiritually examined (ASV margin): The fact that Paul uses this word *anakrino* no less than ten times in this Epistle, though in no other, may suggest that it was a catchword among his critics in Corinth (Barrett). It is a legal term which refers to 'the preliminary examination, preceding the trial proper' (A. Souter). Although the unconverted presume to pass judgment on the gospel after giving it a first hearing, the absurdity of this procedure is at once revealed by their total incapacity to sift its content. 'The unspiritual are out of court as religious critics; they are deaf men judging music' (Findlay).

15: But he that is spiritual judgeth all things, and he himself is judged of no man.

But he that is spiritual examineth all things (ASV margin): It is because the spiritual man is a man whose mind has been illuminated by the Holy Spirit that he has the discernment to evaluate 'all things' in the light of that revelation; whereas the natural man is not only blind to the glory of the gospel, but is also without the ability to reach a right judgment on even the common things of this life because he lacks the perception which would enable him to see their true meaning and purpose (Lenski).

And he himself is examined of no man (ASV margin): As most of this letter is taken up with the sifting of spiritual men, 'no man' must here refer to the natural man. Paul's meaning is that the man who is without the Spirit has no means of judging the spiritual man. 'Since none other possesses the probe of truth furnished by the Spirit of God, the spiritual man stands on a height from which he overlooks the world, and is overlooked only by God. The statement is ideal, holding good of "the spiritual man" as, and so far as, he is such. Where a Christian is carnal [3:1], his spiritual judgment is vitiated; to that extent he puts himself within the measure of the natural man' (Findlay).

16: For who hath known the mind of the Lord, that he should instruct him? But we have the mind of Christ.

Paul makes the prophet's question his own [*Isa.* 40:13]. The Corinthians with all their vaunted wisdom feel free to find fault with the preaching of an inspired apostle. Then perhaps they should go on to instruct the King from whom the ambassador received his message!

'To the Corinthians, Paul brought the mind of Christ and made them share in the divine gospel wisdom. Will they now fall back into their former state and with worldly wisdom tell the Lord how to improve his mind and to make the gospel wisdom what they think it ought to be?' (Lenski). All those who still rely on their own ideas to 'improve' the gospel cannot escape this grave indictment of blasphemy.

But we have the mind of Christ: Since none but Christ knows the mind of God, it is only through the revelation given to him by Christ that Paul is made to share in this knowledge of the divine purpose. 'Thus the minister of a Sovereign could say, after an intimate conversation with his king, I am in full possession of my master's mind. From this moment, therefore, to criticize the servant is to criticize the master' (Godet). The apostles had committed to them a revelation of supreme authority so that afterwards it might spread 'by degrees to the whole church' (Calvin). It is therefore by their response to this declaration of the Lord's once hidden plan of salvation that believers are said to possess 'the mind of Christ', which clearly may not be equated with a state of mindless mysticism [cf. *1 Pet.* 1:13].

CHAPTER THREE

At first Paul's plain preaching of the gospel was due to the fact that the Corinthians were mere babes in Christ, but it is a matter of reproof that he is still unable to feed them with meat. For they had shown how spiritually immature they were by making their favourite preachers the subject of party strife in the church [verses 1–4]. Instead of glorying in men they should understand that ministers are not rivals competing for their loyalty, but fellow-servants engaged in the common task of building God's church. Paul has laid the one true foundation, and now others must take care how they build upon it. The jerry–builder will suffer the disgrace of seeing his work destroyed, but the faithful workman will be rewarded for his labours [verses 5–15]. As the Corinthians are God's temple, they must realize that if any man defiles God's dwelling,-place, God will destroy him [verses 16, 17]. Hence they are to renounce that worldly wisdom which foolishly glories in men. For all things, including their ministers, belong to them, even as they belong to Christ [verses 18–23].

1: And I, brethren, could not speak unto you as unto spiritual, but as unto carnal, as unto babes in Christ.

And I, brethren, 'He reproveth, yet keeps up his love . . . Some have observed in the Old Testament, the *Prophets* in their Sermons were more severe, *Thus saith the Lord*, and they never called their Auditors *Brethren*; but in the *Gospel*, a dispensation of love, there is often *Brethren*, and *I beseech you by the mercies of Christ*' (Anthony Burgess).

Could not speak unto you as unto spiritual, but as unto carnal: Paul reminds his readers that the content of his teaching during the early days of his mission in Corinth was determined by their condition at that time. He could not then address them as spiritual men [2:15], but only as those who were still 'fleshy' in their modes of thought and action. 'The *I could not* is an implicit answer to the disdainful charge of his enemies: "He knew not"' (Godet).

As unto babes in Christ: Immaturity during infancy is normal, but if that condition is unduly prolonged the result is monstrous. The Corinthians had undergone a radical change, a new principle of life had been implanted within them. They were now 'in Christ', but it was not intended that they should remain '*babes* in Christ' for ever [13:11, 14:20]. Life must develop and they are to press on to perfection. It is tragic that so many believers remain in the spiritual kindergarten long after they ought to have been teachers of the gospel [*Heb.* 5:12]. 'Paul's goal was for all babes to become adults [*Col.* 1:28]' (A. T. Robertson).

2: I fed you with milk, not with meat; for ye were not yet able to bear it: nay, not even now are ye able;

It would be quite wrong to infer from this that Paul preached the elementary doctrines to beginners and reserved the advanced teaching for the mature, for he always preached 'the whole counsel of God' [*Acts* 20:27]. The distinction is not between two sets of doctrines but between two ways of presenting the same gospel. 'For the same Christ is milk for babes, and solid food for adults' (Calvin). So our Lord himself condescended to teach the Word to the people in many parables as they 'were able to hear it' [*Mark* 4:33]. But with the words 'nay, not even now are ye able', Paul shatters the spiritual complacency of the Corinthians by an abrupt return to the present tense. 'At one time they were naturally immature without special blame; now their immaturity is a different matter . . . "Now" is cumulative: this inability persists contrary to nature and to expectation' (Lenski).

3: for ye are yet carnal: for whereas there is among you jealousy and strife, are ye not carnal, and do ye not walk after the manner of men?

For ye are yet carnal: When the Corinthians were but babes in the faith Paul said that they were 'fleshy' (*sarkinos*, verse 1); here he accuses them of 'fleshly' behaviour, of walking according to the flesh (*sarkikos*). Although many authorities are doubtful whether there is any difference in meaning between these words, A. T. Robertson says that 'a real distinction seems to be observed' in 1 Corinthians 3:1 and 3:3 (*A Grammar of the Greek New Testament*, p. 158). Paul is blaming them for their unspiritual conduct, for though they have received the Spirit, they are still acting as 'men' [verse 4], i.e. as those who belong to the flesh and are characterized by it.

For whereas there is among you jealousy and strife: 'The proof is from the effects. For since jealousy, disputes and factions are fruits of the flesh, we can be sure that, wherever they are to be seen, there flourishes the root. These evils held sway among the Corinthians; therefore from that Paul shows clearly that they were carnal' (Calvin) [*Gal.* 5:15–26].

Are ye not carnal, and do ye not walk after the manner of men? 'Oh what *Antipodes* are such men to the Scripture! Either lay down the name of a Christian, or else live above what men of the world do. As *Alexander* said to a soldier named *Alexander*, Either lay aside his name, or else do valiant acts' (Burgess).

4: For when one saith, I am of Paul; and another, I am of Apollos; are ye not men?

'Although they did not advance the names and persons of wicked men, but of holy and eminent men, yet by these names of holy men, they made unholy and wicked divisions. Observe, *That when the Devil cannot hurt the Church by a profane and sinful Ministry, then he labours to destroy it by abusing the names and esteem of those who are truly holy and eminent* . . . so the Devil when he cannot destroy souls by stirring up wicked instruments, he will endeavour that men should think of good instruments more than they ought' (Burgess) [cf. 1:12].

5: What then is Apollos? and what is Paul? Ministers through whom ye believed; and each as the Lord gave to him.

These rhetorical questions drive home the folly of making 'ministers' the leaders of parties. Apollos and Paul are merely servants' (*diakonoi:* a word which underlines the lowly character of their service), while the preposition 'through' (*dia*) also marks the purely instrumental character of this service. Moreover, as befits subordinates, 'each' servant was assigned his particular task 'as the Lord gave to him'; and each performed his own duty (Barrett).

6: I planted. Apollos watered; but God gave the increase.

'The Metaphor is easy. As the Gardener sets his herbs, waters them, but he cannot make them grow, he cannot make the least flower that is, though he hath never so much skill: Thus it is here, though they be Ministers of *Seraphical* affections, and *Cherubinical* knowledge, yet they cannot make the Word to prosper, and to increase in the hearer; it is God who doth that, *Isa.* 55:10; 61:11. There you have such similitudes; so that this . . . is an admirable direction to look above the abilities, above the parts and gifts of men: We think, Oh if we have such a Ministry, all would be well! whereas *Apollos* and *Paul* cannot give the increase' (Burgess).

7: So then neither is he that planteth anything, neither he that watereth; but God that giveth the increase.

The emphasis falls on the final word in the Greek sentence, which is 'God'. It is *God* that gives the increase. 'Men are but God's instruments, tools, "agents" (ministers) in performing this work. They do not act in it for God, that is, instead of God; but God acts through them . . . This is Paul's teaching everywhere: that as it is God who created us men, so it is God who has recreated us Christians. And the one in as direct and true a sense as the other. As He used agents in the one case – our natural generation (for none of us are born men without parents) – so He may use instruments in the other, our spiritual regeneration (for none of us are born Christians where there is no Word). But in both cases, it is God and God alone who gives the increase' (B. B. Warfield, 'Man's Husbandry and God's Bounty', *Faith and Life,* pp. 211–21).

8: Now he that planteth and he that watereth are one: but each shall receive his own reward according to his own labour.

All who engage in this spiritual husbandry are in the same honourable employment. So if one plants and another waters, it is all 'one', because both are fellow-labourers under God, who will reward each 'according to his own labour'. 'Wages are measured by labour, not results. And therefore it is all one to you and me, as labourers in God's field, whether He sets us to plough, plant, water or reap . . . The amount of labour, not the department of work, is the norm of our reward. What a consolation this is to the obscure workman to whom God has given much labour and few results; reward is proportioned to the labour, not the results!' (Warfield, op. cit.).

9: For we are God's fellow-workers: ye are God's husbandry, God's building.

We are fellow-labourers in the service of God (Arndt-Gingrich): This alternative rendering of the Greek is to be preferred as being more consistent with context, which stresses the fact that Paul and Apollos are not rivals but joint-workers in God's service. Thus the first part of the verse refers to God's ministers, and the second to God's people. But though both belong to God, he has entrusted his ministers with the task of calling his people to faith in Christ and bringing them to spiritual maturity. 'The Corinthians acted as if these ministers were theirs, to be measured and weighed at pleasure, to be exalted or to be lowered, to be rewarded with praise or to be chastised with criticism. Paul takes these ministers out of their hands, they are God's, doing his work under his special call and commission' (Lenski).

Ye are God's husbandry, God's building: Their work is not completed, but is still in progress. The field is under cultivation; the building is in course of construction. 'The former of these metaphors has been already applied [verses 6–8]: and now the latter is expanded [verses 10–17]. Thus "God's husbandry, God's building" is the link which connects the two paragraphs together. Of the two images "husbandry" implies the organic growth of the church, "building" the mutual adaptation of its parts' (Lightfoot).

10: According to the grace of God which was given unto me, as a wise

masterbuilder I laid a foundation; and another buildeth thereon. But let each man take heed how he buildeth thereon.

Although Paul freely ascribes all the praise to the grace of God, his fickle readers needed to be reminded that the church in Corinth owed its very existence to his labours there. It was he and none other who had laid a foundation as a skilful masterbuilder. It now remains the solemn responsibility of each one who continues the work to see that he builds worthily on that foundation. The apostle 'uses three metaphors to express the respective relations of himself and of other teachers to the Corinthian church. He is planter [3:6], founder [3:10], and father [4:15]. Apollos and the rest are waterers, after-builders, and tutors' (Robertson-Plummer).

11: For other foundation can no man lay than that which is laid, which is Jesus Christ.

Paul is confident that his work will endure because the foundation he laid corresponds with that which is already laid by God. 'The foundation laid by Paul [verse 10] was Christ preached and taught in the work of his crucifixion, and afterwards of his resurrection. The foundation already laid by God [verse 11] was Christ Jesus himself, crucified and risen. The same cornerstone in different fashion was laid by both. *Essentially* by the divine Architect in heaven, *Doctrinally* by his inspired masterbuilder on earth' (T. C. Hammond). This means that Christianity is the historical realization of the eternal purpose of God. It is this fact which manifests the folly of those religious teachers who expect to build an eternal edifice on some other purely temporal foundation. For it is certain that the beliefs which originate in this world are by their very nature quite unable to transcend it. In thus distinguishing himself from the foundation [cf. *2 Cor.* 4:5], Paul may have been implicitly condemning those in Corinth who did not hesitate to identify another apostle with it. If so, it seems reasonable to suppose that some in the Peter-party were claiming that *their* leader was the true foundation of the church, even though Peter's own testimony was very different [cf. *Matt.* 16:16, 18; *1 Pet.* 2:6].

12: But if any man buildeth on the foundation gold, silver, costly stones, wood, hay, stubble;

But whereas some will build upon the true foundation with precious materials, others may think fit to use base materials which will not withstand the testing fire of God's judgment. The first group presents the pure doctrine which is in keeping with the foundation, while the second stands for that teaching which is unworthy of it. 'He doth not by hay and stubble speak of such dangerous and damnable heresies that overthrow the foundation, such are not saved, though by fire, but they bring upon themselves swift damnation [2 Pet. 2:1] but lesser errors and falsehoods, which do not overthrow, yet are no ways agreeable or suitable to the foundation' (Burgess).

13: each man's work shall be made manifest: for the day shall declare it, because it is revealed in fire; and the fire itself shall prove each man's work of what sort it is.

On the Day of Judgment the work of every preacher shall be subjected to the searching scrutiny of the Lord which is here likened to a consuming fire [2 Cor. 5:10, 11]. The key to Paul's imagery is to be found in the prophecy of Malachi which depicts the Lord's sudden coming to his temple in fiery judgment [Mal. 3:1, 2; cf. 2 Thess. 1:8].

Each man's work: 'The unity of structure makes it impossible for men to distinguish the work of one builder from that of another. God only can say where the work of one man ends and that of another begins. The extent no less than the quality of the work will be judged' (Edwards).

And the fire itself shall prove each man's work of what sort it is: The work is *proved* in the expectation that something good will be found in it. 'But it must be kept in mind that Paul does not imply that something good will be found in every instance, a thought definitely excluded by the reference to wood, hay and stubble which will be burnt completely' (Grosheide).

14: If any man's work shall abide which he built thereon, he shall receive a reward.

He whose work survives this stringent test shall receive a wage for work well done. 'This reward cannot be salvation; for the faithful workman was already in possession of this supreme blessing when he was labouring. We have to think then of more particular privileges, such as the joy of being the object of the Master's satisfaction: "Good and faithful servant!"; then the happiness of seeing invested with glory the souls whom a faithful ministry has contributed to sanctify; finally, the possession of a glorious position in the new state of things established by the Lord at his coming: "Thou hast gained ten pounds; receive power over ten cities" [*Luke* 19:17]' (Godet).

15: If any man's work shall be burned, he shall suffer loss: but he himself shall be saved; yet so as through fire.

On the other hand, the man who tries to build with wood, hay or stubble will see all his work destroyed in the fire of divine judgment, and lose the reward he expects to receive. This 'burning up denotes the complete rejection of the work of the unwise builders, their teaching and all that they thought they had accomplished in men's hearts through it' (Lenski). So because it is better to be sure now than sorry later, each preacher should take pains to find out whether he is exercising a fireproof ministry.

But he himself shall be saved: 'The man himself will be saved, though his work will be burned. As a worker he suffers loss; but his salvation is through faith. Yet his salvation even will be through the fire of conflagration that consumes his work. He deserves for his unfaithfulness to forfeit his salvation and perish with the unbeliever. But he is saved as if through the very flames. He is a smoking firebrand' (Edwards). [*Zech.* 3:2; *Jude* 23].

Yet so as through fire: As Godet so clearly shows, no support for the Romish fiction of purgatory can be claimed from this passage. 'This is to forget, − 1. that the fire is allegorical like the building; 2. that it is only teachers who are in question; 3. that the trial indicated is a means of valuation, not of purification; 4. that this fire is lighted at Christ's coming, and consequently does not yet burn in the interval between the death of Christians and that advent; 5. that the salvation of the worker, of which Paul speaks, takes place not *by*, but *in spite of* the fire.'

16: Know ye not that ye are a temple of God, and that the Spirit of God dwelleth in you?

The character of this building is now described: the Corinthians are nothing less than God's temple ('the omission of the article merely concentrates attention on the character of the society, and does not describe them as one of many shrines' – St John Parry). But as is so often the case in this Epistle, the information is conveyed in the form of a question which is fraught with rebuke, 'Know ye not?' [cf. 5:6, 6:2,6:3, 6:9, 6:15, 6:16, 6:19, 9:13, 9:24]. It is indeed a serious matter to build badly upon the true foundation, but to defile the very dwelling-place of God is far worse [verse 17]. Paul's stern warning is evidently addressed to those who are disturbing the unity of the church by their party strife [cf. 1:13: 'Is Christ divided?']. For in virtue of the indwelling presence of the Holy Spirit they all together constitute the true temple of God, whose peace cannot be shattered without sacrilege.

17: If any man destroyeth the temple of God, him shall God destroy; for the temple of God is holy and such are ye.

If any man destroyeth the temple of God, him shall God destroy; That the punishment fits the crime is indicated by the repetition of the verb, for the desecration of the divine sanctuary is a capital offence. Thus he who destroys God's temple will be destroyed by God, i.e. punished 'with eternal destruction' (Arndt-Gingrich).

For the temple of God is holy: As the earthly temple was set apart for holy use and could not be profaned with impunity, so Christians are consecrated to God and cannot be 'defiled by any as instruments in that action, without exceeding great peril and hazard to them that endeavour and attempt any such thing' (Poole).

And such are ye: '*The holy Temple of God under the Gospel, is not any place, though never so adorned or glorious; but persons believing and worshipping of Him according to His will.* This Doctrine hath its great use. For once in God's Church, while Popery and her principles reigned, all the holiness spoken of, preached for, pleaded for principally, was holiness of things, not persons; holy Temples, holy Altars, holy Images; but real, personal holiness, which God commands, was despised and opposed . . . The Temple, the Church of God, are *Persons believing. The Image of God is righteousness and holiness in our lives*' (Burgess).

18: Let no man deceive himself. If any man thinketh that he is wise among you in this world, let him become a fool, that he may become wise.

In conclusion Paul urges the Corinthians to renounce the worldly wisdom which had divided rather than edified the church [verses 18–23]. Each man is warned that his cherished preconceptions are no more than self-deceptions. *'Human conceited wisdom must needs hinder the entertainment of Christ's truth, because it sets itself on the Throne to be Judge, and to determine truth or falsehood according to her own principles.* It makes weights and a standard of its own, and will weigh even what God and the Scripture saith, by its own self' (Burgess). In other words, all *autonomous* thought is *apostate* thought, because the thinking that begins with man can never end with God. Dependent creatures, who have received the candle of reason from God, must be humble enough to think God's thoughts after him.

If any man thinketh that he is wise among you in this world: 'Men must not think to be wise in both spheres; the church's wise are the world's fools, and *vice versa.* The cross is "foolishness" to the world, and he who espouses it a "fool" in its opinion – a *fool* with a *criminal* for his Master; and one can only be a Christian sage – wise after the manner of chapter 2:8ff. – upon condition of bearing this reproach. Paul was crazy in the eyes of the world [4:10; *2 Cor.* 5:13; *Acts* 26:24], but how wise *amongst us!*' (Findlay).

Let him become a fool, that he may become wise: This 'is only in *appearance*, and in the judgment of the world; he speaketh by concession; the world will judge all true Scripture and heavenly wisdom to be foolishness. So that as the world's wisdom is a real folly, but a seeming wisdom: so the Scripture-wisdom, is a real wisdom, but a seeming folly' (Burgess).

19: For the wisdom of this world is foolishness with God. For it is written, He that taketh the wise in their craftiness:

It is because God's judgment of the wisdom of this world is not determined by 'the outward appearance', but is based on his perfect knowledge of all things in their inner reality, that it must be accepted as true [*1 Sam.* 16:7]. 'There are many wise, learned men in the world, whose naked propositions we do more regard than other men's demonstrations. But how much more should we acquiesce in God's assertions? We may justly call all human wisdom mere foolishness, because God doth so' (Burgess). Since the Corinthians found this truth so hard to accept, Paul not only repeats it [cf. 1:20], but also invokes the testimony of Scripture to confirm it [*Job* 5:13]. The words are taken from the speech of Eliphaz who was also a wise man of this world. The apostle uses the statement which is true in itself without in any way endorsing the wrong application that Eliphaz makes of it. Similarly, in addressing the philosophers of Athens Paul felt free to quote the words of heathen poets for he recognized that 'pagan men, in spite of themselves and contrary to the controlling disposition of their minds, as creatures of God confronted with the divine revelation were capable of responses which were valid so long as and to the extent that they stood in isolation from their pagan systems' (Stonehouse) [*Acts* 17:28].

20: and again, The Lord knoweth the reasonings of the wise, that they are vain.

Psalm 94:11 is the second testimony which Paul brings forward to prove his case. Under the inspiration of the Spirit he applies what was originally spoken of 'man' to a particular class of men, for what is true of the vanity of human thought in general is especially relevant to 'the reasonings of the wise'. Such men entertain high hopes for their schemes, but God knows beforehand that these will be void of the expected result. Thus their thoughts are futile because they always leave God out of their reckoning [cf. *Rom.* 1:21].

21a: Wherefore let no one glory in men.

Paul now states the only proper conclusion to be drawn from the preceding argument. This verse is the counterpart of 1:31. It is because the Corinthians are bidden to 'glory in the Lord' that they are forbidden to 'glory in men'. Yet this was precisely what they were doing, for the God–ordained relationship with their teachers was reversed by their partisan applause. For when they said, I belong to Paul or Apollos or Peter, they forgot that by the grace of God these men belonged to them [cf. *2 Cor.* 4:5].

21b: For all things are yours;

22: whether Paul, or Apollos, or Cephas, or the world, or life, or death, or things present, or things to come; all are yours;

23: and ye are Christ's; and Christ is God's.

Having finished his exhortation, Paul is able to end with a passage of great lyrical beauty in which he sets forth the manifold privileges of the people of God in a way that recalls Romans 8:31–39.

For all things are yours: 'The Christian loses this birthright by treating the world or its interests as ends in themselves, i.e. by becoming enslaved to persons [7:23; *2 Cor.* 11:20] or things [6:12; *Phil.* 3:19] . . . The Corinthians, by boasting in men, were forgetting, and thereby imperilling, their prerogative in Christ' (Robertson-Plummer).

Whether Paul, or Apollos, or Cephas: Because God puts his servants at the disposal of the church, they are *all* the property of the congregation [4:1f.]. 'At Corinth they were choosing one of these men and rejecting others. That is foolishness, it is the wisdom of the world, for God gave them all' (Grosheide).

Or the world: God preserves the world so 'that He may attain the ends of His Predestination. Insomuch that there had been no Creation at first, no world at all, nor would there still be any sustentation, or conservation of it, were it not for the Church's sake' (Burgess) [*Rom.* 8:28–30].

Or life, or death: 'This means not merely that the question whether the people of God live or die, is determined with reference to their own good; but also that life and death are dispensed and administered so as best to fulfil the designs of God in reference to the church. The greatest men of the world, kings, statesmen and heroes, ministers, individual believers and unbelievers, live or die just as best subserves the interests of Christ's kingdom' (Hodge).

Or things present, or things to come: The first phrase includes all that can happen to us in this present life; while the second points to the forthcoming transformation, with its eternal consequences.

All are yours: Paul repeats his assertion that 'all things' belong to believers, not only to sum up the preceding enumeration, but also to stress the contrast between this sweeping statement and the phrase with which he immediately qualifies it.

And ye are Christ's: 'The Corinthian readers, exalted to a height outsoaring Stoic pride, are in a moment laid low at the feet of Christ: "Lords of the universe – you are his bondmen, your vast heritage in the present and future you gather as *factors for him*" . . . Our property is immense, but we are Another's; we rule, to be ruled. A man cannot own too much, provided that *he recognizes his Owner*' (Findlay).

And Christ is God's: The official title 'Christ' makes it plain that the reference is to the Son's voluntary or 'economic' subjection to the Father as Mediator. As the Messiah, 1. He received a people from God in the eternal covenant of redemption [*John* 17:2]; 2. He became obedient in life and death to the will of the Father [*Phil.* 2:7, 8]; 3. He is exalted by God to exercise universal lordship as the Head of the redeemed community 'till he hath put all enemies under his feet' [15:24; *Acts* 5:31; *Phil.* 2:9, 10].

'Is Christ thus wholly God's? Then what self–denial, what humility and modesty should we learn hence? Shall Christ not seek His own glory? Shall not He seek to please Himself? Shall not He exalt His own will? Why then are we so apt to magnify our self–glory, our own will, our own advantage? It should shame us who follow such a Christ, to be called by the name of this Christ; How ill do such a Head, and such members agree together? Think of Christ, when pride, vainglory, self–will, stirreth in thee: *If Christ had been thus, there had been no pardon, no salvation for me*' (Burgess).

CHAPTER FOUR

All this means that the Corinthians should regard their ministers as the servants of Christ and stewards of the mysteries of God. Hence Paul is not concerned with how men may estimate the value of his ministry when the only competent judge of his labours is the Lord to whom he is accountable [verses 1–5]. They have no right to prefer one teacher above another when these men have all received their differing gifts from God [verses 6–7]. Paul ironically contrasts the vain spirit that leads them to make such arrogant judgments with his own despised and afflicted state [verses 8–13]. As their one father in Christ, he writes these things not to shame them, but to urge them to follow him [verses 14, 15]. He had sent Timothy to remind them of his teaching, but hopes soon to come in person when his critics shall have full proof of his authority. The character of his visit will be determined by their response to his reproofs: Is he to come with a rod, or in a spirit of meekness? [verses 17–21].

1: Let a man so account of us, as of ministers of Christ, and stewards of the mysteries of God.

A wrong estimate of the servants of Christ has been the occasion of strife in Corinth. Now the apostle proceeds to indicate their true place in the church. The Corinthians are to consider them first of all, not as heads of parties, or even as ministers of the church, but as 'Christ's underlings' (NEB); men without any authority of their own, whose sole business is to execute the commands of their Lord. The word, which originally referred to 'under–rowers', here points to the lowliness of their service. Secondly, they must be recognized as 'God's stewards'; a term showing that they have been dignified with the responsible task of declaring God's 'mysteries' to all men. Accordingly their commission is not to disseminate their own ideas, but to preach a divinely revealed gospel [cf. 2:7].

2: Here, moreover, it is required in stewards, that a man be found faithful.

And in the realm of stewardship, trustworthiness is the principal thing. In the eyes of his master, nothing can compensate for the lack of fidelity in a steward, whatever other good qualities he may be seen to possess [*Luke* 16:1ff.]. The Corinthians presumed to judge ministers by their *gifts*, whereas *faithfulness* is the primary and indispensable requirement. And who but God himself is competent to judge that? 'Responsible not to his fellows, but *to the Lord*, his high trust demands a strict account [*Luke* 12:41–48]' (Findlay).

3: But with me it is a very small thing that I should be judged of you, or of man's judgment: yea, I judge not mine own self.

Since the faithful steward always has in view the final reckoning with his master, whether he stands or falls in the estimation of his fellow-servants is of little moment to him [*Rom.* 14:4; *1 Pet.* 4:10]. Thus as far as he is concerned, Paul regards it as of the smallest consequence that the Corinthians should take it upon themselves to examine his character, motives, and methods. This does not mean that he was not hurt by their criticism, but that he was not moved by it. As he did not receive his message from men, neither their praise nor their blame is to deflect the steward of God's mysteries from his solemn obligation faithfully to fulfil his ministry [*Acts* 20:26, 27; *2 Tim.* 4:2]. Paul's curious reference to 'man's day' (ASV margin) contrasts the judgment of men with the Lord's judgment–day [3:13]. '*That* is the tribunal which the apostle recognizes; a *human* tribunal he does not care to satisfy' (Robertson-Plummer).

4: For I know nothing against myself; yet am I not here by justified: but he that judgeth me is the Lord.

As Calvin points out, Paul is not protesting sinlessness, but claiming that he has carried out his duties as an apostle 'with so much integrity and faithfulness that his conscience did not accuse him in any way'. Nevertheless he refuses to anticipate Christ's judgment on his labours. For though conscience can 'judge' and control conduct in the world, this subjective faculty is powerless to pronounce the final verdict on a man's life. Consequently the word 'justified' here has nothing to do with the sinner's justification by faith [*Rom.* 3:24]; it refers to the judicial acquittal of God's steward when the divine sentence of approval is passed upon his work on the last day [cf. 3:14]. In referring the judgment of his ministry to the Lord, Paul does not mean 'that all ministers are to be given a free hand to do what they think is right until the Lord at last judges them. What Paul says is that men must not usurp the Lord's judgment-seat and judge the Lord's ministers according to their own wisdom. Paul does not for one moment judge himself in this way. Yet the Corinthians were judging their ministers in this manner. Men do it to this day' (Lenski).

5: Wherefore judge nothing before the time, until the Lord come, who will both bring to light the hidden things of darkness, and make manifest the counsels of the hearts; and then shall each man have his praise from God.

The Corinthians must stop passing such premature judgments on the Lord's servants, for only he can judge them, and this he will do at his coming. Yet they were not only guilty of judging what was beyond their jurisdiction, but also of failing to judge that which did fall within its scope [cf. 5:12; 6:1–5]. How foolish they were in pretending to see what they had no means of discerning when they remained blind to what lay before their very eyes!

The brightness of Christ's advent will reveal the true character of those things which were previously hidden by darkness. These are not necessarily *evil* things, but things 'impenetrable to present light'

(Findlay). This infallible verdict will be secured by Christ's perfect knowledge of the hearts of all men, for he alone is able to judge the secret motives which determine the quality of each man's work, whether it be good or evil [*2 Cor.* 5:10].

And then shall each man have his praise from God: 'Then' *every* faithful steward shall receive his *due* praise, and not just the favourite party-leaders! 'The world praises its princes, generals, ambassadors, wise men, artists: God will hereafter praise his ministers' (Bengel).

6: Now these things, brethren, I have in a figure transferred to myself and Apollos for your sakes; that in us ye might learn not to go beyond the things which are written; that no one of you be puffed up for the one against the other.

I have applied all this to myself and Apollos (RSV): i.e. 'I have given this teaching of mine the form of an exposition concerning Apollos and myself' (Arndt–Gingrich). In 3:4–6 Paul expressed himself in terms which showed that no criticism of Apollos was intended, but if Judaizing teachers had arrived in Corinth and were invoking Peter's authority as a cloak for their activities, he could not mention Peter's name without seeming to blame him for their errors [cf. comment on 3:11].

I have done this for your sakes, so that by our example you may learn the lesson, "Not above what is written" (F. F. Bruce): By freely ascribing all the glory to God for the work which he had accomplished through them, Paul and Apollos had not gone beyond the testimony of Scripture [cf. Paul's citation of Jeremiah 9:23, 24 in 1:31]. Accordingly their example did not provide the Corinthians with any excuse for elevating them as the heads of rival cliques within the church. But there were other teachers in Corinth who did not scruple to arrogate to themselves the honour that belonged to God alone.

That no one of you be puffed up for the one against the other: 'To cry up a favourite leader of your own choosing is to betray an inflated self-conceit' (Robertson-Plummer).

7: For who maketh thee to differ? and what hast thou that thou didst not receive? but if thou didst receive it, why dost thou glory as if thou hadst not received it?

Who has distinguished you? (i.e. as compared with others: cf. F. Buchsel, *TDNT*, vol. 3, p. 946). A sharp shaft to puncture the Corinthians' presumptuous conceit, for pardoned sinners can boast of nothing but the *distinguishing* grace of God!

And what hast thou that thou didst not receive? Paul's second 'home-thrust' charges them with ingratitude. Those who owe everything to their generous Benefactor clearly have nothing of *their own* in which they can boast. It is worth recalling that this question had a decisive influence on Augustine. He says that he laboured hard to answer it in terms of human ability, but the grace of God won the day. It was through the challenge of Pelagius and the study of Paul's writings, and especially of this verse and of Romans 9:16, that there 'had crystallized in his mind the distinctively Augustinian doctrines of man's total depravity, of irresistible grace, and of absolute predestination' (Robertson-Plummer).

But if thou didst receive it, why dost thou glory as if thou hadst not received it? The only possible conclusion which can be drawn from the replies demanded by the first two questions is expressed with unassailable logic in this final thrust. Paul intends it to reduce the articulate Corinthians to speechless shame.

8: Already are ye filled, already ye are become rich, ye have come to reign without us: yea and I would that ye did reign, that we also might reign with you.

The Corinthians were behaving as though they had already attained the glories of the coming kingdom, and the emotion which suddenly grips Paul as he contemplates their proud pretensions leads him into a 'long sarcasm' which does not end till verse 13 'where it is extinguished in grief' (Godet).

Already are ye filled: The apostle has been overtaken by his converts, who have reached the goal before him! They need no longer hunger after righteousness, because they have already taken their seats at the Messianic banquet. They are so puffed up with their favourite teachers and their own fancied attainments in knowledge that they feel like those who have feasted to the full.

Already ye are become rich: The thanksgiving [1:5] and the list of gifts in chapter 12 'appear to justify this consciousness of wealth; but ostentation corrupted Corinthian riches; spiritual satiety is a sign of arrested growth: contrast Philippians 3:10–14, and compare Revelation 3:17, "Thou *sayest*, Rich am I, and I have become rich'" (Findlay).

Without us you have become kings (RSV): 'While *we* are still exposed to the dangers, sufferings, and shame of the earthly arena [verse 9], *you* are already reigning in glory with Christ!' Thus the roles have been exchanged: he, the apostle, their "father", must from his lowliness see to what dizzy heights they have attained' (J. Weiss).

Yea and I would that ye did reign, that we also might reign with you: A biting irony which marks an abrupt return to reality. 'Indeed I wish that you did so reign, for then *we* might share *your* triumph!'

9: For, I think, God hath set forth us the apostles last of all, as men doomed to death: for we are made a spectacle unto the world, both to angels and men.

For it seems to me that God means us apostles to come in at the very end, like doomed gladiators in the arena! (Moffatt). As the previous verse echoed the catchwords that recall the Stoic maxim, 'I alone am *rich*, I alone *reign* as king'; so here there is probably an allusion to the Stoic idea of the philosopher's conflict with adverse fate which is played out before the gods. G. Kittel says that in this use 'deity is a spectator of the battle which man himself fights in the proud autonomy of his heroism'.

But because God is pleased to make the *weakness* of his apostles the vehicle of his *divine power* [cf. *2 Cor.* 12:9, 10], those who watch the unequal struggle 'think they see something quite different from that which is really enacted in this *theatre*' (*TDNT*, vol. 3, p. 43). For as Christ achieved victory through the seeming defeat of the cross, so his suffering followers paradoxically triumph in being 'conquered' by the powers which oppose them – to the amazement of angels and men! 'The blood of the martyrs is the seed of the church' (Tertullian). Paul's pathetic description of his own sufferings is a direct challenge to the comfortable security of his readers [verses 9–13]. If the heralds of the gospel are still bearing the cross [*Matt.* 16:24], then how have their converts managed to precede them to glory?

10: We are fools for Christ's sake, but ye are wise in Christ; we are weak, but ye are strong; ye have glory, but we have dishonour.

In this series of striking antitheses, Paul makes his meaning plain by repeating the words, 'fools, wise, weak, strong' [1:25ff., 3:18f.]: 1. 'It is on Christ's account that we are content to be labelled the world's *fools*, yet your union with Christ has made you *wise* in this world!'; 2. 'We confess our personal *weakness*, but you are boasting in your own *strength!*' 3. 'You have saved your reputation in the world: we have completely forfeited ours!'

11: Even unto this present hour we both hunger, and thirst, and are naked, and are buffeted, and have no certain dwelling-place;

12a: and we toil, working with our own hands:

The imaginary exaltation of the Corinthians is now sharply contrasted with the actual sufferings which characterize the life of an apostle 'even unto this present hour'. For fidelity to his commission involved constant hardship [verses 11, 12a] and humiliation [verses 12b, 13]. Although Paul speaks in the plural, it is obvious that his description of these bitter trials is drawn from his personal experience of them [cf. *2 Cor.* 11:23–29]. He knows what it is to go hungry and thirsty, and 'be poorly clothed' (Arndt-Gingrich). Often the victim of violent hands, always treated as a homeless vagabond, he is also guilty of what the Greeks regarded as the supreme indignity of working with his own hands to support himself [*Acts* 18:3 ; *2 Cor.* 12:13].

12b: being reviled, we bless; being persecuted, we endure;

13: being defamed, we entreat: we are made as the filth of the world, the offscouring of all things, even until now.

The present participles denote the habitual treatment meted out to the apostles by their enemies, while the verbs which follow them indicate their habitual response to these cruel acts. They meet insulting abuse with blessings, they hold out under persecution without complaining, and they answer base calumnies with kindly words of entreaty. 'They beseech men not to be so wicked, to return to better feelings, to be converted to Christ' (Godet). In this they followed the teaching and example of their Lord. Yet because meekness was mistaken for weakness, their humility was despised as the mark of an abject, grovelling spirit. Thus in the estimation of the world, the apostles had become the most degraded and despicable of men, the very scum of human society, whose contemptible estate remains unchanged 'even until now'.

14: I write not these things to shame you, but to admonish you as my beloved children.

If what Paul had written might well make the Corinthians hang their heads in shame, that was not his purpose in writing; he wrote to 'admonish' them as his 'beloved children'. Because he loved them, he desired their amendment, and his reproofs were directed towards that end. 'His design was to bring the truth to their minds, and let them see what they really were, as contrasted with what they imagined themselves to be' (Hodge).

15: For though ye have ten thousand tutors in Christ, yet have ye not many fathers; for in Christ Jesus I begat you through the gospel.

'For if you should have ten thousand tutors in Christ, yet you have not many *fathers!*' However many tutors might follow Paul in Corinth, and whatever respect they were entitled to receive from the Corinthians, it could never exceed that which was owed to their *one* father in the faith [cf. 9:2]. 'Paul does not use the title "father" for a Christian minister [cf. *Matt.* 23:9], but keeps the metaphor for the special purpose of describing the relation between an evangelist and his converts' (Barrett).

For in Christ Jesus I begat you through the gospel: It is only in virtue of Paul's union with Christ and by means of the gospel that he sustains this exceptional relation to them. 'He thus excludes beforehand every appearance of boasting in what he says of himself in the last words: *I begat.* – But if it was Christ who acted with His power and word, it was nevertheless through him, Paul (*ego, I*), that He produced this creation. Hence Paul's right and duty to exhort them, and even admonish them as he does' (Godet).

16: I beseech you therefore, be ye imitators of me.

'Then since I am such a father to you, I beseech you to be imitators of me.' Paul has no intention of attracting a partisan following to himself, but rather pleads with the Corinthians to emulate his own example of self–sacrifice in the service of Christ [11:1; *1 Thess.* 1:6;

2 Thess. 3:7–9]. 'Imitation is the law of the child's life . . . It is one thing to say "I am of Paul" [1:12], another to tread in Paul's steps. The imitation would embrace, in effect, much of what was described in verses 9ff.' (Findlay).

> **17: For this cause have I sent unto you Timothy, who is my beloved and faithful child in the Lord, who shall put you in remembrance of my ways which are in Christ, even as I teach everywhere in every church.**

'The father sends a son to sons; but a faithful son, which some of them were not' (Edwards) [*1 Tim.* 1:2]. It was after Timothy had left Ephesus for Corinth via Macedonia that Paul was advised of the grave situation which had arisen there. Accordingly, he sends this letter by sea, expecting it to arrive before Timothy who was travelling more slowly by land [*Acts* 19:22].

Who shall put you in remembrance of my ways which are in Christ: The apostle is confident that the conduct of his faithful son would remind the Corinthians of what had been his own manner of life among them. But it was only because Paul's ways were also those of Christ himself that they became an authoritative pattern for them to follow [*Gal.* 2:20]. 'Paul's *ways* and *teaching* are not the same thing; but the former are regulated by the latter; they will find the same consistency in Timothy' (Findlay).

Even as I teach everywhere in every church: Once again he reminds his readers that they are no more than a part of a much greater whole. They are neither the whole church, nor the most perfect members of it. But 'no more is required of them than is required of other Christians' (Robertson-Plummer).

> **18: Now some are puffed up, as though I were not coming to you.**
>
> **19: But I will come to you shortly, if the Lord will; and I will know, not the word of them that are puffed up, but the power.**

In spite of the confident assertions of his detractors to the contrary, Paul assures the Corinthians that he will indeed visit them shortly, 'if the Lord will', i.e. provided this proposal is in accord with both 'the providential and spiritual government of Christ' (Hodge) [cf. 16:7 with *Acts* 16:7]. Then he will prove whether the arrogant boasts of his opponents are matched by their spiritual power. 'Their lack of the

Spirit's power to transform men's character was the test by which the apostle intended to try the pretensions of the party-leaders [cf. *1 Thess.* 1:5]' (Edwards).

20: For the kingdom of God is not in word, but in power.

In their wordy strife the Corinthians appear to have forgotten that the kingdom of God is something more than boastful talk. As in Romans 14:17, Paul is not giving an exhaustive definition of the kingdom of God, but is bringing one aspect of it to bear on a particular situation. Since the Corinthians were apparently rejoicing in the blessings of the kingdom without him [verse 8], Paul here reminds them that the rule of God in the lives of men cannot be established by mere eloquence. It requires the power of the Spirit to make the preacher's testimony to Christ the means of such a transformation [2:4, 5; *2 Cor.* 5:17].

21: What will ye? shall I come unto you with a rod, or in love and a spirit of gentleness ?

Paul is resolved to come, but they must decide on the character of their meeting with him. Is it to be a painful or a joyous visit? Shall he come with a rod to administer fatherly chastisement, or in love that expresses itself in a spirit of gentleness? The contrast is between the love that is *concealed* in chastening, and the love that is *revealed* in gentleness. He warns them that if they choose to remain defiant, he will not shrink from using the rod. In that event they would certainly lose the sense of his love, but it would not mean that he had ceased to love them [*Heb.* 12:7]. This reference to his right to discipline them as an apostle of Jesus Christ concludes the first part of the Epistle, and serves to introduce 'the subject of the following section, which already stirs his wrath' (Findlay).

CHAPTER FIVE

Paul rebukes the Corinthians for tolerating a scandalous case of incest in their midst instead of removing the offender [verses 1, 2]. As they had neglected their duty, Paul has already judged the man as though present with them, in the hope that the faithful exercise of church discipline will lead to his repentance [verses 3–5]. They have no occasion to glory in view of their deplorable failure to maintain the purity of the church by purging out the old leaven of sin [verses 6–8]. Since they had misunderstood a previous letter which forbad them to associate with immoral persons, Paul now explains that the command had reference to church fellowship, and not to necessary social relationships with unbelievers. It was their responsibility to judge the immoral acts of professing Christians, but the sins of outsiders were to be left to the judgment of God [verses 9–13].

1: It is actually reported that there is fornication among you, and such fornication as is not even among the Gentiles, that one of you hath his father's wife.

Paul expresses the shock of shame which the Corinthians ought to have felt that such a thing should have happened among them. 'Yes, and so heinous a fornication that even the Gentiles utterly condemn what you openly condone!' 'Paul's appeal to this fact is for the purpose of indicating that outside the pale of covenant revelation there was abhorrence of this kind of marital relationship. This implies that the prohibition in question had relevance to mankind in general' (John Murray, *Principles of Conduct*, p. 258).

That one of you hath his father's wife: The offence 'may have been marriage of a stepmother after the father's death, but, since the woman is called "his father's wife" (not widow), and the act is called *fornication*, it is more likely to be a case of immoral relationship with the father's young second wife' (*The New Bible Dictionary*, p. 789). As Paul does not censure the woman, it must be assumed that she was not a Christian but one of the outsiders whom God would judge [verse 13; *Lev.* 18:8, 20:11; *Deut.* 22:30; 27:20].

2: And ye are puffed up, and did not rather mourn, that he that had done this deed might be taken away from among you.

Paul seeks to awaken a sense of shame in the Corinthians who are still inflated with pride when they ought to have been mourning the loss of a brother slain by sin and dead to God. They did not even grieve over the offence, much less reflect that it was their duty to remove the offender from the church [verse 13]. 'Their morbid self–importance, which made them so intolerant of petty wrongs [6:7], made them very tolerant of deep disgrace' (Robertson-Plummer).

3: For I verily, being absent in body but present in spirit, have already as though I were present judged him that hath so wrought this thing,

4: in the name of our Lord Jesus, ye being gathered together, and my spirit, with the power of our Lord Jesus,

5: to deliver such a one unto Satan for the destruction of the flesh, that the spirit may be saved in the day of the Lord Jesus.

But Paul cannot tolerate from a distance what the Corinthians viewed in their midst with complacent indifference, and though absent in body he has already 'judged him that hath *so* wrought *this thing*'. Thus to justify his verdict he has only to point to the shamelessness of the sinner ('so'), and the abominable nature of his sin ('this thing'). The church must give effect to this judgment by meeting together 'in the name of our Lord Jesus', when Paul would be present in spirit to act along with them 'with the power of our Lord Jesus' [cf. Col. 2:5].

To deliver such a one unto Satan for the destruction of the flesh: Calvin rightly says that this is a fitting way to describe excommunication; 'because, while Christ reigns within, so Satan reigns outside, the church'. But the terms of this sentence surely point to something more than the ordinary exercise of church discipline. According to Henry Alford, This 'was a delegation to the Corinthian church of a *special power, reserved to the Apostles themselves*, of *inflicting corporeal death or disease* as a punishment for sin'. As notable examples of this extraordinary power, he cites the cases of Ananias and Sapphira [*Acts* 5:1–11], Elymas [*Acts* 13:8–11], and the blasphemers of 1 Tim. 1:20. The congregation itself could expel the offender – 'but it could not *deliver to Satan for the destruction of the flesh*, without the authorized concurrence of the Apostle's *spirit, with the power of our Lord Jesus*'.

That the spirit may be saved in the day of the Lord Jesus: But though Satan is thus permitted to afflict 'the flesh' (i.e. the body as the instrument of sin), the aim of this punishment was the restoration of the sinner, as it would also serve to maintain the purity of the church. In speaking of 'the spirit' being saved in the day of the Lord Jesus, Paul obviously does not envisage a 'disembodied' state of bliss, for he later teaches that the body is to partake of the salvation of the spirit. And this is why he could not speak of the destruction of 'the body', but only of that of 'the flesh' [cf. 15:50].

6: Your glorying is not good. Know ye not that a little leaven leaveneth the whole lump ?

When the Corinthians can so easily tolerate such flagrant immorality it is evident that they have no ground for boasting. In contrast to their fancied attainments, the low spiritual condition of the whole church is proved by the fact that it is found unashamedly glorying despite the presence in their midst of this particular sin!

A little leaven leaveneth the whole lump, cf. *Gal.* 5:9: 'This proverbial expression is not here intended to express the idea that one corrupt member of the church depraves the whole, because, in the following verses, in which the figure is carried out, the leaven is not *a person,* but *sin.* The idea, therefore, is, that it is the nature of evil to diffuse itself. This is true with regard to individuals and communities' (Hodge).

7: Purge out the old leaven, that ye may be a new lump, even as ye are unleavened. For our passover also hath been sacrificed, even Christ:

As the Jews were obliged to make a thorough search to remove all traces of leaven from their homes before the Passover Feast began, so the Corinthians are completely to remove from their lives every remnant of the sin that belonged to their pagan past. Now they are to be like a freshly mixed lump of dough, to which nothing in the way of yeast has been added. 'The Christian Church is not just the old society patched up. It is radically new' (Leon Morris).

Even as ye are unleavened: It is the indicative of grace ('*ye are* unleavened') that provides the indispensable moral dynamic to fulfil the ethical imperative ('*purge out* the old leaven') (Barrett). [cf. *Rom.* 6:1–11]. Accordingly, they must see to it that their subjective condition corresponds to that objective deliverance from sin which is theirs in Christ.

For our passover also hath been sacrificed, even Christ: 'The Jews made sure that all leaven had been removed before they celebrated their Passover, but Christ our Passover has already been sacrificed, and yet the old leaven remains uncleansed from your house!' To say that this is a sacrificial 'metaphor' does not get rid of the meaning which Paul attached to it. He chose to speak of Christ's death in terms of the Passover sacrifice because he saw that there was the same objective necessity for it. In other words, he views the *death* of Christ as the one sacrifice by which the *life* of his people was secured.

8: wherefore let us keep the feast, not with old leaven, neither with the leaven of malice and wickedness, but with the unleavened bread of sincerity and truth.

Wherefore let us keep festival (ASV margin): Since our Passover Lamb has been sacrificed, 'let us keep perpetual feast' (Lightfoot). 'The Christian's Paschal feast does not last a week, but all his life' (Godet). This character is given to the Christian's life by the enduring efficacy of Christ's death. As befits those who 'are unleavened' [verse 7], the Corinthians must feast all their life long on the unleavened bread of sincerity and truth. Sincerity 'is the harmony of our words and actions with our convictions'; truth 'is the harmony of all these with reality' (Edwards). The leaven of the old life which is forbidden to them is defined as consisting of malice and wickedness. There must be no place in their present experience for that evil disposition and those wicked deeds which characterized their former course [cf. *Rom.* 1:29].

9: I wrote unto you in my epistle to have no company with fornicators;

'That letter, to which he refers, does not exist today. There is no doubt that many others are lost. But we can rest content that the Lord saw to it that sufficient survive to meet our needs' (Calvin). [cf. *John* 21:25 with 20:31]. But some have not scrupled to supply this lack at the expense of the integrity of the letters we do possess. Hence it is confidently affirmed that the lost letter has been 'found' in 2 Corinthians 6:14–7:1, in spite of the fact that there is no manuscript evidence to support this critical flight of fancy! The call in the previous verse for the constant exercise of sincerity and truth may imply that Paul regarded the Corinthians' professed misunderstanding of his previous directive, 'not to mix themselves up together with fornicators', as an excuse for their hesitation to take action against the offender in their midst.

10: not at all meaning with the fornicators of this world, or with the covetous and extortioners, or with idolaters; for then must ye needs go out of the world:

Of course this prohibition did not mean that the Corinthians should avoid all contact with the sinners of this world. Indeed it was impossible to live in a place like Corinth without being in daily touch with those guilty of such vices as fornication, covetousness, and idolatry. But it is one thing to meet them in the market place, and quite another to mix with them in the idol's temple! Paul is not concerned to catalogue every sort of open sinner, but mentions 'three classes as being sufficient for his purpose, namely, that his command concerning fornicators rests on a general principle' (Lenski).

For then must ye needs go out of the world: If the apostle had intended them to shun all sinners, then they would be forced to leave the world – a manifestly absurd conclusion. 'The attempt to get "out of the world", in violation of God's will [*John* 17:15], led to monasticism and its evils' (Fausset).

11: but as it is, I wrote unto you not to keep company, if any man that is named a brother be a fornicator, or covetous. or an idolater, or a reviler, or a drunkard, or an extortioner; with such a one no, not to eat.

No, what I meant when I wrote was this (Bruce): What should have been obvious to the Corinthians is now made explicit: Paul summarily forbids them to have fellowship with any man whose scandalous life belies the name of 'brother'. To the four terms already given he adds two more: the reviler and the drunkard. Godet expresses the opinion that the list is 'an unstudied accumulation' from which order is excluded by disgust. 'With such a one no, not to eat' refers not to the Lord's supper, but to any kind of social intercourse [cf. *2 Thess.* 3:14]. They are to refuse to recognize such a man as a 'brother' in the hope that this may convict him of his sin and lead him to repentance.

12: For what have I to do with judging them that are without? Do not ye judge them that are within?

In the first question Paul harks back to verse 10, and speaks in the first person to express the principle that those outside the communion of the church are beyond its jurisdiction. But in the second question he reminds the Corinthians that it is their responsibility to judge all who do claim to be members of the church [cf. verse 11, 'any man that is named a brother']. While it is not their province to judge the hearts of their fellow–believers, it is their duty to discipline those who fail to walk worthily of the faith they profess.

13: But them that are without God judgeth. Put away the wicked man from among yourselves.

It is not the function of the church to judge outsiders for God judges them. The verb is present because Paul is speaking of disciplinary judging, and not the final judgment [cf. 6:2]. But it is the duty of the church 'to expel the offender, and leave him to God's judgment, he having now become one of *them that are without*' (Morris). The apostle's sharp demand for the expulsion of the incestuous person from the congregation is expressed in words taken from Deuteronomy 17:7, but he changes the verb from the singular to the plural to show that this must be the action of the whole community.

CHAPTER SIX

Another evil for which Paul rebukes the Corinthians is the scandal of bringing their disputes before heathen judges, for those who are destined to judge angels ought to be capable of settling their differences among themselves. Let them suffer wrong rather than inflict it upon their fellow–believers [verses 1–8]. Have they forgotten that evil–doers, such as they once were, shall not enter the kingdom of God? But now that they have been cleansed from these defilements their behaviour must match their new identity [verses 9–11]. All lawful things are not expedient, and liberty is not licence. For though food is for the stomach, the body is not for fornication, but is destined for union with the Lord [verses 12–14]. As believers are therefore members of Christ and temples of the Holy Spirit, this sin is a gross profanation of their bodies, which belong to God and must be used for his glory [verses 15–20].

1: Dare any of you, having a matter against his neighbour, go to law before the unrighteous, and not before the saints?

The necessity of judging those within the church leads on naturally to the scandal of submitting disputes between believers to the judgment of those who do not belong to the church [verses 1–11]. Paul's shocked question is intended to shame the Corinthians. 'Dare' is almost an argument in itself: it is by this grand word that he marks 'the injured majesty of the Christian name' (Bengel). The Jews always settled their differences among themselves since the rabbis held that to take a case before idolatrous judges was blasphemy against the law. But evidently the Greek fondness for litigation had caused the Christians of Corinth to fall below that high standard. They were guilty of this evil because they did not know that it was beneath the dignity of 'the saints' – *those accounted holy through believing* – to call upon 'the unrighteous' – *unjust because unbelieving* – to decide their disputes. Paul is not implying that heathen judges are unjust in their judgments, but is showing that 'to invoke pagan courts to settle lawsuits between believers was a confession of Christian failure. When a dispute between brethren could not be amicably settled by them, the matter should be decided before *the saints*, the church [cf. *Matt.* 18:17]' (Norman Hillyer).

2: Or know ye not that the saints shall judge the world? and if the world is judged by you, are ye unworthy to judge the smallest matters?

Or know ye not? The fact that this question is repeated no less than six times within a few verses gives some indication of the strength of Paul's feeling [cf. verses 3, 9, 15, 16, 19]. He administers this stinging rebuke because their conduct fell far short of their knowledge. Evidently they had been taught that the saints would be associated with Christ in the judgment of the world [cf. *Dan.* 7:22], and yet they had fallen so far beneath their dignity as to call for the arbitration of heathen magistrates! It was a shameful absurdity that those who were destined to judge the world should now confess their incompetence to decide even the smallest matters pertaining to the present age [verse 3]. 'This office the saints will hold by virtue of their perfected knowledge, their completed communion with the judgments of the Great Judge. This is a necessary part of the ultimate triumph of good over evil. Just as the faithful shall reign with Christ as kings [2 *Tim.* 2:12; *Rev.* 22:5], so shall they sit with Him as judges of the world. The thought is an extension of the promise made to the Apostles [*Matt.* 19:28; *Luke* 22:30]: cf. *Rev.* 20:4' (Lightfoot).

3: Know ye not that we shall judge angels? how much more, things that pertain to this life?

These must be 'the angels which kept not their first estate' [*Jude* 6], for there is no mention in Scripture of a judgment of the elect angels. But the omission of the article before the word 'angels' shows that it does not fall within the scope of the apostle's present purpose to specify the class of angels to be judged. 'Paul does not mean to designate these or those angels; he wishes to awaken within the church the feeling of its competency and dignity by reminding it that beings of so exalted a nature shall one day be subjected to its jurisdiction' (Godet).

How much more, matters pertaining to this life! (RSV): It is better to understand this as a concluding exclamation rather than a further question, because it expresses more forcibly the tremendous contrast between mundane affairs and supernatural beings.

4: If then ye have to judge things pertaining to this life, do ye set them to judge who are of no account in the church?

If this is understood as a question, then Paul is drawing attention to the incongruity of appealing to those who are 'of no account in the church', i.e. heathen judges. But it is most unlikely that the apostle would apply such a strong phrase to the civil power without further explanation [cf. *Rom.* 13:1f] and it is therefore preferable to take it as a command: 'set them to judge who are least esteemed in the church' (AV). Paul's tone is sarcastic. 'Since you are to take part in the future judgment of the world, it ought not to be beyond the present capacity of your least *gifted* (and so least esteemed) members to decide such trifling matters among you!' As Edwards remarks, 'He is not justifying their contempt of brethren, but stating it, and in stating it, really rebuking their pride.'

5: I say this to move you to shame. What, cannot there be found among you one wise man who shall be able to decide between his brethren,

6: but brother goeth to law with brother, and that before unbelievers?

'If false pride had not made you blind to your real shame, it would not have been necessary for me to write in this ironical vein' [verse 4]. Paul was not seriously urging the Corinthians to conduct a protracted judicial enquiry, for he regarded such litigation as being quite out of place among brethren. 'Are you then saying, by thus appealing to the judgment of heathen courts, that after all your pretentious claims to wisdom there is not even *one* wise man to be found among you, who shall be able to settle differences between one brother and another?'

And that before unbelievers? 'This is the climax. That there should be disputes about "ordinary matters" is bad; that Christian should go to law with Christian is worse; that Christians should do this before unbelievers is worst of all. It is a scandal before the heathen world' (Robertson-Plummer).

> **7: Nay, already it is altogether a defect in you, that ye have lawsuits one with another. Why not rather take wrong? why not rather be defrauded?**
>
> **8: Nay, but ye yourselves do wrong, and defraud, and that your brethren.**

'In fact before you reach the court, this is altogether a loss, *an utter defeat for you!*' (Arndt–Gingrich). 'You trust to overreach, to gain a victory: it is really a loss, a defeat, before the trial even comes on' (Lightfoot). It is not by engaging in internecine strife and inflicting such grievous wounds upon themselves that the real victory is to be won, but by enduring the wrong and patiently waiving their rights' [13:4; *Matt.* 5:39, 40). In verse 8 Paul contrasts their Christian obligation with the sad fact of their lovelessness. Far from being willing to submit to wrong, they actually inflict it, and that on their brethren!

> **9: Or know ye not that the unrighteous shall not inherit the kingdom of God? Be not deceived: neither fornicators, nor idolaters, nor adulterers, nor effeminate, nor abusers of themselves with men,**
>
> **10: nor thieves, nor covetous, nor drunkards, nor revilers, nor extortioners, shall inherit the kingdom of God.**

The suffering without rebuke of those who were guilty of wronging their brethren in this way proved that the Corinthians had forgotten an elementary truth. This is now brought home to their conscience in the emphatic assertion that '*wrong-doers*' will not inherit *God's* kingdom. The juxtaposition of the italicized words manifests the absurdity of entertaining such an expectation. Yet the danger of their remaining under the spell of this delusion is underlined by the imperative: 'Be not deceived'. If they really thought that gospel liberty was to be equated with lawless licence, then they had better think again. For as righteousness is the fundamental characteristic of God's kingdom, so those whose lives are still characterized by unrighteousness cannot hope to acquire an interest in that kingdom. Paul knows nothing of a mere interim-ethic, an ethical norm which pertains only to the present life, for in fact the 'ethics of the kingdom yet to come determine the morals of the kingdom that now is' (Edwards). He goes on to define the unrighteousness which debars men from any share in the heavenly inheritance in a representative list of sins, each one of which is a violation of the moral law as set forth in the decalogue. It is because this law expresses the divine standard of righteousness that the infringement of any one of its precepts must result in the exclusion of the transgressor from the kingdom of God. This therefore serves to demonstrate the abiding validity of the moral law, and the permanent obligation of all believers to obey it; no longer to secure their justification, but to give evidence of it. 'The law sends us to the gospel for our justification; the gospel sends us to the law to frame our way of life . . . Christ has freed us from the *manner* of our obedience but not from the *matter* of our obedience' (Samuel Bolton, *The True Bounds of Christian Freedom*, p. 72). But as for fornicators, idolaters, adulterers, homosexuals (literally: 'catamites' and 'sodomites'), thieves, the covetous, drunkards, revilers, extortioners – *none* of these shall inherit God's kingdom!

11: And such were some of you: but ye were washed, but ye were sanctified, but ye were justified in the name of the Lord Jesus Christ, and in the Spirit of our God.

And such were some of you: All the Corinthians were sinners in need of salvation, but only some of them had been guilty of such gross sins. The emphasis falls on the fact that all this now lies in the past; you *were* once like that, but by the grace of God you are so no longer [cf. *Eph.* 2:11–13].

But ye had yourselves washed: The verb is in the middle voice and refers to baptism 'in its spiritual meaning; the form of the verb calls attention to the initiative of the Corinthians in getting rid, at the call of God, of the filth of their old life; in baptism their penitent faith took deliberate and formal expression, with this effect' (Findlay). [*Acts* 22:16; *1 Pet.* 3:21]

But ye were sanctified, but ye were justified: Both these verbs direct attention to the action of God which gave their baptism its objective significance. It is not therefore the process of sanctification that is in view. 'Ye were sanctified' means: 'It was then that God claimed you for his own and conferred upon you the status of saints'. Paul puts this before 'ye were justified' because he wishes to stress the act of consecration which had separated them from their former sinful course of self–pleasing. But the latter remains the ground of this consecration, for only those whom God declares just are truly holy.

In the name of the Lord Jesus Christ, and in the Spirit of our God: 'In the name' is the external essential, as 'in the Spirit' is the internal essential of Christian baptism (Lightfoot). C. K. Barrett notes the 'quite unconscious Trinitarianism of the concluding words': *the Lord Jesus Christ, the Spirit, our God.* This is the faith that is confessed throughout the New Testament, for whether 'God is thought of in himself or in his operations, the underlying conception runs unaffectedly into trinal forms' (B. B. Warfield, *Biblical and Theological Studies*, p. 49).

12: All things are lawful for me; but not all things are expedient. All things are lawful for me; but I will not be brought under the power of any.

Apparently while Paul was at Corinth he had asserted the freedom of believers from the restrictions of the ceremonial law in the maxim: 'All things are lawful for me', to which some were now appealing to justify their moral laxity. It is because he does not seek to curb licence by a relapse into legalism that he refuses to retract the principle, though he guards against its further abuse by a double qualification. Thus in upholding his doctrine of liberty, while refusing to minister to licence, Paul here presents in germ a complete Christian ethic, which is 'anti-libertine without being legalistic' (Jean Héring).

'All things are lawful for me,' but not all things are helpful (RSV): 1. The Christian has the liberty to refrain from indulging in those things which are not spiritually helpful to him. 'This gives the *self-regarding*, as 10:23f. the *other-regarding* rule of Christian temperance in the use of things lawful' (Findlay).

'All things are lawful for me,' but I will not be enslaved by anything. (RSV): 2. The Christian has the duty of abstaining from those things which would deprive him of his liberty. 'The reasonable use of my liberty cannot go the length of involving my own loss of it, or of rendering me a slave by reducing me to a thing' (Godet).

13: Meats for the belly, and the belly for meats: but God shall bring to nought both it and them. But the body is not for fornication, but for the Lord; and the Lord for the body:

'Food is meant for the stomach and the stomach for food' – *and God will destroy both one and the other* (RSV): The libertines in Corinth were evidently using this as a slogan to show that sensual indulgence was as natural and necessary to the body, as food was to the stomach. 'If I may gratify one bodily appetite, why may I not gratify another?' (Robertson-Plummer). Paul agrees that food is in itself (*not* as it is offered to idols, chapter 8; 10:25f.) a matter which is morally indifferent [*Mark* 7:15–23]. According to its present constitution the body certainly needs food to nourish it, but God has no permanent plans for the stomach! There is a time coming when the body will neither need food, nor the organs to digest it.

But the body is not for fornication, but for the Lord; and the Lord for the body: This explains why the supposed analogy between food and fornication does not hold good. Since the Greeks tended to think of the body as the temporary prison or tomb of the soul, they could regard the acts of the body as having no necessary connection with the soul's immortal destiny. But according to the biblical teaching man is a living unity of body and soul – a view which has been emphatically endorsed by modern medicine – and there is therefore no basis for maintaining that physical acts are morally indifferent. Paul here teaches that the body as a whole, in contrast to its temporary apparatus, is fashioned for the Lord's use.

Hence to yield it to harlotry is to deny Christ's rights in it and disqualify oneself for a part in his resurrection [verse 14]. The Lord Jesus and 'fornication' contested for 'the bodies of Christian men; loyal to him they must renounce *that*, yielding to *that* they renounce him' (Findlay).

14: and God both raised the Lord, and will raise up us through his power.

Paul will later deal at length with Corinthian doubts about the resurrection [chapter 15]; here he simply affirms that the body unlike its perishable members [verse 13], has a glorious destiny. 'As God raised up Christ, he will also raise the body which has become here below the property and sanctified organ of Christ. The apostle says, "will raise *us* also"; he thus expressly identifies our personality with the body which is to be its eternal organ' (Godet). [*Rom.* 8–11; *Phil.* 3:21]

15: Know ye not that your bodies are members of Christ? shall I then take away the members of Christ, and make them members of a harlot? God forbid.

The repeated question again implies that the Corinthians were not ignorant of the fact, but were far from realizing its implications [cf. 12:12–27; *Rom.* 12:5]. For if the whole body belongs to the Lord [verse 13], then how can *I* possibly unite its members with those of a harlot? Paul speaks to them in these realistic terms in order to bring home the enormity of the sin, while 'God forbid' expresses his personal revulsion against the infamy of such a proposal.

16: Or know ye not that he that is joined to a harlot is one body? for, The twain, saith he, shall become one flesh.

Paul here teaches the promiscuous Corinthians that there is no such thing as casual sex, because the very nature of the sexual act means that the partners become one body. According to Scripture 'this union is more than an incidental function of the members. It is a coming together as one *body*, and it is thus of far–reaching significance for the whole physico–spiritual personal life' (J. Horst, *TDNT,* vol. 4, p. 565). The quotation of God's ordinance [*Gen.* 2:26] at once confirms and serves to advance Paul's argument, for in this context the transition from the ethically neutral word 'body' to 'flesh' is an eloquent reminder of our fallen condition.

17: But he that is joined unto the Lord is one spirit.

As he who joins himself to a harlot is one *flesh* with her, so he who is joined to the Lord becomes one *spirit* with him. Paul speaks of a voluntary attachment which in one case leads to the ultimate degradation, and in the other promotes the highest exaltation, of the human personality. He omits the article before the word 'spirit' in order to contrast it with 'flesh' in the preceding verse, but such a union with Christ presupposes the supernatural work of the Holy Spirit to effect it.

18: Flee fornication. Every sin that a man doeth is without the body; but he that committeth fornication sinneth against his own body.

Flee fornication: As the danger is ever-present, the command is in the present tense. 'Other vices are overcome by resistance [cf. *Eph.* 6: 13; *James* 4:7]. The imagination detracts from the fascination of other sins, but adds fuel to the flame of fleshly lusts . . . Perhaps the close connection in Corinth between impurity and idolatry caused the apostle to give the same warning in reference to idolatry also [cf. 10:14]' (Edwards) [Gen. 39:12].

But he that committeth fornication sinneth against his own body: Although sins like drunkenness and gluttony are an abuse of the body, whose harmful effects it is every man's duty to foresee and avoid, they are still introduced *from without.* 'But fornication is the *alienating of that body which is the Lord's, and making it a harlot's body* – it is sin *against a man's own body,* in its very nature, – against *the verity and nature* of his body; not an *effect on* the body from participation of things without, but a *contradiction of the truth* of the body, wrought *within itself.* When *man and wife* are one in the Lord – united by his *ordinance,* – no such alienation of the body takes place, and consequently no sin' (Alford) [*Prov.* 6:30–32; 7:6–27].

19: Or know ye not that your body is a temple of the Holy Spirit which is in you, which ye have from God? and ye are not your own;

Or know ye not that your body is a sanctuary of the Holy Spirit which is in you (ASV margin): Because each believer is indwelt by the Holy Spirit his body is a veritable sanctuary of God, which must not be dishonoured by the foul sin of fornication. 'The Christian estimate of fornication is thus categorically opposed to the heathen estimate. In the temple of Aphrodite prostitutes were priestesses, and commerce with them was counted a *consecration*; it is an absolute *desecration* of God's true temple in the man himself' (Findlay).

Which ye have from God? The phrase is intended 'to emphasize strongly the superhuman origin of that Spirit whom the believer receives, and the dignity of the body in which this Divine Guest comes to dwell' (Godet) [cf. 1 Thess. 4: 1–8].

And ye are not your own: 'Since your body is the shrine of the Spirit, the very dwelling place of the Deity, it is no longer yours to command; it belongs to Another and that by right of purchase' [verse 20].

20: for ye were bought with a price: glorify God therefore in your body.

There may well be an allusion here to the contemporary practice of sacral manumission. Just as a slave gained his freedom by becoming the servant of the god who purchased him, so the readers were released from their slavery to sin in order to serve the new Owner who had bought them. The aorist tense indicates the once-for-all character of this transaction. Thus 'the redeemed are paradoxically slaves, the slaves of God, for they were bought with a price ... Believers are not brought by Christ into a liberty of selfish ease. Rather, since they have been bought by God at terrible cost, they have become God's slaves, to do his will' (Leon Morris, *The Apostolic Preaching of the Cross*, p. 54) [7:23; cf. *Rom.* 6:18, 22].

Glorify God therefore in your body: They must comply with the command at once. They are not merely to abstain from defiling God's sanctuary, but also to render such service *in* it as truly to glorify him whose property it now is by the double right of creation and redemption.

CHAPTER SEVEN

Paul's advice on marriage here begins his reply to the various questions put to him by the Corinthians. Although the unmarried state has its advantages for those who like himself have the gift for it, it is better to marry than to fall into sin. But voluntary asceticism has no place in marriage, which involves the obligation of maintaining normal sexual relations, unless there be a temporary abstention by mutual consent for devotional purposes [verses 1–9]. Since the experience of salvation does not annul the marriage bond, the Christian must stay with the pagan partner who wishes to continue the relationship, for this may lead to the conversion of the unbelieving partner [verses 10–16]. Faith in Christ does not demand a change in their external condition, and so as a general rule, Paul counsels every man to remain in the state in which he was called. Yet if a slave were given the opportunity to gain his freedom, he should take it [verses 17–24]. During the present distress it is good to avoid the added cares of the married state, especially as this course also leaves the individual free to serve the Lord without distraction. But if any father feels ashamed that his daughter is unmarried, he may let her marry. As marriage is dissolved by death, a widow is free to marry again, but only in the Lord [verses 25–40].

1: Now concerning the things whereof ye wrote: It is good for a man not to touch a woman.

After having dealt with weightier matters concerning which the Corinthians had not deemed it necessary to ask his advice, Paul is now willing to answer a number of questions on which they had sought his guidance in their letter to him [cf. 7:25, 8:1, 12:1, 16:1]. He begins with the subject of marriage because it is closely connected with the previous warning against fornication. What follows is a specific reply to particular problems, and is not an exhaustive statement of his teaching on marriage [cf. *Eph.* 5:22–33]. His discussion of these problems is not at all tentative, but completely authoritative as befits an apostle of Jesus Christ.

It is good for a man not to touch a woman: If this is not a quotation from the Corinthians' letter, it at least appears to represent what was put to Paul in it. But as in 6:12, he repeats the claim only in order to qualify it. He is not saying that celibacy is morally superior to marriage, but that it is commendable in those who have the special gift for it. All such are free wholly to devote themselves to the service of the Lord [verse 32), but if celibacy is good, marriage is natural. It would seem that the licence of some in Corinth had provoked others to the opposite extreme of asceticism. However, as will immediately appear, Paul is no more willing to brand the conjugal relation as unlawful than he was prepared to admit the lawfulness of fornication.

2: But, because of fornications, let each man have his own wife, and let each woman have her own husband.

'But' places a limitation on the preceding statement. Although celibacy is good, it is not expedient in a city so dissolute as Corinth where the temptation to sin abounds. Here the plural 'fornications' points to the variety and extent of its profligacy. In the light of this situation the apostle not merely recommends the unmarried to marry, but positively commands it. Moreover, the form in which the command is expressed at once sanctions monogamy and forbids polygamy. 'Paul does not lay down here the *ground* of marriage, as though it were "ordained for a remedy against sin", but gives a special reason why those should marry at Corinth who might otherwise have remained single' (Findlay).

3: Let the husband render unto the wife her due: and likewise also the wife unto the husband.

4: The wife hath not power over her own body, but the husband: and likewise also the husband hath not power over his own body, but the wife.

The fact that Paul uses the present imperative in verse 3 shows that he regards the mutual recognition of conjugal rights as the normal condition of married life. 'It is not the conferring of a favour, but the payment of a debt' (Robertson-Plummer). For since husband and wife are one flesh, neither has the right to refuse intercourse with the other. Paul insists upon the reciprocal nature of the married relation: '*She* is as much the mistress of his person, as *he* the master of hers' (Findlay).

5: Defraud ye not one the other, except it be by consent for a season, that ye may give yourselves unto prayer, and may be together again, that Satan tempt you not because of your incontinency.

The command 'Defraud ye not' implies that some in Corinth were mistakenly reacting to the sexual vices of their pagan neighbours by practising asceticism within marriage. But Paul, who never falls into the error of countering one evil by endorsing another, will have none of these 'spiritual' unions. 'The apostle teaches that neither party has the right to separate from the other; that no separation is to be allowed which is not with mutual consent, for a limited time, for the purpose of special devotion, and with the definite intention of reunion. Nothing can be more foreign to the mind of the apostle than the spirit which filled the monasteries and convents of the mediaeval church' (Hodge).

That Satan tempt you not because of your incontinency: It is because Paul recognizes that married people are 'incontinent' – for they would have remained unmarried if they had been devoid of sexual desire – that he recommends the regular payment of these marital dues as the best protection against the temptations of Satan. 'Therefore, those who give up intercourse are acting thoughtlessly, indeed as if they had made an arrangement with God for perpetual power of resistance' (Calvin).

6: But this I say by way of concession, not of commandment.

What Paul allows by way of concession is not the resumption of intercourse, but its suspension for a limited period. In marriage sexual relations are the norm, and the only ascetic restraint which he permits (but refuses to impose) is 'this' temporary abstinence for devotional purposes [verse 5].

7: Yet I would that all men were even as I myself. Howbeit each man hath his own gift from God, one after this manner, and another after that.

Paul wishes that all were even as he was himself, viz. that they possessed the same gift of continence which enabled him to remain unmarried, for then they too could devote themselves entirely to the Lord's service [verse 32; cf. *Matt.* 19:11, 12]. However, he freely acknowledges that not all have received this special gift from God, and those who have not must marry. The second part of the verse does not mean that marriage is also one of God's charismatic gifts; it is a creation ordinance which requires no special gift of grace. 'What Paul means is that one Christian has a special gift from God in one direction, another in an entirely different direction. Grace works in all manner of directions as Paul shows *in extenso* in 1 Corinthians 12:8, etc.' (Lenski).

8: But I say to the unmarried and to widows, It is good for them if they abide even as I.

Paul here expresses his conviction that it is good (or to use Edwards' phrase 'morally beautiful') for the unmarried (including the widows who might well wish for a change in their sad lot) to remain as they are; he insists that no stigma is attached to the single state [verse 1].

If they abide even as I: Paul is unmarried (though he may have been a widower, or perhaps was even deserted by his wife after his conversion, cf. verse 15). He has made his own decision, and he is persuaded that others would do well to follow his example, but significantly he leaves the choice open to them. There is no command or even a hint of constraint in the clause.

9: But if they have not continency, let them marry: for it is better to marry than to burn.

This gives evidence of Paul's clear-sighted realism. Those who lack the gift of continency will be unable to acquire it, and so he directs them to marry rather than burn with unsatisfied desire [verse 2].

'Enforced abstinence is valueless if it means being *aflame with passion*, i.e. emotionally distracted by unsatisfied appetite. Sexual desire is natural and marriage is provided for its fulfilment' (Hillyer).

> **10: But unto the married I give charge, yea not I, but the Lord, That the wife depart not from her husband**
>
> **11: (but should she depart, let her remain unmarried, or else be reconciled to her husband); and that the husband leave not his wife.**

Ordinarily, Paul writes on his own authority as an inspired apostle [14:37], but here he appeals to the direct ruling of the Lord himself [*Mark* 10:9, 11, 12]. As the wife is not to leave home, so the husband is not to send her away from it. 'The sense of the double command is that neither a Christian wife nor a Christian husband should disrupt and thus destroy the marriage in which they are joined' (Lenski). Having entered into a permanent bond, it is not open to either partner to settle disagreements by resorting to divorce. Fornication is not mentioned because that would dissolve the marriage relationship [*Matt.* 5:32]. But if, in spite of the command, the wife should desert her husband she is not free to remarry while he lives [*Rom.* 7:3], and must either remain as she is, or else be reconciled to her husband. 'No one will say that such a case was not likely to occur in the Corinthian church, who bears in mind the ease with which a divorce was obtainable in Greece or Rome' (Edwards).

> **12: But to the rest say I, not the Lord: If any brother hath an unbelieving wife, and she is content to dwell with him, let him not leave her.**
>
> **13: And the woman that hath an unbelieving husband, and he is content to dwell with her, let her not leave her husband.**

Paul deals next with the problem of those who became Christians after their marriage and now had a heathen partner [verses 12–16]. His first direction is that such unions are not to be terminated on the initiative of the believing partner. If it is now a *mixed* marriage, it is nevertheless still a *marriage*, and provided the unbeliever is content to live under these changed circumstances then the relationship must be continued. With those who are already Christians before marriage the case is entirely different; they are to marry 'only in the Lord' [verse 39].

Say I, not the Lord: It is noteworthy that though Paul carefully distinguishes between his own words and those of the Lord he regards both as equally authoritative [cf. verse 10 with verse 17]. The 'contrast is not between the inspired teaching of Christ and the uninspired teaching of the apostle but rather between the teaching of the apostle that could appeal to the express utterances of Christ in the days of his flesh, on the one hand, and the teaching of the apostle that went beyond the cases dealt with by Christ, on the other. There is no distinction as regards the binding character of the teaching in these respective cases' (John Murray, *The Infallible Word*, p. 38).

14: For the unbelieving husband is sanctified in the wife, and the unbelieving wife is sanctified in the brother: else were your children unclean; but now are they holy.

Instead of becoming defiled by remaining married to an unbeliever, the holiness of the Christian partner in such a match actually serves to 'sanctify' (i.e. bring within the sphere of spiritual blessing) the unbelieving spouse. 'He stands upon the sacred threshold of the church: his *surroundings* are hallowed. United to a saintly consort, he is in daily contact with saintly conduct: holy association may become holy assimilation, and the sanctity which ever environs may at last penetrate. But the man's *conversion* is not a condition necessary to the sanctity of the subsisting conjugal union' (T. S. Evans, cited in Robertson-Plummer).

Else were your children unclean; but now are they holy: Unless the marriage were thus 'sanctified', their children would be ritually unclean, but as matters stand they are 'holy'. Since the holiness of the children is not inferred from the faith of the believing parent, but from the sanctification of the unbelieving party, it follows 'that the holiness of the children cannot be superior, either as to nature or degree, to that sanctification of the unbelieving partner from which it is derived' (T. E. Watson, *Baptism Not for Infants*, p. 39). Hence if the possession of this 'holiness' authorizes the baptism of infants, then the unbelieving parent through whom it was bestowed would be equally eligible to receive it!

15: Yet if the unbelieving departeth, let him depart: the brother or the sister is not under bondage in such cases: but God hath called us in peace.

On the other hand, if the unbeliever 'is bent on departing', then 'let him begone' (Edwards). With the departure of the unbelieving spouse the marriage ceases to exist, and in such cases the Christian brother or sister is not 'under bondage'. As the desertion of the unconverted partner effectively dissolves the marriage contract, the apostle must mean that the believer is no longer bound by it, and is therefore free to remarry. This further ground for divorce is known as the 'Pauline privilege' (cf. *The New Bible Dictionary*, p. 790).

But God hath called us in peace: Or as C. F. D. Moule suggests: God has called you *into* a peace *in* which he wishes you to live. This peace covers both the case of the believer whose partner is content to remain, and of the believer who makes no attempt to force an unwilling partner to stay.

16: For how knowest thou, O wife, whether thou shalt save thy husband? or how knowest thou, O husband, whether thou shalt save thy wife?

Paul's meaning is a matter of debate, but in view of the fact that he has already referred to the 'sanctity' of such mixed marriages [verse 14], it is preferable to take these questions in an optimistic sense (as in the NEB). Paul is thus encouraging the hope that the living testimony of the Christian wife or husband may lead to the conversion of the pagan partner.

17: Only, as the Lord hath distributed to each man, as God hath called each, so let him walk. And so ordain I in all the churches.

This 'states the general principle which determines these questions about marriage, and this is afterwards illustrated by the cases of circumcision and slavery' (Robertson-Plummer). 'Only' puts limitation on what Paul has just said in verse 15, for Christian liberty is not social anarchy and must not be confused with mere change for change's sake. Hence the apostle insists that every believer's daily walk is to be regulated by two considerations: 1. That every circumstance in life is governed by the glorified Christ; 2. That he is to remain in that station which was his when God called him to salvation. 'Paul does not mean to stereotype a Christian's secular employment from the time of his conversion, but forbids his renouncing this under a false notion of spiritual freedom, or in contempt of secular things as though there were no will of God for him in their disposition' (Findlay).

And so ordain I in all the churches: 'That is, this is the rule or order which I lay down in all churches. The apostles, in virtue of their plenary inspiration, were authorized not only to teach the doctrines of the gospel, but also to regulate all matters relating to practice' (Hodge).

18: Was any man called being circumcised? let him not become uncircumcised. Hath any been called in uncircumcision? let him not be circumcised.

19: Circumcision is nothing, and uncircumcision is nothing; but the keeping of the commandments of God.

If a man is called by God it is of no consequence whether he is a Jew or a Gentile. If he is a Jew, let him not try to become a Gentile by seeking 'to remove the marks of circumcision' [RSV; cf. *1 Macc.* 1:15]; if he is a Gentile, let him not think that he must become a Jew by capitulating to the demands of Judaizers (cf. the fiery polemic of *Gal.* 5:2ff.).

A man's state by birth and inheritance has no bearing on his standing before God, and so he should remain as he is. Under the gospel such externals are of no moment, but the doing of God's will is everything! Lightfoot remarks that those who would contrast the teaching of Paul with that of James, 'or who would exaggerate his doctrine of justification by faith, should reflect on this *keeping of the commandments of God*' [cf. 9:20f.; *Gal.* 5:6, 6:15].

20: Let each man abide in that calling wherein he was called.

Everyone is to remain in the station in which he found himself when he was called (Arndt-Gingrich): Paul here emphatically repeats the principle laid down in verse 17. God's summons to salvation does not overthrow the existing social order, but it gradually leavens the lump through the influence of changed lives. The divine call is not to a new 'vocation'; it rather gives the old job a new meaning (though of course a sinful livelihood would have to be renounced, e.g. *Eph.* 4:28). 'To be a Christian is not something static, but something dynamic. It is to remain one who is called, to abide in that calling wherewith one is called not once, but always. It is always to hear the voice of God from heaven, which calls men to Christ and away from sin and ungodliness' (Grosheide).

21: Wast thou called being a bondservant? care not for it: nay, even if thou canst become free, use it rather.

Paul's point is that a man's social position has no bearing upon his acceptance within the community of faith [cf. 1:26]. Hence the converted slave is called to live as a Christian without being troubled if his emancipation from the slavery of sin brings no improvement of his earthly lot.

But if you can gain your freedom, avail yourself of the opportunity (RSV): But there will be exceptions to this general rule, and the slave who has the opportunity to gain his freedom should take it. Although it is difficult to understand how the author of the Epistle to Philemon could have offered any other advice, many have taken the words in the opposite sense (e.g. Goodspeed: 'Even if you can gain your freedom, make the most of your present condition [as a slave] instead').

22: For he that was called in the Lord being a bondservant, is the Lord's freedman: likewise he that was called being free, is Christ's bondservant.

Since most of those slaves who had been called to faith in Christ would not be offered the opportunity envisaged in verse 21b, the thought of verse 21a is resumed to show why the Christian bondservant should be content with his lot. For though he is still a slave in the eyes of men, he is in a spiritual sense the Lord's freedman. 'A double process is indicated here. Christ first buys us from our old master, sin, and then sets us free. For this enfranchisement see *Rom.* 8:2, *Gal.* 5:1. But observe that a service is still due from the *libertus* to his *patronus*. This was the case in Roman Law, which required the freedman to take his patron's name, live in his patron's house, consult his patron's will, etc.' (Lightfoot).

Likewise he that was called being free, is Christ's bondservant: In each case the paradoxical language points to the same spiritual result, and must mean that freedman and slave stand on the same level before Christ. This is because the free man is in bondage to sin until grace makes him the bondservant of Christ. So 'in effect freedom in Christ and slavery to Christ merely represent two sides of the same moral truth: for subjection to Christ is freedom from sin [*Rom.* 6:18, 22]' (Lightfoot).

23: Ye were bought with a price; become not bondservants of men.

This change to the second person plural shows that Paul now addresses, not just slaves and free men, but the whole church. 'That they have been bought with a price is the proof that they are both the bondmen and the freedmen of Christ. Liberty and service are but the opposite sides of the same fact; for both begin in redemption' (Edwards) [cf. 6:20].

Become not bondservants of men: The precept implies that such servitude to men is abnormal since it infringes the rights of their divine Owner [*Lev.* 25:42, 55]. The Corinthians would revert to this condition of bondage if they allowed worldly modes of thought to determine their attitude to slavery and freedom, circumcision and uncircumcision, marriage and celibacy, or any other social relation. They have been called to Christian freedom, and not to some form of revolutionary emancipation which would be an enslavement rather than a liberation. It was not through the preaching of a 'social' or 'political' gospel that slavery was finally banished from the ancient world, for these 'worldly' messages lack the spiritual dynamic which alone can change the hearts of men and make them truly free.

24: Brethren, let each man, wherein he was called, therein abide with God.

The instruction is given for the third time [verses 17, 20], Yet Paul never indulges in merely sterile repetition. His discussion of this principle is rounded off with the significant addition: 'therein abide with God'. 'The principal idea is not that of abiding *before God* in that state; it is abiding *in that state,* and that *before God.* By these last words, Paul reminds his readers of the moral act which has the power of sanctifying and ennobling every external position: the eye fixed on God, *walking* in his presence. This is what preserves the believer from the temptations arising from the situation in which he is; this is what raises the humblest duties it can impose on him to the supreme dignity of acts of worship' (Godet).

25: Now concerning virgins I have no commandment of the Lord: but I give my judgment, as one that hath obtained mercy of the Lord to be trustworthy.

On the question of virgins Paul has no command from the Lord, nor does he give a definite directive on the matter himself, because in this case neither alternative is sinful. It is not sinful for a virgin to marry and it is not sinful for her to remain single. Therefore he gives instead his inspired advice as 'one that hath obtained mercy of the Lord to be trustworthy', i.e. it is a judgment delivered in the faithful discharge of his commission as an apostle of the Lord Jesus Christ [*1 Tim.* 1:12, 13]. 'On certain details of life and behaviour the Lord has not bound us by *law* to one course of action rather than another. If we follow one course rather than the other we have not sinned because we have not transgressed law' (John Murray, *Principles of Conduct*, p. 71) [*1 John* 3:4].

26: I think therefore that this is good by reason of the distress that is upon us, namely, that it is good for a man to be as he is.

Paul begins by declaring his reason for preferring the single state. He thinks that it is good for a person (man or woman) to remain unmarried in view of 'the impending distress' (Arndt-Gingrich). 'The days of the extensive pagan persecutions were drawing nigh. A girl that married and reared a family might thus be doubly and trebly overwhelmed, for her beloved husband might become involved, or she with him – and what about the children? History records many agonizing cases. Paul thus very properly writes that, in the face of the situation prevailing at that time, "a person" may well prefer to remain alone, untrammelled by tender family ties' (Lenski).

27: Art thou bound unto a wife? seek not to be loosed. Art thou loosed from a wife? seek not a wife.

'Marriage, in the present circumstances of the church, will prove a burden. Although this fact will not justify the dissolution of any marriage, it should dissuade Christians from getting married' (Hodge).

28: But shouldest thou marry, thou hast not sinned; and if a virgin marry, she hath not sinned. Yet such shall have tribulation in the flesh: and I would spare you.

The assurance given here would be inexplicable unless there were some at Corinth who held that marriage was sinful. Paul emphatically rejects this ascetic claim. There is no sin in marrying, but those who marry will find that it involves physical distress, and he would spare them this unnecessary suffering. 'The case of virgins is associated with that of others, in order to show that really there is no difference between them. If virgins sin in marrying, so does a man; if it is because of the impending distress that it is well for all to abstain from marriage, it is well for virgins to do so for the same reason' (Edwards).

29: But this I say, brethren, the time is shortened, that henceforth both those that have wives may be as though they had none;

What Paul is about to say applies to all his readers, whether married or unmarried. 'But, though I counsel none to change their state, I do counsel all to change their *attitude towards* all earthly things' (Robertson-Plummer).

The time is shortened: The reference is to the Second Advent, not to its chronological nearness, but to the special character which the certainty of this event gives to the period which immediately precedes it. 'The underlying idea is none other than that the times preceding the parousia require a unique concentration of the minds of believers upon the Lord and the manner in which they may best please him. The last days are to be days of undivided and most assiduous interest in the Lord and the unparalleled mode in which he may soon come to reveal himself' (G. Vos, *The Pauline Eschatology*, p. 87).

That henceforth both those that have wives may be as though they had none: These words 'must not be taken as an exhortation to neglect marital duties, as the context clearly shows. They imply that it should be constantly kept in mind that marriage is something of this time, not of the proper abiding life of the Christian' (Grosheide) [*Mark* 12:25].

30: and those that weep, as though they wept not; and those that rejoice, as though they rejoiced not; and those that buy, as though they possessed not;

'Sorrows and joys alike are temporary, are transient. In a moment all may be changed. Therefore to one who judges rightly, earthly grief is not over-grievous and earthly joy not over-joyous' (Lightfoot).

As though they possessed not: Although the Christian not only may but must join with unbelievers in buying from the same market-place [cf. 10:25], he differs from them in that he regards earthly goods as a trust and not as his permanent possession [*Luke* 12:19, 20].

31: and those that use the world, as not using it to the full: for the fashion of this world passeth away.

It is because the unbeliever has no higher expectation that he uses the world to the full, but the believer's hope transcends the world and so he is to look upon all temporal things with a sense of spiritual detachment. 'Home with its joys and griefs, business, the use of the world, must be carried on as under notice to quit, by men prepared to cast loose from the shores of time [cf. *Luke* 12:29–36; by contrast, *Luke* 14:18ff]' (Findlay).

For the fashion of this world passeth away: The fascination of the world 'is that of the theatre; but its unreal nature betrays itself in the shifting of the scenes. He appeals to their own observation: "For behold how the scene changes!" Every change proves that the end will come' (Edwards). Therefore, as 'this world in its present form is passing away' (Arndt-Gingrich), believers must not set their hearts upon it, but rather live in the light of its forthcoming transformation [*Rom.* 8:19–23; *2 Pet.* 3:13].

32: But I would have you to be free from cares. He that is unmarried is careful for the things of the Lord, how he may please the Lord:

33: but he that is married is careful for the things of the world, how he may please his wife, v 34: and is divided.

Paul would free the Corinthians from worldly cares so that they might care for the work of the Lord. The unmarried man is free to engage in this work without distraction, but he who is married must also seek to please his wife 'and is divided'. No reproach is implied; he is simply stating a fact. However, as F. W. Grosheide points out, the absolute statements of verses 32–34 are not meant to be taken in an absolute sense. They only serve to show that married people are necessarily and properly so much occupied with the affairs of this world that they cannot fix their minds on the Lord's service with the same single-minded intensity that an unmarried person is able to bring to it.

34b: So also the woman that is unmarried and the virgin is careful for the things of the Lord, that she may be holy both in body and in spirit: but she that is married is careful for the things of the world, how she may please her husband.

In the same way the married woman has the duty of caring for her husband, whereas the widow or virgin is free to 'be holy both in body and in spirit', i.e. she is able to consecrate herself entirely to the Lord's service. Paul says this to encourage and comfort the single woman, and not to cast any reflection upon the married state. There is no justification for interpreting the phrase in an ascetic sense, as though superior holiness were ensured by sexual abstinence.

35: And this I say for your own profit; not that I may cast a snare upon you, but for that which is seemly, and that ye may attend upon the Lord without distraction.

In thus advising the Corinthians of the value of remaining single Paul has nothing but their own spiritual advantage in view. He has no desire to deprive them of their liberty by shutting them up to celibacy. He will not capture them as wild animals are taken by throwing 'a noose' around their necks (ASV margin). His recommendation of the single state is limited to those who have the gift for it; he is far from forbidding marriage [cf. verses 5, 9; *1 Tim.* 4:3].

But for that which is seemly, and that ye may attend upon the Lord without distraction: According to G. G. Findlay, 'seemly' means 'of honourable guise', and covers what belongs 'to the Christian decorum of life'. Paul's language here recalls Luke's account of Martha and Mary [*Luke* 10:38–42]. As Mary chose the one thing needful, he would have them give their undivided attention to the Lord, instead of being 'distracted' by worldly cares as was Martha.

36: But if any man thinketh that he behaveth himself unseemly toward his virgin daughter, if she be past the flower of her age, and if need so requireth, let him do what he will; he sinneth not; let them marry.

Paul now answers the question, 'Should a Christian father give his daughter in marriage?' [verses 36–38] He says that the father is to make his decision only after taking into account the needs of his daughter. 'If the virgin daughter has passed the bloom or flower of her age and she feels the constraint or necessity of marriage, then the father may consider himself as acting in an unbecoming, perhaps shameful and perilous, manner with reference to his daughter if he refuses to give her in marriage. In such an event let the father give her in marriage and let the virgin and her suitor marry; the father has done what is proper and no sin is entailed for any of the persons concerned' (John Murray, *Principles of Conduct*, p. 75).

37: But he that standeth steadfast in his heart, having no necessity, but hath power as touching his own will, and hath determined this in his own heart, to keep his own virgin daughter, shall do well.

But if the father: 1. *standeth steadfast* – being unmoved by the social stigma of his daughter remaining unmarried; 2. *having no necessity* – arising from the natural inclination of the daughter to find fulfilment in marriage; 3. *but hath power as touching his own will* – because his daughter's will is not in opposition to his; 4. *and so hath determined this in his own heart, to keep his own virgin daughter* –THEN, having satisfied these conditions, *he shall do well*.

38: So then both he that giveth his own virgin daughter in marriage doeth well; and he that giveth her not in marriage shall do better.

Thus neither father sins, both do well, but one does better in withholding his daughter from marriage. '1. For the better waiting upon God's work without distraction. 2. For the better bearing of persecution' (Trapp).

39: A wife is bound for so long time as her husband liveth; but if the husband be dead, she is free to be married to whom she will; only in the Lord.

40: But she is happier if she abide as she is, after my judgment: and I think that I also have the Spirit of God.

In conclusion Paul deals with the case of widows. The wife is bound to her husband for as long as he lives, but if he dies she is free to marry again, though only to a fellow–believer in the Lord [*2 Cor.* 6:14]. Yet in Paul's judgment she would be happier (in the sense already described: verses 28, 34, 35) if she did not marry again. 'There is no inconsistency between this and *1 Tim.* 5:14. The "younger widows" come under the rule given in verse 9' (Robertson-Plummer).

I think that I also: An ironical understatement, which invites those Corinthians who claimed the inspiration of the Spirit for their opinions, to reflect upon the fact that Paul also has reason to know that he has God's Spirit [cf. verse 25].

CHAPTER EIGHT

Another matter on which the Corinthians had asked Paul's advice was the lawfulness of eating meat offered to idols. He begins by reminding them that the exercise of knowledge is limited by the higher claim of love [verses 1–3]. It is true that the eating of such food is a matter of indifference to those who know there is but one God and one Mediator, for heathen idols are nothing [verses 4–6]. But to parade this liberty encourages the weaker brother to sin by indulging in that which his conscience condemns. Therefore Paul would rather refuse any food than cause his brother to stumble [verses 7–13].

1: Now concerning things sacrificed to idols: We know that we all have knowledge. Knowledge puffeth up, but love edifieth.

It was virtually impossible for Christians living in a pagan society to avoid all contact with the idolatry which so completely permeated it. Evidently there were those in Corinth who, because of their superior knowledge ('we know that an idol is nothing in the world' – verse 4) felt quite free to eat meat which had been offered to idols, and even accept invitations to attend banquets held in heathen temples. But the believers whom they regarded as less enlightened than themselves were bound by conscientious scruples and could not allow themselves the same liberty. At the very outset of Paul's discussion of this question he uses a word which 'conveys an implicit judgment' (Findlay). He calls it 'the *idol*-sacrifice', whereas the pagan said that it was 'sacrificed to a divinity' (Arndt–Gingrich).

We know that we all have knowledge: Paul begins his reply by ironically endorsing another Corinthian slogan: We know that 'we *all* have knowledge!' But in thus boasting of their knowledge, the 'strong' had overlooked the effect of their liberated conduct on those who were 'weak' [cf. verse 7].

Knowledge puffeth up, but love buildeth up (ASV margin): Paul has no wish to place a premium on ignorance; he rather desires to show the Corinthians that the loveless exercise of knowledge is not constructive but destructive in its effects [verse 11]. In stressing the superiority of knowledge they had failed to appreciate the primacy of love (cf. chapter 13). 'This love "builds up" or "edifies". Instead of fostering pride in our hearts and puffing us up, love considers others, aids them in strengthening their spiritual life and in protecting it from danger' (Lenski).

2: If any man thinketh that he knoweth anything, he knoweth not yet as he ought to know;

The Corinthian know-alls fancied that they knew what the less knowledgeable did not understand, but Paul insists that any man who thinks like that does not yet know as he ought to know. Although such a man is not devoid of knowledge, his whole way of knowing is radically defective because he lacks love [*1 John* 4:8]. For the knowledge which puffs up is not true knowledge, even though the thing known may be true in itself. 'Spiritual pride', says W. G. T. Shedd, is 'the last resort of the Tempter, and whoever is enabled by divine grace to foil him at this point, will foil him at all points' ('Pride Vitiates Religious Knowledge', *Sermons to the Spiritual Man*, p. 282).

3: but if any man loveth God, the same is known by him.

A Christian is not someone who claims to know God through the power of his own will. The soul does not make its own unassisted ascent to God. On the contrary, it is solely because God (the Object of knowledge) has taken the initiative in electing grace and put forth his saving power that a man is enabled to respond to this prior knowledge in grateful love [cf. 13:12; *Rom.* 8:9.9; *Gal.* 4:9; *2 Tim.* 2:19]. Thus to know God is to love him, and this is the fruit of his having first loved us [*1 John* 4:19]. 'Paul would ascribe nothing to human acquisition; religion is a bestowment, not an achievement; our love or knowledge is the reflex of the divine love and knowledge directed toward us' (Findlay).

4: Concerning therefore the eating of things sacrificed to idols, we know that no idol is anything in the world, and that there is no God but one.

Having defined the nature of true spiritual knowledge, Paul resumes the topic introduced in verse 1, and endorses two propositions which were apparently expressed by the Corinthians in their letter to him.

We know that 'there is no such thing as an idol in the world (i.e., an idol has no real existence)' (Arndt–Gingrich): Here the apostle is content to echo the claim that an idol (or rather the imaginary deity it represents) has no real existence; whereas in 10:20 he points out that such deluded worshippers actually sacrifice not to Aphrodite, Serapis, or Aesculapius, but to demons whose existence was all too real.

And that 'there is no God but one' (RSV): Christians are right in affirming that all the gods of the heathen are nonentities, nothing but hollow shams without a vestige of reality [*1 Thess.* 1:9]. 'The *world* reveals the being and power of the One God [*Rom.* 1:20]; idolaters have no living God, but are *without God in the world* [*Eph.* 2:12]' (Findlay).

5: For though there be that are called gods, whether in heaven or on earth; as there are gods many, and lords many;

For indeed, granting the existence of so-called gods, whether in heaven or upon earth, as indeed there are many (such) gods and lords (Findlay): Although believers know that there is only one God, yet in the minds of pagan worshippers the existence of these false gods is real enough. But if Paul denies the actual existence of the deities represented by these idols [verse 4], he nevertheless admits that behind the façade of heathen worship there lurked evil powers upon which it terminated [10:20].

6: yet to us there is one God, the Father, Of whom are all things, and we unto him; and one Lord, Jesus Christ, through whom are all things, and we through him.

Yet to us: 'To us, Christians, there is but one God and one Lord. The inference – which the apostle leaves his readers to draw – is that we, Christians, at least, should not regard meat offered to an idol as either sanctified or polluted' (Edwards).

There is one God . . . and one Lord: Paul here opposes the numerous deities and secondary mediators of heathenism ('Gods a-plenty and Lords a-plenty' – Warfield) with the one *God* [verse 4], and the one Mediatorial *Lord*, Jesus Christ, through whom we are brought near to this otherwise unapproachable God. As in creation all things are *from* the Father *through* Christ, so in the new creation all things (and especially the redeemed) are *through* Christ *unto* the Father [*2 Cor.* 5:17; *Col.* 1:15–22]. When 'Paul says "God the Father and the Lord Jesus

Christ", he has in mind not two Gods, much less two beings of unequal dignity, a God and a Demi-god, or a God and a mere creature, – but just one God. Though Christians have one God the Father and one Lord Jesus Christ, they know but one only God' (B. B. Warfield, *Biblical and Theological Studies*, p. 75).

7: Howbeit there is not in all men that knowledge: but some, being used until now to the idol, eat as of a thing sacrificed to an idol; and their conscience being weak is defiled.

Paul now corrects the assertion of the enlightened: 'We all have knowledge' [verse 1]. There is not in *all* men that knowledge. Some Gentiles have been so accustomed to regard idols as real that, in spite of their conversion, they still cannot get rid of the feeling that, by eating meat sacrificed to idols, they are participating in the worship of heathen gods. Consequently, when the example of their stronger–minded brethren encourages them to eat such food, they become guilty of doing that which their conscience condemns. For 'whatsoever is not of faith is sin' [*Rom.* 14:23].

8: But food will not commend us to God: neither, if we eat not, are we the worse; nor, if we eat, are we the better.

But 'food will not bring us before (the judgment seat of) God' (Arndt–Gingrich): Paul reiterates the conviction of the 'strong' in Corinth and allows its truth. 'Food will not bring us into any relation, good or bad, with God: it will have no effect on the estimate which He will form respecting us, or on the judgment which He will pronounce upon us. It is not one of the things which we shall have to answer for [*Rom.* 14:17]. It is the clean heart, and not clean food, that will matter; and the weak brother confounds the two' (Robertson-Plummer).

Neither, if we eat not, do we lack; nor, if we eat, do we abound (ASV margin): 'Not eating leaves us with no deficit that we should deplore, and eating gives us no balance to our credit to which we may point with pride' (Lenski).

9: But take heed lest by any means this liberty of yours become a stumblingblock to the weak.

But: 'Though food does not affect our relation to God, it may affect our relation to our brethren and so bring us indirectly under the condemnation of God' (Edwards). Therefore love for the brethren must lead the 'strong' to limit this liberty (or right) of theirs, lest by insisting upon their 'rights' ('All things are lawful for me' – 6:12) they should cause the 'weak' to stumble.

10: For if a man see thee who hast knowledge sitting at meat in an idol's temple, will not his conscience, if he is weak, be emboldened to eat things sacrificed to idols?

If then a 'weak' brother sees the knowledgeable Christian dining with his heathen friends before the shrine of an idol, will not his conscience 'be builded up to eat things sacrificed to idols?' (ASV margin). The question is ironical. 'Will you "build up" the weak brother by your enlightened example? You will "build him up" by bringing him to ruin!' Here Paul only has in view the evil effects of this example upon others; he later brands the practice as being in itself sinful [10:14ff.].

11: For through thy knowledge he that is weak perisheth, the brother for whose sake Christ died.

Since Paul speaks of the brother for whom Christ died, it is wrong to assume that 'perisheth' must here signify eternal perdition, for *apollumi* can also refer to temporal loss or ruin (e.g. in *Matt.* 9:17 it is used of bursting wineskins; in *Luke* 15:9, 32 of the lost being found; in *Luke* 15:17 of perishing with hunger; and in *James* 1:11 of fading blossoms). Thus the loveless abuse of knowledge results in the 'wounding' [verse 12] or '*ruining*' of the weak believer—by causing him 'to act against his conscience, and so to commit sin and be in danger of quenching God's Spirit within him' [Alford on *Rom.* 14:15].

12: And thus, sinning against the brethren, and wounding their conscience when it is weak, ye sin against Christ.

The verse gives a vivid description of the violence inflicted upon the conscience while it is weak and so in no condition to withstand the blow: 'how base to strike the weak!' (Findlay).

Ye sin against Christ: A lesson which Paul himself had been taught by the Risen Christ on the road to Damascus [*Acts* 9:4, 5]. 'The principle of union with Christ, which forbids sin against oneself [6:15], forbids sin against one's brother' (Findlay).

13: Wherefore, if meat causeth my brother to stumble, I will eat no flesh for evermore, that I cause not my brother to stumble.

Paul does not specify the kind of meat (in this case: 'meat offered to idols'), because he is stating a principle of universal application which holds good for every kind of eating [cf. *Rom.* 14:14, 17, 21]. The vehemence of Paul's language expresses the strength of his conviction, yet he does not unconditionally renounce his liberty, but abridges it only in the interests of his brother. And what follows shows the Corinthians how far he has gone in this regard [9:1ff.]. 'The strong sought the solution of the question from the standpoint of knowledge and its rights; the apostle finds it from the standpoint of love and its obligations' (C. Holsten).

CHAPTER NINE

Paul answers his critics by affirming that at least the Corinthians have no reason to doubt the reality of his apostleship since they were converted under his ministry [verses 1–3]. And though he had the same right to marry and receive the support of the churches as the other apostles, he had chosen to forego his rights in order to further the gospel by preaching it without charge [verses 4–18]. For though he was free from all men, he curtailed his own liberty by adapting himself to the many he longed to gain for Christ, whether they were Jews, Gentiles, or even the weak! [verses 19–23]. When athletes strive so hard for a corruptible crown, believers must not expect to obtain an incorruptible crown without sacrifice [verses 24–25]. Therefore Paul is always in strict training, lest having preached to others, he should be rejected himself [verses 26, 27].

1: Am I not free? am I not an apostle? have I not seen Jesus our Lord? are not ye my work in the Lord?

Paul establishes his credentials as an apostle by asking four rhetorical questions in the familiar debating style of the day (the *diatribe*), and his use of the negative ('not') implies that the answer he expects to each is 'yes' (W. H. Mare). The *first* question looks back to the previous chapter, and it rebukes those who protest their 'rights' to the ruination of their brothers. As a Christian Paul enjoyed the same freedom as the

Corinthians, but in refusing to exercise that liberty to the full in the interests of the weak he exemplified the doctrine he preached.

The *second* question affirms what some were already inclined to deny, for Paul's critics evidently argued that a full apostle would have insisted upon having all his expenses paid by the church. But love's motives are always misunderstood by loveless hearts. Paul was no less an apostle because he had waived what he had every right to demand from them.

The *third* question underlines an essential feature of his apostleship. The fact that Paul has seen 'Jesus our Lord' made him a witness of the resurrection, and the fact that he saw him 'last of all' [15:8] made him the last member of the apostolic college. It was through that encounter with the Risen Christ on the Damascus road that he was called to salvation and commissioned for service [Gal. 1:15f].

The *fourth* question gives a further proof of his apostleship. The Corinthians were not obliged to believe Paul's testimony that he had seen the Lord as a matter of mere hearsay, since all 'the signs of an apostle' [2 Cor. 12:12] were wrought in their midst, and indeed their own conversion to Christ afforded the most conspicuous proof of this power!

2: If to others I am not an apostle, yet at least I am to you; for the seal of mine apostleship are ye in the Lord.

The Corinthians should have been the very last to dispute Paul's apostleship when they owed their salvation to his work 'in the Lord'. 'The conversion of men is a divine work, and those by whom it is accomplished are thereby authenticated as divine messengers ... This, although valid evidence, and as such adduced by the apostle, is nevertheless very liable to be abused. First, because much which passes for conversion is spurious; and secondly, because the evidence of success is often urged in behalf of the errors of preachers, when that success is due to the truth which they preach' (Hodge).

For the seal of mine apostleship are ye in the Lord: A seal 'is a visible token of something that already exists; thus the Corinthian church does not make Paul an apostle, and his apostleship does not depend on it (any more than on the Jerusalem church – cf. *Gal.* 1:1), but its existence is a visible sign of his apostleship' (Barrett) [*Rom.* 4:11; *2 Cor.* 1:22].

3: My defence to them that examine me is this.

Opinion is divided on whether 'this' refers to what follows or to what precedes. The latter is perhaps the preferable alternative. '"*This*" – referring to verses 1, 2 – "is my answer to those that put me on my defence": I point them to you! . . . Granted the *apostleship* (and this the readers cannot deny), the *right* followed as a matter of course: this needed no "apology"' (Findlay).

4: Have we no right to eat and to drink?
5: Have we no right to lead about a wife that is a believer, even as the rest of the apostles, and the brethren of the Lord, and Cephas?

In Corinth Paul had not exercised his right to be supported by the church, but this forbearance did not mean that he had forfeited that right [*Acts* 18:3; *2 Cor.* 12:13–16]. Then again, if Paul were to marry a believing sister and take her with him on his missionary travels as did most of the apostles, he would be entitled to the same support for himself *and his wife* as these married apostles actually received from the churches.

He might well have imposed this burden on the Corinthians as Cephas (Peter, cf. *Mark* 1:30) appears to have done, but it was to their benefit that he did not. 'The brethren of the Lord' is most naturally explained by supposing that they were the sons who were born to Joseph and Mary after the birth of Jesus [*Matt.* 1:25; *John* 7:5; *Acts* 1:14; *1 Cor.* 15:7]. Paul specially mentions the name of Cephas 'as carrying weight with one partisan section at Corinth. "If your favourite leader does so, surely so may I"' (Fausset).

6: Or I only and Barnabas, have we not a right to forbear working?

Paul's resolve to earn his own living by pursuing the trade he had learned in his youth was evidently shared by Barnabas, his companion on the first missionary journey, but apparently not by the other apostles. But instead of being grateful for his self–sacrifice the Corinthians thought that to engage in such manual labour was beneath the dignity of one who was truly an apostle [*Acts* 18:3, 20:3 4; *2 Thess.* 3:8]. Paul, however, here insists that his voluntary decision to support himself did not mean that he had renounced his right to be wholly maintained by those who benefited from his ministry.

7: What soldier ever serveth at his own charges? who planteth a vineyard, and eateth not the fruit thereof? or who feedeth a flock, and eateth not of the milk of the flock?

The secular occupations Paul mentions to justify his right to maintenance as the equal of the other apostles are themselves types of the Christian ministry. 'The first represents the apostles going forth to wage war with the world; the second represents them, after conquest, planting churches; the third represents their pastoral care of the churches which they have founded. Again, the soldier is a mercenary; the vine–dresser an owner; the shepherd a slave. Yet in all alike labour implies reward' (Edwards) [*John* 21:15–17; *1 Cor.* 3:6, 7; *2 Tim.* 2:3–6].

8: Do I speak these things after the manner of men? or saith not the law also the same?

But Paul does not rest his case on natural analogies alone, and his clinching argument is based upon the testimony of Scripture. He is not merely speaking 'after the manner of men', but is expounding the law of God. Although 'the law' is abolished as a means of obtaining salvation [*Rom.* 3:19ff.], it 'remains a revelation of truth and right [*Rom.* 7:12ff.], and Paul draws from it guidance for Christian conduct [cf. 14:34; *Rom.* 13:8ff.]. The ethics of the New Testament are those of the Old, enhanced by Christ [see *Matt.* 5:17ff]' (Findlay).

9: For it is written in the law of Moses, Thou shalt not muzzle the ox when he treadeth out the corn. Is it for the oxen that God careth,

10: or saith he it assuredly for our sake?

'If God commands men to care for the oxen which tread out the corn, how much more does this principle hold good for ministers who labour to provide men with the Bread of Life?' [*Deut.* 25:4; *Luke* 10:7; *1 Tim.* 5:18].

Calvin says that 'what Paul actually means is quite simple: though the Lord commands consideration for the oxen, he does so, not for the sake of the oxen, but rather out of regard for men, for whose benefit even the very oxen were created . . . You should understand, therefore, that God is not concerned about oxen, to the extent that oxen were the only creatures in his mind when he made the law, for he was thinking of men, and wanted to make them accustomed to being considerate in behaviour, so that they might not cheat the workman of his wages.'

10b: Yea, for our sake it was written: because he that ploweth ought to plow in hope, and he that thresheth, to thresh in hope of partaking.

Yes, it was indeed written for our sake, because the ploughman ought to plough and the thresher to thresh in the hope of having a share of the crop. Thus the *principle* set forth is that the labourer shall partake of the fruit of his labour. 'The oxen cannot understand this even when they feed while threshing. It is said "altogether on our account", and it is a pity if we fail to understand' (Lenski).

11: If we sowed unto you spiritual things, is it a great matter if we shall reap your carnal things?

It is here that Paul applies this principle to the work of the ministry, for this 'sowing' of spiritual things obviously refers to the preaching of the gospel. 'What they owed to him as their spiritual father admitted of no comparison with anything they could do for him in things temporal, though they might *express* it in the supply of his temporal wants' (David Brown).

12: If others partake of this right over you, do not we yet more? Nevertheless we did not use this right; but we bear all things, that we may cause no hindrance to the gospel of Christ.

Paul does not blame the teachers who followed him in Corinth for exercising their right to receive support from the church, but simply points out that the founder of the church had even more right to it than they. But he never availed himself of this right, preferring to endure every kind of privation rather than hamper the progress of the gospel by leaving himself open to the charge of self-seeking.

13: Know ye not that they that minister about sacred things eat of the things of the temple, and they that wait upon the altar have their portion with the altar?

Know ye not? Of course Paul's knowledgeable readers were familiar with the fact that those who served in the Temple in Jerusalem received their living from the Temple; that those who waited on the altar were 'sharers in the altar' (Arndt-Gingrich). The terms Paul uses for 'temple' and 'altar' make it clear that he is not thinking of pagan worship, and he certainly would not have argued for the support of the Christian ministry from such idolatrous practices (cf. 8:10 – 'the place of an idol' – Edwards). 'Paul argues by analogy from the Jewish priest to the Christian minister in respect of *the claim to maintenance;* we cannot infer from this *an identity of function,* any more than in the previous comparison with "the threshing ox"' (Findlay).

14: Even so did the Lord ordain that they that proclaim the gospel should live of the gospel.

'As God enjoined under the law, so also Christ ordained in his church' (Edwards). In writing to Timothy Paul quotes *Luke* 10:7 [*1 Tim.* 5:18]; here he gives its substance. Those who serve Christ in the ministry are to 'live *for* the gospel, and consequently ought also to live *of* the gospel. But woe to the man who claims to live *of* the gospel without living at the same time *for* the gospel!' (Godet).

15: But I have used none of these things: and I write not these things that it may be so done in my case; for it were good for me rather to die, than that any man should make my glorying void.

Although Paul has proved the case for ministerial support, this implies no weakening of his own resolve to remain independent. He first states that he has used none of these privileges. The perfect tense 'affirms a settled position; the refusal has become a rule' (Findlay) [cf. verse 12]. Then Paul hastens to add that he is not writing these things from any ulterior motive. He is not making a subtle bid to secure such financial assistance from the Corinthians in the future. At this point the sentence is broken under the stress of his emotion (in the better attested text):

For I would rather die than – no, no one shall make this boast of mine an empty thing (Barrett): 'He began to say that he *would rather die than be dependent* on Corinthian pay; he ends by saying, absolutely, he *will never be so dependent*' (Findlay).

16: For if I preach the gospel, I have nothing to glory of; for necessity is laid upon me; for woe is unto me, if I preach not the gospel.

This introduces the reason for Paul's refusal to avail himself of these rights. Since he was conscripted into Christ's service against his previous will, he cannot glory in the fact that he preaches the gospel, for he preaches it from necessity rather than choice. A sovereignly determined commission gave him no ground for glorying in the service he was compelled to render. Hence he exclaims, 'Woe is unto me, if I preach not the gospel!' 'Had Paul disobeyed the call of God, his course from that time onwards must have been one of condemnation and misery. To fight against "Necessity" the Greeks conceived as ruin; their *necessity* was a blind, cruel Fate, Paul's *necessity* is the compulsion of Sovereign Grace' (Findlay).

17: For if I do this of mine own will, I have a reward: but if not of mine own will, I have a stewardship intrusted to me.

Had Paul freely chosen to serve Christ, his voluntary labour would have merited a reward. But since he became an apostle under constraint, his position is merely that of a slave who has no part in choosing the stewardship which his master entrusts to him. What Paul means is that he can claim no credit for simply fulfilling the terms of his commission. Preach the gospel he *must*, but he *may* relinquish the pay which he feels a pressed man does not deserve; and so he chooses to receive another reward!

18: What then is my reward? That, when I preach the gospel, I may make the gospel without charge, so as not to use to the full my right in the gospel.

Here we have Paul's paradoxical conclusion: his reward is found in refusing the reward! 'If he wished to exercise his privilege as an apostle for all that it was worth, he would insist upon full maintenance as his reward. But the reward which he prefers and gets is the delight of preaching without pay, of giving the Glad–tidings for nought, and taking no money for them' (Robertson-Plummer).

19: For though I was free from all men, I brought myself under bondage to all, that I might gain the more.

Here the apostle begins to explain how he makes use of his freedom [verses 19–2,3]. In contrast to the proud inflexibility of his Corinthian critics, Paul's seemingly inconsistent behaviour is due to his ardent love for the souls of men. Free from all men, he has used this freedom to make himself the servant of all! Luther gave expression to the same paradox of grace when he said: 'A Christian man is a most free lord of all, subject to none. A Christian man is a most dutiful servant of all, subject to all.'

That I might gain the more: Paul is no universalist. He never did entertain the hope of winning 'the whole wide world for Jesus', nor did he pursue this course to gain more converts than any other apostle, but rather to win 'more than I should have gained if I had not made myself a slave to all' (Robertson-Plummer).

20: And to the Jews I became as a Jew, that I might gain Jews; to them that are under the law, as under the law, not being myself under the law, that I might gain them that are under the law;

Although Paul was no longer 'under the law', because he knew himself to be a new man in Christ [*2 Cor.* 5:17], when he was among Jews he practised the customs he was not obliged to observe in order to gain them for Christ. But if he was always ready to respect Jewish scruples [*Acts* 16:3; 21:16], he was never prepared to sacrifice gospel principles to Jewish prejudice [*Gal.* 2:5]. 'Paul is free from the ceremonial law through the work of Christ but he does not consider it a sin to observe the law, provided this was not done to acquire righteousness' (Grosheide) [cf. *Rom.* 10: 3, 4; *Phil.* 3:2ff]

21: to them that are without law, as without law, not being without law to God, but under law to Christ, that I might gain them that are without law.

But when Paul was with Gentiles he dropped these Jewish customs which would have hindered his preaching the gospel to them. This did not mean, however, that he behaved as though he were under no law at all. On the contrary, all his actions were governed by the knowledge that he was 'subject to the law of Christ' (Arndt-Gingrich). Since Christ has changed Paul's relation to the law by fulfilling it on his behalf, he now recognizes the futility of that legalism which attempts to win salvation by its obedience to the law [*Rom.* 10:4; *Gal.* 3:13; *Phil.* 3:9]. But because gospel freedom is not lawlessness, Paul also acknowledges his abiding obligation to obey the moral law [*Rom.* 6:15, 13:8–10], and is enabled to live out its precepts through the mediation of his Redeemer [7:22, 23] and the power of the Spirit [*Rom.* 8:4]. Grace does not therefore free the believer 'from the requirement of exact obedience, but from that rigour of obedience which the law required as a condition of salvation' (Samuel Bolton, *The True Bounds of Christian Freedom*, p. 40).

22: To the weak I became weak, that I might gain the weak: I am become all things to all men, that I may by all means save some.

Paul next shows how the principle of accommodating himself to the needs of others applies to the actual situation in Corinth [8:13]. 'So well did he enter into the scruples of the timid and half–enlightened [e.g. 8:7, 10; *Rom.* 14:1ff.], that he forgot his own strength [8:4; *Rom.* 15:1] and felt himself "weak" with them: cf. *2 Cor.* 11:29, *who is weak, and I am not weak?*' (Findlay).

I am become all things to all men, that I may by all means save some: 'This does not mean that he will act in an unprincipled manner, or compromise on Christian principles; but he will sacrifice his own legitimate interests and preferences completely, if thereby he may save some' (Hillyer).

23: And I do all things for the gospel's sake, that I may be a joint partaker thereof.

Unlike the selfish Corinthians, Paul does not equate the gospel with a false individualism. It is by devoting himself without reserve to the spiritual welfare of others that he ensures his own participation in the gospel. For though others may be saved through a work which is devoid of love, the preacher who lacks this love will not be saved. As Lenski remarks, Some preachers will think it strange that Paul would lose his own part in the gospel if he did not follow this one method of preaching the gospel [cf. verse 27], for they are sure that *they* will be saved no matter how they decide to preach it!

24: Know ye not that they that run in a race run all, but one receiveth the prize? Even so run; that ye may attain.

25: And every man that striveth in the games exerciseth self–control in

all things. Now they do it to receive a corruptible crown; but we an incorruptible.

Paul selects a familiar figure to enforce the lesson of self–discipline upon his readers, for the famous Isthmian Games were held every two years in their neighbourhood. As befits those who have entered a far sterner contest he exhorts *all* to run as the one victor ran in the Greek games, though of course this does not mean that in the Christian race only *one* wins the prize.

It was well known that every athlete who entered for the games had to undergo ten months' intensive training under the direction of the judges, and was forced to adhere to a strict diet [*2 Tim.* 2:5]. In the same way the Christian athlete must discipline himself to lay aside all that would hinder his progress in the great race to gain the victor's crown ('every weight' as well as every sin: *Heb.* 12:1, 2). 'The pine crown which the judge put on the victor's head in the Isthmian Games, while it was the emblem of glory, was at the same time the emblem of the transitory character of that glory. For the spiritual victor there is reserved an unfading crown!' (Godet) [*2 Tim.* 4:8; *1 Pet.* 5:4]

26: I therefore so run, as not uncertainly; so fight I, as not beating the air:

27: but I buffet my body, and bring it into bondage: lest by any means, after that I have preached to others, I myself should be rejected.

Here Paul lets the careless and self-indulgent Corinthians know that he at least has entered the contest in earnest. He does not run 'as one who has no fixed goal' (Arndt-Gingrich), nor does he box as one who beats the air instead of his opponent, which in this case turns out to be his own body! However, in saying 'I give my body a black eye, and make it a slave' (Lenski), Paul is not providing a proof text for flagellants. He uses this language 'not because the body is necessarily evil, but because it is the weapon with which the law of sin and death fights us and, at the same time, the sphere within which the spiritual powers of evil come within our reach to be bruised and destroyed . . . The Christian victor does not destroy the body, but makes it his slave; so that it now serves the soul which it sought to slay' (Edwards) [*Rom.* 6:12, 13].

Lest by any means, after that I have preached to others, I myself should be rejected (or 'disqualified' – Arndt Gingrich): Paul seeks to awaken the Corinthians from their carnal slumbers by confronting them with this alarming thought. Be he even an inspired apostle, it is not enough to have preached to others if he fails to practise what he preaches. 'A preacher of salvation may yet miss it. He may show others the way to heaven, and never get thither himself . . . A holy fear of himself was necessary to preserve the fidelity of an apostle; and how much more necessary is it to our preservation? Note, Holy fear of ourselves, and not presumptuous confidence, is the best security against apostasy from God, and final rejection by him' (Matthew Henry).

CHAPTER TEN

The danger of believers presuming upon their spiritual privileges is illustrated by God's punishment of the Israelites for their idolatry, fornication, and murmuring. These things are written for our warning. But God will not permit his people to be tempted beyond their strength: there is always a way of escape [verses 1–13]. The Corinthians must flee from idolatry, for to participate in a sacrificial meal is to participate in worship, and they dare not provoke the Lord by holding communion with demons [verses 14–22]. But though they must shun idol–feasts, it is lawful to partake of idol–meats. Yet because love limits liberty, they are to abstain from eating such food in the presence of an over–scrupulous brother. In all things they must seek God's glory, and consult the good of others. This is Paul's own rule which he offers for their imitation [verses 23–11: 1].

1: For I would not, brethren, have you ignorant, that our fathers were all under the cloud, and all passed through the sea;

For I would not, brethren, have you ignorant: Paul does not wish them to overlook the importance of what he is about to say. 'This chapter is to be closely connected with 9:27. In the history of the chosen race we see men becoming *disqualified* and falling short of the promised inheritance. But the warning is the more pointed inasmuch as the danger of the Corinthians and of the Israelites alike lay in contact with idolatry' (Edwards).

That our fathers: The reason Paul uses this phrase in writing to Gentile 'brethren' is to emphasize the continuity of both dispensations [cf. *Rom.* 4.1, 11ff, 11:17f; *Gal.* 3:7, 29; *Phil.* 3:3]. 'The Jewish church is related as parent to the Christian church' (Fausset).

Were all: The example of Israel proves that the possession of great religious privileges does not guarantee immunity from divine judgment. The lesson is underscored by the solemn repetition of the word 'all' which is used five times in the first four verses. 'Those people who *almost all* perished, began with being *all* blessed of the Lord' (Godet).

Under the cloud, i.e. under its guidance: 'The symbol of the divine presence and favour was before their eyes day and night. If any people ever had reason to think their salvation secure, it was those whom God thus wonderfully guided' (Hodge) [*Exod.* 13:21, 22].

And all passed through the sea: 'Would God permit those to perish for whom he had wrought so signal a deliverance, and for whose sake he sacrificed the hosts of Egypt? Yet their carcasses were strewed in the wilderness' (Hodge) [*Num.* 14:29].

2: and were all baptized unto Moses in the cloud and in the sea;

The Israelites 'had themselves baptized into Moses' (middle voice: expressing the voluntary nature of their act) when they crossed the Red Sea under his leadership [*Exod.* 14:31]. Paul's argument is, 'The Corinthians, it is true, have been "baptized", but so also were the Israelites; if the virtual baptism of the latter availed not to save them from the doom of lust, neither will the actual baptism of the former save them' (Fausset).

As Paul appears to have coined this unique expression, 'baptized into Moses', to match his usual formula for baptism ('into Christ', cf. *Rom.* 6:3), the details of the description cannot be pressed. He simply means that the Israelites were surrounded by the cloud and the sea, though they were untouched by either. The point of the comparison both here and in *1 Pet.* 3:20f 'is not passing through the water but deliverance through a flood which separates the saved from the lost' (L. Goppelt, *TDNT*, vol. 8, p. 331).

3: and did all eat the same spiritual food;

The Israelites were not only miraculously delivered from the Egyptian bondage, but they were also miraculously sustained in the wilderness by manna from heaven [*Psa.* 78:24, 25]. This food not only nourished the body, but its supernatural origin ought also to have had the effect of constituting it 'spiritual food' for the soul. It is remarkable, observe Robertson and Plummer, that Paul 'chooses the manna and the rock, and not any of the Jewish sacrifices, as parallels to the Eucharist'.

4: and did all drink the same spiritual drink: for they drank of a spiritual rock that followed them: and the rock was Christ.

The manner in which the Israelites were supplied with water in the desert was no less miraculous [*Exod.* 17:6; *Num.* 20]. If Paul alludes here to the rabbinical legend that the rock from which the water gushed forth at Rephidim accompanied the Israelites on their journey, the word 'spiritual' clearly shows that he does so only to reject it; for as Findlay remarks, 'we must not disgrace Paul by making him say that the pre-incarnate Christ followed the march of Israel in the shape of a lump of rock!'

And the rock was Christ: Although they discerned it not, Christ himself was the author of all their blessings; an assertion which requires his pre–existence and tacitly assumes his Deity by giving him a title which was used of Jehovah in the Old Testament [*Deut.* 32:15; *Psa.* 18:2; *Isa.* 17:10, etc.]. The spiritual similarity of the two covenants, and of the gifts accompanying them, rests on this identity of the divine head of both. The practical consequence is obvious at a glance: Christ lived in the midst of the ancient people, and the people perished! How can you think yourselves, you Christians, secure from the same lot!' (Godet).

5: Howbeit with most of them God was not well pleased: for they were overthrown in the wilderness.

A massive understatement, for of that first generation only Caleb and Joshua lived to enter the land of promise [*Heb.* 3:17]. This does not mean, however, 'that all those who died in the wilderness were also forever damned. Some were saved although they suffered this temporal judgment because of their sins' (Lenski) [cf. 11:30].

For they were overthrown in the wilderness: 'What a spectacle is that which is called up by the apostle before the eyes of the self-satisfied Corinthians: all those bodies, sated with miraculous food and drink, strewing the soil of the desert!' (Godet).

6: Now these things were our examples, to the intent we should not lust after evil things, as they also lusted.

These judgments are not recorded in Scripture as matters of antiquarian interest which have no bearing on the contemporary scene in swinging first–century Corinth. On the contrary, they are beacons set to warn 'us' (all believers) *not* to follow Israel's example in lusting after evil things. The allusion is to their longing after the flesh-pots of Egypt, just as the appeal of good food might tempt the Corinthians to attend idolatrous banquets [*Num.* 11:4–6]. Sin has its genesis in lust and Paul therefore places this first. Unless the first motions of sin's repulsive brood are remorselessly crushed they will *live* to bring forth *death! [James* 1:14, 15].

7: Neither be ye idolaters, as were some of them; as it is written, The people sat down to eat and drink, and rose up to play.

The Corinthians must not fall into idolatry as the children of Israel did when they worshipped the golden calf. Paul aptly quotes Exodus 32:6 because it would call to mind the feasting and licentious dancing which were associated with pagan worship in Corinth; for as the next verse shows, idolatry inevitably leads to immorality [cf. *Rom.* 1:24f].

8: Neither let us commit fornication, as some of them committed, and fell in one day three and twenty thousand.

Paul here recalls the judgment which fell upon the Israelites when they committed fornication with the daughters of Moab at their idol-feasts [*Num.* 25:1–9]. The warning was relevant in a city where the priestesses of the cult of Aphrodite were harlots! Paul gives the number slain as 23,000 whereas Numbers 25:9 has 24,000. But the difference is not important because both figures are obviously round numbers. It is therefore unreasonable to insist upon mathematical exactitude when the figures given are intended only to be approximate: more than 23,000 counted exactly, but not entirely 24,000. Taken in this sense, both figures are correct' (Lenski).

9: Neither let us make trial of the Lord, as some of them made trial and perished by the serpents.

The Corinthians must not presume to put the Lord to the test as did the Israelites, for they complained that he had brought them into the desert to die and despised his provision for their needs. This daring experiment resulted in a punishment which made their complaint a dreadful reality, so that many of them 'lay a-perishing' where they had been bitten by the serpents [*Num*. 21:4–9]. So Paul warns his readers not to try the Lord by resenting the restrictions of their new life in Christ. 'The Christian profession demanded that the Corinthians should forego the old heathen enjoyments. But instead of rejoicing in their deliverance through Christ the Corinthians were dissatisfied and longed for the old pagan celebrations' (Lenski).

10: Neither murmur ye, as some of them murmured, and perished by the destroyer.

Another sin which called down the judgment of God upon the Israelites was their murmuring against his will as this was expressed through the mouth of his servants, Moses and Aaron [*Num*. 16]. Let the Corinthians also beware of this sin, for such murmuring is the audible expression of distrust in God's guidance. 'Voices were beginning to be raised against Paul among the Corinthians; if they remained unchecked, the gravest danger might result' (Lenski). As angels are often mentioned in Scripture as the agents of divine judgment, it is not surprising to find that Paul here refers the destruction of these rebels to the destroying angel of God [cf. *Exod*. 12:23].

11: Now these things happened unto them by way of example; and they were written for our admonition, upon whom the ends of the ages are come.

Paul insists that these Old Testament incidents were recorded in Scripture with a view to the admonition of New Testament saints. It is because the judgments he cites were *exemplary* in their nature that they serve as a lesson for all time.

Upon whom the ends of the ages are come: 'The New Testament dispensation winds up all former "ages". No new dispensation shall appear till Christ comes as judge. The "ends" (plural) include various successive periods consummated and merging together [*Eph*. 1:10: cf. *Heb*. 9:26]. Our dispensation being the consummation of all that went before, our responsibilities are the greater, and the greater our guilt, if we fall short of our privileges' (Fausset).

12: Wherefore let him that thinketh he standeth take heed lest he fall.

In view of the foregoing examples the Corinthians must not presume that the mere possession of the privileges and gifts of the gospel can secure them against the possibility of falling from grace under all circumstances; that they did entertain such an illusory assurance is proved by their dangerously careless walk. 'Our security as it relates to God consists in faith; as it relates to ourselves, in fear' (Fausset).

13: There hath no temptation taken you but such as man can bear: but God is faithful, who will not suffer you to be tempted above that ye are able; but will with the temptation make also the way of escape, that ye may be able to endure it.

But in case the Corinthians should fall a prey to despondency, Paul reminds them that so far they have not been assailed by such superhuman trials as would lead them to doubt God's ability to care for them in the future. They are to find comfort in the fact that God is faithful. This means he will not permit them to be tempted beyond their power; for with the temptation which he appoints, he also makes the way of escape so that they may be able to endure it. God thus tempers the length and strength of the temptation to enable his people to bear it and not be overwhelmed by it. Yet they would certainly 'fall' if they continued to court temptation by yielding to idolatry instead of using God's way of escape.

14: Wherefore, my beloved, flee from idolatry.

Paul softens the tone but not the urgency of his admonition with the tender address 'my beloved'. He keeps up the metaphor of the previous verse, which is that of an army caught in a defile and urged to flee through the mountain pass (Edwards). They are not to stand and fight idolatry with their vaunted knowledge; their only safety is in flight. 'They must not try how near they can go, but how far they can fly' (Robertson-Plummer).

15: I speak as to wise men; judge ye what I say.

Paul speaks without irony. He appeals to them as men with sufficient intelligence to judge the validity of the argument he is about to present to them. 'Ye' is emphatic: 'Do *ye* now judge it; *I* have done so' (Edwards).

16: The cup of blessing which we bless, is it not a communion of the blood of Christ? The bread which we break, is it not a communion of the body of Christ?

Paul argues that if partaking of the Lord's Supper brings the Christian into communion with Christ, then it must follow that those who participate in idol–feasts are thereby brought into communion with demons [verses 16–22]. He mentions the cup first because he intends to enlarge upon the significance of eating sacrificial food [verse 17f.]. Paul does not call attention to the wine, but to the cup which makes it the symbol of Christ's death. It is only because Christ was willing to drain the cup of sin's bitter dregs that in his nail–pierced hands it becomes for us 'the cup of blessing' [*Luke* 22:20, 42]. Believers thus receive this cup from the Lord with thanksgiving, and 'we bless' shows that this 'consecration is the corporate act of the church' (Fausset).

The fact that Paul here refers to the sharing of the cup and the bread as a 'communion' of the blood and body of Christ proves that the Lord's Supper is something more than a memorial meal. For the believer shares in all the benefits of Christ's sacrifice as he partakes of the tokens by which it is recalled but not re-enacted. 'The bread and wine are vehicles of the presence of Christ . . . Partaking of bread and wine is union (sharing) with the heavenly Christ' (F. Hauck, *TDNT*, vol. 3, p. 805).

17: seeing that we, who are many, are one bread, one body: for we all partake of the one bread.

Because there is one bread, we who are many are one body, for we all partake of the one bread (RSV): This punctuation is to be preferred, for it is from the fact that there is but one bread, one Lord, one source of salvation, that Paul deduces the unity of the church. 'We are not said to be one bread; but we are one body because we partake of one bread. The design of the apostle is to show that every one who comes to the Lord's supper enters into communion with all other communicants. They form one body in virtue of their joint participation of Christ. This being the case, those who attend the sacrificial feasts of the heathen form one religious body. They are in religious communion with each other, because in communion with the demons on whom their worship terminates' (Hodge).

18: Behold Israel after the flesh: have not they that eat the sacrifices communion with the altar?

Behold Israel after the flesh: The qualifying phrase 'after the flesh' brings out 'the external character of the Israelitish worship, in opposition to the spiritual worship of the true Israel, the church' (Godet).

Have not they that eat the sacrifices communion with the altar? The same principle held good in ancient Israel. To partake of the sacrifices brought the worshippers into communion with the altar, i.e. with all that it stood for. It is quite unnecessary to maintain that Paul is drawing a parallel between these Jewish sacrifices and the Lord's supper. J. B. Lightfoot decisively rejects the inference of some interpreters, that a comparison of 9:13 with this verse suggests that Paul 'recognizes the designation of the Lord's table as an altar. On the contrary it is a speaking fact, that in both passages he avoids using this term of the Lord's table, though the language of the context might readily have suggested it to him, if he had considered it appropriate. Nor does the argument in either case require or encourage such an inference' (*The Epistle to the Philippians:* 'Dissertation on the Christian Ministry', p. 266).

19: What say I then? that a thing sacrificed to idols is anything, or that an idol is anything?

Paul pauses here to ask, 'Am I contradicting myself?' [cf. 8:4]. Of course not! It is true that an idol lacks the reality attributed to it, and therefore what is offered to it in sacrifice is also devoid of any significance. So because this pagan rite can neither consecrate nor contaminate the food, believers may indeed buy and eat such meat without offence [verses 25, 27]. But to participate in heathen worship is a very different matter!

20: But I say, that the things which the Gentiles sacrifice, they sacrifice to demons, and not to God: and I would not that ye should have communion with demons.

Although the heathen divinities do not exist, it must not be supposed that idolatry is harmless, for it brings the worshipper into communion with demons! Paul's allusion to Deuteronomy 32:17 recalls Israel's departure from the law of God to sacrifice to demons; let not the Christians in Corinth fall into the same grave sin. The point is not what the worshipper intends, but what his worship actually effects.

21: Ye cannot drink the cup of the Lord, and the cup of demons: ye cannot partake of the table of the Lord, and of the table of demons.

Ye cannot: It is a *moral* impossibility for the Corinthians to partake of the Lord's table and of the table of demons. They must realize that these fellowships are mutually incompatible, since the kind of fellowship enjoyed by the guests is always determined by the character of the host at whose table they sit. If therefore they have accepted an engagement to sit at Christ's table, then they are no longer free to accept invitations to have communion with demons! Evidence has been found which shows that a pagan would hold such a meal for his friends in the idol's temple: 'Chairemon invites you to dinner at the table of the Lord Serapis in the Serapeum, tomorrow the 15th at the 9th hour' (*Papyrus Oxyrhynchus*, i. 110).

22: Or do we provoke the Lord to jealousy? are we stronger than he?

Here Paul's language harks back to Deuteronomy 32:21, where the reference is to Israel's idolatry which provoked God's jealous anger. 'If the Corinthians *are* daring Christ's sovereign displeasure by coquetting with idolatry, they must suppose themselves "stronger than he"! As sensible and prudent men they must see the absurdity, as well as the awful peril, of such double-dealing' (Findlay).

23: All things are lawful; but not all things are expedient. All things are lawful; but not all things edify.

Here Paul, returning to the principle of Christian licence in things indifferent, first repeats the slogan of the libertines with the same answer he gave to it in 6:12, but with his second quotation of 'All things are lawful' he returns to the note which was struck in 8:1. He insists that the Christian may not assert his 'rights' to the spiritual detriment of his fellow–believers, but must at all times use his freedom to build up the body to which he belongs. 'A liberty which harms others is not likely to benefit oneself, and a liberty which harms oneself is not likely to benefit others. Cf. 14:26; *Rom.* 14:19'(Robertson-Plummer).

24: Let no man seek his own, but each his neighbour's good.

A succinct statement of the principle by which Christian conduct is to be regulated! Self-seeking love must give place to self-giving love [cf. *Rom.* 15:2; *Phil.* 2:4]. In applying this rule to the question under discussion, 'two cases might present themselves to the Christian: that of a meal in his own house [verses 25, 26], or that of a meal in a strange house [verses 27–30]' (Godet).

25: Whatsoever is sold in the shambles, eat, asking no question for conscience' sake; 26: for the earth is the Lord's, and the fullness thereof.

The 'shambles' was the food market which included the meat market, and in Corinth as in Pompeii, most of the meat sold there would come from the beasts which were sacrificed in the temple that was situated nearby. Paul sides with the strong in affirming that whatever is offered for sale in the market may be eaten 'without raising any question on the ground of conscience' (RSV). Incidentally, this counsel reflects Paul's own emancipation from all Jewish food laws [cf. *1 Tim.* 4:3–5], though among Jews he conformed to their ways to avoid giving needless offence [9:20]. That this is the right attitude towards food is confirmed by his appeal to Psalm 24:1, which was used by the Jews as a 'grace before meat', and perhaps its quotation here already points to the Christian adoption of this practice.

27: If one of them that believe not biddeth you to a feast, and ye are disposed to go; whatsoever is set before you, eat, asking no question for conscience' sake.

A Christian is also free to accept an invitation to share a meal with an unbeliever in his home. 'As the sacrifices lost their religious character when sold in the market, so also at any private table they were to be regarded not as sacrifices, but as ordinary food, and might be eaten without scruple. The apostle did not prohibit the Christians from social intercourse with the heathen. If invited to their tables, they were at liberty to go' (Hodge).

28: But if any man say unto you, This hath been offered in sacrifice, eat not, for his sake that showed it, and for conscience' sake: 29a: conscience, I say, not thine own, but the other's;

But if someone, presumably a fellow–believer with an overscrupulous conscience, should say that the food provided at the meal had been offered in sacrifice, then it must be refused in conformity with the principle laid down in verse 24. It is precisely because his conscience *is* weak that he still calls it 'sacrificial food' rather than 'idol-meat', for to him there is still something 'sacred' about it. He is not yet free of the old heathen superstitions. And so though the strong believer knows that he is free to eat it, he must abstain out of respect for his weaker brother's scruples.

29b: for why is my liberty judged by another's conscience?

30: If I partake with thankfulness, why am I evil spoken of for that for which I give thanks?

This does not mean that the strong Christian is called upon to forfeit his inner conviction concerning the lawfulness of eating such food, but he is voluntarily to restrict his use of this liberty of conscience in the interest of the weaker conscience of his brother. Thus in *principle* Paul is free to eat anything, for he has not surrendered his liberty at the behest of another's conscience; but in *practice* he avoids having his liberty denounced by refusing to exercise it in the presence of the weak. The very fact that he can give thanks for his food proves that he eats it with a clear conscience, but he will not allow that for which he gives thanks to wound the conscience of his weaker brethren.

31: Whether therefore ye eat, or drink, or whatsoever ye do, do all to the glory of God.

The whole discussion is now summed up in this comprehensive principle. Christians are not to consult their own inclinations, but in all their actions the paramount consideration must be the glory of God. It is only when this thought motivates the conduct of men that the best interests of others can be secured. For the showing of love to our neighbour is the corollary of our love to God.

32: Give no occasion of stumbling, either to Jews, or to Greeks, or to the church of God:

'Some may, indeed, *take* offence, namely, wrongfully; we are not to *give* offence. The former no Christian can avoid; the latter all Christians are to avoid' (Lenski). Paul speaks of three categories of existence: Jews, Greeks, and Christians, who are neither Jewish nor Gentile; for the church of God is a new society whose members form a 'new race' (so F. F. Bruce).

33: even as I also please all men in all things, not seeking mine own profit, but the profit of the many, that they may be saved.

Unlike the spiritually immature Corinthians Paul does not live for his own advantage, but for the benefit of the many. He seeks not to please himself, but to please all men in all things in order that they may be saved [9:22]. Of course he could not attain such a holy end by 'pleasing' men in sinful ways. He could never sacrifice principle [*Gal.* 2:5], descend to dissimulation [*Gal.* 2:13, 14], or compromise the truth [*Acts* 20:27], in the interests of gaining more souls for Christ!

11:1: Be ye imitators of me, even as I also am of Christ.

Although Paul did not know Christ after the flesh [*2 Cor.* 5:16], it would be quite wrong to suggest that he took no interest in the earthly life of Jesus. In Romans 15:2f. he directly proposes the example of Christ for the imitation of his readers, and here he urges his own example insofar as he follows that of Christ.

'It is a very important trait, that Paul feels himself to be an imitator of Christ in his practical conduct. He could not say and be this, unless he had a living concrete picture of the ethical personality of Jesus' (J. Weiss).

CHAPTER ELEVEN

Paul next corrects disorders in the worship of the church. He deals first with the decorum and dress of women. It appears that in their new-found freedom they had put off the veil which was then the recognized symbol of their subordination to man. But he insists that equality in grace does not set aside the requirements of the social order which even nature teaches us to respect [verses 2–16]. Secondly, he rebukes them for their disgraceful abuse of the Lord's Supper. This divine ordinance was profaned by their dissension, excesses, and selfishness. To rectify these disorders which had brought grievous judgments upon the church, he reminds them of the nature and purpose of this sacred meal, and warns against the partaking of it unworthily [verses 17–34].

Verse 1 has been placed at the end of the previous chapter where it properly belongs.

2: Now I praise you that ye remember me in all things, and hold fast the traditions, even as I delivered them to you.

This new section of the Epistle is prefaced with a word of praise, though this is later balanced with a word of rebuke [verse 17]. Paul gladly acknowledges that in general the congregation at Corinth remains obedient to the precepts which he had handed down to them. The early church received the oral tradition of the apostles with the same respect that she was to accord to their written testimony, because she recognized in both the voice of her risen and exalted Lord [11:23, 15:2; 2 Thess. 2: 15]. 'We shall search in vain for any suggestion that one possesses a greater measure of inspiration than the other. The one and only source of the teaching was Christ; from him the stream flows, Scripture and "tradition" are blended in one great luminous river of truth, and do not separate into divergent streams till later times. They were at first two forms of the same thing. Both together constitute the Tradition, the Canon or Rule of Faith' (J. F. Bethune Baker cited by N. Geldenhuys, *Supreme Authority*, p. 116).

3: But I would have you know, that the head of every man is Christ; and the head of the woman is the man; and the head of Christ is God.

But Paul wishes the Corinthians to know that though all men are not members of the body of which Christ is the head, every man whether he knows it or not is nevertheless subject to the *headship* or government of Christ. In a less absolute sense every woman is by order of creation under the headship of man, and the equality of the sexes in the realm of grace does not abolish this distinction between them when they become subject to church order and discipline. The Christian women of Corinth will find this truth easier to accept if they remember that as Mediator even Christ himself is subject to God. 'God is the Head of Christ, not in respect of his essence and divine nature, but in respect of his office as Mediator; as the man is the head of the woman, not in respect of a different and more excellent essence and nature, (for they are both of the same nature,) but in respect of office and place, as God hath set him over the woman' (Poole).

4: Every man praying or prophesying, having his head covered dishonoureth his head.

It is not likely that men were actually covering their heads for worship in Corinth. Paul puts the case hypothetically to complete his argument [verse 5]. It is important to note that he first uses 'head' in the literal sense, and then metaphorically of Christ's headship [verse 3]. 'The man that shames his natural head shames also his spiritual head; that is, he that shames himself by wearing a symbol of subjection to the woman, shames Christ, to whom alone God has subjected him' (Edwards).

5: But every woman praying or prophesying with her head unveiled dishonoureth her head; for it is one and the same thing as if she were shaven.

This verse does not necessarily sanction women speaking in church, 'even though possessing miraculous gifts; but simply records what took place at Corinth, reserving the censure till 14:34, 35. Even those "prophesying" women were to exercise their gift rather in other times and places than the public congregation' (Fausset) [Acts 2:18; 21:9].

For it is one and the same thing as if she were shaven: In Greece only immoral women, so numerous in Corinth, went about unveiled; slave-women wore the shaven head which was also a punishment of the adulteress; 'with these the Christian woman who emancipates herself from becoming restraints of dress, is in effect identified. To shave the head is to carry out thoroughly its unveiling, to remove nature's as well as fashion's covering [verse 15]' (Findlay).

6: For if a woman is not veiled, let her also be shorn: but if it is a shame to a woman to be shorn or shaven, let her be veiled.

These imperatives are not to be understood literally; they only show what consistency requires. Let the woman who discards the veil take her defiance of modesty to its logical conclusion. 'If a woman prefers a bare head, she should remove her hair; womanly feeling forbids the latter, then it should forbid the former, for the like shame attaches to both' (Findlay).

7: For a man indeed ought not to have his head veiled, forasmuch as he is the image and glory of God: but the woman is the glory of the man.

Although Genesis 1:27 clearly states that God's image in 'man' includes both sexes, the fact that woman mediately derives her being from man means that she only partakes in the image of God through him [verses 8, 9]. Hence Paul does not here add that woman is the 'image' of man; she is not man's reflection, but his counterpart. 'It follows that he who degrades a woman sullies his manhood, and is the worst enemy of his race; the respect shown to women is the measure and safeguard of human dignity' (Findlay).

8: For the man is not of the woman; but the woman of the man: 9: for neither was the man created for the woman; but the woman for the man:

Paul insists that the facts of creation cannot be reversed or set aside. Man did not take his origin from woman, but woman from man [*Gen.* 2:21–23]; he was not created for her, but she for him [*Gen.* 2:18]. Scripture thus confronts the militant supporters of 'Women's Lib' with 'the fact that the origin and *raison d'être* of woman are to be found in man' (H. Schlier, *TDNT,* vol. 3, p. 679).

10: for this cause ought the woman to have a sign of authority on her head, because of the angels.

Since woman's subjection to man is a divine appointment, she is to cover her head in recognition of the place assigned to her in the created order, and this *veiling* is the *sign* of her 'authority' to approach God in public worship. Paul adds that this is to be done 'because of the angels'. As God's good angels are present when Christians meet together for worship great care must be taken not to offend them by any impropriety [cf. 4:9; *Heb.* 1:14]. Such an offence would occur if women discarded the veil and thereby displayed their disregard for the station given to them by their creation.

11: Nevertheless, neither is the woman without the man, nor the man without the woman, in the Lord.

12: For as the woman is of the man, so is the man also by the woman; but all things are of God.

But though man has been given the superior place, this gives him no right to regard woman as an inferior being, for the sexes are interdependent and neither is complete without the other. The phrase 'in the Lord' points to the sphere where woman's rights are realized as nowhere in heathenism [cf. *Gal.* 3:28; *Eph.* 5:28]. 'As woman was formed *out of* man, even so is man born *by means of* woman; but all things (including both man and woman) are *from* God as their source [*Rom.* 11:36; *2 Cor.* 5:18]. They depend each on the other, and both on Him' (Fausset).

13: Judge ye in yourselves: is it seemly that a woman pray unto God unveiled?

'This is an appeal to their own sense of propriety. The apostle often recognizes the intuitive judgments of the mind as authoritative [*Rom.* 1:32, 3:8]. The constitution of our nature being derived from God, the laws which he has impressed upon it are as much a revelation from him as any other possible communication of his will. And to deny this, is to deny the possibility of all knowledge' (Hodge).

14: Doth not even nature itself teach you, that, if a man have long hair, it is a dishonour to him?

15: But if a woman have long hair, it is a glory to her: for her hair is given her for a covering.

'Nature' here means 'a sense of what is seemly springing from a real distinction in the constitution of things' (Edwards). Natural sentiment is reflected by universal custom. Long hair is felt to be a 'dishonour' to man because it is a contradiction of his manliness, whereas it is the glory of a woman: what is discreditable in the one is delightful in the other' (Findlay). Thus what has been given to woman as a natural covering ought to teach her the propriety of donning the veil in worship.

16: But if any man seemeth to be contentious, we have no such custom, neither the churches of God.

Paul refuses to discuss the matter further with the man who is so contentious as to dispute his conclusion. 'If, after all that the apostle has advanced in maintenance of the modest distinction between the sexes, any one is still minded to debate, he must be put down by *authority* – that of Paul himself and his colleagues, supported by universal Christendom; cf. 14:33, 37ff.' (Findlay).

17: But in giving you this charge, I praise you not, that ye come together not for the better but for the worse.

'This charge' is more likely to refer to the preceding injunction than to what follows. Paul cannot praise them for allowing the women to worship with unveiled heads, but the disorder with which he is about to deal is far more serious, for it means that they 'come together not for the better but for the worse'. 'That is, your public assemblies are so conducted that evil rather than good results. The censure is general, embracing all the grounds of complaint which are specified in this and the following chapters' (Hodge).

18: For first of all, when ye come together in the church, I hear that divisions exist among you; and I partly believe it.

Here Paul begins to press charges against the Corinthians, but though his indictment extends as far as 14:40 there is no 'secondly' forthcoming. He has heard from a reliable but unnamed source that when the church meets together for worship there are 'divisions' among the members.

Its *outward* congregational unity is marred by the unhappy *inward* divisions which separate clique from clique. The apostle seems to be referring to social discrimination rather than to party-spirit, as in 1:10. For in verse 22 the rich are rebuked for refusing to share their food with the poorer members of the church. Paul is reluctant to believe all he has heard to their disadvantage in this matter, but what he is forced to believe is enough to earn his sternest censure. 'There may be schism, where there is no separation of communion. Persons may come together in the same church, and sit down at the same table of the Lord, and yet be schismatics. Uncharitableness, alienation of affection, especially if it grows up to discord, and feuds, and contentions, constitute schism' (Matthew Henry).

19: For there must be also factions among you, that they that are approved may be made manifest among you.

'To the simple divisions which arise from personal preferences or aversions, Paul foresees that there will succeed divisions of a far more profound nature, founded on opposite conceptions of Christian truth. He believes what is told him of the first, because he even expects the second. There will arise among them false doctrines, *heresies*, according to the meaning which the Greek term has taken in later ecclesiastical language, and thence will follow much graver disruptions than the present divisions . . . The Second Epistle to the Corinthians shows in how brief a period this anticipation of the apostle was realized' (Godet). [cf. *Matt.* 18:7; *Acts* 20:29, 30]

That they that are approved may be made manifest among you: Nevertheless there is a divine purpose fulfilled in these heresies which 'are a magnet attracting unsound and unsettled minds, and leaving genuine believers to stand out "approved" by their constancy' (Findlay). Thus those who are approved of God are made known to men [*2 Thess.* 2:11, 12].

20: When therefore ye assemble yourselves together, it is not possible to eat the Lord's supper:

This sets forth the precise nature of the apostle's censure. 'The disorders at Corinth are so serious that when the church meets for the sacrament it is not *the Lord's* supper that is eaten. The disorders have given it a different character. It is no longer the Lord's' (Morris).

21: for in your eating each one taketh before other his own supper; and one is hungry, and another is drunken.

The loveless abuse of the Love–feast (*Agape*) in Corinth was a blatant denial of the fellowship which this common meal was intended to express, for when each selfishly ate his own supper it became morally impossible to eat the Lord's supper. 'Of all imaginable schisms the most shocking: hunger and intoxication side by side, at what is supposed to be the Table of the Lord! This is indeed "meeting for the worse"' (Findlay).

22: What, have ye not houses to eat and to drink in? or despise ye the church of God, and put them to shame that have not? What shall I say to you? shall I praise you? In this I praise you not.

Paul now ironically enquires whether such surfeiting means that the rich have no homes in which to eat and drink, or is it rather that in shaming the poor in this way they are showing their contempt for the congregation *of God*? [*James* 1:9,10; 2:2–9]. Can he praise them for such conduct? 'In this I praise you not!' His restrained response is heavy with blame.

23a: For I received of the Lord that which also I delivered unto you,

For the tradition which I handed on to you came to me from the Lord himself (NEB): 'Paul means by this tradition, without doubt, the message that he had received from the original witnesses. Nevertheless he writes that he has for himself (i.e., as apostle) received the deliverances "from the Lord". He means specifically the ascended Lord. The testimony of the eyewitnesses is for him as apostle the delivered word of the glorified Lord. And as such he himself delivers it to the church of Corinth' (H. Ridderbos, 'The Canon of the New Testament' in *Revelation and the Bible*, p. 194). Oscar Cullmann also points out that the words 'from the Lord' can 'quite well mean a direct communication from the Lord, without it being necessary to think of a vision or to exclude intermediaries through whom the Lord himself transmits the "tradition" . . . (for) it is the united testimony of all the apostles which constitutes the Christian "tradition", in which the "Lord" himself is at work' (*The Early Church*, p. 68) [*1 Cor.* 15: 11; *Gal.* 1: 16].

23b: that the Lord Jesus in the night in which he was betrayed took bread;

24: and when he had given thanks, he brake it, and said, This is my body, which is for you: this do in remembrance of me.

25: In like manner also the cup, after supper, saying, this cup is the new covenant in my blood: this do, as often as ye drink it, in remembrance of me.

Paul begins his account of the Lord's Supper by reminding the thoughtless Corinthians of the poignant fact that Jesus appointed it on the very night of his betrayal by Judas [cf. *Matt.* 26:26f.; *Mark* 14:22f.; *Luke* 22:17f.]. After the Lord had offered a prayer of thanksgiving for the bread, he broke it in token of his bruised and broken body [*Isa.* 53:5]. 'The *breaking* of the bread involves its *distribution*, and reproves the Corinthians at the love feast: "every one taketh before other his own supper"' (Fausset).

This is my body, which is for you: The visible presence of Jesus made it impossible for those who were present at the institution of the Supper literally to identify the bread with his body. 'Jesus takes the bread which is before him, and presenting it to his disciples, he gives it to them as the *symbol* of his body which is about to be given up for them on the cross, and to become the means of their salvation; the verb *be* is taken in the same sense as that in which we say, as we look at a portrait: it is so and so!' (Godet).

This do in remembrance of me: As the celebration of the Passover vividly recalled Israel's historic redemption from the land of bondage, so Christians are bidden to keep on doing this as the means of bringing before their minds the price once paid by Christ to ransom them from their slavery to sin [cf. 5:7].

'The words of Christ contain two distinct but connected ideas. The one implies His presence in the sacrament: "this is my body; this is my blood." The other implies His absence: "in remembrance of me." Both meet in the apostle's word, "communion" [cf. 10:16], which involves, first, that the communicant appropriates Christ, and, second, that the instrument of this appropriation is conscious, voluntary faith. Appropriation of Christ necessitates His real presence; faith implies His equally real absence' (Edwards).

This cup is the new covenant in my blood: The word 'covenant' points to a unilateral disposition made by God in favour of man, and is not to be understood in terms of a mutual agreement made between two parties of equal standing. Christ made the Mosaic covenant 'old' when he referred to his death as the fulfilment of Jeremiah's prophecy of the 'new covenant' [*Jer.* 31:31–34].

The shedding of blood was the basis upon which the distinctive blessings promised under both covenants were bestowed, but the first covenant became 'old' because it rested upon the repeated offering of typical sacrifices which could never take away sins, whereas the second remains 'new' because its gracious provisions have been forever secured by Christ's one real and final atonement for the sins of his people [*Heb.* 9:18–10:14].

This do, as often as ye drink it, in remembrance of me: 'The Lord's supper brings to our *remembrance* Christ's sacrifice once-for-all for the full and final *remission of sins.* Not "do this for a *memorial* of me", as if it were a *memorial sacrifice* . . . a *reminding* the Father of his Son's sacrifice. Nay, it is for our *remembrance* of it, not to *remind* him' (Fausset).

26: For as often as ye eat this bread, and drink the cup, ye proclaim the Lord's death till he come.

This begins Paul's own exposition of the significance of the Supper. In reminding the Corinthians of the solemnity of the occasion it recalls, he rebukes them for the irreverent manner in which they met together to celebrate it. 'The pathos and glory of the Table of the Lord were alike lost on the Corinthians' (Findlay).

For as often as ye eat this bread, and drink the cup: As J. Behm points out, Paul never speaks of eating the body or drinking the blood of Christ, but rather points to the repetition of the whole act by which believers are united with their Lord in intimate table fellowship, so that they participate in the fruit of his work on their behalf. 'The wholly realistic but spiritual and historical understanding of the Lord's Supper which we find in Paul is equally distinct both from a spiritualising which makes the sacrament a mere symbol and from a materialising which sanctifies things and deifies nature' (*TDNT*, vol. 3, p. 740).

Ye proclaim the Lord's death till he come: Paul places the emphasis on the words by which the Lord's death is proclaimed in the Supper, and shows that this testimony to his finished work is to continue 'till he come'. The sacrament therefore not only recalls what was achieved by Christ's death but also looks forward to his return in glory. 'The church crying *Maranatha* testifies to the living, victorious Lord; it not only waits on him but waits for him' (Moffatt) [cf. 16:22].

27: Wherefore whosoever shall eat the bread or drink the cup of the Lord in an unworthy manner, shall be guilty of the body and the blood of the Lord.

Paul solemnly warns the Corinthians that whoever treats the Supper of the Lord as his own supper profanes this means of grace and puts himself alongside those who crucified Christ [verses 21, 29]. The verse condemns the Romish practice of withholding the cup from the laity. 'How could anyone be guilty of drinking the cup of the Lord in an unworthy manner if the cup were not given to him? This is clearly one more instance in which the Church of Rome has taken it upon herself to alter the commands of the gospel' (L. Boettner, *Roman Catholicism*, p. 236).

28: But let a man prove himself, and so let him eat of the bread, and drink of the cup.

29: For he that eateth and drinketh, eateth and drinketh judgment unto himself, if he discern not the body.

Paul says 'Let a man test himself'. This means he must not come to this table in a spirit which is unworthy of it. Let him come with love towards his fellow-believers, so that he can do this in remembrance of the Lord. Such self-examination is necessary because the man who fails to discern the sacred character of this meal, so far from furthering his salvation actually eats and drinks to his own condemnation (not 'damnation' as in AV). Paul refers to the Lord's *once for all sacrificed body,* discerned by the soul in faithful receiving; not present in the elements themselves' (Fausset) [*Acts* 3:21].

30: For this cause many among you are weak and sickly, and not a few sleep.

Paul traces the prevalence of sickness and death among the Corinthians to this failure to discern 'the body', and thus warns them against continuing to profane the Lord's table. 'The mortality at Corinth began at God's house, and that for unworthy communicating. God will be sanctified of all that draw near to him. He loves to be acquainted with men in the walks of their obedience, and yet he takes state upon him in his ordinances, and will be served like himself, or we shall hear from him. What manner of men therefore ought we to be that come so near to God in this holy ordinance?' (Trapp) [*1 Pet.* 4:17].

31: But if we discerned ourselves, we should not be judged.

32: But when we are judged, we are chastened of the Lord, that we may not be condemned with the world.

If the Corinthians would but examine themselves, so that they came to the Lord's Supper in the right spirit, they would not incur these disciplinary judgments [cf. 5:5]. For though they are judged for their sinful conduct, yet this is done in order that they should not have to undergo the sharp verdict of *condemnation* with the world in the last judgment.

33: Wherefore, my brethren, when ye come together to eat, wait one for another.

34: If any man is hungry, let him eat at home; that your coming together be not unto judgment. And the rest will I set in order whensoever I come.

In conclusion Paul appeals to his brethren not to fracture their fellowship by each going 'ahead with his own meal' [verse 21], but to wait for one another. And if any man is too hungry to wait for the others, he should satisfy his appetite at home. Such love feasts 'were not meals to satiate the bodily appetites, but were for a higher and holier purpose: let the hungry take off the edge of his hunger at home: see verse 22' (Alford).

And the rest will I set in order whensoever I come: Matters of less pressing importance concerning the administration of the Lord's Supper could be left until Paul's next visit to Corinth whenever that might be. Since no one can possibly know what things he then intended to set in order it is in vain that Rome appeals to this text to justify her unwritten 'apostolic' traditions! 'If the fixing of the canon (of Scripture) had been carried out by the Church on the tacit assumption that its teaching-office, that is, the *subsequent* traditions, should be set alongside this canon with an *equal normative authority,* the reason for the creation of the canon would be unintelligible' (Oscar Cullmann, *The Early Church,* p. 92).

CHAPTER TWELVE

On the question of spiritual gifts Paul lays down the principle that only those which glorify Christ are of divine origin [verses 1–3]. It is the Holy Spirit who assigns the various gifts of wisdom, knowledge, faith, and tongues to each member for the good of the whole body to which he belongs [verses 4–11]. For in the church as in the human body, every member is useful and necessary, and so none is to be despised. The Corinthians are to recognize that God has set the individual members in their places to form one body as it pleased him. And since this unity involves mutual dependence it must promote mutual love [verses 12–26]. Clearly not all are apostles, teachers, and speakers in tongues, for God's gifts are distributed as he pleases; yet they should earnestly desire his best gifts for use in his service [verses 27–31].

1: Now concerning spiritual gifts, brethren, I would not have you ignorant.

The words suggest that Paul's discussion of the miraculous or charismatic gifts of the Spirit is in response to a question put to him by the Corinthians [cf. 7:1]. He wishes them to understand the common origin and aim of these supernatural endowments, so that they would be able to distinguish between the true and false claimants to the possession of them.

2: Ye know that when ye were Gentiles ye were led away unto those dumb idols, howsoever ye might be led.

Paul here recognizes that religious ecstasy is not a distinctively Christian phenomenon. It is because heathenism also has its ecstatics that a criterion is necessary to prevent the Corinthians in their enthusiasm for these extraordinary manifestations from receiving every ecstatic utterance as the work of the Spirit [cf. the later warning of *1 John* 4:1–3]. Paul says in effect: 'In your pagan days you were helplessly led astray. In your devotion to dumb idols you experienced a form of demonic frenzy which carried you away, for then you had no fixed principle to guide you!' [cf. 10:19ff.].

3: Wherefore I make known unto you, that no man speaking in the Spirit of God saith, Jesus is anathema; and no man can say, Jesus is Lord, but in the Holy Spirit.

Paul thus wishes the Corinthians to grasp the fact that not every form of religious ecstasy is inspired by the Holy Spirit, for no man who is speaking under his influence could possibly say, 'ANATHEMA JESUS', i.e. 'Jesus is accursed!' It would appear that a member of the congregation in Corinth had been guilty of giving utterance to this blasphemy under the mistaken impression that he was making a contribution to the worship of the church.

But since God has already made Jesus LORD, and the Holy Spirit has been given specifically to glorify Jesus as LORD, it is evident that *He* cannot move men to say anything which detracts in the least degree from this DIVINE LORDSHIP [Rom. 10:9]. On the contrary, it is only through the gracious ministry of the Spirit that any man can say that 'Jesus is LORD', for such supernatural confession of faith requires nothing less than a supernatural revelation of its truth [*Matt.* 16:16, 17].

'In stating this first negative criterion, the apostle therefore means to say to the Corinthians: However ecstatic in form, or profound in matter, may be a spiritual manifestation, tongue, prophecy, or doctrine, if it tends to degrade Jesus, to make him an impostor or a man worthy of the divine wrath, if it does violence in any way to his holiness, you may be sure the inspiring breath of such a discourse is not that of God's Spirit' (Godet).

4: Now there are diversities of gifts, but the same Spirit.

5: And there are diversities of ministrations, and the same Lord.

6: And there are diversities of workings, but the same God, who worketh all things in all.

There are distributions of gifts, but the same Spirit; there are distributions of services, and the same Lord; and there are distributions of operations, but the same God who operates all things in all men (Barrett): Paul next corrects the Corinthians for failing to discern the divine unity of purpose in the distribution of spiritual gifts among them. This differentiation had caused rivalry and division in the church, but boasting and jealousy are alike excluded by the realization that the disposition of these gifts is made in accordance with the sovereign will of the Triune God [verse 11]. 'Uniformity of experience and service is not to be expected; unity lies ultimately in the Spirit who gives, the Lord who is served, the God who is at work – the Trinitarian formula is the more impressive because it seems to be artless and unconscious. Paul found it natural to think and write in these terms' (Barrett) [*2 Cor.* 13:14; *Eph.* 4:4–6].

7: But to each one is given the manifestation of the Spirit to profit withal.

To each is given the manifestation of the Spirit for the common good (RSV): Moreover, in the communication to each of a particular gift the Spirit manifests himself for the benefit of all believers. 'When, therefore, the gifts of God, natural or supernatural, are perverted as a means of self–exaltation or aggrandizement it is a sin against their giver, as well as against those for whose benefit they were intended' (Hodge).

8: For to one is given through the Spirit the word of wisdom; and to another the word of knowledge, according to the same Spirit:

9: to another faith, in the same Spirit; and to another gifts of healings, in the one Spirit; 10: and to another workings of miracles; and to another prophecy; and to another discernings of spirits: to another divers kinds of tongues; and to another the interpretation of tongues:

All the gifts listed here were supernatural endowments of the Spirit which were as temporary in their manifestation as was the apostolic office itself; 'the extraordinary gifts belonged to the extraordinary office and showed themselves only in connection with its activities' (B. B. Warfield, 'The Cessation of the Charismata', *Counterfeit Miracles*, p. 23). Hence it is hardly surprising that today we are unable exactly to determine the nature of these gifts and how they were exercised in the apostolic church. Paul begins with the highest of these gifts and proceeds to the least useful of them. Findlay makes the following helpful classification, using 1 Corinthians 14:14–20 as the basis of this discrimination:

I. Gifts which exhibit the Spirit working *through* the mind: The word of wisdom and the word of knowledge.

II. Gifts which exhibit the Spirit working *in distinction from* the mind: Faith, Healing, Miracles, Prophecy, and Discerning of spirits.

III. Gifts which exhibit the Spirit working *in supersession of* the mind: Tongues and their interpretation (the omission of these from the lists of gifts in *Rom.* 12:3–8 and *Eph.* 4:7–11 is significant and should not be overlooked).

1–2. *The utterance of wisdom* and *the utterance of knowledge* (RSV): According to James Dunn, Paul here rebukes Corinthian pride in 'wisdom' and 'knowledge' by confining the gift to the *actual utterance* which reveals some aspect of wisdom and knowledge, and so serves to build up the community (*Jesus and the Spirit*, p. 221). Since these gifts are placed first, a comparison with verse 28 would seem to suggest that they both belonged to the apostolic office; and if the first characterized their inspired proclamation of the gospel [cf. chs. 1–2], the second would presumably describe their role as the inspired teachers of the church.

3. *Faith:* This is not saving faith, for that is not a charismatic gift but is common to every Christian; the reference is to wonder–working faith [cf. 13:2].

4–5. *Gifts of healing and the working of miracles:* That both these gifts were a marked feature of the ministry of Paul and the other apostles is amply illustrated in Dr Luke's history of the early church [for 'healings': see *Acts* 4:22, 30; 9:40; 19:11, 12; 28:7–9; and cf. *2 Cor.* 12:12]. With regard to 'miracles', Calvin inclined to the view that these were the powers by which the apostles subdued demons and executed judgment upon hypocrites or evil–doers [cf. *Acts* 5:1–11, 13:11, 16:18].

6. *Prophecy:* Until the canon of Scripture was complete, the New Testament prophets exercised an important ministry in the primitive church [14:29–32; *Eph.* 4:11]. Prophecy, while employing the intellect, 'has a deeper seat; it is no branch of wisdom or knowledge as though coming by rational insight, but an unveiling of hidden things of God realized through a peculiar clearness and intensity of *faith*, and is in line therefore with the miraculous powers preceding; hence "the prophet" is regularly distinguished from "the teacher"' (Findlay).

7. *Discernings of spirits:* The 'Lord graciously provided for his churches, that some among them should be enabled in an extraordinary manner to discern and judge of them who pretended unto extraordinary actings of the Spirit. And upon the ceasing of extraordinary gifts really given from God, the gift also of discerning spirits ceased, and we are left unto the *word alone* for the trial of any that shall pretend unto them' (John Owen, 'Discourse on the Holy Spirit', *Works*, vol. 3, p. 35).

8–9. *Divers kinds of tongues and the interpretation of tongues:* The fact that these spectacular gifts are completely ignored in the later Epistles suggests that even in the apostolic period they were soon displaced by a more disciplined form of worship which was offered according to recognized 'canons' (cf. Ralph P. Martin, *Worship in the Early Church*, p. 137). It is clear from 14:14–16 that the man who speaks in tongues addresses God under the influence of profound emotion, 'which causes him to *pray, sing* or *give thanks* in an ecstatic language unintelligble to every one who does not share the same emotion, and to which his own understanding, his *nous*, remains a stranger' (Godet).

The interpretation of these mysterious utterances therefore also called for a special gift from the Spirit who had inspired them. Paul forbade tongue-speaking in church unless someone with the gift of interpretation were present, for otherwise the congregation would remain unedified by it [14:19, 27, 28].

'The extraordinary gifts of the Spirit, such as the gift of tongues, of miracles, of prophecy, etc., are called extraordinary, because they are such as are not given in the ordinary course of God's providence. They are not bestowed in the way of God's ordinary providential dealing with his children, but only on extraordinary occasions, as they were bestowed on the prophets and apostles to enable them to reveal the mind and will of God before the canon of Scripture was complete, and so on the primitive church, in order to the founding and establishing of it in the world. But since the canon of Scripture has been completed, and the Christian church fully founded and established, these extraordinary gifts have ceased. But the ordinary gifts of the Spirit are such as are continued to the church of God throughout all ages; such gifts as are granted in conviction and conversion, and such as appertain to the building up of the saints in holiness and comfort' (Jonathan Edwards, *Charity and Its Fruits*, pp. 29–30).

11: but all these worketh the one and the same Spirit, dividing to each one severally even as he will.

All these varied gifts are the work of the *one* Spirit, who suits them to their recipients by individually distributing that which is appropriate to each one in accordance with his own wise will. Paul's insistence upon the sovereign discrimination of the Spirit in the bestowal of spiritual gifts is directed against the envy and pride which these 'inequalities' had provoked among the factious Corinthians [cf. 4:7].

12: For as the body is one, and hath many members, and all the members of the body, being many, are one body; so also is Christ.

As one life flows through all the members of the human body, so all the members of the mystical body of Christ 'are instinct with one personality' (Edwards). Paul's elaboration of this bold figure in the following verses is intended to teach the Corinthians that as the healthy functioning of the natural body demands the harmonious working together of all its constituent parts, so it is also with the church which is the spiritual body of Christ. The unexpected substitution of 'Christ' for that body which exists only in virtue of its relationship to him, does not identify the church with the Divine-human person of Christ' but rather points all believers to him as the common source of their spiritual life. It 'shows how realistic was Paul's conception of believers as subsisting "in Christ", and raises the idea of Church-unity to its highest point' (Findlay).

13: For in one Spirit were we all baptized into one body, whether Jews or Greeks, whether bond or free; and were all made to drink of one Spirit.

Paul can furnish an additional proof of the oneness of the many 'in Christ' by an appeal to the experience of the Corinthians. It was because they were all baptized in one Spirit that those who were once separated from one another by differences of race and rank now formed one body. In representing the Spirit as the element in which this baptism took place, the apostle refers to the spiritual reality of which their baptism in water was the symbol. This verse therefore makes it 'difficult to resist the conclusion that the baptism of the Spirit is not a second and subsequent experience, enjoyed by some Christians, but the initial experience enjoyed by all' (John Stott, *Baptism and Fullness*, p. 39).

And were all made to drink of one Spirit: There is of course no reference to the Lord's Supper, for the verb again points to a *past event*, not a repeated act . . . The two aorists describe the same primary experience under opposite figures (the former of which is *acted* in baptism), as an outward affusion and an inward absorption; the Corinthians were at once *immersed in* (cf. "we were buried with", *Rom.* 6:4) and *saturated with* the Spirit; the second figure supplements the first: cf. *Rom.* 5:5; Titus 3:5,6' (Findlay).

14: For the body is not one member, but many.

Paul is now ready to develop the figure of the body in the interest of demonstrating that each member of it exists for the good of the whole [cf. verse 7]. He insists that the various differences between the members are purely functional; they are not qualitative or 'spiritual'. Hence when all are necessary, there is no need for any member to feel inferior [verses 15–20], and no cause for any member to feel superior [verses 21–25].

15: If the foot shall say, Because I am not the hand, I am not of the body; it is not therefore not of the body.

16: And if the ear shall say, Because I am not the eye, I am not of the body; it is not therefore not of the body.

'In each case it is the inferior limb which grumbles, the hand being of more value than the foot, and the eye than the ear. And Chrysostom remarks that the foot contrasts itself with the hand rather than with the ear, because we do not envy those who are very much higher than ourselves so much as those who have got a little above us' (Robertson-Plummer).

It is not therefore not of the body: This is not a question as in the AV, but an emphatic statement. 'The foot or ear does not sever itself from the body by distinguishing itself from the hand or eye; its pettish argument leaves it where it was' (Findlay).

17: If the whole body were an eye, where were the hearing? If the whole were hearing, where were the smelling?

This is a graphic way of saying that the very existence of the body *as a body* entirely depends upon each member fulfilling the function for which it was designed. So since every member is needed by the body, none should belittle its own role or covet that of another. In other words, our unity in *grace* is expressed through a diversity of *gifts*.

18: But now hath God set the members each one of them in the body, even as it pleased him.

The verse marks a return to reality, for every sane person knows that the human body did not come into being by a spontaneous process of self–development! Each member was given its particular place and function within the body by the creative act of God. 'The eye did not give itself the power of vision, nor the ear its ability to discriminate sounds. Each member occupies in the body the position which God has seen fit to assign it, and which is the most conducive to the good of the whole' (Hodge).

19: And if they were all one member, where were the body?

20: But now they are many members, but one body.

If the whole were one member, it would be a monstrosity and not a body! Every member is important because all are required to enable the body to function as an organic unity. 'In verse 18 the apostle represents the various members as being, so to speak, *inserted* in the body; in verse 19 he represents the body itself as having no organic existence without its members' (Edwards).

21: And the eye cannot say to the hand, I have no need of thee: or again the head to the feet, I have no need of you.

'Up to this point Paul has been showing what the duty of the less honourable members is, viz. to give their services to the body, and not to be envious of the more outstanding members. Now, on the other hand, he is instructing the worthier members not to despise the inferior ones, for they cannot do without them. The eye is a superior part to the hand, yet it cannot treat it with disdain, or scoff at it as a useless thing' (Calvin).

22: Nay, much rather, those members of the body which seem to be more feeble are necessary:

'Nay more, the instant we reflect, we are convinced of the absolute *necessity* of the members which seem to play an altogether secondary part, more secondary even than the hand or the feet. These *weak* parts are no doubt the sensitive organs which are protected by their position in the body, the lungs and stomach, for example, on which, above all, the life and health of the whole body depend' (Godet).

23: and those parts of the body, which we think to be less honourable, upon these we bestow more abundant honour; and our uncomely parts have more abundant comeliness; 24: whereas our comely parts have no need:

'To bestow honour is to put on a covering for the sake of adornment, so that the parts whose exposure would be a shameful thing are decently hidden' (Calvin).

24b: but God tempered the body together, giving more abundant honour to that part which lacked;

25: that there should be no schism in the body; but that the members should have the same care one for another.

In creation God blended together the members of the human body in order that there should be no division of interests within it. This equality was secured when he assigned indispensable functions to its humbler members, for in so doing he bestowed more abundant honour on those parts which were naturally lacking in it. Thus all the members have the same mutual interest in caring for one another, namely, the well–being of that body to which they all belong. Paul is confident that the contentious Corinthians will have no difficulty in discerning the drift of his argument.

26. And whether one member suffereth, all the members suffer with it; or one member is honoured, all the members rejoice with it.

Paul finds a further proof of the unity of the body in the mutual suffering and rejoicing of its members. As to the first, it is evident that when a finger is in pain the whole body suffers with it. And Chrysostom provides a fine illustration of the second: 'When the head is crowned, the whole man feels itself glorified; when the mouth speaks, the eyes laugh and are filled with gladness'. But in the church at Corinth this law of sympathy was conspicuous by its absence. Paul's analogy shows 'how unnatural, abnormal, unreasonable, outrageous it is for the members of the spiritual body of Christ to act in contravention of the very constitution of their own body' (Lenski).

27: Now ye are the body of Christ, and severally members thereof.

Paul concludes the argument with this comprehensive statement. The Corinthians must understand that they sustain the same kind of relation to Christ as that which has been set forth in the preceding analogy. For as they all collectively form the body of Christ, so each is individually a member of it. 'None can claim to be the whole, but none is excluded' (Morris).

28: And God hath set some in the church, first apostles, secondly prophets, thirdly teachers, then miracles, then gifts of healings, helps, governments, divers kinds of tongues.

This begins the apostle's application of the teaching. Just as in the case of the human body, the position of every member within the spiritual organism rests solely upon the appointment of God. The enumeration, first, secondly, thirdly, distinguishes the three outstanding forms of service from five other less useful functions (so Hans

Conzelmann). 'Man may appoint men to offices for which they have not the necessary gifts, but God never does, any more than he ordains the foot to see or the hand to hear. If any man, therefore, claims to be an apostle, or prophet, or worker of miracles, without the corresponding gift, he is a false pretender. In the early church, as now, there were many false apostles, i.e. those who claimed the honour and authority of the office without its gifts' (Hodge).

1–2. *Apostles, prophets:* As in Ephesians 4:11 these are placed first as being of the greatest importance, for it is upon the foundation of their testimony to Christ that the church is built [*Eph.* 2:20]. 'The distinguishing features of an apostle were, a commission directly from Christ: being a witness of the resurrection: special inspiration: supreme authority: accrediting by miracles: unlimited commission to preach and to found churches' (Marvin Vincent). The prophets of the New Testament period were also extraordinarily endowed and exercised an unrepeatable function in that they spoke under the direct inspiration of the Spirit, 'and prior to the completion of the canon they stood to those early churches in such a relation as the written oracles stand to us' (John Eadie).

3. *Teachers:* Whereas *apostles* were 'rendered infallible as teachers and rulers by the plenary gift of inspiration', and *prophets* 'spoke for God as the occasional organs of the Spirit'; *teachers* were 'uninspired men who had received the gift of teaching' (Hodge). Their function was therefore similar to present day ministers [cf. *Eph* 4:11: 'pastors and teachers'].

4–5. *Then miracles, then gifts of healings:* This placing is striking. Those who had these gifts are ranked below teachers, for though teaching is less dazzling than working miracles, it is more edifying. And the building up of the community is the supreme criterion of the usefulness of any gift [14:12, 26].

6–7. *Helps, governments:* Perhaps Paul refers to the ministry of mercy, and the task of church government. 'But when we boil it all down, we *know* nothing about these gifts or their possessors. They have vanished without leaving visible trace' (Leon Morris, *Spirit of the Living God*, p. 63).

8. *Divers kinds of tongues:* 'Last and least' (Edwards). The exciting gift upon which the Corinthians set such store is again firmly placed at the bottom of the list.

29: Are all apostles? are all prophets? are all teachers? are all workers of miracles ? 30: have all gifts of healings ? do all speak with tongues? do all interpret?

Evidently not! But evidently some in Corinth begged to differ from the apostle and thought otherwise. Hence his unwearied insistence upon the fact that all do not speak in tongues. 'All are not, nor can be, any more than all the body can be an ear, or an eye, or a hand, or a foot: you cannot expect, that in a governed body all should be governors; and you see by experience, that all cannot work miracles, prophesy, speak with tongues, or heal those that are sick' (Poole).

31a: But desire earnestly the greater gifts.

But though these gifts are sovereignly bestowed, Paul sees no inconsistency in urging the Corinthians to 'strive for the more valuable gifts' (Arndt-Gingrich). And it is in line with this exhortation that he urges them to seek the gift of prophecy rather than tongues [cf. 14:1–5, 19]. The second part of this verse is placed at the head of the next chapter which it serves to introduce.

CHAPTER THIRTEEN

Paul now proceeds to show the only way in which spiritual gifts can be fruitfully exercised. For without love the greatest gifts are worthless [verses 12:31b–13:3]. Love inspires and animates every grace, as it also excludes every form of sinful self-assertiveness [verses 4–7]. And in contrast to temporary gifts, love, with faith and hope, will last for ever [verses 8–13].

12:31b: And moreover a most excellent way show I unto you.

Paul is not drawing a contrast between love and gifts, but is showing that love is the only way in which gifts can be effectively exercised. For gifts are nothing without the grace of love. The Christian Way is pre-eminently the way of love. This is something which had been sadly overlooked in Corinth.

1: If I speak with the tongues of men and of angels but have not love, I am become sounding brass, or a clanging cymbal.

Paul here first mentions what he considers to be 'last and least' of the gifts because of the Corinthians' exaggerated estimate of its importance. 'According to the Corinthian measuring of the ecstatic life, *glossolalia* (or tongues) comes first as heavenly speech' (H. Conzelmann, *TDNT*, vol. 9, p. 405). He compares the loveless exercise of this gift to the meaningless sounds produced by a noisy gong or a clanging cymbal (instruments which were used to excite the worshippers in the ecstatic cults of Demeter and Cybele). For without love the most impressive display of religious emotion is of no value. And in his insistence upon this truth, Paul is not a whit behind the Apostle of love himself [cf. *1 John*; *Rom.* 13:8–10; *Gal.* 5:6; *1 Thess.* 3:12, etc.].

2: And if I have the gift of prophecy, and know all mysteries and all knowledge; and if I have all faith, so as to remove mountains, but have not love, I am nothing.

Paul further supposes that if he should have the gift of prophecy in such a degree that his inspired insight into all the mysteries of God were matched by an exhaustive intellectual knowledge of them, and that if he should have such wonder-working faith that he could remove mountains (an evident allusion to the Lord's teaching, cf. *Matt.* 17:20), yet even all these powers could not make up for the absence of love in the heart.

I am nothing: Paul's abrupt conclusion of his extended hypothesis brings out the utter destitution of the graceless man, notwithstanding his possession of the most extraordinary gifts.

'Salvation is promised to those who have the graces of the Spirit, but not to those who have merely the extraordinary gifts. Many may have these last, and yet go to hell. Judas Iscariot had them, and is gone to hell. And Christ tells us, that many who have them, will, at the last day, be bid to depart, as workers of iniquity [*Matt.* 7:22, 23]. And therefore, when he promised his disciples these extraordinary gifts, he bade them rejoice, not because the devils were subject to them, but because their names were written in heaven; intimating that the one might be, and yet not the other [*Luke* 10:17]. And this shows that the one is an infinitely greater blessing than the other, as it carries eternal life in it' (Jonathan Edwards).

3: And if I bestow all my goods to feed the poor, and if I give my body to be burned, but have not love, it profiteth me nothing.

Paul next exposes the vanity of every form of self–sacrifice which stops short of surrendering the self to God [*2 Cor.* 8:5]. 'Natural unrenewed men would be glad to have something to make up for the want of sincere love and real grace in their hearts; and many do great things to make up for the want of it, while others are willing to suffer great things. But, alas! how little does it all signify!' (Jonathan Edwards).

And if I should give away in doles of food all my possessions (Robertson-Plummer): Without love, even such a reckless disposition of one's property would not suffice to extinguish the egoism which prompted its seemingly selfless distribution.

And if I give my body to be burned, but have not love: Even to embrace a martyr's death is of no value 'if it is finally orientated to self rather than to God . . . Heroic religious achievements can become a false righteousness of works in which grace is no longer all in all. The desire for one's own cross in martyrdom can obscure the cross of Christ' (K. L. Schmidt, *TDNT,* vol. 3, p. 466).

It profiteth me nothing: This is here substituted for the 'I am nothing' of verse 2, 'because now it is not the worth of the person but of the acts which is in question. What was intended to assure me of salvation, has no value in the eyes of God, whenever the object of it becomes self, in the form of self-merit or of human glory. Love accepts only what is inspired by love' (Godet).

4: Love suffereth long, and is kind; love envieth not; love vaunteth not itself, is not puffed up, 5: doth not behave itself unseemly, seeketh not its own, is not provoked, taketh not account of evil; 6: rejoiceth not in unrighteousness, but rejoiceth with the truth; 7: beareth all things, believeth all things, hopeth all things, endureth all things.

The behaviour of Love is set forth in 'fifteen exquisite aphorisms', which says Findlay, 'run in seven couplets, arranged as one positive, four negative, and two positive verse-lines.' The paragraph then reads:

> *'Love suffers long, shows kindness.*
> *Love envies not, makes no self-display;*

> *Is not puffed up, behaves not unseemly;*
> *Seeks not her advantage, is not embittered;*
> *Imputes not evil, rejoices not at wrong,*
> *but shares in the joy of the truth.*
> *All things she tolerates, all things she believes;*
> *All things she hopes for, all things she endures.'*

This description of love is directly opposed to the spirit in which the Corinthians exercised their gifts. 'The lyric is thus a lancet. Paul is probing for some of the diseases that were weakening the body spiritual at Corinth' (Moffatt).

1. *Love suffereth long:* 'Love to God disposes us to *imitate* him, and therefore disposes us to such long-suffering as he manifests . . . The long-suffering of God is very wonderfully manifest in his bearing innumerable injuries from men, and injuries that are very great and long-continued' (Jonathan Edwards) [*Exod.* 34:6; *Rom.* 2:4].

2. *And is kind:* Such 'was predominantly the character of Christ's ministry, which dispensed deeds of gentle kindness among all the lowly and the needy with whom he came in contact. Thus to God-like "long-suffering" there is added Christ–like "benignity"' (Lenski) [*Acts* 10:38]

3. *Love envieth not:* The opposite positive quality is implied in the eight negatives which follow the first couplet. 'Envy may be defined to be a spirit of dissatisfaction with, and opposition to, the prosperity and happiness of others as compared with our own' (Jonathan Edwards) [*Num.* 11:29]

4. *Love vaunteth not itself:* Love is no 'braggart' or 'windbag' (Arndt–Gingrich). 'Behind boastful bragging there lies conceit, an overestimation of one's own importance, abilities, or achievements' (Lenski) [*Phil.* 2:3, 4].

5. *Is not puffed up:* The Corinthians' besetting sin [cf. 4:6, 18, 19; 5:2; 8:1]. 'There are many ways of manifesting pride; and love is incompatible with them all. Love is concerned rather to give itself than to assert itself' (Morris).

6. *Doth not behave itself unseemly:* Love's behaviour is not contrary to the 'form, fashion, or manner that is proper. When pride puffs up the heart, unseemly bearing and conduct naturally follow' (Lenski) [cf. 11:6–15, 14:40].

7. *Seeketh not its own:* 'Love not merely does not seek that which does not belong to it; it is prepared to give up for the sake of others even what it is entitled to' (Barrett) [10:24, 33].

8. *Is not provoked:* 'Not merely "does not fly into a rage", but "does not yield to provocation": it is not embittered by injuries, whether real or supposed' (Robertson-Plummer) [*Gal.* 5:22, 23].

9. *Taketh not account of evil:* 'Love, instead of entering evil as a debt in its account-book, voluntarily passes the sponge over what it endures' (Godet) [cf. *Philem.* 18].

10. *Rejoiceth not in unrighteousness:* 'To "rejoice at iniquity" when seeing it in others, is a sign of deep debasement [*Rom.* 1:32]' (Findlay).

11. *But rejoiceth with the truth:* The last negative proposition is rounded off with its positive counterpart because Love must take sides with the Truth, which is here personified. 'The false charity which compromises "the truth" by glossing over "iniquity" is thus condemned [*Prov.* 17:15]' (Fausset) [cf. Eph. 4:15].

12. *Covers all things:* Arndt-Gingrich give the first meaning of the word *stego* as '*cover, pass over in silence, keep confidential*', and say that in this verse it refers to 'love that throws a cloak of silence over what is displeasing in another person'.

13. *Believeth all things:* 'All that is not palpably false, all that it can with a good conscience believe to the credit of another' (Fausset) [cf. *Philem.* 21]

14. *Hopeth all things:* While the first pair of 'all things' relate to present experience, the second look more to the future. Here the 'thought is not that of unreasoning optimism, which fails to take account of reality. It is rather a refusal to take failure as final' (Morris). [*2 Cor.* 1:7]

15. *Endureth all things:* This 'is that cheerful and loyal fortitude which, having done all without apparent success, still stands and endures, whether the ingratitude of friends or the persecution of foes' (Robertson-Plummer) [*Eph.* 6:13].

8: Love never faileth: but whether there be prophecies they shall be done away; whether there be tongues, they shall cease; whether there be knowledge, it shall be done away.

Love never ends (RSV): Love never comes to an end. While the gifts of the Spirit are a *means* of grace, divine love is *grace itself*, 'and therefore remains when the means to it cease' (Jonathan Edwards). The argument shifts here to direct polemic. In the previous verses Paul has said that gifts are nothing without love. But now love and spiritual gifts are set in opposition to each other, because gifts are *temporary* whereas love is *eternal*. Thus in contrast to the Corinthians who regarded these gifts as the sign that they had already attained the glories of heaven [cf. verse 1 with 4:8], Paul insists that the possession of the gifts is the proof positive that they are still held fast in the 'not yet' of spiritual immaturity (so Conzelmann).

Prophecies . . . tongues . . . knowledge: These − 'faculties inspired, ecstatic, intellectual − are the three typical forms of Christian expression. The abolition of Prophecies and Knowledge is explained in verses 9ff. as the superseding of the partial by the perfect; they "will be done away" by a completer realization of the objects they seek, − viz., by *intuition* into the now hidden things of God and of man [14:24f], and by adequate *comprehension* of the things revealed. Of the Tongues it is simply said that 'they will *stop*', having like other miracles a temporary significance [cf. 14:22]; not giving place to any higher development of the like kind, they lapse and terminate' (Findlay).

9: For we know in part, and we prophesy in part;

10: but when that which is perfect is come, that which is in part shall be done away.

Our present knowledge is imperfect because it is partial. This is an imperfection of degree rather than quality. What we know of God by revelation is indeed truly known, for it is infallibly communicated. But when this fragmentary disclosure at last gives place to the beatific vision of God in Christ, then 'that which is in part shall be done away'.

11: When I was a child, I spake as a child, I felt as a child, I thought as a child: now that I am become a man, I have put away childish things.

Our progress from infancy to maturity serves to illustrate this truth [verses 9, 10]. Paul does not deny that the child is father to the man, for he was the same 'I' in childhood as he is now in manhood; he merely asserts that as a man he has no desire to become a child again. This means that just as the adult sets aside the nature of the child, so the Christian sets aside the knowledge which seems to be essential now, i.e. in the stage of infancy (so G. Bertram, *TDNT*, vol. 4, p. 919). So though even now we are sons of God, yet we are still little children. Our present views of divine things are not untrue but inadequate. Hereafter things will be very different. 'It is no part of the apostle's object to unsettle our confidence in what God now communicates by his Word and Spirit to his children, but simply to prevent our being satisfied with the partial and imperfect' (Hodge).

12: For now we see in a mirror, darkly; but then face to face: now I know in part; but then shall I know fully even as also I was fully known.

Paul's figure is based on the familiar Old Testament contrast between the ordinary prophets, whose knowledge of the Lord was mediated through visions and dreams, and Moses to whom the Lord directly manifested himself [*Num.* 12:8]. So at present our knowledge of God is indirect: 'we only see the baffling reflections in a mirror' (Moffatt). 'Our present understanding is like peering into a primitive metal mirror with its imperfect reflection [cf. *2 Cor.* 5:7]. But then, in the next life, we shall see face to face [cf. *1 John* 3:2]' (Hillyer). Since such mirrors were made in Corinth Paul's readers would be quick to grasp the point [cf. *2 Cor.* 3: 18].

But then shall I know fully even as also I have been known fully (RV margin): 'As God's direct and all–penetrating knowledge takes into account every one of his children already in eternity and, of course, through all of life, so we, too, shall at last know God directly and completely to the highest degree in which this is possible for his children' (Lenski).

13: But now abideth faith, hope, love, these three; and the greatest of these is love.

Paul concludes by saying that when every gift has passed away [verses 8ff.], this well–known triad of Christian virtues eternally abides [*Rom.* 5:1–5; *Gal.* 5, 6; *1 Thess.* 1:3, 5:8]. But, asks Alford, how can *faith* and *hope* be said to endure to eternity, when faith will be lost in sight, and hope in fruition? With *hope* there is but little difficulty. 'New glories, new treasures of knowledge and of love, will ever raise, and nourish, blessed hopes of yet more and higher, – hopes which no disappointment will blight. But how can *faith* abide, – faith, which is the evidence of things *not seen*, where all things once believed are seen? In the form of *holy confidence and trust*, faith will abide even there. The stay of all conscious created being, human or angelic, is *dependence on God*; and where the faith which *comes by hearing* is out of the question, the faith which *consists of trusting* will be the only faith possible. Thus *Hope* will remain, as anticipation certain to be fulfilled: *Faith* will remain, as trust, entire and undoubting: the anchor of the soul, even where no tempest comes.'

But the greatest of these is love (RSV): Of these eternal virtues love is the greatest, because love alone is divine. 'God does not believe nor hope, but he loves. Love belongs to his essence. Like God himself, it could not change its nature except for the worse. Love is the end in relation to which the two other virtues are only means, and this relation remains even in the state of perfection' (Godet) [*1 John* 4:16, 19].

CHAPTER FOURTEEN

Provided the Corinthians follow the way of love, they are right to desire spiritual gifts, but they should seek prophecy rather than tongues [verses 1–5]. For unless tongues are interpreted, they are mere sounds without meaning, and so bring no benefit to the hearers [verses 6–11]. Because the edification of the church is the standard by which all gifts are to be measured, Paul would rather speak five intelligible words to instruct others than ten thousand in an unknown tongue [verses 12–19]. It was therefore childish to prefer an incomprehensible utterance which hindered the worship of the church to a rational message that helped it [verses 20–25]. In public worship Paul forbids tongues unless an interpreter is present, and then no more than two or three may speak in turn. The prophets must also wait their turn to speak, for God is not the author of confusion [verses 26–33]. Women are not to speak at all in church, but must save any questions for their husbands at home [verses 34, 35]. As the gospel did not originate in Corinth, they are not a law unto themselves, and must see that all things are done decently and in order [verses 36–40].

1: Follow after love; yet desire earnestly spiritual gifts, but rather that ye may prophesy.

The enthusiasm for tongues in Corinth made it necessary for Paul to prepare the ground carefully before dealing specifically with the disorders which had resulted from the indisciplined use of this gift. But having demonstrated the primacy of love, he is now ready to give his practical directions for the orderly conduct of public worship. He sums up the teaching of the previous chapter in the crisp command, 'Pursue after love'. Parry points out that this is a favourite metaphor with Paul for spiritual effort [cf. *Rom.* 9:30, 31; 12:13; *Phil.* 3:12f; *1 Thess.* 5:15; *1 Tim.* 6:11; *2 Tim.* 2:22]. If the Corinthians get their priorities right and put love first, they may indeed eagerly desire spiritual gifts, but they will seek the gift of prophecy rather than tongues. Throughout this extended discussion Paul's point-by-point demonstration of the inferiority of tongues to prophecy 'is such as to pour a douche of ice–cold water over the whole practice' (H. Chadwick, cited by F. F. Bruce). The predictive element is not emphasized in the gift of prophecy as it appears here (in contrast to Agabus, cf. *Acts* 11:28, 21:10): it is *inspired* forth–telling rather than fore–telling. 'Modern *preaching* is its successor, without the inspiration. Desire zealously this (prophecy) more than any other spiritual gift, especially *in preference to* 'tongues', [verses 2ff.]' (Fausset). However, both tongues and prophecy were *speech*, and this shows that Paul gives no place for any gathering together in *silence*, not even in verse 30.

2: For he that speaketh in a tongue speaketh not unto men, but unto God; for no man understandeth; but in the spirit he speaketh mysteries.

This gives the reason for preferring prophecy. It is that the man who speaks with tongues brings no benefit to his fellow–believers [cf. *Eph.* 4:29], for though *God* understands what he says no one else can [verse 9]! 'There was *sound* enough in the *glossolalia* [13:1], but no sense [verse 23]' (Findlay).

But in the spirit he speaketh mysteries: Verse 14 makes it clear that the reference must be to the spirit of the believer as distinguished from his understanding. The ecstatic utterance of such mysteries was therefore a revelation [see note on 2:7], which stopped 'short of disclosure tantalizing the church which hears and hears not' (Findlay).

3: But he that prophesieth speaketh unto men edification, and exhortation, and consolation.

But he who prophesies speaks to *men*, and his intelligible words are a means of edification (or 'building up': see on 8:1), for they serve to encourage and comfort others. Paul uses the terms 'edification' and 'to edify' no less than seven times in chapter 14 [verses 3–5, 12, 26; verses 4 (twice), 17], and this shows that he 'subjects all events of worship to the single and clear criterion of the "edification" of the congregation' (G. Bornkamm, *Early Christian Experience*, pp. 162–3).

4: He that speaketh in a tongue edifieth himself; but he that prophesieth edifieth the church.

There is a striking contrast between the speaker in a tongue who edifies only himself, and the prophet who edifies the whole church. Paul is attacking the selfish individualism of the Corinthians. It is 'wrong for the man who speaks in tongues to edify himself' [verse 4]. This act is not orientated to the community and the brother [verse 17], it is not regarded as service, and consequently it is not dictated by love, but is self–directed' (O. Michel, *TDNT*, vol. 5, p. 141).

5: Now I would have you all speak with tongues, but rather that ye should prophesy: and greater is he that prophesieth than he that speaketh with tongues, except he interpret, that the church may receive edifying.

It is not through any spirit of antipathy or jealousy that Paul so speaks of tongues, for he speaks with tongues more than they all [verse 18]. His aim is rather to help the Corinthians properly to estimate the value of this gift. Although he would have them all speak with tongues, yet it would be even better for them to have the gift of prophecy, because the man who prophesies is 'greater' than he who speaks in a tongue, unless of course he also has the ability to interpret his utterance for the benefit of the congregation. In that case he would do in two acts what the prophet does in one' (Findlay).

6: But now, brethren, if I come unto you speaking with tongues, what shall I profit you, unless I speak to you either by way of revelation, or of knowledge, or of prophesying, or of teaching?

Knowing their exaggerated esteem for tongues, Paul asks the Corinthians to judge what spiritual benefit they would receive from him if he should come to them speaking only in tongues. Would they now be his 'brethren' in Christ, if on his first visit to Corinth he had merely appeared in their midst as a demented ecstatic? [cf. verse 23]. Was it not by means of an address to their understanding in comprehensible speech that the light of the gospel had dawned upon them? [2:2]. And did they now expect to reach Christian maturity by exalting to the premier place a gift which left their highest faculty unedified? [verse 14]. 'There are not four, but only two modes of address contemplated in this verse. Revelation and prophecy belong to one; and knowledge and doctrine to the other. He who received revelations was a prophet, he who had "the word of knowledge" was a teacher' (Hodge).

7: Even things without life, giving a voice, whether pipe or harp, if they give not a distinction in the sounds, how shall it be known what is piped or harped?

Paul next illustrates the importance of intelligibility by three examples: 1. musical instruments [verse 7]; 2. military trumpet and application [verses 8, 9]; 3. human language and application [verses 10, 11]. 'Paul says, "Even the very inanimate things teach us a lesson." Of course there are many noises or crashes to be heard by chance, which have no musical significance. But Paul is speaking here about sounds which are the products of certain technical skill, as though he said: "A man cannot give life to a harp or flute, but he produces sounds, which are adjusted in such a way that they can be picked out. How absurd then that actual men, endowed as they are with intelligence, should utter indistinguishable and unintelligible sounds!"' (Calvin). But some instruments cannot produce a melody and make only a noise, and in 13:1 Paul significantly compares those who speak in tongues with the unmeaning crash of gong and cymbals (so Héring).

8: For if the trumpet give an uncertain voice, who shall prepare himself for war?

9: So also ye, unless ye utter by the tongue speech easy to be understood, how shall it be known what is spoken? for ye will be speaking into the air.

The use of the trumpet in the military realm was well known to Jews and Greeks alike. But if the trumpet is not blown to give notice of a prearranged signal, then not only is its message meaningless, but the lives of the troops who bear it are thereby placed in jeopardy. Paul is stressing the fact that the mere delivery of sound without sense is worse than useless. So the man whose words cannot be understood in church is simply 'speaking into the air'. The use of such a down-to-earth proverbial phrase is very forceful. It is like saying, He is wasting his breath!

10: There are, it may be, so many kinds of voices in the world, and no kind is without signification.

Paul has no idea how many languages there are in the world, but he is convinced that none of them 'is without voice' (ASV margin), i.e. without meaning. Since the whole purpose of language is communication, an utterance which mystifies rather than edifies the hearers is virtually 'voiceless'. And meaningless jumble of sound, had better be inaudible; it is a mere distracting noise. This was just the case with Tongues in a congregation without an interpreter' (Robertson-Plummer).

11: If then I know not the meaning of the voice, I shall be to him that speaketh a barbarian, and he that speaketh will be a barbarian unto me.

The mutual exchange of thought is impossible unless both speak the same language. Otherwise each would regard the other as a 'barbarian', i.e. someone whose speech gave the impression of being nothing more than a meaningless jumble of sounds like 'bar bar'. This derogatory connotation is not absent from Paul's thought here. 'The ecstatic speech which seemed to the Corinthians a matter for such pride turns out to be the means of making them nothing more than barbarians. This would be even worse for a Greek than for us' (Morris).

12: So also ye, since ye are zealous of spiritual gifts, seek that ye may abound unto the edifying of the church.

There is a touch of irony in Paul's admission that the Corinthians are indeed zealous to obtain spiritual gifts (literally, 'spirits' pointing to the various agencies producing these various gifts, cf. 12:10; *1 John* 4:1). Yet what they have failed to grasp is that their individual distribution among them is not for private gratification or personal display (because love 'seeketh not *its own*' – 13:5), but for the *common* good of that one body to which they all belong. 'To this end prophecy should have the preponderance, or tongues be accompanied with interpretation' (Godet).

13: Wherefore let him that speaketh in a tongue pray that he may interpret.

14: For if I pray in a tongue, my spirit prayeth, but my understanding is unfruitful.

'Wherefore' introduces the practical application. Since the church can only be edified by hearing an intelligible message, the man who speaks in a tongue should pray that God would also grant him the ability to interpret this ecstatic utterance. In verse 14 what Paul tactfully supposes of himself condemns what the Corinthians are actually doing. 'For if I pray in a tongue, my spirit prays, but my rational faculty remains unfruitful. His own spirit is edified, but because what is *felt* is not transformed into intelligible speech by his understanding, no benefit is communicated to the congregation. 'The *fruit* of the speaker is found in the profit of the hearer' (Theodoret). It is strange that those who so prided themselves upon their wisdom, 'should need to be told that intellect is not to be ignored, but ought to be brought to full development [verse 20]' (Robertson-Plummer).

15: What is it then? I will pray with the spirit, and I will pray with the understanding also: I will sing with the spirit, and I will sing with the understanding also.

'What then is the upshot of this discussion?' Because the worship of God is an exercise which engages the *whole* man, Paul is resolved to pray and sing not only with the spirit, but also with the understanding. Fervency of spirit must be found in alliance with the illumination of the intellect, and neither is acceptable without the other. 'Rational prayer is not less spiritual than irrational' (Barrett).

16: Else if thou bless with the spirit, how shall he that filleth the place of the unlearned say the Amen at thy giving of thanks, seeing he knoweth not what thou sayest ?

17: For thou verily givest thanks well, but the other is not edified.

The man who speaks in a tongue when the church is at worship is guilty of 'unseemly' behaviour towards his fellow-believers [13:5], because his unintelligible utterance forces them into a place which is not properly theirs, viz., that of the 'unlearned' (i.e., it puts them among those who are 'uninitiated' into God's mysteries). If they could not understand a word of what was said, then it would be a meaningless mockery to express their audible assent to it by the usual 'Amen' [*Neh.* 8:6]. The 'thou' and the 'well' of verse 17 are, as Godet says, 'slightly ironical'. 'Paul estimates the devotions of the church by a spiritually utilitarian standard; the abstractly beautiful is subordinated to the practically edifying' (Findlay).

18: I thank God, I speak with tongues more than you all: 19: howbeit in the church I had rather speak five words with my understanding, that I might instruct others also, than ten thousand words in a tongue.

It is not because Paul is himself a stranger to ecstatic experiences of this kind that he discourages tongues in public worship [cf. *2 Cor.* 12:1–4]. Indeed he speaks 'with tongues *more* than you all'. He surpasses them all in this *mode of speaking*. Had he wished to point to a greater proficiency in foreign languages he would rather have said: 'Because I speak in *more* tongues than you all' (Godet). But he only exercises this gift in private, for he would prefer to speak five sensible words to instruct his fellow–Christians 'than to utter a torrent of words in a tongue' (Morris). Thus it was not through exciting emotional experiences that the apostle sought to edify the Corinthians, but by addressing a rational message to their minds. 'In presenting the Christian gospel we must never, in the first place, make a *direct* approach either to the emotions or to the will. The emotions and the will should always be influenced through the mind. Truth is intended to come to the *mind*. The normal course is for the emotions and the will to be affected by the truth after it has first entered and gripped the mind' (D. Martyn Lloyd–Jones, *Conversions: Psychological and Spiritual,* p. 39).

20: Brethren, be not children in mind: yet in malice be ye babes, but in mind be men.

This exhortation begins a new paragraph. The affectionate address somewhat softens Paul's keen reproof. 'Emulation and love of display were betraying this church into a childishness the very opposite of that broad intelligence and enlightenment on which it plumed itself' (Findlay). Godet also remarks that it is 'characteristic of the child to prefer the amusing to the useful, the brilliant to the solid', and paraphrases the verse thus: 'If you will be children, well and good, provided it be in malice; but as to understanding, advance more and more toward full maturity'.

21: In the law it is written, By men of strange tongues and by the lips of strangers will I speak unto this people; and not even thus will they hear me, saith the Lord.

Paul next introduces a free quotation of Isaiah 28:11, 12 to illustrate the danger of despising a clear revelation (prophecy) in favour of an unintelligible utterance (tongues). 'According to the true interpretation of Isaiah 28:7ff, the drunken Israelites are mocking in their cups the teaching of God through his prophet, as though it were only fit for an infant school; in anger therefore he threatens to give his lessons through the lips of foreign conquerors (11), in whose speech the despisers of the mild, plain teaching of his servants (12) shall painfully spell out their ruin . . . God spoke to Israel through the strange Assyrian tongue *in retribution*, not to confirm their faith but to consummate their unbelief. The *Glossolalia* (speaking with tongues) may serve a similar melancholy purpose in the church' (Findlay).

22: Wherefore tongues are for a sign, not to them that believe, but to the unbelieving: but prophesying is for a sign, not to the unbelieving, but to them that believe.

Apparently there were those in Corinth who regarded speaking in tongues as 'a sign' for believers, i.e. as a proof of their superior spiritual standing and authority. But according to Paul's application of this Old Testament quotation tongues are not a sign of divine pleasure but of divine judgment. For if the Corinthians persist in their perverse preference for the obscure phenomenon of tongues, then they must not be surprised if their unbelieving rejection of prophecy is judicially confirmed by God. 'Paul desires to quench rather than stimulate the Corinthian ardour for Tongues' (Findlay).

But prophesying is for a sign, not to the unbelieving, but to them that believe: 'It is wholly otherwise with prophetic exhortations. These are a sign of faith or of the disposition to believe which already exists in those to whom God thus speaks' (Godet).

23: If therefore the whole church be assembled together and all speak with tongues, and there come in men unlearned or unbelieving, will they not say that ye are mad?

This vividly depicts the disastrous impression which the unbridled exercise of tongues in church would make upon the outsider ('unlearned' here appears without the qualification of verse 16) and upon the unbeliever who came to the service to learn something about the Christian faith. Paul's point is that what outsiders find completely meaningless cannot edify the church; whereas that which builds up the church also serves to convict and convert outsiders [verses 24, 25]. 'If the Tongues are, as many Corinthians think, the highest manifestation of the Spirit, then to have the whole church simultaneously so speaking would be the *ne plus ultra* of spiritual power; but, in fact, the church would then resemble nothing so much as a congregation of lunatics! A *reductio ad absurdum* for the fanatical coveters of Tongues' (Findlay).

24: But if all prophesy, and there come in one unbelieving or unlearned, he is reproved by all, he is judged by all; 25: the secrets of his heart are made manifest; and so he will fall down on his face and worship God, declaring that God is among you indeed.

Tongues may succeed in arousing the scorn of the unbeliever, but only prophecy can make him a believer; a blessedly different result which justifies Paul's critical appraisal of the relative value of these gifts. It is by this inspired preaching that the presence of God among his people is validated in the experience of the unbeliever, for it subjects his inner life to a moral illumination which convicts him of his sin, leads to self–condemnation, and issues in submission to God [cf. *Heb.* 4:12].'What passes in him at such a moment resembles what passed in Paul on the way to Damascus. Struck by this light, he casts himself in the dust, not before man, but before God, acknowledging that such brightness can only proceed from the Holy of holies and the Searcher of hearts; that consequently it is He who speaks by the mouth of those into the midst of whom he has come' (Godet).

26: What is it then, brethren? When ye come together, each one hath a psalm, hath a teaching, hath a revelation, hath a tongue, hath an interpretation. Let all things be done unto edifying.

Having concluded his treatment of spiritual gifts, Paul next shows how they are to be used in the church [verses 26–33]. These detailed directions were necessary because the abundance of gifts possessed by the Corinthians was matched by their eagerness to exercise them. Consequently, spontaneity in worship quickly degenerated into confusion and disorder. In this section Paul is at pains to point out that this unseemly and irreverent behaviour must be rectified at once [verse 33]. E. A. Abbott expands the verse thus: 'Just when ye are assembling for sacred worship, and ought to be thinking of Christ and of Christ's body, the congregation, each one is perhaps thinking of himself, "I have a Psalm", "I have a Doctrine", "I have a Revelation". Have done with this! Let all be done to edification' (cited in Robertson-Plummer).

27: If any man speaketh in a tongue, let it be by two, or at the most three, and that in turn; and let one interpret: 28: but if there be no interpreter, let him keep silence in the church; and let him speak to himself, and to God.

Although there may be many in the congregation ready to speak in tongues, no more than two, or at the most three, should be allowed to do so, 'and that in turn'. Furthermore, if no interpreter is present, the tongue–speaker must keep silent in the church, and exercise his gift privately at home. For without interpretation his gift is of no value to the church. 'One, and one only (*heis* not *tis*), was to interpret; there was to be no interpreting in turn, which might lead to profitless discussion. Moreover, this would be a security against two speaking with Tongues at the same time, for one interpreter could not attend to both' (Robertson-Plummer).

29: And let the prophets speak by two or three, and let others discern.

30: But if a revelation be made to another sitting by, let the first keep silence.

31: For ye all can prophesy one by one, that all may learn, and all may be exhorted;

Similarly, only two or three may prophesy at one church meeting, while those who have the gift of discernment are to judge whether their utterances are really inspired or not [cf. 12:10; *Deut.* 18:22; *1 John* 4:1]. If a direct revelation is received by a prophet who has not been chosen to speak, then the appointed speaker is to give place to him. Eventually all the prophets will have their turn at speaking so that the whole congregation may learn and be strengthened by their distinctive contributions.

When these directions [verses 26–33] are placed in their proper historical perspective it will be seen that they cannot apply to us today, because the great lack which prophecy and tongues were intended to fill in the primitive church was supplied as soon as the canon of Scripture was complete. Therefore those who assert that the apostolic gifts are still continued in the church leave believers at the mercy of a form of soothsaying which cannot be gainsaid because its deluded exponents claim to have received a direct revelation from the Lord! Evangelicals should face up to the fact that such a presumptuous claim places the confused utterances of uninspired men on exactly the same level as inspired Scripture. Now it is granted 'that Scripture does not continue to be written, that it is a closed canon. Once this is admitted, then we must entertain . . . that conception of Scripture taught and pre-supposed by our Lord and his apostles, and insist that it is this conception that must be applied to the whole canon of Scripture. Since we no longer have prophets, since we do not have our Lord with us as he was with the disciples, and since we do not have new organs of revelation as in apostolic times, Scripture in its total extent, according to the conception entertained by our Lord and his apostles, is the only revelation of the mind and will of God available to us. This is what the finality of Scripture means for us; it is the only extant revelatory Word of God' (John Murray, 'The Finality and Sufficiency of Scripture', *Collected Writings*, vol. 1, p. 19).

32: and the spirits of the prophets are subject to the prophets; 33a: for God is not a God of confusion, but of peace.

Unlike the diabolical inspirations of heathenism [12:2], the breathings of God's Spirit do not carry away the prophet without his consent or will, and therefore 'he has no right to make inspiration a pretext for refusing to submit to the rules laid down by the apostle' (Godet). And this must be so, for it would be the height of impiety to attribute the confusion which would result from a prophetic free-for-all to him who is the God of peace.

33b: As in all the churches of the saints, 34: let the women keep silence in the churches: for it is not permitted unto them to speak; but let them be in subjection, as also saith the law.

35: And if they would learn anything, let them ask their own husbands at home: for it is shameful for a woman to speak in the church.

The church in Corinth was not a law unto itself, and was not therefore free to permit what was forbidden in other churches. However, it is not merely on the strength of universal custom that Paul enjoins silence upon the women of Corinth during public worship; it is an authoritative command because it is of divine origin [cf. *Gen.* 3:16]. 'Any act on the part of woman which sets aside her subjection to man is in violation of "the Law", the will of God expressed in creation and stated in his Word. An act of such a nature would be the speaking of women in the public services either in a tongue or in prophecy . . . In many places woman may speak and teach even publicly, but in no place where she will exercise "dominion over a man" by her teaching' (Lenski) [*1 Tim.* 2:12–14] The prohibition is absolute and extends even to the asking of questions. This is to be done at home. It is as *shameful* a thing for a woman to speak in church as it would be to have her hair shorn (the same word as in 11:6).

'To Paul, the human race is made up of families, and every several organism, the church included, is composed of families, united together by this or that bond. The relation of the sexes in the family follows it therefore into the church. To the feminist movement the human race is made up of individuals. A woman is just another individual by the side of the man; and it can see no reason for any differences in dealing with the two. And, indeed, if we can ignore the great fundamental natural difference of sex, and destroy the great fundamental social unit of the family, in the interest of individualism, there does not seem any reason why we should not wipe out the differences established by Paul between the sexes in the church. Except, of course, the authority of Paul. It all, in the end, comes back to the authority of the apostles, as founders of the church. We may like what Paul says, or we may not like it. We may be willing to do what he commands, or we may not be willing to do it. But there is no room for doubt of what he says' (B. B. Warfield, 'Paul on Women Speaking in Church', *The Saviour of the World*, p. 267, Mack Publishing edition). And we may add that if Paul's injunction had been respected and obeyed there would have been no opportunity for charlatans like Aimee Semple McPherson, Ellen G. White, and Mary Baker Eddy to have imposed their noxious wares upon a gullible public!

36: What? was it from you that the word of God went forth? or came it unto you alone?

'Will you obey me? Or, if you set up your judgment above that of other churches, do you pretend that your church is the first FROM which the gospel came, that you should give law to all others? Or are you the only persons UNTO whom it has come?' (Fausset).

37: If any man thinketh himself to be a prophet, or spiritual, let him take knowledge of the things which I write unto you, that they are the commandment of the Lord.

Having concluded his discussion of spiritual gifts (chapters 12–14), Paul now affixes the seal of his authority to what he has written. Let anyone who thinks he is a prophet or spiritually gifted, prove his claim by acknowledging that what the apostle is writing is the *Lord's* commandment. Anyone who fails to recognize the inspiration and authority of Paul's words not only shows that he has no spiritual discernment, but also affords proof positive that he is not of God [*John* 8:47; *1 John* 4:6).

38: But if any man is ignorant, let him be ignorant.

But if any one is ignorant of the source of Paul's authority, he must be left to his ignorance and all it entails. An 'argument likely to have weight with the Corinthians, who admired "knowledge" so much' (Fausset).

39: Wherefore, my brethren, desire earnestly to prophesy, and forbid not to speak with tongues.

The whole discussion is now affectionately summed up in one lucid directive [verses 39, 40]. Paul actively encourages the Corinthians to prophesy, but merely says that they are not to hinder speaking with tongues. 'A vast difference; the one gift to be greatly longed for, the other only not forbidden' (Robertson-Plummer).

40: But let all things be done decently and in order.

Paul's detailed directions in this chapter on the conduct of worship applied to the special circumstances of the church in Corinth. But two principles remain regulative to this day: all things should be done for edification [verse 26], and all things should be done decently and in order. 'The lasting importance of this chapter lies in the fact that Paul sets forth what the character of the divine service must be. That which he writes about that subject is still valid. Furthermore we learn that God the Holy Spirit had endowed the early Christians with special gifts, charismata, and that He guided the ancient church by means of them. We also notice how great the dangers connected with those gifts. That should make us grateful that in the Holy Scriptures of the Old and New Testaments we have all that we need' (Grosheide).

CHAPTER FIFTEEN

After establishing that the truth of Christ's resurrection was a vital part of the gospel which the apostles preached and the Corinthians believed, Paul argues that those who deny the bodily resurrection of believers virtually deny Christ's resurrection and empty the faith of its saving content [verses 1–19]. But now that Christ has been raised as the first–fruits of a new humanity, he has cancelled the curse we inherited from Adam, and ensured the certainty of our resurrection at his coming. Then, having subdued all his enemies, he shall deliver up the kingdom to his Father, that God may be all in all [verses 20–28]. If the Corinthians are right in their shameful denial of this truth, why are they so inconsistent as to practise baptism for the dead, and why does their apostle daily risk his life for the sake of the gospel? [verses 29–34]. Paul refutes the sceptical objections to the resurrection by showing that the relation which the glorified body sustains to our present body is one of vital continuity but not absolute identity, even as the seed that is sown bears no apparent relation to the form that God gives to the plant. So since God organizes matter in an infinite variety of ways, there is no reason to suppose that it is beyond his power to raise to eternal life the body that is sown in corruption. As we inherit our natural life from Adam, so we receive our spiritual life from Christ. And as we have borne the image of the earthy, so we shall bear the image of the heavenly. For flesh and blood cannot inherit the kingdom of God [verses 35–50]. This great change will take place at Christ's coming when the living will be transformed without experiencing death in the same moment that the dead are raised to glory. With this certainty set before them, Paul exhorts the Corinthians to be always abounding in the work of the Lord, because they know that they shall be so gloriously rewarded by him [verses 51–58].

Paul avoids a formal announcement of his last great subject because some in Corinth were disputing the truth of the Resurrection [verse 12]. He adopts this course to ensure the unbiased attention of his readers as he thoroughly rehearses the vital facts of the gospel on which their faith rests [verses 1–11]. Presumably those who embraced this error were influenced by the Greek idea of the body (*soma*) being the tomb (*sema*) of the soul. And because they thought of death as liberating the immortal soul from the shackles of the earthly body, they 'looked for and desired no resurrection; and their formula, perhaps somewhat scoffingly and certainly somewhat magisterially pronounced, was: "There is no rising again of dead men"' (Warfield). Unhappily, these deniers of the Resurrection are not without numerous successors today, including both the 'scholarly' or rationalistic and the 'spiritual' or mystical varieties of unbelief. Hence Paul's masterly treatment of this fundamental article of Christian belief is as much needed now as when it was first written.

> 1: Now I make known unto you, brethren, the gospel which I preached unto you, which also ye received wherein also ye stand,
> 2: by which also ye are saved, if ye hold fast the word which I preached unto you, except ye believed in vain.

Paul gently rebukes the knowledgeable Corinthians by 'making known' to them the gospel which they had already accepted. It is the same gospel which he had preached to them, which they had received, in which they now stand, and through which they are being saved. This process began at the very moment when they believed the word Paul preached to them, but it will be consummated only if they continue to hold it fast (see note on 1:18).

I make known, I say, with what word I preached it unto you, if ye hold it fast (RV margin): This is really an indirect question and it is the climax of the entire sentence. Paul had given the Corinthians a very precise statement of the gospel, and he supposes that they still hold fast this 'form of words' (Barrett), but his assumption can only be endorsed by their own affirmative response.

Except ye believed in vain: Or rather 'without due consideration' (Arndt-Gingrich). Unless they had failed to lay hold of the promised blessings of the gospel by heedlessly rushing into a profession of it. Was his confidence in them ill-founded? Surely not! Paul expects them to say that the reality of their conversion is not open to doubt.

3: For I delivered unto you first of all that which also I received: that Christ died for our sins according to the scriptures; 4: and that he was buried; and that he hath been raised on the third day according to the scriptures; 5: and that he appeared to Cephas; then to the twelve;

For I delivered to you as of first importance what I also received (RSV): Paul passed on to the Corinthians the facts he had received from the eyewitnesses of the vital events of a certain Easter week. For though he is an apostle in virtue of his encounter with the Risen Lord, his knowledge of the earthly life of Jesus was conveyed to him by the testimony of the other apostles. Yet he speaks of this testimony as coming to him directly from the Lord (see note on 11:23). And this is because: '*Transmission by the apostles is not effected by men, but by Christ the Lord himself who thereby imparts this revelation.* All that the Church knows about the words of Jesus, about stories of his life, or about their interpretation, comes from the apostles. One has received this revelation, another that. The apostle is essentially one who passes on what he has received by revelation. But since everything has not been revealed to each individual apostle, each one must first pass on his testimony to another [*Gal.* 1:18; *1 Cor.* 15:11], and only the entire *paradosis* (tradition), to which all the apostles contribute, constitutes the *paradosis* of Christ' (Oscar Cullmann, *The Early Church*, p. 73).

1. *That Christ died for our sins according to the scriptures:* Thus Paul is here clearly quoting a very early tradition, and though he does not actually refer to Christ as the Suffering Servant of God, he obviously sees the work of Christ as the fulfilment of Isaiah 53 (so Oscar Cullmann, *The Christology of the New Testament*, pp. 76, 79). Since 'our sins' were the only reason for Christ's death, this means that he died for us sinners, as the substitutionary sacrifice through whom we receive the forgiveness of sins. 'In other words, there was no gospel known in the primitive church, or in any part of it, which had not this as its foundation – that God forgives our sins because Christ died for them' (James Denney, *Studies in Theology*, p. 104) [cf. *Rom.* 3:24–26; 4:25; *2 Cor.* 5:21; *Gal.* 1:4]

2. *And that he was buried:* That Christ was buried attests both the completeness of his death and the reality of his resurrection. In this indirect reference to the empty tomb, which undoubtedly formed part of the original tradition, 'we have a first indication that the risen Lord, as Paul preached him, possessed a body identical with that in which he had been buried, a body of flesh' (J. A. Schep).

3. *And that he hath been raised on the third day according to the scriptures:* For the second time it is asserted that these events were an exact fulfilment of the prophetic testimony of Scripture. With regard to the difficult phrase 'on the third day', it may be said that it was Christ himself who taught the scriptural necessity of his rising again on the third day [cf. *Luke* 24:46; *Jon.* 1:17; *Matt.* 12:40]. The death and burial of Jesus took place once for all, but having been raised from the dead he remains the Risen One in perpetuity. 'By death and burial he came down to our level, by resurrection he raised us to his' (Robertson-Plummer).

4. *And that he appeared to Cephas; then to the twelve:* The truth of the resurrection was confirmed by unimpeachable witnesses. Peter is placed first because he was the first apostle to see the Risen Lord [*Luke* 24:34]. Then he was seen by 'the twelve'. These words designate 'the college of the apostles, without exact regard to number: actually *ten*, wanting Judas Iscariot, and Thomas absent on the first meeting' (Findlay).

6: then he appeared to above five hundred brethren at once, of whom the greater part remain until now, but some are fallen asleep;

Paul lays stress on the fact that Christ was seen by more than 500 brethren at once, and this meeting is almost certainly to be identified with that recorded in Matthew 28:7, 10, 16. As he writes this letter some twenty years later, most of these witnesses are still able to confirm this testimony with their own lips, 'but some are fallen asleep'. This remarkable expression is not without its point in the argument. Because these men had faced death in the hope of the resurrection through faith in the Risen Christ, they could regard it as nothing more than a sleep [cf. *Acts* 7:60]. 'If there was no resurrection in store for them, how strange was their lot!' (Robertson-Plummer).

7: then he appeared to James; then to all the apostles;

Apart from this verse we should not know that James, the Lord's half-brother [*Matt.* 13:55], owed his conversion to a special resurrection appearance [cf. *John* 7:5]; a fact which explains the presence of 'his brethren' amongst the 120 disciples at Jerusalem [*Acts* 1: 14], and James' subsequent leadership of the church there. Paul met James as well as Peter on his first visit to the Jerusalem church [*Gal.* 1:18f].

Then to all the apostles: Since Paul presumably knew of the absence of Thomas on the occasion mentioned in verse 5, and his consequent scepticism [*John* 20:24ff], he now distinctly says 'that *all* participated in this latter sight, which coincides in point of time with Acts 1:6–12, not John 20:26. The witness of the First Apostles to the resurrection was complete and unqualified' (Findlay).

8: and last of all, as to the child untimely born, he appeared to me also.

Paul is overwhelmed by the thought of the grace manifested to him 'last of all', *as* to one 'untimely born' in the family of the apostles. 'As such a child, though born alive, is yet not of the proper size, and scarcely worthy of the name of man, so 'I am *the least* of the apostles scarcely meet to be called one; a supernumerary taken into the college out of regular course; not led to Christ by gradual instruction, like a natural birth, but by a sudden power, as those prematurely born' (Fausset). Because the idea of a premature birth hardly fits the words 'last of all', many reject this interpretation in favour of the less likely notion that Paul is taking up an insult hurled at him by his opponents (Arndt-Gingrich).

9: For I am the least of the apostles, that am not meet to be called an apostle, because I persecuted the church of God.

Paul can never forget the shameful circumstances which accounted for his violent introduction to the apostolate. He regards himself as 'the least' of this highly favoured band, not in respect of his authority, but because he had been a persecutor of the people of God [*1 Tim.* 1:13–15]. 'The forgiveness of sin does not obliterate the remembrance of it; neither does it remove the sense of unworthiness and ill-desert' (Hodge).

10: But by the grace of God I am what I am: and his grace which was bestowed upon me was not found vain; but I laboured more abundantly than they all: yet not I, but the grace of God which was with me.

It was not by personal merit but by the grace of God that Paul became an apostle after being a persecutor. Nor was this grace bestowed upon him in vain, for he laboured more abundantly than all the rest of the apostles. This point was worth making to a community which was apt to compare him unfavourably with others. Moreover, he refers not simply to his toil but also to its results. For 'by his single labours Paul had extended the kingdom of Christ over a region wider than all the Twelve had traversed up to this date' (Findlay). Yet he does not say this to boast of his own achievements, but to magnify the grace of God without which all his work would have been to no purpose. 'Grace at once made him something and co–operated with him; in the words of the Tenth Article, grace 'prevents (i.e. anticipates) us that we may have a good will, and works with us when we have that good will' (Edwards). [cf. *Phil.* 2,:12, 13]

11: Whether then it be I or they, so we preach, and so ye believed.

After this personal digression [verses 9, 10] Paul sums up the paragraph in an emphatic statement of great importance. Although *each* apostle had his own distinctive contribution to make to the gospel [verse 3], they *all* preached the same gospel [verses 3–5], and this is the good news which *you* believed! Therefore any divergence from these basic beliefs of the gospel cuts a man off from all the blessings of the gospel. 'All the apostles agreed in this testimony; all Christians agree in the belief of it; by this faith they live, in this faith they die' (Matthew Henry).

12: Now if Christ is preached that he hath been raised from the dead, how say some among you that there is no resurrection of the dead?

It is important to note that this argument is addressed to believers. The whole basis of its appeal lies in the Christian experience of the readers, and this is why it has nothing to say about the general resurrection of all men [*Dan.* 12:2]. Paul's line of reasoning here could not be applied to unbelievers: Because you are 'in Christ', you will rise as Christ rose from the dead.

Now if Christ is preached that he hath been raised from the dead: This remarkable expression shows that 'the preaching of Christ *is* the preaching *of his resurrection*' (Findlay). It is through the preaching of the apostolic gospel that the *living* Christ raises dead men to new life. No such power attends the preaching of those whose perverted preference for another 'gospel' leads them to present another 'Christ' [*Gal.* 1:7].

How say some among you that there is no resurrection of the dead? The effect of this unexpected question upon the Corinthians must have been like that of a bomb exploding in their midst! 'How could they deny that dead men rise, when Christ who was a dead man, had risen?' (Warfield). C. K. Barrett makes the likely surmise that the Corinthian error was the same as that of Hymenaeus and Philetus [*2 Tim.* 2:18]. These 'gnostics' affirmed with some plausibility [*Col.* 3:1–4] that the resurrection – which presumably they equated with their regeneration – was past already. But Paul rejects this 'spiritual' deviation from the gospel by insisting that the first resurrection unto eternal life necessarily involved the future resurrection of the body.

13: But if there is no resurrection of the dead, neither hath Christ been raised: 14: and if Christ hath not been raised, then is our preaching vain, your faith also is vain.

But if dead men do not rise, then it is impossible that Christ, who certainly died, can have risen from the dead. The argument involves the true and full humanity of the Lord, and the reassumption of his human body in the resurrection. Paul points out that if this supposition were true, then not only is the apostolic message devoid of reality, but also the faith that is founded upon it. 'Christianity becomes an unreal system of notions, like other phantoms of the theatre, if it is not an interpretation of facts. Faith also is no more faith; for faith must act on an external fact and a living person' (Edwards) [*1 Pet.* 1:3].

15: Yea, and we are found false witnesses of God; because we witnessed of God that he raised up Christ: whom he raised not up, if so be that the dead are not raised.

Moreover, in that case the apostles are discovered to be impostors of the worst kind, for their testimony bears on a false fact which they dared to ascribe to God himself!' (Godet). For they witnessed *against* God 'that he raised up Christ: whom he raised not up, if so be that the dead are not raised'. For Paul the matter at issue is quite simple: '"Either he rose from the grave, or we lied in affirming it" – the dilemma admits of no escape' (Findlay). There is no good news for mankind in the preaching of a myth!

16: For if the dead are not raised, neither hath Christ been raised: 17: and if Christ hath not been raised, your faith is vain; ye are yet in your sins.

Paul restates the thought of verse 13 in order to spell out the fatal consequences which lie hidden in the Corinthian denial of the resurrection. In verse 14 he showed that this error emptied faith in Christ of all *reality*; in verse 17 he emphasizes the complete *futility* of such a faith. 'If there is no resurrection, there is also no redemption, no reconciliation with God, no justification, no life and salvation. If Christ is still dead, then every believer is still dead in trespasses and sins. As long as Christ, our surety, is not released, it is certain that our debt is not paid, we are still liable, no matter how much we may trust in some supposed payment or in some release without payment' (Lenski) [*Rom.* 4:24,25].

18: Then they also that are fallen asleep in Christ have perished.

This depicts the inevitably tragic result of believing what is not objectively true. If Christ was not raised from the dead, then faith in Christ is nothing more than a cruel delusion which will be shattered by the awful reality of death. 'There is a sharp contrast between the two terms: *falling asleep in Christ* and *having perished*. To close the eyes in the joy of salvation, to open them in the torments of perdition! The verb *apolonto*, "perished", cannot designate annihilation, for it is explained by the preceding expression: "to be yet in sins". It denotes a state of perdition in which the soul remains under the weight of divine condemnation' (Godet).

19: If we have only hoped in Christ in this life, we are of all men most pitiable.

If we have turned out to be no more than Christ-hopers and staked on that our whole present life, then we are of all men most pitiable (Vos): Our plight is then most pitiable for two reasons. One is that unrealised hope 'is the most futile and ill-fated frustration of life-purpose'. The other is 'that when this futile hope so engrosses a man as to monopolize him for an unreal world such a state of mind involves the forfeit of all palpable realities of life, a sacrifice at bottom of all this-worldliness for another-worldliness that has no substance' (Vos).

20: But now hath Christ been raised from the dead, the first fruits of them that are asleep.

Paul has made explicit 'the hideous corollaries' which are implicit in the denial by 'some' [verse 12] of 'the possibility of dead men rising' (Warfield). 'But now' is an expression often used by the apostle to introduce important statements [cf. 13:13; *Rom.* 3:21; 6:22; 7:6; *Col.* 1:21], and this triumphant affirmation marks a glorious return to reality. Here he begins to speak of the consequences of Christ's resurrection for believers [verses 20–28]. Throughout the chapter his emphasis is consistently soteriological; he does not refer to God's judgment upon the unbelieving as being outside the scope of his present purpose [cf. *2 Thess.* 1:8, 9]. For the Corinthians have not been appointed to wrath, but unto the obtaining of salvation through the Lord Jesus Christ [*1 Thess.* 5:9].

In designating Christ as 'the firstfruits' Paul firmly puts the resurrection of Christ's people in the future, and thus contradicts the errorists who claim that the resurrection is past already (see note on verse 12). The term 'implies community of nature with the "harvest" to follow; i.e. Christ's resurrection promises the ultimate home-gathering of all God's people. The full harvest was foreshadowed and consecrated by the first sheaf brought as an offering on the day following the sabbath after the Passover [*Lev.* 23:10f.], i.e. on Easter Day, the day of Christ's resurrection. Death with its sting gone [verse 55] is for Christians no more than falling "asleep"' (Hillyer).

21: For since by man *came* **death, by man** *came* **also the resurrection of the dead. 22: For as in Adam all die, so also in Christ shall all be made alive.**

The italics show that there are no verbs, and the omission of the article before each noun stresses its quality. Since it was through man that mankind became mortal [*Rom.* 5:12], through man also is resurrection from death [*Rom.* 5:15, etc.]. This goes deeper than 'firstfruits' in that it points to Christ as the 'beginning', the very principle and root of resurrection–life [*Col.* 1:18]. 'Through man' implies 'that Death is not, as philosophy supposed, a law of finite being or a necessity of fate; it is an event of history, a calamity brought by man upon himself and capable of removal by the like means' (Findlay).

In verse 22 the second 'all' is not coextensive with the first. It is true that there is no exception to the dying in Adam, but that is not Paul's point here; nor does he suggest that there is no exception to the being made alive in Christ. What he *does* mean to say is that as there is no dying outside of Adam, so there is no quickening apart from Christ. 'Both alike are heads of humanity. But they are unlike in this (as also in other things, *Rom.* 5:15), that men are in Adam by nature, in Christ by faith' (Edwards). And just as it needed more than a 'mythical' Adam to produce the concrete reality of universal death, so it requires more than a 'mythical' resurrection of Christ to annul the power of death for all believers [cf. *Rom.* 6:5–11]

23: But each in his own order: Christ the firstfruits; then they that are Christ's, at his coming.

G. Vos rightly maintains that the word *tagma* is not used here in the sense of 'division', 'troup', or 'group' as though several resurrections were involved, for the only point of comparison is that of 'order, sequence of occurrence'. Paul is affirming that in the order of the resurrection Christ as the 'firstfruits' necessarily precedes the final harvest. Probably it had been urged against the apostle's doctrine of the resurrection, that the resurrection of believers ought to take place immediately after their death. To this he replies: 'each in his own order'. Christ must come first because he is the source of the whole process, but the resurrection of his people awaits his return [cf. verses 50–53].

24: Then cometh the end, when he shall deliver up the kingdom to God, even the Father; when he shall have abolished all rule and all authority and power.

'The end' is *the end!* It is true that 'then' need not mean immediately; it could indicate the next significant event. But the two 'when' clauses which follow suggest that it should be taken to mean 'thereupon' (Barrett). Thus, 'the period between the two advents is the period of Christ's kingdom, and when He comes again it is not to institute His kingdom, but to lay it down [verses 24, 28]. The completion of His conquest, which is marked by conquering "the last enemy", death [verse 26], which in turn is manifest when the just arise and Christ comes [verses 54, 23], marks also the end of His reign [verse 25] and the delivery of the kingdom to God, even the Father [verse 24]. This is indubitably Paul's assertion here, and it is in perfect harmony with the uniform representation of the New Testament, which everywhere places Christ's kingdom before and God's after the Second Advent' (B. B. Warfield, 'The Prophecies of St. Paul', *Biblical and Theological Studies*, p. 487).

When he shall have abolished all rule and all authority and power: It was at the cross that Christ won the decisive battle over these hostile powers which seek to oppose the fulfilment of God's saving purpose [*Col.* 2:15; *1 Pet.* 3:22], and he continues the conflict against these enemies throughout his reign [verse 25], until with the resurrection of his people the final victory is won in the war against sin and death.

25: For he must reign, till he hath put all his enemies under his feet.

'Here the kingship of Christ is equivalent to the process of subjecting one enemy after another. After the last enemy, death, has been conquered, there is no further need for the kingdom of Christ: hence it is delivered up to God the Father. Christ's kingdom as a process of conquest precedes the final kingdom of God as a settled permanent state' (G. Vos, *The Kingdom and the Church*, p. 53) [*Psa.* 110: 1].

26: The last enemy that shall be abolished is death.

Death, which is here personified, is the *last* of these enemies to be abolished or brought to nought. The verb is in the present tense and this denotes the certainty of its conquest [verses 53–57]. When Christ returns, his triumph 'over all powers hostile to God and over all that has come into the world through sin will be manifest, and that will mean the full liberation of the people of God from all the consequences of sin, also from temporal death, which means that the resurrection of the body will then take place' (Grosheide) [verse 23].

27: For, He put all things in subjection, under his feet. But when he saith, All things are put in subjection, it is evident that he is excepted who did subject all things unto him.

The final defeat of death, the last enemy, is made certain by the fact that God has put all things under the feet of Christ [*Psa.* 8:6]. How this victory over death was achieved by the Lord is shown by the interpretation which is given of Psalm 8:6 in Hebrews 2:6–18. But when God says in Scripture that he has subjected 'all things' to Christ as Mediator, it is evident that he did not include himself in this subjection. The purpose of the qualification is to prepare the Corinthians for Paul's final statement of what will take place at the end [verse 28].

28: And when all things have been subjected unto him, then shall the Son also himself be subjected to him that did subject all things unto him, that God may be all in all.

When the triumph of Christ the Son is at last complete, he will surrender his mediatorial kingship to the Father from whom he received it. It is clear that Christ cannot divest himself of that sovereignty which belongs to him as the eternal Son, and he will for ever remain the Head of the church which he has redeemed with his blood, but the final consummation of all things will bring his work as Mediator to an end. And this work comes to an *end* simply because the exercise of this office belongs to the *temporal* sphere. 'It was given for Christ's mediatorial mastery of this world, and it is this, when returned to the Father, which makes the glory of God complete' (Raymond O. Zorn, *Christ Triumphant*, p. 123).

That God may be all in all: The termination of the mediatorial office will bring to an end the Son's subordination to the Father in the economy of redemption in order that the one God (Father, Son, and Holy Spirit) may be all in all. From that moment onward 'the Triune God in all three persons conjointly, one God, shall stand supreme amid glorified humanity in the new heaven and the new earth' (Lenski) [*Rev.* 21:3].

29: Else what shall they do that are baptized for the dead? If the dead are not raised at all, why then are they baptized for them?

Paul abruptly turns from this apocalyptic vision of the future to show that the Corinthians' denial of the resurrection is inconsistent with a practice which presupposes a belief in it. For 'if the dead are not raised at all', then is it not the height of absurdity to baptize the living on behalf of the dead? 'The Greeks believed that the souls of the dead were benefited by the funeral honours paid to the body. This widespread feeling would find its way into the church and render the administration of a sacrament on behalf of the dead easy of introduction' (Edwards). Although Paul mentions this practice for the purpose of his argument, the phrase 'what shall *they* do' makes it evident that he is far from giving his approval to it. Moreover, as Hodge points out in his very helpful discussion of this notoriously difficult verse, the entire disappearance of the custom in the orthodox church 'is probably to be referred to the practice having been forbidden by the apostle as soon as he reached Corinth' [cf. 11:34b].

30: why do we also stand in jeopardy every hour?

Moreover, if there is no resurrection, there is no point in enduring hardship and braving danger for the sake of Christ. If the apostles' faith in this fundamental truth of the gospel were misplaced, then they were risking their lives for a dream without substance. They had lost hold of reality to embrace a mirage.

31: I protest by that glorying in you, brethren, which I have in Christ Jesus our Lord, I die daily.

Paul dies daily because the preaching of the gospel exposes him to innumerable dangers [*2 Cor.* 1:8, 9, 11:23]. This he solemnly affirms by the pride that he has in his brethren in Corinth. But though he glories in their faith, he returns all the credit for their conversion to Christ. 'This very name and title is full of the idea of the resurrection. Without the resurrection we should have no "Christ Jesus, our Lord", to commission Paul, to accomplish great things through Paul, to make the Corinthians Paul's glory, pride and joy' (Lenski).

32: If after the manner of men I fought with beasts at Ephesus, what doth it profit me? If the dead are not raised, let us eat and drink, for to-morrow we die.

What would it avail me that, humanly speaking, I 'fought with wild beasts' at Ephesus? (Moffatt): Here Paul uses figurative language to recall a specific occasion during his stay at Ephesus when the violence of the opposition he encountered could be likened to fighting with wild beasts. Certainly from a human standpoint he could gain nothing by risking the speedy dissolution of his life *as man* in this way. 'Paul's point is that, if there is no resurrection, the dead cannot exist as men and that they consequently do not live in the full sense of the word' (Grosheide) [*Psa.* 115:17].

If the dead are not raised. let us eat and drink, for to-morrow we die: This quotation of Isaiah 22:13, LXX, 'describes the reckless indulgence of the despisers of God's call to mourning, – Let us enjoy the good things of life now, for it soon will end. Paul imitates the language of sceptics, to reprove their theory and practice. "If men but persuade themselves that they should die like the beasts, they soon will live like beasts too" (South)' (Fausset)

33: Be not deceived: Evil companionships corrupt good morals.

Paul quotes the heathen poet Menander to convince the Corinthians of the danger of mixing pagan notions with the truth of the gospel. False teaching not only poisons the mind, but also demoralizes the life. 'The doubts of some in the Corinthian church concerning the resurrection of the dead was the consequence of their too intimate intercourse with their heathen neighbours' (Edwards).

34: Awake to soberness righteously, and sin not; for some have no knowledge of God: I speak this to move you to shame.

Awake out of drunkenness righteously (RV margin): 'A startling call, to men fallen as if into a drunken sleep under the seductions of sensualism and heathen society and the fumes of intellectual pride. "Righteously" signifies the *manner* of the awaking; it is *right* the Corinthians should rouse themselves from self–delusion; Paul assails their conscience' (Findlay).

And sin not: Literally, 'and do not go on missing the mark'. Those who prefer independent thought to revealed truth miss the mark set by God for all our thinking. 'This is the worst kind of sinning, for it affects not only our conduct but corrupts the very heart, the source of all conduct' (Lenski) [*Prov.* 4:2, 3].

For some have no knowledge of God: I speak this to move you to shame: 'Some of you are cherishing that ignorance of God which belongs to the heathen; and while it is natural in them, it is a shame to Christians' (Edwards).

35: But some one will say, How are the dead raised? and with what manner of body do they come?

The next aspect of the subject to receive the apostle's animated attention is the nature of the resurrection body [verses 35–49]. The 'gnostic' [cf. verse 12], whose Sadducean objections are here anticipated, is characterized by Godet as 'one of those sages whose whole spiritual stock consists in not knowing God [verse 34]'.

How are the dead raised? and with what manner of body do they come? These are two distinct questions. The first 'intimates *the impossibility of the thing*, and is answered in verse 36; the latter, *the inconceivability of the manner*, answered in verses 37ff. . . . The sceptics advance their second question to justify the first: they say, "The resurrection Paul preaches is absurd; how can any one imagine a new body rising out of the perished corpse – a body suitable to the deathless spirit?"' (Findlay).

36. Thou foolish one, that which thou thyself sowest is not quickened except it die:

The objector is foolish because he is blind to the quickening power of God which is daily displayed before him in nature. To think that what is 'dead' cannot be raised 'is in flagrant contradiction to the facts of experience: "what thou sowest is not made alive except it have died". Death, so far from being an obstacle to quickening, is its very prerequisite' (Vos) [*John* 12:24].

37: and that which thou sowest, thou sowest not the body that shall be, but a bare grain, it may chance of wheat, or of some other kind;

Paul deals at greater length with the second objection. The resurrection is not made impossible by the Corinthians' complete inability to visualize what the resurrection-body will be like. For without previous experience it would be equally impossible to anticipate the appearance of the mature plant from the bare grain that is sown, whether it be wheat or any other kind of seed. 'What right then has a man to argue from the impossibility of provision and pre-imagination, to the presumptuous conclusion that the forthcoming of a new differently-shaped and differently-apparelled body is *a priori* an absurdity?' (Vos).

38: but God giveth it a body even as it pleased him, and to each seed a body of its own.

The body that God now gives to each seed is in accordance with his creative decree [*Gen.* 1:11f]. Thus the identity which exists between the various kinds of seeds and their resultant plants has been established by God and is not due to any necessary natural processes' (Grosheide). From this it is safe to infer that such a God will not be nonplussed by the need to provide a suitable body for the souls of the redeemed.

39: All flesh is not the same flesh: but there is one flesh of men, and another flesh of beasts, and another flesh of birds, and another of fishes.

'If even here, where the general conditions of life are the same, we see such diversity in animal organizations, flesh and blood appearing in so many forms, why should it be assumed that the body hereafter must be the same cumbrous vehicle of the soul that it is now?' (Hodge).

40: There are also celestial bodies, and bodies terrestrial: but the glory of the celestial is one, and the glory of the terrestrial is another.

There is also a *discernible* difference between the glory of bodies celestial and of bodies terrestrial, for as G. Vos notes, *glory* 'is primarily a term of outward manifestation'. If Paul had been speaking of 'angelic bodies' there would have been no difference to note because such beings are not discerned by human vision; the reference is to the heavenly bodies of sun, moon, and stars as the next verse makes perfectly plain.

Nor need we suppose 'that the apostle ascribes life and sensation to them, after the manner of Philo. There is not a trace in the New Testament of the Greek notion that the stars are living creatures' (Edwards).

41: There is one glory of the sun, and another glory of the moon, and another glory of the stars; for one star differeth from another star in glory.

Not only is there a vast difference between the glory of heavenly and earthly bodies, but there are also gradations in glory to be seen among the heavenly bodies themselves. Even so, the God who made all these discernible differences will not be found wanting in the capacity to change the believer's present body that it may be conformed to the body of Christ's glory [*Phil.* 3:21].

42a: So also is the resurrection of the dead.

'Here, strictly speaking, is the answer to the second question of verse 35: *With what body?* Answer: with a body which, far from being the reappearance of the former, will have characteristics of an absolutely opposite kind' (Godet). Robertson and Plummer draw attention to the rhythmical parallelizing (as in Hebrew poetry) of Paul's utterance as he works towards the triumphant conclusion, especially verses 42–49 and verses 51–57.

42b: It is sown in corruption; it is raised in incorruption: 43: it is sown in dishonour; it is raised in glory: it is sown in weakness; it is raised in power: 44: it is sown a natural body; it is raised a spiritual body.

'*Our present life* is the seed–time [*Gal.* 6:7ff], and our "mortal bodies" [*Rom.* 8:10f] are in the germinal state, concluding with death [verse 36], out of which a wholly different organism will spring' (Findlay). As it was through sin that the body became subject to *corruption, dishonour*, and *weakness*, so it is only through redemption from sin that it will attain to the *incorruption, glory*, and *power* of the post-resurrection state [*Rom.* 6:23; 8:11–23; 2 *Cor.* 13:4; *Phil.* 3:21].

But with the fourth contrast between what is sown and raised, Paul reaches a new stage in the argument. It is because he is intent on showing that from the beginning God made provision for a higher kind of body, that he now advances from the contrast between the sinful body and the body restored by redemption to that between the creation–body ('natural' or 'psychical') and the resurrection-body ('spiritual' or 'pneumatic'). For though the body as created by God was sinless, and was not therefore characterized by corruption, dishonour, and weakness, it was nevertheless a *natural* body adapted to earthly conditions of life, and as such was unfit to be the eternal habitation of the *Spirit* [verses 44–49]. This adjective 'spiritual' does not denote a new substance, as though the resurrection-body consisted of 'spirit', and was therefore immaterial or ethereal. It rather points to a new *determination* or *origin*, for it is a body that is brought forth and determined by the divine, heavenly power (so Herman Ridderbos, *Paul*, p. 544).

> **44b: If there is a natural body, there is also a spiritual body.**
>
> **45: So also it is written, The first man Adam became a living soul. The last Adam became a life–giving spirit.**

Paul argues that if one kind of body exists, then so does the other. He views the creation of the natural body as a necessary preparation for its perfection in glory, and finds support for this in Genesis 2:7. His interpretative addition of the words 'first' and 'Adam' emphasizes the preliminary character of God's work in creation. Paul's point is that apart from the entrance of sin into the world Adam needed to be changed.

He was immortal in that he was made in the moral image of God, but in the probationary state under which he was placed by God his body was not fitted for an immortal existence. 'Of this change in the constitution of his body, the tree of life was probably constituted the sacrament. For when he sinned, he was excluded from the garden of Eden, "lest he put forth his hand and take of the tree of life, and eat, and live for ever" [*Gen.* 3:22]' (Hodge).

The last Adam became a life-giving spirit: It is in the light of Christ's redemptive achievement that Paul is able to add his own antithesis to Genesis 2:7 (so Bruce). It was when Christ's *body* was raised and glorified that he became a life-giving *spirit* [cf. *Rom.* 1:4; 8:11; *2 Cor.* 3:17]. For then, 'as the reward for his atoning death, He *received* the promised Spirit in His resurrection and ascension [*Matt.* 28:18; *Acts* 2:33]. He became a life-giving spirit as *the last Adam*, i.e., the last *man*: the unique and exclusive representative of those whom the Father gives Him [*John* 6:37, 17:9], who leads them to that glory which Adam should have obtained for the human race as its first representative [*Rom.* 5:12ff.; *1 Cor.* 15:20ff, 49]' (J. A. Schep, *The Nature of the Resurrection Body*, p. 176).

46: Howbeit that is not first which is spiritual, but that which is natural; then that which is spiritual.

Paul probably had a polemical purpose in making this emphatic assertion, because he reverses the order envisaged by Philo, who held that the ideal, heavenly man was prior to Adam, the earthly and material copy. Accordingly, he insists that the natural man precedes the spiritual man, who is not an archetypal heavenly man but the second man *from heaven* [verse 47]. The reference is not therefore to the pre-existence of Christ, but to that future coming of Christ by which all his people shall be changed [verses 50ff.; *Phil.* 3:21].

47: The first man is of the earth, earthy: the second man is of heaven.

'As *earthy* man is differentiated from what the risen Christ already is and what man will one day be through Him' (E. Schweizer, *TDNT*, vol. 9, p. 478). The real origin of Paul's doctrine of the second man from heaven is not Hellenistic but Jewish. For though he never uses the term Son of Man, his teaching here appears to be based on the Lord's own interpretation of Daniel 7:13 [cf. *Mark* 13:26; 14:62]. Thus Christ coming 'with the clouds of heaven' is seen as the climactic event which will perfect the salvation of his people and usher in the eternal state of glory [verse 23; *Rom.* 8:23; *1 Thess.* 4:16; *2 Thess.* 1:7].

48: As is the earthy, such are they also that are earthy: and as is the heavenly, such are they also that are heavenly.

The comparison is simple when it is remembered that 'bodies' is the main theme of the paragraph (Barrett). All Adam's descendants are of the earth, earthy [verse 47], but at the resurrection those who belong to Christ – the second man from heaven – will then bear his image [verse 49]. The parallel of verse 45 breaks down here, for though man is a 'living soul' like Adam, he will never be a 'life-giving' Creator Spirit like Christ. He will only be a 'spiritual body' (so E. Schweizer, *TDNT*, vol. 9, p. 663).

49: And as we have borne the image of the earthy, we shall also bear the image of the heavenly.

Although there is a variant reading, 'let us bear', the future tense, 'we shall bear', expresses the certainty of the event and is demanded by the context. At present we are forced to live on in a corruptible body, but as F. F. Bruce observes, at the resurrection the Creator's purpose that man should reflect his image [*Gen.* 1:26], will be finally realized when we are conformed to the Man who is himself the image of God [cf. *Rom.* 8:29; *2 Cor.* 4:4].

50: Now this I say, brethren, that flesh and blood cannot inherit the kingdom of God; neither doth corruption inherit incorruption.

What Paul now asserts sums up what he has said about the natural body in the previous verses [verses 44–49]. Such a natural body of 'flesh and blood' *cannot* inherit the kingdom of God because it is evident that the corruptible *does not* inherit incorruption. Hence the present constitution of the body must be changed before it is fit to enter that kingdom in which matter is no longer governed by the soul, but is ruled by the Spirit. The sequel shows that Paul is far from denying the material nature of the resurrection-body; 'our flesh will share in the glory of God, but only after it has been renewed and restored to life by the Spirit of Christ' (Calvin) [cf. *Luke* 24:39].

51: Behold, I tell you a mystery: We all shall not sleep, but we shall all be changed, 52: in a moment, in the twinkling of an eye, at the last trump: for the trumpet shall sound, and the dead shall be raised incorruptible, and we shall be changed.

Paul's exclamation 'Behold' draws the attention of the Corinthians to his revelation of a hitherto undisclosed mystery: it is that the bodies of all believers shall be changed, whether they happen to be dead or alive at Christ's coming. Behind the passive verb 'stands the almighty agent who shall work this miraculous change' (Lenski). Many restrict the pronoun 'we' to Paul and his readers, and gratuitously assume that the apostle expected to be alive at the Parousia, but the reference is general and includes the whole church, i.e. all Christians.

This change will be all but instantaneous, taking place in 'the twinkling of an eye, at the last trump'. The sound of that trumpet at the moment predetermined by God will mark the end of the present age, and consummate the salvation of his people, for then the dead shall be raised incorruptible, and the living shall be changed. As Warfield well says, 'Truly events stay not, when the Lord comes' [cf. *1 Thess.* 4:13–17].

53: For this corruptible must put on incorruption, and this mortal must put on immortality.

This gives the reason why we must be changed. 'It is impossible that corruption should inherit incorruption. This reason applies equally to the quick [living] and to the dead. With regard to both classes it is true that these vile bodies must be fashioned like unto Christ's glorious body' (Hodge) [cf. *2 Cor.* 5: 1–4].

54: But when this corruptible shall have put on incorruption, and this mortal shall have put on immortality, then shall come to pass the saying that is written, Death is swallowed up in victory.

But when . . . then: The resurrection will mark the final 'overthrow of the King of Terrors' (Findlay). This clothing of the saints with immortality will be the fulfilment of 'the farthest reaching of all Old Testament prophecies' [*Isa.* 25:8], since it reverses the sentence of doom that was pronounced in Genesis 3 (A. Dillmann). 'The Scriptures announce how one death (Christ's) devoured the others (ours)' (Luther).

55: O death, where is thy victory? O death, where is thy sting?

The apostle's exultant shout of triumph is a free adaptation of the language of Hosea 13:14. In that day the illusory nature of death's victory will be apparent to all; then its venomous sting will be abolished for ever. T. C. Edwards interestingly notes that Paul never used the word Hades, and that his substitution of Death for it in this passage can hardly have been accidental. For though the grave now claims the *bodies* of believers, their *souls* never enter the shadowy underworld of Hades.[1]

56: The sting of death is sin; and the power of sin is the law:

[1] On the modernist construction of Sheol-Hades see the very fine discussion by L. Berkhof in his *Systematic Theology*, pp. 681–6.

As sin's lethal sting introduced the universal reign of death, so its condemning power is derived from the law of God. If man had not sinned, he had not died [*Gen.* 2:17; *Rom.* 5:12]. Death therefore maintains itself in the sin which calls for condemnation, and in the law which passes sentence upon all who violate its divine sanctions [*Rom.* 7:7ff.]. This means 'that victory over sin is possible only through the propitiation, which is Jesus Christ [cf. *Rom.* 3:25]. The headship of the second Man has no real existence apart from his atonement. Christ acts as a quickening spirit through redemption. In this way the apostle connects the resurrection of believers with the death of Christ as well as with the power of his heavenly life. Thus to make the judicial intent of Christ's death the key–stone of the discussion is an unmistakable sign of Pauline thought' (Edwards).

> **57: but thanks be to God, who giveth us the victory through our Lord Jesus Christ.**

This objective atonement produces subjective results in the lives of all believers. What has been gained for us by Christ is daily being given to us by God [cf. *Rom.* 8:37]. Paul's use of the present tense does not denote the certainty of the future resurrection, but expresses the assurance that even now we have forgiveness of sins. 'If the sting of death is sin, victory over death must be forgiveness of the sin . . . The apostle's purpose is to encourage timid Christians in the conflict against sin with the certain hope of victory at last' (Edwards).

> **58: Wherefore, my beloved brethren, be ye steadfast, unmovable, always abounding in the work of the Lord, forasmuch as ye know that your labour is not vain in the Lord.**

Wherefore: Paul here concludes his great doctrinal argument on a very practical note: it is that the certainty of the resurrection must encourage diligence in present duty. The apostle's method of instruction teaches us that as no exhortation is in place without doctrine, so no exposition of doctrine is complete without exhortation.

My beloved brethren: Despite his severe reproofs, Paul assures the Corinthians that his affection for them remains undiminished.

Be ye steadfast, unmovable: They are to resist the seductive power of unbelief which would overthrow their faith in the doctrine of the resurrection. 'It is implied that an attempt of the kind has been

intentionally made in the Corinthian church, cf. verses 32–34'
(Edwards) [*2 Cor.* 11:2, 3].

Always abounding in the work of the Lord: 'There is perhaps an implied
correction of their disproportionate activity in speculation, cf. 1:18f.
"The work of the Lord" is preparation for the end, in mutual service
and the spread of the Gospel: and the end has been made sure by the
resurrection of the Lord' (St. John Parry).

Forasmuch as ye know that your labour is not in vain in the Lord: It is
because their work is in the Lord that it is not an *empty* expenditure of
energy: 'This is not an activity of external demonstration, wrought in
vacuity, as earthly labour so often is, but serious toil wrought in the
sphere of eternal reality. This is why Paul also uses the present *is*, and
not the future *will be*' (Godet).

CHAPTER SIXTEEN

In the last chapter Paul deals with various practical and personal
matters. He first gives directions concerning the collection for
impoverished fellow–believers at Jerusalem [verses 1–4]. He then
speaks of his travel plans which include a projected visit to Corinth
[verses 5–9]. Meanwhile he urges them to receive Timothy, and informs
them that Apollos will not be visiting the church at this time [verses
10–12]. In his final exhortation to the congregation, Paul expresses
his joy in receiving the delegates from Corinth, and sends the greetings
of the believers in Asia [verses 13–20]. After adding his own greetings,
the apostle pronounces a solemn anathema on anyone who does not
love the Lord, and concludes with the benediction and an assurance of
his love for them all [verses 21–24].

**1: Now concerning the collection for the saints, as I gave order to the
churches of Galatia, so also do ye.**

That Paul was no impractical visionary is shown by his rapid descent
from the sublime truth of the resurrection to the mundane details of
church administration. The familiar introductory formula, 'Now
concerning', suggests that the collection was another matter on which
the Corinthians had requested further guidance. In giving them the
same direction that he gave to the churches of Galatia, Paul lets them
know that they are not the only Gentiles who are asked to contribute

to the support of the poor saints in Jerusalem. 'He proposes the Galatians as an example to the Corinthians, the Corinthians to the Macedonians, the Corinthians and the Macedonians to the Romans; *2 Cor.* 9:2; *Rom.* 15:26. There is great force in examples' (Bengel). Persecution by unbelieving Jews and protracted periods of famine probably account for the dire straits to which these Jewish Christians were reduced. Paul regarded this collection as nothing less than the payment of a debt of gratitude [cf. *Rom.* 15:27]. He also felt that it would 'strikingly demonstrate the solidarity of the Gentile churches with the mother church, and do much to promote unity' (Morris).

> **2: Upon the first day of the week let each one of you lay by him in store, as he may prosper, that no collections be made when I come.**

Upon the first day of the week: This renders it certain 'that that day was already regarded by all Christians as a sacred day, and, as such, the proper day (as we find from *Acts* 20:7) for public worship. In this view, their laying by their weekly sum *on that day* would both stamp the contribution with a sacred character and hallow and stimulate the generous principle itself' (Brown).

Let each one of you lay by him in store: 'Paul trusts the Corinthians: he does not ask them to hand in their collection on a weekly basis, they are allowed to keep the collected money and thus little by little a sufficient amount will be saved up' (Grosheide) [*Matt.* 6:19–21; *Luke* 12:21].

As he may prosper: 'Paul makes the measure of God's blessing to us the measure of our return to him ... At no time does he propose the old Jewish system of tithing to the churches under his care. The only references to tithes found in the New Testament take us back into the Old Testament, *Heb.* 5:7–9, or criticize the Pharisees at Christ's time, *Matt.* 2,3:23; *Luke* 11:42, 18:12. This is quite decisive for us' (Lenski).

That no collections be made when I come: 'Paul would avoid the unseemliness and the difficulty of raising money suddenly, at the last moment; and he wishes when he comes to be free to devote himself to higher matters [cf. *Acts* 6:2]' (Findlay).

> **3: And when I arrive, whomsoever ye shall approve, them will I send with letters to carry your bounty unto Jerusalem: 4: and if it be meet for me to go also, they shall go with me.**

Paul wisely avoids handling the fund himself so that the Corinthians are given no opportunity to question his integrity [cf. *1 Thess.* 2:5]. They are to appoint trustworthy men to deliver their gift, and he will authorize their mission by supplying them with 'letters' (written credentials) addressed to the leaders of the Jerusalem church.

If it seems advisable that I should go also (RSV): This rendering is preferable, for the verse 'does not mean: if the collection is large enough I myself shall go with the delegation, but rather: if circumstances are such that the mission work demands my journeying to Jerusalem they shall go with me. Then letters will not be needed' (Grosheide).

5: But I will come unto you, when I shall have passed through Macedonia; for I pass through Macedonia; 6: but with you it may be that I shall abide, or even winter, that ye may set me forward on my journey whithersoever I go. 7: For I do not wish to see you now by the way; for I hope to tarry a while with you, if the Lord permit.

Paul writes from Ephesus of his future plans. It appears from 2 Corinthians 1:15, 16 that his original intention, presumably announced in the 'lost' letter [5:9], had been to visit them on his way and again on his return from Macedonia. But now he has decided that instead of paying them two flying visits, he will not call at Corinth on his way to Macedonia, because he *prefers* to stay longer with them on his return from Macedonia. This will give him the opportunity of dealing with their problems, and it will give them the privilege of helping him forward on his next journey, wherever that may take him. Thus Paul defers his visit, not from any lack of interest, but rather that he may be able to minister more effectively to them. Yet though this is his settled aim (which was in fact carried out, *Acts* 20:3), they must realize that all his plans are made in subjection to the will of the Lord [*James* 4:15].

8: But I will tarry at Ephesus until Pentecost; 9: for a great door and effectual is opened unto me, and there are many adversaries.

Paul cannot come to them now because his work in Ephesus is not yet finished. At present he must remain in that city not only to grasp the great opportunities he has for effectively preaching the gospel [*2 Cor.* 2: 12; *Col.* 4:3], but also to counter the fierce opposition which the signal success of his mission has aroused [*Acts* 19:9, 13f.]. 'Great success in the work of the gospel commonly creates many enemies.

The devil opposes the most, and makes them most trouble, who most heartily and successfully set themselves to destroy his kingdom' (Matthew Henry).

> 10: Now if Timothy come, see that he be with you without fear; for he worketh the work of the Lord, as I also do: 11: let no man therefore despise him. But set him forward on his journey in peace, that he may come unto me: for I expect him with the brethren.

Since Paul would send this letter by the shortest route, it would reach Corinth before Timothy [4:17], who was to come via Macedonia [*Acts* 19:22]. The somewhat strange request, to ensure that Timothy may stay with them 'without fear', suggests that Paul is afraid that after hearing eloquent preachers like Apollos they may be inclined to belittle this shy and diffident young man [cf. *2 Tim.* 1:7]. Let them then realize that he is working faithfully alongside Paul in the same work for the Lord. Hence no one in Corinth is to despise Timothy. They are to receive him with respect and to send him on his way in peace, for Paul will eagerly await his return with the brethren whom he is now sending to Corinth with this letter (probably Titus and the 'brother' of 2 Corinthians 12:18).

> 12: But as touching Apollos the brother, I besought him much to come unto you with the brethren: and it was not at all his will to come now; but he will come when he shall have opportunity.

Apparently the Corinthians had requested another visit from Apollos, but he refused to accept the invitation even though Paul had urged him to return with the brethren [verse 11]. 'Considering the way in which Apollos had been made a rival to Paul in Corinth, it shows magnanimity on Paul's side to desire his return, and a modest delicacy on the side of Apollos to decline the request' (Findlay) [1:12].

> 13: Watch ye, stand fast in the faith, quit you like men, be strong. 14: Let all that ye do be done in love.

With these five imperatives Paul gathers up the burden of his message as he urges the Corinthians to develop the qualities in which they were sadly deficient. 1. The exhortation to *watchfulness* is directed against their heedlessness and recalls 15:33f. 2. The summons to *stand fast* in the faith rebukes their fickleness and this sums up such passages as

4:17, 10:12, 15:2, 11ff. 3. To *play the man* means that they must give up their childishness, especially as this relates to the question of spiritual gifts, cf. 13:11; 14:20. 4. *'Be strong'* was an appropriate word to those enfeebled by their compromises with paganism, cf. chapter 10. 5. Finally, the demand that *all things be done in love* again touches upon the radical fault of this community, cf. chapters 8 and 13.

15: Now I beseech you, brethren (ye know the house of Stephanas, that it is the firstfruits of Achaia, and that they have set themselves to minister unto the saints), 16: that ye also be in subjection unto such, and to every one that helpeth in the work and laboureth.

It is not because Stephanas and his household are the first to believe the gospel in the province that Paul calls them 'the firstfruits of Achaia', for some were converted through his preaching in Athens [*Acts* 17:34]. But to his mind 'the pledge of a future church came not in Athens, but in Corinth' with the conversion of a whole family (Edwards). Paul singles out this family as worthy of the Corinthians' respect and imitation because their forwardness in service happily matched the priority of their conversion.

'This respectful deference ought to be extended to every one who voluntarily makes himself like those of whom Paul has just spoken; their fellow–labourer by working for the good of the church . . . It is plain from this exhortation that the Corinthians were naturally prone to be lacking in submission and respect to those whom their age, experience, and services naturally pointed out for the veneration of the flock' (Godet).

17: And I rejoice at the coming of Stephanas and Fortunatus and Achaicus: for that which was lacking on your part they supplied.
18: For they refreshed my spirit and yours: acknowledge ye therefore them that are such.

Paul rejoices in the coming of these messengers from Corinth, for 'the lack of your own presence has been supplied by theirs as your deputies' (Brown). This had refreshed Paul's spirit, because the arrival of a delegation, presumably with a letter from the church, showed that the Corinthians, whatever their failings, still acknowledged his authority. Moreover, their own account of the situation in Corinth was not uniformly depressing, but also had its brighter side [1:4f]. In making this fraternal contact with Paul these men minister the same refreshment to the Corinthians. The apostle thus credits them with solicitous feelings that are just like his own' (Lenski). Therefore loyal service like theirs should compel the Corinthians gratefully to recognise the true worth of such men!

19: The churches of Asia salute you. Aquila and Prisca salute you much in the Lord, with the church that is in their house.

All the churches of proconsular Asia send Christian greetings, to which their old friends Aquila and Prisca [*Acts* 18:2, 3], now with Paul in Ephesus [*Acts* 18:18], add special salutations in the Lord, together with the church that gathers in their house. 'As the same expression is used in *Rom.* 16:5, in connection with their names, it is probable that both at Rome and Ephesus, they opened their house as a regular place of meeting for Christians. Their occupation as tent-makers probably required spacious apartments, suited for the purpose of such assemblies' (Hodge).

20: All the brethren salute you. Salute one another with a holy kiss.

Finally, all the brethren at Ephesus salute their fellow believers at Corinth, whom Paul here urges to salute one another with a holy kiss [cf. *Rom.* 16:16; *2 Cor.* 13:12; *1 Thess.* 5:26]. By doing this after having heard Paul's epistle, the Corinthians 'would indicate that they were united with one another and also with the churches of Asia' (Grosheide).

21: The salutation of me Paul with mine own hand.

Paul has finished dictating his letter. It is now time for him to take the pen in his own hand, and write out the last few words himself [verses 21–24]. [cf. *2 Thess.* 3:17] It is a moment charged with deep emotion, and Paul wishes to evoke a corresponding response in the hearts of his beloved Corinthians.

22: If any man loveth not the Lord, let him be anathema. Marana tha.

This would come as a complete surprise and must have produced a profound feeling of shock when it was first read out in church [cf. *Gal.* 1:8, 9]. Truly Paul's letters are powerful! Here he deliberately uses the weaker word for love [*phileo*: cf. *John* 21:15–17] to stigmatize the *heartlessness* of those in whom even human affection for the Lord is wanting. He pronounces his solemn curse upon all who feign a love they do not feel for Christ. 'It is a *spurious* love that is accursed —a cold, false heart which, knowing the Lord, does not really love him' (Findlay).

Marana tha: These two Aramaic words mean, 'Our Lord, come!' [cf. *Rev.* 22:20], and their preservation in a letter addressed to Greek-speaking Christians is 'the Achilles' heel' (A. E. J. Rawlinson) of the fantastic notion that the title 'Lord' was the invention of Hellenistic Christianity (advocated by W. Bousset and R. Bultmann). K. G. Kuhn points out that the untranslated Aramaic term is meaningful only if it was a fixed formula that was well-known in the churches. This means that its origin must be sought only in the Palestinian community, and that it had an important place in the worship of this community. The term is thus 'an important and authentic witness to the faith of the primitive Palestinian community. This confessed Jesus, the exalted Christ, as its Lord. It spoke of Him and prayed to Him as "our Lord". Here then, is the origin of the ascription of the name "Lord", the title *kurios*, to Jesus – a title which in Paul especially takes on profound and comprehensive significance in opposition to the *lords* of the Hellenistic world' (*TDNT*, vol. 4, p. 470) (cf. 8:5).

23: The grace of the Lord Jesus Christ be with you.

'The apostle will not end with a word of warning or severity, but adds the usual benediction. Like a true teacher, as Chrysostom says, he helps not only with counsels, but with prayers' (Robertson-Plummer).

24: My love be with you all in Christ Jesus. Amen.

Here the 'Amen' has been added by a later hand. It is a liturgical addition to the text [cf. NIV]. This is of some importance because its omission makes Paul's last words all the more impressive. For though Paul has found it necessary to administer severe reproofs, in closing he assures the Corinthians that even these were prompted by his love for them 'in Christ Jesus'. 'The last word that is and can be said – in Christ Jesus, in whom both you and I live and are one. It is the ground of the whole Epistle' (St. John Parry).

SOLI DEO GLORIA

BIBLIOGRAPHY AND ACKNOWLEDGEMENTS

The author expresses his grateful thanks to the following authors and publishers who kindly gave permission to reproduce quotations from their copyright works.

BARRETT, C. K., *The First Epistle to the Corinthians* (*BNTC*) (A & C Black, 1971).

BOETTNER, LORAINE, *Roman Catholicism* (Banner of Truth, 1966).

BORNKAMM, GÜNTHER, *Early Christian Experience* (translated by Paul L. Hammer) (Harper & Row, 1969).

BRUCE, F. F., *1 and 2 Corinthians* (*NCB*) (Oliphants, 1971).

CALVIN, JOHN, *The First Epistle of Paul the Apostle to the Corinthians* (translated by John W. Fraser) (Oliver and Boyd, 1960).

CHANTRY, WALTER J., Signs of the Apostles (Banner of Truth, 1976).

CLARK, GORDON H., *1 Corinthians – A Contemporary Commentary* (Presbyterian &Reformed, 1975).

CULLMANN, OSCAR, *The Early Church* (Edited by A.J. B. Higgins) (SCM 1956).

DOUGLAS, J. D., Editor, *The New Bible Dictionary* (IVF, 1962).

DUNN, JAMES, D. G., *Jesus and the Spirit* (SCM, 1975).

EDWARDS, T. C., *A Commentary on the First Epistle to the Corinthians* (Hodder & Stoughton, 1885).

GELDENHUYS, NORVAL, *Supreme Authority* (Marshall, Morgan & Scott, 1953).

GROSHEIDE, F. W., *Commentary on 1 Corinthians* (*NLC*) (Marshall, Morgan & Scott, 1954).

HÉRING, JEAN, *The First Epistle of Saint Paul to the Corinthians* (translated by A. W. Heathcote and P. J. Allcock) (Epworth, 1962).

HILLYER, NORMAN, *Commentary on 1 Corinthians* (NBC Revised) (I V P, 1970).

KITTEL, G. AND FRIEDRICH, G., *Theological Dictionary of the New Testament* Vols. 1–10, translated by Geoffrey W. Bromiley; index by Ronald E. Pitkin) (Eerdmans, 1964–1976).

LENSKI, R. C. H., *The Interpretation of 1 Corinthians* (Augsburg, 1961).

MARE, W. HAROLD, *1 Corinthians* (*EBC*) (Pickering & Inglis, 1976).

MARTIN, RALPH P., *Worship in the Early Church* (Marshall, Morgan & Scott, 1964)

MORRIS, LEON, *1 Corinthians* (*TNTC*) (Tyndale, 1958).

—— *The Apostolic Preaching of the Cross* (Tyndale, 1965).

—— *Spirit of the Living God* (IVP, 1969).

MOULE, C. F. D., *An Idiom-Book of New Testament Greek* (CUP, 1968).

MURRAY, JOHN, *Principles of Conduct* (Tyndale, 1957).

MURRAY, JOHN (contributor to), *The Infallible Word* (Presbyterian & Reformed, 1946).

PARRY, R. ST. JOHN, *The First Epistle of Paul the Apostle to the Corinthians* (*CGT*) (CUP, 1916).

ROBERTSON, A. T., *Word Pictures in the New Testament*, vol. 4 (Broadman, 1931)

ROBERTSON, A. AND PLUMMER, A., *Commentary on 1 Corinthians* (ICC) (T. & T. Clark, 1967).

SCHEP, J. A., *The Nature of the Resurrection Body* (Eerdmans, 1964).

STONEHOUSE, NED B., *Paul before the Areopagus* (Tyndale, 1957).

STOTT, JOHN, *Baptism and Fullness* (IVP 1975).

VINE, W. E., *Expository Dictionary of New Testament Words* (Oliphants, 1958).

VOS, GEERHARDUS, *The Pauline Eschatology* (Eerdmans 1961).

ZORN, RAYMOND O., *Christ Triumphant* (Banner of Truth, 1997).

In addition to these, the following books were consulted:

ALFORD, HENRY, *The Greek Testament* (Rivingtons, 1877).

ARNDT, W. F. AND GINGRICH, F. W., *A Greek–English Lexicon of the New Testament* (University of Chicago Press, 1957).

BENGEL, J. A., *New Testament Word Studies*, vol. 2 (Kregel, 1971).

BERKHOF, L., *Systematic Theology* (Banner of Truth, 1959).

BOLTON, SAMUEL, *The True Bounds of Christian Freedom* (Banner of Truth, 1964).

BROWN, DAVID, *1 Corinthians* (*Popular Commentary on NT*) (T. & T. Clark).

BRUNER, F. D., *A Theology of the Holy Spirit* (Hodder & Stoughton, 1970).

BURGESS, ANTHONY, *A Practical Commentary on 1 Corinthians 3* (London, 1659).

CONZELMANN, HANS, *1 Corinthians* (*Hermeneia*) (translated by James W. Leitch) (Fortress Press, 1975).

CRAIG, CLARENCE T., *The First Epistle to the Corinthians* (*IB*) (Abingdon, 1953).

CULLMANN, OSCAR, *The Christology of the New Testament* (translated by Shirley C. Guthrie and Charles A. M. Hall) (SCM, 1963).

—— *Christ and Time* (translated by Floyd V. Filson), (SCM, 1971).

DAVIES, W. D., *Paul and Rabbinic Judaism* (SPCK, 1970).

DENNEY, JAMES, *Studies in Theology* (Hodder & Stoughton, 1895).

EADIE, JOHN, *Commentary on the Epistle to the Ephesians* (Zondervan reprint of 1883 ed.).

EDWARDS, JONATHAN, *Charity and Its Fruits* (Banner of Truth, 1969).

FAUSSET, A. R., *Commentary on 1 Corinthians* (*JFB*) (Collins, 1874).

FINDLAY, G. G., *Commentary on 1 Corinthians* (EGT) (Eerdmans, 1974).

GODET, F., *Commentary on 1 Corinthians* (T. & T. Clark, 1886).

HENRY, MATTHEW, *Commentary on the Holy Bible* (various editions).

HODGE, CHARLES, *Commentary on 1 Corinthians* (Banner of Truth, 1958).

KENNEDY, H. A. A., *St. Paul and the Mystery-Religions* (Hodder & Stoughton, 1913).

LADD, GEORGE ELDON, *A Theology of the New Testament* (Eerdmans, 1974).

LIGHTFOOT, J. B., *Notes on the Epistles of St Paul* (Zondervan, 1957).

LIGHTFOOT, J. B., *St. Paul's Epistle to the Philippians* (Zondervan, 1953).

LLOYD–JONES, D. M., *Conversions: Psychological and Spiritual* (IVF, 1963).

2 Corinthians

INTRODUCTION

*A*fter staying over eighteen months Paul left the flourishing church he had founded in Corinth for Ephesus (*Acts* 18:18f.), where, it seems, he received disquieting news of the lax conduct of his Corinthian converts. It was to deal with this grave situation that he sent them a letter (since lost) in which he warned them of the serious consequences of such licentious behaviour [*1 Cor.* 5:9]. Following the despatch of that letter, more bad news reached Paul through some of Chloe's household, who informed him that the church was split into factions [*1 Cor.* 1:11], but this was mercifully offset by the arrival of the Corinthian deputies, Stephanas, Fortunatus, and Achaicus [*1 Cor.* 16:17]. For though the letter they presumably brought with them made no reference to these grievous divisions within the fellowship, the fact that the church had taken the trouble to seek his advice on certain points of conduct and worship showed that it still acknowledged his authority [*1 Cor.* 7:1].

By way of reply Paul wrote the Epistle we know as First Corinthians, in which he states that he has already sent Timothy to them as his special envoy [*1 Cor.* 4:17; 16:10]. But when Timothy arrived he was faced with an entirely new situation, for he found that Paul's authority in the church had been undermined by the superior claims put forward by a group of Jewish opponents to the Pauline mission. In view of this fresh crisis Timothy could do nothing but return with the news to Ephesus. On hearing Timothy's report Paul resolved to pay an immediate visit to Corinth, but it appears that this attempt to settle the issue in person met with a humiliating rebuff. The sequel to this 'painful' visit [*2 Cor.* 2:1] was a 'severe' letter of reproof which is also lost to us (it was probably destroyed after it had achieved its object). Although it cost Paul 'much affliction and anguish of heart' to write such a letter [*2 Cor.* 2:4], he knew it had to be done if the rebellious

Corinthians were to be restored to apostolic obedience. Paul entrusted the letter to Titus, but as he anxiously waited to hear how the Corinthians had received it, he was assailed by doubts and beset with danger [2 Cor. 1:8–10].

After the riot in Ephesus brought his work there to an abrupt end [Acts 20:1], Paul hastened to Troas where he had arranged to meet Titus on his return from Corinth [2 Cor. 2:12, 13]. The disappointment of this hope led him to travel on to Macedonia, where at last they met, probably in Philippi or its port, Neapolis. The report that Titus gave to Paul on the Corinthians' response to his letter was largely reassuring. Although the false teachers, who had infiltrated into the church by arming themselves with letters of commendation [2 Cor. 3:1], were encouraging a minority to remain recalcitrant [2 Cor. 12:21], the majority were humbled by the severe letter and had been 'made sorry unto repentance' [2 Cor. 7:9].

Under the inspiration of the Spirit, Paul here gives free expression to the mingled emotions which were aroused in him by this report. It is this deliberate lack of reserve that makes the document we call Second Corinthians the most intensely personal of all Paul's utterances. It is at once a triumphant vindication of his apostolic ministry, and a searing indictment of the pretensions of the 'super-apostles' who were attempting to overthrow his work in Corinth by basely slandering his character and his motives. Thus the purpose of the letter was to prepare the Corinthians for his promised visit. It was written to ensure that when he came to Corinth for the third time it would be in joy and not in sorrow or anger [2 Cor. 2:1; 12:14; 13:1, 2].

If the above is an accurate outline of Paul's relations with the Corinthian church, we have the following sequence of events:

> Paul's first visit [Acts 18:1ff.]
> The previous letter [1 Cor. 5:9]
> 1 CORINTHIANS – c. Spring AD 55
> The painful visit [2 Cor. 2:1]
> The severe letter [2 Cor. 2:4]
> Paul leaves Ephesus and meets Titus in Macedonia [Acts 20:1]
> 2 CORINTHIANS – c. Autumn AD 56
> Paul's third visit [Acts 20:2]

As 'Second' Corinthians is manifestly an intelligible unity, there is no need to accept the modern notion that 2 Corinthians 6: 14–7:1 is a fragment of the 'previous' letter [*1 Cor.* 5:9] and that part of the 'severe' letter is preserved in 2 Corinthians 10:1–13:10, especially as there is no external evidence to show that it was ever circulated in any other form.

CHAPTER ONE

After affirming his divine calling as an apostle of Christ, Paul associates Timothy with himself in greeting the church at Corinth and all the saints of Achaia [verses 1, 2]. Paul blesses God for the comfort received throughout his recent afflictions, by which he is enabled to comfort the Corinthians in their distress [verses 3–7]. He refers to his deliverance from a peril in Asia that made him despair of life, and expresses his confidence in God's future protection through their prayers [verses 8–11]. Apparently the apostle's detractors charged him with inconsistency on the grounds that he had changed his travel plans, but he insists that the real reason for postponing his visit was to spare them [verses 12–24].

1: Paul, an apostle of Christ Jesus through the will of God, and Timothy our brother, unto the church of God which is at Corinth, with all the saints that are in the whole of Achaia:

Paul, an apostle of Christ Jesus through the will of God: Since the Corinthians had questioned his authority so recently, it is not surprising that Paul should begin with the reminder that he is not an apostle of Christ Jesus by human accreditation but by divine appointment [cf. 3:1]. It is through the eternal good pleasure of God that he is such an apostle. Moreover, because he was *directly* called by the risen Christ himself, his apostleship differed radically from that which was exercised by those who were *mediately* commissioned by the church [8:23; *Phil.* 2:25]. And though he counts it a privilege to serve the church [4:5], it is significant that he never speaks of himself as 'an apostle of the church'. All the evidence 'points overwhelmingly to the fact that, *in the highest sense of the word*, only the original apostles and Paul were called and appointed to be the "authorized representatives" of the exalted Lord. Where Barnabas is called an apostle in Acts 14:4, 14 it is clearly in the sense of one being sent by the Church as a fully commissioned missionary but not as an "apostle of Christ" [cf. Acts 13:14] in the highest sense as used of the Twelve and Paul' (Norval Geldenhuys, *Supreme Authority,* pp. 71–72). Thus as it was the unique function of the apostles to be *eye*-witnesses of the resurrection and by their inspired testimony to provide the foundation upon which the church rests, it is evident that they can have no successors in this office.

And Timothy the brother (ASV margin): It is not to share the responsibility of composition that Paul includes Timothy in the address, but to enhance his appeal to the Corinthians. What he writes with all the authority of an apostle also commands the fraternal assent of a fellow–Christian who is also well known to them [*1 Cor.* 1:1]. The linking of Timothy's name with his own is also a tacit rebuke, for it expresses his continued confidence in an envoy they had treated badly (see Introduction), but who nevertheless still had their spiritual welfare at heart.

Unto the church of God which is at Corinth: In writing to this company of believers living in a particular place, Paul reminds them of the dignity that is theirs as *the* church of God, and of their obligations as members of the church *of God.* According to K. L. Schmidt, the designation affords strong support for 'the contention that the Church is not a great community made up of an accumulation of small communities, but is truly present in its wholeness in every company of believers, however small' (cited by P. E. Hughes).

With all the saints that are in the whole of Achaia: Paul addresses the Corinthian church *directly,* and all the Christians in the province *indirectly.* This indicates that he 'was conscious that his written words were significant for the whole Church of God, and not merely for the particular local churches at which they were first delivered' (R. V. G. Tasker).

In the New Testament, sainthood is not the prerogative of a special caste but the privilege of every Christian [cf. *Acts* 9:13]. As each believer is objectively 'holy' in Christ, so he is to be subjectively transformed 'into the same image' [3:18]. But because believers have not yet attained this goal [*Phil.* 3:12], they are not sinlessly perfect, and must continue to trust in the mediation of their righteous Advocate with the Father [*1 John* 1:8–2:1].

2: Grace to you and peace from God our Father and the Lord Jesus Christ.

Grace to you and peace: It is by replacing the ordinary 'hail' of Greek letter writing with the word 'grace' that Paul invests the customary greeting with a deep religious meaning. 'Grace' is the free and unmerited favour of God, and the blessed result of its reception is 'peace'.

From God our Father and the Lord Jesus Christ: The pronoun 'our' advertises the stupendous fact that God the Father is also the Father of believers in virtue of his adoptive grace towards them in the Lord Jesus Christ. The blessings of grace and peace descend to us from God our Father 'as the primal *Fountain*', through Christ 'as the mediatorial *Channel*'; and 'by coupling both Persons in one and the same invocation, their equality in the Godhead is brightly confirmed' (David Brown).

3: Blessed be the God and Father of our Lord Jesus Christ, the Father of mercies and God of all comfort;

Blessed be the God and Father of our Lord Jesus Christ: Paul usually follows his greeting with a thanksgiving for what God has done for his readers, but here he bursts into a jubilant doxology to praise God for the marvellous mercies so recently vouchsafed to himself [verse 4]. As in Ephesians 1:3 and 1 Peter 1:3, the customary Jewish blessing, 'Blessed be God', is given a distinctively Christian content. This remarkable expression indicates that God is both the God and Father of the Lord Jesus Christ. He became his God when the Son was made flesh for our salvation, whereas he is his Father from all eternity. But we cannot call upon God as *our* Father [verse 2], except as we are related to him through the merits and mediation of our Lord Jesus Christ [*John* 14:6].

The Father of mercies: Instead of speaking, as we should, of 'the mercy of God' as an abstract principle, 'Paul speaks of its various concrete manifestations. These reveal the essential nature of the great Father and are therefore taken up into his Name' (J. A. Beet) [*Psa.* 103:13].

And God of all comfort: The word 'comfort' which Paul uses ten times in five verses is not to be understood in any sentimental sense. God comforts his people by encouraging and strengthening them, so that they are not crushed by affliction. Arthur Pink points out that this is an excellency peculiar to the true and living God, for the heathen deities are represented as being so cruel and ferocious that even their own worshippers regard them as objects of dread. Yet 'many believers seem to be as reluctant to go out of themselves to God alone for comfort, as unbelievers are to go out of themselves to Christ alone for righteousness' (*Gleanings from Paul*, p. 68).

4: who comforteth us in all our affliction, that we may be able to comfort them that are in any affliction, through the comfort wherewith we ourselves are comforted of God.

'Affliction' is the distress produced by painful pressure, and this is relieved by the 'comfort' which prevents it from becoming insupportable. Knowing the sustaining strength of God in *all* his affliction qualified the apostle to be of comfort to others in *every kind* of affliction. He did not see this comfort as a blessing to be selfishly kept to himself, but as the divinely given means of helping those in similar straits. Paul would have the Corinthians know that he finds such comforting more congenial than administering the faithful wounds of a friend [*Prov.* 27:6]. For though he had not flinched from this duty, he did not rejoice in it.

5: For as the sufferings of Christ abound unto us, even so our comfort also aboundeth through Christ.

For just as the sufferings of Christ flow over into our lives, so also through Christ our comfort overflows (NIV): There is no thought of sharing in Christ's atoning sacrifice, for the gospel Paul preached was plainly based on the finished work of Christ [*Rom.* 5:8–10; 6:10]. But though the personal sufferings of Christ are past, his sufferings in his people still continue. The unforgettable lesson which Paul learned on the Damascus road was that the glorified Christ reckoned as his own whatever sufferings his people endured for his sake [*Acts* 9:4, 5]. These tribulations are the lot of the Messianic community on earth [*Acts* 14:22], because those who confess their interest in the Messiah cannot avoid their share of the same hatred that reached its climax in his crucifixion [*Heb.* 13:13]. Yet the willing bearers of Christ's reproach always find that their suffering is matched by his comfort. 'As union with Christ was the source of the afflictions which Paul endured, so it was the source of the abundant consolation which he enjoyed. This makes the great difference between the sorrows of believers and those of unbelievers. Alienation from Christ does not secure freedom from suffering, but it cuts us off from the only source of consolation. Therefore the sorrow of the world worketh death' (Charles Hodge).

6: But whether we are afflicted, it is for your comfort and salvation; or whether we are comforted, it is for your comfort, which worketh in the patient enduring of the same sufferings which we also suffer: 7: and our hope for you is steadfast; knowing that, as ye are partakers of the sufferings, so also are ye of the comfort.

The bond which unites Paul with the Corinthians is so vital that whatever befalls him in the service of Christ is experienced with a view to their good. He endures affliction for their encouragement and salvation; he receives comfort for their strengthening, the effectiveness of which is shown in their patient endurance of the same suffering for the sake of the gospel as he himself endures. In verse 7 Paul sums up the paragraph on a note of triumphant hope. It is because the Corinthians are sharers with him both in his sufferings and in his comfort that he has no doubt of their final salvation. They will be enabled to endure to the end, for the comfort is always commensurate with the suffering. 'He does not claim the credit of comforting them: they receive comfort from the same source that he does – from God through Christ' (Alfred Plummer).

8: For we would not have you ignorant, brethren, concerning our affliction which befell us in Asia, that we were weighed down exceedingly, beyond our power, insomuch that we despaired even of life:

Having spoken in a general way of affliction and comfort, Paul now vividly recalls a recent affliction by which he was so excessively weighed down that he even despaired of life. Clearly he had been in mortal peril of some kind, though in the absence of further information it is impossible to identify the nature of this terrible experience. But in the light of Chapter 11:23–26, which reveals something of what the apostle suffered to bring the gospel to the Gentiles [*Acts* 9:16], we can see that he did not exaggerate when he used such expressions as 'death worketh in us' [4:12] and 'I die daily' [*1 Cor.* 15:31]. However, what follows shows that Paul's concern was not to provide a circumstantial account of the danger, but to magnify God's grace in his deliverance from it [verse 9].

9: yea, we ourselves have had the sentence of death within ourselves, that we should not trust in ourselves, but in God who raiseth the dead:

James Denney draws attention to the force of the perfect tense: 'We *had* this experience, and in its fruit – a newer and deeper faith in God – we *have* it still. It is a permanent possession in this happy form.' If Paul now recalls the sentence he had passed on himself in his despair it is only that the Corinthians might learn the blessed lesson he was taught by it. For no trial, however severe, can frustrate the sovereign purpose of God who does in fact work all things together for the good of his people [*Rom.* 8:28].

That we should not trust in ourselves, but in God who raiseth the dead: Thus the affliction that dealt the fatal stroke to all self–trust was sent to inspire undying hope in the God by whose omnipotent power alone the dead are raised to life. It is this capacity to create life where previously death reigned supreme that distinguishes the one true and living God from all the helpless deities of man's invention [*Psa.* 135: 15–18; *Ezek.* 37:1–14; *Rom.* 4:17; *Heb.* 11:19].

10: who delivered us out of so great a death, and will deliver: on whom we have set our hope that he will also still deliver us;

Having experienced so great a deliverance, Paul cannot doubt that the God upon whom he has set his hope will continue to deliver him from whatever perils still lie ahead, until he is finally delivered from suffering and brought to glory [*2 Tim.* 4: 18]. 'Past experiences are great encouragements to faith and hope, and they lay great obligations to trust in God for time to come. We reproach our experiences, if we distrust God in future straits, who hath delivered us in former troubles (Matthew Henry).

11: ye also helping together on our behalf by your supplication; that, for the gift bestowed upon us by means of many, thanks may be given by many persons on our behalf.

Paul here gently reminds the Corinthians that they are not idle spectators of a drama in which they have no part to play. For it is by their joining together in prayer on his behalf that he expects to obtain this deliverance which remains the gracious gift of God, even though its bestowal involves the supplication of many. Yet the great end for which such answers to prayer are given is never secured by the mere reception of the blessing itself, but in that grateful response which magnifies the glory of the Blesser himself. Hence the undeserved favours that descend to us from God must ever ascend to God as a heartfelt paean of praise [cf. 4:15; 9:11].

12: For our glorying is this, the testimony of our conscience, that in holiness and sincerity of God, not in fleshly wisdom but in the grace of God, we behaved ourselves in the world, and more abundantly to you-ward.

Paul can enlist the support of the Corinthians in prayer with confidence. He is satisfied that his conduct both in the world and in their midst is sufficient reply to those who assailed his integrity and impugned his sincerity in order to establish themselves as the new leaders of the church.

For our glorying is this: Since Paul is not ashamed of what the grace of God has wrought in his life, he does not hesitate to counter the empty boasting of his opponents in Corinth with a true glorying in the Lord (contrast 11:18 with 10:17). And this probably accounts for his frequent use of the word 'glorying' or 'boasting' in this Epistle, the various forms of the word appearing some thirty times in it.

The testimony of our conscience: This testimony is true, for he knows the real peace of a conscience pacified by the blood of Christ, and the sure guidance of a conscience enlightened by the Word of God.

That in holiness and sincerity of God, not in fleshly wisdom but in the grace of God, we behaved ourselves in the world: Paul thus freely attributes the 'moral purity' (Arndt-Gingrich) of his conduct and the sincerity of his motives to the grace of God. He has moved in the sphere of this grace ever since the day he renounced all confidence in the flesh, including that fleshly wisdom upon which the Corinthians set such store, and which he had tried so hard to discourage in them [*1 Cor.* 2: 1ff.].

And more abundantly to you-ward: He was of course equally sincere elsewhere, but the Corinthians had been given a better opportunity than most to observe his sincerity. 'He has deliberately put it in this way to show that there was no need for witnesses from a distance, for they themselves were the best witnesses to all that he had said' (John Calvin).

13: For we write no other things unto you, than what ye read or even acknowledge, and I hope ye will acknowledge unto the end: 14: as also ye did acknowledge us in part, that we are your glorying, even as ye also are ours, in the day of our Lord Jesus.

For we write you nothing but what you can read and understand (RSV): Moreover, Paul insists that he is as sincere in his letters as he is in his life. He is not the shifty correspondent his detractors claim him to be, writing one thing and meaning another. He always writes what he means, and means exactly what he writes. 'You don't have to read between the lines of my letters; you can understand them' (Moffatt). But their reception of his letters has shown that they were not always willing to understand the plain meaning of what he had written. The obscurity of Scripture lies not in the supposed difficulty of its message, but in that spiritual insensitivity which cherishes the sins Scripture so clearly condemns.

I hope you will understand fully, as you have understood in part, that you can be proud of us as we can be of you, on the day of the Lord Jesus (RSV): Paul here contrasts 'the imperfect estimate of his sincerity which the Corinthians now have with that which will be theirs when the secrets of all hearts are revealed at the Last Day' (Chrysostom). When they at last realize all that they owe to his ministry, they will be as proud of him as he is of them [*1 Thess.* 2:19, 20].

15: And in this confidence I was minded to come first unto you, that ye might have a second benefit; 16: and by you to pass into Macedonia, and again from Macedonia to come unto you, and of you to be set forward on my journey unto Judaea.

It was on the ground of this mutual confidence that Paul had hoped to pay the Corinthians a double visit, on his way to and from Macedonia, so that they might receive a 'second benefit' and be given the privilege of sending him forward on his journey to Judaea. But as this proposal differs from his original intention of visiting Corinth on his way from Macedonia [*1 Cor.* 16:5], it would seem that Paul made this change in his travel plans *after* the despatch of 1 Corinthians. The fact that he had now changed his mind again and reverted to the original plan was seized upon by his critics as the proof that he was not a man of his word. Paul answers this charge before showing that the Corinthians themselves were to blame for his apparent vacillation [1:23–2:4].

17: When I therefore was thus minded, did I show fickleness? or the things that I purpose, do I purpose according to the flesh, that with me there should be the yea yea and the nay nay?

Was such a change of plan evidence of the fickleness of character attributed to Paul by his opponents in Corinth? Or can the Corinthians believe that their apostle makes his plans in such an unprincipled manner that he has no compunction in affirming one thing at one time and shortly changing to the very opposite? The unjust allegations of his adversaries are not merely echoed but emphatically answered in these indignant questions.

18: But as God is faithful, our word toward you is not yea and nay.

The Corinthians should realize that they could not call in question the trustworthiness of their apostle without also reflecting upon the faithfulness of God who had entrusted him with the gospel. For was it not the height of incongruity to imagine that a faithful God had saved them through the ministrations of a faithless servant? Experience should have taught them above all others that he is not a man of Jesuitical reserve who means 'No' when he says 'Yes'. Thus 'God is faithful in the fact that he sends men to preach whose preaching is not double-tongued, a promise and no performance' (J. Massie).

19: For the Son of God, Jesus Christ, who was preached among you by us, even by me and Silvanus and Timothy, was not yea and nay, but in him is yea.

For the Son of God, Jesus Christ: 'Proof of the unchangeableness of the doctrine from the unchangeableness of the subject of it – viz., Jesus Christ. He is called "the Son of God", to show the impossibility of change in One co-equal with God himself [cf. *1 Sam.* 15:29; *Mal.* 3:6]' (A. R. Fausset).

Who was preached among you by us, even by me and Silvanus and Timothy, was not yea and nay: Paul reminds the Corinthians that they had trusted him and his fellow evangelists, Silvanus (=Silas of *Acts* 18:5) and Timothy, both in their message and their character, for the two went together. 'No mighty yea-Christ could have been transmitted by yea-and-nay heralds' (R. C. H. Lenski).

But in him is yea: The force of the perfect tense is well conveyed by P. E. Hughes: 'In Him *yes* was and continues to be a reality'. The Corinthians had experienced the eternal 'Yes' of God's saving purpose in Christ through the faithful proclamation of this divine affirmative, and so they could not doubt the fidelity of God's messengers without also questioning the reality of their own faith.

20: For how many soever be the promises of God, in him is the yea: wherefore also through him is the Amen, unto the glory of God through us.

Christ is the fulfiller and fulfilment of all the promises of God because he is the sum and substance of them. From Genesis to Malachi – from the *protevangelium*, the first promise of a Redeemer, to prophecy's last witness to his coming – each and every promise finds its affirmation and accomplishment in him [*Luke* 24:44; *Gal.* 3:16; *Heb.* 10:7].

Wherefore also through him is the Amen, unto the glory of God: Christ's 'Yea' to all the divine promises is appropriated by the 'Amen' of faith. In affixing this seal to God's faithfulness, faith gives glory to God [*John* 3:33; *Rom.* 4:20]. It is both through Christ and through those who preach him ('through us') that men are brought to say the 'Amen' of faith. For though Christ is the great awakener of faith, 'his appeal reaches the world through his representatives' (H. L. Goudge) [*Rom.* 10:17].

Through us: 'This connects the thought with the main argument. Is it likely that we should be unfaithful to promises who cause glory to be ascribed to God for his faithfulness?' (Massie).

21: Now he that establisheth us with you in Christ, and anointed us, is God; 22: who also sealed us, and gave us the earnest of the Spirit in our hearts.

Now he that establisheth us with you in Christ: As the Corinthians were divinely constrained to *confirm* Paul's preaching of the gospel with the 'Amen' of faith, so it is no less a work of grace that they with him are being daily *confirmed* in their union with Christ. Nor could they consider the reality of this shared experience without recognizing that he is sincere and consistent in all his relations with them. Moreover, Paul goes on to show that God's *present* work of establishing all believers in Christ is based entirely upon what he has *already* done for them in conversion. For it was then that he anointed, sealed, and gave the earnest of the Spirit to them.

And anointed us, is God: It is in the anointing of his people with the Holy Spirit that God consecrates them to his service and makes them like Christ, the Anointed One *par excellence* [*Luke* 4:18, 19; *1 John* 2:20, 27]. Hence this blessing is bestowed through Christ, 'on whom the oil of gladness, and all the graces of the Spirit are first poured out, and then from him are carried to the meanest member of his body' (David Dickson, on Psalm 133) [cf. *John* 7:39].

Who also sealed us: The sealing of the Spirit is the act by which God marks out a people for himself and secures them unto the day of redemption. The Holy Spirit 'marks those in whom he dwells as belonging to God. They bear the seal of God upon them. *Rev.* 7:2; *2 Tim.* 2:19 . . . He also bears witness in the hearts of believers that they are the children of God. He authenticates them to themselves and others as genuine believers. And he effectively secures them from apostasy and perdition. *Eph.* 1:13; 4:30' (Hodge).

And gave us the earnest of the Spirit in our hearts: The 'deposit' or 'pledge' of the Spirit is at once the foretaste and guarantee of the Christian's interest in the heavenly inheritance [cf. 5:5; *Rom.* 8:23; *Eph.* 1:14]. 'The actual spiritual life of the Christian is the same in kind as his future glorified life; the kingdom of heaven is a present kingdom; the believer is already seated on the right hand of God . . . Nevertheless the present gift of the Spirit is only a *small fraction* of the future endowment. This idea also would be suggested by the usual relation between the earnest-money and the full payment' (J. B. Lightfoot).

23: But I call God for a witness upon my soul, that to spare you I forbare to come unto Corinth.

Having demonstrated the impossibility of any duplicity on his part, the apostle now reveals the real reason for postponing his visit. Since no one else knew what caused him to change his mind, he strongly affirms the truthfulness of his testimony by invoking the punishment of God against himself if what he says is false. In fact it was solely to spare them that Paul stayed away from Corinth in the hope that this delay would give them the opportunity to repent, for he had determined that he would not pay them another painful visit (see further comment on 2:1).

24: Not that we have lordship over your faith, but are helpers of your joy: for in faith ye stand fast.

To guard against any misunderstanding of the word 'spare' [verse 23], Paul assures the Corinthians that he has neither the power nor the desire to exercise any lordship over their faith (though he knows that the 'false apostles' set no such limits to *their* authority – 11:20). But he seeks only to remove those sinful disorders which hinder their true rejoicing. If therefore the pattern of ministry set by the authentic apostles was not that of lording it over the flock [*1 Pet.* 5:3], then how can this power lawfully be claimed and exercised by their pretended successors?

For in faith ye stand fast: 'Well may we disclaim any such undue interference; for ye stand, not on us, but each to his own Master on the footing of his own faith; nor can any one, not even an apostle of Jesus Christ, come in between him and God, the Judge of all' (David Brown) [*Rom.* 14:4].

CHAPTER TWO

Paul now explains why he put off the expected visit. He had determined that he would not come again to the Corinthians with sorrow. And as he could not cause them pain without being grieved himself, he thought it better to write a painful letter than to have another sorrowful meeting with those who ought to give him joy [verses 1–4]. The apostle is satisfied with the censure inflicted by the majority on the man who caused particular offence, and he urges them to forgive and comfort him, just as he has forgiven him in the presence of Christ lest any advantage should be gained by Satan [verses 5–11]. Paul was so anxious to hear how Titus had fared in Corinth that when he failed to find him in Troas, he could not continue preaching there, but went off to seek him in Macedonia [verses 12, 13]. Paul's intense joy on learning that Titus was, after all, the bearer of good news leads him to bless God, who always causes his sincere servant to triumph in Christ [verses 14–17].

1: But I determined this for myself, that I would not come again to you with sorrow.

From this it is clear that Paul had already made one painful visit to Corinth, and since no reference to such a visit is implied in 1 Corinthians, it presumably took place after that letter was despatched [12:14; 13:1f]. Although Paul had no desire to repeat this unhappy experience, he had deferred his visit in the Corinthians' interest, and not simply to escape further personal suffering. His decision was made in the hope that this delay would give them the opportunity to put matters right themselves, following their reception of his 'severe' letter (see comment on verses 3, 4).

2: For if I make you sorry, who then is he that maketh me glad but he that is made sorry by me?

Paul here assures the Corinthians that his own joy is bound up with their spiritual prosperity. 'As the helper of their joy he would receive joy through their faith and obedience. So long as their moral condition compelled him to come, bringing rebuke and pain, they could not be a source of joy to him. If I must needs make you sorry with merited rebuke, who can give me joy save you who are thus made sorry?' (Marvin R. Vincent). Hence the restoration of his joy depended upon their repentance and amendment.

3: And I wrote this very thing, lest, when I came, I should have sorrow from them of whom I ought to rejoice; having confidence in you all, that my joy is the joy of you all.

And I wrote as I did, so that when I came I might not be pained by those who should have made me rejoice (RSV): As the Corinthians' faithful apostle, Paul knew that there was no painless way of dealing with the problem of sin [7:8ff.]. But he wrote them a painful letter to avoid another painful visit, for he hoped that its effect would be such that when he next came to Corinth they would meet in joy, not in sorrow.

For I felt sure of all of you, that my joy would be the joy of you all (RSV): (cf. the 'all' of 13:14) 'Even at this time of revolt he had confidence that they had no real joy apart from his, and would therefore put away what was grievous to him' (Massie).

4: For out of much affliction and anguish of heart I wrote unto you with many tears; not that ye should be made sorry, but that ye might know the love which I have more abundantly unto you.

This is a touching disclosure of what it cost the apostle to write his 'severe' letter. It is impossible to accept the traditional identification of this letter with 1 Corinthians for two reasons:–

1. The discursive style and generally calm tone of 1 Corinthians does not suggest that it was written under the stress of great emotion, as 2 Corinthians undoubtedly was. And this change reflects the crisis which had arisen in the intervening period.

2. It is clear from 2 Corinthians that the 'severe' letter was the sequel to the 'painful' visit. So if the 'severe' letter is taken to be 1 Corinthians, the 'painful' visit must have *preceded* it. But as there is not the slightest hint of such a second visit in 1 Corinthians, it must have taken place *after* its despatch. Hence the 'severe' letter which followed that visit cannot be identified with 1 Corinthians.

Not that ye should be made sorry, but that ye might know the love which I have more abundantly unto you: It gave Paul no satisfaction to make them sorry, but he loved them too much to let them lie down in their sins. Consequently they would not understand his motive in writing the 'severe' letter, unless they saw even this as the fruit of his love for them [cf. *Heb.* 12:11]. 'More abundantly' should not of course be taken to mean that Paul loved the Corinthians more than his converts in other places. It rather refers to the greater demands which they made upon his love by their folly.

5: But if any hath caused sorrow, he hath caused sorrow, not to me, but in part (that I press not too heavily) to you all.

Although the deliberately vague language of this verse makes it difficult for us to identify the culprit, he cannot be equated with the incestuous man of 1 Corinthians 5:1ff, because it appears that his offence was directed against the apostle himself [cf. verse 10]. Evidently Paul refers to the incident which made his second visit to Corinth such a sorrowful one, and we may reasonably suppose that this man took the lead in challenging his authority before the whole church. At the time the Corinthians had failed to stand by Paul, not realizing that an attack on their apostle was also an attack on the church he had founded [cf. *1 Cor.* 3:10,11]. Hence Paul says that the offender has caused sorrow, 'not to me', meaning 'not *only* to me', 'but in some degree (in order not to say too much) to you all' (Arndt-Gingrich).

6: Sufficient to such a one is this punishment which was inflicted by the many; 7: so that contrariwise ye should rather forgive him and comfort him, lest by any means such a one should be swallowed up with his overmuch sorrow.

Awakened to its responsibility by Paul's severe letter and the ministry of Titus, the church had acted to clear itself and punish the rebel [7:11]. In saying that this church censure was imposed by the 'majority' [RSV], Paul does not imply that the minority were disloyal to him. His language in verse 7 rather suggests that they were 'supporters' [*1 Cor.* 1:12, 13] who thought that the punishment was far too lenient! He checks this excessive zeal by showing that the offender's repentance demands their forgiveness. Otherwise there is a grave danger that he might be overwhelmed with too much sorrow. The emphatic placing of 'such a one' at the very end of the sentence gives expression to Paul's compassionate concern for the man. 'The character which Paul here exhibits reflects the image of our heavenly Father. His word is filled with denunciations against impenitent sinners, and at the same time with assurances of unbounded pity and tenderness towards the penitent. He never breaks the bruised reed or quenches the smoking flax' (Hodge).

8: Wherefore I beseech you to confirm your love toward him.

Your love: The vital word is again the last word in the sentence. Instead of agreeing with the rigorists of Corinth, Paul pleads not merely for the formal reinstatement of the offender, but that the congregation should leave him in no doubt of the warmth of their love. For by thus 'loosing' his sin, the church would assure or confirm to him the reality of God's forgiveness [*John* 20:23].

9: For to this end also did I write, that I might know the proof of you, whether ye are obedient in all things.

Paul's purpose in writing the 'severe' letter was to test whether the Corinthians were obedient in all things. And now that they had proved their genuineness by punishing the offender, he is confident that the joyful duty of forgiving this man will command their willing response. Paul does not actually say that they are obedient to him, because he is an apostle whose sole desire is to promote in them the 'obedience of faith' [*Rom.* 1:5; cf. 10:5].

10: But to whom ye forgive anything, I forgive also: for what I also have forgiven, if I have forgiven anything, for your sakes have I forgiven it in the presence of Christ;

The greatness of Paul's character is seen in his ready forgiveness of the rebel and his generous dismissal of the very real injury he himself had suffered. Grace demands that we both forgive and forget, because breaches of fellowship cannot be healed unless even the memory of the offence is blotted out. What a difference it would make if only all believers realized that nursed grievances are nothing less than a canker in the body of Christ!

As there was a danger that the Corinthians might refuse to forgive the man in their belated zeal to defend their apostle [7:11], Paul removes this excuse by assuring them that he had their spiritual welfare at heart [verse 11] when he forgave the wrong in the presence of Christ. And this telling reference to the witness of Christ serves to remind them that their own forgiveness must be equally sincere. 'No man can be severe in his judgment who feels that the mild eyes of Christ are fixed upon him' (Hodge).

11: that no advantage may be gained over us by Satan: for we are not ignorant of his devices.

As the sower of discord among brethren, only Satan stood to gain by a failure to forgive the now repentant wrongdoer. This would give Satan more than his due by allowing him to use the Christian grace of repentance to embitter the church and to drive the man to despair. 'Ignorant' and 'devices' are akin in sound and root; 'we are not without *knowledge* of his *knowing* schemes' (Fausset) [*Eph.* 6:11].

12: Now when I came to Troas for the gospel of Christ, and when a door was opened unto me in the Lord, 13: I had no relief for my spirit, because I found not Titus my brother: but taking my leave of them, I went forth into Macedonia.

Paul now resumes the account of his movements [1:8]. On leaving Ephesus he travelled to Troas where he not only intended to preach the gospel, but also found a favourable opportunity for doing so as he awaited the return of Titus from Corinth [cf. *Acts* 14:27; *1 Cor.* 16:9; *Col.* 4:3]. As P. E. Hughes observes, the expression 'in the Lord' is an evidence of the thoroughly Christ-centred nature of Paul's thought: 'The Lord Christ is both the content of the Apostle's message and also the sphere of his opportunity'.

But when Titus failed to arrive Paul became so anxious about the outcome of the crisis in Corinth that he was unable to continue his work among the people of Troas, and bidding them farewell he crossed over to Macedonia. It was therefore 'a great proof of his very special affection for the Corinthians that his concern for them would not let him rest anywhere, not even in a place that offered great hope of success, till he had news of them' (Calvin).

14: But thanks be unto God, who always leadeth us in triumph in Christ, and maketh manifest through us the savour of his knowledge in every place.

At this point Paul does not stop to explain how his anxiety was relieved by the coming of Titus [7:5ff.], but immediately acknowledges his gratitude to God in a jubilant shout of praise. The figure is probably taken from a Roman triumph which the emperor would grant to a victorious general, the glory of whose conquests was also shared by his staff (cf. F. F. Bruce: 'Now thanks to God, who always gives us a place of honour in Christ's triumphal procession').

The second part of the verse is an extension of the same image, for on such occasions the burning of incense carried the fragrance of victory far and wide. Thus Paul sees his apostolic progress through the world as a continuous triumph, by means of which the knowledge of Christ is spread abroad like perfume. As Christ's loyal lieutenant triumph is assured to Paul 'in every place', even at Corinth, the place where he had appeared to be facing an ignominious defeat!

15: For we are a sweet savour of Christ unto God, in them that are saved, and in them that perish; 16: to the one a savour from death unto death; to the other a savour from life unto life.

As Paul is a chosen vessel filled with the fragrance of Christ, his preaching of the gospel is always a sweet savour to God, no matter whether men 'are being saved' through receiving it, or 'are perishing' in their rejection of it (ASV margin). The gospel divides mankind into two, and only two classes. In the one it is a fatal aroma that ends in death; in the other, a vital fragrance that leads to life. 'The Gospel is preached unto salvation, for that is its real purpose, but only believers share in this salvation; for unbelievers it is an occasion of condemnation, but it is they who make it so . . . The proper function of the Gospel is always to be distinguished from what we may call its accidental function, which must be imputed to the depravity of men by which life is turned into death' (Calvin).

> **16b: And who is sufficient for these things? 17: For we are not as the many, corrupting the word of God: but as of sincerity, but as of God, in the sight of God, speak we in Christ.**

Since these momentous issues of life and death hang upon the preaching of the gospel, who is competent to exercise such a ministry? Who indeed, if not the apostle himself? [3:5]. Certainly not 'the many', those false apostles who sought to establish their own authority in the church at Corinth by disputing that of its founder (cf. the 'some' of 3:1).

For we are not, like so many, peddlers of God's word (RSV): Paul is adequate for the task, for he is not like those cheap-jacks who adulterate the Word of God and sell it for whatever price they can get. 'It is characteristic of these intruders that they go about hawking or peddling the word of God, cheapening and degrading the message by the illegitimate admixture of foreign elements, judaistic or pagan, as a dishonest merchant adulterates wine with water; they seek only their own gain, irrespective of the effect of their teaching on others and careless of the momentous issues which are at stake' (P. E. Hughes).

But as of sincerity, but as of God, in the sight of God, speak we in Christ: This 'completes the inward picture of Paul's preaching. His words spring not from selfish, but from genuine purposes, and from God;

and are such words as men speak when sincere and when moved by God. They are spoken in the presence of God and in union with Christ as their encompassing element' (Beet).

CHAPTER THREE

In claiming to be a competent minister of the gospel, Paul is not commending himself, for he has no need of letters of commendation when all men can read the living testimonial to his ministry in the Corinthians themselves [verses 1–3]. It is God who has made him an able minister of the new covenant, whose abiding glory far excels the temporary splendour of that death-dealing ministry of condemnation which it has replaced [verses 4–11]. Unlike Moses who veiled his face before the children of Israel, Paul delivers his message with the openness and boldness that befits the greater light and liberty which characterize the life-transforming dispensation of the Spirit [verses 12–18].

1: Are we beginning again to commend ourselves? or need we, as do some, epistles of commendation to you or from you?

Are we beginning again to commend ourselves? In thus protesting his sincerity [cf. 2:17], Paul is well aware that his opponents, whose calumnies had forced him to defend his integrity [cf. 5:12; chs. 10–12], would say that he was again indulging a penchant for self-commendation [e.g. *1 Cor.* 4:16; 9:15; 14:18; 15:10].

Or need we, as do some, epistles of commendation to you or from you? But unlike 'some' (who belong to 'the many' of 2:17), Paul does not think that those whom he has begotten through the gospel will suggest that he needs any introduction to them or any commendation from them [*1 Cor.* 4:15]. These false teachers, however, had needed letters of commendation to gain access to the Corinthian church. And they would require similar letters on their departure from it, 'for they were largely dependent on these bills of clearance for profitable marketing of their merchandise in spiritual things' (P. E. Hughes). What Paul condemns is the unprincipled exploitation of this practice by these men; he has nothing to say against the usefulness of such letters in general [*Acts* 18:27; *Rom.* 16:1; *1 Cor.* 16:3].

2: Ye are our epistle, written in our hearts, known and read of all men;

If Paul has no need to flourish any testimonial that could be written with ink, it is because the Corinthians are his credentials. They themselves constitute the 'seal' of his apostleship [*1 Cor.* 9:2]. This living letter is not only indelibly inscribed upon his heart [7:3], it is also *recognized* and *read* by everyone (Bruce). For though outsiders could not inspect Paul's heart, what Christ had written on their hearts through his ministry 'was patent to the world's observation, as it was reflected in their Christian mode of life' (J. H. Bernard) [*Matt.* 5:14; *Rom.* 1:8].

3: being made manifest that ye are an epistle of Christ, ministered by us, written not with ink, but with the Spirit of the living God; not in tables of stone, but in tables that are hearts of flesh.

The Corinthians are indeed Paul's commendatory letter [verse 2], but his part in their conversion was ministerial only. He claims to be no more than Christ's instrument. 'The Lord, so to speak, dictated the letter, and he wrote it. The contents of it were prescribed by Christ, and through the Apostle's ministry became visible and legible in the Corinthians' (J. Denney).

Written not with ink, but with the Spirit of the living God: 'This "writing" which the Corinthians exhibit is no writing with ink on a papyrus roll, but is the mystical imprint of the Divine Spirit in their hearts, conveyed through Paul's ministrations' (Bernard).

Not in tables of stone, but in tables that are hearts of flesh: The superiority of the new covenant over the old dispensation is not that it sets aside the decalogue (the moral law), but that it transfers that law from tables of stone to 'tables that are hearts of flesh' [cf. *Ezek.* 11:19; 36:26]. This is the fulfilment of Jeremiah's prophecy, 'I will put *my law* in their inward parts, and in their heart will I write it' [*Jer.* 31:33]. If, as seems likely, Paul's opponents in Corinth were Judaizers who gloried in the law ('ministers of righteousness' 11:15), it is easy to see how the argument of this chapter would fall upon them with overwhelming force. It is certain that the original apostles did not endorse this teaching with letters of commendation, but their continued observance of the *ceremonial* law led the Judaizers to suppose 'that legalism was of the essence of their religion' (J. G. Machen, cited by Plummer).

4: And such confidence have we through Christ to God–ward: 5: not that we are sufficient of ourselves, to account anything as from ourselves; but our sufficiency is from God;

Thus Paul is confident that his work in Corinth is a standing testimony to the reality of his divine commission. 'This confidence is not mere self-assumption, but a firm assurance, reaching through Christ to the presence of God, and therefore valid in the sight of the searcher of hearts' (J. Waite). But to obviate the charge of boasting Paul clearly disclaims any credit for the gracious work that was done in Corinth, for in and of himself he was quite unequal to the task. The secret of his successful ministry there is not to be found in any natural competence, but solely in the sufficiency of the God who called and equipped him for it [*1 Cor.* 15:10; cf. 4:7].

6: who also made us sufficient as ministers of a new covenant; not of the letter, but of the spirit: for the letter killeth, but the spirit giveth life.

Instead of believing the empty claims of the false apostles, the Corinthians should be the first to acknowledge that Paul has a valid and effective ministry. It is *valid* because he did not appoint himself to it, but can point to the particular occasion when God's commission made him sufficient for it [*Acts* 9:3ff.; 22:12ff., 26:15–18]. It is *effective* because it is the ministry of a new covenant. The very provision of a fresh covenant indicates its superiority over the worn out and obsolete dispensation which it replaces [*Heb.* 8:6–13]. This covenant is not a mutual compact between equals, but a 'unilateral enactment' of which God is the sovereign disposer; and its uniqueness lies in the accomplishing of that which the law demanded but gave no power to perform.

Not of the letter, but of the spirit: for the letter killeth, but the spirit giveth life: The law of God externally engraved on tables of stone is here adversely compared with that same law internally inscribed in the heart of the believer. Sinners confronted by a condemning code could only be killed by it, but the spiritual application of a fulfilled law confers life. Paul neither depreciates the law nor contradicts its plain meaning; he is showing that the natural man's inability to obey it must result in death [*Rom.* 6:23; 7:6–12; *Gal.* 3:10]. The grace of the new covenant 'is life-giving, in that Christ, who as God is the law-giver and as Man is the *only* law-keeper, vicariously endured the sinner's death penalty, ridding us, as it were, of the legal document with its accusing ordinances and nailing it to His cross for all to see [*Col.* 2:14f], and also, by the Pentecostal outpouring of the Holy Spirit, communicated His life and obedience to every trusting heart' (P. E. Hughes).

> **7: But if the ministry of death, written, and engraven on stones, came with glory, so that the children of Israel could not look steadfastly upon the face of Moses for the glory of his face; which glory was passing away:**
> **8: how shall not rather the ministration of the spirit be with glory?**

As Moses descended from the mount his face shone with a glory that testified to the divine origin of the covenant of which he was the mediator, yet death was the unavoidable result of a ministry whose content was only 'engraved in letters on stones' (Lenski). [*Exod.* 34:29–35] But though the ministration of condemnation was so gloriously inaugurated, the fading of this radiance from the face of Moses showed that its glory 'was being done away' (ASV margin). For God always intended to replace it with the abiding and far more resplendent ministration of the spirit. Nevertheless it is the function of the law to convict men of their sin and drive them to faith in the promise [*Gal.* 3:24, 25]. Consequently even the Old Testament saints were saved by their faith in the promise, and not by their obedience to the law [*Rom.* 4:1–8]. For 'by the works of the law shall no flesh be justified in his sight' [*Rom.* 3:20; *Gal.* 2:16]. In effect Paul warns the Corinthians that to give heed to Judaizers who exalt the law at the expense of the gospel is to turn away from that salvation which is theirs by grace through faith alone.

> **9: For if the ministration of condemnation hath glory, much rather doth the ministration of righteousness exceed in glory.**

The ministration of righteousness abounds with greater glory than that which attended the ministry of condemnation, for it is a greater matter to secure the justification of a sinner than to confirm his condemnation. It takes only the letter of the law on slabs of stone to condemn him, but it required the blood of God's own Son and the Spirit's quickening power to make him an heir of an everlasting righteousness [cf. 5:21; *Rom.* 3:19–26; 8:16ff.; *1 Cor.* 1:30].

10: For verily that which hath been made glorious hath not been made glorious in this respect, by reason of the glory that surpasseth.

Although the ministration of the old covenant was truly glorious, yet this seemed as nothing in comparison with the transcendent glory of the new covenant. 'Just as the moon and the stars, though they are themselves bright and spread their light over all the earth, yet vanish before the greater brightness of the sun, so the Law, however glorious in itself, has no glory in face of the Gospel's grandeur' (Calvin).

11: For if that which passeth away was with glory, much more that which remaineth is in glory.

At Sinai the old covenant came *with* glory; the new abides *in* glory as its distinctive element. 'The old dispensation and its ministry were temporary, the new is permanent. There is nothing to intervene, no new revelation, no new economy, between the gospel and its ministry, and the final consummation. Whoever are to be converted, whatever nations are to be brought in, it must be by the preaching of the gospel, "which remaineth", or is to continue, according to Christ's promise, until the end of the world' (Hodge).

12: Having therefore such a hope, we use great boldness of speech,

Since Paul has a sure hope that the glory of the new covenant will abide forever [verse 11], he uses great boldness of speech. For now the full openness of the gospel has superseded the comparative obscurity of the preparatory dispensation. Therefore the unreserved frankness with which he glorifies his ministry is entirely appropriate, even though some should mistake it for self commendation [verse 1]. This 'boldness' or 'openness' of speech that characterizes Paul's ministry stems from the liberty of access to God which he enjoys through Christ [verse 18]. 'He who lifts up his face uncovered to God also turns uncovered to men . . . The apostle can lift up his face openly to God and men because he serves incorruptible glory and kindles unshakeable hope, 3:7ff.' (H. Schlier, *TDNT,* vol. 5, p. 883).

13: and are not as Moses, who put a veil upon his face, that the children of Israel should not look steadfastly on the end of that which was passing away:

As the minister of a covenant whose glory can never be dimmed, it is not for Paul to do as Moses did [*Exod.* 34:33–35, RV]. For after Moses had spoken the words of God to the people it was his custom to cover his face with a veil, which meant that the Israelites could not even look upon the reflected glory of a vanishing order without concealment. But as the revelation vouchsafed to Paul can never be suspended or superseded, no such intervening veil obscures the abiding glory of the gospel. 'His is not a message of condemnation and death, but of grace and mercy and life to every sinner who repents and believes. The eye of faith may gaze upon the everlasting glory of Christ without interruption' (P. E. Hughes).

14: but their minds were hardened: for until this very day at the reading of the old covenant the same veil remaineth, it not being revealed to them that it is done away in Christ.

But their minds were blinded (AV): 'Hardened' is a misleading rendering when 'intellectual obtuseness or blindness is the sense which is most appropriate to this context' (J. Armitage Robinson, p. 265). Thus the veil which hid the face of Moses answered to the spiritual insensibility of those to whom he ministered [*Deut.* 29:4]. 'Unless God give sight as well as light, and enlighten both organ and object, we can see nothing' (John Trapp).

For to this day, when they read the old covenant, that same veil remains unlifted, because only through Christ is it taken away (RSV): This translation is preferable to the less likely alternative which is mentioned in the RV margin and adopted in the ASV text. Paul is saying that the same veil of unbelief prevents the Jews of his day from understanding the real significance of the revelation which was given to them through Moses. For it is only by receiving the One of whom Moses spoke that this veil can ever be removed [*John* 5:46]. 'The Old Testament Scriptures are intelligible only when understood as predicting and prefiguring Christ' (Hodge) [*Luke* 24:44ff.]. The expression, 'old covenant', occurs only here in the New Testament and Paul may well have coined it as a counterpart to the 'new covenant' which Christ inaugurated by his death, cf. *1 Cor.* 11:25 (so H. Seesemann, *TDNT*, vol. 5, p. 720). That Paul could so refer to the religion of his own early manhood as the 'worn out' (*palaios*) covenant affords striking evidence of how completely he dissociated Judaism from Christianity, especially when it is remembered that it had been replaced by the new [*kainos*, cf. verse 6] covenant only thirty years before he wrote this letter (so Bernard) [*Acts* 13:19; *Rom.* 10:1ff.; *Phil.* 3:3ff.].

15: But unto this day, whensoever Moses is read, a veil lieth upon their heart.

The thought of the previous verse is here carried to its climax. As the veil over Moses' face concealed the passing glory of the old covenant from the children of Israel, so today their descendants fail to understand the Book of Moses, even though it is read to them every Sabbath [*Acts* 15:21]. 'Like its author at Sinai, the book is veiled. Or, rather, on the readers' hearts a veil lies. For the hindrance is in themselves' (Beet).

16: But whensoever it shall turn to the Lord, the veil is taken away.

As the subject of the verb 'turn' is unexpressed, 'it' could refer to 'their heart' [verse 15], 'Israel', or 'anyone'. Paul probably means 'anyone' i.e. any Jew, for he is here drawing a general principle from Exodus 34:34, which says that whenever Moses went in before Jehovah to speak with him, he took the veil off.' In the same way, whenever a Jew turns to Christ, the veil is taken away; because it is 'only through Christ' [verse 14], the fulfiller of the law [*Rom.* 10:4], that the impediment of the legal dispensation is removed.

17: Now the Lord is the Spirit: and where the Spirit of the Lord is, there is liberty.

Now the 'Lord' means the 'Spirit' (Bruce): Paul now explains that in this new era of grace, 'the Lord' (i.e. Jehovah, verse 16) whom Moses approached corresponds to the life-giving 'Spirit', who enables us Christians to enter the divine presence 'with unveiled face' [verse 18]'. Although some have claimed that the apostle here virtually identifies the exalted Christ with the Holy Spirit, he is not in fact confusing the distinct identity of their Persons, but is stressing the unity of their work in the economy of redemption. For as every genuine experience of the Spirit must lead to the confession 'Jesus is Lord' [*1 Cor.* 12:3], so here Paul insists 'that what the Spirit does is exactly what the Lord does; the Spirit's work is not an additional or special work beyond the Lord's;

the Spirit is the Lord at work' (F. D. Bruner, *A Theology of the Holy Spirit*, p. 289) [cf. *John* 16:12–16].

And where the Spirit of the Lord is, there is liberty: It is always and only by his Spirit that Christ communicates to men the liberty he died to secure, so that whenever he removes the veil of unbelief from their hearts the bondage of the law gives way to the freedom of the gospel [*John* 8:36, 39; *Rom.* 8:15; *Gal.* 5:1].

18: But we all, with unveiled face beholding as in a mirror the glory of the Lord, are transformed into the same image from glory to glory, even as from the Lord the Spirit.

Whereas Moses alone was privileged to behold the glory of God with unveiled face, now all Christians may always gaze directly upon the full revelation of that glory 'in the face of Jesus Christ' [4:6]. 'We are transformed into the image of the Lord by beholding it, not by reflecting it. The common interpretation is therefore to be preferred: *beholding as in a mirror.* Though in comparison with the unconverted those who are turned to the Lord see clearly, or with an unveiled face, still it is only as in a mirror, *1 Cor.* 13:12. It is not the immediate, beatific vision of the glory of the Lord, which is only enjoyed in heaven, but it is that manifestation of his glory which is made in his word and by his Spirit, whose office it is to glorify Christ by revealing him to us, *John* 16:14' (Hodge).

Are transformed into the same image from glory to glory: This transformation of believers already begins in their present life on earth. As they behold the heavenly glory of Christ in the mirror of his Word, they are progressively changed 'into the same image', and this process of inward renewal issues in the outward refashioning of the life [*Rom.* 12:2]. There is no thought here of mystical deification, for the change into the likeness of Christ is the restoration of the divine image in man at creation, 'and it maintains the characteristically biblical distance between God and man. The initiate has no aristocratic claim to a special experience of God; all Christians participate in the miracle of transformation' (J. Behm, *TDNT,* vol. 4, pp. 758–9).

Even as from the Lord the Spirit: Since such an amazing change clearly demands the exercise of supernatural power, Paul attributes it to the Lord who is the Spirit, and thereby rejects that spurious spirituality which would sever the work of the Spirit from the Lord, whose mission he fulfils in the world [verse 17]. 'Our whole transformation is the work of the Lord in and by and through the Spirit. All Scripture agrees in regard to that' (Lenski).

CHAPTER FOUR

As a minister of the new covenant, Paul has renounced all dishonesty and deceit, and commends himself to every man's conscience by openly proclaiming the truth [verses 1–2]. So if his gospel remains veiled, it is because the god of this world has blinded the minds of the unbelieving, that they might not see the glory of Christ who is the image of God [verses 3–4]. We preach not ourselves but Christ, for God who brought light out of darkness, has illuminated our hearts with the knowledge of his glory in the face of Christ [verses 5–6]. But we have this treasure in earthen vessels to show that its power is of God [verse 7]. It is through the risen life of Jesus that Paul's afflictions benefit the Corinthians, for the death which is at work in him brings life to them [verses 8–12]. He is sustained in these sufferings by the knowledge that he is being inwardly renewed day by day, and by the assurance that his light affliction will lead to an eternal weight of glory [verses 13–17]. Hence he looks not at the temporal things which are seen, but at the invisible realities which are eternal [verse 18].

1: Therefore seeing we have this ministry, even as we obtained mercy, we faint not:

It is not in any spirit of self-sufficiency, but with a lively sense of the distinguishing mercy of God in granting this glorious ministry of the new covenant to one who 'was before a blasphemer and a persecutor', that Paul continues faithfully to discharge it despite all discouragement [*Exod.* 33:19; *1 Tim.* 1:12–16]. As the unworthy recipient of such mercy and such a ministry he does not lose heart, remaining resolute in his refusal to compromise the truth of the gospel to suit Jewish prejudice [verses 2ff.; *Gal.* 5:11; 6:12].

2: but we have renounced the hidden things of shame, not walking in craftiness, nor handling the word of God deceitfully; but by the manifestation of the truth commending ourselves to every man's conscience in the sight of God.

But we have renounced the things that are hidden out of a sense of shame (Arndt-Gingrich): As befits the openness of his ministry, Paul has refused to adopt the tactics of the false apostles who gain their converts by guile, and who try to hide their shame by accusing him of the very things of which they themselves are guilty [12:16].

Not walking in craftiness, nor handling the word of God deceitfully: The apostle plainly contrasts the purity of his own conduct and his honest proclamation of the Word of God with the deceitful practice of these interlopers who robbed the gospel of its power to save by their adulteration of its content in order to enrich themselves [2:17].

But by the manifestation of the truth commending ourselves to every man's conscience: On the contrary, Paul's ministry is marked by 'the open proclamation of the truth' (Arndt-Gingrich), and it is by this transparent fidelity to 'the whole counsel of God' that he expects to commend himself 'to every conscience of men' (literally). For he is confident that the truth, the whole truth, and nothing but the truth must find an echo in every conscience, even if it be sinfully suppressed by many.

In the sight of God: This is added 'because conscience holds us accountable to God. Drop the idea of God, and the vitality of conscience is destroyed. Mere abstract ideas of "right" and "wrong" do not bind the conscience; the idea of God and his judgment does' (Lenski) [1:12; 2:17].

3: And even if our gospel is veiled, it is veiled in them that perish:

In spite of the apostle's claim to preach the truth openly [verse 2], it seems that his opponents in Corinth had said that his message was hopelessly obscure [cf. *2 Pet*.3:16]. If, however, Paul's gospel is veiled, the fault lies not in the obscurity of his preaching, but in the spiritual blindness of those who are on the high road to perdition (ASV margin: 'it is veiled in them that are perishing). 'Those from whom it is hidden must therefore be blind and lacking in every trace of rational understanding. The conclusion is that the blindness of unbelievers in no way detracts from the clarity of his Gospel; the sun is no less bright because blind men do not perceive its light' (Calvin).

4: in whom the god of this world hath blinded the minds of the unbelieving, that the light of the gospel of the glory of Christ, who is the image of God, should not dawn upon them.

In whom the god of this age hath blinded the minds of the unbelieving (ASV margin): It is because Satan has blinded their minds that those who are perishing do not believe the only Word that could save them. And it is by this blinding of the mind that Satan has secured their vassalage to himself as 'the god of this age', though, as dependent creatures, neither he nor they ever succeed in escaping from the lordship and judgment of the one living and true God. As Trapp observes, 'The devil usurps such a power, and wicked men will have it so . . . Their buildings, ploughings, plantings, sailings, are for the devil. And if we could rip up their hearts, we should find written therein, The god of this present world' [cf. *John* 12:31; 16:11; *Eph.* 2:2; *1 John* 5:19].

That they should not see the light of the gospel of the glory of Christ (ASV margin): Unlike the message peddled by the Judaizers, Paul's gospel is a revelation of the glory of Christ [*Acts* 26:13–18]. 'To see this glory is to be saved; for we are thereby transformed into his likeness from glory to glory, 3:18. Therefore it is that Satan, the great adversary, directs all his energy to prevent men becoming the subjects of that illumination of which the gospel, as the revelation of the glory of Christ, is the source' (Hodge).

Who is the image of God: This is the supreme climax. Paul here comes near to the teaching of the Fourth Gospel [*John* 1:18]. What he affirms is not Christ's likeness to the Father, but his essential oneness with the Father. 'He who sees the Son, sees the Father, *in the face* of Christ. The Son exactly represents and reflects the Father' (J. A. Bengel) [verse 6; *Col.* 1:15; *John* 14:9; *Heb.* 1:3].

5: For we preach not ourselves, but Christ Jesus as Lord, and ourselves as your servants for Jesus' sake.

Since Paul was commissioned to preach a gospel which has the glory of Christ for its content, he does not preach himself, as his opponents allege, but Christ Jesus as Lord. Hence those who reject his preaching, repudiate not the preacher but the Christ he preaches. 'To "preach Christ as Lord" is to preach Him as crucified, risen, and glorified, the Lord to whom "all authority in heaven and earth has been given." To confess Him as Lord is to declare oneself a Christian [*Rom.* 10:9; *1 Cor.* 12:3]' (Plummer).

And ourselves as your servants for Jesus' sake: Far from claiming any lordship over their faith [1:24], Paul presents himself as their bond-servant for the sake of the one Master who took upon him 'the form of a servant' [*Phil.* 2:7]. Thus though he is their minister, they are not his masters [*1 Cor.* 7:23]. 'The ideal of a Christian minister, as presented in this pregnant passage, is, that he is a preacher of Christ, and a servant of the church, governed and animated by the love of Jesus' (Hodge).

> 6: Seeing it is God, that said, Light shall shine out of darkness, who shined in our hearts, to give the light of the knowledge of the glory of God in the face of Jesus Christ.

Paul cannot but preach Christ, for God whose first creative word brought light out of darkness [*Gen.* 1:3], is he who shone into his heart in re-creating grace [5:17]. As this spiritual experience is common to all Christians, Paul here stresses the subjective effect of this ('in our hearts') instead of dwelling upon the objective vision of Christ by which it was produced in him, [*1 Cor.* 9:1]. 'For as in His creation of the world God has poured forth upon us the brightness of the sun and has also given us eyes with which to receive it, so in our redemption He shines forth upon us in the person of His Son by His Gospel, but that would be in vain, since we are blind, unless He were also to illuminate our minds by His Spirit' (Calvin).

Moreover, it is only because Paul has been divinely illuminated himself that he can be used by God to turn men 'from darkness to light' [*Acts* 26:18]. For those whose spiritual eyes are still covered by the scales of unbelief obviously cannot reveal Christ to others [cf. *Acts* 9:18]. Although Paul impinges on Hellenistic mysticism in linking God, light, and saving knowledge, he diverges from it in that he does not think in terms of a mystical union and inner light, but primarily in terms of an historical act of salvation and the knowledge bound up with it, 'which is then used by God for missionary transmission' (so A. Oepke, *TDNT*, vol. 4, p. 26).

> 7: But we have this treasure in earthen vessels, that the exceeding greatness of the power may be of God, and not from ourselves;

After Paul has spoken so exultingly of 'the light of the knowledge of the glory of God' [verse 6], it is surprising to find that this treasure is placed in such mean and perishable vessels. The 'majesty of the message is in strange contrast with the weak and buffeted and fragile person of the messenger' (Allan Menzies). The amazing effects produced by the possession of this divine knowledge are evidently 'beyond all measure and proportion' to the means used to diffuse it (Arndt-Gingrich). For it is God's purpose to show that this power cannot be ascribed to the weak vessels in which it is contained, but that it belongs continually to him from whom it comes.

8: we are pressed on every side, yet not straitened; perplexed, yet not unto despair; 9: pursued, yet not forsaken; smitten down, yet not destroyed;

Paul's constant experience as a minister of Christ is now illustrated in a vivid metaphor, expressed in four pairs of participles which form a climax. 'The first clause in each member of the series implies the *earthiness of the vessels*, the second clause the *excellency of the power*' (Fausset).

1. *In every direction pressed hard, but not hemmed in* (Bernard): The apostle thinks of himself as a combatant engaged by an apparently stronger foe whose persistent attacks leave him no room to manoeuvre, yet God does not suffer him to be crushed into a corner [*1 Cor.* 10:13].

2. *Bewildered, but not utterly despairing* (Bernard): Or preserving the play on words: 'confused, but not confounded' (P. E. Hughes). He is often perplexed by the crafty stratagems of his adversary, but God does not permit him to be reduced to blank despair [1:8–10; 7:5ff.].

3. *Pursued, but not forsaken* (i.e. abandoned to the pursuing foe) (Bernard): Although he is hunted by a killer intent on dealing him the death-blow, he is not deserted by God in his extremity [*Josh.* 1:5].

4. *Struck down (as by an arrow), but not destroyed* (Bernard): And even when he is felled by what his enemy takes to be the final stroke, the unexpected power of God ensures that he is far from finished [11:23; *Acts* 14: 9f].

10: always bearing about in the body the dying of Jesus, that the life also of Jesus may be manifested in our body.

This sums up and explains the significance of Paul's afflictions [verses 8, 9]. Here his choice of the word which points to the process of dying (lit. 'the putting to death') shows that the sufferings of Jesus are of necessity reproduced in his apostle [cf. *Acts* 9:16; 14:22]. His devotion to Jesus is the magnet that irresistibly draws the world's hostility upon himself [*Gal.* 6:17]. For the same enmity which reached its culmination in the crucifixion of Jesus now pursues those whom he has chosen out of the world [*John* 15:18–21]. The verse shows that Paul 'taught his converts details in the history of Jesus, especially His sufferings ending in death. Here he assumes that they know' (Plummer).

That the life also of Jesus may be manifested in our body: This discloses the purpose of these sufferings. Paul bears about the *dying* of Jesus in order that the *life* also of Jesus may be manifested in his body. For the inextinguishable resurrection-life of the Jesus who once died is demonstrated in his many deliverances from the jaws of death. It is evident that the distinction made by liberal theologians between the 'Jesus of history' and the 'Christ of faith' was quite foreign to Paul's thought. He 'does not separate the historic Jesus from the glorified Christ. To him it is the same Jesus' (Plummer).

11: For we who live are always delivered unto death for Jesus' sake, that the life also of Jesus may be manifested in our mortal flesh.

Several new elements appear in this explanatory re-statement of the previous verse. 1. It is because Paul is a 'living one', i.e. one whose essential life is the eternal life of Jesus, that the deaths to which he is always being handed over serve to exhibit the triumph of that divine life. 2. The sphere in which this resurrection-life of Jesus is displayed is a body of 'mortal flesh', i.e. a body in subjection to the power of death. 'Christ's followers are in this life delivered unto death, that His life may be manifested in that which naturally is the seat of decay and death. That which is subject to suffering is that in which the power of Him who suffered here is most manifested (W. E. Vine). 3. 'It is for Jesus' sake – because of Jesus – that he suffers. It is only suffering of this kind, which is so abundantly blessed' (H. L. Goudge).

12: So then death worketh in us, but life in you.

A new contrast is brought out by another bold paradox, which links Paul's present theme of 'dying yet living' with the earlier reference to his sufferings in Chapter 1:4–7. Although he knows that death is already at work in him, he is comforted by the fact that his *physical* sufferings have been fruitful in bringing *spiritual* life to the Corinthians.

The apostle thus saw his afflictions as directly contributing to the enrichment of his converts. As a herald of the cross he was glad to accept more than his fair share of suffering in order to benefit them [1:6; *Col.* 1:24].

13: But having the same spirit of faith, according to that which is written, I believed, and therefore did I speak; we also believe, and therefore also we speak;

Since Paul has the same spirit of faith as David had in similar straits ('I believed, and therefore did I speak': *Psa.* 116:10, LXX), he also believes and continues to declare his faith, even though death should soon silence his testimony to the truth [cf. *Acts* 4:20]. This means that Paul and David share the same objective faith. For both Testaments contain the same truth, the Old in the form of promise, the New in the form of fulfilment. 'Hence the spirit of both is identical in defying persecution and death' (Lenski).

14: knowing that he that raised up the Lord Jesus shall raise up us also with Jesus, and shall present us with you.

Paul is fearless in the face of death because he knows that God who raised up the Lord Jesus 'shall raise up us also *with* Jesus'. This obviously does not mean at the same time as Jesus but in virtue of our union with him. For there could be no resurrection of believers apart from his triumph over death [*1 Cor.* 15:23]. And God will raise up Paul together with the believers in Corinth ('us with you') in order to present them 'before the presence of his glory with exceeding joy' [*Col.* 1:22; *Eph.* 5:27; *Jude* 24].

As Paul here speaks of being raised from the dead, some have maintained that this represents a change in his eschatological expectations [cf. *1 Thess.* 4:15, 17]. Yet it is a mistake to assume that the exhortation to live in the light of the imminent (but not *immediate*: cf. *2 Thess.* 2:2; 3:5] return of Christ was based on a categorical assurance that either he or his first readers (in Thessalonica, or elsewhere) would be alive when that event took place. In this respect Paul knew no more than we do ourselves today, for neither the time of his death nor the date of the Parousia was revealed to him [*Matt.* 24:36].

15: For all things are for your sakes, that the grace, being multiplied through the many, may cause the thanksgiving to abound unto the glory of God.

Paul concludes the paragraph by saying that the proximate end of his sufferings [verses 7–13] is the salvation of the Corinthians, while the ultimate result is the glory of God. For 'the more people who come to know the grace of God through the gospel Paul preaches, the more numerous will be the thanksgiving that will be evoked, and the greater the praise that will be offered to God' (R. V. G. Tasker).

16: Wherefore we faint not; but though our outward man is decaying, yet our inward man is renewed day by day.

Wherefore we faint not: This looks back to verse 1. As the minister of a new and superior covenant, who is sustained in all his trials by the hope of the glory to come [verses 14, 15], it is no wonder that Paul does not lose heart.

But though our outward man is decaying, yet our inward man is renewed day by day: As the contrast Paul makes here is between the declining powers of his bodily life and the progressive renewal of his spiritual life, the 'outward man' must not be confused with the unregenerate 'old man' of *Rom.* 6:6; *Eph.* 4:22 and *Col.* 3:9. It is evident that the apostle's afflictions have hastened that process of decay to which his physical life, as at present constituted, is subject. This necessarily includes every faculty which depends upon the body for its proper functioning. On the other hand, what he most essentially *is* by regenerating grace cannot be destroyed, but is being renewed day by day [3:18]. 'The decay of the outward man in the godless is a melancholy spectacle, for it is the decay of everything; in the Christian it does not touch that life which is hid with Christ in God, and which is in the soul itself a well of water springing up to life eternal' (Denney) [*John* 4:14; *Col.* 3:3]

17: For our light affliction, which is for the moment, worketh for us more and more exceedingly an eternal weight of glory;

As the verb 'worketh' also means 'earns', Roman Catholic expositors use the verse as a text on which to hang their doctrine of merit. But though God makes present afflictions the means of obtaining future glory, it is false to infer that they are the meritorious cause of it. 'The spirit of faith which realizes the substance of things not seen inverts the usual relation of ideas. Affliction, generally regarded as a load, has here the quality of lightness. Glory, generally regarded as an ethereal splendour, is a weight. The affliction is not light in itself, but only when put in the balance with the weight, nor momentary in itself, but only when set against eternity . . . The idea in the apostle's mind is that the sufferings of Christ borne by his ministers and followers lead them to glory, even as they led Christ himself to glory, because they are always accompanied by rich supplies of the Spirit and life' (Waite) [*Rom.* 8:17, 18]

> 18: while we look not at the things which are seen, but at the things which are not seen: for the things which are seen are temporal; but the things which are not seen are eternal.

Meanwhile Paul fixes his gaze, not on the things seen, but on the things not seen: for the things which are visible to the eye of sense are transient, but the realities which as yet can only be discerned by the eye of faith are eternal [*Col.* 3:1–4]. 'Note well what it is that will make all the miseries of this world easy to endure; it is that we should transfer our thoughts to the eternity of the kingdom of heaven. If we look around us, a moment can seem a long time, but when we lift up our hearts heavenwards, a thousand years begin to be like a moment' (Calvin).

CHAPTER FIVE

Paul does not lose heart in the midst of his sufferings, because he knows that if death destroys his earthly tent, he has the certainty of receiving from God an eternal, heavenly house at the resurrection [verse 1]. For in this weak earthly body he groans for the glory to come; not that he wished to be found in a disembodied state, but rather to be clothed with his heavenly body so that mortality might be swallowed up in life [verses 2–4]. He owes this confidence to God who gave him the Holy Spirit as the pledge of his glorification [verse 5]. So he is always of good courage, and since he walks by faith and not by sight, he would rather be present with the Lord even if this means absence from the body [verses 6–8]. Paul therefore always aims to please Christ, before whose tribunal all men must at last appear, in order that each may be judged according to his deeds [verses 9, 10]. With that awesome day in view, he faithfully discharges his commission. In saying this he commends not himself, but gives the Corinthians the opportunity to answer those who glory in appearance and not in heart [verses 11, 12]. Whether or not Paul is beside himself, he obeys God in order to benefit them. For the love of Christ constrains him, because he judges that those for whom Christ died should not henceforth live unto themselves, but unto him who for their sakes died and rose again [verses 13–15]. Consequently, he no longer knows any man after the flesh, even though he had once thought of Christ in this worldly way. For if any man is in Christ, there is a new creation, and the old life is displaced by the new [verses 16, 17]. All this is of God, who reconciled us to himself through Christ, and gave us the ministry of reconciliation; namely, that God was reconciling the world unto himself in Christ, not counting their trespasses against them [verses 18, 19]. As an ambassador for Christ, Paul therefore beseeches men to be reconciled to God. For God made him who knew no sin to be sin for us, that we might become the righteousness of God in him [verses 20, 21].

1: For we know that if the earthly house of our tabernacle be dissolved, we have a building from God, a house not made with hands, eternal, in the heavens.

For we know that: Paul is lifted above earthly affliction by this heavenly hope [4:17, 18]. For he knows by immediate revelation, as the Corinthians also know because he had taught it them [*1 Cor.* 15], that if the frail tent in which they live their earthly life is dismantled by death, they have the assurance of receiving from God an eternal and heavenly house. It is only the certainty of this resurrection of the body to life eternal that enables him to contemplate its dissolution with composure.

If: But though Paul is content to die [verses 6–8], he still says 'if' and not 'when', for in the event of Christ's prior return he would not experience death, but instantaneous glorification as in *1 Cor.* 15:51 (see also comment on 4:14).

The earthly tent we live in is taken down (Arndt-Gingrich): A natural image for an itinerant tentmaker [*Acts* 18:3] to use to describe the inferior, insecure, and impermanent nature of the present life. Although recent afflictions [1:8] had made the apostle acutely aware that his 'earthly tent' was being destroyed [4:16], his daily inward renewal by the Spirit was the pledge of its replacement by a glorious and eternal edifice [cf. *Rom.* 8:11].

We have: The present tense expresses the certainty of our possessing it, and must not be pressed to suggest 'the mechanical theory that the body of glory exists now in heaven, in an organic form' (Waite).

A building from God, a house not made with hands, eternal: Since Paul speaks of this body as a building, he appropriately uses the expression 'not made with hands' to point to its divine origin [cf. *Col.* 2:11; *Heb.* 9:11]. It is the *direct* creation of God, an eternal building as contrasted with a perishable tent. This usage makes it appear certain that Paul knew of the charge that was brought against the Lord, that he would destroy the temple made with hands, and in three days build another 'not made with hands' [*Mark* 14:58; cf. *John* 2:19–21].

In the heavens: 'It is practically in heaven: for the power which will raise it is there. When Christ appears from heaven we shall receive our permanent bodily abode. Hence it is also "our dwelling place from heaven", verse 2: Consequently, this building is completely beyond the reach of the uncertainties of earth' (Beet).

2: For verily in this we groan, longing to be clothed upon with our habitation which is from heaven:

For in this earthly tent which is our mortal body, we groan for the glory to come [*Rom.* 8:19–23; *Phil.* 3:20, 21]. Paul longs to be set free from the sufferings and imperfections of this present life, and to have his heavenly habitation 'put on over' his earthly body, 'so that there shall be transformation [*1 Cor.* 15:51f], not death' (J. Massie).

Which is from heaven: The distinguishing properties of the resurrection–body will flow from 'that resurrection–life which resides in "the Lord from heaven". And, as Bengel says, if it be "*from* heaven", the thing meant cannot be heaven itself' (David Brown).

3: if so be that being clothed we shall not be found naked.

Inasmuch as we, having put it on, shall not be found naked (Arndt-Gingrich): This clarifies and confirms the meaning of the previous verse. If Paul is still clothed with his natural body at the Lord's appearing, he will avoid the nakedness of the disembodied state. For then 'his assumption of the new body will be a superinvestment, a process like that of putting on an upper garment' (Waite).

The statement would also have special point for those in Corinth who denied the resurrection of the body [1 Cor. 15:12]. These 'gnostics' maintained that the resurrection was past already, apparently claiming that they had experienced it in conversion or baptism [2 Tim. 2:17, 18]. But to Paul who made no dualistic distinction between the soul and the body, such a bodiless existence held no attractions, and he implicitly condemns this denial of the Christian hope by describing it as a condition of 'nakedness'.

4: For indeed we that are in this tabernacle do groan, being burdened; not for that we would be unclothed, but that we would be clothed upon, that what is mortal may be swallowed up of life.

The burden under which Paul groans is not the mere fear of death, but the separation of the body from the soul by death. Because death is the unnatural disruption of man's being as created by God, he could never be satisfied with a gospel which only provided for the redemption of the soul. He longs for something far richer than the bodiless survival of the soul after death. What therefore concerns him is whether he will have to face 'a *protracted* state of being unclothed, that is "naked" between his possible death and the arrival of the parousia' (Geerhardus Vos). For he cannot regard his salvation as complete until he is clothed with the resurrection body of glory. Thus Paul would prefer to be alive at Christ's coming so that 'what is mortal', i.e. his present mortal body, might immediately be transformed into the body of glory [1 Cor. 15: 53, 54].

5: Now he that wrought us for this very thing is God, who gave unto us the earnest of the Spirit.

It is God who prepared us 'for this very thing', the transformation of the body [verse 4], by the gift of the Holy Spirit whose present transforming work within [3:18; 4:16] is the pledge or first instalment of the glory to come [1:22; *Eph.* 1:14]. Thus 'the present possession of the Spirit is regarded in the light of an anticipation. The Spirit's proper sphere is the future aeon; from thence He projects Himself into the present, and becomes a prophecy of Himself in his eschatological operations' (Vos).

6: Being therefore always of good courage, and knowing that, whilst we are at home in the body, we are absent from the Lord

Since God has guaranteed the future [verse 5], Paul is always of good courage, despite his uncertainty as to whether he will live to see the Lord's return; for his dread of being unclothed by death is offset by the knowledge that as long as he is at home in the body, he is away from his glorified Lord in heaven. For though Christ is always spiritually present with his people [*Matt.* 28:20], they do not enjoy his bodily presence while they remain on earth [*Acts* 3:21]. Now 'He does not show Himself to us face to face, because we are still exiles from His Kingdom and do not yet possess that blessed immortality that the angels who are with Him enjoy' (Calvin).

7: (for we walk by faith, not by sight);

The parenthesis explains the sense in which Paul is 'absent from the Lord'. For while he is at home in the body, the region 'through which he walks is one in which the heavenly things gazed upon are not seen in their actual substance, but only realized, as far as that is possible, by the spiritual discernment of faith [*Heb.* 11:1]. When he migrates to the Lord, he enjoys the sight of the things themselves' (Waite).

8: we are of good courage, I say, and are willing rather to be absent from the body, and to be at home with the Lord.

As Paul was unsure of what was in store for him, he could not count on being alive at the parousia. 'Therefore he says only as much as he could with full certainty profess: to be absent from the body is to be at home with the Lord. Even in case that happened which appeared to him the less desirable, he would still be contented, because in this being with the Lord everything else was potentially given' (Vos) [cf. *Phil.* 1:21–23]

9: Wherefore also we make it our aim, whether at home or absent, to be well–pleasing unto him.

Whether therefore Paul is in the body or out of it at the Lord's return, his constant ambition, and the only lawful one (Bengel), is to win his approval. For whatever the Lord's appointment for him may be, whether it be life or death, his absolute commitment to Christ remains the same [*Rom.* 14:8; *Phil.* 1:20; *1 Thess.* 5:10].

10: For we must all be made manifest before the judgment–seat of Christ; that each one may receive the things done in the body, according to what he hath done, whether it be good or bad.

For Paul makes it his aim to be well-pleasing to Christ because he is to be judged by Christ, and so are the hyper-critical Corinthians!

We must all: Although there is no way of evading the force of this divine 'must' which applies to all men, 'all men do not have minds sufficiently exalted to remember every single moment that they must appear before the judgment-seat of Christ' (Calvin). Paul speaks of the one general judgment of all men by Christ, before whose tribunal even Christians must stand. 'It is impossible to identify a series of distinct and separate judgments' (G. E. Ladd, 'Eschatology', *The New Bible Dictionary*, p. 389) [cf. *Matt.* 25:31–46; *John* 12:48; *Acts* 17:30, 31; *Rom.* 2:16; *2 Tim.* 4:1; *2 Pet.*3:7]

Be made manifest: 'We are at all times, manifest to God; then we shall be so to the assembled intelligent universe and to ourselves; for the judgment shall be not only in order to assign the everlasting portion to each, but to vindicate God's righteousness, so that it shall be manifest to all his creatures, and even to the sinner himself' (Fausset).

Before the judgment-seat of Christ: 'The judgment-seat of God' [*Rom.* 14:10] is also 'the judgment-seat of Christ', because God has ordained that the world shall be judged by the One it condemned [*Acts* 17:31]. 'The judge on this great occasion is to be not God, absolutely considered, but the God-man in his office as mediatorial King. All judgment is said to be, not inherently his, but *committed* to him by the Father. *John* 5:22, 27' (A. A. Hodge, *The Confession of Faith*, p. 390).

In order that each one may receive as his due the things done by means of his body (Plummer): All men are to be judged, but not in the mass. For each man will be individually assessed so that 'there will be exact correspondence between action and requital' (Theodoret, cited by Plummer).

According to what he hath done: That all men will be judged according to their works is the consistent teaching of the New Testament [e.g. *Matt.* 16:27; *Rom.* 2:6; *Rev.* 22:12]. The same principle which seals the doom of the wicked will be used to determine the reward of the righteous. For though salvation is not by works [*Rom.* 3:24], every believer's work will be tested, and whether he is rewarded or suffers loss (but not punishment) will depend on how he has built on the one foundation of grace which is Jesus Christ [*1 Cor.* 3:10–15].

Whether it be good or bad: 'The change to the neuter singular is significant. It seems to imply that, although persons will be judged one by one and not in groups, yet conduct in each case will be judged as a whole. In other words, it is character rather than separate acts that will be rewarded (in the case of believers) or punished (in the case of unbelievers) . . . It is habitual action that will be judged. And this explains the aorist; it is what he did during his lifetime that is summed up and estimated as a total. Human tribunals deal with crime; they have punishments, but no rewards. The Divine tribunal has both' (Plummer) [*John* 5:29].

11: Knowing therefore the fear of the Lord, we persuade men, but we are made manifest unto God; and I hope that we are made manifest also in your consciences.

The purity of Paul's motives in preaching the gospel is guaranteed by the awe which this forthcoming judgment inspires in him. He is prompted to persuade men by the supreme desire faithfully to discharge the Lord's commission, and not by any spirit of self–interest. In fact it is only as a man has this integrity towards God that his preaching can have any real appeal to men, for those who are not faithful to God are never genuine with men.

But we are made manifest unto God: Because Paul knows that God already has a perfect knowledge of his heart, he seeks to be as open before God now as he must be at Christ's judgment-seat [verse 10].

And I hope that we are made manifest also in your consciences: 'Their consciences, rather than their intellects, on which they prided themselves: *conscience penetrates further than the judgment of the flesh;* conscience goes deeper than criticism (Calvin). Paul says "consciences" and not "conscience", because he appeals to the individual conscience of each of them: *the plural has greater weight* (Bengel)' (Plummer).

12: We are not again commending ourselves unto you, but speak as giving you occasion of glorying on our behalf, that ye may have wherewith to answer them that glory in appearance, and not in heart.

In thus defending his ministry Paul is not again indulging in the self-praise with which he was charged by his cynical critics in Corinth [3:1]. But that it should have proved necessary for their father in Christ to supply them with the ammunition to repel these slanders was indeed a reproach to the Corinthians. 'Paul's opponents boasted of what was outward and incidental, personal knowledge of Jesus, connexion with the older apostles, Jewish descent and privilege, learning, eloquence, etc. By "heart" is meant the inward as contrasted with the outward, the essential as opposed to the incidental; so "spiritual reality"' (Massie) [*1 Sam.* 16:7].

13: For whether we are beside ourselves, it is unto God; or whether we are of sober mind, it is unto you.

Like his Master before him, Paul was accused of religious dementia [*Mark* 3:21; *Acts* 26:24], but his 'fanaticism' was for God! Just as the Corinthians should be the last to deny the enlightening effect upon them of his lucid ministry of the gospel! The first part of the verse does not describe a state of religious ecstasy, for though Paul was no stranger to such experiences there is no reason to believe that the Corinthians ever saw him in this condition. On the contrary, he has to inform them of these *private* spiritual experiences [12:1; *1 Cor.* 14:18]. 'For God' and 'for you' are not in opposition, and do not exclude each other as though 'for God' meant 'for him and not for you', and 'for you' meant 'for you and not for God' (Lenski). *All* that Paul did and does is for God *and* for you!

14: For the love of Christ constraineth us; because we thus judge, that one died for all, therefore all died;

It is the love of Christ for Paul which irresistibly impels him to serve God and his people in this way. This is the secret of stability in Christian service. The surpassing love of Christ for us must be reflected in our single-minded devotion to him [*Gal.* 2:20]. This is how Paul defends his conduct before the Corinthians: 'Christ's love claims him in such a way that in relation to others he can no longer exist for himself – in contrast to his opponents, who boast to the Corinthians that they are religious and spiritual, that they are something in themselves' (H. Köster, *TDNT*, vol. 7, pp. 883–4).

Because we thus judge: 'lit., (as) "having judged thus"; implying a judgment formed at conversion, and ever since regarded as a settled truth' (Fausset).

That one died for all, therefore all died: The inescapable meaning of this statement is that the 'all' for whom Christ died are those who also died 'in the person of their representative' (F. F. Bruce) [cf. *Rom.* 5:12ff.; *1 Cor.* 15:22]. 'The nature of the atonement settles its extent. If it merely made salvation possible, it applied to all men. If it effectively secured salvation, it had reference only to the elect. As Dr Warfield says, "The things we have to choose between are an atonement of high value, or an atonement of wide extension. The two cannot go together". The work of Christ can be universalized only by evaporating its substance' (Loraine Boettner, *The Reformed Doctrine of Predestination*, pp. 152–3).

15: and he died for all, that they that live should no longer live unto themselves, but unto him who for their sakes died and rose again.

To die with Christ is 'to die to sin and to rise with him to the life of new obedience, to live not to ourselves but to him who died for us and rose again. The inference is inevitable that those for whom Christ died arc those and those only who die to sin and live to righteousness. Now it is a plain fact that not all die to sin and live in newness of life. Hence we cannot say that all men distributively died with Christ. And neither can we say that Christ died for all men, for the simple reason that all for whom Christ died also died in Christ. If we cannot say that Christ died for all men, neither can we say that the atonement is universal – it is the death of Christ for men that specifically constitutes the atonement. The conclusion is apparent – the death of Christ in its specific character as atonement was for those and those only who are in due time the partakers of that new life of which Christ's resurrection is the pledge and pattern. This is another reminder that the death and resurrection of Christ are inseparable. Those for whom Christ died are those for whom he rose again and his heavenly saving activity is of equal extent with his once–for–all redemptive accomplishments' (John Murray, *Redemption – Accomplished and Applied*, pp. 70–1).

16: Wherefore we henceforth know no man after the flesh: even though we have known Christ after the flesh, yet now we know him so no more.

'Wherefore' points to one consequence of the foregoing statement [verse 15], another is advanced by the same word in the following verse. 'After the flesh' here means '*the external* or *outward side of life*, as it appears to the eye of an unregenerate person' (Arndt-Gingrich). What Paul is saying is that since his conversion he no longer estimates any man according to worldly standards of judgment. For that which was natural to the old mode of living is entirely unnatural to one who has been raised to new life in Christ. But because the Judaizing teachers are not thus constrained by the love of Christ, they still judge 'after the flesh' and are influencing the Corinthians to regard Paul in the same way. Paul knows this tendency must be checked, for when Christians begin to look upon others in a fleshly way, they are 'in the greatest danger of again knowing Christ only in a fleshly way' (Lenski).

Even though we have known Christ after the flesh: Paul does not claim personal acquaintance with Jesus; he disowns his former unworthy estimate of Christ as a blasphemer whose death was merited and whose followers deserved the same treatment [*Acts* 26:9–12]. But the judgment of Saul the unconverted Pharisee and that of Paul the believing Apostle are poles apart.

Yet now we know him so no more: It 'is not the figure of Jesus who once wandered through the fields of Galilee, nor is it the historical picture of the Nazarene, which forms the content of Paul's preaching; but it is the living Lord, who has been exalted out of his humiliation, and who as such is now the Lord of the Church . . . Yet this does not say that Paul preached a different Jesus than the Jesus according to the flesh. Paul preached the same Christ, but Paul now proclaims a Jesus who died, and rose again, and who now sits at the right hand of God, the Father. The difference does not lie in the fact that the one picture is historical and human, whereas the other is super-historical and divine; but it lies in the fact that the history of redemption had progressed, that the Christ according to the flesh is now the Lord of the heavens' (Herman Ridderbos, *Paul and Jesus*, p. 69).

17: Wherefore if any man is in Christ, he is a new creature: the old things are passed away; behold, they are become new.

Wherefore if any man is in Christ, there is a new creation (ASV margin): What Paul has experienced is also true of every man who is in Christ. Because the Christian is in fact a new creation – 'a reborn microcosm belonging to the eschatological macrocosm' (P. E. Hughes) – he not only has a different standard of judgment from the man of the world, but is also the inhabitant of a totally new world. Hence the transformation effected by his union with Christ may not be restricted to his subjective renewal, for it includes his transfer into a world which has assumed a new aspect and complexion. This interpretation is required by the formula 'in Christ', which Paul nowhere uses in an exclusively individual sense: Christ 'is everywhere, where the formula in question occurs, the central dominating factor of a new order of affairs, in fact nothing less than the originator and representative of a new world–order' (Vos) [*Rev.* 21:4, 5].

The old things are passed away; behold, they are become new: 'Old opinions, views, plans, desires, principles and affections are passed away; new views of truth, new principles, new apprehensions of the destiny of man, and new feelings and purposes fill and govern the soul' (Hodge) [*Phil.* 3:7].

18: But all things are of God, who reconciled us to himself through Christ, and gave unto us the ministry of reconciliation;

But all things are of God: All these new things come from God. 'The new creation is no spontaneous development, and it is not man's own work on himself; Apostles do not claim to be the cause of it. It is wholly from God [verse 5; 1:21; 2:14; 4:6, *1 Cor.* 8:6, 11, 12; *Rom.* 11:36]' (Plummer).

Who reconciled us to himself through Christ: 'Reconciliation' in the New Testament sense 'is not something which *we accomplish* when we lay aside our enmity to God; it is something which *God accomplished* when in the death of Christ He put away everything that on His side meant estrangement, so that He might come and preach peace . . . The serious thing which makes the Gospel necessary, and the putting away of which constitutes the Gospel, is God's condemnation of the world and its sin; it is God's wrath, "revealed from heaven against all ungodliness and unrighteousness of men" [*Rom.* 1:16–18]. The putting away of this is "reconciliation": the preaching of *this* reconciliation is the preaching of the Gospel' (Denney).

And gave unto us the ministry of reconciliation: That a former persecutor of the church of God should have been entrusted with 'the ministry of reconciliation' never ceases to amaze Paul. But it is only because God has initiated and completed this great work of reconciliation that there is such a service to perform. 'For unless we can preach a finished work of Christ in relation to sin, a reconciliation or peace which has been achieved independently of us at an infinite cost and to which we are called in a word or ministry of reconciliation, we have no real gospel for sinful men at all' (James Denney, *The Death of Christ*, p. 86).

19: to wit, that God was in Christ reconciling the world unto himself, not reckoning unto them their trespasses, and having committed unto us the word of reconciliation.

That is, in Christ God was reconciling the world to himself (RSV margin): The essence of the good news is that in Christ crucified God was reconciling the world unto himself. The term 'world' is neither to be arbitrarily limited to the elect, nor is it to be indiscriminately extended to each and every man, but it rather points to an 'eschatological' universalism. For as the whole creation was involved in the consequences of the Fall, so the cosmic restoration of all things is secured by Christ's cancellation of the curse of sin [*Rom.* 8:19–21; *Col.* 1:20].

Not reckoning unto them their trespasses, and having committed unto us the word of reconciliation: 'The proof that God was reconciling the world to himself in Christ (i.e. in his death) is that he does not impute to men their trespasses, and that he has established the ministry of reconciliation. The forgiveness of sin and the institution of the ministry are clear evidence that God is propitious. Not to impute sin, is to forgive it. *Rom.* 4, 5; *2 Tim.* 4:16' (Hodge).

20: We are ambassadors therefore on behalf of Christ, as though God

were entreating by us: we beseech you on behalf of Christ, be ye reconciled to God.

So we are ambassadors for Christ (RSV): As the representative of his sovereign, an ambassador delivers only what he has been commissioned to say, so that those who receive his message with contempt offend the king in whose name he speaks. Yet Christ's ambassadors are not quick to take offence on his behalf, and disregarding the obduracy of those to whom they are sent, they *beseech* (the word 'intimates an unusual submission' – Bengel) them to receive the proffered mercy of God. It is important to note that 'the interest of the statement is focused on the (material) authority of the message rather than the (formal) authority of an officer. Paul does not stress the latter even when defending his own apostleship, *Gal.* 1:8; *1 Thess.* 2:7' (G. Bornkamm, *TDNT,* vol. 6, p. 682).

God making his appeal through us (RSV): 'The fact that "God is entreating by us" is a momentous one, and the declaration of it is analogous to the formula of the Hebrew Prophet, "Thus saith the Lord"' (Plummer).

'We beseech on behalf of Christ: "Be reconciled to God!"' (P. E. Hughes): This entreaty is not addressed to the Christians in Corinth, who are here reminded of the content of the apostle's constant appeal to the unconverted. 'The synergistic reasoning is fallacious that, since God tells men to be reconciled, men must have the ability to obey. The imperative is passive; it does not say: "Reconcile yourselves to God!" "Turn thou me, and I shall be turned!" *Jer.* 31:18. Reconcile *thou* me, and I shall be reconciled! Every gospel imperative is full of the divine power of grace to effect what it demands. If it counted on even the least power in the sinner it would never secure the least effect. Jesus calls this the Father's drawing [*John* 6:44; 6:65; 12:32]'(Lenski).

21: Him who knew no sin he made to be sin on our behalf; that we might become the righteousness of God in him.

In this tremendous sentence Paul explains what he means by the words, *'not reckoning unto them their trespasses'* [19]. The non-imputation of sin rests on the fact that Christ our substitute was made sin on our behalf. And it is this objective *satisfaction* for sin that guarantees the reality of the reconciliation which the apostle beseeches men to receive.

Him who knew no sin: 'That is, with a practical knowledge; with an intellectual he did, else he could not have reproved it. We know no more than we practise. Christ is said to "know no sin because he did none' (Trapp) [*John* 8:46; *Heb.* 4:15; *1 Pet.* 2:22; *1 John* 3:5].

He made to be sin on our behalf: Only the One who knew no sin was free to bear its curse for others [*Gal.* 3:13]. As the consequences of sin were charged to Christ's account, he became so closely identified with it that Paul even dares to say that God made him to be *sin.* Nevertheless this is a very different thing from saying that God made him a sinner. For though he exhausted the curse of sin, he was never personally defiled by it. 'While He was personally the object of the Father's everlasting love and complacency, He was officially guilty in our guilt. The paternal and the governmental on the part of God may easily be distinguished and viewed apart. He never was the object of the Father's loathing or aversion, even when forsaken. He never was, what the sinner inevitably is, abhorred, or abominable; because a distinction could always be made between the only begotten Son, the righteous Servant, and the sin-bearing Substitute' (G. Smeaton) [*Isa.* 53:4, 5].

That we might become the righteousness of God in him: The full meaning of our justification is disclosed in the amazing thought that we become 'the righteousness of God' by union with Christ [cf. *Rom.* 5:17, 18, 19]. 'We are made not only the beneficiaries of it; we are made the partakers of it and to such an extent that we are actually identified in terms of it. It is ours in the sense that our identity is defined in terms of it. Just as Christ became so identified with our sins that, though knowing no sin, he was made sin, so we being in ourselves utterly ungodly and therefore knowing no righteousness are so identified with Christ's righteousness that we are made the righteousness of God. In reality the concept is richer than that of imputation; it is not simply reckoned as ours, but it is reckoned to us and we are identified with it' (John Murray, *Collected Writings*, vol. 2, p. 214). The early Christian writer of the Epistle to Diognetus also gave memorable expression to this truth in the rapturous words: 'O sweet exchange. O inscrutable operation. O unexpected blessings: that the lawlessness of many should be hidden in one righteous Person, and the righteousness of One should justify the lawless many' (cited by J. W. C. Wand, *A History of the Early Church*, pp. 61–2).

CHAPTER SIX

As a worker together with God, Paul entreats the Corinthians not to frustrate God's grace in the acceptable day of salvation [verses 1, 2]. In the discharge of his ministry he avoided all offence, proving his sincerity by patiently enduring all the trials which served to enrich others with the gospel [verses 3-10]. Paul speaks so freely because his heart is enlarged towards the Corinthians, and he urges them to enlarge their hearts towards him [verses 11-13]. They also must hold back from any intimate association with unbelievers since fellowship between righteousness and iniquity is impossible. Christians must shun all uncleanness because they are the temple of the living God [verses 14-18].

1: And working together with him we entreat also that ye receive not the grace of God in vain

In the full consciousness that he is working together with God, Paul also appeals to the Corinthians, who have already received the message of reconciliation, that they do not receive this grace of God in vain. This means that there was a danger that the forthcoming judgment [5:10] would disclose a painful discrepancy between their practice and their profession [5:15]. They must see to it that they receive the grace of God *as grace*, and not as legalism or licence, or that day will find them barren of the righteousness which is the fruit of a living union with Christ.

2: (for he saith, At an acceptable time I hearkened unto thee, And in a day of salvation did I succour thee: behold, now is the acceptable time; behold, now is the day of salvation):

This parenthetic appeal to Scripture is made to remind the Corinthians that they have the inestimable privilege of living in the promised season of grace [*Isa.* 49:8]. Here Paul takes the answer that God gives to the prayer of his suffering Servant (Christ) as assuring the salvation of all those for whom he is the chosen Representative. Paul's own comment on the passage consists of an urgent summons to embrace the proffered favour of God in the period appointed by God for its acceptance. He thereby lets the Corinthians know that the privilege of living in such days of gospel opportunity also lays upon them the solemn responsibility of seeing that they do not receive the grace of God in vain [verse 1].

3: giving no occasion of stumbling in anything, that our ministration be not blamed;

The connection is with verse 1, 'we entreat . . . giving no occasion of stumbling'. The consciousness that he is a worker together with God leads the apostle to conduct himself in a manner which is consistent with the ministry he has to exercise. 'Ministers give occasion of stumbling when by their own faults they hinder the progress of the Gospel in those who hear them. Paul claims that he is not of that company and testifies to his careful concern not to stain his apostleship with any taint of disgrace. For this is a trick of Satan – to seek for a fault in ministers which will tend to bring the Gospel into disrepute. For if he succeeds in bringing the ministry into contempt, all hope of progress is gone. Thus the man who wishes to make himself useful in Christ's service must devote all his energies to maintaining the honour of his ministry' (Calvin).

4: but in everything commending ourselves, as ministers of God, in much patience, in afflictions, in necessities, in distresses, 5: in stripes, in imprisonments, in tumults, in labours, in watchings, in fastings;

Paul is not like the false teachers who brandish wordy commendations of themselves [3:1], for his whole life is a constant validation of the message he proclaims. 'In much patience' is that quality of patient endurance which enables the apostle to triumph over trials of every kind. The nine afflictions listed fall into three groups.

In afflictions, in necessities, in distresses: The first 'triplet of trials' provides a climactic description of the general pressures to which he is subjected. 'In *afflictions* (crushings), many ways are open, but they are all difficult; in *necessities* (constraints), one way is open, though difficult; in *distresses* (straits), none is open' (Bengel).

In stripes, in imprisonments, in tumults: He turns next to particular hardships inflicted upon him by other men. His ministry was punctuated by brutal beatings which would have silenced a less determined spirit [11:23–25], frequently interrupted by imprisonments [11:23], and often abruptly halted by mob violence [*Acts* 13:50; 14:19; 16:19; 19:29].

In labours, in watchings, in fastings: Finally, he refers to the hardships he inflicted upon himself in the course of his work. In the cause of Christ he willingly submitted to 'wearing toil, sleepless nights, and hungry days' (Massie) [11:27].

6: in pureness, in knowledge, in long suffering, in kindness, in the Holy Spirit, in love unfeigned, 7: in the word of truth, in the power of God;

Paul has been enabled to endure all these things in virtue of those spiritual graces that constitute the sphere or element in which his ministry moves.

In pureness, in knowledge: In the first pair of graces, Paul significantly couples purity of life and motive with the saving knowledge of the gospel, for both are always found together in all authentic ministry.

In long suffering, in kindness: The injuries inflicted upon Paul by the Corinthians had given him ample opportunity to exhibit his long suffering towards them and to repay their ingratitude with kindness [*1 Cor.* 13:4; *Col.* 3:12].

In the Holy Spirit, in love unfeigned: The holiness, of which the Holy Spirit himself is the author, displays itself in a love that is devoid of the least tincture of insincerity or hypocrisy [*Rom.* 12:9; *1 Pet.*1:22].

In the word of truth, in the power of God: Paul's proclamation of the word of truth was effective because he did not rely on persuasive words of wisdom to make it so, but trusted in the power of God [*1 Cor.* 2:3ff.]. He who is a stranger to the subjective power of the gospel in his own life cannot fittingly communicate its objective truth to others.

7b: by the armour of righteousness on the right hand and on the left. 8: by glory and dishonour, by evil report and good report;

By the armour of righteousness on the right hand and on the left: The sword was held in the right hand, and the shield in the left [cf. *Eph.* 6:13–17]. 'The weapons by which he makes the "power of God" felt are characterized by a righteous temper, and they smite, or ward off smiting, in a righteous cause. They are not "fleshly weapons" [10:3, 4]. Paul's instruments of attack and defence, his sword and his shield, are righteous both as to means and as to end' (Massie).

By glory and dishonour: These opposing estimates of Paul's ministry nevertheless agree in recommending the devotion with which he prosecuted it. 'Some said, "He is beside himself", and others would have plucked out their eyes for his sake, yet both these extremely opposite attitudes were produced by the very same thing – the passionate earnestness with which he served Christ in the Gospel' (Denney).

By evil report and good report: Paul continues faithful to his calling whether slandered in his absence or flattered to his face. '*In proportion as a man has more or less of* glory *or* good report, *in the same proportion has he also more or less of either* disgrace *or* infamy *respectively*' (Bengel).

> 8b: as deceivers, and yet true; 9: as unknown, and yet well known; as dying, and behold, we live; as chastened, and not killed; 10: as sorrowful, yet always rejoicing; as poor, yet making many rich; as having nothing, and yet possessing all things.

As deceivers, and yet true: In the first three couplets Paul has in view the dishonour which was heaped upon him by the evil report of his opponents in Corinth. In branding God's inspired apostle as a purveyor of deceit, these men declared themselves to be the true children of the father of lies, thus proving their own bondage to the arch-deceiver himself [*John* 8:44; *2 John* 7].

As unknown, and yet well known: Paul's credentials may indeed be called in question by men, but he is confident that he is well known to God [*2 Tim.* 2:19]. 'To be unknown to the world matters nothing; it is to be known of God as His own that is all-important' (P. E. Hughes).

As dying, and behold, we live: He is regarded by many as the doomed champion of a lost cause, but just when men are prepared to write him off as finished, all are surprised to find that he goes on living and serving his Lord.

As chastened, and not killed: Leaving these calumnies behind, Paul devotes the remaining four couplets to a paradoxical description of his actual condition. Here he thankfully acknowledges with the Psalmist, that though he is the subject of divine chastening (though never of divine wrath), God has not given him over to death [*Psa.* 118: 17, 18].

As sorrowful, yet always rejoicing: Although constantly surrounded by every kind of grief, nothing could sever him from the source of his continual rejoicing. Thus it was from the cheerless gloom of a Roman gaol that he urged his fellow believers in Philippi to follow his own example: 'Rejoice in the Lord always: again I will say, Rejoice' [*Phil.* 4:4].

As poor, yet making many rich: That the apostle was not well endowed with worldly wealth was evident to all, yet it was given to him to make many rich through his preaching of 'the unsearchable riches of Christ' [*Eph.* 3:8].

As having nothing, and yet possessing all things: 'It is no loss to have nothing and no gain to have everything in the way in which the world has and has not; but to have as Christians have is to have everything, no matter how little they have according to the world's way of having' (Lenski) [*1 Cor.* 3:21ff.].

11: Our mouth is open unto you, O Corinthians, our heart is enlarged.

The emotions aroused in Paul by the complete lack of reserve with which he has spoken of his ministry here overflow in a sudden upsurge of feeling for his beloved converts at Corinth, to whom he addresses the tender appeal: 'O Corinthians' [cf. *Gal.* 3:1; *Phil.* 4:15]. Since such openness of speech only flows from great enlargement of heart, they should no longer doubt the genuineness of his love for them. 'Love, like heat, expands' (Fausset).

12: Ye are not straitened in us, but ye are straitened in your own affections. 13: Now for a recompense in like kind (I speak as unto my children), be ye also enlarged.

Paul here insists that there is no restraint or reserve in his love for them. 'The scanty room was not in him, but in the seat of their own affections, and it hampered *his* free admission to *their* hearts. Even now the feeling in Corinth towards him was not all that he could desire' (Waite). But if even as an apostle he cannot command their love, it is only natural that as their own father in the faith he should expect his love for them to be returned 'in the same way in exchange' (Arndt-Gingrich).

14: Be not unequally yoked with unbelievers: for what fellowship have righteousness and iniquity? or what communion hath light with darkness?

The sudden transition from tender entreaty to stern admonition has led many to suppose that this passage [6:14–7:1] is a misplaced fragment from another letter, and in a number of modern commentaries the text is even re-arranged in accordance with this unproven and indeed unprovable hypothesis! In fact there is no evidence that any copy of the Epistle ever lacked these verses. Certainly the change in tone is abrupt, but the connection is clear enough. As Plummer rightly remarks, 'It is not incredible that in the middle of his appeal for *mutual* frankness and affection, and after his declaration that the cramping constraint is all on their side, he should dart off to one main cause of that constraint, viz. their compromising attitude towards anti-Christian influences.'

Be not unequally yoked with unbelievers: The allusion is to the law which forbade the uniting of animals of different species in the same yoke [*Deut.* 22:10].

'What a picture: a believer with his neck under the unbeliever's yoke! What business has he in such an unnatural, self-contradictory association? What is he, the believer, doing by helping to pull the plough or the wagon of the unbeliever's unbelief? That yoke breaks the necks of those who bear it. God has delivered us from it; can we possibly think of going back to that frightful yoke?' (Lenski). [cf. *Matt.* 11:28-30] Paul follows this command with five rhetorical questions that highlight the absolute incompatibility which exists between Christians and pagans.

For what fellowship have righteousness and iniquity? (literally, lawlessness): While it is true that in this world there are many points of contact between saints and sinners [*1 Cor.* 5:10], it is self-evident that the opposing principles which characterize each class rule out any possibility of a partnership between them. For what fellowship has the *righteousness* of those who are distinguished by their habitual conformity to the law of God, with the *lawlessness* of those who are marked out by their unvarying opposition to it? [*1 John* 3:4,9, 10].

Or what communion hath light with darkness? Since nothing can be more incongruous than light and darkness, the attempt of 'Christians to remain Christians and retain their inward state as such, and yet to enter voluntarily into intimate fellowship with the world, is as impossible as to combine light and darkness, holiness and sin, happiness and misery' (Hodge).

15: And what concord hath Christ with Belial? or what portion hath a believer with an unbeliever?

And what concord hath Christ with Beliar? (ASV margin): This question brings into view the personal rulers behind these qualities and powers. Only the most fundamental antagonism can exist between Christ, who is the personification of righteousness, and Beliar (Satan), who is the personification of lawlessness. 'Christ hath no fellowship with the devil, therefore we ought to have no unnecessary communion with such who manifest themselves to be of their father the devil, by doing his works' (Matthew Poole).

Or what portion hath a believer with an unbeliever? 'As subjects of their respective lords, what "portion" have they together? What the one has, the other has not: righteousness, pardon, spiritual light and life, peace, hope of salvation, a place in heaven. The portions of these two diverge at every point' (Lenski). Obviously, there can be no fellowship between those whose respective destinies are so different. But the antithesis 'must not be interpreted as though it encouraged pharisaic concepts of contamination or invited to eremitic and monastic attempts at segregation from "the world"' (P. E. Hughes).

16a: And what agreement hath a temple of God with idols?

What agreement hath God's sanctuary with idols? (Plummer): This translation is preferable since Paul uses the word which refers to the temple as the very dwelling-place of God. The climax is reached in the final question, which provides the premise for what follows [verses 16b–18]. For it exhibits the utter sinfulness of attempting to find a place for the images of false gods within the imageless sanctuary of God. 'By the introduction of idols the temple ceases to be a temple of God' (Plummer).

16b: for we are a temple of the living God; even as God said, I will dwell in them, and walk in them; and I will be their God, and they shall be my people.

In boldly identifying 'the temple of the living God' (RSV) with the New Testament church (the emphatic 'we' = believers), Paul here condemns the carnal expectations which are fostered by a literalistic interpretation of Old Testament prophecy. 'There cannot be a surer canon of interpretation, than that *everything which affects the constitution and destiny of the New Testament Church has its clearest determination in New Testament Scripture*. This canon, with the grounds on which it is based, strikes at the root of many false conclusions drawn mainly from ancient prophecy, respecting the events of the latter days – conclusions which always implicitly, and sometimes even avowedly, give to the Old the ascendency over the New; and, on the principle which has its grand embodiment in Popery, would send the world back to the age of comparative darkness and imperfection for the type of its normal and perfected condition' (Patrick Fairbairn, *The Interpretation of Prophecy*, p. 158) [cf. *Eph.* 2:21; *1 Pet.* 2:5].

Even as God said, I will dwell in them, and walk in them; and I will be their God, and they shall be my people: The distinctive thought of Leviticus 26:11–12 is that God will dwell *among* his people by means of the material sanctuary, whereas Paul's paraphrase is designed to bring out the fact that under the New Covenant he now dwells *in* them [cf. *Eph.* 2:22]. 'Paul assumes that the ancient promise fulfilled in outward and symbolic form in the ritual of the Tabernacle, is valid now; and assures believers of the inward and spiritual presence of God in themselves. For the entire ritual was an outward symbol of the spiritual realities of the better covenant (Beet) [*Ezek.* 37:27].

17: Wherefore: Come ye out from among them, and be ye separate, saith the Lord, And touch no unclean thing; And I will receive you,

Wherefore: The truth expressed in the foregoing quotation is now also applied in words which are freely drawn from Scripture [verses 17, 18].

Come ye out from among them . . . And touch no unclean thing: God's warning to the returning exiles to leave everything that was unclean behind them in Babylon is here appropriately repeated to those so lately delivered from the idolatry of Corinth [*Isa.* 52:11].

And I will receive you: Such a separation is the necessary preparation for fellowship with God [*Ezek.* 20:34]. 'The Christian life is thus seen to be no barren renunciation, for the believer is separated from the world for no less a purpose than that he may enjoy friendship with God in the blessed company of other faithful people' (Tasker).

18: And will be to you a Father, And ye shall be to me sons and daughters, saith the Lord Almighty.

The final quotation, which combines 2 Samuel 7:14 and Isaiah 43:6, shows that if believers are corporately God's temple, individually they are members of God's family (so Murray Harris). Paul here adapts God's promise to David that his son would build him a house, in order to describe its spiritual fulfilment through David's greater Son [cf. *John* 2:18-22]. Indeed Solomon's words at the dedication of the Temple indicate that he was well aware of its limitations [*1 Kings* 8:27; *Acts* 7:48]. 'It was only when the Christ, born of David's seed, dwelt in the hearts of those who accepted His sacrifice, and submitted themselves to the guidance of His Spirit, that God "became to them really as a Father, and they became His sons and daughters"' (R. V. G. Tasker, *The Old Testament in the New Testament*, p. 95). As the favoured recipients of such great promises, the Corinthians must therefore take care to shun the defilement which would debar them from their benefits [7:1].

CHAPTER SEVEN

After exhorting the Corinthians to purity of life, Paul again urges them to return his love, for he had neither wronged them nor lost confidence in them [verses 1–4]. On resuming the account of his movements, he recalls his anxiety as he awaited the return of Titus, and expresses his joy in their repentance [verses 5–7]. For though his severe letter had made them sorry, he did not now regret sending it, since their godly sorrow had produced such good effects [verses 8–12]. Above all, he rejoiced that the news brought by Titus had confirmed his trust in them [verses 13–16].

1: Having therefore these promises, beloved, let us cleanse ourselves from all defilements of flesh and spirit, perfecting holiness in the fear of God.

As this verse concludes the paragraph begun at 6:14, the chapter division is particularly unfortunate here. In placing the emphasis on the word 'these', Paul underlines the privileges enjoyed by the Corinthians to enforce the obligations of obedience. 'Beloved' intensifies this appeal by conveying the warmth of his feeling for them [cf. 12:19; *Rom.* 12:19; *1 Cor.* 10:14; 15:58; *Phil.* 2:12; 4:1]. It is not from any sense of mock humility that Paul includes himself in his exhortation, for even an apostle must strive to attain the goal of perfection [*Phil.* 3:12–14]. The determinative, decisive act of cleansing is to be realized in the continual and continuing bringing of holiness to completion. Hence he speaks of 'perfecting holiness', not perfected holiness! 'The durative participle excludes sanctification that is attained by one act; moreover, our actions are here stated and not an action by which God totally sanctifies us in one instant' (Lenski). Thus all believers are required by God to cleanse themselves from everything that would defile either body ('flesh') or soul ('spirit'). But those who are unwilling to cleanse themselves from every *stain* of sin only show that they have not been cleansed from the *guilt* of sin. The unsanctified are the unjustified. 'In the fear of God' is 'the motive which is to determine our endeavours to purify ourselves. It is not regard to the good of others, nor our own happiness, but reverence for God. We are to be holy, because he is holy' (Hodge) [*1 Pet.*1:14–17]

2: Open your hearts to us: we wronged no man, we corrupted no man, we took advantage of no man.

Paul now returns to the appeal of 6:11–13. Since the Corinthians occupy so large a place in his affections, surely they can return his love by making room for him in their hearts! That he had harmed no one was made manifest in their consciences [5:11], and therefore he contents himself with a flat denial of the hollow charges which had been brought against him. 'Modestly he leaves them to supply the *positive* good which he had done; suffering all things himself that they might be benefited [verses 9, 12; 12:13]' (Fausset).

3: I say it not to condemn you: for I have said before, that ye are in our hearts to die together and live together.

In thus protesting his innocence, the apostle has no desire to condemn those whom he loves so completely that not even the final crisis of death, much less the vicissitudes of life, can ever erase their image from his heart [cf. 3:2; 6:11]. Paul may put 'death' first because his recent experiences had made it a more likely prospect than life [1:8; 11:23].

4: Great is my boldness of speech toward you, great is my glorying on your behalf. I am filled with comfort, I overflow with joy in all our affliction.

So far from wishing to condemn the Corinthians, Paul has every confidence in them and glories greatly on their behalf. In speaking here of '*the* comfort' and '*the* joy' (translating the article) with which he is filled to overflowing, he evidently refers to the effect produced by the news of their repentance which Titus had brought to him.

5: For even when we were come into Macedonia our flesh had no relief, but we were afflicted on every side; without were fightings, within were fears.

Having concluded his great 'digression' on the glory of the ministry entrusted to him by God, Paul now returns to the point at which he broke off the account of his movements in 2:13. There, he says, 'I had no relief for my *spirit*'; here, 'our flesh had no relief'. This virtually synonymous usage shows that Paul's intense anxiety of spirit as he awaited the coming of Titus also affected his flesh, for the body is the vehicle through which the experience of the spirit finds its expression (so P. E. Hughes).

But we were afflicted on every side; without were fightings, within were fears: The situation is sketched with only three bold strokes, for Paul has no wish to dwell upon past sorrows now. Nevertheless, it is enough to let the Corinthians see something of the severity of his sufferings. For he was not only besieged by those outward troubles which were the usual accompaniment to his ministry, but he was also gripped by inward fears concerning 'the effects of his letter and of the mission of Titus' (Massie).

6: Nevertheless he that comforteth the lowly, even God, comforted us by the coming of Titus;

But God, who comforts the downcast (RSV): The right idea is not conveyed by the word 'lowly'. Paul was depressed and downcast by adverse circumstances. But the 'God of all comfort' [1:3] comforted his much tried servant by the arrival of Titus with the good news from Corinth [*Isa.* 49:13]. 'From this we may gather the most profitable lesson that the more we are afflicted, the greater is the comfort that God has prepared for us. And so this description of God contains a wonderful promise that it is specially God's concern to comfort the miserable and those bowed down to the dust' (Calvin).

7: and not by his coming only, but also by the comfort wherewith he was comforted in you, while he told us your longing, your mourning, your zeal for me; so that I rejoiced yet more.

Determined to savour the word to the full, Paul says that he was not only comforted by the coming of Titus, but also by the comfort Titus had received from the Corinthians. The fact that Titus also needed comforting tells us something of the trepidation he felt as he undertook his difficult mission to Corinth. The comfort dispensed was threefold: 'your longing' refers to the Corinthians' longing to see Paul again and to reassure him of their affection; 'your mourning' to their sorrow for having caused him so much pain; 'your zeal for me' to their ardour in defending him and disciplining the offender [verses 11, 12]. Thus Paul's joy in meeting Titus was greatly increased when he learned how the Corinthians now regarded their apostle.

8: For though I made you sorry with my epistle, I do not regret it: though I did regret it (for I see that that epistle made you sorry, though but for a season), 9: I now rejoice, not that ye were made sorry, but that ye were made sorry unto repentance; for ye were made sorry after a godly sort, that ye night suffer loss by us in nothing.

For though I made you sorry with my epistle, I do not regret it: though I did regret it: The Corinthian revolt had forced Paul to send them a letter he would have preferred not to write, because he knew it would cause them pain (see Introduction and comment on 2:3, 4). But though he cannot now regret the happy consequences of sending this 'severe' letter, he was filled with misgivings after its despatch as he wondered how they would receive it. 'Paul's admission may serve as a great comfort to us. Neither revelation nor inspiration lifted the apostles above their poor "flesh" or human nature (here mentioned twice: 7:1, 5) which asserted itself in hours of weakness and depression in the form of even doubts and regrets' (Lenski).

For I see that that epistle made you sorry, though but for a season: 'Gr. *for an hour.* In sin, the pleasure passeth, the sorrow remaineth; but in repentance, the sorrow passeth, the pleasure abideth for ever. God soon poureth the oil of gladness into broken hearts' (Trapp).

I now rejoice, not that ye were made sorry, but that ye were made sorry unto repentance: Since it gave their spiritual father no pleasure to cause the Corinthians pain, it was only the final result of his letter which brought Paul joy. His regret (*metamelomai*) gave way to rejoicing only when he learned that their sorrow had led to their repentance (*metanoia*). These words differ etymologically in that the former 'lays stress on the affliction or pain that is experienced on the contemplation of our former folly'; while the latter 'points primarily to the change of mind, issuing in amendment, which afterthought brings to us' ('New Testament Terms Descriptive of the Great Change': *Selected Shorter Writings of Benjamin B. Warfield*, vol. 1, p. 267).

For ye were made sorry after a godly sort, literally, 'according to God'. For when they saw their sin in the light of God's Word, they were made sorry 'in a manner agreeable to the mind and will of God; so that God approved of their sorrow. He saw that it arose from right views of their past conduct' (Hodge).

That ye might suffer loss by us in nothing: 'Those who have not experienced true repentance might conceive of it as a great loss; it is always the very opposite, the greatest spiritual gain. The grief of repentance is never loss in any way; not to experience this grief, that is loss indeed' (Lenski) (cf. 'the sorrow of the world', verse 10).

10: For godly sorrow worketh repentance unto salvation, a repentance which bringeth no regret: but the sorrow of the world worketh death.

Here Paul carries over the idea of regretting and not-regretting from verse 8. Such godly sorrow, a right regret for sin, is the essential preliminary to an 'unregrettable repentance', that gracious change of mind which always leads to salvation. Thus *metanoia* (repentance) 'does not properly signify the sorrow for having done amiss, but something that is nobler than it, but brought in at the gate of sorrow' (Jeremy Taylor, *On the Doctrine and Practice of Repentance,* cited by Trench).

But the sorrow of the world worketh death: Those who mourn over their sin turn from it and are saved; those who merely experience remorse over the bitter fruit of sin give way to despair and are lost [e.g. Judas Iscariot, *Matt.* 27:3; Esau, *Heb.* 12:17].

11: For behold, this selfsame thing, that ye were made sorry after a godly sort, what earnest care it wrought in you, yea what clearing of yourselves, yea what indignation, yea what fear, yea what longing, yea what zeal, yea

what avenging! In everything ye approved yourselves to be pure in the matter.

For behold, this selfsame thing, that ye were made sorry after a godly sort: Behold this blessed result and adore what was wrought in you by the grace of God, for you are yourselves an example of the right kind of sorrow and its fruits!

What earnest care . . . yea what avenging! Paul's delight in their repentance is expressed in seven particulars. 1. *Earnest care* refers to the Corinthians' 'zealous concern' for the apostle, 'the concern to make restitution which results from true repentance . . . It is obvious that this *earnestness* is a fruit of the Spirit which the Spirit brings forth through the apostle and his work in the church. Hence *earnestness* denotes a new attitude on the part of the Corinthians' (G. Harder, *TDNT,* vol. 7, p. 566). 2. *Clearing of yourselves* or 'self-vindication' describes their eagerness to show that they did not condone the offence. 3. *Indignation.* This was directed against the one who had taken the lead in defying Paul and at themselves for having listened to him [2:5]. 4. *Fear.* What they feared was not so much the apostle's rod as God's judgments. This is a fear which true repentance always awakens! 5. *Longing* points to their yearning for the renewed favour and return of Paul. 6. *Zeal* relates to their ardour in defending the apostle against his accusers. 7. *Avenging.* Finally, the punishment inflicted upon the offender attested the reality of their repentance [verse 12; 2:6].

In everything ye approved yourselves to be pure in the matter: 'The matter' vaguely refers to what is best forgotten now that the church, through the action taken by the majority of its members, had shown itself to be free of blame in connection with the sin, which at first it appeared to condone.

12: So although I wrote unto you, I wrote not for his cause that did the wrong, nor for his cause that suffered the wrong, but that your earnest care for us might be made manifest unto you in the sight of God.

Clearly, Paul does not mean that he had no concern for the offender (see comment on 2:5), or the one who had suffered the wrong (probably Paul himself), but that this was not the *primary* purpose in writing to them. Here Paul exhibits a common Hebrew mode of thought, in which one of two alternatives is negatived 'without meaning that it is negatived absolutely, but only in comparison with the other alternative, which is much more important. "I will have mercy, and not sacrifice" [*Hos.* 6:6] does not prohibit sacrifice; it affirms that mercy is much the better of the two. cf. *Mark* 9:37; *Luke* 10:20, 14:12, 23:28' (Plummer).

But that your earnest care for us might be made manifest unto you in the sight of God: By putting to the proof their full obedience, Paul aroused their dormant love and loyalty so that in the presence of God they might become aware of how much he meant to them. The issue was not at all a question of personal pique on his part; it involved nothing less than their own future as Christians. For how could they continue in fellowship with Christ while they deliberately remained in a state of alienation from his chosen apostle?

13: Therefore we have been comforted: and in our comfort we joyed the more exceedingly for the joy of Titus, because his spirit hath been refreshed by you all.

Therefore we have been comforted: This rounds off the thought of verse 12. The perfect tense indicates that Paul has been and remains comforted by the report Titus brought back from Corinth [verse 6]. The second part of the verse introduces a new thought which is marked in many modern versions by a new paragraph [cf. RSV, NEB, NIV]. The apostle's joy was augmented by the joyfulness of Titus at the success of a mission that was fraught with the greatest difficulties. But the Corinthians' warm welcome and ready obedience had brought a refreshment to his spirit that was still with him (perfect tense again).

14: For if in anything I have gloried to him on your behalf, I was not put to shame; but as we spoke all things to you in truth, so our glorying also which I made before Titus was found to be truth.

Although Paul did not minimize the gravity of the crisis, he believed that at heart the Corinthians were loyal and true, and he had assured Titus that his mission would be crowned with success. Happily, Paul's confidence in them was justified by the event and so he was not put to shame. This negative has the affirmative meaning: 'Your response more than confirmed my words to Titus' (Lenski).

But as we spake all things to you in truth, so our glorying also which I made before Titus was found to be truth: "'My words *about* you have proved as true as my words *to* you". A delicate hint that they should not have so readily accepted accusations against his genuineness [1:12–14] when he was all the while expressing confidence in them' (Massie).

15: And his affection is more abundantly toward you, while he remembereth the obedience of you all, how with fear and trembling ye received him.

Titus' affection for the Corinthians is intensified as he recalls their willingness to obey the demands he had to make, and their 'nervous and trembling anxiety to do right' (Lightfoot on Philippians 2:12). 'This passage teaches how ministers of Christ should be rightly received. It is not sumptuous banquets or splendid apparel or courteous and honourable salutations or the applause of crowds that give pleasure to a faithful and upright pastor: he has his sufficient joy when the doctrine of salvation is reverently received from his lips, when he can exercise the authority that belongs to him for the upbuilding of the Church, when the people submit themselves to his direction so as to be ruled by Christ through his ministry' (Calvin).

16: I rejoice that in everything I am of good courage concerning you.

'This expression of generous confidence is both a natural conclusion to the present subject and a preparation for the frank exhortation on money matters in chapter 8. It was only after the return to mutual confidence that such matters could be approached' (Massie).

CHAPTER EIGHT

Paul now appeals to the Corinthians to finish the collection for the relief of the saints at Jerusalem, and exhorts them to follow the generous example set by the poor churches of Macedonia [verses 1–6]. As they abounded in every other grace, they should also abound in the grace of giving. In thus calling their attention to the generosity of others Paul issues no commands, for the supreme example of Christ's self-giving should be enough to constrain their ready response. Each must decide how much he ought to give, so that his abundance might help to supply the needs of others [verses 7–15]. Paul informs them that to avoid any occasion of blame, Titus and two approved assistants will help them to complete the fund [verses 16–24].

1: Moreover; brethren, we make known to you the grace of God which hath been given in the churches of Macedonia;

Now we make known to you, brethren: This serves to introduce a topic that deserves their close attention [cf. *1 Cor.* 12:3; 15:1; *Gal.* 1:11]. It concerns 'the collection' [*1 Cor.* 16:1], a collection 'which was not so much for "the *poor* in Jerusalem" as for "the poor in *Jerusalem*"' (K. L. Schmidt, quoted by P. E. Hughes). For it was by this means that Paul hoped to give practical expression to that spiritual unity which both Jew and Gentile now enjoyed in Christ [*Eph.* 2:12–18].

The grace of God which hath been given in the churches of Macedonia: That Paul is able to devote two chapters of this Epistle to the subject of Christian giving without even mentioning the word 'money' is not only something of a *tour de force*, but it also serves to ennoble that which even Christians are apt to consider in a very materialistic manner (Denney). Here, for example, he cites the generosity of the Macedonian churches (which would include those at Philippi, Thessalonica, and Beroea) as an evidence of the grace of God that was still at work in their midst. 'Thus, while holding up human excellence as an example, he shuts out beforehand all human merit' (Beet) [*Eph.* 2:10].

2: how that in much proof of affliction the abundance of their joy and their deep poverty abounded unto the riches of their liberality.

(Namely) *that in a great test of affliction the excess of their joy and their down-to-depth poverty exceeded in the riches of their single-mindedness* (Lenski): Macedonia had been reduced to a state of grinding poverty by the crippling taxes of Rome, and in the case of these Christian communities this condition was made worse by persecution. And though affliction filled them with abounding joy, it reduced them to such dire straits that bounty seemed impossible. 'Yet these two opposites working in combination like an alkali and an acid, brought about an overflowing result which is called "the riches of their single-mindedness". Single-mindedness is that state of heart in which a man does not regard his own slender means nor any selfish consideration, but has his eye fixed exclusively upon his brother's needs. The Apostle says not that the contribution, but that the single-mindedness was rich, because it was *this* that he wished to awaken in the Corinthians. Should it operate upon Corinthian wealth instead of Macedonian poverty, the harvest would be plentiful' (Waite).

> 3: For according to their power, I bear witness, yea and beyond their power, they gave of their own accord, 4: beseeching us with much entreaty in regard of this grace and the fellowship in the ministering to the saints: 5: and this, not as we had hoped, but first they gave their own selves to the Lord, and to us through the will of God.

The single occurrence of the verb 'gave' in verse 5 governs the whole of this elaborate statement, which furnishes further particulars of the liberality of the Macedonians.

1. Their help was on a scale quite beyond their slender resources. 'Despite their deep poverty they insisted on giving far more than anyone could even think they could give. They made a joy of robbing themselves' (Lenski).

2. It was rendered so willingly that they pleaded for the 'favour' (lit. 'grace') of being allowed to 'participate' (lit. 'fellowship') in ministering to the saints. 'They begged the apostle to help them to an opportunity of acting upon the generous desire which God had implanted within them, and so of enjoying the sense of fellowship which "giving and receiving" [*Phil.* 4:15] created' (Massie).

3. The secret of their unexpected generosity lay in their unreserved commitment to the Lord and his apostle. Theirs was no slight contribution, for their gift was not of money merely, 'but of themselves, first and foremost, to the Lord, who gave himself for them [*Gal.* 1:4; 2:20], and also to the apostle, as the minister, through whom Christ's self-sacrifice had been made known to them, and through whom the work of love for the saints was proceeding' (Waite).

> 6: Insomuch that we exhorted Titus, that as he had made a beginning before, so he would also complete in you this grace also.

'This grace' refers to the collection (cf. RSV: 'this gracious work'). It appears that Titus began the task of organizing the collection in Corinth on a former visit, probably before 1 Corinthians was written.

P. E. Hughes suggests that he may have been the bearer of the 'previous' letter mentioned in 1 Corinthians 5:9. Happily, uncertainty on this point does not affect the general sense of the verse, which is well summarized by Fausset: 'As we saw the Macedonians' alacrity in giving, we could not but exhort Titus that, as we collected in Macedonia, so he in Corinth should complete the collection which he had already begun there, lest ye of wealthy Corinth should be outdone in liberality by the poor Macedonians.'

7: But as ye abound in everything, in faith, and utterance, and knowledge, and in all earnestness, and in your love to us, see that ye abound in this grace also.

As Paul rejoiced that in everything the Corinthians were enriched in Christ [*1 Cor.* 1:5], so he desires that they also might abound in the grace of giving. For if they failed 'in this respect, it would falsify his boast that they abound *in everything*. A gentler and more urbane method of incitement to generosity it would be difficult to imagine!' (P. E. Hughes).

8: I speak not by way of commandment, but as proving through the earnestness of others the sincerity also of your love.

Because true liberality is the spontaneous expression of love, Paul refuses to command their charity. Instead he seeks to prove the genuineness of their love by means of the zeal of those in Macedonia. For as Hodge pertinently remarks, 'The real test of the genuineness of any inward affection is not so much the character of the feeling as it reveals itself in our consciousness, as the course of action to which it leads. Many persons, if they judged themselves by their feelings, would regard themselves as truly compassionate; but a judgment founded on their acts would lead to the opposite conclusion.'

9: For ye know the grace of our Lord Jesus Christ, that, though he was rich, yet for your sakes he became poor, that ye through his poverty might become rich.

For ye know: There is no need to command the Corinthians, for they *know* the grand motive to Christian charity. Paul expects their participation in this gracious work as the natural consequence of their experimental knowledge of the grace of Christ.

The grace of our Lord Jesus Christ: The glory of the Giver exhibits the greatness of the grace. It is the grace which comes to them through the infinite condescension of the One who is the *Lord* to whom they owe unqualified obedience, the *Saviour* to whom they owe their salvation, and the *Mediator* through whom they are reconciled to God.

That, though he was rich: 'i.e. though He shared His Father's glory before the world was created (see *John* 17:5), nevertheless He temporarily laid aside this glory in order to "be found in fashion as a man". He did not lay aside His divinity; for there is no doctrine of *kenosis*, or emptying of His Godhead, to be found here any more than in Philippians 2:7' (Tasker).

Yet for your sakes: 'Believers are to consider that Christ impoverished himself *for them* in order that they might be enriched in an immeasurably higher sense than that of worldly riches, and in gratitude, they are to follow his example on a humbler level, by doing an incomparably slighter thing, sacrificing a portion of their worldly substance to supply the natural needs of those who are Christ's' (Waite).

He became poor: The moment when 'he *became* poor' is marked by the aorist tense. It has been thought that this self-impoverishment carries an allusion to the poverty of the Lord's earthly life [*Matt.* 8:20]; 'but the *primary* reference cannot be to this, for the "poverty" of Jesus Christ *by* which we are "made rich" is not the mere hardship and penury of his outward lot, but the state which he assumed in becoming man' (Bernard).

That ye through his poverty might become rich: 'Rich in "redemption through his blood, the forgiveness of sins", rich in "peace with God through our Lord Jesus Christ", rich in "newness of life", in objects to live for and motives to live by; rich in mastery over ourselves, the world, and wicked one, in joy unspeakable and full of glory: "all things are ours, and we are Christ's, and Christ is God's" [*1 Cor.* 3:22,23]' (Brown).

10: And herein I give my judgment: for this is expedient for you, who were the first to make a beginning a year ago, not only to do, but also to will.

And herewith I give my opinion; what I ask is for your advantage, since you took the lead in the matter as far back as last year not only in the doing but even in the willing (Menzies): If Paul does not command [verse 8], he leaves the Corinthians in no doubt of his opinion on the matter. For they had anticipated the Macedonians not only in resolving to make a collection, but also in their eagerness to contribute to it. 'Having thus been beforehand with them it would be to your disadvantage to leave your work half done, seeing that the mere mention of your purpose, chapter 9:2, roused them to such self-denying liberality' (Hodge).

11: But now complete the doing also; that as there was the readiness to will, so there may be the completion also out of your ability.

The Corinthians' initial enthusiasm for the collection must be matched by their determination to bring it to completion. For it would be a sad thing if 'those who were foremost in willing should be hindermost in performing; they must bring their performance into line with their willingness' (Plummer). Paul does not suggest that they should follow the example of the Macedonians by giving beyond their ability [verse 3], but he looks for a contribution according to the measure of their ability [cf. *1 Cor.* 16:2].

12: For if the readiness is there, it is acceptable according as a man hath, not according as he hath not.

God measures the acceptability of the gift in the light of what a man has and the readiness with which it is given. 'For willingness to give is not judged by what you do not have, or, in other words, God never requires that you should contribute more than your resources allow. In this way none is left with any excuse since rich men owe God a large tribute and poor men have no reason to be ashamed if what they give is small' (Calvin) [cf. *Mark* 12:41ff.].

13: For I say not this that others may be eased and ye distressed; 14: but by equality: your abundance being a supply at this present time for their want, that their abundance also may become a supply for your want; that there may be equality:

It is not Paul's object to enrich others by impoverishing the Corinthians. He seeks an equality whereby their present wealth may supply the want of the saints in Jerusalem. Should this situation be reversed at some future date, then it would be for Jerusalem to send relief to them. He is not advocating an equality of goods, but speaks of an equal relief from the burden of want. The Scriptures 'avoid, on the one hand, the injustice and destructive evils of agrarian communism, by recognizing the right of property and making all almsgiving optional; and on the other, the heartless disregard of the poor by inculcating the universal brotherhood of believers, and the consequent duty of each to contribute of his abundance to relieve the necessities of the poor. At the same time they inculcate on the poor the duty of self-support to the extent of their ability' (Hodge) [2 Thess. 3: 10].

15: as it is written, He that gathered much had nothing over; and he that gathered little had no lack.

Paul finds an illustration of the principle of equality in Exodus 16:18. In the wilderness God saw to it that all the Israelites received the same measure of manna, whether they could gather much or little. 'The same equality is now to be established voluntarily in the Christian world. He who in the first instance has received (relatively) much, is not finally to "have more" than others' (G. Delling, *TDNT*, vol. 6, p. 266).

16: But thanks be to God, who putteth the same earnest care for you into the heart of Titus.

As Titus is to lead the delegation entrusted with the responsibility of collecting the Corinthians' gift for the saints in Jerusalem, Paul thanks God for constantly giving Titus the same zeal for their welfare as he has himself. They should realize that this earnest care is in *their* interest, for they would only rob themselves of much spiritual enrichment if they failed to make a worthy contribution to the relief-fund.

17: For he accepted indeed our exhortation: but being himself very earnest, he went forth unto you of his own accord.

When Paul urged Titus to undertake this task, his concern for the Corinthians was such that no persuasion was necessary. He was coming to them of his own accord. 'It was important for his work in Corinth that the Corinthians should know this. It was the best recommendation which Paul could send along with Titus' (Lenski).

Went forth: 'We should say, *he is going* forth; but the ancients put the *past* tense in letter-writing, as the things will have been past by the time that the correspondent receives the letter' (Fausset).

18: And we have sent together with him the brother whose praise in the gospel is spread through all the churches; 19: and not only so, but who was also appointed by the churches to travel with us in the matter of this grace, which is ministered by us to the glory of the Lord, and to show our readiness:

Since Paul does not name the two brethren [verses 18, 22] who are to accompany Titus to Corinth, the attempt to identify them is quite pointless. What he is at pains to point out is that they are both tried and trusted men who have been officially appointed to perform this service by the churches [verse 23]. Moreover, the appointment proves that Paul has no personal axe to grind in forwarding this gracious work. He seeks neither gain nor glory for himself, for his very eagerness to advance such a work of grace serves to manifest the glory of the Lord to whom he is devoted. It seems likely that this particular brother was renowned for his preaching of the gospel, though the reference may be to service of a more general nature.

20: avoiding this, that any man should blame us in the matter of this bounty which is ministered by us:

The collection is organized by Paul, but the money will be collected by Titus and the two messengers who have been appointed by the churches for this purpose. This precaution is necessary to avoid giving anyone an opportunity to accuse the apostle of misappropriating any part of the fund [cf. 12:17, 18]. He encourages the Corinthians to give generously by letting them know that he thinks of their contribution in terms of 'this lavish gift' (Arndt-Gingrich).

21: for we take thought for things honourable, not only in the sight of the Lord, but also in the sight of men.

'This gives the reason for the precaution just mentioned. It was not enough for the apostle to do right, he recognized the importance of appearing right. It is a foolish pride which leads to a disregard of public opinion. We are bound to act in such a way that not only God, who sees the heart and knows all things, may approve our conduct, but also so that men may be constrained to recognize our integrity. It is a general principle regulating his whole life which the apostle here announces' (Hodge) [*Prov.* 3:4, LXX; *Rom.* 12:17].

22: And we have sent with them our brother, whom we have many times proved earnest in many things, but now much more earnest, by reason of the great confidence which he hath in you.

Paul commends the second brother to the Corinthians on the double ground that his earnestness in *many* things has been proved on *many* previous occasions, and that he is now *much* more earnest through the *great* confidence which he has in them (after having heard the good report of Titus). The italicized words show how in the original Paul adds force to this commendation by using the same word four times.

23: Whether any inquire about Titus, he is my partner and my fellow-worker to you-ward; or our brethren, they are the messengers of the churches, they are the glory of Christ.

'Paul extols the three in the highest terms before he sends them off; if anybody in Corinth wishes to know what they are, he is proud to tell. Titus is his partner in the apostolic calling, and has shared his work among them; the other brethren are deputies (apostles) of Churches, a glory of Christ' (Denney). Therefore let the Corinthians receive these duly authorized representatives in a way which befits those whose calling and character are a credit to Christ.

24: Show ye therefore unto them in the face of the churches the proof of your love, and of our glorying on your behalf.

The chapter concludes 'with an exhortation to their liberality, backed with a heap of arguments. 1. It would be an evidence of their love to God, to their afflicted brethren, and to the apostle. 2. It would be a proof of it to those messengers of the churches, and to the churches whose messengers they were. 3. It would evidence that the apostle had not, to Titus and others, boasted on their behalf in vain' (Poole).

CHAPTER NINE

Although aware of the Corinthians' good intentions, Paul had sent the brethren to complete the collection, so that if any Macedonians accompanied him to Corinth he would not be put to shame by finding them unprepared [verses 1–4]. Such preparation was necessary to show that their contribution was freely given and not unwillingly extracted [verse 5]. He encourages them to give bountifully and cheerfully, as the best way of increasing their graces and their means of doing good [verses 6–11]. This ministry to the saints redounds in thanksgiving to God, promotes the mutual love of believers, and exhibits their graces. Hence the apostle thanks God for the priceless boon of Christ, through whom this rich bounty of grace is produced [verses 12–15].

1: For as touching the ministering to the saints, it is superfluous for me to write to you:

Since the word 'for' indicates a continuation of the same subject, the unfortunate chapter division should be ignored. Paul has been speaking in chapter 8 of the need for promptness in making the collection, a promptness which will be a public proof of love [8:24]. 'As to the service itself, the ministering to the saints, about that he need write nothing; they have been inclined for that for some time back: it is their very inclination that leads him to send on the brethren' (Massie) [verse 3]

2: for I know your readiness, of which I glory on your behalf to them of Macedonia, that Achaia hath been prepared for a year past; and your zeal hath stirred up very many of them.

Paul's boasting concerns the readiness with which the Corinthians responded when the matter of the collection was first brought before them. They 'took it up eagerly, and were prepared to contribute at once and actually began [8:10] to contribute. Even the liberality of the Macedonians, for which Paul is so thankful to God, was in great part a result of the example thus nobly set by the Corinthians. All this proves that it is needless for him to write to them *about the collection*. But it does not prevent him from telling them of the liberality of the Macedonians, that the example of those whom their own liberal purpose had aroused might prompt them to complete at once the work they had been the first to begin. Thus example acts and re-acts' (Beet).

3: But I have sent the brethren, that our glorying on your behalf may not be made void in this respect; that, even as I said, ye may be prepared:

But I am sending the brethren, lest the boast I have made of you should be proved an empty one in this particular, that you might be prepared, as I said you were (Menzies): Paul is confident that his boasting on the Corinthians' behalf will be found true in every respect [8:7], except perhaps in this one particular. Of their readiness to will [8:11] he has no doubt, but if this is not matched by a similar alacrity in giving he is afraid that the preparations for the collection will be incomplete when he arrives in Corinth with the envoys from Macedonia. It is to avoid this embarrassment that he is sending Titus and his colleagues in advance so that his confidence in the Corinthians may be fully justified by the event.

4: lest by any means, if there come with me any of Macedonia and find you unprepared, we (that we say not, ye) should be put to shame in this confidence.

Lest if some Macedonians come with me and find that you are not ready, we be humiliated – to say nothing of you – for being so confident (RSV): Paul is warning the Corinthians that when he comes to Corinth he will probably be accompanied by some Macedonians, the representatives of those whose zeal was stimulated by his account of their own enthusiasm for the collection. Let them imagine the disgrace it would be for him, to say nothing of themselves, if this visit found them still unprepared.

5: I thought it necessary therefore to entreat the brethren, that they would go before unto you, and make up beforehand your aforepromised bounty, that the same might be ready as a matter of bounty, and not of extortion.

And not of covetousness (ASV margin): To avoid this disgrace Paul thought it necessary to entreat Titus and his two assistants to 'come beforehand to you and set in order beforehand your blessing, which has been promised beforehand' (Waite). The emphatic repetition makes it impossible for the Corinthians to mistake Paul's meaning. The collection they had promised so long *before* must be completed *before* his arrival in Corinth! And since this fund is intended to minister a blessing to its recipients, let them give generously to it and not in such a manner as would betray a grudging or covetous spirit. 'Love blesses, whereas covetousness takes advantage of the brother by a close scrutiny of the gift, which becomes thereby a gift of covetousness' (G. Delling, *TDNT*, vol. 6, p. 273).

6: But this I say, He that soweth sparingly shall reap also sparingly; and he that soweth bountifully shall reap also bountifully.

As an incentive to liberality Paul reminds the Corinthians of an unvarying principle, the complete equity of which is immediately apparent; it is that the harvest reaped will be proportionate to the seed sown [cf. *Prov.* 11:24, 25; *Gal.* 6:7–10]. 'They who in giving think, not how little they can give, as they would if self-enrichment were their aim, but of benefits to be conferred, will receive back on the same principle. As they to others, so God will act to them' (Beet).

7: Let each man do according as he hath proposed in his heart; not grudgingly, or of necessity: for God loveth a cheerful giver.

The omission of the verb in the original adds force to the sentence. Each man must be entirely free to decide what he will give, for Paul has every confidence that those who have freely received, will freely give [*Matt.* 10:8]. 'There must be real freedom in Christian giving, each individual making the decision in his own heart how much he ought to give. It is far from Paul's intention that a "quota scheme" or a "means test" should be imposed upon the Corinthians' (P. E. Hughes).

Not of grief or of necessity: 'Each is to give what he has purposed in his heart, where he is free and true: he is not to give out of grief, mourning over what he gives and regretting he could not keep it; neither is he to give out of necessity, because his position, or the usages of his society, or the comments of his neighbours, put a practical compulsion upon him' (Denney).

For God loveth a cheerful giver: This is taken from the LXX of Proverbs 22:8 and gives the general sense of the Hebrew: 'He that hath a bountiful (i.e. a good) eye shall he blessed.' It is the man with a generous eye who delights to devise acts of kindness who is blessed of God. For as Trapp well says, 'One may give with his hand, and pull it back with his looks.' God therefore loves the man who gives joyfully, or with hilarity (*hilaron*)! Then let not 'those who give reluctantly, or from stress of circumstances, or to secure merit, imagine that mere giving is acceptable to God. Unless we feel it is an honour and a joy to give, God does not accept the offering' (Hodge).

8: And God is able to make all grace abound unto you; that ye, having always all sufficiency in everything, may abound unto every good work:

The doctrine taught is that abounding grace brings forth abounding good works. The desire to be generous and the means of being generous come from God. So Paul reminds the Corinthians that God is able to make *all* grace abound to them in order that they 'in *all* things at *all* times having *all* sufficiency, may abound to *all* good work' (P. E. Hughes). Paul here gives a Christian meaning to a favourite Stoic word. The inner 'self-sufficiency' of the Stoic made him independent of everything external to himself, but the believer finds his 'self-sufficiency' in the God whose bounty enables him to bestow blessings upon others. 'Enough means not only a sufficiency for oneself but what can also be given to one's brothers. The Christian *self* cannot be considered in isolation. His *self-sufficiency* arises only when the *other* has a share in it' (G. Kittel, *TDNT*, vol. 1, p. 467).

> **9: as it is written, He hath scattered abroad, he hath given to the poor; His righteousness abideth for ever.**

'Righteousness' here means 'benevolence' (RSV margin). Paul cites Psalm 112:9 to prove that a generous-hearted man will never lack the means to express his generosity. 'The man who fears the LORD' and gives to the needy with open-handed beneficence will not be impoverished by his benefactions. His benevolence endures for ever, because God always supplies him with the resources to continue it. Such benevolence is an evidence of righteousness and not a method of attaining it.

> **10: And he that supplieth seed to the sower and bread for food, shall supply and multiply your seed for sowing, and increase the fruits of your righteousness:**

And increase the harvest of your benevolence (RSV margin): The bountiful God who gives 'seed to the sower and bread for food' [*Isa.* 55:10] will abundantly increase your resources that you may scatter abroad acts of beneficence, as a sower scatters seed. The final clause, which is taken from Hosea 10:12, LXX, probably refers 'to the blessings which righteous generosity brings to the giver as well as to the receiver' (Massie).

> **11: ye being enriched in everything unto all liberality, which worketh through us thanksgiving to God.**

The proximate purpose for which they are enriched with this wealth is that 'they may exercise a single-mindedness (see on 8:2), which keeps its gaze undistracted by selfish considerations and fixed solely on doing good to the poorer brethren' (Waite). The ultimate purpose is that those benefited will be led to glorify God by their thanksgiving for this liberality which Paul has encouraged ('through us').

12: For the ministration of this service not only filleth up the measure of the wants of the saints, but aboundeth also through many thanksgivings unto God;

This expands the thought of the previous verse: for this great public service of ministering to the saints will lead to an overflowing of many thanksgivings to God. 'Paul brings out the distinctive feature of Christian charity. Worldly charity is at best happy only in relieving human distress. Pharisaic and work-righteousness charity thinks it is acquiring merit with God. By relieving distress Christian charity delights in the multiplied thanksgivings that will rise to God from the hearts and the lips of those whose distress is thus relieved' (Lenski).

13: seeing that through the proving of you by this ministration they glorify God for the obedience of your confession unto the gospel of Christ, and for the liberality of your contribution unto them and unto all;

The saints at Jerusalem would also see in this ministry a proof of the Corinthians' faith and they would glorify God because their confession of the gospel 'finds expression in obedient subjection to its requirements' (Arndt-Gingrich).

And for the single-mindedness of your fellowship with them and with all (Lenski): Moreover, this tangible proof of the reality of their confession gives evidence of their fellowship not only with the believers in Jerusalem but with all true Christians everywhere. 'Submissive confession of the gospel means single-minded fellowship with all the saints, all of whom so confess and all of whom are in fellowship. The one is never separated from the other. The one is the basis, the other the result. Confession means fellowship, fellowship means confession' (Lenski).

14: while they themselves also, with supplication on your behalf, long after you by reason of the exceeding grace of God in you.

Another blessed result of this ministry will be found in the prayers it will lead their Jewish brethren to offer on their behalf, not only on account of the gift itself, but also because of the exceeding grace of God which it shows is resting upon them. For it was 'a moral miracle that Macedonians and Corinthians should be exhibiting such self-sacrifice for Jews' (Goudge) [*Rom.* 15:25, 26].

15: Thanks be to God for his unspeakable gift.

Thanks be to God for his indescribable gift! (NIV): Words fail the apostle as he contemplates the magnitude of that Gift which is beyond all human computation. There is no doubt that the indescribable gift 'for which the apostle bursts out here into a characteristic doxology is the gift of Christ himself [*John* 3:16] and of salvation in him, thankful appreciation of which had borne such fruit in Christian lives' (Bernard).

CHAPTER TEN

Paul, knowing that some Corinthians still disputed his authority, entreats the church not to persist in that disobedience which would force him to take strong measures against them when he came to Corinth [verses 1–6]. His critics should neither judge him by his humble appearance, nor by their own pretensions, since those who scorned his powerful letters would find that his deeds when present were equally powerful [verses 7–11]. Paul refuses to measure himself by the standards of men, for in preaching the gospel to them he has kept within the measure of his divine commission. And though his missionary mandate extends far beyond Corinth, he commends not himself, but glories only in the Lord whose approval he seeks [verses 12–18].

The marked change of tone which is so evident in chapters 10–13 has led some scholars to conclude that these chapters are part of the 'severe' letter, but the Epistle is manifestly an intelligible unity as it stands. It is all about Paul's promised visit to Corinth. So if the last four chapters were not written at the same time as the first nine, 'we should not expect to find them take up the matter of the proposed visit just where it is left in chapter 9. But this is just what we do find' (Menzies).

In this final part of the Epistle, Paul turns his attention to those who have sown the seeds of dissension in the church at Corinth. False apostles have sought to undermine his authority, and at the same time discredit his gospel, by speaking disparagingly of his 'weakness'. It is therefore entirely natural and eminently sensible that he should answer these attacks and vindicate his apostolic authority before he visits them again. 'The Corinthians must make up their minds, all of them, whether Paul is really their apostle or not. There must be no longer any kind of hesitation about this. It is as their apostle by divine commission that he is going to visit them once again, claiming the allegiance that is his due' (Tasker).

1: Now I Paul myself entreat you by the meekness and gentleness of Christ, I who in your presence am lowly among you, but being absent am of good courage toward you:

Now I Paul myself: This 'is not only the grammatical subject of the sentence, but if one may say so, the subject under consideration; it is the very person whose authority is in dispute who puts himself forward deliberately in this authoritative way' (Denney).

Entreat you by the meekness and gentleness of Christ: The apostle cannot have been as ignorant of the Lord's earthly life as some modern scholars imagine, for this appeal assumes a knowledge of the character of Christ which the Corinthians must have owed to his instruction. Paul knows that he is despised for following the example of him whose 'meekness' of heart [*Matt.* 11:29] was shown by his 'gentleness' in dealing with poor sinners (e.g. *John* 8:1–11), but he hopes that they will not put his courage to the test! [v 2]

I who am humble when face to face with you, but bold to you when I am away! (RSV): This is the only place in the New Testament where 'humble' (*tapeinos*) is used in a bad sense. Paul is echoing the contemptuous accusation of his proud critics who had not learned the Christian meaning of the word. 'They had said that, when he was there, he was a Uriah Heep, very humble and cringing and artful; when he was away from them, he could pluck up his courage and be very resolute – on paper' (Plummer).

2: yea, I beseech you, that I may not when present show courage with the confidence wherewith I count to be bold against some, who count of us as if we walk according to the flesh.

Paul even begs the Corinthians not to force him to display when present that courage which is only attributed when absent [13:10]. Indeed he is resolved to act with the greatest boldness against certain persons who wrongly reckon that his conduct is dictated by purely worldly motives. 'His Corinthian detractors judged him by themselves, as if he were influenced by fleshly motives, desire of favour, or fear of offending, so as not to exercise his authority' (Fausset).

3: For though we walk in the flesh, we do not according to the flesh

Since Paul is a man he is obliged to walk *in* the flesh, but his opponents have greatly misjudged him in thinking that he walks *according to* the flesh. They thought it would be an easy matter to destroy Paul with the carnal weapon in their armoury, but they will shortly discover to their dismay that he neither *walks* nor *wars according to* the flesh. Certainly he will fight these enemies of the gospel to the finish, but not on their terms nor with their weapons [cf. *Eph.* 6:11–18].

4: (for the weapons of our warfare are not of the flesh but mighty before God to the casting down of strongholds);

In the spiritual conflict in which Paul was engaged, he placed no reliance in merely human abilities. He had no confidence in fleshly reasonings, arguments, or stratagems, but trusted solely in the supernatural power of God [*Zech.* 4:6]. The difficult phrase 'before God' (literally, 'to God') either means that the weapons Paul uses are employed in God's service, or more probably that they are 'divinely potent to demolish strongholds' (NEB). The church must learn that the cause of Christ is never advanced by carnal methods, because the strongholds in which sinners entrench themselves will never yield to the bravest display of worldly weapons. It is only before the resistless power of God that the walls of these fortresses fall flat [*Josh* 6:20].

5: casting down imaginations, and every high thing that is exalted against the knowledge of God, and bringing every thought into captivity to the obedience of Christ;

Casting down reasonings (ASV margin): This warfare is not carnal, for the strongholds that Paul is engaged in demolishing are not the *persons* of the unbelieving, but the sinful *reasonings* 'the refuge of lies' –

by which they seek to fortify themselves against the knowledge of God [cf. *Rom.* 1:18ff.]. The military metaphor 'emphasizes the defiant and mutinous nature of sin: sinful man does not wish to know God; he wishes himself to be the self-sufficient centre of his universe' (P. E. Hughes).

And every high thing that is exalted against the knowledge of God: 'Such were the *high towers* of Judaic self-righteousness, philosophic speculations, and rhetorical sophistries, the "knowledge" so much prized by many, which opposed the "knowledge of God" at Corinth. True knowledge makes men humble. Where self is exalted God is not known' (Fausset).

And bringing every thought into captivity to the obedience of Christ: Such a deliverance from the proud ramparts, of 'autonomous' reason has the supremely positive purpose of bringing 'every intention of the mind' (Alford) into subjection to the *obedience of Christ* without which there can be no true *knowledge of God*. But though this is always true of the regenerate in principle, unhappily it is not always so in practice. And Paul intends the Corinthians to see that it was because they had failed fully to submit to the mind of Christ that they 'were being deceived by the specious logic of the false apostles' (P. E. Hughes) [cf. 11:2ff.]

6: and being in readiness to avenge all disobedience, when your obedience shall be made full.

When Paul at last returns to Corinth those who have charged him with uttering empty threats will find to their dismay that he is more than ready to punish the disobedient. Meanwhile he charitably assumes that the church will act obediently, and so he speaks of '*your* obedience'. But as some will act otherwise, he waits in order to give *all* an opportunity of joining the obedient majority. He will not prematurely exact punishment, but delays his coming 'until the full number of those who obey Christ has been "completed", and the remainder have proved incorrigible' (Fausset).

7: Ye look at the things that are before your face. If any man trusteth in himself that he is Christ's, let him consider this again with himself, that, even as he is Christ's, so also are we.

Look at what is before your eyes (RSV): It is preferable to take the verb as an imperative. It recalls the Corinthians to reality. If they will but face the facts, they will see that Paul has given them far more convincing evidence of his apostleship than those who have tried so hard to supplant him [cf. *1 Cor. 9: 1, 2*].

If any one is confident that he is Christ's, let him remind himself that as he is Christ's, so are we (RSV): This is an ironical reference to the arrogant claims advanced by his opponents. Should any one regard himself as an apostle of Christ to whom the church at Corinth must defer, let him also consider that Paul's claim to exercise the same authority is no less emphatic than his own. Moreover, in his case this personal conviction can be substantiated with objective credentials which cannot be matched or gainsaid by these wordy claimants to a superior apostleship. [cf. 3:2; 11:23–28; 12:12-15]

8: For though I should glory somewhat abundantly concerning our authority (which the Lord gave for building you up, and not for casting you down), I shall not be put to shame: 9: that I may not seem as if I would terrify you by my letters.

Paul knows that his critics have accused him of boasting, but even if he were to make higher claims for his ministry he is confident that he would have no cause to be ashamed of his words. He is not like those who must try to bolster up their position with empty boasting, for the reality of his claims is amply borne out by the facts. Because the Lord himself not only appointed him to this office, but his authority as an apostle is always exercised in accordance with the terms of that divine mandate. All his efforts are directed towards the building up of the church, whereas the false apostles used their assumed authority to destroy it. What he says here is no contradiction of verse 5. For though 'we "cast down reasonings", this is not in order to destroy, but to *build up*, by removing hindrances to edification, testing what is unsound, and putting together all that is true in the building' (Chrysostom, cited by Fausset). But Paul refrains from saying anything more about his authority lest he should seem to justify the jibe of his opponents by scaring the Corinthians out of their wits with his letters! A sarcasm which effectively reveals the absurdity of the accusation.

10: For, his letters, they say, are weighty and strong but his bodily presence is weak, and his speech of no account.

It is worth noting that even Paul's detractors were forced to admit that there was nothing weak about his letters. 'The saying is a valuable testimony to the impression the Epistles of Paul at once produced when they were written; they were felt to be grave and important utterances, and they acted effectively, as they were intended to do' (Menzies). It has not since proved necessary to revise this contemporary estimate of the power of Paul's pen.

But his bodily presence is weak, and his speech of no account: They said in effect, 'Paul may write, bold, bluffing letters, but when he appears in person he cannot disguise his weakness and then his speech amounts to nothing!' Thus misjudging Paul's motives, his enemies mistook meekness for weakness [11:21], and branded his artless preaching as being unworthy of the attention of educated Greeks! [11:6; *1 Cor.* 1:17; 2:1–5]

11: Let such a one reckon this, that, what we are in word by letters when we are absent, such are we also in deed when we are present.

Anyone who is tempted to believe that slander should think again. Let him rather count on the fact that Paul's forthcoming visit will prove that he lacks neither the determination nor the courage to discipline the disobedient. Then it would be evident to all that there was no discrepancy whatever between his words and his deeds [13:2, 10].

12: For we are not bold to number or compare ourselves with certain of them that commend themselves: but they themselves, measuring themselves by themselves, and comparing themselves with themselves, are without understanding.

Paul now asks the Corinthians to consider the *character* of the men who have brought such charges against him [verses 12–18]. He ironically confesses that he does not have the courage to class or compare himself with certain of those 'who make self-commendation, unsupported by any corroborating evidence, their title to fame' (Tasker). But the self-satisfied are always the self-deluded, for in adopting their own conduct as the standard of excellence, they prove themselves to be devoid of spiritual understanding. Hence their fancied wisdom was in fact arrant folly! 'Instead of the public standard, they measure themselves by one made by themselves: they do not compare themselves with others who excel them, but with those like themselves; hence their high self-esteem. The one-eyed is easily king among the blind' (Fausset) [*Matt.* 5:20].

13: But we will not glory beyond our measure, but according to the measure of the province which God apportioned to us as a measure, to reach even unto you.

It is not for Paul to compete with those who glory only in themselves, though it is not surprising that those who know nothing of God's standard of measurement are well satisfied to measure themselves by themselves. These false apostles would be trespassing wherever they went, for the very 'gospel' [11:4] they preached was an indisputable proof that no sphere of labour had been marked out for them by God. But Paul's glorying is legitimate for he glories in the Lord who called him and who appointed the bounds of his service.

But according to the measure of the province which God apportioned to us as a measure, to reach even unto you: The Judaizers boasted of gifts they did not possess and battened like parasites on churches which they had not founded. Paul did not indulge in such inordinate boasting and it was his settled practice not to build on another man's foundation [*Rom.* 15:20]. It was he, and not they, who had brought the gospel as far as Corinth; and since his labours there were the instrumental means of bringing the Corinthians to a living faith in Christ, they of all people ought to be the last to doubt the authority of his apostleship over them [*1 Cor.* 9:1,2].

14: For we stretch not ourselves overmuch, as though we reached not unto you: for we came even as far as unto you in the gospel of Christ:

We are not overstretching our commission, as we should be if it did not extend to you (NEB): The apostle is not the intruder at Corinth; this description applied to the self-appointed interlopers who certainly overstretched themselves by thus encroaching upon a sphere which God had clearly assigned to Paul.

For we were the first to reach Corinth in preaching the gospel of Christ (NEB): Paul's point is not merely that he was the first to reach Corinth, but that he was the first to reach it with *the gospel of Christ.* For these emissaries of Jewish legalism who had followed him there brought with them 'another gospel which is not another' [*Gal.* 1:6, 7]. 'They made it their business to follow in Paul's tracks, to steal into his congregations, and then to undermine his gospel work. They had not even a commission from God, to say nothing of a mark of measurement that had been set by God, which they were to reach. Theirs was the devil's work [11:3, 4]' (Lenski).

15: not glorying beyond our measure, that is, in other men's labours; but having hope that, as your faith groweth, we shall be magnified in you according to our province unto further abundance, 16: so as to preach the gospel even unto the parts beyond you, and not to glory in another's province in regard of things ready to our hand.

I do not boast beyond due measure by intruding upon a sphere in which others have been commissioned to labour (Bruce): Paul's 'enemies spoke and acted as if the fruits of his missionary toil had been produced by them. Against this lawless and vaulting ambition he sets his own aspirations' (Waite).

I have good hope that, as your faith increases, my own sphere of labour will be increased the more by your aid, according to the commission which I have been given. That is, I hope to preach the good news in lands farther west than Corinth (Bruce): He hopes that the Corinthians will help him to fulfil his calling, for it is only when increased faith restores them to full obedience that he will feel free to undertake further responsibilities in claiming new territory for Christ [cf. *Rom.* 15:18–24]. This shows that the apostle's missionary strategy was based on the sound principle that the consolidation of existing work must precede further advance (Murray Harris).

But I will not boast beyond due measure by trespassing to someone else's field of labour because it lies ready on my hand (Bruce): The repetition [cf. verse 15a] 'reveals Paul's deep sense of how unjust is his opponents' boasting. While thoughts about the Corinthians, whom he had led to Christ, were that their increasing faith would enable him to break new ground still further off, his opponents were exulting about things in a field allotted by God to Paul, and in reference to work which they found *already done*. With such men Paul dares not compare himself' (Beet).

17: But he that glorieth, let him glory in the Lord.

With this quotation of a favourite text Paul puts his own glorying in the right light, and at the same time passes censure upon his opponents [*Jer.* 9:23, 24; *1 Cor.* 1:31]. The way in which the New Testament writers freely apply or transfer to Christ references in the Old Testament to Jehovah 'is a significant pointer to the fundamental apostolic belief in the pre-existence of Christ in the unity of the eternal Godhead' (P. E. Hughes).

18: For not he that commendeth himself is approved, but whom the Lord commendeth.

Paul has been forced by the attacks made on him to boast about himself, but it was not on this self-praise that he relied. It was ever and only the Lord's approval that he sought, and the manifest blessing which rested upon his work at Corinth and elsewhere proved that he did not lack the tangible tokens of it. The very existence of the Corinthian church was his letter of commendation [3:2]. But his 'assailants had no such confirmation of the praise which they bestowed on themselves' (Plummer). In the final analysis all will be constrained to admit that the Lord's commendation is the only one that matters [*1 Cor.* 4:3, 4], but those who do not seek to please him now will find to their everlasting sorrow and shame that it is too late to do so then.

CHAPTER ELEVEN

Although Paul deprecated self-praise, the attacks of the Judaizers forced him to indulge in this folly, lest they should succeed in seducing the Corinthians from their allegiance to Christ by the false gospel they preached [verses 1–4]. That he was not inferior to these superlative apostles was shown not least by his refusal to accept maintenance from the church. This not only proved his love, but also demonstrated how he differed from the false apostles who gloried only in the guise they assumed [verses 5-15]. Since Paul must boast, he will not exalt himself after the manner of those who would bring them into bondage, but will glory only in his sufferings. He is also a Jew, but the badges of his office consist in his labours, hardships, and the daily burden of his care for the churches. Hence Paul glories in that weakness which began at Damascus when the converted persecutor became the persecuted apostle [verses 16–33].

1: Would that ye could bear with me in a little foolishness: but indeed ye do bear with me.

Paul finds it distasteful to boast about himself, but the tactics of his rivals are forcing him to descend to their level. If he now assumes the fool's mask for a little while, it is because his concern for the Corinthians leads him to expose the folly that is so entirely natural to the men who had deceived them with their great swelling words. In this chapter he sweeps aside the empty boasting of these vocal pretenders to the apostolate with a devastating revelation of what it cost him to be faithful to his commission. With magnificent irony Paul begins by wishing that the Corinthians would bear with him in a little of the folly of self-boasting! But he immediately corrects himself, for after all, such an appeal is quite superfluous when they are so practised 'in enduring the overbearing demeanour of his opponents!' [verse 20]. (Massie).

2: For I am jealous over you with a godly jealousy: for I espoused you to one husband, that I might present you as a pure virgin to Christ.

'This is why he plays the fool', says Calvin, 'for jealousy sweeps a man off his feet.' But the jealousy Paul feels is not for himself or his own reputation, it is a jealousy he endures on God's behalf. His feelings towards the Corinthians are in certain respects analogous to those of Jehovah over faithless Israel [*Hos.* 2:19, 20; 4:12]. For as their spiritual father [*1 Cor.* 4:15], he has betrothed them to one husband, but he is beginning to be fearful for the purity of the prospective bride. 'It is necessary that the bride should concentrate her attention on the "one man" to whom she is engaged, and not open her heart to any other; but there is reason to fear that the Corinthian church is having its attention distracted from the true object, namely, from Christ as he was preached by Paul. He is afraid that this bride is allowing other views to be introduced into her mind, views inconsistent with her first loyalty' (Menzies).

That I might present you as a pure virgin to Christ: 'As, in Eph. 5:27, this presentation of the church to Christ as his bride, is said to take place at his second coming, this passage is commonly understood to refer to that event. Paul's desire was that the Corinthians should remain faithful to their vows, so as to be presented to Christ a glorious church, without spot or wrinkle, on that great day. He dreaded lest they should, in that day, be rejected and contemned as a woman unfaithful to her vows' (Hodge).

3: But I fear, lest by any means, as the serpent beguiled Eve in his craftiness, your minds should be corrupted from the simplicity and the purity that is toward Christ.

Although many of the best manuscripts add 'and purity', this was probably suggested by 'pure' in verse 2 (Barrett). 'Simplicity' [cf. 8:2] refers to the single-minded devotion that the church should have towards Christ. 'What Paul dreads is the spiritual seduction of the church, the winning away of her heart from absolute loyalty to Christ. The serpent beguiled Eve by his craftiness; he took advantage of her unsuspecting innocence to wile her away from her simple belief in God and obedience to him . . . The serpent's agents – the servants of Satan, as Paul calls them in verse 15 – are at work in Corinth; and he fears that their craftiness may seduce the church from its first simple loyalty to Christ' (Denney) [*Gen.* 3:13].

4: For if he that cometh preacheth another Jesus, whom we did not preach, or if ye receive a different spirit, which ye did not receive, or a different gospel, which ye did not accept, ye do well to bear with him.

When the Corinthians bear with the false apostles so well, they should not find it too difficult to put up with their genuine apostle for a little while! 'If' denotes a condition of reality. Paul does not point to any imaginary danger but describes the actual situation in Corinth. Here the actions of one false teacher are representative of all who are like him. He comes of his own volition, as opposed to being commissioned, and sent by God [verses 13-15]. These men 'had simply come, unsent and without divine authorization; and therefore they were no apostles' (P. E. Hughes).

Preacheth another Jesus, whom we did not preach: Paul consigns to a decent oblivion the precise nature of his opponents' teaching, but it is hardly likely that he would have overlooked a defective Christology without comment. On this assumption the contrast would not be between their human Jesus and his heavenly Christ. It would seem a far more reasonable surmise to suggest that in transforming the gospel into a scheme of salvation by works, these Jewish legalists in effect preached 'another Jesus' even though they held to an orthodox view of his Person, including the confession of his Deity.

Or if ye receive a different spirit, which ye did not receive: An ironical allusion to the powerlessness of the Judaizers to impart the Holy Spirit. They are dispensers of a different spirit, a spirit which is consonant with the doctrine taught. It is the spirit 'which gendereth to bondage' [*Gal.* 4:24, 25; 5: 1, 4].

Or a different gospel, which ye did not accept: It was in connection with Paul's preaching of Jesus as the Saviour of sinners that the Corinthians received the Spirit through whom they were able to accept the one authentic gospel. 'The will of man is passive in RECEIVING the "Spirit"; but it is actively concurrent with the will of God (which goes before to give the good will) in ACCEPTING the "Gospel"' (Fausset). But to give heed to a man who preaches *another* Jesus is to receive a *different* spirit and to accept a *different* gospel!

You put up with it well enough! (Arndt-Gingrich): A cutting reflection on their disloyalty to him. '*He* had to plead for their toleration, but they had no difficulty in tolerating men who by a spurious gospel, an unspiritual conception of Christ, and an unworthy incapacity for understanding freedom, were undermining his work, and seducing their souls' (Denney).

5: For I reckon that I am not a whit behind the very chiefest apostles.

For I reckon that I am in nothing behind the superlative apostles! (Waite): It is difficult to believe that Paul would speak so scathingly of the Jerusalem apostles; his scorn is directed at the Judaizers who presumably claimed their authority to propagate a *different* gospel [verse 4]. 'What a pity you find it so easy to tolerate these superfine apostles when my credentials are in no way inferior to theirs!' Paul is not seriously comparing himself with the *false* apostles [verse 13], 'but speaking with incisive bitterness of the supposed position of inferiority which they had tried to assign to him' (Waite).

6: But though I be rude in speech, yet am I not in knowledge; nay, in every way have we made this manifest unto you in all things.

This concession to the criticism of his enemies is also tinged with irony. If Paul's speech was devoid of the ornamental flourishes of a man trained in the art of rhetoric, its content was certainly not deficient in knowledge as the Corinthians had good cause to know [cf. *1 Cor.* 2]. But it is the mark of an infantile mind to be more concerned with the wrappings than the contents of the parcel! Unlike the pretenders to apostolic status, Paul possesses a divine commission to manifest the truth to every man's conscience [4:2]. He has made known this knowledge without the slightest reserve, freely declaring the whole counsel of God to all who would listen to him.

7: Or did I commit a sin in abasing myself that ye might be exalted, because I preached to you the gospel of God for nought?

Or perhaps the Corinthians prefer these false gospellers because they have had to pay for the privilege of being deceived by them? Evidently Paul's opponents had said that his refusal to accept maintenance from the Corinthians was a tacit admission of his amateur status, for a proper apostle would have received it as a right! [verse 12; cf. *1 Cor.* 9:4–19]. 'Christ's pure Gospel without price and the corrupted doctrine of the Judaizers at a cost [11:20]; his self-abasement and their self-glorification; his emancipation and their enslaving of the community, are pointed contrasts' (Waite).

8: I robbed other churches, taking wages of them that I might minister unto you;

Paul even 'robbed' other churches, i.e. 'accepting support so that I might serve you' (Arndt-Gingrich). He accepted a subsistence from the poorer Macedonian churches, which were not receiving the benefits of his ministry, in order that he might minister the gospel without charge to the Corinthians. Paul rubs in this truth and makes it smart 'to drive out their mean ingratitude. For what is meaner than to slander a benefactor for bestowing his benefaction *gratis?*' (Lenski).

9: and when I was present with you and was in want, I was not a burden on any man; for the brethren, when they came from Macedonia, supplied the measure of my want; and in everything I kept myself from being burdensome unto you, and so will I keep myself.

While ministering to the Corinthians Paul ran short of funds, probably because the demands they made on him meant that he could not work long enough at his trade to support himself [*Acts* 18:3]. Yet even then no one found him a 'burden' —a wor d derived from *narke*, the torpedo fish which benumbs anyone who touches it; 'hence to be idle to the detriment of another person (like a useless limb)' (Vine) – for his needs were met by the unstinted generosity of the brethren from Macedonia. Thus during the whole of his mission to Corinth Paul studiously avoided taking any financial assistance from the Corinthians, and whatever the mercenary-minded Judaizers might say about it, he would maintain this independence on his forthcoming visit.

10: As the truth of Christ is in me, no man shall stop me of this glorying in the regions of Achaia.

Paul, conscious of the fact that he speaks in conformity with the truthfulness of Christ, here avers that 'this boasting will not (let itself) be stopped' (Arndt-Gingrich). Despite the desperate attempts of his enemies to stop (i.e. to block by barricade or damming up) the flow of his boasting about preaching without payment, they will not succeed either in Corinth or indeed throughout all Achaia.

11: Wherefore? because I love you not? God knoweth.

It would seem that the false apostles had insinuated it was because Paul cared so little for the Corinthians that he refused to take their money, whereas *they* had enough affection for them to receive it! Can they really find it in their hearts to believe that he is too proud to be indebted to those to whom he is indifferent? If they did not know him better than that, there is One who does. God, before whom no secrets are hid, takes full cognizance of the strength of his feeling for them, and knows the real reason for his refusal to accept their support.

12: But what I do, that I will do, that I may cut off occasion from them that desire an occasion; that wherein they glory, they may be found even as we.

And I will keep on doing what I am doing in order to cut the ground from under those who want an opportunity to be considered equal with us in the things they boast about (NIV): Paul's rivals will be disappointed if they hope that their criticism of his disinterestedness will induce him to follow their lead in accepting money from the Corinthians. For he is determined not to afford them any pretext for claiming that their nefarious work of deception has even a semblance of equality with the authentic ministry which he exercises. 'Paul was too capable a strategist to surrender such a position to the enemy. It would never be by any action of his that he and they found themselves on the same ground' (Denney).

13: For such men are false apostles, deceitful workers, fashioning themselves into apostles of Christ.

Not a few have questioned the apostle's wisdom in using such 'intemperate' language, but as Bengel finely observes, 'the indifferentism, which is so pleasant to many in the present day, was not cultivated by Paul. He was no pleasant preacher of toleration'. But the truth is always intolerable to those who are distinguished by their easy toleration of every conceivable deviation from the faith 'once for all delivered unto the saints' [*Jude* 3]. Today when every babbler of error is almost certain to be hailed as an apostle of Christ by a degenerate Christianity, it is high time for those who remain faithful to the testimony of Jesus to sound no uncertain note of warning. The moment is long overdue for professed Evangelicals to stop fêting the traducers of their Lord and to recognize these men for the deceitful workers they are.

Fashioning themselves into apostles of Christ: They changed their outward appearance by assuming the guise of Christ's servants, but their essential character as the slaves of Satan remained unchanged. 'They pose as something which they are not, and in doing so they deceive those who through gullibility or inexperience are more ready to give credence to plausible impostors than to remember the sound teaching and warnings of him who is their true apostle' (P. E. Hughes).

14: And no marvel; for even Satan fashioneth himself into an angel of light.

It is no wonder that those who are in reality opposed to Christ should wish to be taken for his apostles, for in this they are merely following the practice of their true master! Satan's masquerading by deceit as a messenger of light, i.e. as the herald of true knowledge, is but the pattern of his conduct as the deceiver, from his first dealings with mankind in the Garden of Eden [verse 3]. Because it is only by posing as the champion of truth that the prince of darkness is able to persuade men to swallow his lies.

'Satan is most hurtful to the church, when he opposes it by subtlety and creeping; when he comes not as an open enemy, but an appearing friend. He is never so much a devil, as when he appears in white, and transforms himself into an angel of light. He does more hurt by creeping into, than breaking into, the church. False apostles and seducers in the church have been more hurtful to it by fraud, than bloody and paganish persecutors by force. Satan has gained more victories by using the one as sunshine to dazzle the eyes, than by raising the other as wind to blow in the faces of the faithful' (William Jenkyn, *The Epistle of Jude*, p. 78).

15: It is no great thing therefore if his ministers also fashion themselves as ministers of righteousness; whose end shall be according to their works.

It is therefore no great thing, 'if Satan's power to present himself in a guise foreign to his real nature should also be found in those enlisted in his service. Appearing as *the ministers of righteousness*, i.e. eloquent advocates of the Pharisaic doctrine that men can put themselves right with God by their own unaided efforts, they are in fact deceivers of others because they are themselves deceived' (Tasker) [cf. *Acts* 13:39; *Rom.* 10:3; *Gal.* 2:21; *Phil.* 3:6, 9] But their end will be according to their Satanic deeds, and not according to their apostolic pretensions! [5:10]. Then those who thought that they were saved by 'works' will discover to their eternal confusion that these were not sufficient to secure them a place among the redeemed.

16: I say again, Let no man think me foolish; but if ye do, yet as foolish receive me, that I also may glory a little.

In returning to the theme of 'boasting', Paul again makes clear his extreme reluctance to indulge in the same folly as the Judaizers [verse 1]. He wishes the Corinthians to understand that though such boasting is natural to the false apostles, he is only acting a part which has been forced upon him by their accusations. But if they insist on regarding him as a fool, then let them *also* listen to a little of *his* foolishness.

After all, this should be no hardship to those who are so ready to welcome fools with open arms!

17: That which I speak, I speak not after the Lord, but as in foolishness, in this confidence of glorying.

I speak not after the Lord: To regard this as a disclaimer of either the authority or the inspiration of the Lord is not only to discount the value of Paul's utterance for the church but also to do him a grave injustice. Lenski brings out the true meaning of the verse: 'This foolish boasting will not follow the norm and principle of Jesus, for it will be done, not, indeed, "*in* folly", yet "*as in* folly". It will look like folly. It will thus stoop to a lower norm than Jesus used. If it were done in actual folly it would, of course, be stooping to sin; since it is done only in apparent folly it is not sin but is ethically on a lower plane than the one on which Jesus moved.' This explains why Paul is so reluctant to glory, but he is going to do so in order to bring the Corinthians to their senses.

18: Seeing that many glory after the flesh, I will glory also.

After the flesh here means to 'boast of one's outward circumstances, i.e. descent, manner of life, etc. [cf. verse 22]' (Arndt-Gingrich). Since his opponents wax eloquent in extolling their external advantages, Paul will meet them on the same ground to show the Corinthians that even at this low level of boasting he is not a whit behind these superlative apostles! [verse 5].

19: For ye bear with the foolish gladly, being wise yourselves.

Foolish . . . being wise: 'The Greek antithesis is "senseless, sensible". The irony cuts at the Corinthian self-sufficiency, which blinds them to what real folly is. "Foolish are these boasters; but you plume yourselves on your shrewdness in accepting them. So you will, I am sure, accept me when I talk like them"' (Massie).

20: For ye bear with a man if he bringeth you into bondage, if he devoureth you: if he taketh you captive, if he exalteth himself, if he smiteth you on the face.

Paul knows that the Corinthians will put up with him when they are so patiently enduring the indignities which are being heaped upon them by these tyrannical teachers! Not only have they suffered these things, for all the 'ifs' denote reality, 'but the conditional form also implies that they are ready to have it repeated again and again' (Lenski). 1. *They were being enslaved.* In forfeiting Christian liberty for the yoke of Jewish legalism, they were exchanging their spiritual freedom for abject bondage [*Gal.* 2:4; 5:1]. 2. *They were being exploited.* 'Devours' vividly describes the rapacious exactions of the Judaizers which they justified on the grounds of apostolic rights! [cf. *Luke* 20:47]. 3. *They were being ensnared.* This word pictures them as caught by the crafty cunning of these unscrupulous hunters of the souls of men. 4. *They were being dominated.* The false apostles made free use of their usurped authority to lord it over the Corinthians. 5. *They were being humiliated.* To crown it all, it would seem that their new masters even resorted to physical violence. This was doubtless done 'under the pretext of divine zeal. The height of insolence on their part, and of servile endurance on yours [*1 Kings* 22:24; *Neh.* 13:25; *Luke* 22:64; *Acts* 23:2; *1 Tim.* 3:3]' (Fausset).

21a: I speak by way of disparagement, as though we had been weak.

To my shame I admit that we were too weak for that! (NIV): This final shaft brings Paul's biting satire to a shattering climax. He might well have said, 'What a disgrace *for you* to have received such fellows *gladly!*' Instead he says, 'No, the disgrace is mine, for *we* were too *weak* to treat you like that!' [cf. 10:10]. Yes, these 'false apostles know how real apostles ought to act so as to impress you with what real apostles are; *we* – why, we did not even know how to act as apostles' (Lenski). This makes the Corinthians realize the full shame of their disloyalty as nothing else would.

21b: Yet whereinsoever any is bold (I speak in foolishness), I am bold also.

Paul's lengthy preamble is over. Although the task is disagreeable, the moment has come when for the sake of the Corinthians he must cast modesty aside and launch into his 'foolish' boasting. This he does in the full confidence that he is well able to match any claim put forward by his rivals. For 'the grounds on which they show their audacity are as much mine as theirs' (Massie).

22: Are they Hebrews? so am I. Are they Israelites? so am I. Are they the seed of Abraham? so am I.

That Paul should place this proud claim in the forefront of his apology would seem to indicate that his antagonists were Palestinian Jews who boasted of the purity of their descent in order to confine the Corinthians within the straitjacket of their Judaistic 'gospel'. But he insists that his own pedigree is in no sense inferior to theirs; he has inherited exactly the same privileges, though of course he attached a very different value to them [cf. *Rom.* 4:9–18].

The three questions form a climax, – '"Hebrews" referring to the *language* and *nationality*; "Israelites", to the *theocracy* and *descent from Israel,* the "prince who prevailed with God" [*Rom.* 9:4]; "the seed of Abraham", to the *claim to a share in the Messiah* [*Rom.* 9:7; 11:1]. Cf *Phil.* 3:5, "an Hebrew of the Hebrews"; not an Hellenist or Greek-speaking Jew, but a Hebrew in tongue, sprung from Hebrews' (Fausset).

23: Are they ministers of Christ? (I speak as one beside himself) I more; in labours more abundantly, in prisons more abundantly, in stripes above measure, in deaths oft.

Are they ministers of Christ? . . . I more: 'i.e. I am more a minister of Christ than they, not I am more than a minister of Christ. "The more a man suffers", says Bengel. "the more he ministers"' (Goudge). As a minister of Christ Paul is far beyond them, because they are not ministers of Christ at all [verses 13, 15]; so here he does not say 'So am I.'

I speak as one beside himself: Paul thus interrupts his boasting, because he knows that 'to glory about so sacred a matter as the service of Christ is downright madness' (Plummer).

Through hard toils in abundance, through imprisonments in abundance, through stripes beyond measure, through deadly perils on many occasions (Massie): The reality of Paul's ministry is so completely beyond the empty claims of the false apostles that no comparison between them is possible. They had brought letters of commendation [3:1], but he bears on his body 'the marks of Jesus' [*Gal.* 6:17]. Paul finds the badges of his office in what he has suffered for Christ, but the Judaizers are mere verbalizers. They have no such credentials to offer.

24: Of the Jews five times received I forty stripes save one.

Paul's revealing account of the terrible sufferings he had endured up to the time of writing this Epistle conveys a vivid impression of his extraordinary labours and forms a valuable supplement to the very selective outline of his life in Acts. On no less than five occasions he was sentenced by the Jews to be beaten within an inch of his life. Forty strokes was the maximum punishment which could be inflicted short of the death penalty [*Deut.* 25:3], and this was later reduced to thirty-nine for fear of a miscount. 'Notice that the Jews, even in cruelty and injustice to a servant of God, were scrupulously careful to obey in an insignificant detail the letter of the Law. Cf. *Matt.* 23:23' (Beet) [*Matt.* 10:17]

25: Thrice was I beaten with rods, once was I stoned, thrice I suffered shipwreck, a night and a day have I been in the deep;

Of the three occasions when Paul was beaten by the Roman authorities we only have a record of the one at Philippi [*Acts* 16:22, 23, 37]. As Plummer points out, the fact that Paul 'was thrice treated in this way is evidence that being a Roman citizen was an imperfect protection when magistrates were disposed to be brutal'. Although Luke gives an account of the stoning at Lystra [*Acts* 14:19], he does not mention these shipwrecks, which of course took place before that recorded in Acts 27, but Paul made many voyages – P. E. Hughes calculates at least eighteen - and sailing was a risky business in those days.

A night and a day I have been adrift at sea (RSV): This means that Paul was in (not under) the sea, probably clinging to some fragment of the wreck, in imminent peril of his life for twenty-four hours before being rescued. The tense may indicate that a recent experience is here vividly recalled.

26: in journeyings often, in perils of rivers, in perils of robbers, in perils from my countrymen, in perils from the Gentiles, in perils in the city, in perils in the wilderness, in perils in the sea, in perils among false brethren;

A graphic description of the many hazards Paul continually faced in the prosecution of his apostolic commission, of which the last would be the most distressing [cf. *Gal.* 2:4, where the same word is used of the Judaizers). The pseudo-apostles also braved the dangers of first-century travel to reach Corinth with their false gospel, but none of *their* perils were like Paul's. 'Paul's were perils that were met with on *apostolic* journeys, theirs were perils such as the Pharisees encountered when they compassed sea and land to make one proselyte; "and when he is made, ye make him two-fold more the child of hell than yourselves", *Matt.* 23:15' (Lenski). How like the cultists today!

27: in labour and travail, in watchings often, in hunger and thirst, in fastings often, in cold and nakedness.

I have laboured and toiled and have often gone without sleep; I have known hunger and thirst and have often gone without food; I have been cold and naked (NIV): In addition to these perils, the physical privations Paul endured would have served to quench the ardour of a less indomitable spirit than his. The 'fastings' referred to here were not religious, though they were voluntary in the sense that Paul often went without food because his work left him no time to eat. 'When we remember that he who endured all this was a man constantly suffering from infirm health [4:7–12; 12:7-10; *Gal.* 4:13, 14], such heroic self-devotion seems almost superhuman' (Conybeare and Howson).

28: Besides those things that are without, there is that which presseth upon me daily, anxiety for all the churches.

It is more likely that the opening phrase means: 'besides the things that I do not mention' (Plummer). Paul could say much more along the same lines, but he wants the troublesome church in Corinth to understand that all these trials are as nothing compared with the daily pressure of his anxiety for all the churches. He regards this as his real burden; his other troubles are only the incidental extras he receives by way of a bonus! His evaluation is intended to startle the Corinthians, especially when it is contrasted with the callous indifference of the selfish hirelings they had been so ready to welcome as their true shepherds.

29: Who is weak, and I am not weak? who is caused to stumble, and I burn not?

Paul's deep concern for the churches leads him to sympathize with the weak and to wax indignant against their seducers. He feels their weakness as though it were his own. Christian love is gentle and bears patiently with the weak, but carnal pride ruthlessly takes advantage of their weakness to impose its own will on them. Thus the weak Corinthians had succumbed to the boastful strength of the Judaizers!

If anyone is made to stumble, does my heart not blaze with indignation? (NEB): 'It was not to Paul a matter of indifference when any of the brethren, by the force of evil example, or by the seductions of false teachers, were led to depart from the truth or to act inconsistently with their profession. Such events filled him not only with grief at the fall of the weak, but with indignation at the authors of their fall' (Hodge).

30: If I must needs glory, I will glory of the things that concern my weakness.

This verse looks both ways. It sums up what has gone before [verses 23–28], and is the preface to what follows [12:5–10]. Paul had promised to join his adversaries in the foolishness of boasting, but his boasting has been of a very different character from theirs. For he does not boast of his achievements, but always of the things that concern his weakness. 'He set out to boast; see how he has done it! he has brought forward the very things a boastful person would have said nothing about. There is a boast for you! The Corinthians, carried away by the boasting of those other people, are now to look at this boast too, and see what they think of it' (Menzies).

31: The God and Father of the Lord Jesus, he who is blessed for evermore knoweth that I lie not.

This solemn assurance vouches for the veracity of all that he has said and all that he has yet to say concerning his weakness, and was doubtless intended to counter the calumnies which were circulated about the reliability of his word [1:17]. As befits the servant of the One who cannot lie, Paul speaks only what God *knows* to be the truth [cf. *Rom.* 9:5 and see comment on 1:3].

32: In Damascus the governor under Aretas the king guarded the city of the Damascenes in order to take me: 33: and through a window was I let down in a basket by the wall, and escaped his hands.

Many have wondered why Paul should have decided to mention his escape from Damascus at this particular point. The most reasonable explanation would seem to be that this experience marked the beginning of his 'weakness'. The name of Damascus was indelibly engraved upon the tablet of his memory because it was 'there that the persecutor became the persecuted' (Waite). What a contrast there was between his arrogant approach to the city, and his humiliating exit from it! [cf. *Acts* 9:1, 2, 23–25] Moreover, this account of Paul's inglorious escape is also in pointed contrast to the experience which he is about to describe [12:2ff.]. 'The man who experienced the ineffable "ascent" even to the third heaven was the same man who had experienced the undistinguished "descent" from a window in the Damascus wall' (P. E. Hughes).

Damascus was not part of the Nabataean kingdom which bordered it, but the governor (or ethnarch) of King Aretas had jurisdiction over the large Arabian colony in the city. In seeking to silence a notorious troublemaker, the Jews successfully enlisted the help of the governor who made arrangements for his clandestine arrest. 'The ethnarch had no authority to arrest Saul openly, as he would have had if Damascus had at this time been part of Aretas's realm' (F. F. Bruce, *Commentary on the Book of Acts*, p. 204).

CHAPTER TWELVE

Paul here discloses that though he had been favoured with inexpressible revelations, yet he chose rather to glory in his weaknesses in case any man accounted him to be above that which could be seen and heard [verses 1–6]. To prevent his being filled with pride by these proofs of God's favour, he was given a painful affliction from which he thrice prayed to be delivered. But instead of granting his request, the Lord assured him that the power of his grace is made perfect in man's weakness. Therefore he gladly glories in his weaknesses that the power of Christ may rest upon him [verses 7–10]. Paul blames the Corinthians for forcing him to become a fool by boasting when they had been given ample proofs of his apostleship. If they were less privileged than other churches, it was only in his refusal to be a burden to them [verses 11–13]. Before he comes on his third visit he assures them of his unchanging affection, and reminds them that they are well qualified to rebut the attacks which have been made on his integrity [verses

14–18]. But he fears lest when he comes he should find many grave disorders still unresolved, to his sorrow and theirs [verses 19–21].

1: I must needs glory, though it is not expedient; but I will come to visions and revelations of the Lord.

I am obliged to boast (NEB): Paul introduces his final boast with a fresh apology. Such boasting is not delightful, but it is necessary. It is with the greatest reluctance that he brings forward an experience about which he has kept silent for fourteen years, and the only reason he does so now is in order to relate its sequel [verses 7–10]. Hence his purpose is again to reduce his boast to a 'boasting in weakness' (Massie).

It does no good (NEB): i.e. it is not useful or helpful. 'He means that he expects to confer no spiritual profit upon the Corinthians by telling them about this phenomenal experience of his' (Lenski).

But I shall go on to tell of visions and revelations granted by the Lord (NEB): The construction indicates the Lord as the source of the visions and revelations. The plural indicates that Paul is no stranger to those ecstatic experiences of which the super-apostles had evidently boasted to the Corinthians. Of the many revelations vouchsafed to him, he selects one that marked a turning-point in his life, yet what he heard clearly impressed him more than anything he may have seen [verse 4]. The visions Paul received had a revelatory function, but not every revelation that was made to him was visually mediated.[1]

2: I know a man in Christ, fourteen years ago (whether in the body, I know not; or whether out of the body, I know not; God knoweth), such a one caught up even to the third heaven.

The man Paul knows intimately is of course himself, but he chooses to speak in the third person to avoid the appearance of boasting in what he is now forced to relate [verses 5, 6]. 'Another person might shout: '*I, I,* have been in Paradise!' and exalt himself above all his fellow

---

[1] *It is important for Christians today to grasp the fact that the gospel would be incomplete if extra-Biblical revelations were necessary to supplement its teaching.* Revelation is the interpretation of a redemption which is partly objective and partly subjective. Revelation keeps pace with the objective acts of redemption, the incarnation, the atonement, and the resurrection of Christ, but it does not accompany the *subjective application* of that redemption to the individual in regeneration, conversion, justification, and sanctification. This explains why redemption extends further than revelation. To insist

men. Another man might tell about it on every possible occasion. Paul kept it a secret for fourteen years' (Lenski). As this Epistle was written in AD 56, fourteen years before would mean that this took place around AD 43, possibly towards the end of Paul's sojourn at Tarsus [*Acts* 9:30; 11:25]. If so, the experience would have inwardly prepared him to obey the outward call of Barnabas to engage in the momentous work of preaching to the Gentiles at Antioch [*Acts* 11:16; cf. *Acts* 10:9–29].

Whether in the body, I know not; or whether out of the body, I know not; God knoweth: 'Ignorance of the mode does not take away the certain knowledge of the thing' (Bengel). Since Paul confessed his ignorance as to whether he was in or out of the body at the time, speculation on the matter is quite pointless, for we can hardly expect to establish what he himself was unable to determine. What satisfied him, should satisfy us too: '*God* knoweth'.

Such an one caught up: 'The same word describes how surviving Christians will be "caught up" to meet the descending Lord [*1 Thess.* 4:17]' (Massie).

Even to the third heaven: As Calvin sensibly remarks, Paul is not here drawing fine philosophical distinctions between the different heavens, but uses three as a perfect number to indicate what is highest and most complete. Thus 'not content with using the simple word heaven, Paul adds that he had reached its utmost height and innermost chambers'.

3: And I know such a man (whether in the body, or apart from the body, I know not; God knoweth), 4: how that he was caught up into Paradise, and heard unspeakable words, which it is not lawful for a man to utter.

---

upon revelation 'accompanying subjective-individual redemption would imply that it dealt with questions of private personal concern, instead of with the common concerns of the world of redemption collectively' (condensed and quoted from *Biblical Theology* by Geerhardus Vos, p. 14). This means that inspiration, in the full apostolic meaning of the word, ceased when the canon of Scripture was brought to completion. Without such *apostolic* inspiration there can be no *infallible* revelation. The only revelation from God which Christians still await is the Revelation of Jesus Christ at his second Coming. And that will be objective enough to satisfy everyone that it has really taken place! See also 'The Finality and Sufficiency of Scripture' in *Collected Writings of John Murray*, vol. 1 (Banner of Truth, 1976), and the Chapter 'Is Scripture Complete?' in Walter Chantry's *Signs of the Apostles* (Banner of Truth, 1976).

The solemn repetition in verse 3 prepares the way for some additional information about the same experience. Although Paul offers no description of Paradise, he knows he has been there. The first Paradise in Eden was 'lost' through sin, but through the triumph of grace that lost glory is 'regained' in the Paradise of heaven [cf. *Luke* 23:43; *Rev.* 2:7]. What Paul heard was incommunicable, but he preached an intelligible message of salvation. 'Paul was not a "gnostic", but a witness; salvation, according to his teaching, came not through a mystic vision, but through the hearing of faith' (J. G. Machen, *The Origin of Paul's Religion*, p. 265).

Which it is not lawful for a man to utter: 'If anyone retorts that in that case what Paul heard was superfluous and useless, for what good was there in hearing something that had to be held back in perpetual silence, my answer is that this thing happened for Paul's own sake, for a man who had awaiting him troubles hard enough to break a thousand hearts needed to be strengthened in a special way to keep him from giving way and to help him to persevere undaunted' (Calvin).

5: On behalf of such a one will I glory: but on mine own behalf I will not glory, save in my weaknesses.

'On behalf of one, who in all this was entirely passive and recipient, without exertion or merit of his own, he will boast, but not on behalf of his personal self, his own will, work and service, except with regard to his infirmities. He has already in mind the infirmity of verse 7; the correlative of his visions and revelations' (Waite).

6: For if I should desire to glory, I shall not be foolish; for I shall speak the truth: but I forbear, lest any man should account of me above that which he seeth me to be, or heareth from me.

If I should choose to boast, it would not be the boast of a fool, for I should be speaking the truth (NEB): Paul cuts short his glorying even though he could say a great deal more, all of which would be nothing but the sober truth. 'Even in his great humility Paul takes care to leave no false impressions. He *was* something by the grace of God [*1 Cor.* 15:10]. It would be falsehood to deny it even by implication, an implication which one might falsely deduce from the emphasis which Paul puts on his weakness as being his only boast' (Lenski).

But I refrain, because I should not like anyone to form an estimate of me which goes beyond the evidence of his own eyes and ears (NEB): It is significant that Paul thus refuses to make mystical experience a ground for claiming apostolic authority, when his opponents had clearly made much of their imaginary visions to enhance their standing in Corinth. 'Paul places no such value on ecstasy, nor does he imply that he was nearer to God then – when caught up into Paradise – than at other times under normal conditions. This is an important observation, which should set us on our guard against all forms of "mysticism" and exceptional experiences which are made the basis for some claim in a matter of Christian doctrine or practice' (Ralph P. Martin, *Daily Bible Commentary*, vol. 4, p. 200).

> **7: And by reason of the exceeding greatness of the revelations, that I should not be exalted overmuch, there was given to me a thorn in the flesh, a messenger of Satan to buffet me, that I should not be exalted overmuch.**

It should not be forgotten that self-deification is the great goal of fallen man [*Gen.* 3:5], and even believers need to be protected against assuming that their spiritual privileges are their own prerogatives. 'How dangerous must self-exaltation be, when the apostle required so much restraint!' (Bengel).

There was given to me a thorn in the flesh: The gift was entirely unsolicited by Paul, but with the gift he was also given the grace to receive it as a favour! Of this 'thorn' we know no more than Paul tells us here. That it was a recurring painful physical affliction is certain, but an exact diagnosis of the condition is impossible. Our ignorance remains even if Galatians 4:13–14 may be legitimately linked with this verse. The most plausible guesses all fall short of final certainty. If it had been spiritually profitable for us to know the nature of this malady God would have told us. As it is, Paul's thorn in the flesh becomes 'by its very lack of definition, a type of every Christian's "thorn in the flesh" not with regard to externals, but by its spiritual significance' (P. E. Hughes).

A messenger of Satan to buffet me: The case of Job furnishes a helpful parallel [*Job* 2:7], for it shows that it was within God's wise and holy purpose to prove the fidelity of his servant by sending Satan to do the evil work in which he takes a fiendish delight [cf. *Luke* 13:16]. Satan could not touch a hair of Job's head without leave, for absolutely nothing lies outside the scope of God's sovereignty. All God's creatures are subject to his ruling and over-ruling; and even the work of Satan is overruled so that it assists in bringing to pass the divine purpose, though Satan on his part uses his utmost powers to thwart that purpose.

That I should not be exalted overmuch: The divine purpose in this affliction is repeated for emphasis. Satan's malice is always frustrated by God and made to minister a blessing *to his people.* The 'all things' of Romans 8:28 admits of no exceptions.

8: Concerning this thing I besought the Lord thrice, that it might depart from me.

On three occasions Paul made it a matter of earnest entreaty that the Lord Jesus would deliver him from the attacks of this messenger of Satan. In moments of physical suffering it is natural to seek relief from the One who is 'touched with the feeling of our infirmities' [*Heb.* 4:15], 'and the Greek word for "besought" is one frequently used of the appeals of the sick in the Gospels' (Goudge).

9: And he hath said unto me, My grace is sufficient for thee: for my power is made perfect in weakness. Most gladly therefore will I rather glory in my weaknesses, that the power of Christ may rest upon me.

And he hath said unto me: 'The perfect tense denotes that what the Lord said was a *standing* answer valid for the Apostle's whole life' (Waite).

My grace is sufficient for thee: for my power is made perfect in weakness: Two thoughts intertwine here: 1. You will get no more, Paul's request being denied [verse 8], and 2. You need no more, since 'my power is made perfect in weakness' (H. Conzelmann, *TDNT,* vol. 9, p. 395). Christ's grace is sufficient in that it does not banish weakness, but overcomes it by making it the vehicle of his royal power. None is too weak to be of service to Christ, but many are too strong to be used by him [*1 Cor.* 1:27]. It is because the Lord will have all the glory that he uses those who are acutely aware of their own weakness [*1 Cor.* 2:3]. Paul thus reaches the climax of the entire Epistle in this revelation of the secret of his power, a secret whose meaning was far beyond the understanding of his boastful rivals. For the self-sufficient must ever remain strangers to the power of that grace which is manifested only in conscious weakness.

Most gladly therefore will I rather glory in my weaknesses: This unexpected answer resulted in a complete reversal of Paul's attitude towards his thorn in the flesh, so that he was now prepared to welcome the weaknesses which made his dependence upon the power of Christ so complete. But it is important to distinguish between Paul's weaknesses which were given him [verse 7], and 'a joyless theology of insecurity' that encouraged men to try to accumulate merit before God through sufferings which were self-inflicted (so P. E. Hughes).

That the power of Christ may rest upon me: Literally, 'may pitch its tent upon me', i.e. 'dwell in me as in a tent, as the shechinah dwelt of old in the tabernacle. To be made thus the dwelling-place of the power of Christ, where he reveals his glory, was a rational ground of rejoicing in those infirmities which were the condition of his presence and the occasion for the manifestation of his power' (Hodge).

10: Wherefore I take pleasure in weaknesses, in injuries, in necessities, in persecutions, in distresses, for Christ's sake: for when I am weak, then am I strong.

For Christ's sake: These are the all-important words which qualify the five preceding nouns. 'Only a morbid fanatic can take pleasure in the sufferings he inflicts upon himself; only an insensitive fool can take pleasure in the sufferings that are the consequences of his folly; and only a convinced Christian can take pleasure in sufferings endured *for Christ's sake*' (Tasker).

For when I am weak, then am I strong: This paradox of grace is the principle of all effective service. Paul had early learned that the treasure of the gospel is committed to frail earthen vessels, in order to show that the power belongs to God alone [4:7–10]. This is a hard lesson for us to learn, yet it brings great encouragement with it. For though we can accomplish nothing in our own strength, mountains are moved by weak men who trust in Christ's power.

11: I am become foolish: ye compelled me; for I ought to have been commended of you: for in nothing was I behind the very chiefest apostles, though I am nothing.

Paul admits that he has become a fool, but this foolishness was forced upon him by the disloyalty of the Corinthians. For if instead of receiving the slanders of his detractors, they had rushed to his defence, he would not have been compelled to descend to the folly of boasting in order to rescue them from the toils of false doctrine. 'It is a debt we owe to good men, to stand up in the defence of their reputation; and we are under special obligation to those we have received benefit by, especially spiritual benefit, to own them as instruments in God's hand of good to us, and to vindicate them when they are calumniated by others' (Matthew Henry).

For in nothing did I fall short of the superlative apostles, nothing though I am (Waite): '"Nonentity" though I am, you have had ample proof that I did not fall short of these precious "apostles" of yours!' The charge hurled at Paul is a boomerang, for he has boasted of nothing but his own 'nothingness'. Yet this nothingness has been used as the vehicle of divine power in Corinth, whereas the self-inflated pretensions of these super-apostles have been productive of nothing more than the works of the flesh. 'The difference between this statement and that of 11:5, is that there he asserted a general and standing non-inferiority, whereas he here asserts a non-inferiority proved in his actual ministry among them (aorist). Hence the clause is a transition-link to the appeal to facts [12ff.] with which they were acquainted' (Waite).

12: Truly the signs of an apostle were wrought among you in all patience, by signs and wonders and mighty works.

The signs that mark a true apostle were performed among you (but you paid no attention) (Arndt-Gingrich): The miraculous element in Paul's ministry should have convinced the Corinthians of the reality of his apostleship. For apostolic signs were the visible authentication of an apostolic commission. 'We no longer have the apostles with us and therefore the supernatural gifts (the communication of which was an essential part of "the *signs* of an apostle" (*2 Cor.* 12:12) are absent' (Arthur Pink, *The Holy Spirit*, p. 179). It is obvious that such an appeal would have been ludicrous if the Corinthians had never witnessed such signs. By his use of the passive, Paul shows that he was but the instrument through whom the power of God was manifested in their midst. 'In all patience' is the element *in* which these signs were wrought.

By signs and wonders and mighty works: 'He calls them *signs* because they are not merely meaningless spectacles but are designed to instruct men. He calls them *wonders* because by their novelty they should rouse and astonish, and he calls them powers or *mighty works* because they are more evidently examples of divine power than those which we discover in the ordinary course of nature' (Calvin) [cf. *Acts* 2:22; *2 Thess.* 2:9; *Heb.* 2:4]

13: For what is there wherein ye were made inferior to the rest of the churches, except it be that I myself was not a burden to you? forgive me this wrong.

Thus the ministry the Corinthians received from Paul was in no respect inferior to that which the rest of the churches received, unless it was in regard to his refusal to accept maintenance from them. With cutting irony he asks their forgiveness for this wrong! 'In my nothingness I did not ask even a penny of support. Pardon me for the great loss which you thus suffered!' (Lenski).

14: Behold, this is the third time I am ready to come to you; and I will not be a burden to you: for I seek not yours, but you: for the children ought not to lay up for the parents, but the parents for the children.

Paul is now ready to pay them his third visit and he will not be a burden to them this time any more than he was on his two previous visits, the first of which took place when he founded the church, and the second 'painful' visit towards the end of his stay in Ephesus [cf. 2:1 and see *Introduction*].

For I seek not yours, but you: Paul has a far greater goal in view than a share of their wealth; he seeks their full salvation through the grace of God in Christ Jesus. He cares not for their goods so long as he can gain their souls. His concern is not for the wool, but for the sheep [cf. *1 Pet.* 5:2].

Children . . . parents: As their spiritual father [*1 Cor.* 4:14, 15), Paul does not seek earthly treasure *from* them, but rather seeks to lay up heavenly treasure *for* them!

15: And I will most gladly spend and be spent for your souls. If I love you more abundantly, am I loved the less?

Paul's more than fatherly affection for the Corinthians was proved by his willingness to spend and 'be spent out' (ASV margin) for the good of their souls. But it would be an unhappy irony if his increasing love resulted in a diminishing return from them. 'That would be a strange kind of return to make, a strange instance of inverse proportion!' (Plummer).

16: But be it so, I did not myself burden you; but, being crafty, I caught you with guile.

That Paul himself had never been a burden on the Corinthians' resources could not be disputed by anyone, but his detractors had not been above hinting that he had profited from them in other ways. The insinuation was that 'with my natural craft, I caught you by my ostentatious disinterestedness, and then all the more successfully plundered you through my agents' (Massie).

17: Did I take advantage of you by any one of them whom I have sent unto you? 18: I exhorted Titus, and I sent the brother with him. Did Titus take any advantage of you? walked we not in the same spirit? walked we not in the same steps?

Paul throws down the challenge in the confidence that the transparent honesty of his assistants speaks for itself. Titus appears to have visited Corinth at least three times: first to start the collection [8:6a]; then as the bearer of the 'severe' letter; and finally to complete the collection [8:6b, 16–24]. As the false apostles had questioned the financial integrity of Paul's representatives [verse 16], these verses must refer to the first visit of Titus, and perhaps 'the brother' who was his companion on that occasion was also chosen by Paul to help in the completion of the gracious work [8:22]. By appealing to the success of Titus in winning the Corinthians' trust, Paul would also have them know that the character and conduct of the messenger was a faithful reflection of the apostle upon whose instructions he had acted.

19: Ye think all this time that we are excusing ourselves unto you. In the sight of God speak we in Christ. But all things, beloved, are for your edifying.

Have you been thinking all along that we have been defending ourselves to you? (NIV): Paul's self-vindication is complete but he does not want the Corinthians to run away with the idea that he stands before their tribunal in the hope of securing a favourable verdict.

We have been speaking in the sight of God as those in Christ (NIV): It is not to *men* that Paul holds himself accountable [*1 Cor.* 4:3], for it is in the sight of God and in union with Christ that he so speaks [cf. 2:17].

And everything we do, dear friends, is for your strengthening (NIV): 'So far as his authority in Corinth was undermined, so far were they tottering and it was necessary to reconsolidate *his* position in order that *theirs* might be restored and secured' (Waite).

> **20: For I fear, lest by any means, when I come, I should find you not such as I would, and should myself be found of you such as ye would not; lest by any means there should be strife, jealousy, wraths, factions, backbitings, whisperings, swellings, tumults;**

Although Paul has spoken so sternly, it has been with a view to their edification, for he fears that when he comes he may find them in a different state than *he* would wish, i.e. still wallowing in the same sins which had called forth his severe reproofs. In that case, they would find him to be other than *they* would wish, i.e. severe in punishing their misconduct. He gently gives expression to his fear in the hope that they will take the opportunity to remove all occasion for such severity before he arrives in Corinth. The list of vices seems to be arranged in four pairs: contention and envying; fits of temper and party-intrigues; open slander and secret gossip; swellings of pride and grave disorders.

> **21: lest again when I come my God should humble me before you, and I should mourn for many of them that have sinned heretofore, and repented not of the uncleanness and fornication and lasciviousness which they committed.**

Having once visited them in sorrow [2:1], Paul fears a further humiliation may be in store for him on his return to Corinth. 'Nothing brings a Christian teacher into the dust so much as the defection of those whom he has looked on as fruits of his labour and as his crown of rejoicing' (Beet). He therefore wonders whether he will find that many, having relapsed into their old pagan ways, remained impenitent under his reproofs. His coming will discover whether he must mourn over them as those who are spiritually dead.

CHAPTER THIRTEEN

On Paul's third visit the unrepentant shall have an unwelcome proof of his authority in the punishment he will not fail to administer [verses 1–4]. But instead of forcing him to provide them with such proofs, they will do better to prove the reality of their own faith [verses 5, 6]. He prays that they may be so restored that severity will not be necessary, even if he is thus made to appear weak. He would far sooner write severely to them than deal severely with them when present, because his power was given to build up and not to cast down [verses 7–10]. He closes the letter with a final exhortation, greetings, and his farewell prayer for them all [verses 11–14].

1: This is the third time I am coming to you. At the mouth of two witnesses or three shall every word be established.

Paul abruptly announces the imminence of this *third* visit. That he *is* coming is certain, but the manner of his visit will depend upon the Corinthians' attitude towards him. He wishes no one to be in the slightest doubt of his determination to deal with the recalcitrant in accordance with the principles of justice laid down by Moses and endorsed by Christ [*Deut.* 19:15; *Matt.* 18:16]. 'Paul's word is intended as a warning. He has just mentioned repentance [12:21]. He hopes that there will be no unrepentant sinners with whom he must deal when he arrives. They will get a fair trial, indeed, but a trial they will get' (Lenski).

2: I have said beforehand, and I do say beforehand, as when I was present the second time, so now, being absent, to them that have sinned heretofore, and to all the rest, that, if I come again, I will not spare;

As Bengel notes, there is in the text, 'an uninterrupted chiasmus throughout the three members of the sentence', which P. E. Hughes sets out as follows:

I have said beforehand	*and*	*I do say beforehand*
when I was present the second time	*and*	*now being absent*
to them that have sinned heretofore	*and*	*to all the rest*

Paul has already warned those who were leading sinful lives at the time of his second visit that if he came again he would not spare them, and now he reiterates the warning to all others whom he may find in the same sinful state when he arrives in Corinth for the third time.

If I come again: The meaning is, 'when I come this time' (NEB). It would be ridiculous to take the 'if' as expressed uncertainty over the much-advertised visit. 'All that is meant is that the punishment depends on the coming, whenever that takes place' (Massie).

I will not spare: Paul hopes that it will not be necessary to provide the Corinthians with the proof that he means what he says [verses 7, 10], but those who disregard this final warning must realize that they leave their apostle with no alternative [verse 3].

3: seeing that ye seek a proof of Christ that speaketh in me; who to you-ward is not weak, but is powerful in you:

This is closely connected with the previous verse ('I will not spare; seeing that . . .'). Since the Corinthians demand a proof that Christ speaks in Paul, they shall have what they want! It is possible that there is an implied contrast with his opponents' claim to be the true spokesmen of Christ. Thus Waite comments: 'The words *in me* are obviously emphatic, and show that the Christ who spoke *in him* is contrasted with the Christ which spoke in the Judaizers. In accordance with their entire system, they ascribed the weakness shown on his second visit to the Christ whom he preached and who, being not a legal, but a spiritual Christ, they said was powerless to enforce obedience to law. Thus they challenged his Christ to a proof of his power. The libertines by their defiance did the same thing, for if they did not take up the taunt of the Judaizers, they clearly counted upon the same weakness for escaping punishment altogether'.

Who to you-ward is not weak, but is powerful in you: 'Of Christ's power *towards* and *among* the Corinthians, Paul has already given full proof, viz. [12:12] the miracles wrought in their midst and [3:2] the spiritual effects of the Gospel in their hearts. He will now add the more terrible proof of special punishment' (Beet).

4: for he was crucified through weakness, yet he liveth through the power of God. For we also are weak in him, but we shall live with him through the power of God toward you.

As it was in virtue of his self-assumed weakness that Christ was once crucified, so it is in virtue of the power of God that he now lives for ever as the triumphant Son of Man. It would be folly to presume on a temporary weakness, and to forget the present reality of Christ's power to punish as well as to save. For 'the cross does *not* exhaust Christ's relation to sin; he passed from the cross to the throne, and when he comes again it is as Judge' (Denney).

If Paul has experienced in full measure what it means to be weak in Christ, he is no stranger to that divine power which is made perfect in weakness. Thus though his 'painful' visit was marked by a weakness which the Corinthians despised, when he comes again he will act towards them with a power which will command their respect! Thus the believer's future inheritance is not in view here.

5: Try your own selves, whether ye are in the faith; prove your own selves. Or know ye not as to your own selves, that Jesus Christ is in you? unless indeed ye be reprobate. 6: But I hope that ye shall know that we are not reprobate.

Instead of putting Paul's apostleship to the proof [verse 3], the Corinthians should be testing the genuineness of their own faith in Christ! If, as Paul expects, most of them find that this self-examination confirms the reality of their attachment to Christ, then it must also show that he has exercised an authentic ministry among them [3:2; *1 Cor.* 9:2]. In this passage 'reprobate' is not used in the theological sense of being judicially abandoned to everlasting perdition; it means 'failing to pass the test, unapproved, counterfeit' (Souter). 'They ought to recognize Christ as a power in themselves – unless indeed they, being counterfeit Christians, cannot recognize him because he is not there' (Massie). But should any among them prove to be such counterfeit Christians, Paul hopes to convince them that at least *he* is not a counterfeit apostle! For faithfulness to his commission will compel him to mete out condign punishment to the faithless in Corinth.

7: Now we pray to God that ye do no evil; not that we may appear approved, but that ye may do that which is honourable, though we be as reprobate.

Paul, however, prays that the Corinthians may do that which is noble and right, for he has no desire to demonstrate his apostolic authority by inflicting punishment. His first concern is not with his own reputation, but with the spiritual well-being of his converts. Hence if none deserved punishment he would not be disappointed, even though in failing to carry out a threatened judgment he might *seem like* a counterfeit apostle!

8: For we can do nothing against the truth, but for the truth.

For, as Paul explains, he has no power to act against the truth, but only for the truth. Should he come to Corinth and find that their conduct was in conformity with the truth of the gospel, there would be no occasion to demonstrate his power in punishing the disobedient. But he would be opposing the truth, if he preferred them to do wrong because it gave him the opportunity of proving his power.

9: For we rejoice, when we are weak, and ye are strong: this we also pray for, even your perfecting.

The apostle has no desire to appear strong among them, but is glad to be weak when their strength in well-doing requires no punishment or censure. In fact, the burden of his prayer for them is that they might be restored to spiritual wholeness. The word used here denotes 'a resetting of what has been broken and dislocated, and hence a restoration of harmonious and efficient functioning. It carries no suggestion of what is known theologically as "perfectionism"' (P. E. Hughes).

10: For this cause I write these things while absent, that I may not when present deal sharply, according to the authority which the Lord gave me for building up, and not for casting down.

'He would not write to them severely from a distance [10:10] except for the purpose of avoiding severity of action when present. With all his resolve to punish, with all the authority which the Lord gave him to punish, he will do anything rather than punish. This he expresses by repeating what he said in 10:8, that the true end for which his authority was given was to build up and not to pull down. However necessary or beneficial chastisement may be, it is still "a pulling down", because it is, in the form here contemplated by him, plucking out stones, for a season at least, from the temple of the Lord. It is that evil which he prays they may not bring about [verse 7]' (Waite).

11: Finally, brethren, farewell. Be perfected; be comforted; be of the same mind; live in peace: and the God of love and peace shall be with you.

Mend your ways, heed my appeal (RSV): The apostle's farewell exhortation sums up his message to the Corinthians. Their many deficiencies must be amended, for the wholeness (or holiness) of the body to which they belong depends upon the harmonious working together of its many members (cf. the meaning of 'perfecting' in verse 9). But if this desirable end is to be attained in Corinth, they must so heed his appeal as to act upon it.

Be of the same mind; live in peace: They must seek to be 'of the same mind in the Lord' [*Phil.* 4:2], for they can only live in peace when they set their minds on the same thing. To have the mind of Christ is to banish that selfish way of thinking which always fosters strife.

And the God of love and peace shall be with you: 'We have here the familiar Christian paradox. God's presence produces love and peace, and we must have love and peace in order to have his presence. God gives what he commands. God gives, but we must cherish his gifts. His agency does not supersede ours, but mingles with it and becomes one with it in our consciousness. We work out our own salvation, while God works in us' (Hodge) [*Phil.* 2:12, 13]. Thus the believer becomes actively engaged in doing the will of God through the enabling power of the same Spirit by whom he was first quickened.

12: Salute one another with a holy kiss. 13: All the saints salute you.

The kiss of peace was the customary greeting among friends in the East, and its early adoption by believers invested it with a deeper meaning. It was a holy kiss because it expressed the communion they enjoyed through their sharing together in the peace of God, and was exchanged before the Lord's Supper as a sign of mutual forgiveness. [cf. *Rom.* 16:16; *1 Cor.* 16:20]. But later abuses brought the practice into disrepute, and it was eventually abandoned by the Western church. 'It is not a command of perpetual obligation, as the spirit of the command is that Christians should express their mutual love in the way sanctioned by the age and community in which they live' (Hodge).

As an expression of the church's unity, Paul follows his usual practice of sending the greetings of the 'saints' [cf. *1 Cor.* 1:2] with whom he is in touch when despatching the letter, i.e. the Christians of Macedonia.

14: The grace of the Lord Jesus Christ, and the love of God, and the communion of the Holy Spirit, be with you all.

'Remarkable it is that an Epistle written under a tempest of conflicting emotions, breathing in some places indignation, reproach, and sadness, at being driven to self-vindication against worthless detractors who should never have been listened to – that precisely this Epistle is the one that closes with the richest and most comprehensive of all the benedictions in the New Testament, the one which the Christian church in every land and of every age has found, and will find as long as the world lasts, the most available for public use, as a close to its worship' (Brown)

The grace of the Lord Jesus Christ: The Pauline gospel is summed up in the word which is his distinctive signature in every epistle. He who was once the implacable enemy of gospel grace is now its doughtiest defender. As the unworthy recipient of God's grace, he is inexorably opposed to the self-sufficient moralism by which it is subverted, always insistent that it comes to helpless sinners as the unmerited favour of God in Christ. It cannot be bought; it cannot be earned; it must be received as a free gift. Hence the order here is the order of Christian experience, for it is only through the grace of the Lord Jesus Christ that sinners come to know the love of God for them. The full title sets forth the majesty of the Mediator. 'Lord' points to his essential Deity, 'Jesus' underlines his genuine humanity so willingly assumed for our salvation, while 'Christ' tells us that he is the Messiah, the anointed fulfiller of the promised redemption.

And the love of God: Although God loved his people with an everlasting love, his holiness could not overlook the reality of their fearful fall into sin. In the resolution of this dilemma at the cross, the divine wisdom comes to its sublimest expression. It is there that all the attributes of God are seen to harmonize in the dread judgment that vindicated his justice even as it published his mercy. Thus the eternal love of God was the secret source of that matchless grace through which there is now manifested the marvel of the Father's adopting love.

And the communion of the Holy Spirit: Apart from the cross there can be no real understanding of God's love, while the only lasting fellowship between men is the fellowship of sinners redeemed by Christ's blood. It is the work of the Holy Spirit to bring about this fellowship by applying the benefits of that redemption to the hearts of God's people. It is therefore upon his gracious work that the individual and corporate spiritual life of believers entirely depends.

Be with you all: Here is the measure of Paul's magnanimity; his love embraces *all* the Corinthians, even those who have been the most disaffected towards him.

'The distinct personality and divinity of the Son, the Father, and the Holy Spirit, to each of whom prayer is addressed, is here taken for granted. And therefore this passage is a clear recognition of the doctrine of the Trinity, which is the fundamental doctrine of Christianity. For a Christian is one who seeks and enjoys the grace of the Lord Jesus, the love of God, and the communion of the Holy Ghost' (Hodge).

SOLI DEO GLORIA

BIBLIOGRAPHY

ARNDT, W. F. AND GINGRICH, F. W., *A Greek-English Lexicon of the New Testament* (University of Chicago Press, 1957).

BARRETT, C. K., *The Second Epistle to the Corinthians* (*BNTC*) (A. & C. Black, 1973).

BEET, J. A., *2 Corinthians* (Hodder & Stoughton, 1882).

BENGEL, J. A., *Gnomon of the New Testament* vol. 3 (T. &T. Clark, 1857).

BERNARD, J. H., *2 Corinthians* (*EGT*) (Eerdmans, 1974).

BOETTNER, LORAINE, *The Reformed Doctrine of Predestination* (Presbyterian & Reformed, 1965)

BROWN, DAVID, *2 Corinthians* (*Popular Commentary on the NT*) (T. & T. Clark, 1882).

BRUCE, F. F., *An Expanded Paraphrase of the Epistles of Paul* (Paternoster, 1965).

—— *1 and 2 Corinthians* (*NCB*) (Oliphants, 1971).

—— *Paul: Apostle of the Free Spirit* (Paternoster, 1977).

BRUCE, F. F., *The Acts of the Apostles* (*NICNT*) (Marshall, Morgan and Scott, 1956).

BRUNER, F. D., *A Theology of the Holy Spirit* (Hodder & Stoughton), 1971).

CALVIN, JOHN, *2 Corinthians–Philemon* (St Andrew Press, 1964).

CHANTRY, WALTER J., *Signs of the Apostles* (Banner of Truth, 1976).

DENNEY, JAMES, *2 Corinthians* (*EB*) (Hodder & Stoughton, 1894).

—— *The Death of Christ* (Tyndale, 1964).

DICKSON, DAVID, *The Psalms* (Banner of Truth, 1959).

DOUGLAS, J. D. (Editor), *The New Bible Dictionary* (IVP, 1962).

FAIRBAIRN, PATRICK, *The Interpretation of Prophecy* (Banner of Truth, 1964).

FAUSSET, A. R., *2 Corinthians* (*JFB*) (Collins, 1874).

FILSON, FLOYD V., *The Second Epistle to the Corinthians* (*IB*) (Abingdon, 1953).

GELDENHUYS, NORVAL, *Supreme Authority* (Marshall, Morgan & Scott, 1953).

GOUDGE, H. L., *2 Corinthians* (*WC*) (Methuen, 1927).

GUTHRIE, DONALD, *New Testament Introduction* (Tyndale, 1970).

HARRIS, MURRAY J., *2 Corinthians* (*EBC*) (Zondervan, 1976).

HENRY, MATTHEW, *Commentary on the Holy Bible* (various editions).

HODGE, A. A., *The Confession of Faith* (Banner of Truth, 1958).

HODGE, CHARLES, *2 Corinthians* (Banner of Truth, 1959).

HUGHES, PHILIP E., *2 Corinthians* (*NICNT*) (Marshall, Morgan & Scott, 1961).

JENKYN, WILLIAM, *Exposition of the Epistle of Jude* (James & Klock, 1976).

KITTEL, G. AND FRIEDRICH, G., *Theological Dictionary of the New Testament*, vols. 1–10 (Eerdmans, 1964–1976) (translated by Geoffrey W. Bromiley; index by Ronald E. Pitkin).

LENSKI, R. C. H., *The Interpretation of 1 & 2 Corinthians* (Augsburg, 1961).

LIGHTFOOT, J. B., *Notes on the Epistles of St Paul* (Zondervan, 1957).

MACHEN, J. G., *The Origin of Paul's Religion* (Eerdmans, 1925).

MARTIN, R. P. (contributor), *Daily Bible Commentary*, 4 (Scripture Union, 1974).

MARTIN, R. P. (contributor), *New Testament Foundations – 2* (Paternoster, 1978).

MASSIE, J., *1 & 2 Corinthians (CB)* (Caxton, n.d.).

MEETER, JOHN E. (Editor), *The Shorter Writings of B. B. Warfield,* vol. 1 (Presbyterian & Reformed, 1970).

MENZIES, ALLAN, *2 Corinthians* (Macmillan, 1912).

MURRAY, JOHN, *Redemption – Accomplished and Applied* (Banner of Truth, 1961)

—— *Collected Writings,* vol. 1 (Banner of Truth, 1976).

—— *Collected Writings,* vol. 2 (Banner of Truth, 1977).

PINK, ARTHUR W., *Gleanings from Paul* (Moody, 1967).

PLUMMER, ALFRED, *2 Corinthians (ICC)* (T. & T. Clark, 1915).

POOLE, MATTHEW, *A Commentary on the Holy Bible,* vol. 3 (Banner of Truth, 1963).

RIDDERBOS, HERMAN, *Paul and Jesus* (Presbyterian & Reformed, 1957).

ROBINSON, J. ARMITAGE, *St Paul's Epistle to the Ephesians* (James Clarke, n.d.).

SMEATON, GEORGE, *The Apostles' Doctrine of the Atonement* (Banner of Truth, 1991).

SOUTER, A., *A Pocket Lexicon to the Greek New Testament* (Oxford, 1956)

TASKER, R. V. G., *2 Corinthians (TNTC)* (Tyndale, 1958).

TASKER, R. V. G., *The Old Testament in the New Testament* (SCM, 1946)

TRAPP, JOHN, *Commentary on the New Testament* (Sovereign Grace, 1958).

TRENCH, R. C., *Synonyms of the New Testament* (James Clarke, 1961).

VINCENT, MARVIN R., *Word Studies in the New Testament* (Macdonald, n.d.).

VINE, W. E., *Expository Dictionary of New Testament Words* (Oliphants, 1958).

VOS, GEERHARDUS, *Biblical Theology* (Banner of Truth, 1975).

—— *Pauline Eschatology* (Eerdmans, 1961).

WAND, J. W. C., *A History of the Early Church* (Methuen, 1937).

WAITE, JOSEPH, *2 Corinthians (Speaker's Commentary)* (John Murray, 1881).

Galatians

INTRODUCTION

*T*he identity of the Galatians is a relatively modern problem, for among ancient interpreters it was universally assumed that they were a people of Celtic descent who lived in that part of Asia Minor which once formed the old kingdom of Galatia. But it is doubtful whether Paul penetrated so far north as Ancyra (now Ankara), Tavium, or even Pessinus, and we have no record that any churches were founded in those regions. Most scholars therefore now think, thanks largely to the work of Sir William Ramsay, that Paul uses the term to designate the existing Roman province of Galatia, which included those towns in the south which he and Barnabas had visited on the first missionary journey [*Acts* 13–14].

If this view, commonly known as the South Galatian theory, is accepted it becomes possible to date the letter before the Council of Jerusalem [*Acts* 15]. It is suggested that Paul wrote it either on his return to Syrian Antioch, or even perhaps while actually *en route* to the Council in AD 48 or 49. This would make the Epistle to the Galatians the earliest of Paul's extant letters, and it is not without significance that its theme is in complete harmony with the principle so boldly enunciated in his first sermon to the Galatians at Pisidian Antioch [*Acts* 13:38, 39]. The advantage of adopting this early date is that by identifying Galatians 2:1ff. with the 'famine relief visit' of Acts 11:27–30 rather than with Paul's attendance at the Council, it avoids the difficulty of explaining why he did not appeal to a decision which would have settled the point at issue in the Galatian churches [*Acts* 15:19–29]. With his customary acumen Calvin regarded this difficulty as the conclusive reason for maintaining that the Epistle was written before that Council was held.

Thus we arrive at the following probable sequence of events. When Paul had worked with Barnabas for about a year in Antioch [*Acts*

11:26], they were commissioned by the church there to carry the famine relief fund to Jerusalem. In the course of this visit the Jerusalem apostles fully recognized that Paul and Barnabas had a divine vocation to take the gospel to the Gentiles [*Gal.* 2:1–10]. Some time later they were sent out by the church at Antioch on the first Gentile mission during which they established churches at Pisidian Antioch, Iconium, Lystra, and Derbe. Shortly after their return to Syrian Antioch, the misguided enthusiasm for the law shown by certain emissaries from the Jerusalem church caused a breach in table-fellowship between Jewish and Gentile believers so that even Peter and Barnabas no longer deemed it expedient to eat with the Gentiles. Although in itself this seemed a small matter, Paul had no hesitation in publicly opposing such a separation, for he could see that nothing less than the gospel was at stake [*Gal.* 2:11–14]. As if this were not enough, Paul now learned that Judaizers had also appeared among his recently won converts in Galatia demanding their submission to all the requirements of the law including circumcision. In the Galatian Epistle Paul personally combats this subversive teaching, and not long afterwards the Council of Jerusalem officially outlawed it, but to win the victory over legalism was to cost the apostle a life-long struggle against these 'zealots for the law', whose ubiquitous activities threatened to stifle the faith of the infant church.

Of the Epistle's importance there is happily no doubt whatever, for as Luther so rightly insisted, the mastery of its message is basic to a true understanding of the Christian faith. In this brief letter there is distilled for us the quintessence of Paul's gospel. Here we are brought face to face with a man whose burning words express the measure of his care for the purity of that gospel and for the safety of his readers. And in days of widespread doctrinal decline we would do well to remember that there can be no genuine pastoral concern for the souls of men without a similar zeal to maintain and defend 'the faith which was once for all delivered unto the saints' [*Jude* 3].

CHAPTER ONE

In this letter Paul's salutation is notable for the omission of his customary thanksgiving, and for the emphasis he places on the divine commissioning which made him an apostle of God's grace [verses 1–5]. He at once expresses his surprise that the Galatians are so quickly deserting the truth for the false gospel of the Judaizers, and twice pronounces his solemn anathema on anyone who preaches another gospel [verses 6–9]. As Christ's servant, he is no man-pleaser since he received neither the gospel nor his office from men, but immediately from God [verses 10–12]. He could receive nothing from Christians before his conversion, because his zeal for the traditions of the fathers made him a bitter persecutor of the church. And when it pleased God to reveal his Son in him, he did not seek the approval or advice of the Jerusalem apostles, but went to Arabia and Damascus [verses 13–17]. When he visited Jerusalem three years later, he had stayed a fortnight with Peter, but did not then meet any other apostle except James the Lord's brother. And his subsequent departure for Syria and Cilicia meant that he had no personal contact with the Christians of Judæa, who nevertheless glorified God for turning their former persecutor into a preacher of the gospel [verses 18–24].

1: Paul, an apostle (not from men, neither through man, but through Jesus Christ, and God the Father, who raised him from the dead),

Paul, an apostle (not from men, neither through man: As the Judaizers had discredited Paul's teaching and gained the ear of the Galatians for their false gospel by denying the divine origin of his apostleship, this fiery letter to his fickle converts aptly begins with an emphatic assertion of the unique authority of his commission. With his third word, 'not', he launches into his sustained polemic. His calling was neither from men as an *ultimate* nor through man as a *mediate* authority, for no human source or agency could have given him that infallible authority which was his as an apostle of Christ. Mere men cannot make an apostle, and no human representative can convey the grace and gifts which the office demands. This is sufficient to explode the myth of apostolic succession so carefully cherished by the Papacy, since 'it is the property of an Apostle to be called immediately by Jesus Christ, hence it follows, that the authority, Office, and function of Apostles ceased with them, and did not pass by succession to any other' (William Perkins).

But through Jesus Christ, and God the Father: The fact that a single preposition ('through') is here used to govern both nouns indicates that Paul conceived of Jesus Christ and God the Father as together sustaining the one supreme source of his apostolic authority. No higher source of authority could be envisaged, while all thought of any lower intermediary is ruled out.

Who raised him from the dead: The exceptional character of his ministry was born of this conviction which had been indelibly stamped upon his heart by that divine encounter on the road to Damascus. 'As surely as God the Father had raised His Son Jesus from the dead and given Him glory, so surely had the glorified Jesus revealed Himself to Saul His persecutor to make him His Apostle' (G. G. Findlay). Thus it was by the sheer supernaturalism of his calling that he differed from the rest of the apostles. For they were appointed by Christ during the time of his humiliation, whereas Paul had received his commission from the exalted and glorified Christ.

2: and all the brethren that are with me, unto the churches of Galatia:

The brethren who are with Paul as he writes were evidently his fellow missionaries. They share in full measure his anxiety to recover the Galatians from their apostasy. He says 'all the brethren' to express their unanimity in the faith, yet avoids naming them in case his readers should think that the validity of his message depended upon their support. And it is in keeping with his insistence upon the independence of his apostleship of men that he adheres to the first person singular throughout this letter [cf. *1 Thess.* 1, 2: 'Paul and Silvanus and Timothy . . . *we* give thanks to God']. The curtness of his address is remarkable and reflects his anger at their swift defection from the one true gospel. For though he still calls them 'churches', their corrupted faith is unworthy of any commendation. The plural shows that this was a circular letter, and according to the South Galatian theory (see Introduction), the churches to which it was sent were those at Pisidian Antioch, Iconium, Lystra, and Derbe.

3: Grace to you and peace from God the Father, and our Lord Jesus Christ,

'In this Pauline greeting, "grace" designates the undeserved favour of God, and "peace" the profound well-being of the soul which is the result of it' (J. G. Machen). This characteristic salutation therefore served to remind these erring Galatians of what they once gladly confessed. Grace alone had given them peace with God, a peace which they had put at risk by their dangerous dalliance with legalism. For the compromise of grace always leads to the forfeiture of peace. Hence they must learn afresh that it took nothing less and required nothing more than the achievement of 'grace' so freely conferred upon the undeserving, to give the assurance of an interest in that 'peace' with God which was purchased by the blood of Christ [Eph. 2:11–18].

From God our Father, and the Lord Jesus Christ (ASV margin): The reading 'our' is probably to be preferred here [cf. NIV]. Once again the use of a single preposition ('from') presents God the Father and Christ the Lord as the sole source of this 'grace' and 'peace'. This not only places them on the same plane of divine equality, but also underlines the fact that the knowledge of God as 'our' Father is inseparably conjoined with the redemptive mediation of the Lord Jesus Christ.

4: who gave himself for our sins, that he might deliver us out of this present evil world, according to the will of our God and Father:

Who gave himself for our sins: This unusual extension of the greeting is an arresting announcement of the theme of the Epistle and the purpose of the gospel. It was to save sinners that Christ freely gave himself up to the suffering and death of the cross. The magnitude of the sacrifice which our sins called forth manifests the supreme folly of looking elsewhere for their forgiveness. It is high time the Galatians made up their minds concerning the sufficiency of Christ's sacrifice to save them from their sins, and that without the addition of their obedience to the superseded rites of the Mosaic law. Paul would have them know that his gospel – the free justification of the sinner through Christ crucified – means nothing to those for whom it does not mean everything. For as there were no half-measures in the sacrificial self-giving of Christ, so there can be no half-hearted acceptance of the message of salvation [*Gal.* 2:21; 3:1]. 'The Judaizers are dead and gone, but not the issue that they raised. Faith or works – that is as much as ever a living issue . . . Paul in Galatians was fighting the age-long battle of the Christian Church. "Just as I am, without one plea but that thy blood was shed for me" – these words would never have been written if the Judaizers had won' (J. G. Machen, *The New Testament*, pp. 129–130).

To rescue us from the present evil age (NIV): No mere pedlars of religious reforms could deliver mankind from its helpless bondage to the prince of darkness. It called for an Almighty Saviour to liberate those held captive by the entrenched powers of evil. As John Calvin says, this one word 'evil' is a thunderbolt which lays low all human pride. For 'apart from the renewal brought about by the grace of Christ, there is nothing in us but unmixed wickedness. We are of the world, and until Christ rescues us from it, the world reigns in us and we live unto it'. This rescue does not immediately remove believers from what is now an alien environment; it is rather a spiritual emancipation from any part in the curse, character, and condemnation that belongs to the present age [*John* 17:15; *1 John* 2:15, 16]. Christ thus sacrificed himself for our sins, so that we might be rescued from our bondage to an evil world [cf. 4:9; 5:1].

According to the will of our God and Father: There is nothing fortuitous in this deliverance because it is the historical outworking of the eternal purpose of him who is at once our God and Father. 'Therefore we have not been delivered by our own will or exertion [*Rom.* 9:16] or by our own wisdom or decision; we have been delivered because God has had mercy on us and has loved us. As it is written in another passage [*John* 1:13]: "Who were born, not of blood nor of the will of the flesh nor of the will of man, but of God". It is by grace, then, and not by our merit that we have been delivered from this present evil world' (Martin Luther).

5: to whom be the glory for ever and ever. Amen.

It is in this letter alone that Paul finds himself unable to add any word of thanksgiving for the faith of his readers [verse 6]. Instead he concludes his greeting with a fervent ascription of praise to God for that glory which essentially belongs to him and which therefore must endure throughout the endless ages of eternity. By inviting the Galatians to join in this adoration, the final 'Amen' virtually becomes a summons to return to the faith from which they had so quickly declined.

6: I marvel that ye are so quickly removing from him that called you in the grace of Christ unto a different gospel; 7: which is not another gospel; only there are some that trouble you, and would pervert the gospel of Christ.

I am astonished that you are so quickly deserting him who called you in the grace of Christ and turning to a different gospel – not that there is another gospel (RSV): Paul is amazed to learn that the Galatians are forsaking the gospel so quickly after their conversion. As he writes they are in the very act of turning from it, and the urgency of his address is dictated by the hope of bringing them to a better mind before the process of apostasy is complete. To recover them from the brink of spiritual disaster, it was necessary to show them the true nature of their defection. This was no less than a deserting of 'him' (the Galatians know very well that he means 'God') who is the author of that call which came to them through the preaching of the apostle. But the distinctive feature of the gospel which they had inexcusably overlooked is that this calling by God to salvation is ever and only 'in the grace of Christ'.

Thus the essence of their folly was that they were guilty of 'abandoning the position of grace, i.e., the relation towards God which made them the objects of the grace of Christ and participators in its benefits, to put themselves under law, which could only award them their sad deserts' (Ernest De Witt Burton). They were forfeiting these inestimable privileges by turning to a *different* gospel. Such a gospel is really no gospel at all, for though it assumes the name of gospel it is so completely emptied of any power to save that it is of an entirely different kind from the one authentic gospel preached by Paul.

Only there are some that trouble you, and would pervert the gospel of Christ: These Judaizers have successfully infiltrated the churches of Galatia by dignifying a different doctrine with the name of gospel, but to receive another gospel is to embrace another faith [*2 Cor.* 11:4]. Although the Galatians have not yet succumbed to this false teaching, Paul lets them know that they are being confused and unsettled by those who wished so completely to change the character of Christ's gospel that it no longer belonged to him. Since 'the gospel preached by them was conformity to the Mosaic ritual, it was in antagonism to that gospel which has Christ for its theme, for by its perversion it would render "Christ of none effect". Whatever would derogate from the sufficiency of Christ's gospel, or hamper its freeness, is a subversion of it, no matter what guise it may assume, or how insignificant the addition or subtraction may seem' (John Eadie).

8: But though we, or an angel from heaven, should preach unto you any gospel other than that which we preached unto you, let him be anathema.

But even if we, or an angel from heaven, should preach to you a gospel contrary to that which we preached to you (RSV): As God is the author of the gospel, so gospel authority is never inherent but always derived. It is only as the messenger remains faithful to the divine message that he speaks with divine authority. Neither Paul nor his colleagues are free to alter the message they were commissioned to declare. Hence even if they, or indeed an angel from heaven itself, should present the Galatians with a gospel whose content was contrary to that which they had preached to them, they could not hope to escape the divine 'anathema'. The word literally means 'devoted', but it is used here in the bad sense of being devoted to destruction [cf. *Deut.* 7:26].

Let him be accursed (RSV): i.e. by God and as such rejected with abhorrence by all true believers. No words could more plainly exhibit the awful doom that must overtake anyone, whether apostle or angel, who takes it upon himself to preach as God's message of salvation what is in fact a complete perversion of the one true gospel. As no crime is worse than this, so no judgment is heavier. But this 'will not justify our thundering out anathemas against those who differ from us in lesser things. It is only against those who forge a new gospel, who overturn the foundation of the covenant of grace, by setting up the works of the law in the place of Christ's righteousness, and corrupting Christianity with Judaism, that Paul denounces this' (Matthew Henry).

9: As we have said before, so say I now again, If any man preacheth unto you any gospel other than that which ye received, let him be anathema.

As we have said before, so say I now again: This is a reminder that they had been warned on a previous occasion against giving heed to false teaching, probably on his return visit when Barnabas was his companion [*Acts* 14:21ff]. 'It is therefore no surprise to Paul to learn, as he does now, that Judaistic propaganda is going on in Galatia: what does surprise him, as he says in verse 6, is that it is achieving so immediate and so signal a success' (G. S. Duncan).

If anyone is preaching to you a gospel contrary to that which you received, let him be accursed (RSV): In passing from an improbable supposition [verse 8] to a condition of reality, Paul does not shrink from applying the same divine sentence of condemnation to what is now actually taking place in Galatia. He might well marvel that they should be so willing to listen to a message which was a flagrant contradiction of the gracious good news they had heard and received from him. Only those who are blind to the glory of the gospel and the seriousness of the situation blame the apostle for the severity of his language. 'As there is only one God, so there can be only one gospel. If God has really done something in Christ on which the salvation of the world depends, and if He has made it known, then it is a Christian duty to be intolerant of everything which ignores, denies, or explains it away. The man who perverts it is the worst enemy of God and men' (James Denney, *The Death of Christ*, p. 66).

10: For am I now seeking the favour of men, or of God? or am I striving to please men? if I were still pleasing men, I should not be a servant of Christ.

'For' advances the reason for this severity. Evidently the Judaizers had represented him as a man who had no scruples in relaxing what they regarded as the essential requirements of the gospel in order to gain Gentile converts more easily. But surely no one who is intent on currying favour with men approaches them with anathemas! Is the man who utters such strictures really the ingratiating compromiser his opponents make him out to be? Then let the Galatians acknowledge that he never seeks the favour of *men* at the cost of losing the approval of GOD. As Bengel tersely comments: 'Regard is to be had to God alone.'

If I were still pleasing men, I should not be a servant of Christ: If, while Paul claimed to be the bondservant of a Master to whom he owed absolute obedience he nevertheless sought to please men, his devotion to Christ would be no more real than the sham service of his accusers [cf. 6:12, 13]. 'No one can serve Him who makes it his study to be popular with men. For to His servant His will is the one law, His work the one service, His example the one pattern, His approval the continuous aim, and His final acceptance the one great hope' (Eadie) [*Matt.* 6:24].

11: For I make known to you, brethren, as touching the gospel which was preached by me, that it is not after man.

In still addressing the erring Galatians as his 'brethren' (nine times in this Epistle), Paul appeals to that bond of union which was forged between them through the preaching and receiving of the gospel of God's grace. If he finds it necessary to make known to them what they already know, it is because they are now listening to an entirely different message which has made them forget the distinctive character of this gospel. In contrast to those who had followed him, the gospel preached by Paul is not 'after man'. It was not invented or developed by man, but is as supernatural in its origin as it is in its effects [3:2]. 'It is above man's devising, to be received and handed on in its integrity, neither diminished nor increased' (A. Lukyn Williams).

12: For neither did I receive it from man, nor was I taught it, but it came to me through revelation of Jesus Christ.

It would seem that the apostle's critics in Galatia had charged him with claiming an authority he did not possess, for they said that he preached only a garbled version of the gospel which he had received at second-hand. But Paul insists that his gospel was not 'from man', because it had not come to him through any human intermediary; it was neither transmitted by tradition, nor conveyed by instruction. On the contrary, the gospel came to Paul through the transforming experience of an immediate revelation of the Risen Christ. It was this divine disclosure which convinced the erstwhile persecutor that the object of his hatred had been none other than the Son of God himself! [*Acts* 9:5] Thus he received the gospel, of whom Christ is the sum and substance, and the commission to preach it, in that moment when his soul was illuminated by the blinding vision of his Conqueror [1:16].

13: For ye have heard of my manner of life in time past in the Jews' religion, how that beyond measure I persecuted the church of God, and made havoc of it:

Paul's third 'for' [verses 10, 12] introduces evidence to prove that there was nothing in his former career which predisposed him towards the faith he now proclaimed. The Galatians had heard, probably in the first place from his own lips, of his boundless persecuting zeal against those whom he once regarded as the guilty followers of a blasphemous impostor, but who were in fact those whom he had come to recognize as the true people (*ekklesia*) *of God*. Paul's use of the expression here shows that he had not only learned to think of each local assembly of believers as 'the church of God' in that particular place, but had also already learned to regard the entire body of believers as constituting the one universal church. Hence this was the term 'which came most naturally to his lips when he was speaking of his persecution of the Christians' (Burton). His application of this title to believers further shows that he already regarded them as the chosen people of God, and this indicates 'how fully, in his thought, the Christian church had succeeded to the position once occupied by Israel' (Burton) – [cf. 6:16].

Nothing short of a divine intervention could have turned such an audacious opponent into an outspoken champion of the faith he had tried so hard to destroy [*Acts* 8:3; 9:1, 13, 14; 22:4, 5; 26:10,11]. The implied contrast between his former practice and his present faith is significant because it shows that Christianity was no offshoot of Judaism. The gospel he presented to the Galatians could not have sprung from the religion of petrified legalism he had renounced; it was the proper development of that Old Testament hope which was fulfilled in the Messiah whom Judaism had seen fit to reject.

14: and I advanced in the Jews' religion beyond many of mine own age among my countrymen, being more exceedingly zealous for the traditions of my fathers.

This violent fanaticism was the expression of Paul's zeal for the traditions of Judaism, in devotion to which he outstripped all his contemporaries [*Phil.* 3:4– 6]. These traditions were those rules and regulations which purported to interpret the law of God, but which had really corrupted it into a crippling system of moral casuistry [cf. *Matt.* 5:21ff.; 15:3, 6; 23:1ff.]. Thus for as long as he followed the traditions of his fathers, he remained a stranger to Israel's ancestral *faith* and the avowed enemy of the Deliverer upon whom it was centred [4:4, 5]. When therefore conversion to Christ made so ardent a Jew as Paul break with this religion, how could the Gentile Galatians imagine that submission to its demands was necessary to complete the gospel?

15: But when it was the good pleasure of God, who separated me, even from my mother's womb, and called me through his grace, 16: to reveal his Son in me, that I might preach him among the Gentiles;

As Bengel well says, 'The *good pleasure* of God is the farthest point which a man can reach, when inquiring as to the causes of his salvation'. Thus it was only when the time of God's antecedent purpose of grace was fulfilled that Paul was called to salvation and service. His furious career as a persecutor was then abruptly terminated and the whole course of his life entirely changed [verse 16b.f]. The fact that Paul's calling meant a complete upheaval in his life sharply distinguishes him from the other apostles, who did not have to make such radical break with their past.

Moreover, they came to complete commitment to Christ 'only after much vacillation and a long course of instruction by Him. In the case of Paul we find no evidence of either vacillation or instruction' (K. Rengstorf, *TDNT*, Vol. I, p. 438). The apostle's affinity with Jeremiah probably here leads him consciously to adopt the prophet's language in describing his own call to service [cf. *Jer.* 1:5]. Paul is affirming his independence of men. His commission is neither derived from men nor subject to their control, for before he was even born God had set him apart to preach the gospel to the Gentiles!

To reveal his son in me: There is always an *objective* element in revelation without which it would be nothing more than a formless mysticism. For Saul this was the real appearance of the Risen Christ on the Damascus road; for us it is the record of the same Christ as infallibly revealed in the inspired Scripture. But the *subjective* appropriation of this revelation of the Son of God always calls for the inward penetration of the Spirit. For 'no man can say that Jesus is Lord but by the Holy Spirit, [*1 Cor.* 12:3]. Hence Paul does not merely say that it pleased God to reveal his Son 'to me' but 'in me' [*2 Cor.* 4:6].

That I might preach him among the Gentiles: The Christ who was privately revealed to Paul now had to be publicly proclaimed by him among the Gentiles. There is no preaching that is worthy of the name unless Christ is set forth in all the glory of his Person and all the fullness of his saving power. '*In this encounter with the person of the exalted Christ is to be found the starting point of Paul's apostolic preaching, as well as the real significance of his conversion, and it is this confrontation to which he appeals again and again to justify his preaching of Christ*' (Herman Ridderbos, *Paul and Jesus*, p. 46).

16b: straightway I conferred not with flesh and blood: 17: neither went I up to Jerusalem to them that were apostles before me: but I went away into Arabia; and again I returned unto Damascus.

Having received such a revelation from *God*, Paul at once decided that he would not consult with mere 'flesh and blood', an expression emphasizing the weakness and frailty of *men;* 'whose intelligence is limited and their counsel moulded by the constitution of their material clothing' (J. A. Beet). Indeed so far was he from acknowledging any dependence upon the authority of the Jerusalem church that he did not even go to visit those who were, in point of time but not of standing, apostles before him. For what Paul needed was not conference with men but communion with God, and so after only a few days [cf. *Acts* 9:19: 'certain days'] with the disciples in Damascus he travelled east to seek the solitude of the Nabatean desert. It is probable that his stay there was comparatively short, for on his return to Damascus he entered upon an extended period of evangelistic activity [*Acts* 9:20; cf. verse 23: 'many days'].

18: Then after three years I went up to Jerusalem to visit Cephas, and tarried with him fifteen days.

Then: The pointed repetition of this word draws attention to certain salient incidents which show the real nature of Paul's relations with the church in Jerusalem: 'his first introduction to them [verse 18], his departure to a distant sphere of labour [verse 21], and his return to Jerusalem with Barnabas [2:1]' (Frederic Rendall).

What Paul is concerned to stress is that it was not until *three years* after his conversion that he went up to Jerusalem to meet Peter with whom he spent *fifteen days.* After having exercised an independent commission for three years his visit was too late to seek Jerusalem's recognition of his calling, and it was too short for him to be looked upon as Peter's disciple. But the fact that Paul did not receive his *gospel* from an acknowledged superior does not mean that he failed to receive any part of the *gospel-tradition* from an honoured colleague. No doubt it was during this visit that he heard of the resurrection appearances to Peter and James from their own lips (cf. F. F. Bruce, *Tradition Old and New*, p. 32). He makes no mention of the advocacy of Barnabas which secured this introduction, for it had no bearing on his inner convictions regarding the reality of his apostleship [cf. *Acts* 9:26–29]. Paul's argument is that he 'enjoys the same apostolic authority as those who were apostles before him [*Gal.* 1:17], because he, like them, received his commission and his gospel directly from the Lord' (G. E. Ladd, 'Revelation and Tradition in Paul': *Apostolic History and the Gospel,* p. 230).

19: But other of the apostles saw I none, save James the Lord's brother.

The only other apostle whom Paul met on his first visit to Jerusalem after his conversion was James the Lord's brother. Although James was not a believer during the public ministry [*John* 7:5], a particular appearance of the Risen Lord was the means of his conversion [*1 Cor.* 15:7], and he was now one of the 'pillars' [2:9] of the church in Jerusalem. The only sensible explanation of the word 'brother' is that this James was the son of Mary by Joseph [*Matt.* 1:25], and therefore the Lord's younger brother [cf. *Mark* 6:3].

'Can we characterize it otherwise than as a contumacious setting up of an artificial tradition above the written Word, if we insist upon it that "brother" must mean, not brother, but either cousin or one who is no blood-relation at all; that "first-born" does not imply other children subsequently born; that the limit fixed to separation does not imply subsequent union?' (J. B. Mayor, *The Epistle of St James,* p. lv).

20: Now touching the things which I write unto you, behold, before God, I lie not.

Such a solemn confirmation of the truthfulness of this account would not have been necessary unless the Galatians had been told a very different story. 'It would seem that a totally different account of his visits to Jerusalem after his conversion, and of the relation he sustained to the elder apostles, had been in use among the Judaists, to undermine his independent authority and neutralize his teaching' (Eadie).

21: Then I came into the regions of Syria and Cilicia.

Paul did not spend the whole fortnight in conversation with Peter! He preached so boldly in the city that he again put his life in jeopardy [*Acts* 9:28, 29]. At this time the Lord appeared to Paul in a vision, and told him to leave Jerusalem for the Jews there would not receive his testimony, 'And he said unto me, Depart: for I will send thee forth far hence unto the Gentiles' [*Acts* 22:17–21]. It was therefore in accordance with this divine commission that Paul departed for regions far removed from the influence of the Jerusalem apostles [*Acts* 9:30, 11:25, 26]. 'The name of Syria is placed before Cilicia, though the ministry at Tarsus preceded at Antioch: for the latter was by far the more important and prolonged ministry. A further reason for placing Syria first was the subordinate position of Cilicia: for Roman Cilicia was, like Judaea, only a district of the great province of Syria, separately administered by an imperial procurator at Tarsus' (Rendall).

22: And I was still unknown by face unto the churches of Judaea which were in Christ:

Because of this swift departure for distant places Paul remained personally unknown to the churches in Judaea (as distinguished from the church in Jerusalem), though they had heard much of him [verse 23]. The fact that Paul was at once called to labour elsewhere took away all semblance of dependence upon the Jerusalem apostles, for had he worked under their direction he would have become a well-known figure among the Christians of Judaea.

In Christ: This is what distinguishes the Christian church from the Jewish synagogue. Either a church *in* Christ or *no* church! Paul emphasizes the relationship which makes the church what it is: the body of Christ [*Eph.* 1:22, 23].

23: but they only heard say, He that once persecuted us now preacheth the faith of which he once made havoc; 24: and they glorified God in me.

Thus hearsay was Paul's only link with the Judaean Christians. Reports kept reaching them of how he who was once notorious for his persecution of believers was now famous for preaching the faith he had vainly attempted to suppress. 'It is a striking proof of the large space occupied by "faith" in the mind of the infant Church, that it should so soon have passed into a synonym for the Gospel. See *Acts* 6:7' (J. B. Lightfoot).

As they kept hearing reports of Paul's missionary work, so they kept on glorifying *God* (placed last for emphasis) as the evident Author of this amazing transformation *in* Paul. When those who had only suffered from the attentions of a persecutor recognized the hand of God in his ministry, how could those who had only benefited from the labours of an apostle even begin to doubt it? Moreover, the acknowledgement that the faith Paul now preached was the same as their own showed that the pseudo-faith of the Judaizers was not the apostolic faith of the church.

CHAPTER TWO

On Paul's second visit to Jerusalem fourteen years later he was accompanied by Barnabas, and Titus, who, though a Greek, was not circumcised despite the pressure of the Judaizers. For Paul was determined to maintain the freedom of Gentile converts from the bondage of the law [verses 1–5]. As for the Jerusalem apostles they added nothing to Paul's ministry, and their recognition of his mission to the Gentiles clearly showed that they regarded him as an equal partner in the Lord's work [verses 6–10]. Paul gave further proof of his apostolic authority when he publicly rebuked Peter at Antioch for his inconsistent separation from the Gentiles [verses 11–14]. He took this stand because he saw that Jews who were saved by faith in Christ could not ask Gentiles to place any reliance on the law for their acceptance with God. Union with Christ means that Paul's obedience is secured through faith in the Son of God who loved him and gave himself for him. But to seek righteousness by the law is a denial of God's grace and makes Christ's death a thing of nought [verses 15–21].

1: Then after the space of fourteen years I went up again to Jerusalem with Barnabas, taking Titus also with me.

When Paul was next in Jerusalem he had been an apostle for fourteen years. Two brief contacts in fourteen years hardly proved his alleged dependence upon the authority of the Jerusalem church! As the second visit took place in AD 46, this would suggest AD 33 as the probable date of his conversion according to the ancient 'inclusive' system of reckoning. 'The grand moment of his life was his conversion, and it became the point from which dates were unconsciously measured – all before it fading away as old and legal, all after it standing out in new and spiritual prominence ... Had this verse occurred immediately after 1:18, we might have said that the fourteen years dated from the first visit to Jerusalem; but a paragraph intervenes which obscures the reference, and describes some time spent and some journeys made in various places. It is natural, therefore, to suppose, that after a digressive insertion the apostle recurs to the original point of calculation – his conversion' (Eadie).

I went up again to Jerusalem with Barnabas: This must refer to the projected 'famine relief visit' of *Acts* 11:29f. and its later accomplishment, *Acts* 12:25. Calvin saw clearly that it could not be identified with the visit to attend the Council of Jerusalem recorded in *Acts* 15, and therefore judged that the Epistle was written before it was held. For he said, Paul 'would never have alluded to that journey, undertaken with the consent of all believers, without mentioning its occasion and its memorable outcome'. Barnabas had been sent by the Jerusalem church to investigate the thriving work among the Gentiles at Syrian Antioch. On seeing much evidence of the grace of God in their midst, he determined to seek the assistance of Paul whom he brought from Tarsus. Their first opportunity to report on the progress of the Gentile mission came when they were entrusted to bring this gift from the 'Christians' of Antioch [*Acts* 11:19–30].

Taking Titus also with me: The presence of Titus was to give rise to a debate, the importance of which was out of all proportion to his subordinate position in the party. For he was a Gentile, and perhaps Paul took him along to see whether brotherly love for a fellow-believer would triumph over Jewish prejudice.

2: And I went up by revelation; and I laid before them the gospel which I preach among the Gentiles but privately before them who were of repute, lest by any means I should be running, or had run, in vain.

It was in consequence of a revelation that I went up at all (Moffatt): As it took a vision to make Paul leave Jerusalem [*Acts* 22:21], so it required a similar revelation from the Lord to induce him to return. He was no stranger to such revelations, for the Lord who called him, also constantly guided him in the way he should go. Perhaps this was made known to him through the prophecy of Agabus [*Acts* 11:28], though a direct revelation seems more probable. What Paul wants the Galatians to know is that it was not with any feeling of dependence that he went up to this earthly seat of power and influence, for the source of his authority, no less than that of the other apostles, was Jerusalem above.

And I set before them the gospel which I preach among the Gentiles – privately, I mean, to the 'men of repute' among them (Bruce): Compare also NEB. Although other business had brought Paul to Jerusalem, he welcomed the opportunity privately to acquaint the leaders of the church with the exact nature of the message he had always preached, and still did preach among the Gentiles. It is not likely that Paul would have submitted his gospel for the approval of the *members* of the Jerusalem church, though it was necessary to secure the sanction of its *leaders*; not to validate his message, but to avoid the tragedy of a split between the Gentile and Jewish wings of the church. In itself there is nothing ironical in the term 'men of repute', but its repeated use in this passage [verse 6] suggests an awareness of the exaggerated esteem in which these men were held by the Judaizers, who had probably told the Galatians that Paul was not one of the 'pillar' apostles [verse 9].

Lest by any means I should be running, or had run, in vain: The stadium foot race is one of Paul's favourite metaphors when speaking of his apostolic calling [*1 Cor.* 9:24, 26; *Phil.* 2:16; *2 Tim.* 4:7]. He feared that his strenuous missionary efforts would be in vain if the authorities in Jerusalem failed to endorse the 'free' gospel the Gentiles had received from him. For to insist upon Gentile compliance with the demands of the ceremonial law would in effect introduce them to 'another' gospel [1:7].

> **3: But not even Titus who was with me, being a Greek, was compelled to be circumcised: 4: and that because of the false brethren privily brought in, who came in privily to spy out our liberty which we have in Christ Jesus, that they might bring us into bondage: 5: to whom we gave place in the way of subjection, no, not for an hour; that the truth of the gospel might continue with you.**

But even Titus, who was with me, was not compelled to be circumcised, though he was a Greek (RSV): It was not to be expected that Paul's choice of an uncircumcised Greek for his companion would meet with universal approval in Jerusalem. Thus the presence of Titus constituted a test-case, and the fact that he was not compelled to be circumcised, though this was strongly pressed by the Judaizers, really amounted to a declaration of principle. 'The apostle is showing that he had not laboured in vain, – that the very point which characterized his gospel was gained, that point being the free admission of uncircumcised Gentiles into the church; for even in Jerusalem the circumcision of Titus was successfully resisted, – the enemy was worsted even in his citadel' (Eadie).

But because of false brethren (RSV): Paul's meaning is plain enough, though the connection is broken under the stress of emotion. The Jerusalem apostles are not the culprits who caused this controversy, but certain false brethren ('sham-Christians', NEB) whose representations may well have caused these 'pillars' to waver, not realizing that a vital principle was at stake. As Lightfoot says, this view of the matter is 'consistent with the timid conduct of Peter at Antioch shortly after [2:11], and with the politic advice of James at a later date [*Acts* 21:20]. It was the natural consequence of their position, which led them to regard tenderly the scruples of the Jewish converts.'

Secretly brought in, who slipped in to spy out (RSV): 'The metaphor is that of spies or traitors introducing themselves by stealth into the enemy's camp . . . The camp thus stealthily entered is the Christian Church. Pharisees at heart, these traitors assume the name and garb of believers' (Lightfoot).

Our freedom which we have in Christ Jesus (RSV): Not merely freedom from the Mosaic ritual, but included within it justification by faith without the deeds of the law. 'Its element of being is "in Christ Jesus", not by Him though He did secure it, but in Him through living faith, and in Him by fellowship with Him. By Him it was secured to us, but in Him we possess it' (Eadie).

That they might bring us into bondage (RSV): It was the intention of the Judaizers to bring all Gentile converts under the yoke of the law, but it was Paul alone who saw that the adoption of this error would reduce Christ's 'free men' to a condition of abject slavery [5:1].

To them we did not yield submission even for a moment, that the truth of the gospel might be preserved for you (RSV): Paul did not pause to deliberate the issue. His resistance to this demand was immediate and unyielding. He would not sacrifice 'the *truth* of the gospel' – the truth which is the gospel's distinctive element – simply to soothe the ruffled feelings of *false* brethren! Thus Titus the Greek was not circumcised so that the gospel might be preserved in its integrity for the Gentiles, including the Galatians ('you').

> **6: But from those who were reputed to be somewhat (whatsoever they were, it maketh no matter to me: God accepteth not man's person) – they, I say, who were of repute imparted nothing to me:**

And from those who were reputed to be something (RSV): Having dealt with the question of Titus, Paul takes up the thread of verse 2. But now the 'men of repute' have become 'those who are looked up to as authorities', a description that 'is depreciatory, not indeed of the Twelve themselves, but of the extravagant and exclusive claims set up for them by the Judaizers' (Lightfoot).

What they once were, it maketh no matter to me: God accepteth not man's person (ASV margin): The fact that these men had known Jesus 'after the flesh' [2 *Cor.* 5:16] made no difference to Paul, though it meant everything to his opponents, who were wholly preoccupied with an external glorying in the flesh [cf. 6:13]. 'Paul simply means that the noble position which the apostles held did not prevent his having been called by God and raised suddenly from being nothing to becoming their equal. Although the difference between them had been great, it was nothing in God's sight, for He does not accept persons and His calling is not influenced by any prejudice' (Calvin).

Those, I say, who were of repute added nothing to me (RSV): 'that is to say, they neither modified his teaching nor added to his authority' (W. E. Vine). When Paul laid before these 'authorities' the gospel he preached among the Gentiles, they accepted it without amendment or addition. This meant that in requiring the Galatians to submit to circumcision, the Judaizers were seeking to enforce what the Jerusalem apostles had never enjoined.

> **7: but contrariwise, when they saw that I had been intrusted with the gospel of the uncircumcision, even as Peter with the gospel of the circumcision**

But on the contrary when they saw that I had been entrusted with the gospel to the uncircumcised as Peter with the gospel to the circumcised (Burton): But far from condemning Paul's practice, the Jerusalem apostles endorsed it for they perceived that God had entrusted him with the task of taking the gospel to the Gentiles, even as Peter's sphere was to preach it to the Jews, though this was not a hard and fast division of labour [e.g. Acts 10:34ff.; 13:16ff.]. Jew and Gentile both received the *same* gospel, but 'circumcision formed the point of difference. The Jew might practise it, for it was a national rite; but it was not to be enforced on the Gentile' (Eadie).

8: (for he that wrought for Peter unto the apostleship of the circumcision wrought for me also unto the Gentiles);

For it was evident that the same God who worked by Peter in his mission to the Jews also worked by Paul in his mission to the Gentiles. In each case the manifestation of divine power was the incontrovertible proof of a divine commission. In thus reminding his converts of the effectiveness of his ministry, Paul tacitly rebukes them for their disloyalty in listening to the false claims of the Judaizers.

9: and when they perceived the grace that was given to me, James and Cephas and John, they who were reputed to be pillars, gave to me and Barnabas the right hands of fellowship, that we should go unto the Gentiles, and they unto the circumcision;

And when they perceived the grace that was given to me: At this momentous private meeting [verse 2] Paul's stirring exposition of his gospel evidently made a powerful impression upon these 'pillars' of the Jerusalem church. 'They came to a knowledge of the divine gift enjoyed by Paul, implying that they had not distinctly understood it before. If they added nothing to Paul [verse 6], he certainly added something to them' (Eadie). The undeserved favour of God to which Paul owed his commission is here underlined by his use of the word 'grace' [cf. *Eph.* 3:8].

James and Cephas and John, they who were reputed to be pillars: It is in accord with the important part that James [1:19] was later to play in the Council of Jerusalem that his name is placed first [*Acts* 15]. For while Peter was the leader in missionary work among the Jews, James seems to have early attained a position of great influence in the church at Jerusalem. As in the early chapters of Acts, John (mentioned only here in Paul's Epistle) again appears as Peter's associate. Paul recognizes these men to be *pillars,* 'being such as God made use of in the first founding and building of the gospel church; as also to bear it up', but qualifies this by the word *reputed,* 'because the false teachers had magnified their ministry, but disparaged his' (Matthew Poole).

Gave to me and Barnabas the right hands of fellowship: In a day when it is deemed expedient to suppress the truth in the interests of church unity, it is worth noting with J. G. Machen that it is only by having the gospel in common that there is any basis for fellowship at all. In extending the right hands of fellowship to Paul and Barnabas, the Jerusalem leaders acknowledged that they were serving the same Lord, and preaching the same gospel. Such mutual 'fellowship' in the gospel was indeed a far cry from the 'inferior' position assigned to Paul by the Judaizers!

That we should go unto the Gentiles, and they unto the circumcision: 'The so-called "division of labour" between Paul and the original apostles was not, strictly speaking, a division of labour at all; its purpose was not negative; it was not meant at all as a limitation of the field of one party or of the other; it did not mean that Paul was not to preach to Jews or that Peter was not to preach to Gentiles; it did not mean that Paul was not to preach in Palestine or that Peter was not to preach outside of Palestine. But it meant that so far, according to the plain meaning of God, Paul had been sent predominantly to the Gentiles and the original apostles to the Jews; and that, therefore, unless both Paul and the original apostles continued their work, the cause would suffer' (Machen).

10: Only they would that we should remember the poor; which very thing I was also zealous to do.

'Only' they said, 'please go on remembering the poor'; and in fact I had made a special point of attending to this very matter (Bruce): The only request made by these 'authorities' was that Paul and Barnabas should go on remembering the needs of the poor, which was the very thing that had brought them up to Jerusalem! [Acts 11:29ff.; 12:25] Although Gentile believers were generally poor, they were relatively better off than their Jewish brethren, whose economic distress was made worse by religious discrimination. Paul uses the singular pronoun 'I' because the point at issue in Galatia turned on what the Jerusalem apostles

had said to *him*, while the past tense ('had made') points back to the decision to send this aid, 'for though it was during the Jerusalem visit that the relief-work came to visible manifestation, the instigation of it lay in the past in Antioch' (Duncan).

11: But when Cephas came to Antioch, I resisted him to the face, because he stood condemned.

When Paul later returned to Antioch after the first missionary journey, he had to rebuke Peter publicly for the inconsistency of his conduct in hiding his real convictions [*Acts* 10:28], by which 'he stood quite self-condemned' (Bruce). 'In this debated matter of Gentile freedom, while others stumbled or advanced with unsteady step . . . Paul moved onwards without hesitation or pause, and by his single courage and consistency secured to the churches a liberty which, though it might be grudged or suspected in many quarters, could not be withdrawn, but has descended as an invaluable legacy to modern times. As he knew Peter's character, it must have cost him a pang to confront him whose name stands first in all the catalogues of the apostles; but the claims of truth were paramount' (Eadie).

12: For before that certain came from James, he ate with the Gentiles; but when they came, he drew back and separated himself, fearing them that were of the circumcision.

For before certain individuals from James arrived he had been in the habit of eating his meals with the Gentiles (W. Hendriksen): The arrival of envoys from James made Peter have second thoughts about the wisdom of openly fraternizing with the Gentile believers in Antioch. It seems that news of this had reached Jerusalem and was causing a grave scandal, especially since it had become known to unbelieving Jews in the city. James therefore appealed to Peter to desist from this practice to save further embarrassment to the church in Jerusalem. (So F. F. Bruce in *New Testament History*, p. 267). However, these men doubtless exceeded their brief when they insisted upon circumcision as a condition of salvation [*Acts* 15:1], for James would not have gone back on his earlier agreement with Paul [2:9].

But when they came he gradually drew back and separated himself (Burton): The tenses 'give a graphic picture of Peter's irresolute and tentative efforts to withdraw gradually from an intercourse that gave offence to the visitors' (Rendall). Under the influence of these representations Peter's loyalty to his convictions was worn away until he acted a part to save his reputation [verse 12]. So easily did the apostle who opened the door of faith to the Gentiles [*Acts* 10:34ff.] change like a chameleon into Peter the Pharisee, the separated one! 'The whole incident is remarkably characteristic of Peter – ever the first to recognize, and the first to draw back from, great principles and truths' (Henry Alford).

Fearing the circumcision party (RSV): So much for the stability of that 'Rock' upon which Rome claims to build! In once more falling a prey to moral cowardice [*Mark* 14:66ff.], Peter proved that 'the fear of man bringeth a snare' [*Prov.* 29:25]. (Cf. his later stand for the truth: *Acts* 15:7ff.)

13: And the rest of the Jews dissembled likewise with him; insomuch that even Barnabas was carried away with their dissimulation.

And the rest of the Jews joined him in playing the hypocrite, so that even Barnabas was carried along by their hypocrisy (Hendriksen): Such was the power of Peter's bad example that not only was it followed by the other Jewish believers in Antioch, but even Paul's trusted colleague, so recently returned from the first mission to the Gentiles, was swept away by the strong current of this hypocrisy. The word 'even' highlights the gravity of the crisis, and also shows how the unexpected defection of Barnabas must have cut Paul to the quick. This one lapse of Barnabas, who had been such a true 'son of encouragement' to Paul [*Acts* 9:27; 11:25f.], demonstrates 'the danger of theological compromise, the besetting sin of loving natures' (R. A. Cole).

'If Peter and Barnabas had changed their views, hypocrisy could not have been laid to their charge. But with their opinions unchanged, they acted as if they had been changed; therefore are they accused of dissimulation . . . This dissimulation, so wide and powerful, was compromising the freedom of the gospel, for it was subverting the doctrine of justification by faith; and therefore the apostle, who could on fitting occasions "to the Jews become a Jew", was obliged to visit it with immediate and stern rebuke' (Eadie).

14: But when I saw that they walked not uprightly according to the truth of the gospel, I said unto Cephas before them all, if thou, being a Jew, livest as do the Gentiles, and not as do the Jews, how compellest thou the Gentiles to live as do the Jews?

But when I saw that they were not pursuing a straight course in accordance with the truth of the gospel (Hendriksen): Only Paul saw that Peter's conduct was such a contradiction of his convictions that it was bound to lead many astray. Although Peter's error was not doctrinal but practical, Paul perceived that its implications were harmful to the truth of the gospel, which they were both committed to uphold. Hence Paul did not hesitate to withstand even an apostle of such prestige as Peter.

I said unto Cephas before them all: 'This example teaches us that those who have sinned publicly must be chastised publicly, so far as it concerns the Church. The aim is that their sin may not, by remaining unpunished, do harm by its example. And elsewhere [*1 Tim.* 5:20] Paul expressly says that this should be observed in regard to elders, because the office they hold makes their bad example more harmful' (Calvin).

'If you, though a Jew, live like a Gentile and not like a Jew, how can you compel the Gentiles to live like Jews?' (RSV): These are the actual words Paul used, while the following verses recall his general argument especially as it related to the contemporary situation in Galatia. If Peter, though born and bred a Jew, normally ignored Jewish food taboos and mixed freely with Gentiles, then it was quite unreasonable of him to *compel* the Gentiles to conform to these customs and live like Jews: 'i.e. practically oblige them, though such was not his intention. The force of his example, concealing his true principles, became a species of compulsion' (Lightfoot).

15: We being Jews by nature, and not sinners of the Gentiles, 16: yet knowing that a man is not justified by the works of the law but through faith in Jesus Christ, even we believed on Christ Jesus, that we might be justified by faith in Christ, and not by the works of the law: because by the works of the law shall no flesh be justified.

We ourselves, though by nature Jews and not 'Gentile sinners' (Hendriksen): The purpose of this concessive statement is to strengthen what follows: 'Though we are Jews by descent, and not Gentiles who as such are regarded by us from our elevation as sinners, yet our Judaism, with all its boasted superiority, could not bring us justification. Born and bred Jews as we are, we were obliged to renounce our trust in Judaism, for it was powerless to justify us. Why then go back to it, and be governed by it, as if we had not abandoned it at all?' (Eadie). In verse 16, Paul establishes this vital truth of the gospel in three propositions of increasing emphasis.

Yet knowing that a man is not justified by the works of the law but through faith in Jesus Christ: The apostle first makes the general statement that *a man* (i.e. any man) is not justified by the works of law but only through faith in Jesus Christ. 'Yet knowing' shows that he is not revealing some new truth for the first time; he is reminding Peter of what they as apostles of Christ are both committed to uphold. As 'law' here lacks the article, some have thought that a wider reference is intended, but to the Jewish mind there was only one law, and that was the law which God had given them through his servant Moses. Paul's contribution to the doctrine of justification may be gauged from the fact that he is responsible for twenty-nine of the thirty-nine occurrences of the verb 'justify' in the New Testament. J. I. Packer also defines what justification means to Paul: it is '*God's act of remitting the sins of guilty men, and accounting them righteous, freely, by His grace, through faith in Christ, on the ground, not of their own works, but of the representative law-keeping and redemptive blood-shedding of the Lord Jesus Christ on their behalf* ('justification': *The New Bible Dictionary*, p. 682). Here the preposition 'through' points to faith as the sole *means* by which the sinner is enabled to lay hold of Christ and all his saving benefits.

Even we believed on Christ Jesus, that we might be justified by faith in Christ, and not by the works of the law: The second statement sets forth what Paul and Peter both knew from personal experience. For despite our pedigree and privileges, we have committed ourselves to Christ for salvation, so that we might be justified 'out of' faith in him, and not 'out of' the works of the law. This change of preposition is probably intended to bring out the contrast between faith and works (so D. Guthrie). Consequently, 'even we' Jews who once thought we had righteousness by works of law, became just like the ignorant 'Gentile sinners' [verse 15] who trusted in nothing but the doing and dying of Christ on their behalf.

Because by the works of the law shall no flesh be justified: Finally, Paul quotes Scripture to show that the principle of non-justification by the works of the law is of universal application [*Psa.* 143:2]. To achieve righteousness by the law is far beyond the power of frail flesh, because all men stand condemned by their inability to fulfil its comprehensive demands. Although the words 'by works of law' are not in the Psalm, there is 'a basis for them in the preceding line, "Enter not into judgment with thy servant", which gives to the words that Paul has quoted the sense, "no man can be justified if judged on a basis of merit, all grace and mercy on God's part being excluded"' (Burton).

17: But if, while we sought to be justified in Christ, we ourselves also were found sinners, is Christ a minister of sin? God forbid.

Paul now asks: 'But if we Jews, in seeking to be justified in Christ apart from the works of the law, thus turn out to be no better than "Gentile sinners" [verse 15], is Christ then a minister of sin?' Since we have renounced *law-keeping* as the ground of our justification, and thereby placed ourselves on the same level as Gentile *law-breakers,* are the Judaizers then right to conclude that this 'lawless' doctrine makes Christ a promoter of sin? Paul does not stop to argue the point, but at once repudiates the very suggestion that Christ could be regarded as the author of sin.

18: For if I build up again those things which I destroyed, I prove myself a transgressor.

Paul tactfully uses the first person singular to set forth the consequences of Peter's inconsistency. Peter had torn down by his preaching and conduct the idea that works contributed to a man's justification, but his renewed submission to Jewish dietary laws was virtually a building up again of that erroneous opinion. For in yielding to the demands of the Judaizers, Peter had given occasion for others to suppose that he looked upon such obedience to the law as an essential supplement to faith in Christ. His conduct thus belied his faith and fostered the impression that justification might be attained by an amalgam of grace and works. But God's holy law demands far more than the paltry, piecemeal 'fulfilment' that guilty sinners can bring to it! [verse 21; 3:10]. Since the very completeness of the divine code called for Christ as its perfect Fulfiller, 'reconstruction of the same materials is in respect of the law not only a tacit avowal of "sin" in having pulled it down, but is a real and definite "transgression" of all its deeper principles' (C. J. Ellicott) [verse 19].

19: For I through the law died unto the law, that I might live unto God.

For I through the law died unto the law: The emphatic 'I' shows that Paul is calling upon his own experience to explain the preceding assertion. Paul died to the law as a legal demand in the person of his Saviour who satisfied its claims and endured its curse on his behalf [verse 20; 3:13]. 'As our Representative in whom we were chosen and in whom we suffered, He yielded himself to the law, which seized Him and nailed Him to the cross. When that law seized Him, it seized at the same time all his in Him, and through the law they suffered and died to it . . . And now certainly, if the law, avenging itself on our guilt, has in this way wrought our release from itself – has set us for ever free from its yoke, and we have died to it and have done with it; then he who would re-enact legalism and bring men under it, proves himself its transgressor, nay, opposes its deepest principles and its most gracious design' (Eadie) [*Rom.* 6:6–13; 7:1–6].

That I might live unto God: But freedom from the law is not lawlessness. The supreme purpose for which Christ confers life and liberty is that those thus redeemed may no longer live unto themselves but unto God. And this dedication to God is expressed by their delight in his law as *their rule of duty.* For though Paul had died to the condemning power of the law, he did not see himself as being 'without law to God, but under law to Christ' [*1 Cor.* 9:21].

Now believers are free from the law in four respects. 'First, in respect of the accusing, and damnatory sentence of the law, Romans 8:1. Secondly, in respect of the power of the law, whereby as an occasion it provoketh and stirreth up the corruption of the heart in the unregenerate, Romans 7:8. Thirdly, in respect of the rigour of the law, whereby it exacteth most perfect obedience for our justification. Thus *Paul* here saith, that *he is dead to the law.* Lastly, in respect of the obligation of the conscience, to the observation of ceremonies, *Col.* 2:20. Thus are all persons justified by the faith of Christ, free from the law' (Perkins).

20: I have been crucified with Christ; and it is no longer I that live, but Christ liveth in me: and that life which I now live in the flesh I live in faith, the faith which is in the Son of God, who loved me, and gave himself up for me.

With Christ I have been crucified: This explains the previous verse and shows how Paul died to the law. 'Paul uses the perfect tense in speaking of his having died with Christ, that is, in speaking of something that once took place and has not lost its power since. This thing that has happened somewhere else in the past does not refer to Paul's subjective experience, but to the death of Christ. The believers, by virtue of their corporate belonging to Him, were included in that dying' (Ridderbos).

And it is no longer I that live, but Christ liveth in me: Paul's meaning is not that his own personality has ceased to exist, but that it is so transformed by Christ's living in him that he no longer recognizes his former sinful self (*John* 15:4, 5). Having experienced so great a deliverance from legalism, Paul could never travel that road again. But the Galatians, who are on the brink of such a fatal relapse, must learn that submission to a regime of law would sever their union with the Christ who was the sole source of their spiritual life [*Col.* 3:4].

And that life which I now live in the flesh I live in faith, the faith which is in the Son of God: Faith is the secret of Paul's new life, and it is a faith which rests on the Son of God himself. '*Faith*, not the *flesh*, is the real element in which I live. The phrase, "the Son of God", reminds us that his divine Sonship is the source of his life-giving power' (A. R. Fausset). It is therefore because the Christian life is a life of faith in the Son of God that it excludes all reliance upon oneself or one's works.

Who loved me, and gave himself up for me: Paul's whole life is dominated by the thought that the Son of God so loved him that He willingly gave Himself up to death for him (i.e. in his stead). Such personal pronouns express the very essence of saving faith. 'No matter who else were loved, He loved me; no matter for whom other He gave Himself, He gave Himself for me. Is it any wonder, then, that my life even now is a life of faith in Him, and no longer one in legal bondage? . . . He must deny himself and forget all his previous history, before he could turn his back on that cross where the Son of God proved the intensity and self-denying nature of His love for him in that atonement which needs neither repetition nor supplement. "Wilt thou bring thy cowl, thy shaven crown, thy chastity, thy obedience, thy poverty, thy works, thy merits? What shall these do?" (Luther)' (Eadie).

21: I do not make void the grace of God: for if righteousness is through the law, then Christ died for nought.

The apostle's concluding statement is a ringing affirmation of his determination to uphold the grace of God in the face of all temporising expedients. It is, as Machen rightly says, the key verse of the Epistle and expresses its central thought. It was because Paul refused to make void God's grace that he did not stand by in silence when the truth of the gospel was compromised by Peter's dissimulation [verse 11]. For he realized that if righteousness could be attained through the law, then Christ died in vain. If his sacrifice did not secure our *complete* salvation, then he died to no purpose! 'The Judaizers attempted to supplement the saving work of Christ by the merit of their own obedience to the law. "That", says Paul, "is impossible; Christ will do everything or nothing: earn your salvation if your obedience to the law is perfect, or else trust wholly to Christ's completed work; you cannot do both; you cannot combine merit and grace; if justification even in the slightest measure is through human merit, then Christ died in vain"' (Machen).

CHAPTER THREE

Having refuted the claims of the Judaizers from personal experience [1:10–2:21], Paul next shows that such reliance on the deeds of the law is not in accord with the testimony of Scripture [3:1–4:31]. Since the Galatians had become Christians by believing the gospel, it would be the height of folly if they now reverted to the law, and exchanged the blessings of the Spirit for the works of the flesh [verses 1–5]. For as Abraham was justified by faith, so his blessing belongs to those who share his faith [verses 6–9]. The law could do no more than bring all men under its curse, from which we were redeemed by Christ who took our curse upon himself, so that we might receive the promised blessing through faith [verses 10–14]. And as even the covenants of men cannot be modified, it is evident that God's promise to Abraham has an abiding validity which could not be made void by the later provisions of the law [verses 15–18]. This does not mean that the law has no function, for its purpose was to prepare the way for Christ. The law shuts up all under sin, and thus acted as our tutor to bring us to Christ. But now that faith has delivered us from its strict supervision, we are all sons of God and Abraham's true spiritual heirs, for in Christ all human distinctions have ceased to count [verses 19–29].

1: O foolish Galatians, who did bewitch you, before whose eyes Jesus Christ was openly set forth crucified?

O senseless Galatians, who has bewitched you – you who had Jesus Christ the crucified placarded before your very eyes? (Moffatt) Paul's passionate remonstrance is an appeal to the Galatians' spiritual experience. Their senseless folly in giving credence to the perverted gospel of the Judaizers showed such 'an unworthy lack of understanding' (Vine), that to speak figuratively, they seemed like those hypnotized by some malign spell. For what else could explain their removing from the gospel of 'Christ crucified' [*1 Cor.* 1:23; 2:2] when this truth has been placarded so plainly before them in Paul's preaching? The reference is to spiritual perception and not of course to any visual representation of Christ [cf. verse 2: 'the *hearing* of faith'). 'This is the indictment against the Galatians: all this placarding was so plain to the eye, and yet they acted as though they could not see, had no sense to read, could not think what this meant. "Crucified crucified – crucified!" – even a little thinking should suffice to turn the Galatians against all Judaizers. The entire Scriptures are so placarded, yet men even preach on them and see nothing in the cross except noble martyrdom [*2 Cor.* 4:3, 4]' (R.C. H. Lenski).

2: This only would I learn from you, Received ye the Spirit by the works of the law, or by the hearing of faith?

The Galatians could return but one answer to this question. They had received the Spirit not by obeying the law but by believing the gospel. It was through the hearing of faith they came to know that Spirit without whom no man can say 'Jesus is Lord' [*1 Cor.* 12:3] – 'that Spirit which enlightens, sanctifies, certifies of sonship, makes intercession for us as being in us, seals us, and is the earnest and first-fruit! However, they were now being mesmerized by the 'Higher Life' teaching of the Judaizers which promised far greater blessings than these, if only they would fully yield them to God by obeying the demands of his holy law! But since the reception of the Spirit is nothing less than a receiving of Christ in all the fullness of his saving grace, only those who fail to see the greatness of the initial bestowment can be deceived by the teaching that God's free grace can be *supplemented* by our obedience. 'So the error of the Judaizers is a very modern error indeed, as well as a very ancient error. It is found in the modern Church wherever men seek salvation by "surrender" instead of by faith, or by their own character instead of by the imputed righteousness of Christ, or by "making Christ master in the life" instead of by trusting in His redeeming blood' (Machen).

3: Are ye so foolish? having begun in the Spirit, are ye now perfected in the flesh?

Are ye so foolish? having begun in the Spirit, do ye now make an end in the flesh? (ASV margin): This is really one question which reveals the extent of the Galatians' folly by pointing a double contrast. Their good beginning in the faith is contrasted with the tragic completion proposed by the Judaizers, and the life-giving power of the Spirit is contrasted with the futility of ending with the flesh. 'They are insane men who do not understand what the Spirit or the flesh is. The Spirit is whatever is done in us through the Spirit; the flesh is whatever is done in us in accordance with the flesh and apart from the Spirit . . . By "flesh" he does not mean sexual lust, animal passions, or the sensual appetite, because in this passage he is not discussing sexual lust or other desires of the flesh. No, he is discussing the forgiveness of sins, the justification of the conscience, the attainment of righteousness in the sight of God, and liberation from the Law, sin, and death. And yet he says here that after they have forsaken the Spirit, they are now being ended with the flesh. Thus "flesh" is the very righteousness and wisdom of the flesh and the judgment of reason, which wants to be justified through the Law. Therefore whatever is best and most outstanding in man Paul calls "flesh", namely, the highest wisdom of reason and the very righteousness of the Law' (Luther).

4: Did ye suffer so many things in vain? if it be indeed in vain.

Have you had such remarkable experiences in vain? (Arndt-Gingrich):

This translation is preferable as the idea of suffering or persecution is quite foreign to the context. Paul asks whether they will contradict their experience of that more abundant life which Christ had brought to them by his Spirit? Having experienced Christian freedom, will they now be guilty of relapsing into Jewish legalism?

If it be indeed in vain: This is added because Paul cannot bring himself to believe that their good beginning in the faith was after all to no purpose. Thus he shows them that he still hopes that his appeal will lead to their amendment.

5: He therefore that supplieth to you the Spirit, and worketh miracles among you, doeth he it by the works of the law, or by the hearing of faith?

In verse 2 Paul reminds the Galatians of their reception of the Spirit; here he directs their attention to God as the Giver of the Spirit. He uses the present tense not specially to refer to their present experience of the Spirit, but to characterize God as the Supplier of the Spirit. Thus Eadie explains: 'God, whose prerogative it is to give the Spirit and work miracles, – does He, is He in the habit of giving the one and doing the other by the works of the law or by the hearing of faith?' it was impossible for the Galatians to evade the force of this question. They knew from personal experience that the law-message of the Judaizers was powerless to impart the spiritual graces and gifts they had received by believing the message of faith! Paul's insistence upon the 'hearing of faith' as the *exclusive* means through which God bestows the Spirit therefore leads to the inescapable conclusion that they would forfeit their great spiritual privileges by declining to the 'works of the law' (F. D. Bruner).

6: Even as Abraham believed God, and it was reckoned unto him for righteousness.

This appeal to the Galatians' experience [verses 1–5] is now confirmed by the testimony of Scripture [*Gen.* 15:6]. As Paul's doctrinal argument is largely centred upon the example of Abraham [verses 6, 7, 8, 9, 14, 16, 18, 29; 4:22], it seems reasonable to assume that he is refuting the false conclusions which the Judaizers had drawn from the patriarch's life (see comment on verse 7). But Paul quotes this verse to show that Abraham's acceptance with God was found through believing the divine promise [*Gen*. 15:5], for his faith was 'reckoned' or credited to him for righteousness.

This means that 'the non-righteous Abraham stood before the divine tribunal acquitted and accepted as truly as if he had possessed a personal righteousness through uniform obedience. His faith, not as an act, but as a fact, put him into this position by God's own deed, without legal fiction or abatement . . . He was lifted into acceptance with God, however, not on account of his faith, but through it laying hold of the promise. That faith had no merit; for what merit can a creature have in believing the Creator's word? – it is only bare duty, – but Abraham's trust in God introduced him into the promised blessing. His faith rested on the promise, and through that faith he became its possessor or participant. That promise, seen in the light of a previous utterance, included the Messiah; and with all which it contained, and with this as its central and pre-eminent object, it was laid hold of by his faith, so that his condition was tantamount to justification by faith in the righteousness of Christ' (Eadie) [cf. *Gen*. 12:3; *John* 8:56].

7: Know therefore that they that are of faith, the same are sons of Abraham.

This begins the apostle's answer to the argument of the Judaizers, who evidently taught that Gentiles who wished to be blessed with Abraham must receive the covenant-sign by which their participation in covenant-blessing would be assured [*Gen*. 17:1–14]. But the mere reception of an external sign does not automatically confer internal grace [cf. 6:15]. Paul's use of the imperative 'Know ye' shows that he is determined to teach the Galatians the lesson of *Gen*. 15:6 [verse 6] – a verse the Judaizers doubtless omitted to quote! For as Abraham's faith, which antedated his circumcision by many years, was the vital factor in his acceptance with God, so the possession of the same justifying faith is ever that which distinguishes his true 'sons' from those whose connection with him is purely physical [*Matt*. 3:9; *John* 8:39; *Rom*. 2:28, 29]. 'Not those who are descended from Abraham by ordinary generation, not those who have united themselves to Abraham's descendants by circumcision and the keeping of the law of Moses, certainly not those who have tried – vainly – to attain merit with God by any kind of observance of God's law, but those who have the same faith as that which Abraham had are his true sons and the true heirs of the promises which God gave to him' (Machen).

8: And the scripture, foreseeing that God would justify the Gentiles by faith, preached the gospel beforehand unto Abraham, saying, In thee shall all the nations be blessed.

Paul now passes to another aspect of the same truth. It is no novelty that the Gentiles are saved by faith, for this was revealed to Abraham. 'It was not, however, the Scripture (which did not exist at the time) that, foreseeing God's purposes of grace in the future, spoke these precious words to Abraham, but God himself in his own person.' The apostle therefore could only attribute such an act to Scripture because he habitually regarded it 'as the living voice of God' (B. B. Warfield, *The Inspiration and Authority of the Bible*, pp. 299, 345) [cf. *Rom.* 9:17]. Here the present tense, which underlies 'would justify', points to God's method of justifying by faith as the unchanging principle of the divine government.

Paul can say that God's first promise to Abraham was a prior preaching of the gospel [*Gen.* 12:3], because it showed that the pattern of future blessing for the world would be found in connection with 'believing Abraham' [verse 9]. Hence the nature of the Gentiles' union with Abraham ('in thee') was not what the Judaizers had supposed, for they were joined to him by faith and not by circumcision! So God, foreseeing his 'own gracious and uniform process of justifying the Gentile races through faith, made it known to Abraham, even while disclosing to him the blessing of his own promised and direct posterity. God revealed it, not to some heathen prince or priest, one of the Gentiles himself, but to the father of the Jewish race' (Eadie).

9: So then they that are of faith are blessed with the faithful Abraham.

So that the men of faith are blessed with the faithful (believing) Abraham (Burton): Thus only those who are also characterized by faith enjoy community of blessing with believing Abraham. The present tense shows that Gentile believers are not only given the prospect of future bliss, but are blessed by God – declared righteous – the moment they trust Christ for salvation. Since in both dispensations, the old and the new, the one Saviour has but one people, the summit of blessing is found in company with faithful Abraham!

10: For as many as are of the works of the law are under a curse: for it is written, Cursed is every one who continueth not in all things that are written in the book of the law, to do them.

Having established the truth of justification by faith from Scripture, Paul now confronts his bemused readers with three more texts which exhibit the folly of replacing the principle of faith with reliance upon the works of the law [verses 10–12]. Submission to the demands of the legalizers, far from bringing the Galatians the promised blessing, would actually place them under a curse, since all who break God's law are justly exposed to God's wrath. This means that if they remove from the blessings of faith, then they must incur the curse of the law. For to merit salvation by personal obedience is not an option that is open to violators of the law. Therefore sinners who wish to find acceptance with God must sue for grace and seek an interest in the justifying righteousness of Christ. The Scripture cited confirms that the law can bring only a curse to those unable to render exact and unvarying obedience to all its commands [*Deut.* 27:26].

It is important to realize that the Judaizers divorced the law from the context of grace in which it had been given to Israel, for under the old economy the law remained subservient to the promise [3:17]. Consequently Israel's assent to all the curses pronounced on Mount Ebal is inexplicable apart from the promised Redeemer who was to be born 'under the law' [4:5], in order that he might exhaust its curse on their behalf [3:13]. And the fact that Christ would come to bear that curse for them 'was daily demonstrated to them by their sacrifices' (Herman Hoeksema, *Reformed Dogmatics,* p. 404).

11: Now that no man is justified by the law before God, is evident: for, The righteous shall live by faith;

Having shown that salvation by law-keeping is impossible because man is disabled by sin, Paul goes on to prove from Scripture that in fact justification has never been by works but always by faith. And since it is God who established this connection between faith and salvation, it is evident that those who rely on the works of the law have no hope of securing a favourable verdict before the divine tribunal.

The righteous shall live by faith: Although the original Hebrew word is more accurately rendered as 'faithfulness', such fidelity in the face of mortal danger is only made possible by faith in the promises of God. So Paul is not guilty of distorting the prophet's message when he sees this faith as the *abiding principle* in the life of the righteous man. 'In Habakkuk 2:4 this faith is not set in contrast to the works of the law, however, but over against the arrogance and self-confidence of the wicked. Positively seen, though, the faith intended in Habakkuk 2 and Galatians 3 is essentially the same. It is a resting in God without regard to human care and effort' (Ridderbos) [cf. *Rom.* 1:17; *Heb.* 10:38].

12: and the law is not of faith; but, He that doeth them shall live in them.

And the law is not of faith: It is because the apostle knows that 'the law' and 'faith' are mutually exclusive principles that he challenges the 'both/and' of the false gospel with the 'either/or' of God's Word. For to seek justification by obedience to the law is to renounce any interest in Christ's free salvation. The real point at issue between Paul and the Judaizers is well summarized by Machen. 'Paul said that a man (1) first believes on Christ (2) then is justified before God (3) then immediately proceeds to keep God's law. The Judaizers said that a man (1) believes on Christ and (2) keeps the law of God the best he can, and then (3) is justified.' The difference was not simply a matter of hair-splitting distinctions. It 'was the difference between two entirely distinct types of religion; it was the difference between a religion of merit and a religion of grace. If Christ provides only a part of our salvation, leaving us to provide the rest, then we are still hopeless under the load of sin' (Machen, *Christianity and Liberalism*, p. 24).

But, He that doeth them shall live in them: As with Paul's quotation of Deuteronomy 27:26 [verse 10], when the principle set forth in Leviticus 18:5 was artificially isolated from its original setting in what was essentially a covenant of grace, it became a sentence of condemnation. Since Israel was merely the recipient of God's undeserved favour, their obedience to the law could not earn the blessings they already enjoyed. And though the retention of the inheritance was suspended upon Israel's obedience, it would be a mistake to interpret this condition in any legalistic sense. It rather typically represents the truth that the reception of grace must always be recorded in the register of gratitude. 'But the Judaizers went wrong in inferring that the connection must be *meritorious*, that, if Israel keeps the cherished gifts of Jehovah through observance of his law, this must be so, because in strict justice they had *earned* them' (Geerhardus Vos, *Biblical Theology*, p. 143). Thus Paul's polemic is directed against the legalism which demanded obedience to the law as a *condition* of salvation [cf. *Acts* 15:24].

13: Christ redeemed us from the curse of the law, having become a curse for us; for it is written, Cursed is every one that hangeth on a tree:

Christ: The absence of any connecting particle is significant. 'Coming after all that has been said about the curse, the abrupt introduction of the name of Christ suggests the appearance on the scene of one who alone can deal with so tragic a situation' (Duncan).

Redeemed us: The word 'redeemed' focuses attention upon the cost of the deliverance wrought by Christ. He paid the price to set men free from the bondage of sin. This was no mere token payment, but a full satisfaction of the claims of divine justice. It was only because Christ was not in debt to the law himself that he could undertake to pay the debt of those who were under its condemning curse. Here the word 'us' can no more be restricted to Jews than the 'we' of the following verse limits the gift of the Spirit to Gentiles. This 'us' not only includes Paul and the Galatians, but also embraces all believers, whether Jews or Gentiles. For Gentiles, no less than Jews, needed to be ransomed from the curse of a broken law, though it was only written in their hearts [cf. *Rom.* 2:12–16].

From the curse of the law, having become a curse for us: The curse of the law means that every infraction of the law's demand must be visited with the wrath of God, so that in becoming the surety of a sinful people Christ was made in this official respect the object of divine wrath [*Matt.* 27:46]. No words could more clearly express the penal and substitutionary nature of Christ's death. 'Without deliverance from this curse there could be no salvation. It is from this curse that Christ has purchased his people and the price of the purchase was that he himself became a curse. He became so identified with the curse resting upon his people that the whole of it in all its unrelieved intensity became his. That curse he bore and that curse he exhausted. That was the price paid for this redemption and the liberty secured for the beneficiaries is that there is no more curse' (John Murray, *Redemption – Accomplished and Applied,* p. 44).

For it is written: Cursed is every one that hangeth on a tree: Crucifixion was not a Jewish punishment, and the quotation from Deuteronomy 21:23 originally referred to the hanging of the dead bodies of flagrant sinners on the tree of shame to show that they were accursed of God. 'So the very means of Christ's death showed it to be an accursed death. His being hanged on a tree proved that He was made a curse. The manner of the death, besides being in consonance with prophecy, was a visible proof and symbol of its real nature; for "He bore our sins in His own body on the tree". He bore the curse of a broken law, and the mode of His death signally showed that He became a curse, for, by being suspended on a stake, He became in the express terms of the law a curse. *Acts* 5:30, 10:39; *1 Pet.* 2:24' (Eadie).

14: that upon the Gentiles might come the blessing of Abraham in Christ Jesus; that we might receive the promise of the Spirit through faith.

In two final clauses Paul states the gracious consequences of Christ's vicarious bearing of the curse. Both cover the same ground, the second establishing what is meant by the first.

That upon the Gentiles might come the blessing of Abraham in Christ Jesus: As Christ bore the curse to fulfil the promise made to Abraham that in him all nations would be blessed [verse 9], so this blessing of Abraham comes upon the Gentiles only 'in Christ Jesus' – through the faith that comes to them [verses 23, 25], and not by their becoming 'Jews' [5:2]! Because Christ's death which brought deliverance from the curse also 'put an end to the typical and national economy from which the Gentiles were excluded, and introduced a new dispensation without distinction of race or blood' (Eadie) [verses 26–29; cf. *Eph.* 2:11–18].

That we might receive the promise of the Spirit through faith: This harks back to verse 2. It is the comprehensive boon of the promised Spirit received through faith *in conversion* that confers the blessing of Abraham in full measure on both Jews and Gentiles. For it is the Spirit who puts men 'in Christ Jesus' and makes them sons of God by giving them the saving faith that was in Abraham, whose trust in God's Word made him the 'father' of all believers.

15: Brethren, I speak after the manner of men: Though it be but a man's covenant, yet when it hath been confirmed, no one maketh it void, or addeth thereto.

As Paul begins to explain the true relation of the law to the promise, he appeals to his erring 'brethren' to follow his argument, which he illustrates with 'an example from everyday life' (NIV). He argues thus: even in human affairs when a legal 'disposition' of property is once ratified, its provisions cannot be set aside or modified in any way. This being so, how much more does the same principle hold good with God's sovereign 'disposition' of gospel grace, which has the unconditional character of a one-sided grant. 'So legal Judaism could make no alteration in the fundamental relation between God and man, already established by the promises to Abraham; it could not add as a new condition the observance of the law, in which case the fulfilment of the promise would be attached to a condition impossible for man to perform. The "covenant" here is one of free grace, a *promise* afterwards carried into effect in the gospel' (Fausset).

16: Now to Abraham were the promises spoken, and to his seed. He saith not, And to seeds, as of many; but as of one. And to thy seed, which is Christ.

Having shown the immutability of God's covenant, Paul now proceeds to identify those included within the scope of its oft-repeated promises. He insists that the true heirs of Abraham are not his natural descendants, for Christ is the 'seed' in whom alone these promises are fulfilled. This dictum has its objective basis in the distinction which God himself made between Ishmael and Isaac. For Abraham was told that 'in Isaac shall thy seed be called' [*Gen.* 21:12; *Rom.* 9:7; cf. 4:28–31]. Moreover, it was later revealed to Isaac and Rebekah that the line of promise would be continued through Jacob and not Esau [*Gen.* 25:23; *Rom.* 9:8–13]. But if the promise did not embrace all the natural progeny of Abraham, it obviously could not be limited to the spiritual remnant of Israel, because it was centred upon Christ in whom all the nations were to be blessed. It therefore included all who would he brought to faith in Christ, whether Jews or Gentiles, for these alone are the true sons of believing Abraham [verses 26–29]. Thus the promised Messiah, 'the seed of the woman' [*Gen.* 3:15], is the sum and substance of the promise, not as an individual, but as the Christ 'embodying at the same time His church – the Head with its members in organic unity' (Eadie).

17: Now this I say: A covenant confirmed beforehand by God, the law, which came four hundred and thirty years after, doth not disannul, so as to make the promise of none effect.

This resumes the thought of verse 15. Paul's meaning is that what holds good for human covenants must apply in a pre-eminent degree to God's covenant. It is evident that the law which came so long after the promise cannot nullify the provisions of grace. But the Judaizers are placing the law above the promise, 'for they make obedience to the law the condition for obtaining the salvation granted by the promise' (Ridderbos). A possible solution to the problems of chronology raised by this verse is put forward by E. J. Young, who suggests that the apostle's thought here is that the whole patriarchal period of the giving of the promise was separated from the period of the giving of the law by Israel's long sojourn of 430 years in the land of bondage (*Thy Word Is Truth*, pp. 177–80) [cf. *Exod.* 12:40].

18: For if the inheritance is of the law, it is no more of promise: but God hath granted it to Abraham by promise.

For if the inheritance is of the law, it is no more of promise: This unsound premise prepares the way for the irresistible conclusion which immediately follows it. If the inheritance is due to law, it clearly cannot be conferred by promise. Paul uses the same kind of argument in *Rom.* 4:13f. His reasoning serves to show that the law and the promise are contradictory principles which cannot be combined, for 'that which is of grace, and of the promise, is of free love; that which is of works, and the law, is wages, and a reward of debt' (Poole).

But God hath granted it to Abraham by promise: But the fact of the matter is that God freely bestowed the inheritance on Abraham by way of promise. Here the perfect tense shows that the gift of God retains its character as the free grant of grace which remains in force for ever. Paul thus overthrows the false claims of the Judaizers by confronting the Galatians with this great historical fact which cannot be gainsaid. The covenant of grace that God established with Abraham could not be rescinded by the coming of the law, which was never intended to be the means of attaining the promised salvation. For what is earned by obedience cannot be received as a gift! 'The state of grace and favour with God here, and of glory hereafter, is the inheritance, portion, and heirship of the Lord's people, there being no temporal worldly inheritance which can sufficiently furnish the heart with satisfaction, *Psa.* 4:6, 7, of which spiritual and heavenly inheritance the land of Canaan was a type; for the apostle, speaking of justification, and all the spiritual blessings which flow from it, calleth them the inheritance by way of excellency' (James Fergusson) [cf. *Heb.* 11:8ff.].

19: What then is the law? It was added because of transgressions, till the seed should come to whom the promise hath been made; and it was ordained through angels by the hand of a mediator.

What then is the law? It was added because of transgressions: Paul here anticipates the inevitable objection, What then is the function of the law? His astonishing reply still further emphasizes the inferiority of the law to the promise. It was added alongside the promise, for the subordinate and temporary [verse 23] purpose of bringing transgressions to light! 'For through the law cometh the knowledge of sin.' This axiom of the apostle's teaching was learned through the crucible of his own experience [cf. *Rom.* 3:20; 4:15; 5:20; 7:7, 13). Men 'may *sin* in ignorance, but they *transgress* only when they have a recognized standard of what is right, and it was to provide such a standard that the Law was brought in' (Duncan).

Till the seed should come to whom the promise hath been made: The law was added in order to prepare for the coming of Christ 'by so deepening the sense of sinfulness that men, convicted of so often breaking it, could not look to it for righteousness, but must be "shut up unto the faith which should be afterwards revealed"' (Eadie).

And it was ordained by angels through an intermediary (RSV): Whereas the Jews gloried in the angelic mediation of the law, Paul speaks of it in disparagement, because of the distance it placed between God and men [cf. *Deut.* 33:2; *Psa.* 68:17; *Acts* 7:53; *Heb.* 2:2]. 'The Promise was given directly by God to Abraham; the Law was given indirectly, and indeed doubly so (a) by means of angels (b) through Moses ... Luther expresses the thought of our passage when he writes, "The Law is the voice of the servants, but the Gospel is the voice of the Lord Himself"' (Williams). Thus the Divine Mediator of the gospel cannot be compared with the purely human intermediary through whom the law was given.

20: Now a mediator is not a mediator of one; but God is one.

Now an intermediary does not exist for one party alone (Arndt-Gingrich): It is doubtless because the Judaizers had laid great stress upon the importance of Moses that Paul does not even mention him by name. Having said that the law was given through an intermediary [verse 19], the apostle now tersely states that such an intermediary presupposes the existence of at least two other parties between whom he is to mediate. 'The Law then is of the nature of a contract between two parties, God on the one hand, and the Jewish people on the other. It is only valid so long as both parties fulfil the terms of the contract. It is therefore contingent and not absolute' (Lightfoot).

But God is one: This emphasizes the unilateral character of the covenant of grace. 'Unlike the law, the promise is absolute and unconditional. It depends on the sole decree of God. There are not two contracting parties. There is nothing of the nature of a *stipulation*. The giver is everything, the recipient nothing' (Lightfoot).

21: Is the law then against the promises of God? God forbid: for if there had been a law given which could make alive, verily righteousness would have been of the law.

In case it should seem that Paul is seeking to exalt the promise by depreciating the law, he boldly asks whether the law is contrary to God's promises, an inference which he at once repudiates with disgust. As the same God gave both the promise and the law it is evident that there can be no conflict between them. The law is itself holy for it makes known the will of a holy God, but it has no power to confer the righteousness it demands. Had there been given a law which could have imparted life to the spiritually dead, then righteousness would have been by the law. But the true function of the law, which only pronounces a curse upon the disobedient, is to drive sinners to trust in the promise [verse 22]. 'The implication of the statement is the fact that law is always given, it is never produced by man himself. All evolutionary origin of law is denied. The passive includes the agent: there must always be the divine Lawgiver. This is true also of the law written in the hearts of Gentiles which is greatly blurred by the darkening effect of sin' (Lenski).

22: But the scripture shut up all things under sin, that the promise by faith in Jesus Christ might be given to them that believe.

But the Scripture declares that the whole world is a prisoner of sin (NIV): But so far from righteousness being of the law, the verdict of the law as embodied in the Scripture quoted in verse 10 [*Deut.* 27:26] had exactly the opposite effect and locked up all men under the condemnation of sin [*Rom.* 3:19].

That the promise by faith in Jesus Christ might be given: 'It may be thou thinkest that all this is a preparation to thy damnation; but it is not. For it is contrariwise a preparation to thy salvation. For the law with a loud voice in thy heart, proclaims thee a sinner, and threatens thee with perdition: but the end of all this is, that Jesus Christ may become a Saviour unto thee, so be it thou wilt come unto him, and believe in him. For he saves no sheep, *but the lost sheep*, and *he calls not just men, but sinners to repentance*' (Perkins).

To them that believe: 'The Galatians were ready to admit that those who believed would be saved, but they doubted whether faith *alone* was sufficient; hence the Apostle interposes the limitation in reference to the thing promised ("the promise by faith"), and virtually repeats it in reference to the recipients. The promise was of faith, not of law; the receivers were not doers of the law, but believers' (Ellicott).

23: But before faith came, we were kept in ward under the law, shut up unto the faith which should afterwards be revealed.

Now before this faith came, we were kept in custody under law, being locked up with a view to the faith that was to be revealed (Hendriksen): Before *the* faith came ('note article, meaning the faith in verse 22 made possible by the historic coming of Christ the Redeemer' – Robertson), we Jews were kept under guard by the law. 'When the Mosaic law held all the Jews under guard as it did, it thereby stopped every mouth and declared the whole world guilty and subject to God's judgment' (Lenski). Paul does not deny the existence of either grace or faith under the old economy, but to those whose attention was being turned back from the grace now so fully manifested in Jesus Christ, he could only point out its privative or negative aspect. 'With a view to the faith that was to be revealed' shows that there was a beneficent purpose in this temporary bondage to the law. But if the Galatians, who enjoyed the noonday of gospel light, now reverted to the regime of law, they would lose their liberty and find themselves under its condemning constraint without hope of a reprieve [5:1].

24: So that the law is become our tutor to bring us unto Christ, that we might be justified by faith.

So the law became our custodian (to conduct us) to Christ (Hendriksen): The word translated as 'custodian' means literally 'boy-leader'. He was the man, usually a slave, whose duty it was to take the boy or youth 'to and from school and to superintend his conduct generally; he was not a "teacher" (despite the present meaning of the derivative "pedagogue")' (Arndt-Gingrich). There is no exact English equivalent, though 'schoolmaster' (AV) quite definitely conveys the wrong impression. For the word refers not to the impartation of knowledge, but to that strict discipline which was exercised by the law during the period of immaturity. Thus for the Galatians to make 'progress' after the fashion of the Judaizers would return them to a state of spiritual nonage! This custodial function of the law was not in the repression of sins; it was given to produce such convictions of guilt and helplessness as prepared for faith in Christ as the sole redeemer from its curse [verse 13]. But it is important to recognize that the reference is not 'to the individual experience under the law as bringing men individually to faith in Christ. For the context makes it clear that the apostle is speaking, rather, of the historic succession of one period of revelation upon another and the displacement of the law by Christ' (Burton). [cf. verses 23a, 25a]

That by faith we might be justified (Hendriksen): That stern supervision was intended to lead to this happy result, 'the emphatic "by faith" serving to suggest and enhance the contrast with the non-justifying and merely pedagogic "law"' (Ellicott).

25: But now that faith is come, we are no longer under a tutor.

But now that this faith has come we are no longer under a custodian (Hendriksen): With this triumphant note of assurance Paul begins to remind the Galatians of the great privileges that are theirs in Christ, for to speak of the coming of *the* faith is to refer to him who is its object. They are no longer minors under austere constraint, but Christ's free men. For Christ has brought to an end the wardship of the law so that in him the church has become of age. 'God makes us adults, causes us to come of age ... by sending His Son. Sonship as immediacy to the Father is rather different from dependence on even the best pedagogue' (G. Bertram, *TDNT*, vol. 5, p. 620) [cf. 4:4–6].

26: For ye are all sons of God, through faith, in Christ Jesus.

Paul speaks of the liberty of sonship and not of the discipline of childhood. 'The sudden change from the first to the second person plural betokens an extension in the point of view from Israel to the Gentile world. The Epistle has been dealing since 3:17 with the position of Israelites under the Law before the Advent of the Christ. But that event brought Gentiles also within the scope of God's revealed promises and of his blessings in Christ. So the apostle turns to his converts, largely enlisted out of Gentiles, with the assurance, "Ye are all sons of God, whatever your antecedents." Their adoption is assumed, as their possession of the gifts of the Spirit is assumed in 3:2. The Spirit of adoption, of which they were conscious within their hearts, assured them that they were sons of God [cf. *Rom.* 8:15, 16]' (Rendall).

27: For as many of you as were baptized into Christ did put on Christ.

Baptized into union with him, you have all put on Christ as a garment (NEB): Why should the Galatians now submit to circumcision when they have already clothed themselves with Christ in baptism? 'You have all put on' (middle voice) denotes responsible action, for in their obedience to the command of Christ they had given conscious expression to their faith in him [*Matt.* 28:19]. 'The figure of changing garments attests to the inner spiritual change. We strip off the clothes of the old life to be clothed with the garments of Christ's righteousness through faith-baptism [note the same figure in *Psa.* 132:9; *Isa.* 61:10, 64:6; *Zech.*3:3]' (Samuel J. Mikolaski).

28: There can be neither Jew nor Greek, there can be neither bond nor free, there can be no male and female; for ye all are one man in Christ Jesus.

Since faith is the bond of union with Christ, differences of race, rank, and even sex no longer divide. The thought is not that these distinctions have ceased to exist, but that in Christ they have ceased to matter. In this spiritual relationship, the natural son of Abraham enjoys no advantage over the pagan Greek, the slave is in no sense the inferior of the free man, and the man's privilege is no greater than the woman's. It is an affirmation of religious equality, and not a programme for social reform.

Paul avoided such a direct approach because he knew that men must be renewed before society could be changed. While the 'social' gospel is powerless to leaven the lump, religious revival has always resulted in social progress.

For ye are all one in Christ Jesus (AV): 'The unity is organic, not unconscious or fortuitous juxtaposition, but like the union of all the branches with the root, and through the root with one another. There may be many disparities in gifts and graces, but there is indissoluble oneness in Christ Jesus, its only sphere, or through union to Him, its only medium' (Eadie) [*Eph.* 2:15].

29: And if ye are Christ's, then are ye Abraham's seed, heirs according to promise.

Doubt is not implied by 'if' which assumes a condition of reality. The promises of the Judaizers notwithstanding, circumcision cannot make the Gentile Galatians the heirs of Abraham. In fact that privilege is already theirs in virtue of the faith which has brought them into saving union with Christ. They are heirs, not by works of law, but 'according to promise'.

'With this last link in the chain, it becomes clear in what sense Christ could be called the seed of Abraham [verse 16]: in a corporative sense, that is, as Head of the body and of the new covenant. Always and again this one thing is reconfirmed: that belonging to the seed of Abraham is not determined by physical descent, but by faith. Essentially, in principle, the seed of Abraham is spiritual seed' (Ridderbos).

CHAPTER FOUR

Abraham's true heirs were held under the law during the time of their minority, but this guardianship ceased when Christ came, and now all believers have received the adoption of sons [verses. 1–7]. Hence it would be the height of folly if the Galatians renounced the privileges of sonship by returning to the rudiments of legalism [verses 8–11]. Paul touchingly recalls their former eagerness to receive him and his gospel, which he contrasts with their inconsistency in welcoming the Judaizers, and expresses his longing to see Christ restored in them [verses 12–20]. The apostle finds further support for his argument in the history of Hagar and Sarah, which illustrates the difference between legal bondage and Christian freedom. As the son of the servant was displaced by the son of the free woman, so those who follow the law cannot receive the inheritance which belongs to the children of promise [verses 21–31].

1: But I say that so long as the heir is a child, he differeth nothing from a bondservant though he is lord of all; 2: but is under guardians and stewards until the day appointed of the father.

Paul now takes up the word 'heir' to illustrate the inferior state of the people of God under the law. For though they were indeed the sons of God, they were sons in the time of their minority. The child is 'his father's trueborn son. In time he will be full owner. Meanwhile he is as subject as any slave on the estate. There is nothing he can command for his own. He is treated and provided for as a bondman might be; put "under stewards" who manage his property, "and guardians" in charge of his person, "until the day fore-appointed of the father". This situation does not exclude, it implies fatherly affection and care on the one side, and heirship on the other. But it forbids the recognition of the heir, his investment with filial rights . . . The case supposed, we observe, is not that of a *dead* father, into whose place the son steps at the proper age. A grant is made by the father *still living*, who keeps his son in pupilage till he sees fit to put him in possession of the promised estate' (G. G. Findlay). Thus the point of Paul's argument is that with the coming of Christ, the time set by the Father for investing believers with the full rights of sonship has arrived [verses

4–6], and the state of subjection to 'guardians' and 'stewards' which characterized the legal economy has been left behind.

3: So we also, when we were children, were held in bondage under the rudiments of the world:

The RSV rendering 'elemental spirits of the universe', without even a marginal note, is regarded by Oswald T. Allis as a particularly striking example of the 'dogmatism' of that version. For as Bruce Metzger points out, 'a better translation is "rudimentary notions of the world", referring to elementary religious observances [verses 9–10; *Col.* 2:8, 20]' (*The New Oxford Annotated Bible: Revised Standard Version* (OUP, New York, 1973, p. 1413). Furthermore there is nothing to show that 'the cosmic elements, the stars, or related spirits etc., played any particular role in the Galatian churches', and it seems that Paul himself contributed the phrase in both Galatians and Colossians (G. Delling, *TDNT*, vol. 7, pp. 684–5). See also George Eldon Ladd's note on *STOICHEIA* in his *Theology of the New Testament*, pp. 402–3.) As Paul appears to equate this expression with 'the tradition of *men*' in Colossians 2:8, it seems fairly certain that the term 'world' bears an ethical meaning and refers to *mankind* as alienated from the life of God. Thus William Hendriksen interprets these 'worldly rudiments' as *elementary teachings regarding rules and regulations, by means of which, before Christ's coming, people, both Jews and Gentiles, each in their own way, attempted by their own efforts, and in accordance with the promptings of their own fleshly (unregenerate) nature, to achieve salvation*. The worldly man, whether he lives within or beyond the pale of special revelation, is under bondage to these regulations because he always regards salvation as a reward to be earned, and never as a gift to be received.

4: but when the fulness of the time came, God sent forth his Son, born of a woman, born under the law.

But when the fulness of the time came: The 'servitude' of the heir lasts 'until the day appointed of the father' [verse 2], i.e. the moment determined by God's eternal decree. Our 'spiritual bondage expires with the advent of the fulness of the time – God's set time. The nonage of the church was the duration of the Mosaic covenant. But not till the last moment of its existence, when its time was filled like a reservoir with the last drop, was it set aside, and the ripe or full age of the church commenced – "the time is fulfilled", *Mark* 1:15. The fulness of the time was also the fittest time in the world's history' (Eadie).

God sent forth his Son: This points to an eternal relationship. As the object of the Father's love, the pre-existent Son always enjoyed filial fellowship with God [*2 Cor.* 8:9; *Phil.* 2:6]. 'The Son's going out from God on his mission is seen in his becoming man. He did not cease to be the Son of God when he became man. He did not drop his deity, which is an impossible thought. He remained what he was and added what he had not had, namely a human nature, derived out of a woman, a human mother. He became the God-man' (Lenski).

Born of a woman: In accordance with the divine decree, the Son of God entered the world of men by being 'born of a woman'. The apostle does not say, 'born of a virgin', for he is stressing the humiliation of Christ, his likeness to us, a likeness which he voluntarily assumed for our redemption. 'Paul is thinking not of the difference, but of the identity of Christ's birth and our own. We are carried back to Bethlehem. We see Jesus a babe lying in his mother's arms – *God's Son a human infant,* drawing his life from a weak woman!' (Findlay).

Born under the law: It was with the express purpose of liberating those who were under the curse of the law that Christ by his birth became subject to all the law's demands. As the surety of a sinful people he came to pay their debt to the law of God, not only to fulfil all its *precepts* as our representative [*Matt.* 3:15, 5:17], but also to exhaust its *penalty* as our substitute [3:13].

5: that he might redeem them that were under the law that we might receive the adoption of sons.

These two final clauses set forth two gracious purposes of God in the plan of salvation. They correspond to the clauses of the previous verse in an inverted order (chiasmus): 'The Son of God was born a man that we might receive the adoption of sons; He was born under the law that he might redeem them which were under the law' (Lightfoot).

The first gracious purpose of God was the removal of the great hindrance to our adoption. The primary reference is to the Mosaic law. Jesus was born under that law which gave the most perfect and exact expression to the claims of God upon man. It was by exhausting the curse of the highest law that Christ redeemed his people from all bondage to any kind of law [3:13]. Hence his sacrifice has ushered in the era of liberty from which there can be no reversion to the tutelary bondage of the Mosaic covenant. 'The description *under Law* includes Gentiles as well as Jews: for though they had not *the Law*, they were not without Law to God [cf. *Rom.* 2:14]: they had indeed been expressly specified in 3:14 as included in the redemption from the curse of the Law' (Rendall).

The second gracious purpose of God was the bestowal of the unspeakable privilege of our adoption into the family of God [*1 John* 3:1]. He who was the Son by nature willingly took the form of a servant, so that we who were *by nature* the servants of sin might become sons by the adoption of *grace!* His Father is now our Father, for he has ascended to heaven not only as the natural Son returned home to the Father, but also as the triumphant Son of Man who took his place in glory on our behalf [*John* 20:17; *Heb.* 2:11, 12].

6: And because ye are sons, God sent forth the Spirit of his Son into our hearts, crying, Abba, Father.

To prove that you are sons, God has sent into our hearts the Spirit of his Son (NEB): The Galatians must realize that the presence of the Spirit is the proof of their adoption [3:2]. They are not minors under discipline, but have been endowed with all the rights and privileges of sonship. As God sent forth his Son to accomplish redemption [verse 4], so he sent forth 'the Spirit of his Son' to apply its benefits to the hearts of his people. The significance of this title, which occurs only here in the New Testament, is that it shows that the activity of the Spirit is never divorced from the Son whom he was sent into the world to glorify [*John* 16:14]. This means that the objective blessings of justification cannot be separated from their realization through the gift of the Spirit. The passage affords no encouragement whatever to any conception of a two-stage faith which relegates justification to the 'primary' stage of Christian experience, and urges believers to strive after the 'higher life' of the Spirit. It is the express teaching of the apostle that this assurance of sonship is certified to believers by the Spirit in conversion, and not in some subsequent experience [cf. *Eph.* 1:13, NIV].

Crying, Abba, Father: The research of Joachim Jeremias has shown that though the Jews never dared to address God in this intimate way, Jesus always used this form (except in the cry of dereliction on the cross, Matt. 27:46), and taught his disciples to do the same. It is only in virtue of the new relationship given by *God* through the *Son* and actualized by the *Spirit* that men can joyfully cry, 'Abba, dear Father'. Hence the mere fact that Gentile Christians accepted this Aramaic word into their prayers 'shows how conscious they were of the new element which had been given them in the cry of "Abba"' (J. Jeremias, *The Prayers of Jesus*, p. 65).

> *'Abba, Father', Lord, we call Thee –*
> *Hallowed Name! – from day to day;*
> *'Tis Thy children's right to know Thee,*
> *None but children 'Abba' say.*
> *This high glory we inherit,*
> *Thy free gift through Jesus' blood;*
> *God the Spirit, with our spirit,*
> *Witnesseth we're sons of God.*
>
> Robert Hawker

7: So that thou art no longer a bondservant, but a Son; and if a son, then an heir through God.

Thus the evidence of sonship is to be seen in that filial consciousness which is produced by the gift of the Spirit. Paul 'changes to the singular to drive the point home to each one. The spiritual experience [3:2] has set each one free. Each is now a son and heir' (Robertson).

Through God: This 'carries to a climax the emphatic repetition of "God" observed in verses 4 and 6. "*God* sent his Son" into the world; "*God* sent" in turn "his Son's Spirit into your hearts". God then, and no other, has bestowed your inheritance. It is yours by his fiat. Who dares challenge it?' (Findlay).

8: Howbeit at that time, not knowing God, ye were in bondage to them that by nature are no gods:

Paul here contrasts the former ignorance of the Galatians with their present knowledge. Now that they have come to know the one living God they enjoy the liberty of sons, but before their conversion they were held in abject bondage by imaginary deities of man's invention. The phrase 'by nature are no gods' determinatively discriminates between the true God and all other so-called gods. 'False worship given to God, presupposeth a false opinion of God: and a false opinion of God sets up an idol, or false god, in the room of the true God. For it is not sufficient to conceive some true things of God, but we must precisely conceive him, as he hath revealed himself, without addition or detraction. And thus did the wisest of the Galatians worship false gods' (Perkins) [*1 Cor.* 8:4–6].

9: but now that ye have come to know God, or rather to be known by God, how turn ye back again to the weak and beggarly rudiments, where unto ye desire to be in bondage over again?

Paul corrects himself since the Galatians had only come to know God through his prior knowledge of them. Salvation is wholly of God 'whose gracious fore-knowing and fore-appointing of us to eternal life is the ground and foundation of our illumination and conversion, our love to him a reflex of his love to us' (John Trapp).

But now . . . how turn ye back again? 'By *rudiments* we are to understand Circumcision, the Jewish Sacrifices, and all the ceremonies of the law of *Moses*. And it may not seem strange, that they are called impotent and beggarly rudiments. For they must be considered three ways, with Christ, without Christ, and against Christ. With Christ, when they are considered as types and figures of Christ to come, and as signs of grace by divine institution for the time of the Old Testament. Without Christ, when they are used only for custom, whether before or after the death of Christ. Against Christ, when they are esteemed as meritorious causes of salvation, and the justification of a sinner is placed in them, either in whole or in part: as though Christ alone were not sufficient. In this respect *Paul* calls them impotent and beggarly rudiments.

'And *Paul* having said, that the Galatians returned again to the rudiments of the law, in the next words he shows how they do it: namely, by *serving them again*. They served or yielded service to them three ways: In opinion, because they judged them to be necessary parts of God's worship, and means of their salvation. In conscience, because they subjected their consciences to them. In affection, because they placed part of their affiance in them for their justification and salvation. It may be demanded, how the Galatians can be said to return again to the rudiments of the law, and serve them again, that were never used to them before? *Answer.* In the speech of *Paul* there is that which is called *Catachresis*, that is, a kind of speaking somewhat improper in respect of fineness and elegancy. The like we have, *Ruth* 1:22, when *Ruth* is said to return to Judea with *Naomi*; and yet she was never there before. Nevertheless, the speech in sense is most significant and proper. For *Paul* (no doubt) signifies hereby, that when the Galatians subjected themselves to the rudiments of the law, and placed their salvation in part even in them, they did in effect and in truth as much as return again to their old superstitions, and serve again their false gods' (Perkins).

10: Ye observe days, and months, and seasons, and years.

Paul sees in the eagerness of the Galatians to embrace the legalistic observance of Jewish religious festivals a conspicuous example of their sad decline from the freedom of the gospel. It seems reasonable to assume with Burton that the Judaizers had adopted the adroit course of first presenting to them the least objectionable requirements of the Jewish law, and that they were now urging them to receive circumcision [cf. 5:2, 3, 12; 6:12,13]. Since Paul is rebuking Gentiles for subjecting themselves to Jewish ordinances *and that with a view to acquiring merit before God*, it is evident that the verse furnishes no argument against the obligation to observe the Christian Sabbath. 'Yet all superstitious observation of days is unlawful, as being here condemned, either expressly or by consequence' (Fergusson) [*Col.* 2:16].

11: I am afraid of you, lest by any means I have bestowed labour upon you in vain.

I am afraid for you, lest I might have expended my labour on you in vain (Arndt-Gingrich): Although Paul hopes that the Galatians have not heard the gospel in vain [3:4], their present conduct certainly puts a large question mark over the effectiveness of his work in their midst. In thus frankly expressing his fear for their safety, he intends to rouse them from their legal stupor to the evangelical grace of repentance. 'There is something peculiarly affecting in these simple words of the apostle. He had laboured, laboured too with apparent success; but now, through the exertion of false teachers, the fruits of his labour seem in extreme hazard of being completely blasted. How happy would it be for Christ's church if ministers in general were of the apostle's spirit – "jealous over their people with a godly jealousy!"' (John Brown) [*2 Cor.* 11:2]

12a: I beseech you, brethren, become as I am for I also am become as ye are.

Even to contemplate the possibility of his having laboured among the Galatians to no purpose is so distressing to Paul that he breaks into a passionate personal appeal [verses 12–20]. "'As I, though a zealous Jew by birth [1:14], in my life among you cast out Jewish habits, so do ye; for I am become as ye are" – viz., in not observing legal ordinances. "My laying them aside among Gentiles shows that I regard them as *not at all contributing to justification or sanctification.* Do you regard them in the same light, and act accordingly". His observing the law among the Jews was not inconsistent with this, for he did so to win them, without compromising principle [*1 Cor.* 9:20, 21]. But the Galatian Gentiles, by adopting legal ordinances, showed they regarded them as needful for salvation (Fausset).

12b: Ye did me no wrong: 13: but ye know that because of an infirmity of the flesh I preached the gospel unto you the first time: 14: and that which was a temptation to you in my flesh ye despised not, nor rejected; but ye received me as an angel of God, even as Christ Jesus.

Despite the distressing circumstances under which Paul brought the gospel to the Galatians, he reminds them that they did him no harm at that time. For though the sight of a man in such bodily weakness could well have caused them to turn away from him and his message in contempt, they had received him so warmly that they might have been welcoming an angel of God, or even Christ himself! How sadly different was their attitude towards him now!

We have no means of knowing the nature of Paul's infirmity, still less whether it is to be connected with his 'thorn in the flesh' [*2 Cor.* 12:7]. But evidently illness forced him to change his travel plans, for it was 'because of a physical ailment' (Arndt-Gingrich) that he came to preach in their area. There is also uncertainty over the meaning of the phrase 'the first time'. It could either mean 'originally' (NEB) or 'on that former occasion' (Hendriksen), pointing to the first of two visits. Perhaps the first alternative is preferable, though the second is not incompatible with the sequence of events suggested in the Introduction, for if that view is correct Paul would have visited the Galatians *twice* on the first missionary journey [cf. Acts 14:21].

15: Where then is that gratulation of yourselves? for I bear you witness, that, if possible, ye would have plucked out your eyes and given them to me.

Where then is your felicitation of yourselves? (Lightfoot): Paul asks the Galatians what has become of the happiness they once felt in his ministry. They then congratulated themselves because the apostle had brought them the good news of God's free grace in Christ. But they lost their joy when they began to give heed to the law-message of the Judaizers. The question thus underlines the folly of exchanging the blessings of grace for the treadmill of works. It is precarious to assume from the second part of the verse that Paul was afflicted with some form of eye disease like ophthalmia. He simply means that at the time of their conversion they thought so highly of him, they would have deemed no sacrifice too great to make on his behalf. 'For had it been possible to benefit me by plucking out the most precious member of your body, you would have done so!' [cf. *Psa.* 17:8; *Matt.* 5:29].

16: So then am I become your enemy, by telling you the truth?

Is it possible that the Galatians who once regarded themselves as greatly blessed in knowing Paul have now come to think of him as their enemy? Is he their enemy simply because he is too good a friend to refrain from telling them the truth they would prefer not to hear? The important lesson which this verse teaches us is that we cannot be selective with the truth of God. We cannot choose what we like and reject what we dislike of the apostolic teaching. 'No, the apostles of Jesus Christ have authority in everything they teach, whether we happen to like it or not' (John Stott).

17: They zealously seek you in no good way; nay, they desire to shut you out, that ye may seek them.

These people are zealously courting you for no commendable purpose: on the contrary, they want to isolate you, in order that you may zealously court them (Hendriksen): Paul's genuine concern for the spiritual welfare of his converts is in sharp contrast to the selfish and sinister motives of his rivals for their affections, the Judaizers, whom he does not condescend to name here. While they now pay court to the Galatians, their intentions are far from honourable. For when the churches have been cut off from all contact with the apostle of their liberty, they will become entirely dependent upon these taskmasters of bondage. Such is ever the technique of the cultist!

18: But it is good to be zealously sought in a good matter at all times, and not only when I am present with you.

Now (it is) commendable to be zealously courted in connection with a commendable cause (and this) always (Hendriksen): Paul here gives abstract expression to a truth which must command their ready assent. Zealous courting is good provided the suitor pursues an honourable course in an honourable way. Now whereas the Judaizers had cast dishonour upon the Galatians by seeking to seduce them from the truth for their own selfish gain, Paul had brought honour to them by courting them with honourable intentions in a supremely honourable cause, the gospel. And what is honourable at one time must also be honourable at all times!

And not only when I am present with you: Paul now lets the Galatians see that this principle applies no less to the wooed than it does to the wooer. For a faithful suitor demands constancy in his beloved whether he happens to be present or absent. Yet no sooner had Paul turned his back than the fickle Galatians began to respond to the dishonourable overtures of those who designed to pervert the purity of their faith. 'If the Apostle be thus jealous, how much more then is Christ himself jealous, who hath espoused himself to his Church? This plainly shows, that he cannot brook either partner, or deputy. And therefore his sacrifice on the cross must stand without the sacrifice of the Mass, his intercession without the intercession of Saints, his merits without the merit of works, his satisfaction without any satisfaction of ours. He will have the heart alone, and all the heart, or nothing: and he will not give any part of his honour to any other' (Perkins).

19: My little children, of whom I am again in travail until Christ be formed in you –

My little children: This mode of address so common in *John* is not used elsewhere by Paul. Here the diminutive is expressive both of 'the tenderness of the Apostle and the feebleness of his converts' (Lightfoot). His spontaneous outburst of tender affection for his erring children has the irresistible appeal of being completely genuine. Their spiritual birth had once involved him in painful travail, but now their threatened defection has brought on those birth-pangs for the second time! Not as though they needed a second conversion, but rather that Christ might be so completely formed in them that they would be for ever immune from the insidious germs of false doctrine. He is not satisfied to see them assume a mask of Christ; his eager desire is that they may fully know the inner reality of Christ living within their hearts. As Calvin well says, 'If ministers wish to do any good, let them labour to form Christ, not to form themselves, in their hearers.' Hence they must labour so to teach the Word of God 'in demonstration of the Spirit and of power' that men may come to know the Christ of whom it testifies.

20: but I could wish to be present with you now, and to change my tone; for I am perplexed about you.

This upsurge of affection for his converts makes Paul wish he were now present with them so that he could change his tone. For with the obstacle of distance removed, he would be able to assure them of his love even as he sought to disabuse them of their errors. 'Paul could put his heart into his voice. The pen stands between them. He knew the power of his voice on their hearts. He had tried it before' (Robertson). He confesses his perplexity as he wonders how best to continue his exhortation, and restore their faith in the one gospel from which they had so sadly declined.

21: Tell me, ye that desire to be under the law, do ye not hear the law?

At this point Paul does indeed change his tone. 'He will tell his "children" a story!' (Findlay). He challenges those who desire to be under the law to hear what the law (i.e. the Pentateuch) is really saying to them through the history of the two sons of Abraham. He would have them learn that the law has in it far more than the specific commands of a vanished ceremonialism; it also contains in germ the grace that is now openly proclaimed to them in the gospel. Thus the spiritual lessons which the apostle draws from this story are firmly based upon the historical facts. He simply makes patent what is latent in the narrative.

22: For it is written, that Abraham had two sons, one by the handmaid, and one by the free woman.

This is not a direct quotation but a summary of the facts (recorded in Genesis 16 and 21) which show that it is possible to be a son of Abraham in more than one sense. For Abraham had two sons, one by the slave woman and one by the free woman. And what they were by birth made all the difference to their respective destinies. Neither the unbelief which proposed its own fulfilment of God's promise nor the opposition of the natural seed could frustrate God's elective purpose of grace [*Gen.* 16:2; 21:9]. So though he was the elder son, the inheritance was not for Ishmael, because unlike Isaac, he was not born free.

23: Howbeit the son by the handmaid is born after the flesh; but the son by the free woman is born through promise.

Not only were these the sons of different mothers, but there was also a significant difference in the manner of their begetting. The son who was born after the ordinary course of nature is here contrasted with the son who was born through promise. One birth was natural, the other was supernatural in that God intervened in a miraculous way to enable Abraham and Sarah to have Isaac long after all hope of any purely human fulfilment of the promise had been extinguished [*Gen.* 21:7; *Rom.* 4:19–21; *Heb.* 11:11]. This child who was brought to birth by the exercise of divine power therefore becomes the fitting symbol of all who are supernaturally born of the Spirit [cf. verse 29].

24: Which things contain an allegory: for these women are two covenants; one from mount Sinai, bearing children unto bondage, Which is Hagar.

Which things contain an allegory: This means 'to express or explain one thing under the image of another' (Ellicott). Calvin castigates

Origen and those like him for having 'seized this occasion of twisting Scripture this way and that, away from the genuine sense. For they inferred that the literal sense is too meagre and poor and that beneath the bark of the letter there lie deeper mysteries which cannot be extracted but by hammering out allegories'. This single example of allegorizing by the apostle therefore affords no lawful precedent to give our imaginations free rein with the text of Scripture. Paul was inspired; we are not! Moreover, Paul's use of allegory is very different from Philo's ingenious speculations. 'The simple historical facts are not explained away as if they had been portions of a mere allegory, like the persons and events in Bunyan's *Pilgrim*; but these facts are invested with a new meaning as portraying great spiritual truths, and such truths they were intended and moulded to symbolize' (Eadie).

For these women are two covenants: The free woman represents the Abrahamic covenant of promise and the slave woman represents the Sinaitic covenant of law. As Paul sees these women in terms of two contrasted series of concepts, the differences between them can be grasped more easily if they are arranged in parallel columns:

Hagar, the slave woman	Sarah, the free woman
Ishmael, the natural child,	Isaac, the spiritual heir,
'born after the flesh'	'born after the Spirit'
The Old Covenant	The New Covenant
The earthly Jerusalem	The heavenly Jerusalem
The bondage of the law	The freedom of the gospel

One from Mount Sinai, bearing children unto bondage: Although God 'gave his law to Israel in a context of grace, that law was unable to save anyone. Besides, when it is, nevertheless, viewed as a force by means of which a person achieves deliverance and salvation, as the Jews and Judaizers actually viewed it, then it enslaves. It then not only leaves men in their bondage but more and more adds to their heavy burden' (Hendriksen) [see comment on 3:12, 23; cf. *Matt.* 11:28, 29; *Rom.* 8:15].

Which is Hagar: With this shattering identification Paul lets his infatuated readers know that they may indeed become the sons of Abraham by means of law. Yes, 'the Law will make you his sons by Hagar, whose home is Sinai – not Israelites, but *Ishmaelites!*' (Findlay).

25: Now this Hagar is mount Sinai in Arabia, and answereth to the Jerusalem that now is: for she is in bondage with her children.

Now Hagar stands for Mount Sinai in Arabia (NIV): 'The thought "Hagar" (not the word and not the woman as such, but the thought of bondage suggested by her) corresponds to Mount Sinai, situated in a desert land and far away from the land of promise generally, and Jerusalem in particular' (Williams).

And corresponds to the present city of Jerusalem (NIV): Thus Hagar, Sinai, and present-day Jerusalem all belong together in the same rank or category. It was Sinai and not Canaan that Paul saw in Jerusalem, for it was no longer the capital of the land of *promise* but had become the metropolis of *legalism*. A terrible indictment indeed!

For she is in bondage with her children: This is the 'justification of the parallelism just affirmed between Hagar and Jerusalem. As Hagar, a slave, bore children that by that birth passed into slavery, so the Jerusalem that now is and her children, viz., all the adherents of legalistic Judaism which has its centre in Jerusalem, are in bondage to law' (Burton).

26: But the Jerusalem that is above is free, which is our mother.

In his haste to apply the truth Paul does not stop to complete the figure by naming Sarah as the other mother. The contrast he draws is not between *present* bondage and *future* bliss, since he is showing the Galatians that believers even now enjoy that liberty which descends to them from Jerusalem above. In other words, the 'eschatological salvation is not awaited in an indefinite future but has come already. We who believe in Christ are children of our mother, the Jerusalem which is above, verse 31' (E. Lohse, *TDNT*, vol. 7, p. 337).

'What he calls heavenly is not shut up in heaven, nor are we to seek for it outside the world. For the Church is spread over the whole world and is a pilgrim on the earth. Why then is it said to be from heaven? Because it originates in heavenly grace. For the sons of God are born, not of flesh and blood, but by the power of the Holy Spirit. The heavenly Jerusalem, which derives its origin from heaven and dwells above by faith, is the mother of believers' (Calvin).

27: For it is written, Rejoice, thou barren that bearest not;
Break forth and cry, thou that travailest not:

For more are the children of the desolate than
   of her that hath the husband.

That the glory of the church far surpasses the temporary favours once
vouchsafed to an earthly Zion is proved by an appeal to Isaiah 54:1,
according to the Septuagint (the most influential Greek translation of
the Old Testament). The preceding verses in Isaiah, chapter 52:13–
53:12, clearly teach that the grounds of this rejoicing are found in the
redemptive accomplishments of the Lord Jesus Christ. It is because
Paul sees the barren Sarah and exiled Israel as fitting symbols of the
fructifying power of the divine promise that he aptly applies the passage
to the church's experience of the power of her exalted Saviour.

'Paul calls the church barren because her children are not born by
means of the Law or works or any human efforts or powers but in the
Holy Spirit through the Word of faith. This is purely a matter of being
born, not of doing any works. Those who are prolific, on the other
hand, labour and strain greatly in travail; this is purely a matter of doing
works, not of giving birth. But those who try to achieve the status of
sons and heirs by the righteousness of the Law or by their own
righteousness are slaves, who will never receive the inheritance even
though they work themselves to death with their great effort; for they
are trying, contrary to the will of God, to achieve by their own works
what God wants to grant to believers by sheer grace for Christ's sake.
Believers do good works; but they do not become sons and heirs
through this, for this has been granted to them by their birth. Now
that they have become sons for Christ's sake, they glorify God with
their good deeds and help their neighbour' (Luther).

28: Now we, brethren, as Isaac was, are children of promise.

Now you, brothers, like Isaac, are children of promise (NIV): The
implication is that if the Galatians insist on behaving like those born
'after the flesh' they will forfeit the status that is theirs by grace, for
they are 'children' only by virtue of the promise. 'In Isaac this became
apparent from the circumstances of birth; in believers it becomes
apparent in the quickening, the regenerating, of the Spirit [cf. verse
29]. But in both instances, God's power and sovereign grace is the
cause of the birth . . . The household of Abraham is the prototype of
the church of God. The promise which accrued to him is the secret of

the maintenance of the church. Ishmael's and Isaac's birth represents the two attitudes towards the promise: that of human self-vindication and that of faith' (Ridderbos).

29: But as then he that was born after the flesh persecuted him that was born after the Spirit, so also it is now.

Paul next shows that Ishmael's mockery of the infant Isaac gave evidence of such malice that it could be called nothing less than a persecution of the heir of promise. The reference is to Genesis 21:9 which should read 'laughing at him' (NEB) and not 'playing' with him (RSV). It would seem that Ishmael made Isaac's name ('laughter'), which was given to him in holy joy, the butt for his unholy ridicule. Thus Isaac 'was laughter to his mother in one sense, but to his brother in a very different sense – the one laughed for him, the other at him' (Eadie).

So also it is now: The Judaizers doubtless held up the gospel of God's grace to the same ridicule. 'The persecution of the church by Judaism gave proof of the Ishmaelite spirit, the carnal animus by which it was possessed. A religion of externalism naturally becomes repressive. It knows not "the demonstration of the Spirit"; it has "confidence in the flesh". It relies on outward means for the propagation of its faith; and naturally resorts to the secular arm. The Inquisition and the *Auto-da-fé* are a not unfitting accompaniment of the gorgeous ceremonial of the Mass. Ritualism and priestly autocracy go hand in hand' (Findlay) [cf. *2 Cor.* 10:3–5].

30: Howbeit what saith the scripture? Cast out the handmaid and her son: for the son of the handmaid shall not inherit with the son of the free woman.

Paul's question challenges his converts to apply this Scripture to the deplorable crisis in the Galatian churches. Sarah's demand for the expulsion of Hagar and Ishmael was a truly prophetic word, for it gave expression to the sentence of God [*Gen.* 21:10, 12]. As the Scripture is a living word, it still pronounces this same verdict upon all those who have no higher birth than Ishmael's. So that all the Galatians will accomplish by succumbing to the blandishments of the Judaizers is their own exclusion from any share of the inheritance of grace.

'The Law and the Gospel cannot co-exist; the Law must disappear before the Gospel. It is scarcely possible to estimate the strength of conviction and depth of prophetic insight which this declaration implies. The Apostle thus confidently sounds the death-knell of Judaism at a time when one-half of Christendom clung to the Mosaic law with a jealous affection little short of frenzy, and while the Judaic party seemed to be growing in influence and was strong enough, even in the Gentile churches of his own founding, to undermine his influence and endanger his life. The truth which to us appears a truism must then have been regarded as paradox' (Lightfoot).

31: Wherefore, brethren, we are not children of a handmaid, but of the free woman.

The practical conclusion the Galatians are to draw from this allegory is now expressed in the simplest form. Since they are children of the free woman they must act accordingly, and not submit to any form of bondage: '"not of *any* bondwoman" whether of Judaism or some form of heathenism, for there are *many*, "but of *the* free woman, the lawful spouse, the Church of Christ, *which is one*"' (Lightfoot).

CHAPTER FIVE

Paul warns the Galatians not to forfeit their freedom in Christ, for if they consent to circumcision they would exchange justifying grace for the condemnation of the law [verses 1–6]. He reminds them of their good beginning through believing the preaching of the cross, and denounces the preachers of circumcision who are now leading them astray from the truth [verses 7–12].

Yet liberty must not be confused with licence, and they are to use their freedom to serve one another in love [verses 13–15]. To walk by the Spirit is to be free from the lust of the flesh, but they must desist from the works of the flesh if they would bring forth the fruit of the Spirit [verses 16–26].

1: For freedom did Christ set us free: stand fast therefore, and be not entangled again in a yoke of bondage.

The ASV rightly makes a separate paragraph of this verse, for it serves the double function of summing up the whole of Paul's doctrinal argument [chapters 3, 4], and of providing the point of transition for his ethical argument [chapters 5, 6].

For freedom did Christ set us free: In making this emphatic affirmation Paul was not indulging in needless repetition, for the Galatians were in dire danger of despising their birthright. The statement virtually amounts to the challenge: 'Did Christ set us free that we might be slaves? No, but that we might be free!' He thus blames them for overlooking the purpose of Christ's great sacrifice, for it was to liberate guilty sinners from the curse of the law that he died and rose again [3:13; 22–25]. This freedom became a reality in their experience through the power of the Spirit, who had invested them with the liberty of sons by applying the all-sufficient merit of that redemptive accomplishment to their hearts [3:2; 4:6]. Hence their falling back into bondage was 'inexplicable and inexcusable' (Ridderbos). As the nature of this freedom is defined by all that has gone before, so all that follows shows that it must not be confused with lawless licence.

Stand fast therefore, and be not entangled again in a yoke of bondage: The whole of the apostle's appeal to the Galatians is contained in this urgent charge to maintain their freedom, and to stand firm against the efforts of the Judaizers to bring them again under a yoke of bondage. The force of 'again' is well noted by Lightfoot: 'Having escaped from the slavery of Heathenism, they would fain bow to the slavery of Judaism' [cf. 4:9]. Those who have been liberated by Christ to serve him in perfect freedom must not yield themselves in servile submission to *any* such yoke of slavery [cf. *Matt.* 11:29, 30 with 23:4].

2: Behold, I Paul say unto you, that if ye receive circumcision, Christ will profit you nothing.

'Behold' is a sharp summons to pay heed to a warning of the highest moment, the unique authority of which is demonstrated by the emphatic 'I Paul'. He will not mince his words, for the salvation of his converts is at stake. Already they have surrendered much of their freedom to the demands of the Judaizers [4:10], and now they are on the brink of submitting to that rite which would be 'the sacrament of their excision from Christ' (Huxtable cited by Findlay). They cannot have Christ *and* circumcision; they must choose circumcision *or* Christ. As Ridderbos points out, this does not mean that circumcision is of itself an impediment to Christ, but the legalist demand that those who were never subject to the law of Moses should receive it *as a condition for obtaining salvation* perverted the gospel by challenging the sufficiency of Christ's work. 'Many do profess Christ who shall receive no saving advantage by him, especially they who rely upon any thing besides him, or jointly with him, as the meritorious cause of their salvation: for saith he, "If ye be circumcised, Christ shall profit you nothing"' (Fergusson).

3: Yea, I testify again to every man that received circumcision, that he is a debtor to do the whole law.

'Again' repeats the warning of the previous verse. But this time Paul solemnly assures every man who is contemplating circumcision that this act will not only sever his connection with Christ, but will also place him under an obligation to keep the whole law. He who is not content to owe his salvation entirely to grace becomes a debtor to do the whole law, which is 'impossible for man to keep in part, much less *wholly* [*James* 2:10]; yet none can be justified by it, unless he keep it *wholly* [3:10]' (Fausset).

4: Ye are severed from Christ, ye who would be justified by the law; ye are fallen away from grace.

The severity of the apostle's language is meant to disabuse the Galatians of their misguided enthusiasm for the law. For to seek justification by one's own works according to law, implies a severance from Christ as the provider of righteousness, and a non-reliance upon God's grace as the source of our salvation. 'Christ's method of justification is wholly of grace, and those who rely on law and merit are in opposition to grace – are fallen out of it. The clause has really no bearing on the doctrine of the perseverance of the saints, or on their possible apostasy' (Eadie). Those who are saints take heed of such warnings and persevere in their calling; those who are not often show it by publicly separating themselves from that domain of grace to which they never truly belonged.

5: For we through the Spirit by faith wait for the hope of righteousness.

For it is by faith that we wait in the Spirit for the righteousness we hope for (Moffatt): Far from seeking to supplement our faith by any *work* [verse 4], 'we' who believe God's promise simply *wait* in the Spirit for the hoped-for righteousness. Thus the Spirit who unites us with Christ enables us to live in earnest expectation of our final salvation. According to the New Testament believers do not wait for a second experience of the Holy Spirit, imperfectly received in conversion. They rather wait 'in the Spirit' for the inheritance, which is assured to them through their present experience of the Spirit [cf. *Rom.* 5:5; 8:23f; *Eph.* 1:13f; 4:30].

Although believers are already justified, their righteous standing before God has yet to be revealed, and this is therefore still the object of their hope [*Col.* 1:5; *2 Tim.* 4:8]. But legal justification has no future, and is present only in the legalist's imagination. 'Justification by faith is present, and also stretches in sure "hope" on to eternity. Righteousness, now the believer's hidden possession, shall then *shine out* as glory' [*Matt.* 13:43; *Col.* 3:3, 4] (Fausset).

6: For in Christ Jesus neither circumcision availeth anything, nor uncircumcision; but faith working through love.

For in Christ Jesus: This verse is of outstanding importance since it establishes the spiritual nature of the Christian faith. As the very source of Paul's life was union with Christ (he uses the phrase 'in Christ' some 160 times in his letters), he could no longer define religion in terms of external marks and carnal ordinances [cf. *Phil.* 3:4–6]. Hence he speaks here of that vital *spiritual* relationship in which faith is all-important, and the externals of the *flesh* are a matter of complete indifference. The phrase shows that it takes more than a formal assent to certain truths about Christ to make a man a Christian, for it is only through union with a *living* Saviour that Christianity becomes in the truest sense of the word a *living* religion.

Neither circumcision availeth anything, nor uncircumcision: 'The uncircumcised has nothing to boast of over the circumcised; if both be in Christ, their condition is equal – is influenced neither by the presence of the mere external rite, nor by the want of it' (Eadie).

But faith working through love: 'This is the new *creature* [6:15]. He joined *hope* with *faith*; now he joins with it *love*. In these the whole of *Christianity* consists' (Bengel). For though the law commands love, only faith can beget love, and thus provide us with the moral dynamic to fulfil the law [verse 14; *Rom.* 13:8–10]. As Lightfoot points out, these words bridge over the gulf which seems to separate the language of Paul and James, since both see faith as 'a principle of practical energy, as opposed to a barren, inactive theory'. Paul praises the true faith which is fruitful in every good work, whereas James condemns the false faith which is barren of any good work [*James* 2:20].

7: Ye were running well; who hindered you that ye should not obey the truth?

When the Galatians were running well they were obeying the truth. Their right belief was shown in right conduct. But the Judaizers had hindered them, for their preaching of works had broken up the highway of free grace and halted their progress [cf. 3:2f; *Heb.* 12:1]. 'The man who yields his mind to the influence of the truth as it is in Jesus, finds all he needs in Christ – he does not go about to establish a way of justification of his own, but submits to God's method of justification, through the faith of Christ. All halting in the Christian course originates here. While the mind yields itself up to the influence of the truth, the Christian runs well; but whenever this influence is resisted, he is hindered' (John Brown).

8: This persuasion came not of him that calleth you.

That persuasion, that draws you away from the truth, does not come from him who calls you (Arndt-Gingrich): 'The Judaistic arts and arguments were not in harmony with the effectual calling of God. The one is persuasion – art and arguments – on merely human and specious principles; the other is "calling", the summons of God to life and truth in Christ. The apostle goes back in idea to "Who hindered you?" – the Judaizers are present to his mind from this question on through several verses and to the end of the twelfth verse. It is their work which he thus pictures; their "persuasion" was the preaching of another gospel, the bewitching of the Galatians' (Eadie). [3:1]

9: A little leaven leaveneth the whole lump.

This is a proverbial saying which Paul uses in a different connection in *1 Cor.* 5:6. There it refers to the leavening effect of one man's sin upon the whole church; here it is applied to the doctrine of the Judaizers. 'A little legalism, mixed with the gospel, corrupts its purity. To add ordinances and works in the least degree to justification by faith, is to undermine the *whole*' (Fausset). The danger for the Galatians in accepting their *persons* lay in receiving their false *principles*. It is the Word of God, and not a pleasing presence, that is the touchstone by which every teacher is to be judged [*Isa.* 8:20]. And the contemporary church will never recover the pure gospel until she learns to reject those who bring her a different gospel, even though they may have the ability to present error in an attractive guise [cf. *2 Cor.* 11:13–15]

10: I have confidence to you-ward in the Lord, that ye will be none otherwise minded: but he that troubleth you shall bear his judgment, whosoever he be.

I on my part am persuaded in the Lord with respect to you, that you will not adopt a different view (from mine): In spite of the ready reception the Galatians had given the Judaizers, Paul believes that disenchantment will follow this temporary success. He has confidence that his converts will adhere to the one true gospel. This persuasion 'rests not on any innate goodness of theirs, but solely on *their* and *his* relation to Christ, *their* and also *his* Lord. It is that Lord who, having begun a good work in the Galatians, will carry it on toward completion' (Hendriksen) [*Phil.* 1:6].

But he that troubleth you shall bear his judgment, whosoever he be: The singular 'he' does not designate a particular person, but simply supposes that what is true of an individual is also true of the class he represents. For anyone who burdens the church with false teaching shall not escape being burdened with a crushing judgment. In that day all who have recklessly perverted the gospel shall discover to their eternal sorrow that 'it is no light thing to scatter the leaven of false doctrine' (Lenski).

11: But I, brethren, if I still preach circumcision, why am I still persecuted? then hath the stumbling-block of the cross been done away.

Apparently the Judaizers had even appealed to the 'example' of Paul in their attempts to persuade the Galatians to receive circumcision. But if he were *still* (temporal: as he was before his conversion) the advocate for circumcision, why is he *still* (logical: in that case) being persecuted? That he proclaims a very different message is proved by the fact that his preaching does not attract the applause of the circumcised, but provokes them to such fury that they persecute him in every place.

This leads to the ironical conclusion that the offensiveness of the cross, that which aroused such violent opposition, has been removed. The persecuted apostle was, however, the living proof that the offence of the cross remained, as did its power to save [6:17]. He resolutely refused to adapt his preaching to the prejudices of his kinsmen after the flesh, and presented them with a crucified Messiah as the supreme fulfilment of their national hope. 'Worldly Wiseman, of the town of Carnal Policy, turns Christian out of the narrow way of the Cross to the house of legality. But the way to it was up a mountain, which, as Christian advanced, threatened to fall on and crush him, amidst lightning flashes from the mountain ('*Pilgrim's Progress*': *Heb.* 12:18–21)' (Fausset).

12: I would that they that unsettle you would even go beyond circumcision.

I wish those who unsettle you would mutilate themselves! (RSV): This may not be watered down to a wish that the Judaizers might be cut off from the communion of the church. It is rather an expression of deep disgust with those who are unsettling the Galatians with an emasculated message: these people had better complete the process by following the example of the priests of the pagan cult of Cybele which had its home in Galatia! The fierceness of this outburst is born of Paul's passionate desire to keep the gospel free from all self-engendered additions which would denature it. 'Such a mutilation of the gospel stands for Paul on one and the same level as the most despicable pagan practices, by means of which men tried to assure themselves of the favour of the gods' (Ridderbos) [cf. *Phil.* 3:2: 'beware of the "mutilation" party' – Bruce].

13: For ye, brethren, were called for freedom; only use not your freedom for an occasion to the flesh, but through love be servants one to another.

For ye, brethren, were called for freedom; This verse echoes the challenge of 5:1, and like that verse it also marks a point of transition in the argument. 'For' looks back to verse 12 and justifies the scorn poured on the Judaizers – 'for' you (emphatic) were not called for bondage but freedom! Yet this freedom, as Paul at once goes on to show, is not a liberty in licence, but the liberty of love [verses 13–26].

Only use not your freedom for an occasion to the flesh: The qualification introduces an urgent warning. The Galatians must be on their guard against the abuse of this freedom, which would provide the flesh with a bridgehead that would allow sin to recapture lost ground. In this passage 'the flesh' has an ethical meaning, and 'it obviously signifies the depraved inclinations which are natural to man in his present state, and which, though subdued, are by no means extinguished even in the regenerate' (Brown).

But through love be servants one to another: Being free from the servitude of legalism, they are to regard themselves as bound by the claims of love. Forsaking the selfish individualism of lawless licence, they are constantly to seek the welfare of one another through that self-giving love which delights to express itself in mutual service.

14: For the whole law is fulfilled in one word, even in this: Thou shalt love thy neighbour as thyself.

For the whole law has found its full expression in a single word (Arndt-Gingrich): Paul's insistence that the law must find its proper expression in the life of believers is very striking when it is remembered that thus far the entire argument has been directed against the encroachments of legalism. With an unerring grasp of the principles at stake, he denounces the slavish spirit that vainly seeks justification by the law, while enjoining the fulfilment of the law by that love which is the fruit of faith. A similar thought is expressed in *Rom.* 13:9, where the demands of the Decalogue are 'summed up' in this one word. 'Love, then, is both the *summary* (interpretive epitome or condensation) and the *realization in practice* of the entire God-given moral law, viewed as a unit' (Hendriksen).

Even in this: Thou shalt love thy neighbour as thyself: It is significant that the apostle should enforce the abiding validity of the moral law by an appeal to a book which his opponents doubtless regarded as the stronghold of their ceremonialism [*Lev.* 19:18]. Here '*love to God* is presupposed as the root from which *love to our neighbour* springs'

(Fausset). All right believing in God is visibly reflected in right behaviour towards men [*1 John* 4:20, 21]. The skeleton of Christian doctrine is essential but this must be enfleshed by the living reality of Christian love, which is the love that *recognizes, considers, and cares* for the needs of our neighbour [cf. *Luke* 10:25–37] (Cf L. H Marshall, *The Challenge of New Testament Ethics*, pp.106–7).

15: But if ye bite and devour one another, take heed that ye be not consumed one of another.

It seems reasonable to assume that it was no imaginary danger that called forth this strong warning. There was a tragic disparity between the obligation to fulfil the law by mutual love and the bitter dissensions about the law which prevailed among the Galatians and threatened to destroy their spiritual life. Let them take heed, for the moral savagery that delights to bite and devour could lead to nothing but mutual destruction. Even defenders of the truth must be careful about their spirit and manner in controversy.

16: But I say, Walk by the Spirit, and ye shall not fulfil the lust of the flesh.

The Geneva Bible has the heading: *He sheweth them the battel betwixt the Spirit and the flesh; and the frutes of them bothe.* In these verses there is no hint of the 'Victorious Life' teaching of C. G. Trumbull, 'Let go and let God'. (For an incisive criticism of this teaching, see Warfield's fine article 'The Victorious Life' in *Perfectionism*, pp. 349–99.) On the contrary, the apostle's teaching is that all Christians are engaged in a constant warfare in which they are called to resist the unlawful demands of the 'flesh' by responding to the rightful claims of the 'Spirit'. To frustrate the desire of the 'flesh' believers are instructed to 'walk by the Spirit'. They are to do the walking, but they are to do it by the power of the Holy Spirit [verses 18, 25]. 'To be sure, we do not act in our own power, but only in so far as the Spirit graciously gives us power and ability to act. It is not as though the Spirit works partially in us, setting us in motion, whereupon we do the rest . . . Rather, it is a balance in which the Spirit is completely sovereign and man is completely responsible: a hundred-hundred proposition, as contradictory as that may seem' (Edwin Palmer, *The Holy Spirit*, pp.

96, 179). 'Ye shall not fulfil' is the assurance that the flesh will fail to achieve the complete domination it desires [cf. verse 17b].

17: For the flesh lusteth against the Spirit, and the Spirit against the flesh; for these are contrary the one to the other; that ye may not do the things that ye would.

Unbelievers know nothing of the struggle depicted here, for it is only the Spirit who can prompt those desires which are contrary to the flesh. Hence 'Spirit' must refer to the Holy Spirit, 'for the human spirit in itself and unaided does not stand in direct antagonism to the flesh' (Lightfoot). Thus it is because the Spirit and the flesh are irreconcilably opposed to each other that there is a continual conflict going on within the believer.

So that ye cannot do the things that ye would (AV): Is Paul here saying that the flesh prevents our complete obedience to the promptings of the Spirit, or that the presence of the Spirit enables us to resist the cravings of the flesh? In view of the assurance given in verse 16 it would seem that the latter meaning is preferable. 'To walk by the Spirit of God ensures that we do no longer as we please (i.e. fall to the false freedom of carnal impulse). Rather, we live in freedom which triumphs over such impulses. This is not freedom which steers an uncertain middle course between evil impulses and obedience to religious rules, but a new way which transcends them both' (Mikolaski).

18: But if ye are led by the Spirit, ye are not under the law.

It is because believers are led by the Spirit that they are not under the law. As the Galatians experienced release from the curse and bondage of the law through receiving the Spirit in conversion, so victory over the flesh was to be experienced by the Spirit's inward leading and strengthening. Hence the privilege of being led by the Spirit also involved the duty of responding to that leading, which if resisted would rather ensure the ascendancy of the flesh [*Rom.* 8:1–14]. 'If one is to offer resistance in the struggle between Spirit and flesh, one must be in the service of the Spirit and not in that of the law. That the demand of the law remains [verse 14] is not denied, of course. The issue, in short, is the strength, the power, that is necessary for the fulfilment of the law' (Ridderbos).

19: Now the works of the flesh are manifest, which are these: fornication, uncleanness, lasciviousness, 20: idolatry, sorcery, enmities, strife, jealousies, wraths, factions, divisions, parties, 21: envyings, drunkenness, revellings, and such like; of which I forewarn you, even as I did forewarn you, that they who practise such things shall not inherit the kingdom of God.

Now the works of the flesh are manifest: 'The flesh concealed betrays itself by its own works, so that its discovery is easy . . . *The works,* in the plural, because they are divided and often at variance, and even singly betray the flesh. But *the fruit,* being good, verse 22, is in the singular, because it is united and harmonious. Compare *Eph.* 5:11, 9' (Bengel).

Which are: immorality, impurity, indecency (Hendriksen): 1. *Sexual sins.* 'The flesh is never made more manifest than it is by the besmirching and degrading sins of the flesh. Any society that begins by regarding them with indifference very shortly becomes enslaved by them. 'In nothing did early Christianity so thoroughly revolutionize the ethical standards of the pagan world as in regard to sexual relationships' (Duncan). Now that 'permissiveness' is an accepted norm this note needs to be sounded again in no uncertain manner.

Idolatry, sorcery: 2. *False religion.* Man in his rebellion against his Creator remains incurably religious, and he seeks to satisfy this instinct by making his own deities. He much prefers these lifeless puppets to the one true living God, because they allow him to pull the strings. In the same way magic is man's unlawful attempt to manipulate unseen spiritual forces to his own advantage. In an age which is not ostensibly religious, there has been a remarkable proliferation of false gods and a terrifying revival of occult arts and practices. Besides the parasitic growth of many new cults, the 'secular' gods of Communism, Scientism, and Humanism are worshipped with a fervour approaching religious ecstasy, while the increasing popularity of witchcraft, spiritism (alias Spiritualism), clairvoyance, astrology, and horoscopes heralds a relapse into the Dark Ages.

Enmities, strife, jealousies, wraths, factions, divisions, parties, envyings: 3. *Sins of ill-will.* The largest group affords mournful proof of the depravity of the human heart [*Jer.* 17:9]. Lightfoot sees an ascending scale in the arrangement of these 'violations of brotherly love'.

Cherished 'enmities' lead to 'strife', which finds expression in 'outbreaks of jealousies', 'outbursts of anger', and 'unscrupulous intriguing'. These in turn lead to the point where the contending parties separate and form either temporary 'divisions' or permanent 'parties'. The final 'envyings' is 'a grosser breach of charity than any hitherto mentioned, the wish to deprive another of what he has' [cf. *Prov.* 14:30].

Drunkenness, revellings: 4. *Intemperance.* To conclude Paul lists the sin of drunkenness and the revellings which are its natural accompaniment. 'Komos, the Revel, was made a god, and his rites were carried on quite systematically, and yet with all the ingenuity and inventiveness of the Greek mind, which lent perpetual novelty and variety to the revellings' (William Ramsay). And such orgiastic excesses are by no means unknown today!

And such like: This is by no means an exhaustive catalogue of the works of the flesh but only a representative list.

I warn you, as I warned you before, that those who do such things shall not inherit the kingdom of God (RSV): The gospel Paul preached was no form of cheap and easy believism, for it demanded and provided for the radical reformation of the whole life. In dealing with pagan Gentiles who were ignorant of the moral law, the apostle was always careful to warn them of the fatal consequences of continuing in sin that grace may abound [*Rom.* 6:1ff.]. Here he again reminds the Galatians that those who deny Christ's present reign of grace by their persistence in such sins shall not inherit the kingdom of God at the end of the age [cf. *1 Cor.* 6:9, 10].

22: But the fruit of the Spirit is love, joy, peace, longsuffering, kindness, goodness, faithfulness, 23: meekness, self-control; against such there is no law.

But the fruit of the Spirit: Of a very different character is that supernatural 'fruit' whose *organic development* springs from the one living root of the Spirit [cf. *John* 15:4, 5]. This 'fruit' includes 'those ethical qualities and spiritual experiences which were not popularly thought of as evidences of the Spirit's presence, but which, to the mind of Paul, were of far greater value than the so-called *charismata*. See *1 Cor.* chapters 12–14, especially 12:31, chap 13, and 14:1' (Burton). The harvest of the Spirit falls into three triads which may be roughly classified as follows: 1. *Spiritual graces*; 2. *Social conduct;* 3. *Personal discipline.*

Love: The greatest Christian grace appropriately heads the list. Love is the animating principle 'of all the other graces – greater than faith and hope, for "God is love"; love to God and all that bears his image, being the essence of the first and second tables of the law, – all the other graces being at length absorbed by it as the flower is lost in the fruit. *1 Cor.* 13; *Rom.* 12:9' (Eadie).

Joy: This is not *joie de vivre,* the mere feeling of physical well-being. It is a spiritual joy that is not extinguished by the most adverse circumstances. So Paul and Silas, though beaten and in prison, sang hymns to God at midnight [*Acts* 16:25]. The ultimate object of all Christian preaching is to bring men that joy which is unattainable by any other means [*John* 15:11]. As Raymond Stamm points out, next to Paul's letters, this spirit of joy which is brought forth by the gospel is nowhere better illustrated than in Luke's writings [e.g. *Luke* 2:10, 15:10, 24:52; *Acts* 5:41, 8:8, 8:39, 13:48, 52, 15:31].

Peace: The primary reference here is to the believer's assurance of peace with God through faith in Christ; it is the blessing of a conscience that has been pacified by the knowledge that Christ has satisfied all the claims of divine justice on its behalf [Rom. 5:1]. The Galatians must learn that to doubt the sufficiency of Christ's sacrifice is to lose all sense of peace with God, for the conscience can find its rest in no other doctrine but this. But no outward storms can disturb the inward calm of those who are guarded by the 'peace of God, which passeth all understanding' [Phil. 4:7].

Longsuffering: 'The word means "long-temperedness" and refers to the endurance of wrong and exasperating conduct on the part of others without flying into a rage or passionately desiring vengeance. One of the great ethical qualities of God celebrated in Holy Scripture is that He is "slow to anger" and Paul here suggests that the spiritual man shares in this characteristic of God' (L. H. Marshall).

Kindness: As God is kind even to the unthankful and the evil [Luke 6:35], so believers are to reflect the divine kindness by treating others in the way God has treated them [Eph. 4:32].

Goodness: This is the goodness that *benefits* others even as Christ 'went about doing good' [*Acts* 10:38]. Thus in this triad which deals with the believer's relations with his fellowmen we have another ascending scale: 'longsuffering' is *passive*, 'patient endurance under injuries inflicted by others'; 'kindness', *neutral*, 'kindly disposition towards one's neighbours' not necessarily taking a practical form; 'goodness', *active*, 'goodness, beneficence' as an energetic principle (Lightfoot).

Faithfulness: 'It is clear from the subordinate place assigned to *pistis* that it does not here denote the cardinal grace of faith in God which is the root of all religion, but rather good faith in dealing with men, and due regard to their just claims' (Rendall).

Meekness: This is not spineless weakness, but the gentleness of a strength which has been brought under control, as a horse is made obedient to bit and bridle. As meekness is thus the mark of the man who has been mastered by God [*Num.* 12:3], so the secret of all effective service is found in willing submission to Christ's yoke [*Matt.* 11:29, 30].

Self-control: This is the grace which gives victory over the desires of the flesh [verse 16]. It is a virtue that is exercised by the Christian and which produces in him the desire to 'bring into captivity every thought to the obedience of Christ'. Thereby he 'escapes the corruption that is in the world by lust' [*2 Cor.* 10:5; *2 Pet.* 1:4].

Against such there is no law: While law, whether written or unwritten, must condemn the works of the flesh, all these graces, and others like them, are condemned by no law. In fact, as the fruit of the Spirit, they are in principle a fulfilling of the law's demand [verse 14]. Thus, 'where the Spirit reigns, the law has no longer any dominion. By moulding our hearts to His own righteousness, the Lord delivers us from the severity of the law, so that He does not deal with us according to its covenant, nor does He bind our consciences under its condemnation. Yet the law continues to perform its office of teaching and exhorting. But the Spirit of adoption sets us free from subjection to it' (Calvin) [verse 18; *1 Tim.* 1:9].

24: And they that are of Christ Jesus have crucified the flesh with the passions and the lusts thereof.

And those who belong to Christ Jesus have crucified the flesh with its passions and desires (RSV): Paul is reminding the Galatians of the moment in their experience when they made a definitive break with the flesh and its sinful desires. In their conversion they made this radical breach with sin by identifying themselves with the Christ who was crucified to secure their release from the dominion of the flesh. This 'does not mean that since that moment the flesh can no longer bring an influence to bear, but rather that its corruptness is acknowledged and is assigned to death, not by the cross of Christ alone, but by the believers themselves also' (Ridderbos). As they then recognized that the flesh was crucified with Christ, so now they must put to death its passions and desires as having no longer any right to live.

25: If we live by the Spirit, by the Spirit let us also walk.

'Walk' here means to walk in line, and 'may imply a more studied following of a prescribed course' (Ellicott). Calvin's fine comment on this verse shows that it was not without reason that Warfield called him 'the theologian of the Holy Spirit'. He says, 'Now in his usual way, Paul draws an exhortation out of the doctrine. The death of the flesh is the life of the Spirit. If God's Spirit lives in us, let Him govern all our actions. There will always be many who impudently boast of living in the Spirit, but Paul challenges them to prove their claim. As the soul does not live idly in the body, but gives motion and vigour to every member and part, so the Spirit of God cannot dwell in us without manifesting Himself by the outward effects. By "life" is here meant the inward power, and by "walk", the outward actions. Paul means that works are witnesses to spiritual life.'

26: Let us not become vainglorious, provoking one another, envying one another.

Walking by the Spirit must quench the natural tendency to turn spiritual privileges into an occasion for boasting, by which fellow-believers are provoked to envy the assumed pre-eminence. In this exhortation Paul may have had the situation in Galatia very much in mind [verse 15], but the vainglorying he deprecates is not to be limited by it. 'Experience of the mission-field and of religious "revivals" reveals how prone it is to arise where the emphasis on the life of the Spirit has not yet led to a realization of its ethical implications. Paul has often to warn his churches against it [cf. notably *Phil.* 2:1ff.]' (Duncan). The exhortation has an intimate bearing on what follows.

CHAPTER SIX

Paul exhorts the Galatians to restore those who fall, and to bear one another's burdens [verses 1–5]. They should support their teachers liberally, and are not to become weary in well-doing, for in due season they shall reap what they have sown [verses 6–10]. In a final warning against the Judaizers he contrasts their selfish motives with the self-denying love which springs from an interest in Christ crucified [verses 11–16]. He enforces this appeal by reminding them of his own sufferings, and closes the Epistle with the benediction [verses 17, 18].

1: Brethren, even if a man be overtaken in any trespass, ye who are spiritual, restore such a one in a spirit of gentleness; looking to thyself, lest thou also be tempted.

My brothers, if one of your number is caught off his guard by some sin, those among you who are spiritual men must restore him in a spirit of gentleness (Bruce): Mindful of man's frailty and Satan's subtlety, Paul recognizes that not all who seek to walk by the Spirit will always do so without stumbling. In such cases, those who are noted for their consistent obedience to the Spirit's leading [5:16, 18, 25] must gently restore their fallen brother. The word 'restore' shows that this is no task for the spiritually inexperienced. It is used to describe the work that calls for special skill, e.g. setting a broken limb, and mending nets [*Matt.* 4:21]. 'To "restore such an one", is to use the appropriate means of convincing him of his error and sin, and bringing him back to the path of truth and righteousness' (Brown).

Looking to thyself, lest thou also be tempted: A striking transition from the plural to the singular. Each of you must watch *himself*, for none is immune from temptation. Therefore a censorious spirit is out of place in those who are subject to the same weaknesses [*Matt.* 7:2–5].

2: Bear ye one another's burdens, and so fulfil the law of Christ.

The primary reference is to the duty of sharing the spiritual burdens by which fellow-believers are oppressed, though other burdens are not excluded (cf. for example verse 6). The precept is well illustrated by Chrysostom: 'He who is quick and irritable, let him bear with the slow and the sluggish; and let the slow, in his turn, bear with the impetuosity of his fiery brother: each knowing that the burden is heavier to him who bears it than to him who bears with it.' Paul sees in this mutual burden-bearing the active manifestation of the love that fulfils the law of Christ. Against the legalism that would seek to fulfil the law in its own strength, Paul sees the capacity to fulfil that same law as being given to believers by Christ through the Spirit [5:16]. As Ridderbos says, 'The new element is not the content of the law, although Christ's coming and His work modified it, but in the root of obedience, namely, Christ'.

3: For if a man thinketh himself to be something when he is nothing, he deceiveth himself.

'For' indicates the close connection with the previous verse. Self-importance 'based on self-ignorance is the grand hindrance to the duty of mutual burden-bearing. If a man thinks himself so perfect that he can have no burden which others may carry with him, or for him; if he regards himself so far above frailty, sin, or sorrow, that he neither needs nor expects sympathy nor help, – he will not readily stoop to bear the burdens of others' (Eadie). Such a one is sadly self-deceived for the flattering estimate he entertains of himself has no basis in reality. He believes he is something, when in fact he is nothing!

4: But let each man prove his own work, and then shall he have his glorying in regard of himself alone, and not of his neighbour.

But let each one test his own work; then his reason to boast will be in himself alone, and not in (comparing himself with) someone else (Hendriksen): 'It is not what we gain by detracting from others, but what we have without any comparison, that is truly praiseworthy' (Calvin). Instead of indulging the Pharisaic pride which exalts self by looking down on others, each is to bring his own work to the test [*Luke* 18:11]. This is all he is qualified to do, since this self-knowledge cannot be applied as a standard to test another's work [*2 Cor.* 10:2]. Every man is to find the basis for boasting in himself, for he alone knows what God's grace has wrought in his life. Hence his glorying will be a glorying in the Lord [verse 14; *1 Cor.* 1:31].

5: For each man shall bear his own burden.

For each person will have to bear his own load (Hendriksen): Or 'shoulder his own pack' (J. B. Phillips). The thought again follows on from the preceding verse: 'everyone is to concern himself about his own burden, rather than to compare himself complacently with others' (Arndt-Gingrich). For each has his own burden of sin and weakness which ought to lead him to be charitable towards others. The word used here 'was applied to the pack usually carried by a porter or soldier on the march . . . It is necessary to distinguish this from the heavy loads to which verse 2 refers as needing the help of Christian brethren for the relief of overtaxed carriers' (Rendall).

6: But let him that is taught in the word communicate unto him that teacheth in all good things.

Let him who is taught the word share all good things with him who teaches (RSV): This is probably to be connected with verse 2: 'I spoke of bearing one another's burdens. There is one special application I would make of this rule. Provide for the temporal wants of your teachers in Christ' (Lightfoot). In pagan religion there were *priests* who levied dues on the sacrifices they offered, but no *teachers* who would have had to rely on a system of voluntary contributions for their support. 'Hence the duty of supporting teachers or preachers had to be continually impressed upon the attention of all Paul's converts from Paganism. The tendency to fail in it was practically universal; it was connected with a universal fact in contemporary society; perhaps it was not unconnected with a universal characteristic of human nature' (Ramsay). [cf. *1 Cor.* 9:11f.; *1 Tim.* 5:17f.] It was not pagan ritual that changed the ancient world, but the communication of a message which demanded the understanding of faith and issued in a moral transformation of the character. An *ex opere operato* faith, whether heathen or 'Christian', is always an ethically sterile thing.

7: Be not deceived; God is not mocked: for whatsoever a man soweth, that shall he also reap.

God is not mocked: 'That of which the apostle speaks is not a ridicule of God which he will not leave unpunished, but an outwitting of God, an evasion of his laws which men think to accomplish, but, in fact, cannot' (Burton). This stern warning sums up the appeal of the whole letter. Let the Galatian fascination for law find a healthy outlet in the contemplation of this immutable law of God's moral government! Although the seeds of legalism may be fair in the blade, they shall not fail of their appointed reward. Full maturity will reveal a fruitlessness that must be swept down by the avenging sickle of divine wrath. Men are the dupes of their own sinful self-love, believing that what they regard as a truism in the natural world has no application in the spiritual realm. On the contrary, the forthcoming harvest will inexorably reveal the value or otherwise of what has been sown in the present life and vindicate the justice of the respective judgments they call forth [5:19–23]. For the equity of the law of sowing and reaping is manifestly beyond reproach.

> **8: For he that soweth unto his own flesh shall of the flesh reap corruption; but he that soweth unto the Spirit shall of the Spirit reap eternal life.**

That God is not mocked when men deceive themselves is shown by the fact that the future life only brings to fruition the seed sown here. 'Unto his own flesh' indicates that sin is no alien principle coming to man from without, but is entirely *natural* to him and is essentially *selfish* in its aims. Hence the man who sows 'unto his own flesh' with a view to fulfilling its desires must of the flesh reap 'corruption' [cf. *1 Cor.* 3:17; *2 Pet.* 2:12]. This is to experience 'eternal destruction from the face of the Lord' [2 Thess. 1:9], and is the opposite of 'eternal life' [verse 8b]. Thus the term 'corruption' shows that this awful infliction of divine wrath is 'not an *arbitrary* punishment of fleshly-mindedness, but is its *natural* fruit' (Fausset). [cf. *Rom.* 8:12,13].

On the other hand, he who sows 'unto the Spirit' (i.e. who obediently follows the leading of the author of his spiritual life) shall reap the harvest of eternal life from the selfsame Spirit [*Rom.* 8:11]. The function of the Holy Spirit in the future life is twofold. He is the source of resurrection-life and the 'element' in which it shall be lived. 'He produces the event and in continuance underlies the state which is the result of it. He is Creator and Sustainer at once, the *Creator Spiritus* and the Sustainer of the supernatural state of the future life in one' (Geerhardus Vos, *The Pauline Eschatology*, p. 163).

> **9: And let us not be weary in well-doing: for in due season we shall reap, if we faint not.**

And let us not lose heart (Arndt-Gingrich): Paul now presents the Galatians with the grand incentive to unwearied perseverance in well-doing: 'We shall reap, if we faint not.' 'The great cause of weariness in well-doing is a deficiency in faith, and a corresponding undue influence of present and sensible things . . . Nothing is so much calculated to produce languor as a suspicion that all our exertions are likely to be fruitless; and nothing is better fitted to dispel it than the assurance that they shall assuredly be crowned with success' (Brown) [*1 Cor.* 15:58]

10: So then, as we have opportunity, let us work that which is good toward all men, and especially toward them that are of the household of the faith.

We have now the 'season' for *sowing*, as there will be hereafter the 'due season' [verse 9] for *reaping*. In one sense the whole of life is the season of opportunity; and in a narrower sense, there occur in it especially convenient seasons. The latter are lost in looking for 'still more convenient seasons [*Acts* 24:25]. We shall not always have the opportunity "we have" now. Satan is sharpened to the greater zeal in evil-doing by the shortness of his time [*Rev.* 12:12]. Let us be sharpened to the greater zeal in well-doing by the shortness of ours' (Fausset).

And especially toward them that are of the household of the faith: As every right-minded man does well to his own family [*1 Tim.* 5:8], so believers must do the same to those who belong to the household of the faith – i.e. those who are made members of God's household in virtue of their faith in Christ [*Eph.* 2:19].

11: See with how large letters I write unto you with mine own hand.

This verse marks the point at which Paul takes up the pen from his amanuensis to write the final admonition in his own hand. By these large letters he would impress upon the Galatians the supreme importance of remaining faithful to the gospel of God's redeeming grace in which Christ is set forth as the sinner's all-sufficient Saviour. 'The boldness of the handwriting answers to the force of the Apostle's convictions. The size of the characters will arrest the attention of his readers in spite of themselves' (Lightfoot).

12: As many as desire to make a fair show in the flesh, they compel you to be circumcised; only that they may not be persecuted for the cross of Christ.

It was not because the Judaizers were genuinely concerned for the spiritual welfare of the Galatians that they pressed them to receive circumcision, but because they desired 'to make a fair show in the flesh'. It was in the sphere of 'the flesh' (the body) that this fleshly (non-spiritual) glorying showed itself. Their unspiritual mind was revealed by their preoccupation with 'a specious outward show'. 'The whole expression describes those to whom it refers as desiring to stand well in matters whose real basis is physical rather than spiritual' (Burton).

The Jews were implacably opposed to the preaching of the cross, for it offered the Gentiles salvation without obliging them to become Jewish proselytes, thus destroying their religious pre-eminence by placing them on a level with the Gentile world. To escape this enmity the Judaizers compromised the gospel by insisting that Gentile converts should submit to circumcision in token of their allegiance to the law. As the missionaries of a Jewish ecumenism, tolerated alike by pagan Rome and unbelieving Jerusalem, these Judaizers therefore adroitly avoided the scandal of the cross. 'But this syncretistic mixture of law and gospel veiled the cross and its salvation, so free and fitting to mankind without distinction of race or blood; so that their profession was deceptive, perilous in its consequences, and prompted and shaped by an ignoble and cowardly selfishness; it was a "fair show", but only in the sphere of fleshly things, and assumed on purpose to avoid persecution' (Eadie).

13: For not even they who receive circumcision do themselves keep the law; but they desire to have you circumcised, that they may glory in your flesh.

These zealous advocates for circumcision do not themselves feel bound by the yoke they were asking others to accept, for like all hypocrites they were motivated by purely external considerations [cf. *Matt.* 23:4]. Although they honoured the law with their lips, they showed no corresponding concern to obey it in their lives, and the only reason they desired to impose this outward mark upon the Gentiles was to make them members of their party. All their powers of persuasion were directed to this end in order that their glorying in a Gentile surrender to a carnal rite might transform the fanatical opposition of the Jews to the gospel into a complacent acceptance of their activities.

14: But far be it from me to glory, save in the cross of our Lord Jesus Christ, through which the world hath been crucified unto me, and I unto the world.

In emphatic contrast with the boasting of the Judaizers, which has its sphere and basis in the mere material flesh of men, the apostle sets forth as *his* ground of boasting, the central fact of his gospel, the cross of Christ [cf. *1 Cor.* 1:18ff.]. '*The world* as used here is an epitome of everything outside of Christ in which man seeks his glory and puts his trust' (Ridderbos). It is through the cross that the world has been crucified unto Paul, and he unto the world. This instrument of his union with Christ was also the symbol of his separation from the world. So that in his reckoning the world was as dead to him, as he was in the estimation of the world. If the world now had nothing but contempt for him, it was because it recognized that he no longer belonged to it as he once did [2:20]. 'Men to whom the world is not crucified, are certainly not believers; and men professing Christianity, who are not "crucified to the world" – men whom the world loves and honours, have cause to stand in doubt themselves. Where the Cross holds the place in the heart which it did in the apostle's, and exercises the influence over the character and conduct it did in him, it will be equally clear that the world is crucified to the individual, and he to the world' (Brown).

15: For neither is circumcision anything, nor uncircumcision, but a new creature.

Since nothing external can effect a saving change in man, his outward state is a matter of indifference; circumcision is no help and uncircumcision is no hindrance [5:6]. Man's need can only be met by a 'new creation' (ASV margin): 'The spiritual renewal springs out of living union to Christ, and it is everything. For it re-enstamps the image of God on the soul, and restores it to its pristine felicity and fellowship. It is not external – neither a change of opinion, party, or outer life.

Nor is it a change in the essence or organization of the soul, but in its inner being – in its springs of thought and feeling, in its powers and motives – by the Spirit of God and the influence of the truth. "All old things pass away; behold, all things are become new", *2 Cor.* 5:17. This creation is "new" – new in its themes of thought, in its susceptibilities of enjoyment, and in its spheres of energy; it finds itself in a new world, into which it is ushered by a new birth' (Eadie).

16: And as many as shall walk by this rule, peace be upon them, and mercy, and upon the Israel of God.

And as many as shall walk by this rule, peace (be) upon them and mercy, even upon the Israel of God (Hendriksen): It is upon as many as shall walk by this rule, and not upon as many as desire to make a fair show in the flesh [verse 12], that the peace and mercy of God shall rest. Such blessings are exclusive to the new Israel of God, even to those who have found a new standard of life in Christ. For only those thus quickened by Christ are able to 'walk in newness of life' [cf. *Rom.* 8:1, 2]. 'Those who walk by the rule of the spirit are declared to be indeed the true Israel of God, not the Jews who have the name of Israel, but are really only the children of Abraham after the flesh' (Rendall) [3:29; *Phil.* 3:3].

17: Henceforth let no man trouble me; for I bear branded on my body the marks of Jesus.

Henceforth let no man trouble me; for I bear on my body the marks of Jesus (RSV): Paul is confident that he will hear no more of the empty pretensions of the Judaizers, for he bears on his body the marks of what it cost him to bring the gospel to the Galatians [cf. *Acts* 14:19]. The suggestion that the expression is borrowed from the pagan practice of branding slaves or of religious tattooing is wholly inappropriate to an apostle of Christ. 'The scars on Paul's body belonged to Jesus, were like the wounds he himself suffered, for Paul's scars were truly suffered because of Christ. Compare *2 Cor.* 1:5; 4:10; *Col.* 1:24. A far later age invented "stigmata of Jesus", a reproduction of the marks of the five wounds in the hands, the feet, and the side of Jesus. These "stigmata" are either violent pains in these parts of the body or marks that turn red and, in some cases, bleed. All of these peculiar phenomena are pathological and have nothing to do with Paul's scars' (Lenski).

18: The grace of our Lord Jesus Christ be with your spirit, brethren. Amen.

Apart from the solemn 'Amen', 'so let it be', 'brethren' is Paul's last word to the Galatians. It is at once a word of affection and appeal. He accounts them as his brethren still, and has confidence that their future conduct will justify this address. 'He prays not only that grace may be bestowed upon them freely, but that they may have a proper feeling of it in their minds. It is only really enjoyed by us when it reaches to our spirit. We ought therefore to ask that God would prepare in our souls a habitation for his grace. Amen.' (Calvin).

Soli Deo Gloria

BIBLIOGRAPHY

Alford, Henry, *The Greek Testament* (Rivingtons, 1865).

Allis, Oswald T., *Revision or New Translation?* (Presbyterian & Reformed, 1948).

Arndt, W. F.–Gingrich, F. W., *A Greek-English Lexicon of the New Testament* (University of Chicago Press, 1957).

Bengel, J. A., *New Testament Word Studies* (Kregel, 1971).

Boice, James Montgomery, *Galatians* (*EBC*) (Pickering & Inglis, 1976).

Brown, John, *Exposition of Galatians* (Banner of Truth, 2001).

Bruce, F. F., *An Expanded Paraphrase on the Epistles of Paul* (Paternoster, 1965).

—— *New Testament History* (Nelson, 1969).

—— *Tradition Old and New* (Paternoster, 1970).

Bruner, F. D., *A Theology of the Holy Spirit* (Hodder & Stoughton, 1971).

Burton, Ernest De Witt, *Galatians* (*ICC*) (T. & T. Clark, 1921).

Calvin, John, *Galatians-Colossians* (Saint Andrew Press, 1965).

Cole, R. A., *Galatians – Introduction and Commentary* (*TNTSC*) (Tyndale, 1965).

DENNEY, JAMES, *The Death of Christ* (Tyndale, 1964).

DUNCAN, GEORGE S., *Galatians* (*MNTC*) (Hodder & Stoughton, 1934).

EADIE, JOHN, *Galatians* (Zondervan, n.d.).

ELLICOTT, CHARLES J., *Galatians* (Longmans, Green, 1867).

FAUSSET, A. R., *Galatians* (*JFB*) (Collins, 1874).

FERGUSSON, JAMES, *A Brief Exposition of the Epistles of Paul* (Banner of Truth, 1978).

FINDLAY, G. G., *Galatians* (*EB*) (Hodder& Stoughton, 1888).

GUTHRIE, DONALD, *Galatians* (*NCB*) (Nelson, 1969).

—— *New Testament Introduction* (Tyndale, 1970).

HENDRIKSEN, WILLIAM, *Galatians* (NTC) (Banner of Truth, 1969).

HENRY, MATTHEW, *Commentary on the Holy Bible* (various editions).

HOEKSEMA, HERMAN, *Reformed Dogmatics* (Reformed Free Publishing, 1966).

JEREMIAS, JOACHIM, *The Prayers of Jesus* (SCM, 1967).

KITTEL, G.–FRIEDRICH, G., *Theological Dictionary of the New Testament,* vols. 1–10 (Eerdmans, 1964–76).

LADD, GEORGE ELDON, *A Theology of the New Testament* (Eerdmans 1974).

—— in *Apostolic History and the Gospel* (Paternoster, 1970).

LENSKI, R. C. H., *The Interpretation of Galatians* (Augsburg, 1961).

LIGHTFOOT, J. B., *Galatians* (Zondervan, 1962).

LUTHER, MARTIN, *Lectures on Galatians, 1519, 1535* (Concordia, 1963–4).

McDONALD, H. D., *Freedom in Faith* (Pickering & Inglis, 1973).

MACHEN, J. GRESHAM, *The New Testament* (Banner of Truth, 1976).

—— *Christianity and Liberalism* (Victory Press, n.d.).

MARSHALL, L. H., *The Challenge of New Testament Ethics* (Macmillan, 1946).

MAYOR, J. B., *The Epistle of James* (Zondervan, n.d.).

MIKOLASKI, SAMUEL J., *Galatians* (*NBC*-Revised) (IVP, 1970).

MOFFATT, JAMES, *Love in the New Testament* (Hodder & Stoughton, 1929).

MURRAY, JOHN, *Redemption – Accomplished and Applied* (Banner of Truth, 1961).

PACKER, J. I., in *The New Bible Dictionary* (IVP, 1962).

PALMER, EDWIN H., *The Holy Spirit* (Presbyterian & Reformed, 1964).

PERKINS, WILLIAM, *Commentarie on Galatians* (London, 1617).

POOLE, MATTHEW, *Commentary on the Holy Bible* (Banner of Truth, 1963).

RAMSAY, WILLIAM M., *Historical Commentary on the Epistle to the Galatians* (Hodder & Stoughton, 1900).

RENDALL, FREDERIC, *Galatians* (*EGT*) (Eerdmans, 1974).

RIDDERBOS, HERMAN, *Galatians* (*NLC*) (Marshall, Morgan, & Scott, 1954).

—— *Paul and Jesus* (Presbyterian & Reformed, 1957).

ROBERTSON, A. T., *Word Pictures in the New Testament,* vol. 4 (Broadman, 1931).

SKILTON, JOHN H., *Machen's Notes on Galatians* (Presbyterian & Reformed, 1972).

STAMM, RAYMOND T., *The Epistle to the Galatians* (*IB*) (Abingdon, 1953).

STOTT, JOHN R. W., *Only One Way* (IVP, 1973).

TRAPP, JOHN, *Commentary on the New Testament* (Sovereign Grace Book Club, 1958).

VINE, W. E., *An Expository Dictionary of New Testament Words* (Oliphants, 1958).

VOS, GEERHARDUS, *Biblical Theology* (Banner of Truth, 1975).

—— *Pauline Eschatology* (Eerdmans, 1961).

WARFIELD, B. B., *Calvin and Augustine* (Presbyterian & Reformed, 1956).

—— *Perfectionism* (Presbyterian & Reformed, 1958).

—— *The Inspiration and Authority of the Bible* (Marshall, Morgan & Scott, 1959).

WILLIAMS, A. LUKYN, *Galatians* (*CGT*) (CUP, 1910).

YOUNG, E. J., *Thy Word Is Truth* (Banner of Truth, 1963).

Ephesians

INTRODUCTION

Of the four Epistles which date from Paul's first imprisonment in Rome, Ephesians, Colossians, and Philemon bear the marks of having been written at about the same time, while Philippians is probably best placed near the end of that period of captivity. Ephesians is the most majestic of Paul's letters, but because it is also the most general and least personal of them, not a few have questioned its authenticity. Such scepticism fails to recognize that a change of purpose can account for an author's change of style. Specific problems are dealt with in Colossians and Philemon, but Ephesians contains no hint that the apostle has any particular situation in mind. Yet even the vagueness of its temporal setting serves to enhance its universal appeal, as Paul here gratefully contemplates all things in the light of God's eternal election. Moreover, his sustained use of the language of exalted praise is admirably adapted to the sublime unfolding of its lofty theme – the glorious destiny which belongs to the church in virtue of her union with Christ.

Those who deny the apostolic authorship not only fly in the face of the great weight of evidence that supports it, but are also bound to maintain that an unknown imitator of greater genius than his supposed model was successful in foisting a 'pious' forgery upon a church which was famous for its spiritual discernment [*Rev.* 2:2]. And though much has been made of the fact that in Colossians there are close links with no less than 78 of this Epistle's 155 verses, these ideas are not reproduced in any mechanical fashion as would be the case with a mere forger, but they receive the fresh development which only their originator could give to them.

The absence of the words 'at Ephesus' from the best manuscripts is probably an indication that Paul intended the Epistle to be read by a group of churches around Ephesus. This 'circular letter' theory also explains the verses which imply that the writer and readers have not met [1:15; 3:2, 4], and the omission of any personal greetings. It therefore seems likely that 'Ephesians' is the letter 'from Laodicea' to which the apostle refers in Colossians 4:16.

Paul was prompted to write these two great 'Prison Epistles' by the disturbing news Epaphras had brought to him of the situation in Colosse, where the rise of a heresy which dethroned Christ and denied the sufficiency of his work threatened to overthrow the faith throughout the Lycus Valley [*Col.* 2:8ff.]. As a good physician of souls Paul sent the right antidote to counteract the poison of error (Colossians), and the right tonic to build up the faith of all believers in Asia Minor (Ephesians). Tychicus, who was entrusted with both letters, evidently took the encyclical to the churches where it was to be read [6:21; *Col.* 4:7]. Probably the address was left blank in the original letter, so that this could be orally filled in by the reader at each particular place.

It was Paul's refusal to discriminate against Gentiles in favour of Jews which had brought him to Rome 'as the prisoner of Jesus Christ' [3:1; cf. *Acts* 21:17ff.; 22:21–24], and in this Epistle he explains the once secret but now revealed mystery of the unity of Jews and Gentiles in the one body of Christ [2:11ff.; 3:2ff.]. This unity was the purchase of Christ's blood, whose death broke down the dividing wall of the legal economy and so made peace between them [2:14, 15].

Thus it is in the apostle's exposition of the essential meaning of the New Covenant, both in its blessings [chs. 1–3] and its duties [chs. 4–6], that we have his spiritual testament to the church. It is the charter which teaches us that the church is the society of the future, for as the Bride of Christ it is the one society to which the future belongs.

CHAPTER ONE

After greeting his readers [verses 1, 2], Paul bursts into a great thanksgiving to God for all the blessings of salvation in Christ – election, redemption, and the assurance of the promised inheritance through the gift of the Holy Spirit [verses 3–14]. The opening doxology thus strikes the note of adoring worship which is evident throughout the first half of the Epistle. This praise is followed by the apostle's prayer for further spiritual blessings. He is thankful for their faith and love, but he prays for increased wisdom and understanding to enable them to realize that the power of God at work in them is the same power which raised Christ from the dead and made him the Head of the church which is his body [verses 15–23].

1: Paul, an apostle of Christ Jesus through the will of God, to the saints that are at Ephesus, and the faithful in Christ Jesus:

It is important to note that the abiding significance of all that follows is determined by the validity of Paul's opening appeal to the fact of his apostleship. He is conscious that his words possess unique authority for the whole church of God, because he knows that he is 'an apostle of Christ Jesus through the will of God'. The word 'apostle' (or 'sent one') connects the one who is sent (Paul) with the Sender (Christ) and thus draws attention to the special charge which authorizes the mission; whereas the ordinary Greek word for 'send' merely links the sender with the recipient (K. Rengstorf, *Theological Dictionary of the New Testament*, vol. 1, p. 398). What Paul claims is that the grace of apostleship was conferred upon him through the initiative of God and the direct call of Christ. And it was the *personal* appearance of the Risen Lord to Paul which transformed the persecutor into a *witness* who was now *sent forth* to preach the very gospel he had tried to overthrow [cf. *Acts* 26:16, 17: 'unto whom I send (*apostello*) thee']. 'From this it appears clearly how the Sovereign Lord himself changed, called and appointed Paul to be his "apostle" in the fullest sense of the word – one clothed with the authority and endued with the power of his Sender, to go forth and act as his representative in the fulfilling of the commission given to him' (J. Norval Geldenhuys, *Supreme Authority*, p. 63).

As already noted in the Introduction, the traditional view that this Epistle was the peculiar property of the Ephesian church cannot be sustained by the evidence, which rather points to its wider circulation among the churches around Ephesus. Yet even though Ephesus was not the Epistle's only destination, it is better to retain the words 'at Ephesus' than to omit them, as does the RSV, because this message was sent to Christians living in particular places. For the church of Christ would be nothing more than a vague idea without its visible manifestation in definite localities. But instead of using the term 'church,' Paul here chooses to remind his readers of the dignity and duty that is theirs as 'the saints' and 'faithful' who are 'in Christ Jesus.' The root of both designations is found in Israel's consecration and consequent calling to faithful service [*Exod.* 19:5, 6]. As Israel was brought into the sphere of covenant blessing to obey God's commands [*Lev.* 19:2], so the new Israel of God has now been chosen to serve him in holiness of heart and life [cf. *1 Pet.* 2:9 where *Israel's* distinctive titles are transferred to the *church*; *Rom.* 6:22; *2 Cor.* 7:1].

Such obedience is possible only because they are 'in Christ Jesus', who is not only their personal Saviour but also the Head of this new community, into which they have been incorporated by grace. It is not too much to say that the whole of Paul's experience and teaching of Christ is summed up in the phrase 'in Christ Jesus,' upon which the Epistle itself is but one large comment. The key to its meaning is found in Christ as the Head of the new creation through his redemptive achievement as the second Adam [note that the first time 'in Christ' occurs in Romans is in 6:11, following the teaching of *Rom.* 5:12–21]. Thus a corporate relationship is here in view, for our individual salvation in Christ also makes us members of the church which is his body [1:23; 2:15]. Truly, 'the New Testament knows nothing of a solitary Christianity' (John Wesley).

2: Grace to you and peace from God our Father and the Lord Jesus Christ.

As in all Paul's Epistles the conventional greeting is replaced by the prayer that those who read his words may be enriched with the twin blessings of 'grace' [1:6, 7; 2:5, 7, 8; 3:2, 7, 8; 4:7, 29; 6:24] and 'peace' [2:14, 15, 17; 4:3; 6:15, 23]. He wants them to enjoy the free favour of God in Christ and the deep peace which flows from it. In an Epistle which dwells upon the essential unity of all believers in Christ, this combination of Greek and Jewish forms of greeting is especially appropriate. The linking together of the Father and the Son under a single preposition ('from') evidently assumes their complete equality. While it would be a startling offence to associate the name of the greatest reformer, saint, or even apostle with the name of God in this way, there is one reason why it is not blasphemous to speak of God and Christ as the joint-bestowers of all grace and peace to men. It is because 'Jesus Christ is God. Being God, and for that reason only, he can be linked in this stupendous fashion with God the Father and can be separated from the whole universe of created things' (J. Gresham Machen, *The Christian Faith in the Modern World,* p. 224).

3: Blessed be the God and Father of our Lord Jesus Christ, who hath blessed us with every spiritual blessing in the heavenly places in Christ;

The stately elevated style of Ephesians is due to the fact that most of the apostle's teaching in this Epistle, particularly in the first three chapters, is expressed in the language of prayer. Although the long opening doxology [verses 3–14], recalls the form of the Jewish *berakah* (blessing), it has a distinctively Christian content. In three stanzas of unequal length, Paul here gratefully surveys the grace of God in our salvation, as he progressively describes the work of the Father [verses 3–6], Son [verses 7–12], and Holy Spirit [verses 13–14], punctuating each section with a phrase that points to the glory of the Father's sovereign initiative [verses 6, 12, 14].

Blessed be: This first word of heartfelt praise strikes the keynote of Paul's great thanksgiving. As the absolutely 'blessed' (*eulogetos*) One, God is infinitely worthy of that ascriptive praise which acknowledges him as the sole source of every blessing, even though it can add nothing to his essential blessedness [cf. *Luke* 1:68; *2 Cor.* 1:3; *1 Pet.*1:3]. For while God blesses us by his *deeds of grace* ('with every spiritual blessing'), we can only bless him by our *words of gratitude.*

The God and Father of our Lord Jesus Christ: This single mention of the name of God shows that he is the subject of the entire sentence [verses 3–14]. God is from eternity the *Father* of the Son, but it was not until the Word was made flesh for our salvation that he also became his *God* [*John* 21:17]. And we are taught here to bless God for this provision of his grace, because it is only through the merits of *our* Mediator that we are brought to know God as *our* Father [cf. verse 5: 'having foreordained us unto *adoption as sons* through Jesus Christ unto himself'].

Who hath blessed us: Or rather 'who blessed us,' the aorist tense pointing to the time when God called us to faith in Christ, an event which the 'even as' of verse 4 traces back to our election. The idea 'is that in calling us to Christian faith God blessed us, and that the great deed of blessing which thus took effect in time had its foundation in an eternal election' (S. D. F. Salmond). Consequently no one ever becomes a believer by the power of his own choice [*John* 1:13], but only because the Father draws him to Christ [*John* 6:44].

With every spiritual blessing: The nature of God's decisive act of 'blessing' is here described. This includes 'every *spiritual* blessing' [cf. 5:19], i.e. all those blessings that are brought by the Spirit, and that lead to life in the Spirit [verses 13, 14; *Rom.* 8:1–27; *Gal.* 4:6; 5:22–23]. 'All, and yet but one blessing; to note that spiritual blessings are so knit together, that they all make up but one blessing; and where God gives one, he gives all' (John Trapp).

In the heavenly places in Christ: Union with Christ has made the believer an inhabitant of two worlds. Spiritually he is already raised and seated with Christ 'in the heavenly places' [2:6], though meanwhile he lives in the body on earth as a stranger and pilgrim whose true citizenship is in heaven [*Phil.* 3:20; *Heb.* 11:13]. Paul's use of the phrase here shows that these spiritual blessings have their origin in heaven, and it is from heaven that our enthroned Head [1:20] dispenses this largesse to his members on earth. Thus we are blessed by God because we are 'in Christ.' The blessings have their source in our election 'in Christ,' and they were secured for us by his death; but they become ours in actual possession only in virtue of our vital union with him.

4: even as he chose us in him before the foundation of the world, that we should be holy and without blemish before him in love:

Even as he chose us: This presents election as the sole ground of all the blessings vouchsafed to believers. It was not that they chose God, for they became believers only because God first chose them. The verb 'chose' '*always* has, and must *of logical necessity* have, a reference to others to whom the chosen would, without the *choosing out*, still belong' (H. A. W. Meyer). And it was from the mass of fallen humanity that God chose out *for himself* (middle voice) a people whom he formed to show forth his praise [*Isa.* 43:21; *1 Pet.* 2:9,10]. In the divine decree which contemplated the race as ruined by the fall, God thus chose to save some to the praise of his mercy, while leaving the non-elect to suffer the consequences of their sin to the praise of his justice [*Rom.* 9:17–23].

'Us' joins Paul with his readers, and it expresses the apostle's adoring wonder at the inscrutability of God's choice, unprompted as it is by any foreseen merit in those so chosen to receive an eternal inheritance [*Rom.* 9:11, 13, 16].

In him: The brief phrase conveys a vital truth, for it was only in their worthy Redeemer that such a choice of the unworthy could be made. God's election, says Calvin, is like 'a registering of us in writing' in which 'Jesus Christ serves as a register. It is in him that we are written down and acknowledged by God as his children. Seeing, then, that God had an eye to us in the person of Jesus Christ, it follows that he did not find anything in us which we might lay before him to cause him to elect us.'

Before the foundation of the world [cf. *2 Tim.* 1:9]: This proves that our election in Christ was no historical afterthought but the eternal resolve of unfettered sovereignty. 'Salvation is no precarious half-measure but a foundation laid in heaven' (E. K. Simpson). The acceptance of this truth leads to an unshakeable confidence in God even as it withers all confidence in the flesh [*1 Cor.* 1:27–31].

That we should be holy and blameless before him (RSV): As the emphasis throughout this passage is upon the spontaneous love of the Father, it is more appropriate to link 'in love' with the act of foreordaining his people to sonship [verse 5] than to read 'blameless before him in love' [verse 4], which less fittingly attributes the primary reference to love in the Epistle to our secondary response.

The ultimate purpose of our election in Christ was that we should be perfectly holy and without blame before him who is the searcher of every heart. Such spiritual perfection clearly pertains to the heavenly state, but because God's decree not only determines the *end* but also includes the *means* of attaining that end, he moves and enables the elect to persevere and progress in holiness until what was begun in grace is at last consummated in glory [cf. *Phil.* 2:12, 13; *2 Thess.* 2:13]. From this it follows, 'First, that individuals, and not communities or nations, are the objects of election; secondly, that holiness in no form can be the ground of election. If men are chosen to be holy, they cannot be chosen because they are holy. And, thirdly, it follows that holiness is the only evidence of election. For one who lives in sin to claim to be elected unto holiness, is a contradiction' (Charles Hodge) [*2 Pet.* 1:3–11].

5: having foreordained us unto adoption as sons through Jesus Christ unto himself, according to the good pleasure of his will,

Having in love foreordained us unto adoption as sons through Jesus Christ (ASV margin): Clearly this is no coldly conceived decree, for nothing but predestinating *love* can account for our adoption into the family of God as his sons! This elevation of us by grace to the status and privileges of sonship could be effected only through the redemptive mediation of the One who is the Father's Son by nature [*Rom.* 8:29]. The experience of this filial relationship is a present reality in the life of believers [*Rom.* 8:15; *Gal.* 4:5], though its unveiling in glory remains as the hope of the future [*Rom.* 8:23; *1 John* 3:1–3].

Unto himself: The phrase discloses the *goal* of God's foreordination of us to the standing of sons. It is to bring us 'to himself, into perfect fellowship with him, into adoring, loving relation to himself as the true end and object of our being' (Salmond).

According to the good pleasure of his will: These words signify something more than the determination of bare sovereignty, for the reference to God's 'good pleasure' brings out the fact that his gracious resolve to save the elect was wholly grounded in the free delight with which he *fore-loved* them [*Rom.* 8:29].

6: to the praise of the glory of his grace, which he freely bestowed on us in the Beloved:

To the praise of the glory of his grace: The heaping up of such genitival phrases is a striking feature of this letter, in which Paul so often struggles against the limitations of language as he endeavours to express the unutterable riches of God's grace. 'To' here shows that the glory of God is the great end in our election, and this consists in our ever increasing recognition ('the praise') of the manifested excellence ('of the glory') of God's undeserved bounty towards us ('of his grace').

Which he freely bestowed on us in the Beloved: Paul again prompts our praise of God's unmerited favour by making a play on the word grace, for 'freely bestowed' really means 'be-graced' (Bruce). Thus he speaks of the 'grace' [verse 6a] with which God 'be-graced' us in the Beloved. All the grace of God is lavished upon us in the supreme gift of his Son [*Rom.* 8:32]. We are beloved of God only in the Beloved, in whom he is well pleased [*Matt.* 3:17; 17:5; cf. *Col.* 1:13: 'the Son of his love'].

As the title 'Saviour' regards our Lord from the point of view of men, so 'the Beloved' tells us what he is 'from the point of view of God – He is God's unique One, the object of his supreme choice, who stands related to him in the intimacy of appropriating love' (B. B. Warfield, *The Lord of Glory*, p. 246).

7: in whom we have our redemption through his blood, the forgiveness of our trespasses, according to the riches of his grace,

The necessary consequence of God's eternal election is seen in Christ's saving work, for those who are chosen by the Father are the very ones who are redeemed by the Son [verses 7–12]. 'If, then, redemption be in order to accomplish the purpose of the sovereign election of some, then it is certain that Christ died in order to secure the salvation of the elect, and not in order to make the salvation of all men possible' (A. A. Hodge, *The Atonement*, p. 370).

In whom we have redemption through his blood: 'In whom' exclusively ascribes redemption to the unique achievement of God's beloved Son, in whom alone 'we have our redemption.' Modern attempts to reduce the meaning of this word to the idea of mere deliverance are here ruled out by the qualifying phrase 'through his blood.' Those who limit 'redemption' to an act of emancipation empty the word of its saving content, for our release from the bondage of sin was a great *rescue by ransom* wrought out for us by the One who paid the price to set us free [cf. *Mark* 10:45; *Rom.* 3:24; *Heb.* 9:12; *1 Pet.*1:18, 19]. The 'final' redemption of 1:14 and 4:30 still rests upon this initial ransoming, the effects of which stretch into the future to secure our ultimate deliverance from the power and presence of evil in all its forms [*Luke* 21:28; *Rom.* 8:23]. 'Through his blood' poignantly recalls the violent and shameful death that Christ willingly endured as the appointed substitute of those who constitute the church, which he loved and came into the world to purchase at the cost of his all [5:25; *Acts* 20:28; *1 Cor.* 6:20].

The forgiveness of our trespasses: This linking of 'forgiveness' with the death of Christ proves that the cancellation or remission of the penalty due to sin is based upon his payment of that debt on our behalf [*Matt.* 26:28]. For 'sin is forgiven only as it is borne' (James Denney). The plural 'trespasses' draws attention to the many false steps, or deviations from God's standard of absolute righteousness, for which we daily stand in need of his forgiving grace. And this forgiveness, or sending away of our sins [*Psa.* 103:12], we are said to *have* (present tense) in Christ. 'We are ever needing, and so are *ever having it*, for we are still "in him," and the merit of his blood is unexhausted. Forgiveness is not a blessing complete at any point of time in our human existence, and therefore we are still receiving it' (John Eadie) [*1 John* 1:7–9]. The perfection of God's provision in Christ shows the folly of those who seek the remission of sins by other methods of their own devising. Hence this inclusive faith demands the exclusive confession that 'there is none other name under heaven given among men, whereby we must be saved' [*Acts* 4:12].

According to the riches of his grace: This is the *measure* of God's limitless generosity towards us in Christ: it is '*according to* the riches of his grace.' 'Riches' is one of Paul's favourite words [*Rom.* 2:4; 9:23; 11:12, 11:33; *2 Cor.* 8:2; *Phil.* 4:19; *Col.* 1:27], which is also much in evidence in Ephesians [verse 18; 2:7; 3:8, 16]. He uses it here to underscore the fact that God's securement of our free forgiveness was a costly matter. As Thomas Goodwin says, 'Thou needest not bring one penny. God is rich enough.' It is well that it is so, for how can beggars bring anything towards the forgiveness of their sins? Nothing but the overwhelming munificence of God's grace can suffice for that!

8: which he made to abound toward us in all wisdom and prudence;

The profusion of God's grace in Christ is next stated to be received by us in the form of 'all wisdom and prudence.' It is because Christ 'was made unto us wisdom' [*1 Cor.* 1:30] that we have the spiritual understanding to discern and appropriate the divine realities which remain hidden from the unbelieving [verse 19], and the prudence or practical intelligence to apply that wisdom to all the varying situations of our life. 'Wisdom is the knowledge which sees into the heart of things, which knows them as they really are. Prudence is the understanding which leads to right action' (J. Armitage Robinson).

9: making known unto us the mystery of his will, according to his good pleasure which he purposed in him

This overflowing of God's grace towards us 'in all wisdom and prudence' took effect in the disclosure of 'the mystery of his will.' In the New Testament a 'mystery' is not an unexplained riddle, but a divine secret which, though proclaimed to all, is understood only by those whom the Spirit of God enlightens [*Mark* 4:11; *1 Cor.* 2:7–16]. Thus God's plan of salvation, once the secret of his unfathomable will, is now being revealed to all included within its scope. For it is through the worldwide preaching of the gospel that this mystery is made known to the elect who are given ears to hear and hearts to receive it [cf. *Acts* 13:48; 16:14; 18:9, 10]. But there is one aspect of that plan which engages the particular attention of the apostle in Ephesians and Colossians, namely, the amazing inclusion of Gentiles as well as Jews within the same household of faith [2:11–22; 3:3–9; *Col.* 1:26, 27].

The manifestation of the mystery was 'according to his good pleasure'. It was God's special delight to reveal the secret of his love to the sons of men, and as Paul never tires of pointing out, it was a love which embraced them in the Beloved. Hence he adds, 'which he purposed *in him*'. The Father's purpose was *in the Son*, 'inasmuch as it was to take effect through the Son, incarnate, sacrificed, and glorified; and further, as it concerned a church which was to be incorporated "into Christ"' (H. C. G. Moule) [*Rom.* 8:28, 29].

10: unto a dispensation of the fullness of the times, to sum up all things in Christ, the things in the heavens, and the things upon the earth; in him, I say,

With a view to a dispensation belonging to the fullness of the times: 'Dispensation' (*oikonomia*) is a word that primarily refers to house-management, and the meaning here is that God has entrusted Christ with the 'administration' of that purpose which is the good pleasure of his will [verse 9]. Just as a great landowner appoints a manager to put into execution his plans for the estate, so the Father has given Christ full authority to administer and bring to completion the entire plan of salvation [*Matt.* 28:18]. 'The fullness of the times' points forward to this epoch of consummation, whereas in Galatians 4:4 'the fullness of the time' covers the more restricted period of Christ's first advent.

To sum up under one head all things in Christ, the things in the heavens, and the things upon the earth: Paul now explains that the object which God had in view was the summing up of all things in Christ. This is one of several verses in Ephesians and Colossians in which the apostle sets forth the cosmic significance of Christ's person and work [verses 20–22; *Col.* 1:15–20]. No doubt this teaching was directed against the heretical speculations of those 'gnostics' whose superior 'knowledge' had relegated Christ to an inferior rôle through the unlawful exaltation of a host of angelic intermediaries. Although opinion is divided over the precise meaning of 'to sum up' [*anakephalaioo*: used only here and in *Rom.* 13:9], the rendering 'to sum up under one head' is not unlikely in a passage that goes on to speak of Christ as the Head of the church [verse 22]. It would seem that Paul has two headships in mind: Christ's sovereign headship of the cosmos, and his redemptive headship of the church [*Acts* 20:28]. When it is recognized that the church does not include 'all things,' the danger of confusing the saving effects of Christ's work with its cosmic consequences is avoided. The passage does not teach the universal salvation of all men; it states that God will sum up the whole creation under Christ through whom 'all things' shall find their true coherence and unity [cf. *Rom.* 8:19–23]. Thus the apostle's reference is to 'the entire harmony of the universe, which shall no longer contain alien and discordant elements, but of which all the parts shall find their centre and bond of union in Christ. Sin and death, sorrow and failure and suffering, shall cease. There shall be a new heaven and a new earth' (J. B. Lightfoot).

In him, I say: This is to be connected with the following verse.

11: in whom also we were made a heritage, having been foreordained according to the purpose of him who worketh all things after the counsel of his will;

It was in fulfilment of God's eternal design that in Christ 'we' – i.e. *all* believers as represented by Paul and his readers – were actually 'made a heritage,' or taken for God's inheritance. This rendering is preferable to that of the AV, 'in whom also we have obtained an inheritance,' because it is more consistent with the context which speaks of 'God's own possession' [verse 14] and 'his inheritance in the saints' [verse 18]. The apostle's appropriation of this Old Testament title for Christian use indicates the spiritual fulfilment in the church [*Gal.* 6:16] of that election which had singled out national Israel as God's peculiar possession [cf. *Deut.* 4:20; 9:29; 32:9]. 'That God should be his people's portion is easy to be accounted for, for he is their joy and felicity; but how they should be his portion, who neither needs them, nor can be benefited by them, must be resolved into the wondrous condescensions of free grace. *Even so, Father, because it seemed good in thine eyes* so to call them and count them' (Matthew Henry on *Deut.* 32:9).

Since believers may never ascribe their privileged position to the power of their own choice [*John* 1:13], Paul again states that God's foreordination was the cause of this saving change [verse 5]. Thus the calling out to faith in Christ of God's heritage (which consists of those elect Jews and Gentiles who together make up the universal church) takes place 'according to the purpose of him who worketh all things after the counsel of his will.' In God's execution of his great plan of salvation nothing is left to 'chance,' and nothing is contingent upon the will of the creature, because nothing is exempted from his sovereign control. For God 'works' (his energy is dynamically operative in) '*all* things,' not arbitrarily but intelligently, in order to fulfil what he had determined to accomplish in the eternal 'counsel' of his grace [*Rom.* 8:28].

12: to the end that we should be unto the praise of his glory, we who had before hoped in Christ:

To the end that we should be to the praise of his glory, we who beforehand had centred our hope in Christ (Hendriksen): It is more in keeping with the inclusive scope of the passage to regard the verse as giving expression to the common Christian hope in Christ's return than to restrict 'we' to the priority of the Jewish hope in the Messiah. Those who do so are bound to maintain that the 'you' of the following verse refers to Gentile believers, but such a division would limit 'the praise of his glory' to Jews and apportion 'the Holy Spirit of promise' to Gentiles! It is therefore preferable to accept the interpretation offered in Moule's paraphrase: 'That we should contribute to the glory of God, at the appearing of Christ; welcomed then as the once patient and expectant believers in his promise while still it tarried' [*Rom.* 8:24,25].

13: in whom ye also, having heard the word of the truth, the gospel of your salvation, – in whom, having also believed, ye were sealed with the Holy Spirit of promise;

Paul's majestic opening sentence approaches its climax with the change of address which thankfully recalls his readers' participation in the gift of the Holy Spirit through the gracious act of God [verses 13, 14]. The main thought of the verse is: *in whom* (in Christ) *ye* (Ephesians) *also* (in common with all other Christians) . . . *were sealed.* The connection is difficult because the construction is broken by the apostle's characteristic insistence upon the necessity of faith. And his teaching is that the believing and the sealing always go together. As there is no sealing without believing, so there is no believing without sealing. Hence this is not an experience reserved for a favoured few; *it is the birthright of all believers!*

Having heard the word of the truth, the gospel of your salvation: But as no one can believe in him of whom he has never heard, Paul first refers to the preaching through which the Ephesians had been brought to faith in Christ [*Rom.* 10:14–17]. Objectively, this message is 'the word' that has the truth for its essential content [*Col.* 1:5]; and subjectively, it became 'the gospel' or good news of *their* salvation when they believed it for themselves [*Rom.* 1:16].

In whom, having also believed, ye were sealed with the Holy Spirit of promise: 'Having believed' is the coincident aorist participle and Paul's use of it here shows that they were not sealed *after*, but *when* they believed (exactly as in *Acts* 19:2: 'Did ye receive the Holy Spirit *when ye believed?*'). This distinction is important because it means that the two verbs must be seen as the two sides of the same event: in the moment when they believed, they were also sealed. Hence the sealing is not represented as a process, but as a definite act which was at once complete. Moreover, the further use of 'in whom' indicates the impossibility of separating the experience of being 'in Christ' from the sealing which is common to all believers [cf. the universal language of *2 Cor.* 1:21, 22].

It is not necessary to read any reference to baptism into the text to explain what this sealing means. In the ancient world visible seals were used to attest as genuine, to mark ownership, and to keep secure. But as this seal cannot be seen, its presence may be known only by its characteristic effects [*John* 3:8]. So believers are authenticated as the children of God by the inward witness of the Spirit [*Rom.* 8:16]. And it is because they are sealed by a living Person who can be grieved by sin, that they may lose for a time this subjective assurance of their salvation, even though they remain objectively sealed unto the day of redemption [4:30]. Consequently, the adjective 'holy,' placed emphatically at the end of the clause, points to the kind of separation which is always demanded by him, whose essential attribute is holiness [cf. *Rom.* 8:1–14]. He is also the 'promised' Spirit, whose advent ushered in the long-awaited era of gospel grace. 'It is clear that what is in view here is not the extraordinary or miraculous gifts of the Spirit, but that bestowal of the Spirit in which all believers shared, which was the subject of the great Old Testament prophecies [*Joel* 2:28–32; *Isa.* 32:15; 44:3; *Ezek.* 36:26; 39,29; *Zech.* 12:10], and of which a new heart, a new spirit, was to be the result' (Salmond).

14: which is an earnest of our inheritance, unto the redemption of God's own possession, unto the praise of his glory.

Paul enlarges on the theme of the believer's assurance of final salvation, already implied in the concept of sealing, by stating that the Holy Spirit is also 'an earnest' of our inheritance. This is the deposit that is given as the guarantee that the full amount will be paid later. It is not simply a pledge, which might be different in kind, but the first instalment. 'In other words the thing given is related to the thing assured – the present to the hereafter – as a part to the whole. It is the same in kind' (Lightfoot). So the gift of the Holy Spirit is the beginning of salvation, the first instalment of the Christian's future inheritance. The same truth is expressed under a different metaphor in Romans 8:23, where the Spirit is compared to 'the first-fruits' of the final harvest.

As Lightfoot further observes, 'The actual spiritual life of the Christian is the same in kind as his future glorified life; the kingdom of heaven is a present kingdom; the believer is already seated on the right hand of God . . . Nevertheless the present gift of the Spirit is only a *small fraction* of the future endowment. This idea also would be suggested by the usual relation between the earnest-money and the full payment.' Thus we must recognize in the gift of the Spirit the indisputable proof of God's determination to honour all the obligations he has assumed towards us under the covenant of grace [*Phil.* 1:6]. Yet it would be a grave mistake to conceive of this gift in any static sense, for our present realization of future glory admits of spiritual increase *in this world* [cf. comment on verse17 and 3:16].

Unto the redemption of God's own possession: This looks forward to the day of ultimate deliverance when God shall finally claim us as his special possession [*Mal.* 3:17; *1 Pet.* 2:9]. Paul's language in this passage clearly shows that he is thinking of the church as the new Israel, for he applies to Gentiles the very terms – 'promise,' 'inheritance,' 'possession' – which were used to describe Israel's peculiar privileges. Now it is by *our* possession of the Spirit that we are already marked out as *God's* own possession. And this means that it is only by receiving the Spirit, who is the very essence of the new covenant [*Gal.* 3:14], that a man is made a member of the new Israel and participates in the blessings of the new age.

Unto the praise of his glory: We must never confuse God's glory with the vain egoism of man's boasting. For since God is God he could set no higher object before himself than the complete manifestation of his own glory. Thus the fulfilment of his purpose of grace in the salvation of the elect shall eternally redound to the praise of his glory, which is the great end of all creation [*Rev.* 4:11].

15: For this cause I also, having heard of the faith in the Lord Jesus which is among you, and the love which ye show toward all the saints;

Filled with thanksgiving by the knowledge that the Ephesians share in the blessings just enumerated [verses 3–14], and having heard of their continued progress since he last saw them, Paul now begins his great prayer for their further enlightenment [verses 15–23]. Those who deny Paul's authorship of the Epistle regard 'having heard' as a proof of their argument that the writer was not personally acquainted with his readers [as in *Col.* 1:4]. But this assumes too much, for the same language is used in Philemon 4, 5 and Paul certainly knew Philemon! 'May one not *hear* of friends from whom one has been absent for five years?' (Lenski). Obviously, one may hear about persons whom one has met (the Ephesians, Philemon) as well as about persons whom one has never met (the Colossians).

Note that the Ephesians showed the reality of their 'faith' in the Lord Jesus by the sincerity of their 'love' toward all the saints. 'Faith is but an empty name if it does not fructify in love. Faith in Christ is only a

delusion if it issues not in love for those who are his' (Arthur W. Pink)
[*1 John* 3:14; 4:20, 21].

16: cease not to give thanks for you, making mention of you in my prayers;

It is very striking that Paul never congratulates his readers on their
faith, but always thanks God for it.[1] And this is because every genuine
conversion is a signal instance of the putting forth of God's almighty
power [cf. verses 19, 20 with 2:1, 5]. But Paul not only regarded the
Ephesian Christians as a constant cause for thankfulness to God, he
also saw them as standing in need of his continual prayers on their
behalf. 'How much of the Apostle's work for his converts consisted in
the holy labour of special intercessory prayer, with thanksgiving! In
his Roman lodging this was the case, perhaps, even more than ever'
(Moule).

**17: that the God of our Lord Jesus Christ, the Father of glory, may give
unto you a spirit of wisdom and revelation in the knowledge of him;**

Paul here prays that God, who is the fountain of all grace and the
Father of glory, may give his readers the wisdom and revelation of the
Spirit which will increase their knowledge of him (i.e. God). It is as
the God of our Mediator, the Lord Jesus Christ, that God is seen to
be the sole source of grace for sinful men [cf. 1:3]. Moreover, there is
an intermingling of grace in the sublime title, Father of glory; for God
is not only the One to whom all glory belongs, but also the bestower
of the glory by which his children are enlightened and transformed
[*Psa.* 84:11; *2 Cor.* 3:18; 4:6].

---

[1] A fact which is entirely in harmony with the teaching of the opening doxology. Cf.
the *Westminster Confession of Faith*, ch. 10, sections 1 and 2: 'All those whom God
hath predestinated unto life, and those only, he is pleased, in his appointed and accepted
time, effectually to call, by his Word and Spirit, out of that state of sin and death in
which they are by nature, to grace and salvation by Jesus Christ; enlightening their
minds spiritually and savingly to understand the things of God; taking away their
heart of stone, and giving unto them an heart of flesh; renewing their wills, and by his
almighty power determining them to that which is good; and effectually drawing them
to Jesus Christ; yet so as they come most freely, being made willing by his grace. This
effectual call is of God's free and special grace alone, not from any thing at all foreseen
in man; who is altogether passive therein, until, being quickened and renewed by the
Holy Spirit, he is thereby enabled to answer this call, and to embrace the grace offered
and conveyed in it.'

The fact that 'Spirit' lacks the article is no reason to exclude a personal reference to the Holy Spirit, for only he can impart wisdom and revelation to men. The apostle's request is that believers may have more of the Spirit as the Spirit of wisdom, so that they may have an enlarged understanding of that wisdom which must be not only preached *to us* but also revealed *in us* [*1 Cor.* 2:10ff]. For we are blind and understand 'nothing of God's spiritual grace, unless he opens our eyes and takes away the veil that is upon them, and even gives us a new sight which we do not have. For our eyes are worse than put out until he enlightens them by his Holy Spirit' (Calvin).

And it is through this endowment that they will acquire a greater knowledge of God. As J. Armitage Robinson rightly points out, this is not abstract knowledge, but 'knowledge directed towards a particular object' in the sense of perceiving, discerning, and recognizing God as 'the God of our Lord Jesus Christ, the Father of glory.' It is therefore a warm personal knowledge of God as he is revealed in Christ [*John* 14:6]. Philosophy comes to us with the man-centred message, 'Know thyself'; whereas the *summum bonum* of the inspired Word is, 'Know thy God'.

18: having the eyes of your heart enlightened, that ye may know what is the hope of his calling, what the riches of the glory of his inheritance in the saints,

19: and what the exceeding greatness of his power to us-ward who believe, according to that working of the strength of his might,

In Scripture 'the heart' denotes what a man is in his deepest self; it is the seat of his intellectual, religious, and moral life. It is because man is inwardly blinded by sin that the light which is within him is darkness until the Spirit shines into his heart in re-creating grace [*Matt.* 6:23; *2 Cor.* 4:6]. But as this initial illumination is only the beginning of what must be a continuous process, Paul prays that the Ephesians may enjoy such further enlightenment of the inner vision as will enable them to grasp the three great realities of their faith.

That ye may know what is the hope of his calling: 1. It is the eternal choice of God that makes this an *effectual* calling and a *certain* hope. Hence it is with no fragile confidence in their own resources that believers are to face the future, but with the assured hope that the God, who called them to eternal life in Christ by giving them the earnest of the Spirit [verse14], will soon invest them with the promised glory [*Rom.* 15:13].

What the riches of the glory of his inheritance in the saints: 2. Although God's people are called to a glorious inheritance, Paul here returns to the amazing thought that they are also an inheritance for God [verses 11, 14]. They are 'his own possession, in whom he will display to the universe the untold riches of his glory. We can scarcely realize what it must mean to God to see his purpose complete, to see creatures of his hand, sinners redeemed by his grace, reflecting his own glory' (F. F. Bruce).

And what the exceeding greatness of his power to us-ward who believe, according to that working of the strength of his might: 3. The Ephesians must not only have in view God's past calling and God's future inheritance, but also realize God's power in their present experience; for the continued progress of believers in the way that leads to glory entirely depends upon the exceeding greatness of that *power*, whose measure is further defined by an awkward but impressive accumulation of synonyms. According to T. K. Abbott, this *working* or actual exercise of the *strength* of God's inherent power is that *might* which overcomes all resistance. Thus Paul's request is that believers may recognize that the power which awakened them from the sleep of death will invincibly bring them to heaven, for it is the same power which raised Christ from the dead [verse 20].

20: which he wrought in Christ, when he raised him from the dead, and made him to sit at his right hand in the heavenly places;

As the Word made flesh Jesus can speak of raising himself by his own power [*John* 2:19, 21; 10:17, 18], but Paul always refers the resurrection of our Head to the direct act of God because this set the seal of divine approval upon Christ's work for us [cf. *Rom.* 4:24, 25; 8:34]. Without this act of omnipotent power the apostles would have had no gospel to preach [*1 Cor.* 15:14, 15]. 'Had he not emerged from the tomb, all our hopes, all our salvation would be lying dead with him unto this day . . . The resurrection of Christ is thus the indispensable evidence of his completed work, his accomplished redemption' (B. B. Warfield: 'The Resurrection of Christ a Fundamental Doctrine,' *Selected*

Shorter Writings, vol. 1, p. 200). And it is because believers already know the power of Christ's resurrection that they enjoy the consequent assurance of participating in the resurrection of the just [*Rom.* 8:11, 23].

An equally important place is given to the exaltation of Christ by the New Testament writers who see it as the fulfilment of what was foretold in Psalm 110:1 [cf. *Acts* 5:31; 7:56; *Rom.* 8:34; *1 Cor.* 15:25; *Phil.* 2:9–11; *Col.* 3:1; *Heb.* 1:3; 8:1; 12:2; *Rev.* 5:1–14]. This sharing of God's throne at once demonstrates the divine dignity of Christ and proclaims his universal lordship [*Heb.* 1:13; *1 Pet.*3:22]. He is represented as seated, not to denote his permanent posture in heaven [*Acts* 7:56; *Rev.* 2:1], but to show that he has finished the work of redemption and entered upon the exercise of that power which belongs to his heavenly state [*Acts* 3:21]. And though Christ's people are to see in his glorification the pledge of their future glory, Paul's special concern in Ephesians is not with the ultimate but the *present* consequences of this enthronement for believers [1:3, 2:6; cf. *Col.* 3:1ff].

21: far above all rule, and authority, and power, and dominion, and every name that is named, not only in this world, but also in that which is to come:

22a: and he put all things in subjection under his feet,

Paul affirms Christ's lordship over all created powers, probably with a sidelong glance at the false teaching in Asia Minor that denied the finality of Christ's mediation by paying homage to angels [*Col.* 2:18]. In comparing this enumeration of angelic orders with that given in Colossians 1:16, Lightfoot insists that no stress can be laid on the sequence of names, as though Paul were formulating a precise doctrine of the celestial hierarchy. He clearly has no patience with this elaborate angelology, and brushes aside these speculations without remarking upon how much or how little truth there may be in them. For the one fact which every believer must hold fast is that the exalted Christ is far above 'every name that is named' [*Phil.* 2:9]. 'The decisive point for Paul is that in no regard, whether as fate, or nature, or intermediate beings, or servants of God, can these powers either separate the Christian from Christ or lead him to Him' (W. Foerster, *TDNT*, vol. 2, p. 573).

Furthermore, this supremacy belongs to Christ 'not only in this age, but also in that which is to come.' Paul's adoption of the Jewish concept of the two ages was modified by his teaching that in the experience of believers the future had already invaded the present age [1:3, 2:6; Phil. 3:20].

Hence it is the function of faith to acknowledge the reality of Christ's rule during the very period when all the unbelieving are blind to it – a lesson which is enforced by Paul's quotation of Psalm 8:6 [cf. Heb. 2:6ff].

And he put all things in subjection under his feet: After Christ's triumph over principalities and powers on the cross [Col. 2:15], God exalted him to the throne of the universe and put all things under his feet. Despite present appearances to the contrary, the victory of the cross has secured the final doom of Satan and his hosts, though in the meanwhile believers must contest his usurped power well knowing that the ultimate issue of this spiritual warfare is not in doubt [6:11, 12; Rom. 16:20; 1 Cor. 15:25]. Paul here shows that David's words find their proper fulfilment in the Son of Man whose conquest of sin and death has invested him with a domination far more glorious than that which was lost to the race through Adam's fall.

22b: and gave him to be head over all things to the church, 23: which is his body, the fulness of him that filleth all in all.

Paul further states that this universal lordship is exercised for the benefit of the church: God gave *him* – who is over all things – to be Head 'to' (or rather 'for') the church. 'Christ therefore has power over all things in heaven and on earth, and in a specific sense he is the King over his church, which he rules by his grace and Spirit and Word. The relation between this power over all things and his sovereignty over his church is such, that he employs the former to the preservation and salvation of the latter' (Herman Hoeksema, *Reformed Dogmatics,* p. 627). This headship of Christ means: 1. He is the sole ruler of the church [5:23ff], so that it must refuse submission to the alien yoke of state or pope; 2. He is the sole source of its life and strength, so that it receives from him that nourishment which promotes the growth of the whole body [4:15, 16].

Which is his body: The final development of this familiar Pauline metaphor is reached in Colossians and Ephesians. When the church is compared to the body of Christ in the earlier Epistles it is the crucified body of Christ that is in view [*1 Cor.* 10:16f.; 11:23–27], whereas here the emphasis is upon the risen and glorified body [though the cross is not forgotten, cf. 2:13ff.; *Col.* 2:14, 15]. What immediately follows shows that Paul is not speaking of the *outward witness* of the church, but of its *inward union* with Christ its Head. In Ephesians the main stress is placed on what the church receives from Christ and on its internal growth. This is certainly the prerequisite for its active service, but a different image is used to express that thought [cf. 6:10–20].

The fulness of him that filleth all in all: A profound phrase whose meaning is the subject of much dispute. Some say that the church fills up that which is lacking in Christ who would be in some sense incomplete without his body; while others maintain that it is Christ who fills the church. The idea that the church is the complement of Christ is not favoured by the context, which is concerned with what Christ is to the church and not what the Church is to Christ. 'All that Christ has from God, the power, the gifts, the grace, he passes on to the church . . . The church has nothing to give Christ of herself, by which what is lacking in him could be filled up. Instead, it is the church that is filled with him [cf. 3:19], becoming a partaker of all that he owns and is, for the purpose of continuing his work' (Stig Hanson, *The Unity of the Church in the New Testament*, pp. 128–9).

CHAPTER TWO

Paul next reminds his readers of how they had been delivered by the grace of God from the deadness of their former walk in trespasses and sins, and quickened into a new life in Christ so that they are now able to walk in those good works which God had prepared for their doing [verses 1–10]. The apostle then goes on to show that this individual experience of salvation has the most far reaching corporate consequences. As Gentiles they were formerly aliens from the commonwealth of Israel, but now in Christ they are fellow-citizens with believing Jews and full members of the household of God. This spiritual unity was achieved by Christ's reconciling death which abolished the dividing wall that stood between them and created one new man, so that Jews and Gentiles are knit together into a holy temple in the Lord [verses 11–22].

1: And you *did he make alive*, when ye were dead through your trespasses and sins,

The chapter begins with one grand sentence, which celebrates the greatness of the grace that raised the readers from the sepulchre of their sins [verses 1–10].

And you did he make alive: An emphatic address which says in effect: '*You* were the unworthy objects of distinguishing mercy!' But as Paul actually makes no reference to God's quickening grace until he has first made clear their abject plight by nature [verses 1–3], it is better to omit the italicized words supplied by the translators to ensure a smoother reading. It is vital to grasp the significance of the apostle's method [cf. *Rom.* 1–3], because an inadequate doctrine of sin always leads to slight views of grace and also leaves ajar the door that admits error. '"Never was there a heresy, but it had something to do with an insufficient estimate of sin." And an insufficient estimate of the "thing which God hateth" is not only the parent of speculative error; it is the secret death of true spiritual joy' (Moule, *Ephesian Studies*, p. 70).

When ye were dead through your trespasses and sins: 'Trespasses and sins' are two plurals which vividly recall the multiplied aggravation of their guilt before God. But if the terms are not used synonymously, then 'trespasses' would indicate the deliberate transgression of the law, while 'sins' would point to the 'missing of the mark' set for them by God. Being dead while they lived, their activity was then the activity of death [verses 2,3]. This deadness made them insensible of their separation from the life of God [4:18] and of his just condemnation of their wayward walk [verse 3], even as it also left them without either the ability or the inclination to arise from the tomb [verse 5]. Thus they were destitute of all *spiritual* life, 'having no hope,' because they were 'without God in the world' [verses 11, 12].

2: wherein ye once walked according to the course of this world, according to the prince of the powers of the air, of the spirit that now worketh in the sons of disobedience;

Paul uses the verb 'to walk' as a graphic metaphor to denote deliberate progress in a particular direction. Here it points to the voluntary adoption of a life-style which was utterly opposed to the standard set for man by God [cf. 4:17–19]. Hence the spiritually *dead* are in a state of *active* opposition to God, for which they are justly held responsible.

According to the course of this world: The former conduct of the readers was in complete conformity to the transient norm of worldly life, and was a total contradiction of the spiritual norm of the kingdom of God. So that while they embraced the corrupt and debased standard of 'this present evil world' [*Gal.*1:4], they walked in nothing but trespasses and sins.

According to the ruler of the kingdom of the air (Arndt-Gingrich): Although they had chosen to live in this way, and were certainly accountable for their actions, they could not have chosen otherwise. For at that time they were under Satan's sway, and served him as the willing captives of his realm [*Col.* 1:13; *2 Tim.* 2:26]. Some say that 'air' should be understood figuratively, but William Hendriksen presents a convincing argument for its literal meaning. He concludes: 'This passage, in conjunction with others [3:10, 15; 6:12], clearly teaches that God has tenanted the supermundane realm with innumerable hosts, and that in its lower region the minions of Satan are engaged in their destructive missions.'

Of the spirit that now worketh in the sons of disobedience: According to F. F. Bruce, this means that Satan is the governing power behind the 'spirit of the age' [cf. *1 John* 5:19], which is so powerfully at work in 'the sons of disobedience'. As this Hebraism indicates, the disobedience is not incidental but innate. It describes those whose lives are wholly characterized by disobedience. Paul's reference to the *present* activity of this spirit in the unregenerate serves to remind believers of their gracious deliverance from its enslaving power.

3: among whom we also all once lived in the lusts of our flesh, doing the desires of the flesh and of the mind, and were by nature children of wrath, even as the rest:-

Among these we all once lived in the passions of our flesh (RSV): It was among these sons of disobedience that 'we all' – Paul as well as the Ephesians – who now believe, once lived in the same bondage to the imperious dictates of our 'flesh'. Here the word has its full ethical meaning, viz. fallen human nature as alienated from God and under the dominion of sin. 'At one time "our flesh" governed us completely. It is its nature to produce nothing but sinful desires and appetites that call for sinful satisfaction' (Lenski).

Following the desires of body and mind (RSV): As the RSV correctly indicates, 'flesh' now receives the more restricted meaning of 'body' from its juxtaposition with 'mind'. Thus the lusts of the flesh are not limited to the sins of the *body*, but also include the sins of the *mind*. 'Both are under the same dominion of sin, and together constitute that natural life in the flesh which is enmity against God' (John Macpherson) [*Rom.* 8:7, 8].

And we were, in our natural condition (as descendants of Adam), children of wrath (Arndt-Gingrich): This reveals the spring of our corruption. For what man *does* can only be explained by what man *is*; his personal transgressions are the result of inborn depravity. So through Adam's one act of disobedience [Rom. 5:12ff] we are born 'children of wrath' – another Hebraism which shows that we deserve nothing but wrath. And since nothing evokes God's wrath but sin, it is evident that *original sin* must be something more than a mere theological figment!

Like the rest of mankind (RSV): At one time we believers were just like all the rest! The ultimate reason for this contrast is that God has chosen us in love [1:4, 5], and has thus made us to differ from 'the rest', who by nature were the same as ourselves. Up to the time of our conversion there was no difference. The contrast therefore is between nature and grace.

4: but God, being rich in mercy, for his great love wherewith he loved us,

'But God' points to the Author of this transition from wrath to grace. It was not simply the misery of our plight which called forth God's mercy, for he left multitudes to perish in their sin [*Rom.* 9:15, 16]. No, the reason we received these riches of mercy was because of the greatness of that love which he bore towards us 'in Christ'. And as God never acts ineffectively, it is a degradation of the gospel to depict him as *helplessly* pleading with men to respond to his love! For at the very outset of this letter Paul makes it crystal clear that God's love always reaches its intended objects [1:3–14]. 'Us' here means 'we who now believe', it is through faith that we are brought to realize our interest in the eternal covenant of grace. Until we believe there is nothing to distinguish us from other men, for we are 'by nature children of wrath, even as the rest'. Scholars have commented upon the confessional character of this passage [verses 1–10] but we must recognize that the ability to make such a statement of faith is the result of God's quickening grace [verse 5]. Scripture does not present us with a God whose hands are tied until man chooses to believe the gospel; it declares that God will assuredly call the elect to saving faith through the preaching of the gospel to every creature [*Isa.* 55:11; *Acts* 13:48].

5: even when we were dead through our trespasses, made us alive together with Christ (by grace have ye been saved),

Even when we were dead through our trespasses: Paul is about to introduce the verb which (in the Greek) has been held back from verse 1, but before doing so he introduces another modifier to heighten the contrast between our former deadness and the power of God's grace. For it is marvellous that God should quicken dead men who are worthy of nothing but everlasting damnation. As John Trapp says, Paul repeats himself because we find his doctrine so difficult to believe. We are apt to think 'better of ourselves than there is cause for, and can hardly be persuaded that we are dead in sins and trespasses, and lie rotting and stinking in the graves of corruption, much worse than Lazarus did after he had lain four days in his sepulchre.'

God . . . made us alive together with Christ: At last we are given the *compound* verb which shows that God's act of quickening united us *with* Christ [cf. verse 6: 'raised up *with*' and 'made to sit *with*']. These remarkable verses set forth our present participation in Christ's heavenly life more clearly than any other passage in the New Testament. As the article in the original indicates ('the Christ'), Christ is here considered in his official relation to us. Accordingly his resurrection is seen as the pledge and pattern of our spiritual quickening. When he was physically raised, all his people were *ideally* raised in him; and because of this prior union with him, they are, in regeneration, *actually* quickened and raised with him (Eadie).

By grace have ye been saved: Paul's characteristic parenthesis further emphasizes the grace by which our salvation has been secured. 'Nothing else than grace could give life to the dead, but grace could indeed do even that' (Salmond). Here it is important to note the force of the perfect tense, which points to a present state as the continuing result of a past action. Salvation is complete with respect to our deliverance from the death of sin, but incomplete with respect to what is still reserved for us [*Rom.* 8:24].

6: and raised us up with him, and made us to sit with him in the heavenly places, in Christ Jesus:

It is because Christ is our Head, both in the judicial and organic sense of the word, that he did not ascend to heaven in any private capacity, but as representing all the elect. As the Head of his own, he bore all our iniquities and obtained eternal righteousness. His righteousness is our righteousness; his death is our death; his resurrection is our resurrection. And so in that legal sense his ascension is our ascension. We sit with him in heavenly places. But he is also our Head in an organic sense. As we are his members we can never be separated from him. Hence he could not return to heaven without taking us with him. And because we are already spiritually present with him, we know that he will soon draw us to himself [*1 John* 3:2]. Thus all who are regenerated by the Spirit partake of the heavenly life of their Lord, so that they now fix their affections on things above [*Col.* 3:1–4] [condensed from Herman Hoeksema's *Reformed Dogmatics*, pp. 425–6, and *The Triple Knowledge*, vol. 2, pp. 74–76]. 'Your head is in heaven; if your heart be there too, you are members of his mystical body . . . Christ may lose members [hypocrites], as he is head of a visible church, but not as he is head of a mystical body' (Thomas Manton, *Exposition of John 17*, pp. 168, 226).

In Christ Jesus [cf. 1:13]: The concluding phrase qualifies the whole statement. 'This quickening, this resurrection, this seating of us with him take effect in so far as we are *in* him as our Representative, having our life and our completeness in our Head' (Salmond).

7: that in the ages to come he might show the exceeding riches of his grace in kindness toward us in Christ Jesus:

This verse shows us that the manifestation of God's glory is the chief end of our salvation. 'The purpose of God for his church, as Paul came to understand it, reaches beyond itself, beyond the salvation, the enlightenment and the re-creation of individuals, beyond its unity and fellowship, beyond even its witness to the world. The church is to be the exhibition to the whole creation of the wisdom and love and grace of God in Christ' (Francis Foulkes). Since 'the ages to come' is simply 'a plural of immensity' (Vos), the meaning is that only eternity will suffice for the complete display of the surpassing riches of God's grace in that kindness which he has shown us 'in Christ Jesus'. Here again the richness of the thought accounts for the apparent extravagance of the language. It is probable that in using the word 'kindness' Paul had in mind God's special act of kindness in giving Christ to be 'the saviour of the body' [2:13, 16; 5:23].

8: for by grace have ye been saved through faith; and that not of yourselves, it is the gift of God;

'For it is by *this* grace that you have been saved.' With this re-assertion of what has already been parenthetically stated in verse 5, Paul exultantly attributes the Ephesians' salvation to the solitary achievement of God's grace. 'Through faith' in no way detracts from the grace which bestows this priceless boon upon us, for the preposition used (*dia*) shows that faith was only the instrumental means of our receiving it. 'The hands of all other graces are working hands, but the hands of faith are merely receiving hands' (Goodwin).

And that not of yourselves, it is the gift of God: Ever jealous of God's glory, Paul adds that even this faith is not self-generated; it is the gift of God! When we are thus dependent upon God for the very capacity to embrace the gospel, then clearly faith can contribute nothing to our salvation. There are sound arguments for this interpretation, which completely rules out 'the most refined doctrine of conditional merit' (G. C. Berkouwer, *Faith and Justification*, p. 490). To insist that 'that' is neuter and 'faith' is feminine is not decisive against this view, which recognizes an advance in Paul's reasoning; whereas he merely repeats himself if 'that' is referred to 'salvation' rather than 'faith'. To say: 'You are saved by faith; not of yourselves; your salvation is the gift of God; it is not of works,' is simply to say the same thing without making any progress. But to say: 'You are saved through faith (and that not of yourselves it is the gift of God), not of works,' greatly increases the force of the passage (Charles Hodge).

9: not of works, that no man should glory.

This is a familiar Pauline antithesis. It is an axiom of his gospel that God's grace leaves no room for man's merit, so that all boasting is absolutely excluded. That the glory of this salvation 'belongs wholly to God and in no degree to man, and that it has been so planned and so effected as to take from us all ground for boasting, is enforced on Paul's hearers again and again, in different connections, with anxious concern and utmost plainness of expression [cf. *Rom.* 3:27; *1 Cor.* 1:29, 4:7; *Gal.* 6:14; *Phil.* 3:3, etc.]' (Salmond).

10: For we are his workmanship, created in Christ Jesus for good works, which God afore prepared that we should walk in them.

The proof that salvation is 'not of works' is given in the emphatic affirmation: '*His* workmanship (*poiema*) are we.' The only other occurrence of this word in the New Testament is in *Rom.* 1:20, where it refers to the natural creation ('the things that are made'); whereas here it is used of the new creation [cf. verse 15; 4:24]. As Christians owe their very existence to God's re-creative fiat, they can glory in nothing but the handiwork of grace. So Paul triumphantly exclaims, *He* has made us what we are!

But though salvation is not *of* works, yet we are created anew *for* good works, 'just as a tree may be said to be created for its fruit' (Alford). This ability to do those works which God adjudges to be good is not native to ourselves, for it is only 'in Christ Jesus' that this miraculous renewal has taken place [*2 Cor.* 5:17]. And as such good works are the indispensable *evidence* of new life, this text must banish all slothfulness and stir us to earnest endeavour [*Rom.* 12:1]. There is no excuse for indolence when God has previously prepared even the very works for our performance! God long before made ready our course of well-doing, so that we are in no position to boast of the good works that flow from our union with Christ. There is no need to prepare the works at this late date; all we need do is to walk in them. 'All the works are ready, they only await the living doers and their doing' (Lenski).

11: Wherefore remember, that once ye, the Gentiles in the flesh, who are called Uncircumcision by that which is called Circumcision, in the flesh, made by hands;

In this section Paul reaches the very heart of his message, as he explains how Christ our peacemaker secured the unity of the church by that sacrifice which abolished the age-old enmity between Jews and Gentiles [verses 11–12].

Wherefore remember: As those who were once pagan Gentiles, the readers are here exhorted to remember with gratitude the great change that grace has wrought in their condition [verse 12], and especially to reflect upon the marvellous difference their new standing before God has made in their relations with Jews who share their faith in Christ.

That formerly ye Gentiles in the flesh called (in contempt) Uncircumcision by the so-called Circumcision in the flesh, a circumcision merely physical, made with hands (Abbott): This puts Jews and Gentiles on exactly the same level of need so that neither party can lord it over the other. The heathen Gentiles were despised by the Jews for being outside the pale of God's covenant; while the Jews, though in touch with the means of grace, had not profited from their privileges because they trusted in the outward sign of the covenant [*Rom.* 2:28, 29], knowing nothing of that circumcision of the heart of which the prophets spoke [*Deut.* 10:16; *Jer.* 4:4]. Yet in Christ both Jews and Gentiles now know the blessed spiritual reality of the 'circumcision made without hands' [*Col.* 2:11], by which they have become members of the same body [verses 14–18]. The fact is that in Christ Jesus 'neither circumcision availeth anything, nor uncircumcision but a new creature' [*Gal.* 6:15].

12: that ye were at that time separate from Christ, alienated from the commonwealth of Israel, and strangers from the covenants of the promise, having no hope and without God in the world.

That ye were at that time separate from Christ: This is what has well been called 'the first tragic predicate'. Paul calls upon them to remember that in their former heathen state they had no connection with Christ, for unlike the Jews they did not look for the coming of the Messiah. Thus their complete separation from Christ, without whom there is no salvation, was the foundation of all the other miseries described in the four following clauses.

Alienated from the commonwealth of Israel: As alien Gentiles they were without the privileges of citizenship within the chosen community to whom God had made himself known 'in many and various ways' [*Heb.*

1:1, RSV]. And this exclusion from Israel, the sole recipient of the light of God's special revelation [*Rom.* 3:2], left them in the darkness of nature's night.

And strangers from the covenants of the promise: Consequently at that time they were ignorant of the *one* promise of salvation which God had confirmed to Abraham and his seed in several covenants. The one-sided character of these testaments of grace is shown by the fact that they are never called anything but *God's,* never Abraham's covenant or Israel's covenant!

Having no hope: This means that they were utterly without hope. They were engulfed by despair because they had no hope beyond the fragile tenure of their house of clay. It was this blank finality of death that robbed their present existence of any meaning. Hence they either squandered their days in cynical scepticism or 'squalid profligacy'.

And without God in the world: This was the 'deepest stage' of their misery, for though they believed in the gods of their own invention, they were destitute of the true knowledge of God [*John* 17:3]. For every man who is not taught by God's Word 'builds and forges absurd conceits of his own, and we know that man's mind is like a store of idolatry and superstition; so much so that if a man believes his own mind it is certain that he will forsake God and forge some idol in his own brain' (Calvin) [*Gal.* 4:8].

13: But now in Christ Jesus ye that once were far off are made nigh in the blood of Christ.

But now in Christ Jesus: Another 'but' [cf. verse 4] marks the amazing contrast between their former lost condition and their present privileges in Christ Jesus, the personal name being added here to emphasize their personal interest in him as Saviour.

Ye that once were far off are made nigh: The words are taken from *Isa.* 57:19 [cf. also verse17], and 'were frequently used by Rabbinic writers with reference to proselytes, who were said to be "brought near"' (Abbott). Such converts merely came over from paganism to Judaism, but in Christ Jesus these Gentile believers had been brought into fellowship with God himself.

In the blood of Christ: By this one sacrifice for sin, Gentiles who were 'far off' and Jews who were 'nigh' [verse 17], are both reconciled to

God in that blood of the new covenant which has made them fellow-citizens in the same commonwealth of grace. Once again the word 'blood' bears eloquent testimony to the infinite cost of this reconciliation [1:7]. Indeed the whole gospel is centred upon it, for 'apart from shedding of blood there is no remission' [*Heb.* 9:22]. Thus nothing less than the blood of the Surety shed in vicarious sacrifice was required to redeem his spiritual seed [*Isa.* 53:10–12; *Mark* 10:45; *Acts* 20:28].

14: For he is our peace, who made both one, and brake down the middle wall of partition, 15: having abolished in his flesh the enmity, even the law of commandments contained in ordinances; that he might create in himself of the two one new man, so making peace;

For he is our peace, who made both one: 'For' shows that the implications of the previous verse are about to be explained [verses 14–18]. Paul does not merely say that peace is the result of Christ's death, but confesses on behalf of all believing Jews and Gentiles that the risen Lord is in his own person '*our* peace'. 'Made both one' points to the definite act by which this peace was procured, though Christ's 'separated' members only enter into the experience of their unity through faith in the promise [cf. *Gal.* 3:26–29].

And has broken down the dividing wall of hostility (RSV): Paul probably alludes to the wall in Herod's temple beyond which no Gentile might pass on pain of death, because the very fact that he was now a prisoner in Rome had arisen from the false charge of having taken Trophimus, an Ephesian, past this barrier [*Acts* 21:29]. It is no argument against this to say that the wall was still standing when this letter was written. For Paul could see in the union of Jews and Gentiles 'in one body' [verse 16] that Christ's death had already broken down the hostility of which that barrier was the visible symbol. As the apostle to the Gentiles [3:1ff.], he realized more clearly than anyone else that this mutual hatred was formed by the dividing wall of the law [verse 15], which fenced off the Jews from the rest of mankind. To the Jews the law was the bastion of their privileges from which they looked down on the 'unclean' Gentiles with unmingled contempt; while to the Gentiles it was the outlandish rampart of an assumed superiority behind which 'the enemies of the human race' practised their abominable rites. Their reconciliation was therefore a miracle of grace, and that was objectively achieved when Christ broke down this wall of Jewish particularism [cf. *Mark* 15:38]. For when he secured their peace with God he also united them in the bond of peace.

By abolishing in his flesh the law of commandments and ordinances (RSV): Hodge's comment is very much to the point: 'The law was not abolished by Christ as a teacher; but by Christ as a sacrifice. It was not by his doctrine, but by his blood, his body, his death, his cross, that our deliverance from the law was effected. The doctrine of the passage, therefore, is that the middle wall of partition between Jews and Gentiles, consisting in their mutual enmity, has been removed by Christ's having, through his death, *abolished the law in all its forms, as a rule of justification*, and thus, opening one new way of access to God, common to Jews and Gentiles' [cf. *Rom.* 10:3, 4; italics added].

That he might create in himself of the two one new man, so making peace: Christ's purpose in breaking down the hostility that divided Jew and Gentile was that he might create in himself 'one new man' [cf. 4:13], a phrase which stands for the totality of the new creation as summed up in its Creator [2 *Cor.* 5:17]. Thus it is by uniting Jew and Gentile in *one church* that Christ makes peace between them, having reconciled both to God [verse 16].

16: and might reconcile them both in one body unto God through the cross, having slain the enmity thereby:

From the consequences that Christ's death has for men Paul turns to the fundamental change it effected in their relation to God. It is only because God is reconciled to men through the propitiation of the cross that they can be at peace with one another, for it was there that Christ slew the divine enmity against sin which had resulted in their estrangement from God [cf. 2:3; 5:5f]. 'His death satisfied justice, it propitiated God, i.e. removed his wrath, or his enmity to sinners; not hatred, for God is love, but the calm and holy purpose to punish them for their sins' (Charles Hodge).

The completeness of this reconciliation is indicated by the phrase 'in one body,' which does not refer to Christ's crucified body but to the church as his body [1:23]. This continued emphasis upon the corporate significance of Christ's objective achievement is important in showing that the church has an *ideal existence*, which is progressively realized as

Jews and Gentiles are reconciled to God and to one another by the joyful discovery of their joint-membership within the one body of Christ [verses 17, 18].

17: and he came and preached peace to you that were far off, and peace to them that were nigh:

After having explained the meaning of the cross, Paul does not leave us to imagine that the subjective application of the benefits Christ purchased by his death are then left to 'chance'! On the contrary, he expressly affirms that Christ himself is the preacher of this peace both to the 'far off' Gentiles and the Jews who were 'nigh'. And this he does, 'having come' as he promised in the Spirit [*John* 14: 18], so that his voice continues to be heard through the authentic proclamation of the apostolic gospel [*Isa.* 57:19; *Rom.* 10:15]. This divine initiative is indispensably necessary, for such is the inability of the natural man that neither the pagan Gentiles nor the externally privileged Jews would ever have 'decided' to come to Christ – *he had to come to them!* ' "Go!" is still his command to us for our mission work. This going is his coming' (Lenski).

18: for through him we both have our access in one Spirit unto the Father:

This teaches us that it is in communion with the Father that the great goal of reconciliation is reached. Although Paul previously spoke of the act which made of Jew and Gentile 'one new man' [verse 15], here he says 'we *both*' which acknowledges that the outward distinctions remain, though religiously they have ceased to matter [cf. *Gal.* 3:28]. For through the one Mediator [*1 Tim.* 2:5] they both now enjoy the same access in one Spirit [*1 Cor.* 12:13] to the one Father [4:6] – a statement which shows that the doctrine of the Trinity is not a dead dogma but a living development of the Christian experience of salvation. These privileges are vastly superior to those possessed by the Jews under the law, for then they had no right of immediate access to God and their worship lacked the filial confidence by which the gospel economy is characterized. 'As that right is ours only *through* Christ, so it is made ours in actual experience only *in* the Spirit, and Jew and Gentile have it alike because it is one and the same Spirit that works in both. So both have continuous access to God from whom once they were far removed, and to him, too, in the benign character of the *Father* whom they can approach without fear' (Salmond).

19: So then ye are no more strangers and sojourners, but ye are fellow-citizens with the saints, and of the household of God:

'So then' introduces the conclusion that Paul would have his Gentile readers draw from the facts just adduced [verses 19–22]. For though they were once excluded from 'the commonwealth of Israel' [verse 12], they are no longer 'strangers' – aliens without the rights of residence – or even 'sojourners' – tolerated outsiders living in a community to which they did not properly belong. Now that they are the free-born citizens of 'the Israel of God' [*Gal.* 6:16] they have been placed on a level of perfect equality with 'the saints,' i.e. with all other believers, whatever their natural descent [*Gal.* 3:9]. As Abbott says, 'The word does not refer to personal holiness, but to membership of the spiritual commonwealth to which Jewish and Gentile Christians alike belong'. And what is even more amazing, they have been brought into 'the household of faith' [*Gal.* 6:10], not as servants or slaves, but as full members of the Father's family, his children by the adoption of grace!

'In any part of the Christian church all national distinctions are swept away, and we are no more foreigners and strangers, but fellow citizens of the saints and of the household of God . . . God has levelled down the Jews and made them stand in the same class as the Gentiles . . . He has levelled up the outcast and despised Gentiles and has admitted us to all the privileges of his ancient covenant, making us to be heirs of Abraham . . . He has given us all the blessings which belong to Abraham's seed, because we, too, possess like precious faith as the father of the faithful himself had . . . oh, what a blessing it is that all racial, national, and ceremonial distinctions have gone forever, and that Christ is all in all to all who believe in him' (C. H. Spurgeon).

20: being built upon the foundation of the apostles and prophets, Christ Jesus himself being the chief corner stone;

You are built upon the foundation laid by the apostles and prophets (NEB): Paul here takes an important step forward in his development of the 'house' image. Advancing from the thought of family-members dwelling within God's household [verse 19], he now sees the believing

Gentiles as built into the very fabric of that house which is indwelt by God himself [verse 22]. Thus in contrast to the provisional nature of temples made with hands [*Acts* 7:48], the New Temple (i.e. the church) is the permanent edifice because it is a living organism [*1 Pet.* 2:5]. Although the Greek is ambiguous, it is preferable to understand the apostolic proclamation of *CHRIST* as the foundation upon which the church is built (the verb is a passive which points to God as the true author of this work). The unique task assigned to the apostles and prophets proves that they can have no successors today, for clearly this foundation could only be laid once [cf. *1 Cor.* 3:10, 11]. Like the apostles with whom they are classed, the New Testament prophets [3:5; 4:11; *Acts* 13:1] also exercised an unrepeatable function in that they spoke under the direct inspiration of the Spirit, 'and prior to the completion of the canon they stood to those early churches in such a relation as the written oracles stand to us' (Eadie).

And Christ Jesus himself is the foundation-stone (NEB): Many scholars explain this in terms of the key-stone which holds the final arch of the building in place, but it seems more appropriate to adhere to the traditional view of the foundation stone. However, this is no ordinary foundation-stone because the whole building *grows* out from it [verse 21]. Paul may well have had in mind the rabbinic tradition which regarded the foundation-stone of Zion [*Isa.* 28:16] as the embryonic centre from which God created the world. The physiological features falsely attributed to that stone can be truly predicated of Christ as the foundation-stone of the church which is his new creation. 'He creates it, sustains it, imparts harmony and unity to it, just as he determines its "shape" and growth' (R. J. McKelvey, *The New Temple*, p. 204).

21: in whom each several building, fitly framed together, groweth into a holy temple in the Lord;

In whom all the building (AV): 'In whom each several building' must be rejected because a multiplicity of buildings is completely at odds with the thought of the passage, which speaks only of two parts (Jew and Gentile) which are made one. Hence Paul says that it is in Christ that the whole building, into which his Gentile readers have been incorporated, is 'being fitly joined together.' The only other occurrence of this compound verb in the New Testament is found in 4:16, where it more naturally refers to the harmonious growth of the members of the body. But as the word was used of the mason's art in preparing stones for the building this technical meaning may be in view here.

In stating that the *building* is growing into a *temple,* Paul does not mean that the church will not become a temple until its growth is complete. For, as McKelvey suggests, we have here two distinct images which convey two different ideas. 'Viewed as the building the church is still under construction; viewed as the temple, however, it is an inhabited dwelling' (*The New Temple,* p. 117). In the church there is the *spiritual* fulfilment of what was signified by the inner sanctuary of the temple in Jerusalem, for the glory of God is manifested among the redeemed who are a *holy* community in virtue of their vital union with the Lord.

22: in whom ye also are builded together for a habitation of God in the Spirit.

And it is in Christ that 'ye also' – you Gentiles as well as believing Jews – 'are being built together' (compound verb found only here in the New Testament) into a habitation of God which is realized *in* the Spirit. Paul is not enforcing a duty; he is describing the greatness of their privilege as constituent members of God's habitation. No higher view of the church is possible, but we are intended to reach this height and not fall sadly short of it! 'The Father makes choice of this house, the Son purchaseth it, the Holy Ghost taketh possession of it. This happiness he best understandeth that most feeleth. The cock on the dunghill knows it not' (Trapp).

CHAPTER THREE

This truth that the Gentiles are equal heirs with Jews of the same inheritance was hidden from former generations, but now has been revealed to the apostles and prophets; and Paul, despite his own unworthiness, has been entrusted with the key role of preaching Christ to the Gentiles, and of making known this mystery to all men [verses 1–9]. It was God's eternal purpose that even the angelic powers should come to know his many-splendoured wisdom through the church in which all the redeemed are united in their Redeemer [verses 10–12]. Paul's prayer for his readers is that they might be given the inner spiritual strength and steadfast love which would lead to a greater knowledge of the love of Christ, even though this can never be fully comprehended. He concludes with another doxology to God for the manifestation of his power in the church [verses 13–21].

1: For this cause I Paul, the prisoner of Christ Jesus in behalf of you Gentiles,

So far the Epistle has been strangely impersonal, for Paul has been wholly taken up with God's great salvation and the Gentiles' part in it. 'It is only as he reaches a resting-place in his thought, that he hears as it were the clink of his chain, and remembers where he is and why he is there: *I Paul, the prisoner of Christ Jesus for you, the Gentiles'* (J. Armitage Robinson). At this point the construction is broken as the apostle pauses to explain the significance of his ministry [verses 2–13], before resuming the thread with a repeated 'for this cause' in verse 14.

Paul wishes his imprisonment to be understood in terms of persons: he serves *Christ* by ministering to the *Gentiles*. He is not ashamed to confess that he is a 'prisoner' in such an honourable cause, but he does not regard himself as Caesar's captive. He is *Christ's* prisoner: 1. Because he knows that he is not detained at Caesar's pleasure, 2. Because he belongs to Christ no less in captivity than when he is at liberty [*Rom.* 8:35f.]. The Ephesians ought to be among the first to acknowledge that Paul is a prisoner for the sake of Gentile freedom, for his arrest in Jerusalem followed the uproar caused by the false charge that he had taken with him into the temple an Ephesian believer named Trophimus [*Acts* 21:29].

2: if so be that ye have heard of the dispensation of that grace of God which was given me to you-ward;

For surely you have heard (NEB): The expression Paul uses assumes that his readers *have* heard, though it is vague enough to cover those who have *only* heard (e.g. converts who joined the church after he left Ephesus, and believers in other churches). As in *Col.* 1:25 'the dispensation' was the stewardship that God gave to Paul along with the requisite grace to fulfil it. He neither received the office from man, nor did he preach according to his own wisdom. For though men may take to themselves the name of 'apostle', the fact that they so conspicuously lack 'the signs of an apostle' shows that this is a mere sham without substance. Moreover, this grace was not a private gift for Paul to keep to himself [cf. 4:12]; it was bestowed upon him for the benefit of the Gentiles. After surveying Paul's use of the word 'grace' in connection with his ministry to the Gentiles, J. Armitage Robinson concludes that it is impossible to doubt that it is 'dominated by the thought of the admission of the Gentiles to the privileges which had been peculiar to Israel. Grace was given to the Gentiles through his ministry: grace was given to him for his ministry to them'.

3: how that by revelation was made known unto me the mystery, as I wrote before in few words,

Paul is about to explain the mystery to which he referred at the beginning of the Epistle (see note on 1:9), but even now he holds back the disclosure of what this mystery is until its dramatic announcement in verse 6. The apostle's reticence is no mere literary device; his purpose is to draw forth the adoring wonder of the Gentiles for the surpassing riches of God's grace towards them. Saul the Pharisee was such an extraordinary choice for *the* apostle to the heathen that nothing could have fitted him for this office but that overwhelming revelation on the Damascus road which secured his unconditional surrender to the divine will [*Gal.* 1:16]. It was therefore 'by special instruction that he comprehended the worldwide adaptations of the gospel, and gave himself to the work of evangelizing the heathen' (Eadie) [*Acts* 22:21].

As I have written above in brief (Moule): The reference is not to some previous letter, but to the immediately preceding paragraphs in which he urged his Gentile readers to remember what they were and what they have now become, equal members with Jewish Christians of the one church of God [2:11–22].

4: whereby, when ye read, ye can perceive my understanding in the mystery of Christ;

Paul is therefore confident that as they read what he has written above they will perceive his insight into 'the mystery of Christ', i.e. his inspired interpretation of the gospel through which the meaning of this mystery is revealed. Verse 8 confirms that there is nothing boastful in this statement; Paul is simply drawing attention to the significance of what has been committed to him. For it is incredible that the recipient of such a revelation would be unaware of its supreme value, and would take no pains to impress its importance upon those to whom he was authorized to communicate it. In writing to the Colossians who were confronted by the perils of a false 'gnosis' Paul was concerned to stress that aspect of the mystery which would counteract these claims, viz. the personal indwelling of Christ in every believer [*Col.* 1:27]; whereas in this letter he brings out the corporate dimensions of the mystery, viz. that Christ is the Head of the church in which Jews and Gentiles are united as fellow-members of the same body.

> **5: which in other generations was not made known unto the sons of men, as it hath now been revealed unto his holy apostles and prophets in the Spirit;**

The privileges of living in the age of gospel grace are great indeed, for this mystery was not made known to men of former generations as clearly as it has now been revealed by the Spirit to his apostles and prophets (see note on 2:20). There is beautiful parallelism in this statement – temporal, revelational, and personal:

which in other generations	*as it hath now*
was not made known	*been revealed*
unto the sons of men,	*unto his holy apostles and prophets.*

Critics have seized upon the word 'holy' as un-Pauline, but a glance at the above arrangement will suffice to show that there is no incongruity in describing the apostles and prophets as 'holy' when they are contrasted with the rest of mankind ('the sons of men'). That the Gentiles were to be included within the scope of divine blessing was the promise first given to Abraham and repeatedly confirmed throughout the old Testament, but that its fulfilment would make of Jews and Gentiles 'one new man' was a truth so astonishing that it could not be disclosed until their reconciliation had been objectively secured (2:16, 17: cf. Denney's remark: Reconciliation 'is a work which is *finished*, and which we must conceive to be finished, *before the gospel is preached*'). And not even these apostles and prophets of the new covenant would have received the Gentiles into the church on equal

terms with the Jews without the evident persuasion of the promised
Spirit [*Acts* 10:44, 45; 11:15–17; 15:8–12].

**6: to wit, that the Gentiles are fellow-heirs, and fellow-members of the
body, and fellow-partakers of the promise in Christ Jesus through the
gospel,**

Here Paul at last makes an explicit declaration of the content of this
long-hidden mystery. It is that the Gentiles are *fellow*-heirs with the
Jews, being *fellow*-members with them of the body, and *fellow*-partakers
with them of the promised salvation [another triad of compounds
beginning with *syn:* cf.. 2:5, 6]. 1. 'Fellow-heirs' means that though
their interest in the inheritance was only recently revealed, yet theirs
was no second-rate blessing for they inherited equally with the earlier
sons. 2. 'Fellow-members' was coined by Paul and it means
'concorporate.' 'In relation to the Body, the members are "incorporate":
in relation to one another they are "concorporate", that is, sharers in
the one Body' (J. Armitage Robinson). 3. 'Fellow-partakers shows that
they are now 'joint-sharers' in 'those covenant-promises from which
they had once been excluded [2:12]' (Bruce).

In Christ Jesus through the gospel: All these privileges are now enjoyed
by the Gentiles '*in* Christ Jesus', for the sole depository of salvation is
the One in whom it was objectively accomplished; but it was '*through*
the gospel*', the preaching of the good news, that they actually entered
into the possession of this salvation – a fact which highlights the
importance of preaching [verse 7].

**7: whereof I was made a minister, according to the gift of that grace of
God which was given me according to the working of his power.**

Unworthy and unfitted as he was for the work, Paul nevertheless
became a minister of his gospel by the gift of that grace which so
powerfully equipped him for God's service. His commission to preach
the gospel to the Gentiles was the gift of God's grace, even as the ability
to fulfil that ministry called for the mighty energizing of God's power.
For to transform 'a Jew into a Christian, a blasphemer into a saint, a
Pharisee into an apostle, and a persecutor into a missionary' was such a
change as could only be wrought by the omnipotence of grace [1:19]
(Eadie). We must learn from this that the true and able ministers of the

new covenant are not self–appointed, for it is by God's grace that they are called and empowered to preach the gospel. So, 'let us at this day understand that whenever it pleases God to raise up men of skill who have the gift of teaching us, it is a sure indication that he has pitied us already, and intends to call us to the inheritance of salvation' (Calvin).

8: Unto me, who am less than the least of all saints, was this grace given, to preach unto the Gentiles the unsearchable riches of Christ;

Some scholars see the hand of an imitator in this profound expression of self-abasement, but those with saner judgment insist that the utterance is entirely characteristic of the apostle. The shameful remembrance of his career as a persecutor is quite sufficient to account for it [cf. *1 Tim.* 1:12–16]. It does not really go beyond *1 Cor.* 15:9; 'for there he declares himself not only the least of the apostles, but not meet to be called an apostle; here he does not say that he is not meet to be reckoned amongst the saints' (Abbott). So though he accounts himself 'less than the least', he still claims to be a saint!

Paul thus regards it as the greatest mark of grace that he was given the task of preaching to the Gentiles, whose complete bankruptcy presented no problem to the One whose resources are illimitable [cf. *Rom.* 11:33]. These 'unfathomable' riches of Christ 'are the fullness of the Godhead, the plenitude of all divine glories and perfections which dwell in him; the fullness of grace to pardon, to sanctify and save; every thing in short, which renders him the satisfying portion of the soul' (Charles Hodge).

9: and to make all men see what is the dispensation of the mystery which for ages hath been hid in God who created all things;

And to make all men see what is the plan of the mystery hidden for ages in God who created all things (RSV): Another purpose of Paul's preaching is to enlighten all men (Jews as well as Gentiles) through the setting forth of God's eternal plan of redemption. This is the mystery which for ages has been hidden in God, that is to say, from the moment that there were any created intelligences from whom it could be concealed. It is this age-long concealment which makes the present revelation of the mystery of such momentous importance for all mankind [*Heb.* 2:3]. It is vital to grasp the fact that there is nothing provisional or temporary about the gospel. It is God's last word to men. Hence its publication is the eschatological event which ushers in the period of the end-time [*Rom.* 16:25, 26]. Paul was so acutely conscious of the absolute *finality* of the gospel that he addresses those who are privileged to live in the days of its disclosure as the ones 'upon whom the ends of the ages are come' [*1 Cor.* 10:11]. And in case any are inclined to find fault with the timing of this revelation, Paul here adds that it is God 'who created *all things*', since this is 'a fact which involves his perfect right to adjust all things as he will' (Alford).

10: to the intent that now unto the principalities and the powers in the heavenly places might be made known through the church the manifold wisdom of God,

In verse 8 Paul contrasted the greatness of his calling with his own unworthiness, and then showed that the design of his mission was to preach to the Gentiles and to enlighten all men concerning the long-hidden mystery of redemption. And now he states that this takes place in order that the church thus formed might now furnish the heavenly world with a dazzling display of the 'many-splendoured wisdom of God' (Bruce). That good angels are meant is suggested by the exalted nature of the passage, and confirmed by the thought that 'evil angels more naturally recognize the *power*, good angels the *wisdom* of God' (Ellicott). The amazing announcement that even the angels obtain the knowledge of God's wisdom 'through the church' should surely give us pause for thought. For it is in the New Testament *ecclesia* – chosen by God, redeemed by Christ, and sanctified by the Spirit – that there is at last revealed to the angels' wondering gaze the consummation of God's eternal purpose [cf. *1 Pet.*1:12]. 'In different ways had God dealt with men, with the Jew in one way and with the Gentile in another, in the long course of the ages. But in all these he had had one great end in view. Now in the *church* the realization of that end is seen, and in that great spiritual harmony angels can perceive the manifoldness and majesty of that divine wisdom which by ways so diverse had been working to this great result' (Salmond).

11: according to the eternal purpose which he purposed in Christ Jesus our Lord:

When Paul sees in the establishment of the church nothing less than the fulfilment of God's eternal purpose, then it is clearly something more than a mere 'parenthesis' in the plan of God! In contrast to the theories of men, Scripture teaches that nothing can succeed that which stands at the climax of redemptive history [cf. *Heb.* 12:22–24]. 'The past *ages*, angelic, paradisaic, patriarchal, Mosaic, prophetic, have led up to the Universal Church, in its spiritual reality, as their goal' (Moule). *Which he purposed in Christ Jesus our Lord:* Although some recent versions give the verb 'made' the historical sense of 'wrought out' (e.g. RSV: 'realized'), it is preferable to take it as meaning that God 'formed' this eternal purpose in him whom we know as 'Christ Jesus our Lord', since the tense would appear to point back to the origination of that grand design.

12: in whom we have boldness and access in confidence through our faith in him.

The experimental character of Paul's concluding affirmation shows why he chose to use the full title, 'Christ Jesus our Lord', in the previous verse. For he would not have us forget that it is only 'in him' that we can approach God in the confidence that we have 'boldness and access'. This is the openness of children before their Father [2:18], and it is realized through our faith in Christ, who is himself the objective ground of that privilege. Thus, 'we may always come boldly to God's throne, assuring ourselves that his majesty will no more be terrifying to us, seeing he shows himself a Father towards us in the person of his only Son. We see then that St Paul's intention is to keep us close to Jesus Christ' (Calvin).

Paul's masterly survey of the significance of his work among the Gentiles within the plan of God is helpfully summarized by Lenski as follows:

1. The divine purpose going back to eternity.
2. Formed in Christ Jesus, our Lord.
3. Standing veiled in all past ages yet standing nonetheless.
4. Revealed in gospel preaching to all men including the Gentiles.
5. Establishing the church of the New Testament with its wonderful universality.

6. Unveiling even to the angels in heaven the wonderful wisdom of God contained in the divine purpose from its inception onward.

7. Putting us believers into possession of the enjoyment of the highest earthly communion with our heavenly Father.

13: Wherefore I ask that ye may not faint at my tribulations for you, which are your glory.

The greatness of Paul's heart is shown by the measure of his concern for his readers. As Christ's prisoner for the Gentiles he can glory in tribulations [3:1], so he gives no thought to himself. Instead he asks that they may not lose heart at what he endures on their behalf! In fact if they share his perspective they will see that these tribulations are their glory, for it was in the worthwhile cause of securing their freedom that his liberty had been sacrificed. So they must not become discouraged as though the Gentile mission were disgraced rather than advanced by his sufferings. Indeed this Epistle was the proof that their apostle could minister a special blessing to them, and the whole church of God, even from a Roman prison.

14: For this cause I bow my knees unto the Father, 15: from whom every family in heaven and on earth is named.

'For this cause' harks back to verse 1, where the phrase refers to the preceding exposition of the unity of Jews and Gentiles in one body through the cross [2:11–22]. And now, after having explained his part in this great work [verses 2–13], Paul again follows teaching by prayer [verses 14–21; cf. 1:15–23]. 'He mentions his prayers for them, not only to testify his love for them, but also that they themselves may pray. For the Word is sown in vain, unless the Lord fertilizes it by his blessing. Therefore let pastors learn from Paul's example, not only to admonish and exhort people, but also to seek from the Lord success for their labours, that they may not be unfruitful' (Calvin, *Commentary*). Although standing was the usual posture for prayer among the Jews [*Matt.* 6:5; *Luke* 18:11, 13], the urgent intensity of Paul's supplication is indicated by the words 'I bow my knees unto the Father' [cf. *Luke* 22:41; *Acts* 20:36, 21:5].

Of whom the whole family in heaven and earth is named (AV): Many scholars claim that the absence of the article demands the translation 'every family', but C. F. D. Moule rightly hesitates to accept this ruling and claims that 2 Timothy 3:16 'is most unlikely to mean *every inspired scripture*, and much more probably means *the whole scripture (is) inspired*'. In this case 'the whole family' is required by the context, which has the unity of the church as its dominant concept [cf. 2:14, 16, 18, 19, 21; 3:6]. In view of the apostle's unwearied insistence upon this fact, it would be very strange if he now began to speak of a multiplicity of families, thus raising but not resolving interesting speculations about the 'angelic' families in heaven! What Paul has in mind is the entire company of the redeemed which makes up 'the Father's family' (Hendriksen). 'The name this great family bears always indicates its Father. This family is the *Una Sancta*. A part of it is already in heaven, the other part is still on earth' (Lenski).

16: that he would grant you, according to the riches of his glory, that ye may be strengthened with power through his Spirit in the inward man; 17a: that Christ may dwell in your hearts through faith;

Here we have the content of what many consider to be the most sublime of all Paul's prayers. 'The riches of his glory, are the sum of God's manifested perfections, not merely his grace or his power, but all his attributes as these are harmoniously exercised in the salvation of his people. Thus the measure of the gift for which Paul prays on behalf of the Ephesians is nothing short of those perfections of God which are revealed now in their glorious fullness and inexhaustible wealth [cf. 1:7, 18; 2:4,7]' (Salmond).

It is evident from this prayer that conversion is but the beginning of the work of grace in the believer. The apostle did not regard the seal of the Spirit as an end in itself, but as the guarantee of continued spiritual progress [1:13, 14]. He therefore prays that those who have received this initial bestowment of grace may be further strengthened 'with power through his Spirit' [see also comment on 5:18]. The Christian 'has not yet begun to conceive of the rich heritage unto which God has begotten him unless he perceives that it is his privilege, his duty, his rightful portion, to be strong with the strength of the divine Spirit. The devil seeks to persuade us that God would have his children remain frail and feeble in this life, but that is one of his many lies. God's revealed will for us is the very reverse, namely, "Be strong in the Lord, and in the power of his might" [6:10]' (Pink).

'The inward man' is neither the soul as opposed to the body, nor the rational as distinguished from the sensual principle of life; it is the essential man who delights in the law of God [*Rom.* 7:22], the hidden self whose daily renewal is contrasted with the declining powers of the outward man [*2 Cor.* 4:16]. But as Paul nowhere represents the renewing as an automatic process, he prays that the indwelling presence of Christ may be realized 'through faith', for even the subjective side of salvation depends upon this further gift of grace [2:8; *Phil.* 1:29].

Calvin has some searching words on the importance of a real heart knowledge of Christ: 'For many men have him in their mouth, and even also in their brain, as they hear him, and they think they acquit themselves well when they can prattle about him, but in the meanwhile there is no living root in them. It is not enough then to have some vague knowledge of Christ, or to engage in airy speculations, as they say, and to be able to talk a lot about him, but he must have his seat in our hearts within, so that we are unfeignedly joined to him, and with true affection. That is the way for us to be partakers of God's Spirit.'

17b: to the end that ye, being rooted and grounded in love, 18: may be strong to apprehend with all the saints what is the breadth and length and height and depth, 19a: and to know the love of Christ which passeth knowledge,

Paul mixes his metaphors but his meaning is plain. So basic is the grace of love to the Christian that it may be compared with the roots of a tree or the foundation of a building [cf. *Col.* 2:7 and NEB: 'deep roots and firm foundations']. This doubling of participles emphasizes the primacy of love, just as the perfect tense points to the establishment and continuance in love as the essential condition for an increase in our knowledge of Christ's love. Between our spiritual strengthening and the enlargement of our spiritual understanding there is an intermediate link of love. 'The Spirit does not immediately work this enlargement of mind in us; he immediately works love, and only through working this love, enlarges our apprehension. The Holy Ghost "sheds love abroad in our hearts". Love is the great enlarger. It is love which stretches the intellect. He who is not filled with love is necessarily small, withered, shrivelled in his outlook on life and things. And conversely he who is filled with love is large and copious in his apprehensions. Only he can apprehend with all saints what is the breadth and length and height and depth of things' (B. B. Warfield, *Faith and Life*, pp. 275–6).

May be strong to apprehend with all the saints what is the breadth and length and height and depth, and to know the love of Christ which passeth knowledge: It is Paul's desire that the Ephesians, not as an isolated community but in company with all believers, may be fully able to comprehend the immensity of that love which is far beyond their knowledge! The solution to this paradox lies in taking note of the difference between what is possible and impossible. Paul prays for an increasing *experimental* knowledge of Christ's love because it is not unknowable; but he also recognizes that finite souls can never possess an *exhaustive* knowledge of an infinite love. Despite the misdirected ingenuity of some patristic interpreters, no mystical meaning may be imposed upon the four different dimensions, which 'are introduced with no other purpose than the simple and consistent one of setting forth the surpassing magnitude of Christ's love for us' (Salmond).

19b: that ye may be filled unto all the fullness of God.

The words which form this astonishing climax are easy to read, but who can fathom their meaning? Yet at least we should not allow our familiarity with the words to blunt our appreciation of the boundless nature of Paul's concluding request. It is that they may be filled 'unto' all the fullness of God, a preposition which 'suggests the idea of a continuous process, a progressive and enlarging experience' (Pink). This is no unattainable ideal, but the great goal which is to be realized in union with Christ, through whom alone the divine fullness can be communicated to the sons of men [*Col.* 2:9]. 'Absolute perfection is the standard to which the believer is to attain. He is predestinated to be conformed to the image of the Son of God, *Rom.* 8:29. He is to be perfect as man, as God is perfect as God; and the perfection of man consists in his being full of God; God dwelling in him so as absolutely to control all his cognitions, feelings, and outward actions' (Charles Hodge) [cf. 4:13]. This therefore means that even when he is eventually filled with all the fullness of God, man does not himself become divine but remains a creature whose glory consists in eternally reflecting the glory of his Creator.

20: Now unto him that is able to do exceeding abundantly above all that we ask or think, according to the power that worketh in us, 21: unto him be the glory in the church and in Christ Jesus unto all generations for ever and ever. Amen.

Now to him who is able to do infinitely more than all we ask or imagine (Hendriksen): In the final petition the limits of human thought and language were reached, but no such limitation can be placed upon God's infinite resources. In this magnificent doxology Paul therefore gives sublime expression to the truth that God not only has absolute ability, but that he exercises that ability towards believers in a manner which far transcends their highest aspirations and utmost imaginings. Paul uses the compound 'infinitely more' (*huperekperissou*) because nothing less than this intensified superlative is adequate to describe the fullness of God [verse 19] which is now freely poured out, on the ground of Christ's finished work [4:8], in the gift of the Spirit ('according to the power that worketh in us').

According to the power that worketh in us: 'Those who have been raised from the dead, who have been transformed by the renewing of their minds, translated from the kingdom of darkness into the kingdom of God's dear Son, and in whom God himself dwells by his Spirit, having already experienced a change which nothing but omnipotence could effect, may well join in the doxology to him who is able to do exceeding abundantly above all we can ask or think' (Hodge).

Unto him be the glory in the church and in Christ Jesus: God is the one to whom all glory belongs, but it is only because he was pleased to manifest that glory to the praise of his grace that we can glorify him as we ought. Thus Paul says, Let God be glorified 'in the church', for the community of the redeemed is the body of Christ; 'and in Christ Jesus', the divine Head of the church who alone makes its praise acceptable to God.

Unto all generations for ever and ever. Amen: The meaning of this remarkable expression appears to be that the church's praise shall endure throughout the present age 'unto all generations' of believers, and then throughout the ages to come (i.e. to all eternity). 'Amen' in Scripture indicates far more than intellectual assent. 'It always involves an energetic demand for faith since it seals something that pertains to Christ and salvation' (Lenski). Therefore if we would truly endorse the promise of God in Christ our 'Amens' must register the ardent conviction of our hearts.

CHAPTER FOUR

This begins the practical section of the Epistle in which the apostle exhorts believers to live as befits their high calling in Christ (ch. 4–6). They must be careful to cherish the graces of lowliness, patience, and love, which make it possible to maintain the unity of the Spirit. For the church is one body, having one hope, inspired by one Spirit, acknowledging one Lord, one faith, one baptism, and one Father of all [verses 1–6]. This unity is not achieved by a drab uniformity, but through the ascended Christ's bestowal of a rich diversity of gifts, all of which are designed to edify the church [verses 7–13]. Instead of being unsettled by the shifting stratagems of error, believers are to attain spiritual maturity by speaking the truth in love, so that they will receive through the appropriate contribution of each member such nourishment from Christ their Head that the whole body will be built up in love [verses 14–16]. With this great end in view, they are to abandon the patterns of thought and conduct which characterized the old life, and remembering that they have put on the new man, they must now live by new standards [verses 17–24]. This means discarding the things which grieve the Holy Spirit, especially lying, anger, stealing, and harmful speech; and replacing them with kindness and gentleness as found in God's treatment of them in Christ [verses 25–32].

1: I therefore, the prisoner of the Lord, beseech you to walk worthily of the calling wherewith ye were called,

The second part of the Epistle begins with this chapter. And as usual in Paul, 'therefore' marks the logical transition from doctrine to its practical application in the lives of believers [cf. *Rom.* 12:1; *Col.* 3:1; *1 Thess.* 4:1]. It should be noted that Paul neither dragoons his readers into submission, nor cajoles them by flattery, but always *appeals* for the obedience their gospel-allegiance demands, for such is the mode of address that befits those who are the children of the King.

In 3:1 Paul refers to Christ as the author and originator of his captivity, but here he regards it as the consequence of his union with Christ and of his devotion in his service. Hence it is as the Lord's *faithful prisoner* that he exhorts them to walk 'worthily' of their high calling [*Col.* 1:10]. This comprehensive principle offers us sure guidance in all doubtful situations which are not covered by specific precepts: 'which course of action will be most worthy of the calling with which God has called us?' (Bruce).

'The calling which is wholly of God comes first, and a corresponding life is looked for as the fitting and appropriate fruit of that calling. Their walking can never render them worthy of the calling of God which is theirs of free grace; but having been enlightened and strengthened, as Paul had prayed that they might be, they are to bring forth fruits in the life, which will give evidence of the presence of the Holy Spirit and the indwelling of Christ in their hearts' (Macpherson).

2: with all lowliness and meekness, with longsuffering, forbearing one another in love; 3: giving diligence to keep the unity of the Spirit in the bond of peace.

In verse 2, Paul states four graces which should attend this walk, and in verse 3 specifies the particular direction in which they are to be exercised. Believers are to walk 'with *all* lowliness and meekness', for without humility of mind [*Phil.* 2:3] and the forbearance that is inspired by love, they will not be able to bear 'with longsuffering' the faults and failings of others, and so 'keep the unity of the Spirit in the bond of peace' [cf. *Phil.* 4:2].

Lowliness found no place in heathen ethics since it was thought of as a form of abject grovelling. That it became a primary Christian virtue is entirely due to the example and teaching of Christ [*John* 13:4ff], whose sinless humility consisted in taking the form of a servant and rendering a perfect obedience to God [*Phil.* 2:5–8]. With us lowliness also consists in taking our proper place before God, but because we are sinners as he was not, in our case this means 'the esteeming of ourselves small, inasmuch as we are so; the thinking truly, and because truly, therefore lowlily, of ourselves' (Trench).

Meekness is again primarily meekness towards God; it is not weakness but the grace which is the opposite of all self-assertiveness.

For it is in submitting ourselves to God that we are given the strength to serve others. Longsuffering and forbearance are both divine perfections which are to find their finite reflection in us. As God is slow to anger, so we are to be longsuffering by enduring provocations without quickly giving way to passion. And this is made possible by a loving forbearance that is the fruit of God's gracious dealings with us.

It is in this way that believers are to make every effort to preserve that unity already established by the Spirit in the bond of peace. As 'the unity of the Spirit' is the gift which enables men to recognize one another as members of the same body, so 'the bond of peace' inevitably recalls the objective achievement by which their reconciliation was secured. 'That "peace" with God, and in him with one another, which is in fact Christ himself [2:14], in his sacrifice and his presence, is to form the "bond" which shall maintain you in a holy union of spiritual hope and aim' (Moule).

> **4: There is one body, and one Spirit, even as also ye were called in one hope of your calling; 5: one Lord, one faith, one baptism; 6: one God and Father of all, who is over all, and through all, and in all.**

Having urged his readers to preserve their God-given unity, Paul immediately adds a sevenfold description of its unique basis, which may well echo an early confession of faith. He insists that *all* believers:

(i) belong to *one body*, because they are indwelt by *one Spirit*, and are joined in *one hope*;

(ii) are united with *one Lord* through *one faith* confessed in *one baptism*;

(iii) have *one God and Father* who has made them the children of his grace.

1. *One body:* The one body is the one church of Christ. It remains an invisible body to the extent that it includes all Christ's members and excludes all false professors, but this does not mean that it is without any visible manifestation in the world. For the Lord adds to the church those whom he calls out from the world [*Acts* 2:47]. Thus when the elect in Corinth were converted they formed the church in that city [*Acts* 18:10, 11; *1 Cor.* 1:2]. And it was because Paul recognized the grace which had given them this corporate identity that he laboured to preserve its peace, purity, and unity. Yet it is believers who make up

this body, and not the sum total of local visible churches. Thus because each member of the body is directly related to the Head, the church must never be regarded as a 'mediating institution' which comes between the soul and the Saviour (Edmund Clowney) [*1 Tim.* 2:5].

2. *One Spirit:* Just as the human body has many members which are joined together in virtue of its common life, so the unity of Christ's members in one body is realized through the one Spirit who indwells them all [2:18; *Rom.* 8:9; *1 Cor.* 3:16]. 'This fact prevents any view of the church as a mere organization; for the presence of the Spirit constitutes the church, and is the basis of its unity' (Foulkes).

3. *One hope:* Although they were once strangers without hope [2:12], the call of God's grace gave them the assured hope of an heavenly inheritance [1:18], a foretaste of which they had already received in the gift of the Spirit [1:14]. 'The fact that, when they were called out of heathenism, one and the same *hope* was born in them, is a fact in perfect keeping with the unity of the Christian body and the unity of the divine Spirit operating in it, and the one confirms and illumines the other' (Salmond).

4. *One Lord:* In gladly confessing 'Jesus is Lord', the early Christians gave voice to the uniqueness of the Person in whom they had found their salvation [*1 Cor.* 12:3; *Phil.* 2:11]. And since this title is his by the right of redemption [*1 Cor.* 6:20], to know the one Lord is to own and obey but one will [*1 Cor.* 7:23]. Hence no true Christian can regard Christ as a mere man who attained a dubious kind of divinity, for he is the one Lord from whom all other lordship is derived and to whom it is accountable [*1 Cor.* 8:6]. It is this common confession which binds men together as nothing else can. 'Where there is "the same Lord" [*Rom.* 10:12], Jews and Gentiles, black and white, rich and poor, great and small, are yoked together' (Foulkes).

5. *One faith:* Because there is one Lord, there can be only one faith in him, one way of being saved by him. It therefore follows that this subjective trust in Christ, this believing in him, is exactly the same for all, whether Jew or Gentile. For there is no way to the Father save through him who is the way, the truth, and the life [*John* 14:6].

6. *One baptism:* The one faith which unites the believer with one Lord is visibly confessed in one baptism [*Rom.* 6:3; *Gal.* 3:27]. Baptism, and not the Lord's Supper is mentioned, because this is the initiatory

rite in which *all* are joined by one Spirit to the one body [cf. *1 Cor.* 12:13]. The repeated 'all' of this verse shows that the gift of the Spirit is not reserved for a privileged minority in the church, but is bestowed upon every believer without distinction. In the New Testament it is only in connection with John's baptism that Spirit-baptism is contrasted with water-baptism [cf. *Acts* 19:2, 3]. For in the experience of the early church the work of the Spirit in conversion and the gift of the Spirit in baptism were so closely associated that they were regarded as constituent parts of the same event. And this is why the apostles nowhere exhort believers to be baptized with the Spirit, though Paul directs them to 'be filled with the Spirit' [see comment on 5:18].

7: *One God and Father of all, who is over all, and through all, and in all:* The final item in the series is a triad which crowns the two previous triads. As their Creator, God is the Father of all men, but this 'all' speaks of his special relation to all the sons of faith, who are united to him by the double tie of creation and redemption. 'The apostle does not refer to the dominion of God over the universe, or to his providential agency throughout all nature. Neither is the reference to his dominion over rational creatures or over mankind. It is the relation of God to the church, of which the whole passage treats. God as Father is over all its members, through them all and in them all. The church is a habitation of God through the Spirit. It is his temple in which he dwells and which is pervaded in all its parts by his presence . . . This is the climax. To be filled with God; to be pervaded by his presence, and controlled by him, is to attain the summit of all created excellence, blessedness and glory' (Charles Hodge).

7: But unto each one of us was the grace given according to the measure of the gift of Christ.

But the unity of the body does not mean that its members are characterized by a drab uniformity, for each was given by the exalted Christ in sovereign wisdom that measure of grace which manifests itself in his particular gift [verse 16; cf. *1 Cor.* 12:4ff]. And as this grace 'is not bestowed upon us to diffuse and lose itself in our separate individualities' (Findlay), every member must recognize that this distribution of diverse gifts is made for 'the building up of the body of Christ' [verse 12]. Paul thus establishes three facts: (1) Because 'the grace' is given to *each one*, 'nobody in the church need feel that he is of no use or without a task'; (2) because it is a *divine gift* it is not a thing the Christian can grasp by himself; (3) this grace *is different* in various members, 'All have not gifts of equal size and nature, but the gift is under all conditions such as Christ has decided' (Hanson).

8: **Wherefore he saith,**

When he ascended on high, he led captivity captive, And gave gifts unto men.

Wherefore he saith: '*Who* says it (cf. 5:14) is obvious of itself, namely, *God*, whose word the Scripture is' (Meyer).

When he ascended on high: Psalm 68:16 celebrates the arrival of the ark of the Lord in Jerusalem, whose dignity is not derived from its physical height, but from its spiritual elevation as God's designated dwelling-place. The verse quoted shows that it is after the conquest of the enemy's citadel that Jehovah 'ascends' the earthly sanctuary of Mount Zion to share the spoils of victory with his people [*Psa.* 68:18]. But Paul sees that these words have found a still higher fulfilment in Christ's triumphant ascension to the seat of universal sovereignty in heaven, from whence he dispenses the gifts of his grace upon the church [verse 7].

He led captivity captive: The captives in the Victor's train are not the redeemed, but the vanquished powers of evil. For at the cross 'captivity' itself was taken captive, and the hellish rule of these hostile powers over mankind was broken [*Col.* 2:15; *Heb.* 2:14; cf. *Mark* 3:27].

And gave gifts unto men: It is in order to set forth the true Messianic application of this passage that Paul here diverges from both the Septuagint and the Hebrew text which read: 'received gifts for (among) men'. But the difference is more apparent than real,[1] for 'what Christ receives mediatorially he receives to bestow on his people, as Peter reminded his hearers on the day of Pentecost [*Acts* 2:33]. They are blessed with all spiritual endowments in and through him. N.T. quotations of O.T. passages are also authoritative interpretations of the significance of these passages. The Spirit of God knows his own letter-

---

[1] It is worth noting with Derek Kidner that this change 'summarizes rather than contradicts the psalm, whose next concern is with the blessings God dispenses [19ff., 35]' [*Psalms 1–72*, p. 242].

press better than the most lynx-eyed modern critic, so often "all eyes and no sight"' (Simpson).

9: (Now this, He ascended, what is it but that he also descended into the lower parts of the earth?

Now, the word 'ascended' implies that he also descended to the lowest level, down to the very earth (NEB): As this ascension was the return of the One whose proper abode is heaven [cf. *John* 3:13, NEB: 'whose home is in heaven'], it must also imply his previous descent to the earth, a descent in which he plumbed the lowest depth of humiliation for the sake of those he came to save. Thus we have here a pregnant reference to the same sequence which is fully described in *Phil.* 2:6–11. 'Now *this* ascension whereby he, as Victor over Satan, sin, and death, re-entered heaven in the full merits of his atoning sacrifice would never have been possible had he not first descended from the glories of heaven to earth's shame and suffering' (Hendriksen).

10: He that descended is the same also that ascended far above all the heavens, that he might fill all things.)

He who descended is no other than he who ascended far above all heavens, so that he might fill the universe (NEB): There is no reference here to a diffused and ubiquitous physical presence, but to a 'pervading and energizing omnipresence' (Ellicott). Paul is showing that the object of Christ's exaltation to the highest place that heaven affords 'was that he might enter into regal relation with the whole world and in that position and prerogative bestow his gifts as he willed and as they were needed. He was exalted in order that he might take kingly sway, fill the universe with his activity as its Sovereign and Governor, and his church with his presence as its Head, and provide his people with all needful grace and gifts' (Salmond) [verse 11; cf. 1:23].

11: And he gave some to be apostles; and some, prophets; and some, evangelists; and some, pastors and teachers;

Among the gifts bestowed upon the church by the ascended Christ ('he' is emphatic), Paul here mentions in order of importance the *persons* whom he gave to serve the church at large as apostles, prophets, and evangelists, while those who have the task of pastor and teacher are evidently the resident overseers of local congregations. In stating that such men are *Christ's gift,* Paul doubtless intends to evoke the *church's gratitude.* 'That we have ministers of the gospel is his gift; that they excel in necessary gifts is his gift; that they execute the trust committed to them, is likewise his gift' (Calvin).

1. *Apostles:* Here, as in 2:20, the word is used in the highest sense. 'The distinguishing features of an apostle were, a commission directly from Christ: being a witness of the resurrection: special inspiration: supreme authority: accrediting by miracles: unlimited commission to preach and to found churches' (Vincent).

2. *Prophets:* These were also extraordinarily endowed, 'not only in the more special sense [as Agabus, *Acts* 11–28], but in the more general one of preachers and expounders, who spoke under the immediate impulse and influence of the Holy Spirit, and were thus to be distinguished from the teachers' (Ellicott) [cf. 2:20].

3. *Evangelists:* Of lower rank than the apostles under whom they worked, these men were itinerant preachers whose task was to spread the gospel in new places, as did Philip in Samaria and Caesarea [*Acts* 8:5 ff]

4. *Pastors and teachers:* The construction here shows that the ministers of particular churches are assigned the dual function of guiding and feeding the flock over which they have been set [*Acts* 20:28]. 'No man is fit to be a pastor who cannot also teach, and the teacher needs the knowledge which pastoral experience gives' (Vincent).

12: for the perfecting of the saints, unto the work of ministering, unto the building up of the body of Christ:

To equip God's people for work in his service, to the building up of the body of Christ (NEB): As the NEB's omission of the first comma shows, the purpose for which Christ gave *these men* is that *all* God's people should be perfectly fitted for the particular service that each is to contribute to the building up of the body of Christ. In other words, Christ has appointed the ministry of the Word as the means by which all members of the church are equipped for Christian service in the world [cf. 4:25–32; 5:21–6:9]. Thus Christ gave men to be the servants of the Word, so that through their ministry his Body might be built up. 'From this it is plain that those who neglect this means and yet hope to become perfect in Christ are mad. Such are the fanatics, who invent secret revelations of the Spirit for themselves, and the proud, who think that for them the private reading of the Scriptures is enough, and that they have no need of the common ministry of the church' (Calvin).

13: till we all attain unto the unity of the faith, and of the knowledge of the Son of God, unto a full-grown man, unto the measure of the stature of the fullness of Christ:

Till we all attain unto the unity: Since this 'all' is the totality of the redeemed, it is clear that the purpose for which Christ gave the means of grace will be achieved only when the whole church has reached its appointed goal. And this will be attained 'when the members of the church have all come to their proper unity and maturity in their Head' (Salmond).

Of the faith, and of the knowledge of the Son of God: This 'unity of the faith' is something more than a common assent to the objective truth of the gospel; it is that living unity among believers which is produced by their shared *experience* of 'the knowledge of the Son of God'. Paul uses this title here to bring out the essential and eternal dignity of the One with whom believers are thus united. They are already *individually* united with the Son of God [*Gal.* 2:20], but they must constantly strive to realize their *corporate* unity in him, even though they know that its consummation belongs to the state of glory [cf. 5:27].

Unto a full-grown man, unto the measure of the stature of the fullness of Christ: Paul envisages the unity of the church in its final form by likening it to a 'full-grown' man, whose 'stature' corresponds to the 'full measure' of Christ. 'This perfect form is achieved when all who are appointed to it by the divine plan of salvation belong to the church. The emphasis is on the words *we all* [verse 13a]. The church, which is the body of Christ, represents in its perfected form the fullness of Christ' (J. Schneider, *TDNT*, vol. 2, p. 943).

14: that we may be no longer children, tossed to and fro and carried about with every wind of doctrine, by the sleight of men, in craftiness, after the wiles of error;

In the climax of the previous verse Paul set forth the ultimate goal of Christian growth, and he now states both negatively [verse 14] and positively [verses 15, 16] how that great end is to be attained. For Christ gave us the ministry of the Word [verses 11, 12], so that we may be no longer like naive children who are easily led astray from the truth. Paul's warning against spiritual immaturity is continued in a nautical image; he expects his readers to have such a firm grasp of the gospel that they will not be tossed about by the waves and winds of false doctrine, which are already unsettling their fellow-believers in nearby Colosse [cf. *Col.* 2:8].

The second half of the verse shows that Paul cannot speak of the dangers of false teaching without also describing the devious arts of those who propagate it. First, he uses the word 'sleight', which literally means 'dice-playing', to expose the trickery which underlies their plausible pretensions. And secondly, in drawing attention to their craftiness 'in deceitful scheming' (Arndt-Gingrich), he seems to suggest by his repetition of the word in 6:11 ('the *wiles* of the devil') that they owe this capacity to lead men into error to their real master [cf. *John* 8:44].

15: but speaking truth in love, may grow up in all things into him, who is the head, even Christ; 16: from whom all the body fitly framed and knit together through that which every joint supplieth, according to the working in due measure of each several part, maketh the increase of the body unto the building up of itself in love.

But maintaining the truth in love (J. Armitage Robinson): It is preferable to adopt this rendering because Paul is here contrasting the truth with error [verse 14]. But just as error and deceit always go together, so truth and love are inseparably conjoined 'as the twin conditions of growth' (J. Armitage Robinson). 'Truth without love lacks its proper environment and loses its persuasive power; love without truth forfeits its identity, degenerating into maudlin sentiment without solidity, feeling without principle' (R. M. M'Cheyne).

May grow up in all things into him: It is simpler to refer this back to the 'full-grown' man of verse 13 than to link it with the next phrase, which involves the difficulty of explaining how we can grow into Christ as the Head. When we thus take the words as complete in themselves, they point to a process of growth in which the members are to reach perfect conformity with Christ. According to Paul, individual development is subordinated to the growth of the whole body, and this means that Christ's gifts are imparted not for private edification, but so that each member may be able to make his distinctive contribution to the building up of Christ's body [cf. *1 Cor.* 12].

Who is the head, even Christ: It is because the significance of Christ cannot be contained within one metaphor that Paul now advances to the thought of the Head. For though Christ is the whole body because all the members are in him [*John* 15:1; *Rom.* 12:5; *1 Cor.* 12:12], he is far more than the sum total of his members! He is also the Head of the body, 'which stands over against him no matter how much it is also one with him' (E. Schweizer, *TDNT*, vol. 7, p. 1080).

From whom the whole body, joined and knit together by every joint with which it is supplied (RSV): It is from Christ the Head that the whole body derives its life, nourishment, and well-ordered growth [cf. *Col.* 2:19]. And the fact that Paul assigns the key role in this process to 'every joint' leads R. P. Martin to suggest an identification with Christ's gift of the ministry [verse 11], through which the Word of his grace reaches all the members ('each several part').

According to the proportionate working of each several part (Abbott): Thus the vertical descent of Christ's grace finds its expression in the horizontal harmony of the members. Paul sees this spiritual truth illustrated in the growth of a healthy body in which there are no disproportionate developments. For each part receives that measure of grace which determines its proper contribution to the functioning of the whole body.

Maketh the increase of the body unto the building up of itself in love: Paul's remarkable conclusion is that the church thus acquires the power to grow and build *itself* up, though he is careful to add that this is only achieved in caring love. This means that there is no room in the church for a selfish individualism that neglects the need to serve its fellow-members. 'As every member in a body has a task to fulfil, and exists for the sake of the body as a whole, so has every Christian a function in the church, however different it may be, and only if each one's gift is placed in the service of the whole, i.e. if love is allowed to be the superior principle, is the unity and growth of the church promoted' (Hanson).

17: This I say therefore, and testify in the Lord, that ye no longer walk as the Gentiles also walk, in the vanity of their mind,

Having shown the readers the glory of the body to which they belong, Paul is at last ready to enforce the consequences of that union in terms of everyday conduct [thus resuming the exhortation begun at verse1]. They must not mistake this for mere human advice, for he speaks with apostolic authority, 'identifying himself with Christ and giving the exhortation as one made by Christ himself' (Salmond).

That ye no longer walk as indeed the Gentiles walk, in the vanity of their mind (Bruce): As befits those who are members of 'the Israel of God' [*Gal.* 6:16], they must no longer live as they once did [2:12] and as the unenlightened heathen still do. Paul's diagnosis of the evils of paganism is intended to put them on their guard against any relapse into what were now alien patterns of thought and behaviour. First he focuses attention upon the darkening effects of sin upon the mind. The Gentiles led frustrated, fruitless lives because their minds were 'fixed on futile things' (Arndt-Gingrich). With this one word Paul exhibits the folly of the ancient world's empty reliance upon its own wisdom to find the meaning of life. Idolatry was the root cause of such vanity of mind [*Rom.* 1:21], for all who forsake the living God inevitably worship objects which are void of value, and thus condemn themselves to a purposeless existence.

18: being darkened in their understanding, alienated from the life of God, because of the ignorance that is in them, because of the hardening of their heart;

Being darkened in their understanding: The heathen pursue this futile course because their understanding is in a state of darkness. The retina of reason has been obscured by sin so that the light of revelation makes no impression upon it. Yet they consider this culpable condition of darkness to be normal and proudly claim the ability to see [*Matt.* 6:23; *Rom.* 1:19–22]. 'Many a present-day "scientist" claims to know, but knows nothing as he ought to know it' (Lenski).

Being . . . alienated from the life of God: This is co-ordinate with the previous clause and shows that the darkening of the understanding necessarily involves a state of alienation from God, who is the sole source of spiritual life [*John* 17:3; *1 John* 5]. It is evident that such an estrangement must have the direst consequences, for to be thus deprived of the highest blessedness [2:12] also entails death in trespasses and sins [2:1].

Because of the ignorance that is in them: Paul is not content to say that the miserable state of the heathen was due to their ignorance; he traces it to the ignorance 'that is in them', which suggests that it belongs to their very nature. 'It is not an acquired ignorance that is due to absence of light and information; it is an original ignorance that is in them from the start, the ignorance of inborn sin' (Lenski).

Because of the petrifaction of their heart (Lenski): This is the ultimate cause of their alienation. That they have no feeling for God is due to the rock-like hardness of their heart. 'This is what is wrong with the natural man; yes, he is blind and ignorant, but worse, his heart is stone [compare *Ezek.* 11:19]' (Lenski). What then but divine omnipotence can suffice to change it?

19: who being past feeling gave themselves up to lasciviousness, to work all uncleanness with greediness.

Paul now states the ethical consequences of this religious alienation. The inner petrifaction of the heathen was outwardly registered in their callous conduct. Impiety and impurity always go hand in hand, but those who make this terrible surrender to uncleanness may not complain when God justly confirms them in their vile choice [cf. *Rom.* 1:24]. 'With greediness' denotes the reckless rapacity that breaks through all restraints and violates all rights in its unlawful quest for satisfaction in *uncleanness!* History vouches for the accuracy of this frightful description of the shameless debauchery in which the Gentile world was sunk.

20: But ye did not so learn Christ;

'But' is in emphatic contrast, as Paul reminds his believing readers that they did not (in their conversion: aorist tense) so learn Christ. This makes it clear that becoming a Christian involves more than the learning of a doctrine. It is nothing less than the learning of Christ as Saviour and Lord, which means that authentic discipleship includes the dynamic that enables a man to lead a disciplined life [cf. *Matt.* 11:28–30]. It is therefore as Christ's disciples that they have learned to renounce the way of darkness and death and to follow his way of light and life. In the next four verses the full consequences of this learning of Christ are gratefully recalled [verses 21–24]. 'Usually we learn subjects, not persons; but the Christian's choicest lesson-book is his loveworthy Lord. Instruction about him falls short of the mark; personal intimacy is requisite to rivet the bond of union with the Saviour' (Simpson).

21: if so be that ye heard him, and were taught in him, even as truth is in Jesus:

'If so be' implies no doubt but takes it as certain that they both heard Christ and were taught in union with him. 'Christ himself is the Christians' Teacher, even if the teaching is given through the lips of his followers; to receive the teaching is in the truest sense to hear him' (Bruce) [cf. *Acts* 1:1].

Even as truth is in Jesus: In using the name of Jesus by itself [only here in this Epistle, cf. *Phil.* 2:10], Paul draws attention to the Incarnate Saviour as the very embodiment of truth. It is because Jesus is the truth in all its saving fullness that we can be said to 'learn him' [*John* 14:6].

22: that ye put away, as concerning your former manner of life, the old man, that waxeth corrupt after the lusts of deceit; 23: and that ye be renewed in the spirit of your mind, 24: and put on the new man, that after God hath been created in righteousness and holiness of truth.

So that ye have put off, according to the former manner of life, the old man who is corrupted according to the lusts of deceit (Murray): The translation followed in verses 22–24 is that given by John Murray in his *Principles of Conduct*, pp. 214–5, to which the interested reader is referred for its grammatical justification. It is not in harmony with Paul's teaching elsewhere to interpret this passage in terms of an exhortation. It rather sets forth the *result* of the Ephesians' learning of Christ: they have put off the old man and have put on the new man! That such a decisive change is in view here, and that it provides the *basis* of the ensuing exhortation [verses 25–32], is apparent from the parallel passage in *Col.* 3:9, 10, where believers are admonished, 'Lie not to one another', precisely because they 'have put off the old man with his doings'. Moreover, in *Rom.* 6:6 we have the conclusive statement that 'our old man was crucified with him', from which it is clear that the old man is neither ailing nor dying, but dead and gone forever! Finally, we must reflect upon the implications of Paul's characterization of the old man, who has his pattern in 'the former manner of life' [as described in verses 17–19] and 'is corrupt according to the lusts of deceit'. The contrast Paul draws with the words, 'But ye did not so learn Christ', shows that he does not think of believers as answering to such a description! [cf. verse 24].

And are being renewed in the spirit of your mind (Murray): The consequence of their having put off the old man is that they are being progressively renewed in the spirit of their mind. Although the Spirit is the unnamed agent behind this 'being renewed', what is stressed here is that it is by the transformation of the governing spirit of the mind that this renewal is taking place [cf. *Rom.* 8:16 for this distinction between the Holy Spirit and the human spirit]. Regeneration adds nothing to the properties and processes of the mind as a functioning organism, but the mind's character or prevailing bent is so entirely changed by this renewing of its motivating spirit that the result can only be described as a new creation.

And have put on the new man who after God has been created in righteousness and holiness of the truth (Murray): The subject of this process of renewal is here identified with the new man they became when they put on Christ [*Gal.* 3:27]. The new man has been created after the likeness of God [*Gen.* 1:27] in that righteousness and holiness which are born of the truth of the gospel [*1 Pet.* 1:23]. And it is because such a *definitive breach* with the old life has been made that believers are urged to bring their behaviour into conformity with the new identity which is theirs in Christ [2:10; *2 Cor.* 5:17]. It is this objective sanctification already possessed in Christ [*1 Cor.* 1:30] that lays upon them the solemn obligation to live a righteous and holy life [*1 Pet.* 1:16]. For clearly it is monstrous for those who are now in union with Christ to present again their 'members unto sin as instruments of unrighteousness' [*Rom.* 6:13; cf. *1 Cor.* 6:15ff]. John Murray sums up his illuminating discussion of these verses by drawing this important conclusion: 'The believer is a new man, a new creation, but he is a new man not yet made perfect. Sin dwells in him still, and he still commits sin. He is necessarily the subject of progressive renewal . . . But this progressive renewal is not represented as the putting off of the old man and the putting on of the new . . . It does mean the mortification of the deeds of the flesh and of all sin in heart and life. But it is the renewal of the "new man" unto the attainment of that glory for which he is destined, conformity to the image of God's Son' (*Principles of Conduct*, p. 219).

25: Wherefore, putting away falsehood, speak ye truth each one with his neighbour; for we are members one of another.

Wherefore having put off then once for all falsehood in its every form, speak ye truth each one with his neighbour (Salmond): Paul wishes believers to understand why they must speak the truth; it is because they finished with all falsehood when they put off the old man [verse 22]. The genesis of all sin lay in the acceptance of the devil's lie, and this outright rejection of God's Word made 'truth' a relative concept for the old man, whose whole life was lived under the dominion of deceit. But it is as those who have for ever renounced all duplicity that believers must continually speak the truth ['in love', verses 15, 16] to one another [*Zech.* 8:16].

For we are members one of another: Lying is never beneficial, but always injurious in its effects. Hence it would be in the highest degree unnatural for fellow-members of the same body to harm one another in this way [*Rom.* 12:5]. As Chrysostom strikingly remarks, 'If the eye sees a serpent, does it deceive the foot? if the tongue tastes what is bitter, does it deceive the stomach?'

26: Be ye angry, and sin not; let not the sun go down upon your wrath:
27: neither give place to the devil.

Be angry, but do not sin (Arndt-Gingrich): A quotation of *Psa.* 4:4 according to the Septuagint. 'The easiest charge under the hardest condition that can be. Anger is a tender virtue, and must be warily managed. He that will be angry and not sin, let him be angry at nothing but sin' (Trapp) [cf. *Mark* 3:5].

Let not the sun go down upon your wrath: Yet even righteous anger may not be cherished [verse 31], but must be dismissed before the day is over. It seems likely that Paul's imagery here was influenced by the second part of Psalm 4:4: 'Commune with your own heart upon your bed, and be still'. It is interesting to compare this verse with James 1:19 as they place a double restraint upon this dangerous emotion: Christians are not only to be *slow* to anger but also *quick* to overcome it! (cf. G. Stählin, *TDNT*, vol. 5, p. 421).

And give no opportunity to the devil (RSV): Or '*do not give the devil a chance* to exert his influence' (Arndt-Gingrich). 'We are neither to cherish anger, nor are we to allow Satan to take advantage of our being angry. Anger when cherished gives the Tempter great power over us, as it furnishes a motive to yield to his evil suggestions' (Charles Hodge).

28: Let him that stole steal no more; but rather let him labour, working with his hands the thing that is good, that he may have thereof to give to him that hath need.

With Paul the demand to desist from vice is always an occasion for enjoining the practice of the opposite virtue. So here the condemnation of what is wrongly gained by stealing leads to the positive teaching that the believer may not eat the bread of idleness but is to earn an honourable living [*2 Thess.* 3:6–12]. Hence not only must the former thief no longer steal; he must now use his hands to engage in honest toil so that he may have the means to help his needy brother [*Gal.* 6:10]. 'The Christian philosophy of labour is thus lifted far above the thought of what is right or fair in the economic field; it is lifted to the place where there is no room for selfishness or the motive of personal profit at all. Giving becomes the motive for getting' (Foulkes).

29: Let no corrupt speech proceed out of your mouth, but such as is good for edifying as the need may be, that it may give grace to them that hear.

No bad language is to escape the lips of believers, who are to produce evidence of the reality of a cleansed heart by the purity of their speech [*Luke* 6:45]. Shunning the defiling utterance that destroys, they are to speak words that will build up, wisely chosen to suit the occasion so that they may be the means of blessing those who hear them. 'Even words good in themselves must be introduced seasonably, lest they prove injurious instead of useful. Not vague generalities, which would suit a thousand other cases equally well or ill: our words should be as nails fastened in a sure place, words suiting the present time and the present person' (Fausset).

30: And grieve not the Holy Spirit of God, in whom ye were sealed unto the day of redemption.

'And' indicates that this exhortation is closely connected with the preceding injunction. Since the Spirit specially claims to control the speech of believers [5:18f], he is grieved when his sanctifying work in them is hindered by their abuse of the very gift which should further it. And to make them realize the enormity of the offence, Paul writes, the *Holy* Spirit *of God*. 'It is not an influence that these sacrileges stifle, but a sacred Person they repel' (Simpson). At first sight it is perhaps surprising that Paul should choose to base his appeal for obedience upon the *security* of believers [1:13, 14]. 'Men may think that a stronger appeal might be based on fear lest we fall from the Spirit's keeping; as if Paul should rather have said, Because you can be kept only by the Spirit, beware lest you grieve him away by sinning. But Paul's actual appeal is not to fear but to gratitude. Because you have been sealed by the Spirit unto the day of redemption, see to it that you do not grieve, bring pain or sorrow to this Spirit, who has done so much for you' (B. B. Warfield, *Faith and Life*, pp. 294–5).

31: Let all bitterness, and wrath, and anger, and clamour, and railing, be put away from you, with all malice:

This terse but telling arrangement of terms is in itself a powerful dissuasive against any indulgence in such sins. Paul thus shows how one sin leads to another. For 'bitterness' nurses the hatred which finds expression in 'anger' and 'wrath', and these induce unbridled denunciation and violent cursing. *All* these together with *all* 'malice' – the frightful animus which inspires this evil speaking – 'are to be put away in every kind and degree – in germ as well as maturity – without reserve and without compromise' (Eadie).

32: and be ye kind one to another, tenderhearted, forgiving each other, even as God also in Christ forgave you.

Paul follows the negative with the positive. Believers must also show themselves to be of another spirit, always manifesting mutual kindness and tenderness of heart, and freely forgiving one another's faults and failings without grudging. This is not put forward as a counsel of perfection, but as the only practical norm for maintaining fellowship among those who have not yet been made perfect [*Matt.* 18:21, 22]. The supreme motive for this waiving of the petty debts of our fellow-men is furnished by what God did in Christ to secure our discharge from the immense debt of sin. Thus we are to forgive 'even as' we have been forgiven [*Matt.* 18:33]. 'Observe that the cross of Christ is the sole medium of gospel forgiveness. All pardons pass through Immanuel's hands. God's evangel exhibits a miracle of mercy that should ensure large-heartedness in its recipients; but that mercy is essentially *cruciform*' (Simpson).

CHAPTER FIVE

The apostle insists that believers must strive to be like God as the true children of their heavenly Father. They must be distinguished by the purity of their lives in contrast to the immorality of those who will incur God's wrath. They must not only refuse to have fellowship with such people but must expose the real nature of their evil deeds[verses 1–14]. He also directs them to walk wisely, to make good use of the time, and to understand the Lord's will for them. Instead of indulging in riotous revelry, they are to be filled with the Spirit, whose gracious presence is evidenced in the joyful thanksgiving and reverent worship which promotes the Christian grace of mutual submission [verses 15–21]. The mention of this general principle leads Paul to speak of the submission which wives owe to their husbands. This injunction is illustrated by Christ's relation to his church, which is compared to that of the husband to the wife. As the church is subject to Christ, so the wife should be subject to her husband. And just as Christ loved the church and gave himself up for it, so the husband should love his wife. The comparison not only ennobles the marriage relationship itself, but also provides Paul with the opportunity to expound his doctrine of the church: Christ is the Saviour of his body the church, which he cleansed by his sacrifice so that he might present it to himself without blemish. And he cares for it in the same way as a man nourishes his own flesh [verses 22–33].

1: Be ye therefore imitators of God, as beloved children; 2: and walk in love, even as Christ also loved you, and gave himself up for us, an offering and a sacrifice to God for an odour of a sweet smell.

Although these verses are usually regarded as rounding off the preceding exhortation, it is preferable to understand them as providing the foundation of the following admonition against filthiness [verses 3–14]. Having shown how believers should treat one another, Paul is now ready to instruct them on their behaviour in a world which is full of temptations for the unwary [verses 6, 7]. But before giving them detailed counsel, he wants them to grasp the fact that they cannot remain distinct from the world unless they cherish their new identity, and keep in mind the cost of their deliverance from its evil ways [*Gal.* 1:4]. Hence the bold call to become 'imitators of God, as beloved children'. As it is natural for children to imitate their parents, so the children of grace must always seek to reflect the perfections of their heavenly Father [cf. *1 Pet.*1:14–16]. 'We can be only "imitators", but we are to be that always' (Lenski).

And walk in love, even as Christ also loved you: This 'limitation' of God is to be shown in a life of love, which finds its motive and model in Christ's self-giving love. Obviously we cannot copy God in his creative or redemptive work, but our experience of his love towards us in Christ must lead us to walk before him in love – an exclusive relationship which bars us from all lust [verses 3–7].

And gave himself up for us, an offering and a sacrifice to God: What Paul briefly indicates here is fully expounded in Hebrews, where it is demonstrated that Christ's surrender to the death of the cross on our behalf was in fact the priestly offering of himself to God as the complete sacrifice for sin [cf. *Heb.* 9:14]. In one great transaction our Mediator then fulfilled all that was signified by the typical ceremonies prescribed under the law [cf. *Heb.* 10:1–10].

For an odour of a sweet smell: In words that recall Genesis 8:21, Paul expresses the acceptability of this sacrifice to God. We who have been reconciled to God by the sweet fragrance of Christ's sacrifice can never return to a life that reeks with the vile stench of sin.

3: But fornication, and all uncleanness, or covetousness, let it not even be named among you, as becometh saints;

But immorality and impurity of any kind, or greed, let it not even be mentioned among you (Hendriksen): This rigorous demand to shun every form of moral laxity is an emphatic condemnation of a course of living which was all but universal in the ancient Gentile world. Paul insists that the Christian community must be so sharply distinguished from the surrounding corruption that its members should be above even the suspicion of indulging in such degrading practices. In view of the present context, 'greed' [cf. 4:19] is more likely to refer to uncontrolled sexual desire than to avarice. What the world calls romantic love is really the obsessive lust that gratifies itself without regard to the injury that is done to others. But Christians must cherish a higher standard of living than this [cf. *1 Thess.* 4:6].

As becometh saints: 'The title "saints" makes prominent their relation to God. The apostle thus employs a term that brings out the peculiar unfitness of the slightest approach to impurity on the part of those who profess to be related to the God of holiness [cf. *1 Cor.* 6:15]' (Macpherson).

4: nor filthiness, nor foolish talking, or jesting, which are not befitting: but rather giving of thanks.

Believers must also be on their guard against spreading the contagion of filthiness by sinful language. Hence Paul exhorts them to abstain from all foul, foolish, and facetious talk ['filthiness' is used here in the same sense as 'shameful speaking' in *Col.* 3:8]. As Trench points out, 'foolish talking' means more than idle words; it is that 'talk of fools' which is foolishness and sin together. He further observes that 'jesting' is wit enlisted in the service of sin, and recalls the line of Plautus, the Roman comic poet, in which an old profligate boasts that his clever ribaldry is just what was to be expected of one who was born in Ephesus! Paul effectively condemns such sinful speech by mildly stating that it does not befit believers, who are rather to express their gratitude to God in words of thanksgiving. It is this that 'lifts us above the vileness of worldlings. Amid our Father's blessings with hearts and lips full of thanksgiving, these filthy vices will not even be named among us' (Lenski).

5: For this ye know of a surety, that no fornicator, nor unclean person, nor covetous man, who is an idolator, hath any inheritance in the kingdom of Christ and God.

'If *pleonexia* is simply "covetousness", the question is, why should this, any more than fornication and impurity, be singled out to be called idolatry?' (Abbott). But this difficulty disappears if the word is given the wider meaning advocated in 4:19 and 5:3. Then we have a natural climax: 'For you are well aware of the fact that no immoral or impure person, or greedy man who is an idolater (because he makes sex his god!) has any inheritance in the (one) kingdom of Christ and God.' Although it is grammatically possible to regard Paul as here identifying Christ with God (as in *Titus* 2:13), such a reference would appear alien to the context. Nevertheless, we should not fail to note that the one who can be linked together with God under one definite article is no mere created being, but the very Son of God himself.

6: Let no man deceive you with empty words: for because of these things cometh the wrath of God upon the sons of disobedience.

Let all believers be on their guard against being deceived by anyone who should try to excuse or even advocate the practice of these vices. For such 'empty words' are quite 'alien to the *solidity* of the immoveable *facts* that the body cannot sin without sin of the spirit; that body and spirit alike are concerned in eternal retribution; that the wrath of God is no figure of speech, and that his love cannot possibly modify his holiness' (Moule, *CB*). This wrath is the righteous reaction of God in manifesting his active displeasure against sin. There is a partial disclosure of God's wrath in the present experience of 'the sons of disobedience' [cf. 2:2], who live in wilful rebellion against his revealed will [*Rom.* 1:18ff], though its final outpouring awaits the last day [*Rom.* 2:5].

7: Be not ye therefore partakers with them;

'Lest by infection of their sin ye come under infliction of their punishment' (Trapp). Rather they must stand entirely aloof from these workers of iniquity as befits those who have been called to share in a very different destiny [cf. 3:6].

8: for ye were once darkness, but are now light in the Lord: walk as children of light

It is only in terms of an absolute antithesis that Paul can adequately express the contrast between what his readers once were and what they are now [verses 8–14]. Formerly they were 'darkness', immured in a darkness that was all their own; now they are 'light', but this enlightenment is theirs only in the Lord. And they must so abide in him that no darkening by sin will prevent them from being the clean reflectors of this light to others [*Matt.* 5:14].

Walk as children of light: Having been thus delivered from the dominion of darkness they are to evidence the reality of this blessed change by walking as children of light [cf. *Col.* 1:12f; *1 John* 1:5–7]. This exhortation teaches us that light is never given for mere intellectual illumination, but always to promote practical obedience. Our daily conduct must make credible our confession of faith in Christ. For though man cannot look into the heart, he does closely observe the outward appearance we present to the world [cf. *1 Sam.* 16:7].

9: (for the fruit of the light is in all goodness and righteousness and truth),

The purpose of this parenthesis is to show what it means to walk as children of light. The moral fruit of the light is seen in every form of 'goodness and righteousness and truth', which are the opposite of all 'malice' [4:31], unrighteousness, and falsehood. The entire Christian ethic is summed up in the good, the right, and the true. As the light never changes, so this standard remains constant in every age. 'The only progress possible is to enter more deeply into these three. It is one of the lies of our time that we have progressed beyond them' (Lenski).

10: proving what is well-pleasing unto the Lord;

Those who are bidden to 'walk as children of light' [verse 8] will make it their constant aim to find out and follow that which 'is well-pleasing unto the Lord', i.e. Christ [cf. *Rom.* 12:2]. 'The believer is not to prove and discover what suits himself, but what pleases his divine Master. The one point of his ethical investigation is, Is it pleasing to the Lord, or in harmony with his law and example?' (Eadie).

11: and have no fellowship with the unfruitful works of darkness, but rather even reprove them; 12: for the things which are done by them in secret it is a shame even to speak of. 13: But all things when they are reproved are made manifest by the light: for everything that is made manifest is light.

And have no fellowship with the unfruitful works of darkness: The incongruity of such an association is apparent, for 'what fellowship has light with darkness?' [*2 Cor.* 6:14ff]. It is plainly absurd to expect 'the fruit of the light' [verse 9] to flourish in the midst of darkness, that ethically sterile sphere whose only products are the barren works of death [cf. *Rom.* 6:21].

But rather expose them: for of the things which are done of them in secret it is a shame even to speak (J. Armitage Robinson): Rather, since they 'are now light in the Lord' [verse 8], they must let their light so shine forth that it shows up the real nature of those deeds of darkness which are too shameful even to mention. 'So the meaning is that the Christian, by a life so essentially different from those around him, rather than by reproof in speech, is to "expose" their sins' (Foulkes).

But all things when they are exposed by the light are made manifest (J. Armitage Robinson): When the light of God breaks in to *expose* these works for what they are, this *conviction* of sin will lead men to forsake the darkness and turn to the light [as explained in *John* 3:20, 21].

For whatsoever is made manifest is light (J. Armitage Robinson): This manifestation therefore leads to a transformation. For as the light of the gospel first disclosed and then dispelled the former darkness of Paul's readers [verse 8], so they may now be used to bring the same enlightenment to their heathen neighbours. Thus, as F. F. Bruce helpfully paraphrases it, 'Whatever abandons the darkness and is made manifest by the light belongs henceforth to the light.'

14: Wherefore he saith, Awake, thou that sleepest, and arise from the dead, and Christ shall shine upon thee.

Wherefore he saith, At first sight it is remarkable that the same phrase which introduced the words of Scripture [4:8] should be used here to introduce what appears to be part of a Christian hymn. But the difficulty disappears when we see that such snatches of sacred song only found a place in the written Word of God because they were first inspired by the Holy Spirit [cf. '*spiritual* songs', verse19]. The quotation is in the form of a metrical triplet:

> *Awake, O sleeper,*
> *From the grave arise.*
> *The light of Christ upon you shines* (Martin).

The most likely setting of this exhortation is baptism, which was known in the later church as 'enlightenment'. As the congregation sang these lines, the convert would emerge from the water in the confidence that he had quit the grave of sin for a new life in Christ [cf. *Rom.* 6:4ff; *Col.* 2:12]. 'Paul harks back to this experience as a reminder to his readers to fulfil now their baptismal profession by walking in Christ's light and by stirring themselves to active witness' (R. P. Martin, *NBC*).

15: Look therefore carefully how ye walk, not as unwise, but as wise;

The word 'therefore' shows that the exhortation of verse 8 is here resumed. In view of the evils which surround them and their responsibility towards those who are without the light of saving truth [cf. *Col.* 4:5], believers are to give the most careful consideration to their conduct. They must walk 'not as unwise, but as wise'. The unsaved are the unwise who behave unwisely because they either follow a course of unthinking worldliness, or rely on that worldly wisdom which God has reduced to foolishness. But something better is to be expected of those whose wisdom has its root in the knowledge of God and its fruit in obedience to his will [cf. *Psa.* 111:10].

16: redeeming the time, because the days are evil.

Buying up the opportunity (ASV margin): 'As wise merchants, trading for the most precious commodity, and taking their best opportunity. The common complaint is, We want time; but the truth is, we do not so much want it, as waste it' (Trapp). So believers must not take after the unwise who heedlessly fritter away their brief span, but are rather to buy up every opportunity that presents itself for the doing of God's will in the world.

Because the days are evil: 'If these days so evil afforded any opportunities of doing good, it was all the more incumbent on Christians to win them and seize them. The very abundance of the evil was a powerful argument to redeem the time, and the apostle writing that letter in a prison was a living example of his own counsel' (Eadie)'

17: Wherefore be ye not foolish, but understand what the will of the Lord is.

This amplifies the summons to walk wisely which was given in verse 15. If believers are to redeem the time they must not lapse into the senseless behaviour which belonged to their former state, and this can be avoided only if they clearly grasp what the will of the Lord is [cf. verse 10]. Thus in every situation the Christian's paramount concern must be to discern and do the will of Christ his *Lord.* 'Others may direct their minds to other questions such as: "What will bring me earthly gain, honour, pleasure, ease, etc.? What do others say, advise, do?" This is not only wrong, it is folly, senselessness. He is a fool who asks thus and determines his judgement and his life accordingly' (Lenski).

18: And be not drunken with wine, wherein is riot, but be filled with the Spirit;

An outstanding example of such 'want of sense' is drunkenness [verse 17], which Paul emphatically contrasts with the filling of the Spirit. 'Men are said to be filled with wine when completely under its influence; so they are said to be filled with the Spirit, when he controls all their thoughts, feelings, words, and actions' (Charles Hodge). But whereas a filling of wine results in debauchery and dissipation, the Spirit's fullness is manifested in the spiritual graces which are described in verses 19–21. In this masterly fashion the apostle combines a needful warning on the danger of over-indulgence in wine with the directive to receive the one safeguard against this temptation [cf. on the sinful abuse of wine, *Rom.* 13:13; *1 Cor.* 11:21; *1 Tim.* 3:8; *Titus* 2:3]. Thus instead of the riotous revelry of the tippler in his cups, there is to be the sensible enjoyment of the Spirit whose presence is always marked by the grace of 'self-control' [*Gal.* 5:23].

Believers are here commanded to go on being filled with the Spirit, but are nowhere exhorted to be baptized (or sealed) with the Spirit because this blessing was conferred upon them in conversion [*1 Cor.* 12:13; cf. 1:13, 4:30]. The difference between the baptism and the fullness of the Spirit is illustrated by the state of the church at Corinth when Paul first wrote to the believers there. For though they had been baptized with the Holy Spirit, and were richly endowed with the gifts of the Spirit, they were not filled with the Spirit. And throughout the Epistle the apostle rebukes them for their unspiritual conduct in walking as men [compare, for example, verse 21 with the behaviour reflected in *1 Cor.* 3:13; 11:20–22].

To be filled with the Spirit thus involves our submission to the control of the Spirit in every aspect of our lives. This is not an optional extra for the 'keen Christian', but a demand which is binding upon all believers. It means that we must avoid grieving or quenching the Spirit, and that we are to be always sensitive to his promptings. In short, there must be a continuous appropriation of the Spirit's fullness. Clearly this is not a once-for-all experience. For it is to the extent that this filling is known by Christians that the greater beauty of Christian living will be displayed in them [see comment on verses 19–21].

19: speaking one to another in psalms and hymns and spiritual songs, singing and making melody with your heart to the Lord; 20: giving thanks always for all things in the name of our Lord Jesus Christ to God, even the Father; 21: subjecting yourselves one to another in the fear of Christ.

In these verses the present participles ('speaking', 'singing and making melody', 'giving thanks', and 'subjecting') depend on the main verb of the previous verse ('be filled'), and thus describe the blessed consequences of the Holy Spirit's fullness.

Speaking one to another in psalms and hymns and spiritual songs: As the parallel passage in *Col.* 3:16 indicates, the fellowship of believers is founded upon their mutual submission to 'the word of Christ' whose reception is marked by the response of praise [cf. the punctuation of RSV, NEB]. Hence this verse does not mean that believers receive instruction solely by means of song! The importance of singing in the worship of the early church is illustrated in a letter written by Pliny to the Emperor Trajan about AD 112. He reports that the Christians of his province gathered regularly on a fixed day before dawn to sing antiphonally 'a hymn to Christ as God'. It is doubtful whether these terms can be clearly distinguished. 'Psalms' may point to the Christian adoption of the Old Testament Psalter, but in *1 Cor.* 14:26 an ecstatically inspired hymn is evidently in view. 'Hymns' were probably like the samples of Christian praise that seem to be embedded in the New Testament [cf. verse14; *Phil.* 2:6–11; *Col.* 1:15–20; *1 Tim.* 3:16]. 'Spiritual songs' are so designated to show the source of their inspiration. However, if as some scholars think, 'spiritual' covers all three terms, then the richness of the early church's worship is expressly attributed to the prompting of the Holy Spirit.

Singing and making melody with your heart to the Lord: 'With', not 'in' your heart (as in AV), because the exhortation is not to silent, but to *heartfelt* worship ('with *all* your heart,' RSV). In congregational singing the outward expression of praise must not outrun the spirit of inward devotion. As the mouth sings the words, so the heart is to be lifted up to the Lord. For spiritual worship demands spiritual men [*John* 4:24].

Giving thanks always for all things in the name of our Lord Jesus Christ to God, even the Father: Another mark of the fullness of the Spirit is a constant sense of thankfulness to God for 'all things' [cf. *Rom.* 8:28]. These 'sovereign dispensations are a matter of gratitude, not for murmuring . . . The mixed yarn of life, woven in the loom of heaven by the Father of mercies, traces a perfect design for those "in Christ" and their thanksgivings should reascend to him through their mediatorial All-in-all' (Simpson).

Subjecting yourselves one to another in the fear of Christ: Finally, reverence for Christ must prompt believers to subject themselves to one another [cf. *John* 13:1–17]. For unless personal pride is mortified it is impossible to maintain that mutual fellowship which is the fruit of Christian humility [*1 Pet.* 5:5]. 'Humble submission is such an important part of Christian behaviour that the verb occurs 32 times in the New Testament. Not self-assertion but self-submission is the hallmark of the Spirit-filled Christian . . . We should submit to others right up to the point where our submission to them would mean disloyalty to Christ' (John Stott).

22: Wives, be in subjection unto your own husbands, as unto the Lord.

The wives to their own husbands as to the Lord! (Lenski). Beginning with marriage Paul now enjoins the kind of submission that is required in *particular* relationships [verses 22–23; 6:1–4, 5–9]. The thought is so closely connected with the previous verse that it has to supply the verb which this sentence lacks. In pagan society the inferiority of women and their lawful subjugation by men was taken for granted. The apostle here challenges this 'fact of life' with the teaching which transformed the status of women in every society that accepted it. He bids every Christian wife so to subject herself to her *own* husband (not all men) that she regards this voluntary (not enforced) submission as a *part* of her obedience to Christ. 'The idea is that the will of God who arranged the marriage relation at creation is likewise the will of the Lord Christ for Christian wives' (Lenski).

23: For the husband is the head of the wife, as Christ also is the head of the church, being himself the saviour of the body.

This advances the reason for such wifely subjection. It is found in the headship that makes man the ruling partner in the marriage relation, an arrangement not only established by creation but also endorsed in redemption. For Paul's astounding analogy likens a husband's headship over his wife to Christ's headship over the church [1:22]. Certainly no higher view of the marriage bond can be imagined than this sublime conception which makes *obedience* a matter of devotion, and *authority* an expression of love.

Being himself the saviour of the body: 'i.e. Christ is the Saviour of his church, implying that so likewise the husband is given to the wife to be a saviour to her, in maintaining, protecting, and defending her; and therefore the wife, if she regard her own good, should not grudge to be subject to him' (Poole) [cf. verses 29–30].

24: But as the church is subject to Christ, so let the wives also be to their husbands in everything.

As the church gladly submits to the rule of Christ her head, even so wives should be subject to their husbands in everything pertaining to their legitimate authority as *husbands*: 'everything not contrary to God' (Fausset). Christian wives must understand that equality within the sphere of grace [*Gal.* 3:28; *1 Pet.*3:7] does not set aside the God-given order for marriage. 'In the state of sin the divine and blessed order is disturbed in two directions: wives seek to rule their husbands and refuse loving self-subjection; husbands tyrannize their wives often to the point of enslaving them. Endless woe results. Christianity restores the divine order with all its happiness' (Lenski).

25: Husbands, love your wives, even as Christ also loved the church, and gave himself up for it;

Turning now to husbands, Paul tells them to love their wives with the same kind of self-giving love which Christ showed for the church when he gave himself up to the death of the cross. In *Gal.* 2:20 the apostle uses the same verbs to confess his own interest in Christ's death, whereas here the whole church is viewed as a collective person: the Bride to whom the heavenly Bridegroom betrothed himself in this costly covenant of love [cf. *John* 3:29]. This remarkable image has its roots in the Old Testament where Jehovah's covenant with Israel is described in terms of the marriage relationship [*Hos.* 2:16; *Isa.* 54:5]. The rabbis traced this union back to the covenant at Sinai, where the law became the marriage contract, and Moses led the bride to God. The gospel sequel shows that the age of law has given place to the reign of grace, for the church is the Bride who is saved and sanctified by the Bridegroom's own blood [*Acts* 20:28], and Paul sees himself as taking over the rôle of Moses in leading the bride to her husband [*2 Cor.* 11.2].

'The church's obedience to Christ, which is the wife's model for her duty to her husband, may fall short of what it should be; there are no shortcomings about the love of Christ for his church, which is here prescribed as the model for the Christian husband's love for his wife. By setting this highest of standards for the husband's treatment of his wife, Paul goes to the limit in safeguarding the wife's dignity and welfare' (F. F. Bruce).

26: that he might sanctify it, having cleansed it by the washing of water with the word,

That he might sanctify it, cleansing it by the washing of the water with (the) word: The immediate purpose for which Christ gave himself up was that he might sanctify and cleanse the church. The verbs are coincident in time, so that the aorist participle 'cleansing' expresses the way in which this sanctification was secured. Paul speaks of an objective accomplishment, and not of a subjective process. For in its most fundamental sense sanctification 'is not something that is worked up, but something that is rather sent down . . . Holiness is not so much acquired as conceded . . . it is less an activity than a status' (J. K. S. Reid, *A Theological Word Book of the Bible*, p. 217). Thus in verses 25–27 our attention is directed to the action of Christ; nothing is said of the activity of the church because this Bride provides her Husband with no dowry but receives everything from his nail-pierced hands [cf. *Heb.* 13:12].

'The washing of the water' evidently refers to baptism, but it is unique in that it speaks of the baptism of the church rather than of individuals. The salvation that is signified by baptism is conferred upon all the elect in connection with the word which the Spirit uses as his sword [6:17]. This 'word' is not a baptismal confession or formula, an idea which is in any case at variance with the corporate image used here; but the whole gospel, the preached message of salvation [cf. *Rom.* 10:8a].

27: that he might present the church to himself a glorious church, not having spot or wrinkle or any such thing; but that it should be holy and without blemish.

That he might himself present to himself the church, glorious (Salmond): This states the ultimate purpose of Christ's sacrifice [cf. *Col.* 1:22; *Rev.* 19:7, 21:2]. 'The thought is of the heavenly Bridegroom welcoming the glorified Bride at the Marriage Feast hereafter. True, she is now "his Spouse and his Body"; but the manifestation then will be such as to be, in a sense, the Marriage as the sequel to the Betrothal. The words "present to himself" suggest that the Bride is not only to be welcomed then by her Lord, but welcomed as owing all her glory to his work, and as being now absolutely his own' (Moule, *CB*).

Not having spot or wrinkle or any such thing; but that it should be holy and without blemish: Here the future glory of the church is first figuratively set forth in negative terms, and then literally expressed by the corresponding positive terms. At that great day Christ's *bride* shall be manifested in all the flawless beauty of unfading perfection, and this consummation of the *church* is the fulfilment of 'the original purpose of election formed before the foundation of the world' (Charles Hodge) [cf. 1:4; *Jude* 24].

28: Even so ought husbands also to love their own wives as their own bodies. He that loveth his own wife loveth himself.

Since Paul is a preacher of the gospel rather than a teacher of ethics, the response he asks for always assumes the reception of grace. So here it is Christ's love for the church that provides the pattern for the husband's love of his wife. Consequently 'ought' expresses not moral obligation, but spiritual indebtedness. It is because this word indicates the response to be expected from an experience of salvation, that such apostolic injunctions never 'lead into externally imposed legalism' (F. Hauck, *TDNT*, vol. 5, p. 564). In thus exhorting husbands to love their wives 'as their own bodies', Paul already seems to have in mind the words of *Gen.* 2:24 [cf. verse 31].

He that loveth his own wife loveth himself: Paul follows the plural with the singular to bring the point home to every individual husband. As husband and wife share the same life whatever 'is done to one is done to both. This is not an appeal to the selfish principle of self-love, but the laying down of the law of community of interests' (Macpherson).

29: for no man ever hated his own flesh; but nourisheth and cherisheth it, even as Christ also the church; 30: because we are members of his body.

This teaches us that it is not only a man's *duty* to love his wife, but also entirely *natural* that he should do so. For no man in his right mind ever hates his own flesh, but rather feeds it and tenderly cares for its every need. So she who is 'one flesh' [verse 31] with him may justly expect to receive the same attention that he lavishes upon himself. In demanding the *God-given* rights of women in a world which generally regarded them as mere chattels, Paul is revealed as something more than the woman-hater his detractors allege him to be! It may also be noted that the passage offers cold comfort to those who wish to make their ascent to God by climbing the ladder of asceticism, for clearly only a fanatic hates his own flesh [cf. *Col.* 2:23].

Even as Christ also the church; because we are members of his body: Once again Christ's example in caring for the church's every need is invoked as the pattern upon which the husband's behaviour towards his wife is to be modelled. This Christ does because we are members of his body [cf. 4:7ff.]. 'We are veritable parts of that body of which he is head, and this is the reason why he nourishes and cherishes the church' (Salmond).

31: For this cause shall a man leave his father and mother, and shall cleave to his wife; and the two shall become one flesh.

As the ASV indicates, 'for this cause' belongs to *Gen.* 2:24, which Paul now quotes to confirm the teaching of the previous verses [verses 28, 29a] and to exhibit the source of his imagery. This Scripture shows that the sanctity of the marriage bond is grounded in the intimacy of its union. It is because the two become one flesh that the violation of that bond is so great a sin [cf. *1 Cor.* 6:16]. The significance of the verb order is succinctly noted by Derek Kidner: '"Leaving" before "cleaving"; marriage, nothing less, before intercourse. So this question, as well as divorce, was settled "from the beginning" [*Mark* 10:6ff.]' (*Commentary on Genesis*, p. 66).

32: This mystery is great: but I speak in regard of Christ and of the church.

Paul has quoted Genesis 2:24 in its literal meaning and he returns to this sense in verse 33, but here he reveals its *mystic or hidden* significance (so Thayer, p. 420; cf. NEB, 'It is a great truth that is hidden here'). Thus the apostle's extended analogy is based upon his inspired understanding of this Scripture, where he finds in the union of husband and wife a pre-figuration of the union of Christ and the church. For 'the meaning of that primary institution of human society, though proclaimed in dark words at the beginning of history, could not be truly known till its heavenly archetype was revealed, even the relation of Christ and the Ecclesia' (F. J. A. Hort). As the following verse shows, Paul's purpose is not speculative but practical: it is that this exalted conception may enrich and ennoble every Christian marriage.

33: Nevertheless do ye also severally love each one his own wife even as himself, and let the wife see that she fear her husband.

Nevertheless: 'Howbeit – not to dwell on this matter of Christ and the church, but to return to what I am treating of' (Abbott);

Do ye also severally love each one his own wife even as himself: The 'also' is important for it alludes to the example of Christ, and means 'in you also, as in Christ, *love* is to be fulfilled'. Consequently the authority of the husband must be exercised in love. *Every* husband is *always* to love his *own wife* as being part and parcel of *himself.*

And let the wife see that she respects her husband (RSV): It is important to understand that Paul's prescription for the ideal marriage is based upon the Christ-church relationship. Wives must be subject to their husbands because the church is under the control of Christ. Hence he 'never tells wives that they are to love their husbands . . . The reason is that which he gives: Christ loves the church, but it is for the church to obey and submit to Christ' (C. Chavasse, cited by R. P. Martin).

CHAPTER SIX

Here further guidance is given on family relationships. Paul exhorts children to obey their parents, and he tells fathers to exercise restraint in the nurture of their children [verses 1–4]. Slaves are to regard their work as a service to Christ, while masters must avoid threatening since their heavenly Master shows no partiality in his judgments [verses 5–9]. The final exhortation is a rousing call to prepare for battle. Believers must put on the whole armour of God in order to stand against the powers of darkness which oppose them [verses 10–17]. The apostle requests his readers to pray that he may be given boldness to preach the mystery of the gospel, and urges them to continue in prayer for all the saints. He warmly commends his messenger Tychicus, and closes the Epistle with the benediction [verses 18–24].

1: Children, obey your parents in the Lord: for this is right.

Paul next deals with the mutual duties of children and parents [verses 1–14]. His use of the phrase 'in the Lord' makes the natural obligation of children to obey their parents a summons to religious service. They are to recognize that in obeying their parents, they are obeying Christ. 'Not merely natural instinct, but religious motive should prompt children to obedience, and guard them in it . . . Filial obedience is "right"; it has its foundation in the very essence of that relation which subsists between parents and children. Nature claims it, while Scripture enjoins it, and the Son of God exemplified it' (Eadie) [*Luke* 2:51].

2: Honour thy father and mother (which is the first commandment with promise), 3: that it may be well with thee, and thou mayest live long on the earth.

'Honour thy father and mother,' which is a commandment of the greatest importance with a promise attached (Arndt-Gingrich): Paul confirms this injunction by an appeal to the abiding authority of the moral law [*Exod.*

20:12; *Deut.* 5:16], while he makes the promise universal in its scope by taking away the local reference to Canaan – an inspired adaptation that teaches us to distinguish the enduring *substance* of the moral law from the historical *accidents* that belonged to its Old Testament form. Thus each child must honour father and mother as worthy of equal respect and obedience. This is a commandment of primary importance to which is attached the promise of a long and blessed life. 'Obedient children sometimes die, as ripe fruit falls first. But the promise of longevity is held out – it is a principle of the divine administration and the usual course of providence . . . Filial obedience, under God's blessing, prolongs life, for it implies the possession of principles of restraint, sobriety, and industry, which secure a lengthened existence' (Eadie) [cf. *Prov.* 10:27].

4: And, ye fathers, provoke not your children to wrath: but nurture them in the chastening and admonition of the Lord.

On the other hand, fathers (upon whom the responsibility for the family primarily rests) also have a duty towards their children. This 'is given first *negatively*, as avoidance of all calculated to *irritate* or *exasperate* the children – injustice, severity and the like, so as to make them indisposed to filial obedience and honour' (Salmond).

But bring them up in the discipline and instruction of the Lord (RSV): Paul's *positive* directive to fathers is that they are to train their children in the *Christian* way, giving them the training that is of Christ, proceeding from him and prescribed by him' (Salmond). This means that fathers are not only to treat their children fairly but also firmly; repressive harshness and weak indulgence are alike to be avoided [cf. *1 Sam.* 3:13]. Rather they are to guide them by discipline and instruction. *Discipline* is 'the training by act' which Trench refers to 'the laws and ordinances of the Christian household, the transgression of which will induce correction'; whereas *instruction* is 'the training by word – by the word of encouragement, when this is sufficient, but also by that of remonstrance, of reproof, of blame, where these may be required'.

5: Servants, be obedient unto them that according to the flesh are your masters, with fear and trembling, in singleness of your heart, as unto Christ;

It is because Paul's 'household code' is based on the general principle stated in 5:21 that he first speaks to those in a position of dependence, wives, children, and now *servants* [verses 5–8], before dealing with those who are placed in authority over them, husbands, fathers, and *masters* [verse 9]. Although many modern versions rightly translate 'slaves', it is perhaps preferable to retain 'servants' because the exhortation 'embodies principles applicable to all posts of subordination' (Simpson). If Paul had preached 'the social gospel' he doubtless would have encouraged slaves to repudiate their position, with disastrous consequences, yet in sending the converted slave Onesimus back to his master as 'a brother beloved' [*Philem.* 16] he set forth the great principle of religious equality before God which undermined and eventually brought about the abolition of slavery. So here the apostle asks for that heart-obedience which only the redeemed man is able to render to his master. As the adoption of this ethic led to a transformation of the slave/master relationship, so its widespread absence from the modern industrial scene is diagnosed by John Murray as 'our basic economic ill' (*Principles of Conduct*, p. 103).

With fear and trembling: Not in servile fear of man, but in the fear of God. Christian slaves 'were not to tremble lest anything unpleasant might happen to themselves, but lest their Lord's name should be brought into disrepute through them' (Bruce).

In singleness of your heart, as unto Christ: Paul insists that it is the duty of servants always to obey their earthly masters with conscientious care and sincerity of purpose, as those who are well assured that in so doing they are serving their heavenly Master [cf. *Col.* 3:22–24].

6: not in the way of eyeservice, as men-pleasers; but as servants of Christ, doing the will of God from the heart; 7: with good will doing service, as unto the Lord, and not unto men:

Not in the way of eyeservice, as men-pleasers: 'The vice was venial in slaves; it is inexcusable, because it darkens into theft, in paid servants; and it spreads far and wide. All scamped work, all productions of man's hand and brain which are got up to look better than they are, all fussy parade of diligence when under inspection, and slackness afterwards, and all their like, which infect and infest every trade and profession, are transfixed by the sharp point of this precept' (Alexander Maclaren).

But as servants of Christ, doing the will of God from the heart: This is the antidote for such shoddy service. When the worker regards himself as the bond-slave of Christ his work is always well done. For the most humdrum job becomes a vocation when it is looked upon as the doing of God's will.

With good will doing service, as unto the Lord, and not unto men: No labour is servile when the Lord's approval is the paramount consideration. The most willing service to men is rendered by those who are bent on pleasing Christ!

8: knowing that whatsoever good thing each one doeth, the same shall he receive again from the Lord, whether he be bond or free.

'This verse presents for the encouragement of the slave, the elevating truth that all men stand on a level before the bar of Christ . . . In this world some men are masters and some are slaves. In the next, these distinctions will cease. There the question will be, not, Who is the master? and Who the slave? but who has done the will of God?' (Charles Hodge). Thus in the Day of Judgment every believer will be rewarded according to the good that he has done [the converse truth is stated in *Col.* 3:25]. And as every good work is the fruit of grace, so the promised reward is also the reward of grace.

9: And, ye masters, do the same things unto them, and forbear threatening: knowing that he who is both their Master and yours is in heaven, and there is no respect of persons with him.

And, ye masters, do the same things unto them: 'Perform your reciprocal duty' (Calvin). For masters are also under an obligation to their servants [cf. *Col.* 4: 1: 'that which is just and equal']. 'This is what Paul means by the term "the same things"; for we are all ready enough to demand what is due to ourselves; but when our own duty comes to be performed, every one tries to plead exemption' (Calvin).

Giving up your threatening: 'Your' is literally 'the' – the article hinting at its common occurrence: 'the too habitual threatening'. Paul 'singles out the prevailing vice and most customary exhibition of bad feeling on the part of the master and in forbidding this naturally includes every similar form of harshness' (Ellicott).

Knowing that he who is both their Master and yours is in heaven, and that there is no partiality with him (RSV): This heavenly Master 'is not a judge who "takes the face", sees who a man is and decides his case with partiality, in favour of the one who is a lord and master, rich and powerful, in disfavour of one who is a poor slave and powerless' (Lenski) [*James* 5:1ff].

10: Finally, be strong in the Lord, and in the strength of his might.

As in 1:19 with which this verse is vitally connected, the final phrase is not to be reduced to 'in his mighty strength', but has the full force of 'in the active efficacy of the might that is inherent in him' (Salmond). Paul now draws the Epistle to its practical conclusion. He charges his readers to stand fast against all the powers of evil, acquitting themselves like soldiers who are divinely strengthened and equipped to engage in this conflict [verses 10–20]. This command is of primary necessity, for the finest armour is wasted on the soldier who has no will to fight. And as the armour is spiritual, so is this courage; 'for physical courage and intellectual prowess are often, alas! allied to spiritual cowardice. Moreover, soldiers have an invincible courage when they have confidence in the skill and bravery of their leader; and the power of his might, in which they are strong, has proved its vigour in routing the same foes which they are summoned to encounter. As the Captain of salvation, "He spoiled principalities and powers, and triumphed over them"' (Eadie) [*Col.* 2:15].

11: Put on the whole armour of God, that ye may be able to stand against the wiles of the devil.

Put on the whole armour: To be fully furnished for the fight the Christian must put on the *whole* armour of God. '*He must be armed, in every part* cap-à-pie, *soul and body,* the powers of the one, and the senses of the other, not any part left naked. A dart may fly in at a little hole, like that which brought a message of death to Ahab, through the joints of his harness, and Satan is such an archer, who can shoot at pennybreadth' (William Gurnall) [cf. *Rom.* 13:12, 14].

Of God: This is the armour that God provides; it is not of man's devising. 'Instead of relying on the arms which God has provided, men have always been disposed to trust to those which they provide for themselves or which have been prescribed by others. Seclusion from the world (i.e. flight rather than conflict), ascetic and ritual observances, invocation of saints and angels, and especially, celibacy, voluntary poverty, and monastic obedience, constitute the panoply which false religion has substituted for the armour of God' (Charles Hedge) [cf. *Col.* 2:18–23].

That ye may be able to stand: '"To stand" is the key-word of the passage. The present picture is not of a march, or of an assault, but of the holding of the fortress of the soul and of the church for the heavenly King. Bunyan's "Mr Standfast" is a portrait that may illustrate this page' (Moule, *CB*) [cf. verses 13, 14].

Against the wiles of the devil: All the resources of divine grace are required to stand firm against the prince of darkness, an adversary of superhuman strength and guile, whose greatest triumph is to make men doubt his existence! The devil 'useth arts and stratagems, as well as force and violence, and therefore, if any part of your spiritual armour be wanting, he will assault you where he finds you weakest' (Poole) [cf. 4:14; *2 Cor.* 11:3, 13, 14].

12: For our wrestling is not against flesh and blood, but against the principalities, against the powers, against the world-rulers of this darkness, against the spiritual hosts of wickedness in the heavenly places.

It is because the forces arrayed against believers are not merely human opponents, men of flesh and blood like themselves, but the massed legions of the evil one, that they must put on the whole armour of God. And to show the absolute necessity for this divine provision, Paul, as it were, parades the devil's army in review, using each of the four designations to set forth a different aspect of this dreadful host. The term 'principalities' is probably meant to indicate that these fallen angels have retained the rank of ruling dignitaries. That this is no empty title is shown by the fact that these rebellious spirits are also called 'powers', which suggests that they are invested with the authority to exercise such rule. The third phrase defines the sphere of their dominion: the world in its present state of darkness is the realm over which they exert their usurped sway within the limits permitted them [cf. *Dan* 10:13, 20]. Finally, 'the spirit-forces of evil' (Moffatt) points to an invisible horde whose 'appetite for evil only exceeds their capacity for producing it' (Eadie). The domain of this army appears to be located in a region above the earth but below the highest heavens [cf. 2:2]. The reason why Paul uses 'in the heavenlies' and not 'in the air' here may be his wish to 'bring out *as strongly as possible* the superhuman and superterrestrial nature of these hostile spirits' (Meyer).

13: Wherefore take up the whole armour of God, that ye may be able to withstand in the evil day, and, having done all, to stand.

Since Christians must contend against such formidable adversaries, it is essential that they take up the 'panoply' (i.e. 'the full armour of a heavily armed soldier' – Arndt-Gingrich) of God.

> *Stand then in his great might,*
> *With all his strength endued;*
> *And take, to arm you for the fight,*
> *The panoply of God.*
>
> Charles Wesley

That ye may be able to withstand in the evil day [cf. 5:16]; The Christian soldier must be thoroughly prepared in order that he may be able to withstand any sudden assault that is launched against him. 'The evil day' is the day when the conflict is most severe. It is any day of which it can be said 'This is your hour, and the power of darkness' [*Luke* 22:53].

And, having done all: Some maintain that the meaning is, 'after proving victorious over everything' (Arndt-Gingrich). But *'after you have done or accomplished everything'* (Arndt Gingrich) in preparing for the battle is preferable. For it is unlikely that Paul would first speak of the result of the combat and then urge his readers to put on the armour piece by piece [verses 14–17].

To stand: The central idea of the passage is not progress or conquest, but that of standing firm in the faith. 'The scene is filled with the marshalled hosts of the Evil One, bent upon *dislodging* the soul, and the church, from the one possible vantage-ground of life and power – union and communion with their Lord' (Moule, CB).

14: Stand therefore, having girded your loins with truth, and having put on the breastplate of righteousness,

In order that the Christian soldier may take his stand in readiness for the fight, he must first have put on the complete armour of God, which Paul now enumerates.

1. *He must brace himself with the belt of truth*, which most commentators, including Calvin, take to be sincerity of heart. This subjective interpretation is inadequate because not even Christian virtues constitute the armour that God provides. Nothing less than the objective realities of the gospel will afford the believer the divine protection he requires to resist the devil's wiles. Accordingly, 'truth' is to be understood as the dependable reality that has come to us in the gospel [cf. *John* 14:6]. This 'is something which the believer can put on like the protective apron of the soldier. He can make active use of it in withstanding the assaults of evil' (A. Oepke, *TDNT*, vol. 5, p. 308).

2. *He must put on the breastplate of righteousness*, which in view of the ethical context is also generally explained in the subjective sense of living righteously. 'But this is no protection. It cannot resist the accusations of conscience, the whispers of despondency, the power of temptation, much less the severity of the law, or the assaults of Satan. What Paul desired for himself was not to have on his own righteousness, but the righteousness which is of God by faith [*Phil.* 3:8, 9]. And this, doubtless, is the righteousness which he here urges believers to put on as a breastplate. It is an infinitely perfect righteousness, consisting in the obedience and sufferings of the Son of God, which satisfies all the demands of the divine law and justice; and which is a sure defence against all assaults whether from within or from without'(Charles Hodge).

15: and having shod your feet with the preparation of the gospel of peace;

And have your feet shod with the stability of the gospel of peace (Moffatt): 3. Here again opinion is divided on the meaning of the word *'preparation'*, which may refer to a readiness to preach the gospel [*Isa.* 52:7]; but in the Greek version of *Psa.* 88:15 [*Psa.* 89:14 in our versions] it has the sense of a 'prepared foundation', and this is more in harmony with the idea of standing unmoved against the foe. So if we would have a 'firm footing' (NEB) for the fight, we must put on these heavily-studded shoes of the gospel of peace [cf. 2:14ff]. Thus we are prepared for the war with Satan by the realization of our peace with God! Such peace does not exempt us from active service, but rather sustains us in it. For as no soldier stands firm in the day of battle unless his morale is high, so believers must be assured of their acceptance with God before they can withstand the assaults of the great adversary of their souls [*Rom.* 5:1].

16: withal taking up the shield of faith, wherewith ye shall be able to quench all the fiery darts of the evil one.

4. *'In addition to all'* the believer must take up the shield of faith. Here the protection afforded the heavy infantryman by the large, oblong shield, four by two and a half feet, is likened to the faith with which the Christian is able to quench all the flaming missiles that are hurled at him by the tempter. This faith is neither self-generated (carnal self-confidence) nor reflexive (faith in our faith), but is the gift of God (cf. 2:8) by which we are enabled to lay hold of Christ and all his saving benefits. It is therefore a faith which is as objective as the shield with which it is compared. The subjective aspect of faith is covered by the command to take up and use this shield in quenching all the devil's fire-tipped darts.

'As burning arrows not only pierced but set on fire what they pierced, they were doubly dangerous. They serve here therefore as the symbol of the fierce onsets of Satan. He showers arrows of fire on the soul of the believer; who, if unprotected by the shield of faith, would soon perish. It is a common experience of the people of God that at times horrible thoughts, unholy, blasphemous, sceptical, malignant, crowd upon the mind, which cannot be accounted for on any ordinary law of mental action, and which cannot be dislodged. They stick like burning arrows; and fill the soul with agony. They can be quenched only by faith; by calling on Christ for help. These, however, are not the only kind of fiery darts; nor are they the most dangerous. There are others which enkindle passion, inflame ambition, excite cupidity, pride, discontent, or vanity; producing a flame which our deceitful heart is not so prompt to extinguish, and which is often allowed to burn until it produces great injury and even destruction. Against these most dangerous weapons of the evil one, the only protection is faith. It is only by looking to Christ and earnestly invoking his interposition in our behalf that we can resist these insidious assaults, which inflame evil without the warning of pain' (Charles Hodge).

17: And take the helmet of salvation, and the sword of the Spirit, which is the word of God:

5. In this case Paul uses a different verb which specifically indicates (though not in contrast to the other pieces of armour) that *the helmet of salvation is to be 'received' as a gift from God*. As in verse 14 the apostle evidently has in mind Isaiah 59:17, where God is depicted as the Warrior who 'wears the helmet of salvation as the Worker and Bringer of salvation' (Foulkes). This is therefore the helmet of victory, for we receive it as an objective assurance that the decisive battle has been already fought and won on our behalf. So in putting it on we are subjectively trusting in that salvation which is at once given and promised, which is ours both in present possession and future prospect [cf. *1 Thess.* 5:8]. And since it is the function of the helmet to protect the soldier's head and ensure his clear vision through its visor, so this 'given' salvation must fill the Christian's mind and keep his eyes fixed upon the glorious goal that is set before him. We must at all times remember the objective character of God's salvation, and not become unhealthily obsessed with our own subjective spiritual states. We have to preserve the balance Luther showed in his great hymn, 'A safe stronghold our God is still', which though it speaks of his experience, puts the whole emphasis on the outward and upward, upon God (cf. James Philip's brilliant and heart-warming exposition in *The Christian Warfare and Armour,* pp. 83–97).

And the sword of the Spirit which is the spoken word of God (Hendriksen): 6. *The only offensive weapon in the Christian's armoury is the sword of the Spirit, which is identified with the Word of God* [cf. *Heb.* 4:12]. For it is only by this means that the powers of darkness are put to flight. What is in view is the special utterance of God that is exactly fitted to repel the tempter's attack on any particular occasion. Just as Christ routed the devil by appealing to particular texts of Scripture [cf. *Matt.* 4:4, 7, 10], so the Christian must learn to wield the sword of the Spirit with such effect that he is able to parry all the deadly thrusts of the enemy. 'All scripture is given by inspiration of God' [*2 Tim.* 3:16], but it is only through knowing it for ourselves that it becomes the sword of the Spirit in our hands. The Christian is invincible when armed with this Excalibur whose power belongs to the Spirit who inspired it; yet it is he and no one else who is commanded to do the fighting! Unhappily, many are now using the Bible as a sword to do the devil's work in the world. The aggressive cultists of our day are not taught of the Spirit, but simply come to Scripture for the authority to propagate the ideas they wish to impose upon the sacred text. So in their case the Word of God is the sword upon which they commit spiritual suicide, taking down their deluded followers with them into the pit! [*Rev.* 22:18, 19].

18: with all prayer and supplication praying at all seasons in the Spirit, and watching thereunto in all perseverance and supplication for all the saints.

7. *This state of spiritual preparedness* ['Stand therefore', verse 14] *would not be complete without the weapon of 'all-prayer'*, and though Paul now drops the metaphor he clearly wishes his readers to understand that persevering prayer [*Luke* 18:1] is essential to the success of this warfare.

> *Restraining prayer, we cease to fight;*
> *Prayer makes the Christian's armour bright;*
> *And Satan trembles when he sees*
> *The weakest saint upon his knees.*
> William Cowper.

In the Spirit [cf. *Jude* 20]: This is added because 'true prayer is both the suitor's own and the Spirit's work. The sincerity and intension of soul pertain to the human petitioner; the potency, inspiration and freedom of utterance and access [2:18] spring from "the secret touch of the Spirit" (Gurnall), generating a glow of holy emotion in the suppliant's soul' (Simpson).

And watching thereunto in all perseverance and supplication for all the saints: 'The conflict of which the apostle has been speaking is not merely a single combat between the individual Christian and Satan, but also a war between the people of God and the powers of darkness. No soldier entering battle prays for himself alone, but for all his fellow-soldiers also. They form one army, and the success of the one is the success of all. In like manner Christians are united as one army, and therefore have a common cause; and each must pray for all' (Charles Hodge).

19: and on my behalf, that utterance may be given unto me in opening my mouth, to make known with boldness the mystery of the gospel,

Although an apostle, Paul was always careful to ask his fellow-believers to pray for him, and here he requests them to pray that God will speak through his lips, enabling him boldly to proclaim 'the mystery of the gospel' [for which see comment on 3:9]. 'Like the early apostles [*Acts* 4:29] his prayer was not for success, nor for deliverance from danger or suffering, but for boldness in proclaiming the gospel of God that was entrusted to him' (Foulkes).

20: for which I am an ambassador in chains; that in it I may speak boldly, as I ought to speak.

For which I am an ambassador in a chain (ASV margin) [cf. *2 Cor.* 5:20]: 'Ambassadors were inviolable by the law of nations, and could not, without outrage to sacred right, be put in chains. Yet Christ's ambassador is *in a chain!*' (Fausset). Pending the hearing of his appeal to Caesar, Paul was allowed to hire his own lodging in Rome, but was kept chained to the soldier who guarded him [*Acts* 28:16,20].

That I may declare it boldly, as I ought to speak (RSV): 'It' meaning the message of the gospel [cf. *Col.* 4:4]. Thus Paul invokes their prayers on his behalf that he may fearlessly discharge his commission despite his chain [cf. *Acts* 28:30, 31].

21: But that ye also may know my affairs, how I do, Tychicus, the beloved brother and faithful minister in the Lord, shall make known to you all things: 22: whom I have sent unto you for this very purpose that ye may know our state, and that he may comfort your hearts.

The close verbal similarity of this personal postscript with that found in Colossians 4:7, 8 is best explained 'by the supposition that the apostle wrote the two conclusions together, when both letters had been written and were about to be despatched' (Foulkes). For after having addressed the Colossians it would be natural for Paul to add the word 'also' when virtually repeating the same message to the Ephesians. The bearer of these epistles and of all the news from Rome is Tychicus [*Acts* 20:4], Paul's beloved brother and faithful helper 'in the Lord' whose ministry is certain to encourage and strengthen their hearts.

23: Peace be to the brethren, and love with faith, from God the Father and the Lord Jesus Christ.

As Paul writes to those who are believers, his closing prayer for them is that their faith may be accompanied by the graces of peace and love. 'It is evident that the peace here intended is peace among themselves as brethren, and that love is not the love of God manifested toward them, but the Christian grace of brotherly love, which is the only true basis of peace in the community' (Macpherson). And the apostle makes this the subject of prayer because such graces will not be manifested on the horizontal level unless they descend from heaven as blessings conjointly bestowed by God the Father and the Lord Jesus Christ.

24: Grace be with all them that love our Lord Jesus Christ with a love incorruptible.

It is with this beautiful benediction that the great apostle fittingly concludes his 'spiritual testament' to the church. 'The benediction is upon those who love Christ with an incorruptible love. They love him who first loved them; and this love, which they have experienced and which has produced their love, has imparted to them and to their love that same incorruptibility which belongs to him and to his love. Their love is not of the earth earthly. It is heavenly, of heavenly origin and of heavenly quality. That love which is of Christ and in Christ can know no decay' (Macpherson).

SOLI DEO GLORIA

BIBLIOGRAPHY AND ACKNOWLEDGEMENTS

Quotations have been selected from the following books, and the author expresses his grateful thanks to the authors and publishers who kindly gave permission to reproduce quotations from their copyright works.

ABBOTT, T. K., *The Epistles to the Ephesians and to the Colossians* (*ICC*) (T. & T. Clark, 1897).
BERKOUWER, G. C., *Faith and Justification* (Eerdmans, 1972).
BRUCE, F. F., *The Epistle to the Ephesians* (Pickering & Inglis, 1961).
—— *An Expanded Paraphrase on the Epistles of Paul* (Paternoster Press, 1970).

CALVIN, JOHN, *Commentary on Ephesians*, (St Andrew Press, 1965).

DENNEY, JAMES, *The Death of Christ* (Tyndale, 1964)

EADIE, JOHN, *Commentary on the Epistle to the Ephesians* (Zondervan reprint of 1883 ed.).

ELLICOTT, C. J., *St Paul's Epistle to the Ephesians* (Longmans Green, 1868).

FAUSSET, A. R., *Ephesians (JFB)* (Collins, 1874).

FINDLAY, G. G., *The Epistle to the Ephesians (EB)* (Hodder & Stoughton, 1892).

FOULKES, FRANCIS, *Ephesians – Introduction and Commentary (TNTC)* (Tyndale Press, 1963).

GELDENHUYS, J. NORVAL, *Supreme Authority* (Marshall, Morgan & Scott, 1953).

GOODWIN, THOMAS, *Exposition of Ephesians (1–2:10)* (Sovereign Grace Book Club, n.d.).

GURNALL, WILLIAM, *The Christian in Complete Armour* (Banner of Truth, 1964).

HANSON, STIG, *The Unity of the Church in the New Testament – Colossians and Ephesians* (Almquist & Wiksells, 1946).

HENRY, MATTHEW, *Commentary on the Holy Bible* (various editions).

HODGE, A. A., *The Atonement* (Evangelical Press, 1974).

HODGE, CHARLES, *Commentary on Ephesians* (Banner of Truth, 1964).

HOEKSEMA, HERMAN, *Reformed Dogmatics* (Reformed Free Publishing, 1966).

—— *The Triple Knowledge* (Reformed Free Publishing, 1966).

KIDNER, DEREK, *Genesis (TOTC)* (Tyndale 1967).

—— *Psalms 1–72 (TOTC)* (Tyndale, 1973).

KITTEL, GERHARD & FRIEDRICH, GERHARD (eds.), *Theological Dictionary of the New Testament,* vols. 1–9 (Eerdmans, 1964–74).

LENSKI, R. C. H., *The Interpretation of Ephesians* (Augsburg, 1961).

LIGHTFOOT, J. B., *Notes on the Epistles of St. Paul* (Zondervan, 1957).

—— *Colossians and Philemon* (Zondervan, 1961).

—— *Philippians* (Zondervan, 1968).

MCKELVEY, R. J., *The New Temple* (OUP, 1969).

MACPHERSON, JOHN, *Commentary on Ephesians* (T. & T. Clark, 1892).

MACHEN, J. G., *The Christian Faith in the Modern World* (Eerdmans, 1970).

MANTON, THOMAS, *Exposition of John 17* (Banner of Truth, 1959).

MARTIN, RALPH P., *Ephesians* (*NBC*) (IVP, 1970).

—— *Worship in the Early Church* (Marshall, Morgan & Scott, 1974).

MORRIS, LEON, *The Apostolic Preaching of the Cross* (Tyndale, 1965).

MOULE, C. F. D., *An Idiom-Book of New Testament Greek* (CUP, 1968).

—— *The Epistle to the Ephesians* (*CB*) (CUP, 1889).

—— *Ephesian Studies* (Pickering & Inglis, n.d.).

MURRAY, JOHN, *Principles of Conduct* (Tyndale, 1957).

PINK, ARTHUR W., *Gleanings from Paul* (Moody Press, 1967).

POOLE, MATTHEW, *A Commentary on the Holy Bible*, vol. 3 (Banner of Truth, 1963).

RICHARDSON, ALAN (ed.), *A Theological Word Book of the Bible* (SCM, 1957).

ROBINSON, J. ARMITAGE, *St Paul's Epistle to the Ephesians* (James Clarke, n.d.).

SALMOND, S. D. F., *The Epistle to the Ephesians* (*EGT*) (Hodder & Stoughton 1903).

SIMPSON, E. K., *The Epistle to the Ephesians* (*NLC*) (Marshall, Morgan & Scott, 1957).

STOTT, JOHN, *Baptism and Fullness* (IVP, 1975).

THORNWELL, J. H., *Collected Writings*, vol. 2 (Banner of Truth, 1974).

TRAPP, JOHN, *Commentary on the New Testament* (Sovereign Grace Book Club, 1958).

TRENCH, R. C., *Synonyms of the New Testament* (James Clarke, 1961).

VINCENT, M. R., *Word Studies in the New Testament* (MacDonald, n.d.).

VOS, GEERHARDUS, *The Pauline Eschatology* (Eerdmans, 1961).

WARFIELD, B. B., *The Shorter Writings*, vol. 1 (Presbyterian & Reformed, 1970).

The following books were also consulted:

ALFORD, HENRY, *The Greek Testament* (Rivingtons, 1859).

ARNDT, W. F. AND GINGRICH, F. W., *A Greek-English Lexicon of the New Testament* (University of Chicago Press, 1957).

BARTH, MARKUS, *Ephesians* (*AB*) (Doubleday, 1974).

BEST, ERNEST, *One Body in Christ* (SPCK, 1955).

CALVIN, JOHN, *Sermons on the Epistle to the Ephesians* (Banner of Truth, 1973).

CLOWNEY, EDMUND P., *The Doctrine of the Church* (Presbyterian & Reformed 1969).

DABNEY, R. L., *Systematic Theology* (Banner of Truth, 1985).

DUNN, JAMES D. G., *Baptism in the Holy Spirit* (SCM, 1970).

GUTHRIE, DONALD, *New Testament Introduction* (Tyndale, 1970).

HENDRIKSEN, WILLIAM, *Ephesians* (*NTC*) (Banner of Truth 1972).

LLOYD-JONES, D. M., *Exposition of Ephesians*, 8 vols. (Banner of Truth, 1972–82).

MACDONALD, H. D., *The Church and Its Glory* (Henry Walter, 1973).

MARTIN, RALPH. P., *Ephesians* (*BBC*) (Marshall, Morgan & Scott, 1972).

MITTON, C. LESLIE, *Ephesians* (*NCB*) (Oliphants, 1976).

MURRAY, J. O. F., *The Epistle to the Ephesians* (*CGT*) (CUP, 1889).

PHILIP, JAMES, *The Christian Warfare and Armour* (Victory Press, 1972).

THAYER, J. H., *A Greek-English Lexicon of the New Testament* (Evangel Publishing, 1974).

THOMAS, L. R., *Does the Bible Teach Millennialism?* (Reiner Publications, n.d.).

WARFIELD, B. B., *The Person and Work of Christ* (Presbyterian & Reformed 1950).

—— *The Lord of Glory* (Evangelical Press, 1974).

—— *Faith and Life* (Banner of Truth, 1974).